BUILDING A SACRED MOUNTAIN

中臺之頂
大竹林之寺
大聖文殊真身
大聖文殊真身殿
大福聖之寺
大建安之寺

BUILDING A SACRED MOUNTAIN

The Buddhist Architecture of China's Mount Wutai

WEI-CHENG LIN

A China Program Book

University of Washington Press | Seattle and London

ART HISTORY
PUBLICATION INITIATIVE
This book is made possible by a collaborative grant from the Andrew W. Mellon Foundation.

MM
Publication of this book has been aided by a grant from the Millard Meiss Publication Fund of the College Art Association.

This book was also supported in part by the China Studies Program, a division of the Henry M. Jackson School of International Studies at the University of Washington, and by the University of North Carolina at Chapel Hill.

Printed and bound in the United States of America
Design by Barbara E. Williams; typeset by BW&A Books, Inc.
Cartography by Deborah Reade
Composed in Dante, typeface designed by Giovanni Mardersteig and Charles Malin
17 16 15 14 5 4 3 2 1

Frontispiece is a detail of Plate 10: Mount Wutai west wall mural, Mogao Cave 61. Courtesy of Dunhuang Academy.

University of Washington Press
PO Box 50096, Seattle, WA 98145, USA
www.washington.edu/uwpress

Library of Congress Cataloging-in-Publication Data
Lin, Wei-Cheng, 1969-
Building a sacred mountain : the Buddhist architecture of China's Mount Wutai / Wei-Cheng Lin. — First [edition].
pages cm — (Art history publication initiative)
Includes bibliographical references and index.
ISBN 978-0-295-99352-2 (hardback)
1. Wutai Mountains (China)—History. 2. Buddhist architecture—China—Wutai Mountains. 3. Buddhist monasteries—China—Wutai Mountains. 4. Buddhism and culture—China—Wutai Mountains. I. Title.
DS793.W8222L56 2014
951'.17—dc23 2013031629

The paper used in this publication is acid-free and meets the minimum requirements of American National Standard for Information Sciences–Permanence of Paper for Printed Library Materials, ANSI Z39.48–1984.∞

To my parents

CONTENTS

ACKNOWLEDGMENTS

It has been a long, twelve-year journey since I started the first research on Mount Wutai. A journey that I could never have completed without the guidance, support, and good wishes of colleagues, friends, and family along the way.

No one has provided me with more intellectual and moral support than my mentor Wu Hung, who was my advisor in this project in its early stages. No one has done more to encourage and push me to reconsider how Buddhist architecture could be defined and studied in relation to the history of the sacred mountain. I owe him the intellectual inclination, as well as the skills, to think historically, holistically, and creatively. To him, this book is offered, although I know he thinks it should have been completed years ago.

I am also indebted to Yen Chüan-ying and Katherine Taylor, who helped me conceptualize this project and who advised me in the subsequent research and writing. My great appreciation also goes to the rest of my University of Chicago community: Joel Snyder, Richard Neer, Katherine Tsiang, and Hans Thomsen for their advice at various stages of this project; and my Chicago colleagues Delin Lai, Yudong Wang, Catherine Stuer, Sun-ah Choi, and Seunghye Lee, as well as the late Cong Liu, among others, for the many conversations and discussions we shared; from them I learned a great deal in intellectual maturity and collegial relations.

Many of my teachers, colleagues, and friends have read or heard parts of this work, and offered their honest and valuable comments. I am truly grateful for Michael Nylan's correction of my use of the term *zhenrong*; Yumin Lee's kind words on my study of Mogao Cave 61; insightful opinions from an anonymous reader of *Artibus Asiae* regarding the icon of the "new-mode" Mañjuśrī; and much feedback and encouragement from Wendi Adamek, Raoul Birnbaum, Sheng-chih Lin, Shu-fen Liu, Amy McNair, Liang-wen Pan, Shou-chien Shih, Michelle Wang, and Dorothy Wong. During my several trips to China, I could not have accomplished much at all without timely and generous help from Chai Zejun, Li Qingquan, Li Yuqun, Zhang Zong, and Zheng Yan. Special thanks are owed to Shi Jinming, the director of Shanxi Provincial Museum, whose enthusiastic assistance made each of my trips to Shanxi much easier and more enjoyable. Fan Jinshi, Peng Jinzhang, and Zhao Shengliang of Dunhuang Academy were also wonderful supporters of my project during my research trips in Dunhuang.

My colleagues in the Triangle Area have provided me with their unfailing support in the past five years since I arrived in Chapel Hill. My thanks go to Stanley

Abe, Glaire Anderson, Jan Bardsley, Paroma Chatterjee, Eduardo Douglas, Pika Ghosh, Jim Hirschfield, Li-ling Hsiao, Michelle King, Cary Levin, Charles D. Orzech, Mary Sheriff, Daniel Sherman, Wenhua Shi, and Jiayun Zhuang. Beyond creating a rich and stimulating intellectual environment, these colleagues have helped me in various ways through the difficult times and frustrations I encountered while writing my book. Hsi-chu Bolick, East Asian bibliographer at the University of North Carolina at Chapel Hill, deserves a special note for never failing to answer any of my requests. I also benefited from the Carolina Asia Center, the Program in Medieval and Modern Studies, and the University Research Council of UNC at Chapel Hill for their research support, which made the completion and publication of my book possible.

I would also like to express my appreciation to those who have generously assisted me in preparing my manuscript and illustrations. I owe much to Shih-shan Susan Huang for sharing many useful tips about publishing a first book, and Jason Steuber for his expertise and advice in the publication business. Thanks also to Beverly Foit-Albert, Guo Zhicheng, Jungmin Ha, Sonya Lee, Li Yuqun, Puay-peng Ho, Sun Xiaogang, Katherine R. Tsiang, Yen Chüan-ying, Zhang Zong, Zhao Shengliang, and Zhao Xiaoxing, as well as the Academia Sinica, Daigoji, Dunhuang Academy, Seiryōji, and Wenwu Press, for permitting me to use their images. In particular, I am very grateful to Lin Zhu for granting me the right to use Liang Sicheng's drawings, and to Fu Xinian who graciously let me use his drawings of Foguang Monastery. I also appreciate Chia-ling Chen, Dora C. Y. Ching, Annie Feng, Guo Daiheng, Alexandra Harrer, Shih-ming Pai, Sarai Mai, Mei Mei, and Wang Guixiang for their help with acquisition of image permissions. At the University of Washington Press, I am fortunate to have worked with Lorri Hagman and her excellent staff, and appreciate their patience and effort in guiding me through the stressful but valuable learning process of producing a book. I also wish to thank the two anonymous readers of my manuscript for their careful and thoughtful comments, which greatly improved the quality and arguments of the book. Thanks also go to Margaret McCormack, Deborah Reade, and Carol Wengler for their assistance with various aspects of the production, to Barbara Williams and her team for managing the production so patiently and professionally, and to Maura High for her meticulous and excellent copyediting that truly improved the overall quality of the book.

Last, this book bears my utmost gratitude to my parents, for their unceasing love and support throughout my career. They never fail to encourage me by letting me know they care for whatever I do and have confidence that I will succeed. Without their support, the long journey would not have been completed. My final thanks is reserved for my wife, Kim, whose unconditional support and untiring proofreading of my manuscript many, many, many times over are forever remembered. Also not forgotten is that in the past busy years of my career, she has been a wonderful and dedicated mother to our son, Joseph, who has learned to say, "Baba, you should go write your book," when he wants me to let him be. To all of you, I am forever grateful.

CHRONOLOGY OF CHINESE DYNASTIES

Shang	ca. 1600–ca. 1045 BCE
Zhou	1045–256 BCE
Western Zhou	1045–771 BCE
Eastern Zhou	770–256 BCE
Spring and Autumn (Chunqiu)	770–476 BCE
Warring States (Zhanguo)	475–221 BCE
Qin	221–206 BCE
Han	202 BCE–220 CE
Western Han	202 BCE–9 CE
Xin (Wang Mang's Usurpation)	9–23
Eastern Han	25–220
Three Kingdoms	220–65
Wei	220–65
Shu Han	220–63
Wu	222–80
Western Jin	265–317
Eastern Jin	317–420
Southern Dynasties	420–589
Liu Song	420–79
Southern Qi	479–502
Liang	502–57
Chen	557–89
Northern Dynasties	386–581
Northern Liang	398–439
Northern Wei (Tuoba)	386–534
Eastern Wei	534–49
Western Wei	535–56
Northern Qi	550–77
Northern Zhou	557–81
Sui	581–617
Tang	618–907
Liao (Khitan)	916–1125
Five Dynasties	907–1279
Song	960–1279
Northern Song	960–1127
Southern Song	1127–279
Yuan	1260–368
Ming	1368–644
Qing	1644–911

BUILDING
A SACRED
MOUNTAIN

Early Buddhist Monastic Architecture in Context

All mountains, whether larger or smaller, have gods and spirits. If the mountain is large, the god is great; if the mountain is small, the god is minor.

—Ge Hong, *Master Who Embraces Simplicity* (Baopuzi)

Mountain cults in China may have developed long before the creation of the written word.[1] Since antiquity, mountains were thought to embody the mythical and primordial power and energy that created cosmological order, structured geographical hierarchy, and sanctioned political authority. Soaring between heaven and earth, mountains were considered not only places inhabited by the divine but divinities themselves.[2] As China's dynastic history unfolded, mountains with extraordinary features found their way onto the imperial map as physical and territorial markers and anchors of the land under heaven within which the emperor ruled.[3] Mountains received sacrifices and revealed the heavenly mandate, for the greater a mountain was, the more spiritually potent it became, as the epigraph taken from Ge Hong's *Master Who Embraces Simplicity* emphasizes. The myth, the imagined, and the imaginary were forged to cultivate the natural into something admirable, awesome, and sacred; myth and history in this case were equally important in the formation of what has been termed Chinese mountain culture (*shan wenhua*).[4] After Buddhism arrived in China in the first century CE, however, this culture, with its conception of mountains and the practices of mountain cults, was significantly modified, and took a very different trajectory.

Never before in China had a mountain cult been established because a specific, named deity was said to reside in the mountain and assist and benefit religious practitioners. Mount Wutai was the first to be accorded recognition as *the* Buddhist "sacred mountain," and it was granted this status because the bodhisattva Mañjuśrī, or Wenshu Pusa, one of the great bodhisattvas of Mahayana Buddhism, was believed to live there.[5] This recognition, in a land where Buddhism was initially a foreign religion, began no earlier than the fifth century CE and continued into the Tang dynasty (618–907), as Mount Wutai developed not only as the domicile of the bodhisattva but eventually as one of the most important Buddhist centers in Tang China, drawing pilgrims from neighboring nations such as India, the birthplace of Buddhism.[6] The importance and popularity of the new "sacred mountain" cult at Mount Wutai is evident in the restructuring of Buddhist sacred geography after the identification of Mount Wutai as a Buddhist mountain, when Buddhism's geographic center in India gradually shifted to China from the fifth through the tenth centuries.[7] What is more, Mount Wutai was only the first of four mountains recognized in premodern China as associated with specific Buddhist bodhisattvas, and the pattern by which it was built into a Buddhist sacred site became the model for the later three.[8] It is not an overstatement to say that Mount Wutai occupied one of the most prominent positions in China's religious geography and played a paramount role in the early Buddhism of medieval China, from the end of the Han dynasty (202 BCE–220 CE) until the end of the tenth century.[9]

Mount Wutai's development into a Buddhist sacred mountain involved a complex historical process that domesticated and localized the sacred presence of the foreign deity in ways that show how Buddhism was realized, practiced, and expressed in the religious landscape of medieval China. When the history of Mount Wutai is examined against long-standing Chinese mountain culture, several fundamental questions arise: How was Mount Wutai, a native mountain whose early history was relatively unknown, converted into a Buddhist mountain? How was its natural terrain sanctified in Buddhist terms and its sacrality revealed to believers? And what did the transformation of the site and maintenance of its sacrality entail? Did monastic architecture, built or unbuilt (e.g., in visionary experience), help establish Mount Wutai as *the* sacred mountain by reconfiguring and reconceiving its topography and thus affirming its sacrality?

Studies of sacred sites have often begun with issues related to pilgrimage, placing much emphasis on the history and legends of site, saints, or miraculous events.[10] Concepts such as rites of passage or *communitas* have also been evoked, focusing on the transformative experience of pilgrimage to the site but not on the site itself.[11] A sacred site, however, also belongs to a spatial category—located at a geographical place, characterized by its topographic features, and delimited in a specific space—such that the sacrality of the site is also necessarily bound and explicated in spatial concepts and physical terms.

It was a deeply rooted view in ancient Chinese mountain culture that all mountains were potentially numinous and potent. At least two sets of determinants influenced the construction of sacred mountains. First were their intrinsic qualities. Mountains inspired spiritual associations by virtue of their extraordinary topographies—tremendous mass and height or unusual features such as grottos, caverns, chasms, and so on—suggesting not only solidity and endurance but also a mythical interior of secret treasures, energy, or power. Also, mountains were surrounded by clouds and emitted vapors, as if they were breathing, so were thought of as the source of life that nurtures all things and beings. Mountains, moreover, contain spectacular rock formations and harbor strange flora and fauna. All these natural and physical characteristics are intrinsic to mountains and can be cultivated, revealed, and explored. The second set of qualities is extrinsic. They include apparitions and visions peculiar to the mountain; relics, images, or texts originating elsewhere yet miraculously uncovered there; or steles, shrines, or other buildings that mark the site—all exterior to the mountain proper but weav-

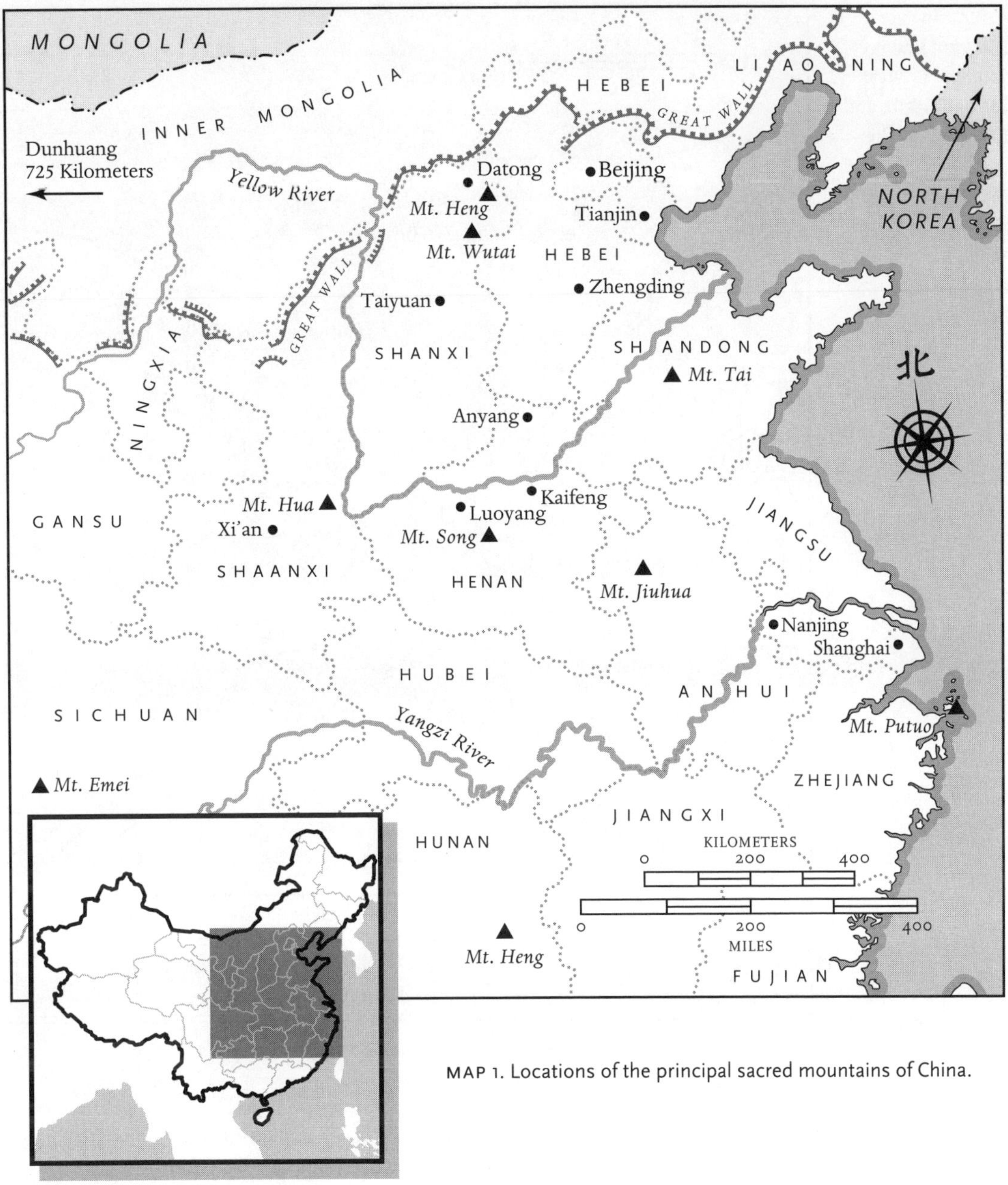

MAP 1. Locations of the principal sacred mountains of China.

ing layers of significance into the mountain topography. These also bring about particular viewpoints—bureaucratic, historical, and religious or related to myth, memory, and imagination—in dialogue with intrinsic characteristics to provide the language with which sacred mountains can be described and their sacrality defined.

Located in present-day Shanxi Province in northern China (map 1), the sacred area of Mount Wutai extends over an extensive mountainous region, approximately 336 square kilometers in size.[12] Although it is referred to as a mountain

MAP 2. The area of Mount Wutai, bounded by West, Central, North, and East Peaks in the north and the South Peak in the south.

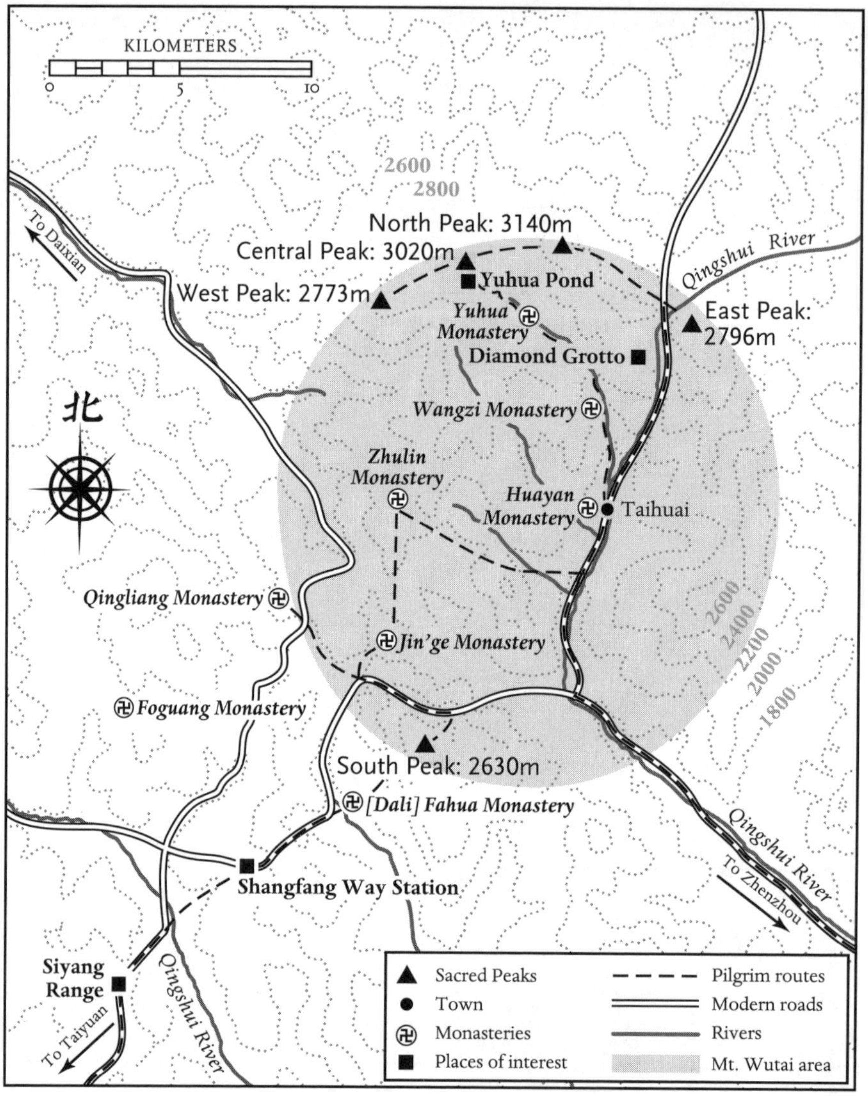

(*shan*), Mount Wutai is actually a cluster of mountains with five towering peaks, each with a high and roughly domed or terrace-like grassy mountaintop—as indicated in its Chinese name, Wutaishan, which literally means "mountain of five terraces." Although not corresponding exactly to the cardinal directions, the five peaks have since the mountain's earliest history been designated based on their relative positions: Western, Central, Northern, and Eastern Peaks clustered in the north, and the Southern Peak in the far south (map 2). The highest of the five peaks is the Northern Peak at 3,140 meters above sea level; the lowest, the Southern Peak at 2,630 meters. Together, the five peaks encircle and demarcate the area known as Mount Wutai.

Mount Wutai's prominent topography would have appeared to Buddhist practitioners in medieval China as more than merely natural; it would have also had some numinous and spiritual quality. Ennin (794–864), a Japanese pilgrim monk, who arrived at Mount Wutai in 840, was deeply moved when he first saw the sacred mountain: "[As soon as] I saw the Central Peak while heading toward the northwest, I prostrated myself on the ground and worshiped it. Here was the realm presided over by Mañjuśrī. Its five [sacred] peaks were round and tall, yet without vegetation, shaped thus like overturned bronze bowls. Gazing at them from afar, my tears rained down involuntarily. Plants and flowers that grew here were rare and different from elsewhere; how extraordinary this place was!"[13] The looming peaks were unmistakably the five sacred markers of the holy domain where the rare flora grew; but the power of the extraordinary place lay, more importantly, in the presiding bodhisattva, who had come to reside at the mountain site and whose presence its landscape evoked. As Ennin concluded: "This is Mount Qingliang [Mount Wutai], the Golden World [Pure Land of Bodhisattva Mañjuśrī], who manifests himself right here for our benefit."[14]

Indeed, the process of Mount Wutai's changing identity from native mountain to a Buddhist sacred site can be characterized as a shift from a *place*-oriented conception to a *presence*-oriented one. As has been suggested by scholars, hagiography in miraculous legends, acts, or visions necessarily includes a spatial dimension, which establishes the meaning and spiritual import of sacred topography.[15] The conversion of Mount Wutai involved a historical process of reappropriating, reinterpreting, or even replacing the intrinsic determinants of the sacred site with extrinsic ones.[16] Thus the initially foreign deity, Bodhisattva Mañjuśrī, was seen and located in the native mountain through ritual, vision, and architecture. In this regard, the monastic architecture at Mount Wutai was built not so much to partake in the numinous qualities intrinsic to the sacred site as to construct and construe the sacrality of the site by virtue of its own built environment. Buddhist architecture was one of the primary, if not the most prominent, means of cultural and material intervention through which Mount Wutai was developed into the first Buddhist sacred mountain in medieval China.

In recent years, studies of Chinese sacred geography have departed from the earlier practice of separating the sacred and the profane into exclusive categories,[17] instead seeing the sacred as constructed and contested by various influxes, not only religious or spiritual but also sociopolitical and historical. In addition, studies on space and place have contributed analytical terms and methodologies for understanding how the sacred could be valorized in spatial experience and localized in place.[18] This "spatial turn," which recognizes the critical role of space and place in the perception and conception of the sacred, is also coupled with a strong emphasis on the temporal aspect of the sacred geography; that is, in recognizing the multiple histories and multivalent significance of a sacred site as it evolves and fluctuates in the *longue durée,* as we know from several recent studies.[19] The different religious traditions coexisting at Mount Heng (Hengshan), also known as the Southern Sacred Peak (Nanyue), has been analyzed from a microhistorical viewpoint. A "cultural stratigraphy" has been proposed to account for the multilayered narratives of pilgrimage that have accumulated around Mount Tai (Taishan), or the Eastern Sacred Peak (Dongyue). Likewise, attention has been drawn to the "complex amalgam" of nature, history, religion, and human experiences in the historical development of Mount Emei (Emeishan) as a Chinese sacred mountain.[20] This book shares with those studies a view of sacred geography as multifaceted, requiring an approach both contextual and interdisciplinary to unravel its complexity. Architecture—its site, space, image, and built environment—provides a critical point of access to this complexity, as well as to the essential concepts, practices, and history of Chinese sacred mountains.

This use of architecture as the primary lens of investigation is also apt for my topic, particularly in the context of the broader religious and material culture of this period. Medieval China, already enthusiastic for material luxuries, developed a fascination with the material world without negating the potential of that world as the agent, sign, form, or embodiment of the divine.[21] Material objects or things were not rejected but often considered indispensable to the understanding and attainment of the immaterial. For example, it was thought that miracle-performing relics could inspire the "corporeal imagination" and living icons could elicit a "visceral vision"; in these cases, the corporeal and visceral rendered the sacred and potent more immanent and experiential.[22] In the same vein, architecture was not simply the building of structures; it was material-spatial construction that could structure and represent the divine presence in its fullest manifestation. By extension, the larger, built environment of a monastic complex and the mountain landscape, reconfigured and reconceived by the building of monasteries, could also reveal the manner in which the devotee perceived the divine.[23] An icon from Mount Wutai depicting Mañjuśrī mounted on the back of a lion was known as the "icon of the true presence of Mañjuśrī" (*Wenshu zhenrong xiang*). Despite its materiality, the statue was believed to be able to manifest the true divinity of the bodhisattva. A monastic structure or "image hall" was then built to enshrine the icon at the very place where the bodhisattva was recorded to have been frequently encountered. Named after the icon, this image hall was called the Cloister of Mañjuśrī's True Presence (Wenshu Zhenrong Yuan), its purpose to locate the amorphous presence of the divine, realized not only in the materially bound icon but also in the space of the physical building. The hall was built on the highest ground of the monastery, at the very center of the sacred mountain area. In this symbolic and spatial functionality, the architecture mediated the ways in which the icon would be perceived, approached, and venerated, while the icon itself, in the built environment of the monastery, would in turn make the faithful feel as if they were in Mañjuśrī's true presence, at the center of his terrestrial domicile.

Monastic architecture, in its multiple capacities and functionalities, is the key to Mount Wutai's sacrality, as it developed from a natural mountain into a Buddhist one. Serving as it did a new belief system, the Buddhist monastery, as an instance of Chinese architecture, cannot be properly discussed except in the context of the new religion. Since China had never before produced a separate building style or tradition exclusively for Buddhism, a monastery could be so identified only by the monastic functions it served or the divinity it accommodated. Thus, as I examine the roles that monastic architecture played in transforming Mount Wutai, I will use the history of the sacred site to provide contextual frameworks in which this architecture can be analyzed and defined. It is in such an intercontextual investigation that we begin to see the emergence of the sacral architecture, or architecture of the sacred,[24] in medieval China, one that was developed and built alongside the rise of Buddhism.

Beyond Physical Structure: Foguang Monastery in Its Modern and Historical Context

By its most straightforward definition, architecture is the art or practice of designing and constructing buildings, and it concerns itself most directly with the physical form, building material, and architectonic structure of buildings, built or unbuilt (as in the case of architectural plans, representations, the imagination, etc.). Architecture also refers to various "ideas" of the building—as dwelling or living space, sacred or secular, real or utopian.[25] Sacral architecture incorporates both these definitions, in that it goes beyond physical structure, encompassing building as defined, portrayed, or revealed in text, legend, image, or vision in direct relation to the discourse of sacrality. Monasteries are often discussed as mere architectural "containers" for the actions of a religious community. Yet, as Buddhist textual records testify, a monastery is also described in terms such as the setting of the natural or urban landscape; its contents of relics, statuary, paintings, and powerful deities that fill the architectural space; and the history accrued through such means as hagiography, divine presence, and imperial recognition.[26] Monastic architecture in this regard is not just a building structure but an integral component in dialogue and dialectic relation with other monastic components, which together gave form and substance to the monastery as a religious/sacred institution—in medieval China, as elsewhere.

A diary left by an unnamed pilgrim who traveled to Mount Wutai in the early tenth century includes an itinerary of his visit. Although fragmentary, it provides a glimpse into one of the most famous monasteries of the sacred site, the Monastery of Buddha's Radiance (Foguangsi):[27]

> After traveling for forty *li* I arrived at Foguang Monastery. At night on the twenty-seventh day of the fifth lunar month, I witnessed [at the monastery] luminous lanterns in a cloud form [flying] in the dark [sky] eighteen times. Meanwhile [I also worshiped at] the Main Buddha Hall, a building with a seven-bay facade, containing a Buddha triad in the middle, flanked by Bodhisattva Mañjuśrī on one side and Bodhisattva Samantabhadra on the other. At the Maitreya Pavilion, a three-story building with a seven-bay facade, [I venerated] seventy-two worthies, ten thousand bodhisattvas, and sixteen Lohans. There were also the relics pagoda of Monk Jietuo [561–642] and another one for Suozigu [n.d.]. They were said to have been Mañjuśrī and Samantabhadra reincarnated [in this world]. The grand building of the Constant Abiding

> [Changzhu] Cloister had a five-bay facade; its upper story was used as a sutra repository, and the lower section, living quarters for the assembly, daily lodging more than five hundred people. In addition, the monastery also had many other rooms, corridors, halls, various structures, and several other cloisters; there were simply too many to count every meritorious devotion and ritual taking place inside the monastery.[28]

As suggested in this pilgrim's account, the monastic architecture at Foguang Monastery appeared as part of its overall religious scene and landscape. Not separate from visions (e.g., flying lanterns), icons, or legends, the "sacral architecture" included the ritual ensemble and the ambience, helping the practitioner envision the transcendent reality of Mount Wutai and experience the holy presence of the presiding bodhisattva.

Focusing beyond the physical building and its textual representation, therefore, this book tracks and analyzes the building of the monastic architecture of the site from idea to actuality as a process of thinking, expression, and practice of the religion. Also, because representation operates in motifs and vocabularies, how the monastery was represented cannot be separated from the motifs and vocabularies with which it was discussed and built, nor the motifs and vocabularies from the monastery. It is thus important, when we consider the study of medieval Chinese architecture, to do so with this new set of agendas in mind.

To students of Chinese architecture, Mount Wutai will not be unfamiliar, for it retains one of the nation's oldest surviving timber structures, the Great Buddha Hall (Da Fodian) at Foguang Monastery (plate 1), the same monastery visited by the tenth-century pilgrim quoted above.[29] Dating from 857, the Great Buddha Hall is one of only four timber structures surviving from Tang-era China, and it is the grandest in scale and highest ranked in structural style. It was brought to light in 1937 by members of the Institute for Research in Chinese Architecture (Zhongguo Yingzao Xueshe) led by the preeminent architectural historian Liang Sicheng (1901–72).[30] Its "discovery" in the modern era as the then earliest surviving example of Chinese traditional timber structure guaranteed it attention then, and continues to attract it today. Its reentry into history in the 1930s, however, also brought it into a completely different context. Architectural historians since Liang Sicheng have focused on its timber-frame structure. The building was studied carefully, its structure examined and compared with the official medieval building manual, *Treatise on Architectural Methods* (Yingzao fashi), promulgated in 1103, with regard to its building method and formal features.[31] Liang produced precise and detailed diagrams (figs. I.1a, I.1b) to illustrate the structural principles and form, facilitating a more abstract analysis, which transformed an age-old building craft into a modern discipline. With its striking profile and style, the Great Buddha Hall at Foguang Monastery embodies the excellence of its historical heritage, in which it serves as the "iconic prototype" of its own architectural tradition and pedigree.[32] For Liang Sicheng and many of his colleagues and later students, rather than merely a Buddhist monastic complex, Foguang Monastery was more importantly

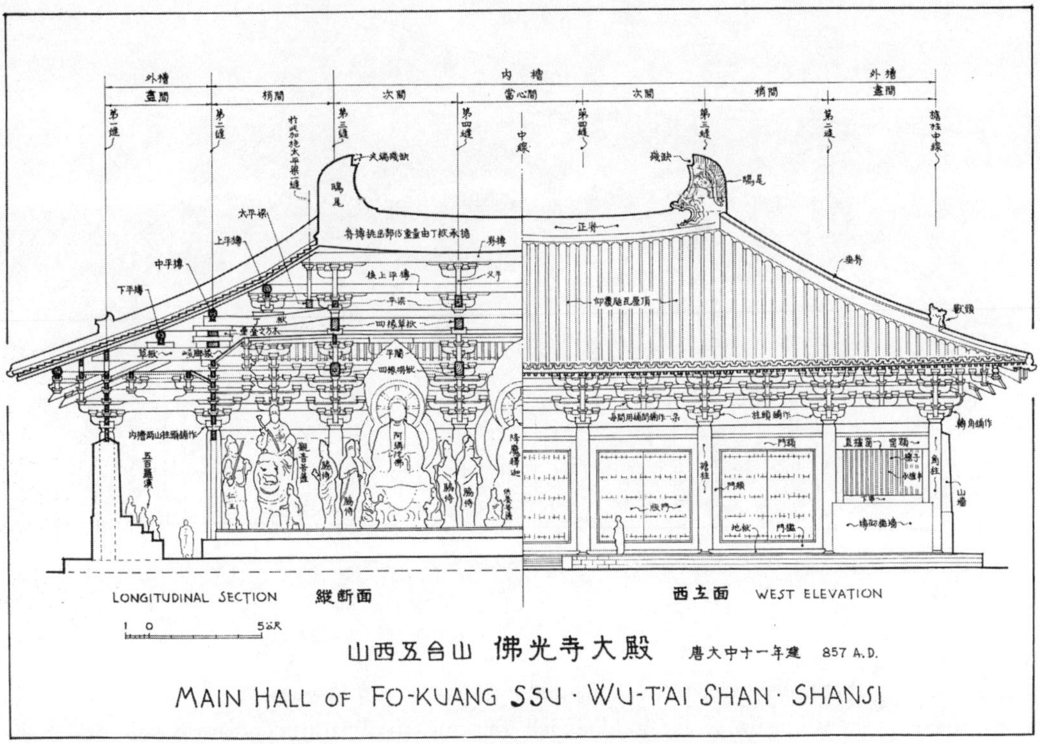

FIGURE I.1a. Section and elevation of the Great Buddha Hall, Foguang Monastery, Mount Wutai. 857 CE. From Liang, *A Pictorial History of Chinese Architecture*, fig. 24j. Diagram courtesy of Lin Zhu.

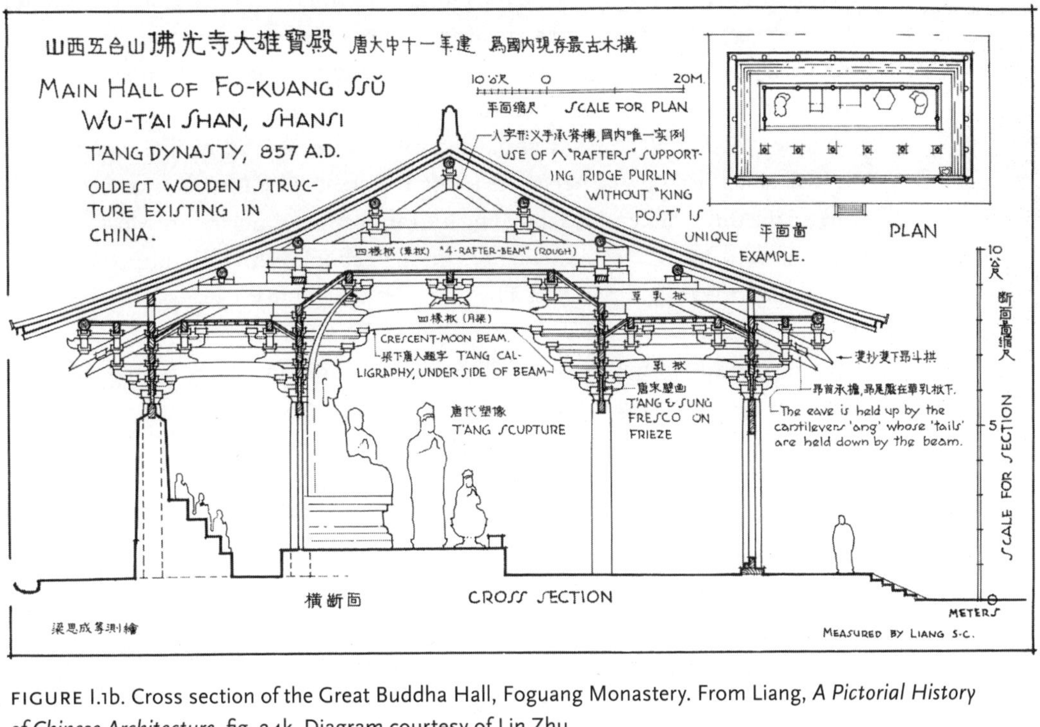

FIGURE I.1b. Cross section of the Great Buddha Hall, Foguang Monastery. From Liang, *A Pictorial History of Chinese Architecture*, fig. 24k. Diagram courtesy of Lin Zhu.

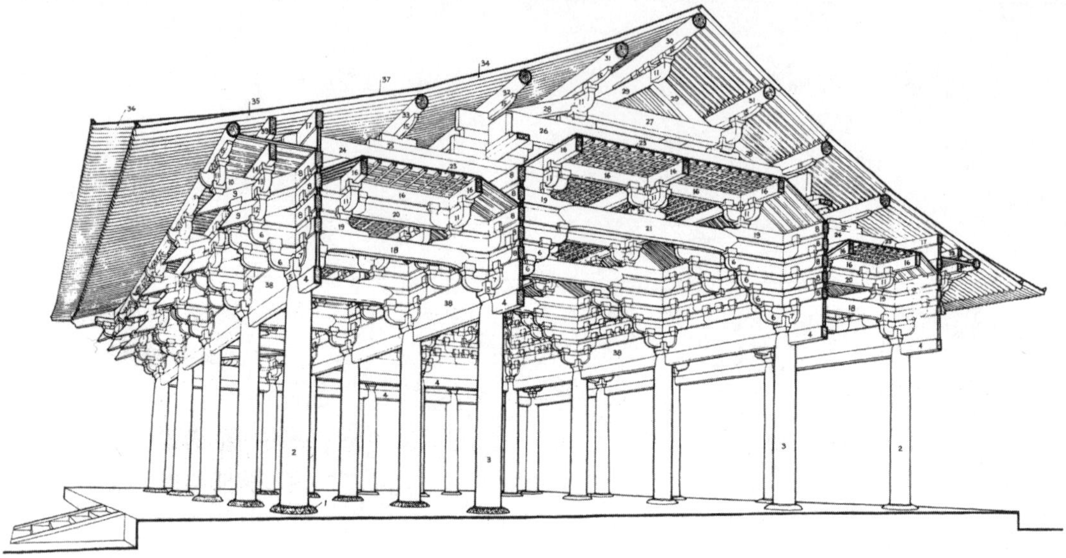

FIGURE I.2. Orthogonal view of the Great Buddha Hall, Foguang Monastery. After Fu Xinian, "Wutaishan Foguangsi jianzhu," fig. 4. Diagram courtesy of Fu Xinian.

a *locus classicus* in China's architectural history. It is in this new, modern context that the significance of the building was discovered anew.

While the Great Buddha Hall continues to captivate scholars as a cultural relic, the modern discovery of Foguang Monastery also raises questions. The Great Buddha Hall was investigated in an analytic framework that was largely predetermined by a focus on its structural system and historical evolution, and the terms of analysis were much aligned with the modernist emphasis of Liang Sicheng's times on structural rationalism and formalism.[33] After Liang's death in 1972, though the historical circumstances greatly changed, the structural approach and vocabulary that Liang introduced continued to be dominant. The structural framework of Chinese wooden buildings is visualized even more rigorously, illustrated in the fully detailed orthogonal perspective (fig. I.2) created by Liang's students, which turned the three-dimensional building into an abstract simulacrum. Most recently, from 2004 to 2006, a research team from the School of Architecture at Tsinghua University (the program founded by Liang Sicheng in 1946), using X-ray scanning tools, conducted a scientific investigation of the Great Buddha Hall, measuring each structural component and its current condition and revealing different modular systems used throughout the building.[34] We have gained much more knowledge since 1937 about the structural skeleton of the Buddha Hall and its importance in the history of Chinese wooden architecture, but at stake is the cultural and religious context inscribed in the skin of the building, so to speak, which has faded almost into oblivion.

The Great Buddha Hall is a single-story structure, seven bays across and four bays deep, standing on a foundation of 34 by 17.66 meters.[35] It matches the scale of the main image hall described in the travel diary of the tenth-century pilgrim. As the diary recorded, the Great Buddha Hall contains the original triad of the three Buddhas, Śākyamuni, Amitābha, and Maitreya, flanked by two bodhisatt-

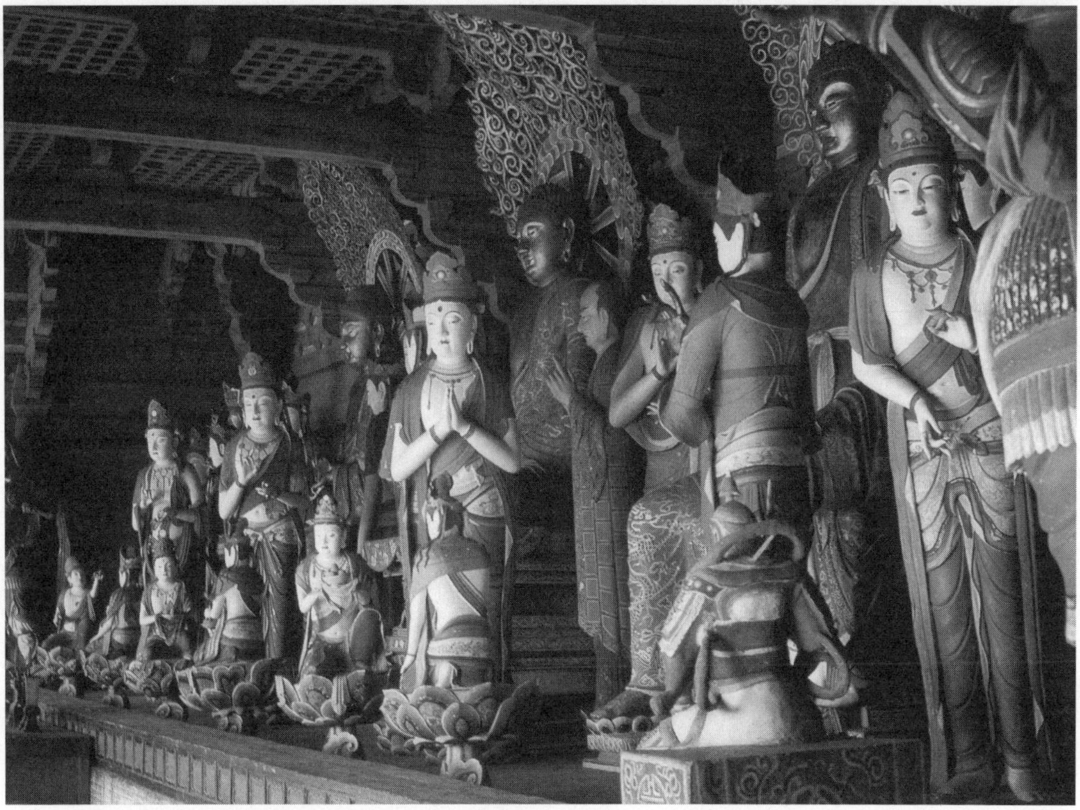

FIGURE I.3. Main icons enshrined in the Great Buddha Hall, Foguang Monastery. 857 CE. The central three main deities visible in back row, from right to left, are the Buddhas Maitreya, Śākyamuni, and Amitābha; they are in turn flanked by the bodhisattvas Mañjuśrī at the farther end of the altar and Samantabhadra at the closer end outside the picture. Each of the three main Buddhas is also flanked by two attending (standing) bodhisattvas and two kneeling bodhisattvas presenting offerings. From Chai and Chai, *Shanxi gudai caisu*, 37. Photograph by permission of Wenwu Press.

vas, Mañjuśrī and Samantabhadra (fig. I.3). Also surviving at Foguang Monastery (fig. I.4) are an early-Tang relics pagoda (*shenta*), likely one of the two pagodas mentioned in the diary, and two sutra pillars (*jingchuang*), one of which bears the date 857 and engravings of a *dhāraṇi* sutra pivotal in the history of Mount Wutai.[36] A smaller structure, the Hall of Mañjuśrī (Wenshu Dian), enshrining a statue of Mañjuśrī riding a lion (fig. I.5), was built in 1137 during the first revival period in the monastery's post-Tang history. The statue, in an iconic style of the bodhisattva's "true presence" specifically tied to the sacred mountain, may have been the reason Foguang Monastery was later renamed the Chan Monastery of the True Presence of Buddha's Radiance (Foguang Zhenrong Chanyuan), as stated on the large Ming-period plaque hanging over the central entrance of the Great Buddha Hall (fig. I.6; see also fig. C.2).[37]

Stepping outside the monastery in 1937, Liang Sicheng was awed by the magnificent view of the mountains surrounding the Tang monastic complex. A similar

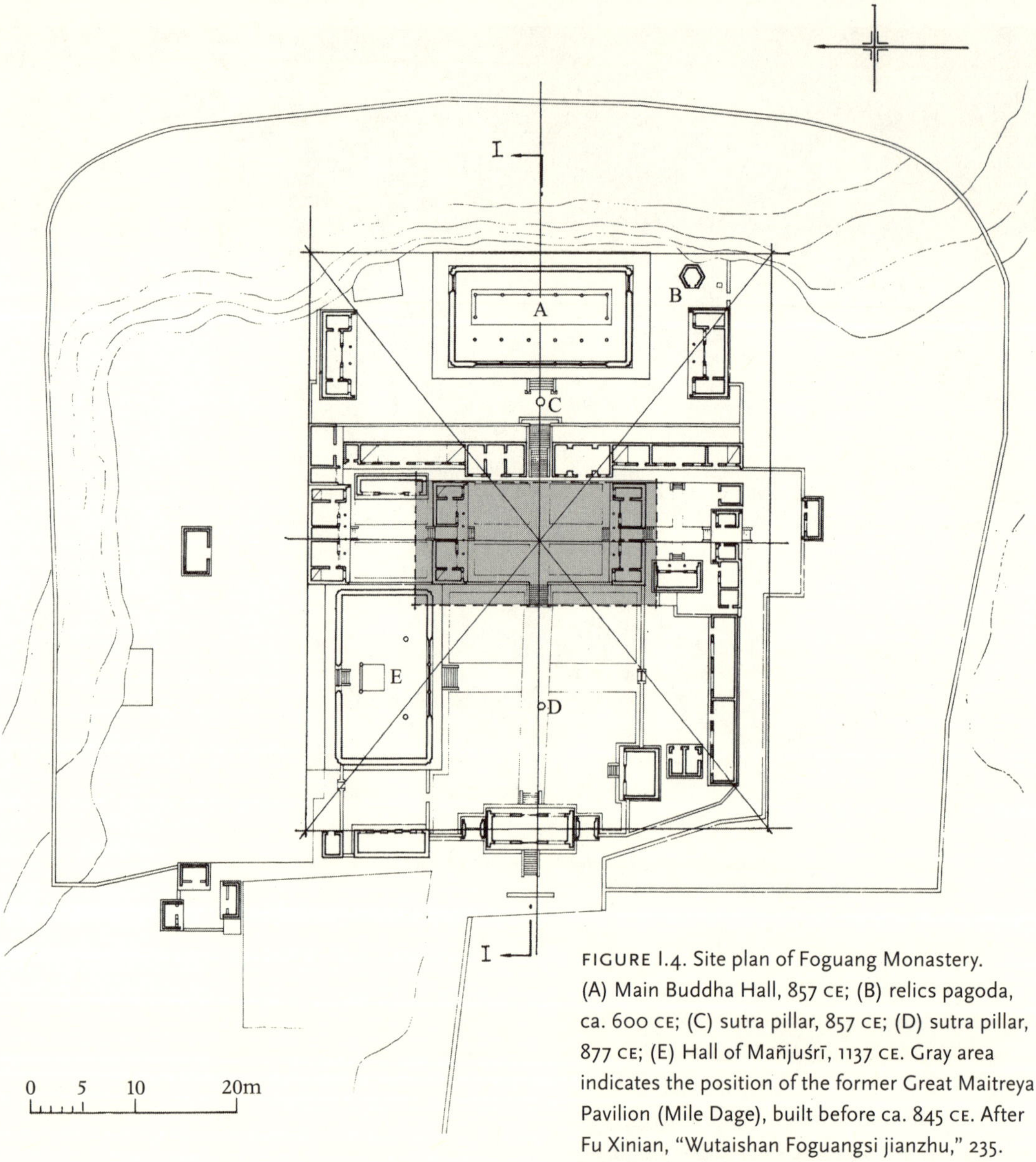

FIGURE I.4. Site plan of Foguang Monastery. (A) Main Buddha Hall, 857 CE; (B) relics pagoda, ca. 600 CE; (C) sutra pillar, 857 CE; (D) sutra pillar, 877 CE; (E) Hall of Mañjuśrī, 1137 CE. Gray area indicates the position of the former Great Maitreya Pavilion (Mile Dage), built before ca. 845 CE. After Fu Xinian, "Wutaishan Foguangsi jianzhu," 235. Diagram courtesy of Fu Xinian.

landscape also inspired Zhencheng (1546–1617), author of the Ming gazetteer of Mount Wutai, to describe the monasteries at the sacred site in 1595: "Of the monasteries at Mount Wutai, some are embraced amid the five peaks, some emerge between mountains, some arise from rocky peaks, and some soar high atop the clouds. Pavilions and towers of monasteries appear in the misty air; temple bells chime and resound in the smoke of incense fragrance. The Golden Pavilion floats aloft as if a heavenly city manifests itself. . . . In such an inconceivable realm the sacred land looms miraculously."[38] Chiming bells, smoking incense, and monastic buildings were all part of the sacred landscape of Mount Wutai, creating a reli-

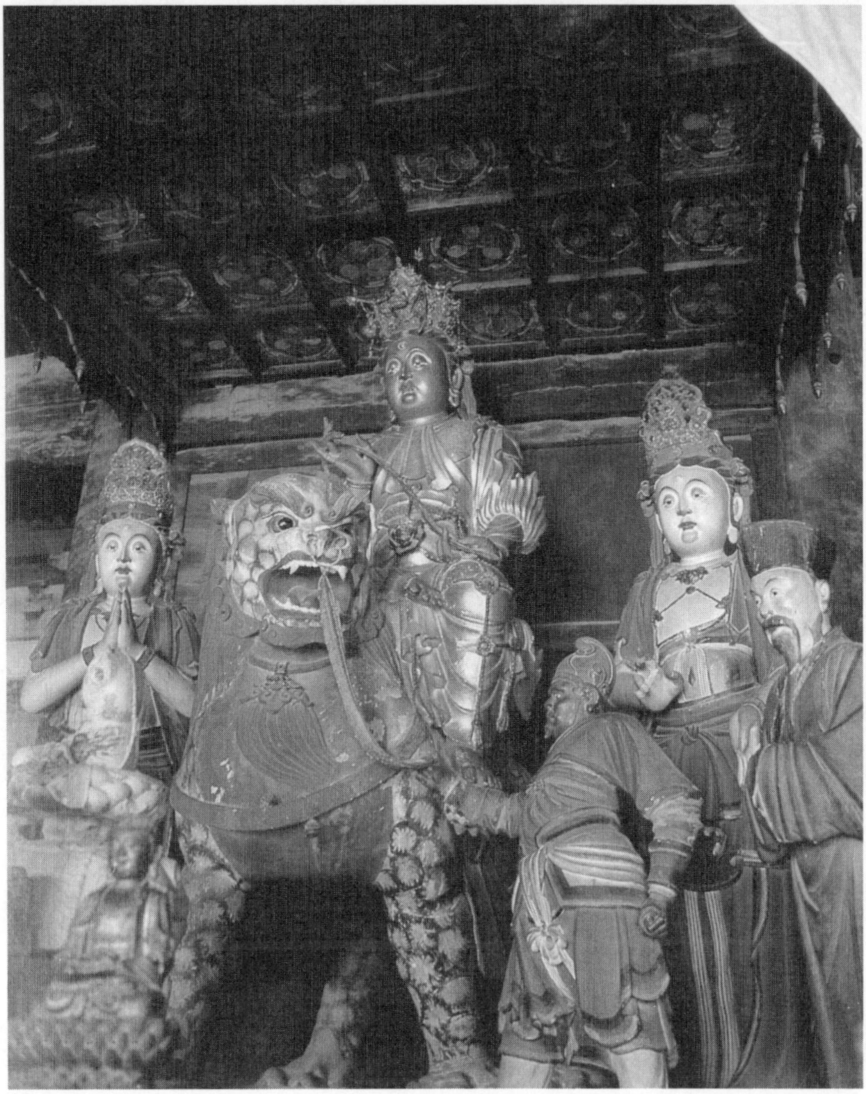

FIGURE I.5. The "true-presence" (*zhenrong*) icon of Mañjuśrī riding a lion, Hall of Mañjuśrī (Wenshu Dian), Foguang Monastery. 1137 CE. From Liang, "Ji Wutaishan Foguangsi de jianzhu," *Wenwu cankao ziliao*, pl. 42.

gious aura and aspiring to the inconceivable. But only through monasteries did the sense of the sacredness of the site become more perceivable and experiential.

The intimate correlation between the mountain and monasteries at Mount Wutai is suggested in an enormous mural that depicts a panorama of Mount Wutai inside a tenth-century image cave in Mogao near Dunhuang, an important Buddhist center lying at the western border of Tang China, approximately three thousand kilometers from Mount Wutai.[39] Ten building complexes labeled as "great" (*da*) monasteries are depicted across the width of the mural, and among them is a walled cloister enclosing a two-story building and identified in the accompanying cartouche as Foguang Monastery (plate 2). Neither isolated from the surroundings nor separated from a large monastic network, Foguang Monastery was built within the sacred terrain of Mount Wutai and the historical matrix of the site. Yet Foguang Monastery as depicted in the mural bears no resemblance to any of the existing

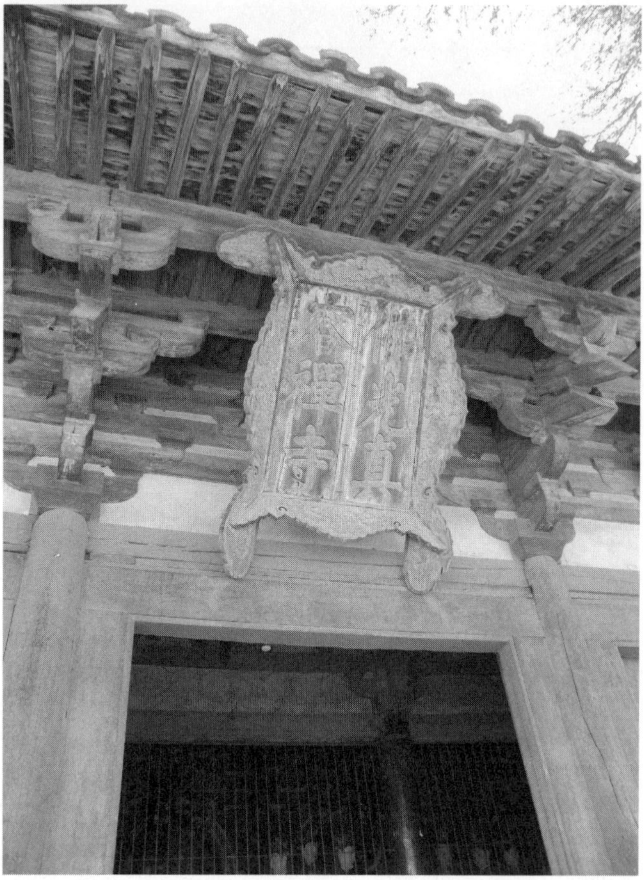

FIGURE I.6. Name plaque inscribed "The Chan Monastery of the True Presence of Buddha's Radiance," over the entrance to the Great Buddha Hall, Foguang Monastery. 1614 CE. Photograph by author.

structures; in fact, the Mount Wutai in the visual representation yields no obvious cartographic reference to its reality except for the five sacred peaks. As a representation, however, the mural with its visual vocabularies and tropes (see chapter 6) was meant to transform the sacred site into an "image" that mediates between viewer and the depicted architecture, spatial practice, spiritual experience, and the evoked visions, all together as a holistic experience. Integrated in the cohesive and hegemonic landscape of the sacred mountain, the monastic architecture in both reality and imagery served to structure physically, symbolically, and representationally the access to the sacrality of the site.

To address the gap between our understanding of Chinese Buddhist monasteries and the ways monasteries were represented in history as sanctified institutions or numinous sites,[40] this book brings both textual and visual representations of the monastery into discussion. Yet monasteries at Mount Wutai were also physical structures built at the mountain site as part of the religious landscape in both architectural and topographic terms. The physical site, topography, and building structures, forms, and practices all substantiate the perceptual representation and conceptual discourse of monasteries. Outside the scope of this study are the building styles, structural details, and trades involved in timber-frame architecture in medieval China, the analysis of which would in any case be limited by the small number of examples surviving from this early period. Instead, I concentrate on identifying the ways in which the Buddhist "sacral architecture" developed in medieval China, in order to illuminate both the ontological and contextual roles of monasteries—as built, recorded, visualized, or imagined—in the historical trajectory in which Mount Wutai was transformed into *the* sacred mountain.

Toward an Intercontextual Study of Monastic Architecture at Mount Wutai

Even before the excursion taken by Liang Sicheng and his colleagues into the mountainous area of Mount Wutai in 1937, several Japanese scholars had already ventured to the sacred site, photographing mountain scenery and monastic buildings, including the Great Buddha Hall of Foguang Monastery. As early as the 1920s, Japanese scholars in Buddhist history and art and architectural history had published articles about Mount Wutai.[41] What most interested them were the long-standing history of the sacred mountain and the structures and artifacts surviving in situ that witnessed the rise and fall of the ancient site. Their photographs and writings depicted monasteries at Mount Wutai as part of the site's religious history, activities, and topography (fig. I.7). But detailed research on specific monasteries or a historical overview of monasteries built at Mount Wutai had not yet been attempted.

The first monograph to take a more inclusive approach, aiming to provide a historical survey of Mount Wutai's past and present, is the landmark work *Godaisan* (Mount Wutai), coauthored by two Japanese scholars, Ono Katsutoshi (1905–88) and Hibino Takeo (b. 1914) in 1942.[42] Realizing the enormous spatial expansion of the mountain range and the wealth of its visible and invisible histories and legends, Ono and Hibino decided to divide their book into two sections: the first gives a history of the site (*rekishi*), and the second, their personal observations of Mount Wutai as they found it, written in the form of travelogue (*kikō*).[43] Brought together, the two halves ably recapitulate the long history of Mount Wutai. Informative and historical as it is, however, this first book-length research on Mount Wutai fits better in the category of the traditional gazetteer, although supplemented and updated with photographs, building diagrams, site plans, maps, and bibliography. The two different sections also testify to the fact that Mount Wutai in the early twentieth century was already a very different site from the medieval one that the authors tried to retrieve.

At the start of the Qing dynasty (1644–1911), indeed, Mount Wutai was revitalized after a short period of decline but with a rather different religious outlook.[44] The Manchu emperors, pious believers of Tibetan Buddhism (which like Chinese Buddhism regards Mount Wutai as an extremely important sacred site), supported the monastery authorities and sponsored extensive building projects in the mountains, converting major monasteries into centers of Tibetan Buddhist practice throughout the seventeenth and eighteenth centuries. The increasing presence of Tibetan Buddhism decisively changed the practices, traditions, and schools with

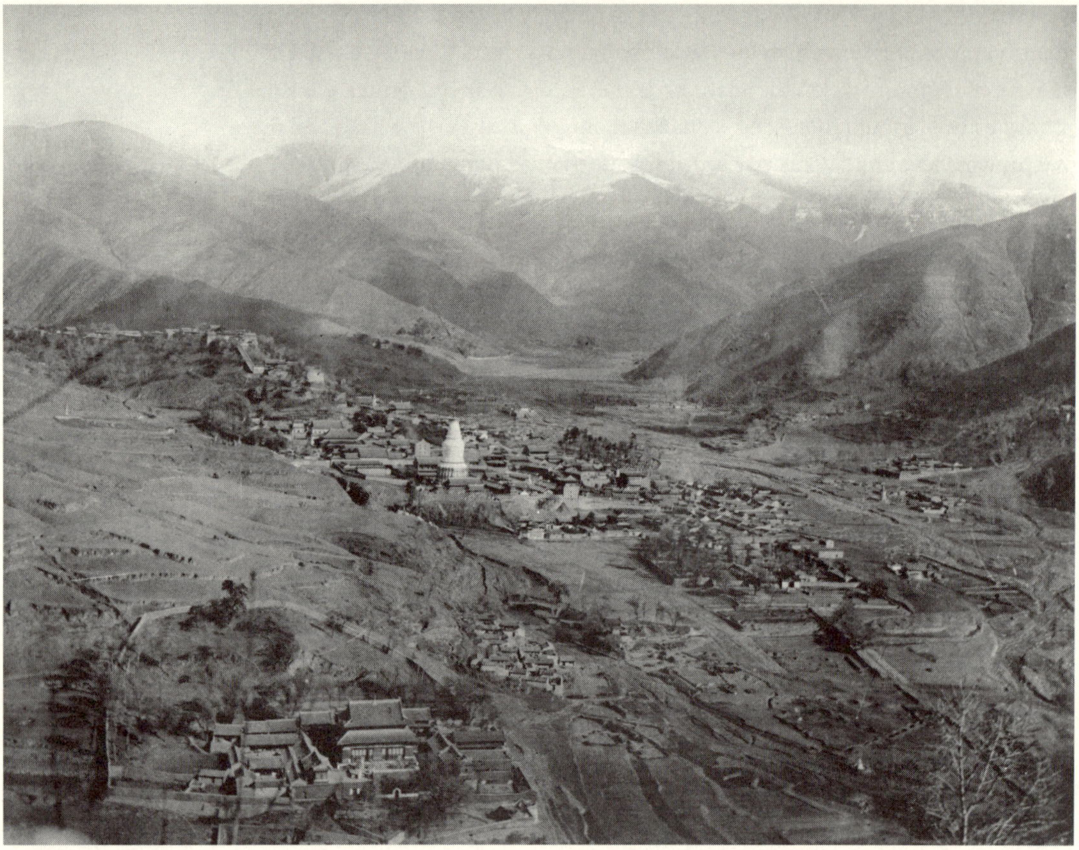

FIGURE I.7. View of the valley and the town of Taihuai, the geographic center of Mount Wutai and the site of its largest monastic complex, Great Huayan Monastery (Da Huayansi), during the Tang period. Early 20th century. From Tokiwa and Sekino, *Shina bukkyō shiseki*, vol. 5, pl. 4.

which the monasteries had previously been associated. Over time, Mount Wutai was altered so much that its present state little resembles the well-documented religious landscape when the sacred mountain cult first flourished in the Tang dynasty; the physical structure remains, in the five peaks, the famous (numinous) places, and buildings and icons such as the Great Buddha Hall and statues inside Foguang Monastery. The challenge for any historical project of the sacred mountain is how to reinstate its historical past and reconstruct the earlier context buried under layers of its new political and religious fabric.[45]

Accordingly, this book examines the monastery in three critical and interrelated contexts. First, monasteries at Mount Wutai were built foremost as efficacious places of practice. The monastic layout, icons, buildings, and topography were all important constituents of each monastery, organized to create a liminal space for encountering the divine and collaboratively aspiring to the transcendent. Second, monasteries at the sacred mountain were never isolated; they were part of a large network created by different factors, most prominently the pilgrimage. The monastic network or system restructured the ways in which mountain terrains were conceived and the sacred topography was configured. Third, each monastery was bound by the physical context of Mount Wutai—its five peaks, orientation, and range—but as a sacred site, it could not be deciphered or comprehended without monasteries that functioned as the "spatial syntax" of its sacred topography. Monasteries at Mount Wutai were not only the context of the religious practice but also the content and components of the larger sacred mountain context.

More broadly, "building a sacred mountain" as a topic of inquiry considers space, place, and building as interrelated notions, which address different ways in which monastic architecture served as a cultural intervention in the process of site making.[46] To a greater degree than other genres of art or artifacts, a building is inextricably tied to the site upon which it stands, and yet, unlike some other sacred objects (texts, relics, icons, etc.),[47] its presence and immobility activate the divine and saturate the space, turning the initially unqualified site into a particular place. Moreover, architecture in its actuality is site-specific, and since it can't be moved, it necessarily entails travel (as in pilgrimage) across space, establishing a broader spatial relation and hierarchy critical to the experience and imagination. More specifically, in Buddhism, the pilgrimage journey was often taken metaphorically as a path (*mārga*) to get from "this shore" to "the other," from this world to the next. In this regard, the liminality of the sacred mountain was not only temporal but also spatial in its topography and architecture, and those who traveled to Mount Wutai could experience the divine presence in that liminal space. The totality of the interrelations among space, place, and building made Mount Wutai more perceivable as a sacred site. Sacrality, after all, is "a category of emplacement."[48] And it is through a conception of this totality that it became possible to reproduce a Mount Wutai that takes *place* elsewhere, and by extension, to reconceptualize Mount Wutai as a particular kind of place—that of "the" monastery.

To explore the multiple contextual and functional roles of the monastery in building a sacred mountain at Mount Wutai, the book's chapters revolve around twin foci: monastery and mountains. Each focus has its separate tradition and history, within the larger context of Buddhist expansion in China, for certainly, monasteries had already been built at mountains elsewhere in China when Mount Wutai became identified as a Buddhist sacred mountain. The book is thus conceived to explore the intricate and changing relations between monastery and mountains that not only led to the building of Mount Wutai but also developed it into one of the most important features of Buddhism in medieval China.

Chapters 1 and 2 answer two related questions: How was "building" monasteries at Mount Wutai from the fifth and sixth centuries onward different from the earlier building efforts, and why may these monasteries be seen as the pivotal means of intervention that changed people's perception of the mountains? In answer, I will show the monastery as a particular place where the practitioner began to encounter and understand the presence of the initially foreign divinity, and posit that Mount Wutai, recognized as *the* sacred mountain, was developed against a specific historical and regional background. Chapters 3, 4, and 5 reconstruct the history of the bodhisattva cult at Mount Wutai during the seventh through the ninth centuries. Each of these chapters, using one major monastery as the focus of analysis, takes on a particular factor—topography, vision, and iconography—in its exploration of how the monastery was conceived and built to mediate critical aspects of the bodhisattva cult at the sacred mountain. Together these three chapters suggest that the development of Mount Wutai during the period when the bodhisattva worship climaxed is a history of its sacral architecture. From a different viewpoint, chapter 6 investigates the pilgrimage at Mount Wutai. As a kind of "spatial practice," the increasingly popular pilgrimage conceptually transformed the mountain site—its five sacred peaks and monasteries—into a structured totality, conducive to both literary and visual representation. Eventually Mount Wutai could no longer be experienced without the mediation of this representation, the "metamonastery," which reveals the divine origin and presence, vision, ideology, and history—the essential components and qualities of monasteries that built Mount Wutai into the Buddhist sacred mountain.

As the first monograph dedicated to the early history of Mount Wutai in medieval China, *Building a Sacred Mountain* posits a complex historical process that involved factors both intrinsic and extrinsic to the mountains, arguing that this complexity cannot be properly unraveled without taking into account the functioning and ontological role of the monastery in the transformation of Mount Wutai into a sacred mountain. The book thus offers a methodological departure from previous scholarship on Mount Wutai by shifting the focus of analysis from the site to the sight of divinity and from mountains to the monastery, a shift that enables us to investigate both the religious and the cultural inventions that made Mount Wutai a sacred site. In using the monastery as an analytical lens, the discussion is not limited to the physical structure of architecture but includes icons, murals, space, and ritual, as well as topography and vision, stressing not only the monastery's material properties and liturgical functions but also its visionary and discursive potentials as understood in medieval Buddhism. To a great extent, *Building a Sacred Mountain* challenges the current scholarship in the history of traditional Chinese architecture by introducing an intercontextual strategy or approach—architecture is always a context itself and the content of a larger context—to explore the multivalent significance of Buddhist architecture other than just its building structure. The timber frame of a monastic structure can be distinguished in terms of regional or period style and practice, but often not its particular religious or spiritual meaning, which, in a historical process, was layered onto the structure by inscribing, naming, decorating, or spatializing it for particular monastic purposes. In examining the layers of meanings of monastic architecture at Mount Wutai, this book provides an alternative perspective from which to study and write the history of Chinese sacral architecture in medieval China.

CHAPTER ONE

Building the Monastery, Locating the Sacred Presence

Upon seeing the building, one is inspired to take vows to become a Buddhist; looking at it, one no longer thinks of returning. A building as such that increases one's meritorious rewards and promotes one's goodness is called "monastery."

—Daoshi, *Jade Grove of the Dharma Garden* (Fayuan zhulin)

In 248 CE, during the Three Kingdoms Period (220–65), a monk of Sogdian ancestry named Kang Senghui (d. 280) arrived in Jianye, present-day Nanjing, the capital of the Wu Kingdom in the south. Buddhism was not yet popular then in southern China, and Kang, determined to establish the practice there, "built a hermitage, set up images, and performed rituals."[1] One version of the story tells that when he was interrogated by the suspicious Wu ruler, Sun Quan (182–252), who demanded evidence to prove the divinity of the foreign god he worshiped, Kang replied, "It has been more than a thousand years since the Thus-Come-One [*rulai*][2] passed away, but the bone relics he left behind still shine divinely and beyond measure. Long ago King Aśoka erected as many as 84,000 stupas [to hold the Buddha's relics], for building stupas was the means to manifest the salvific influence [of the Buddha] bequeathed to later generations."[3] Kang was referring to the tale of the Indian king Aśoka (ca. 304–232 BCE), the devout and ideal Buddhist ruler who, with the help of *yakṣas* (nature spirits), distributed the relics of the Buddha throughout the Indian subcontinent in a single day in order to promote Buddhism.[4] Sun was skeptical but was willing to build a stupa if Kang could indeed produce relics and prove himself; if he failed, he would receive due punishment. After Kang performed several concentrated rituals and said prayers in a quiet room for twenty-one days, his entreaties were answered: relics miraculously appeared, rattling in a bottle and emanating a five-color radiance. Sun Quan held up the bottle and tipped the relics onto a bronze tray, but they smashed the tray as soon as they struck it. Sun was awed, uttering, "Such a rare omen!" Keeping his promise to enshrine the relics, Sun subsequently built a stupa, which then became the first Buddhist monastery, named Monastery of the First Built (Jianchusi).[5]

While the story is a fabrication written retrospectively to account for the early patronage and spread of Buddhism in southern China, it nonetheless epitomizes the basic components and pattern of reception, understanding, and practice of this initially foreign religion in the first centuries after its arrival in China. It also points to the importance

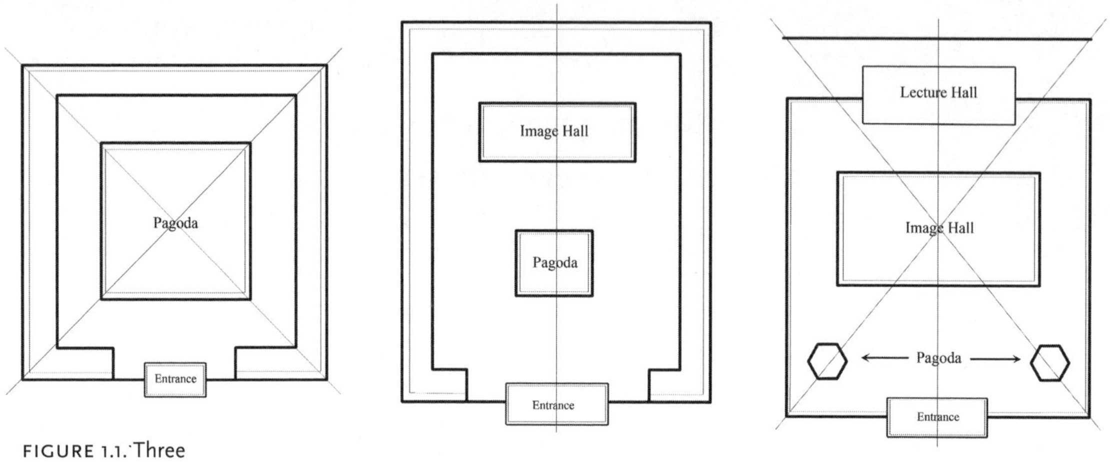

FIGURE 1.1. Three basic layouts of early Buddhist monastic compounds based on the position of the stupa or pagoda and its relation with the main image hall. Diagram by author.

of the divine presence in the origin of the monastery, as manifested in the tangible form of images and relics, as well as to a particular architecture built to accommodate the Buddhist divinity. Before Buddhism, neither relics nor images were worshiped religiously in China, nor was the stupa (or pagoda, its narrower and taller counterpart in East Asia) a traditional building type. In the centuries following the founding of Jianchu Monastery, other monasteries were built and various forms of practice developed, including liturgical ritual, precept observation, and icon-focused meditation and visualization, along with prolific translation of sutras and the production of images. All this activity firmly established Buddhism as a "practice religion" in China.[6] Monastic architecture in China also developed, beginning with the pagoda for enshrining relics. At the same time, Buddhist monasticism became more and more elaborate, following monastic regulations and liturgical procedures devised to assist practitioners to see and comprehend the divine presence of the Buddha in a monastic, that is, ritualistic environment. As the architectural layout and space of the monastery evolved, it was increasingly perceived as a sanctioned, effective field of religious practice. By the end of the sixth century it was within the four walls of the monastery that the divine was observed, venerated, and reenacted. In other words, monastic practice was intimately correlated with architecture during this early period in the shaping of Buddhist monasticism, centered on the conception and experience of the divine presence.

Scholarly research on Buddhist monastic architecture in its initial stage in China is relatively sparse—understandably, since there is a lack of surviving material.[7] The primary approach has been textual, augmented by evidence from archaeological sites and building remains. Much of the research has also looked at the building types of early Indian Buddhist construction—stupa, *caitya* (worship hall), and *vihāra* (assembly hall)—and how these were transmitted eastward and eventually adapted to a Chinese architectural style and vocabulary. The general consensus among scholars is that monastic architecture developed in three stages, transitioning from a stupa/pagoda-centered layout, to a binary plan of pagoda and additional Buddha (image) hall, to a monastic precinct centered on the Buddha hall (fig. 1.1).[8] In terms of spatial configuration, the earlier plan centered on a stupa/pagoda gradually gave way to an axial plan, with a symmetrical disposition of buildings within a four-sided enclosure—in accordance with long-standing practices in Chinese architecture.

While this account of early monastic architecture is viable and its general conclusion still holds, the implications in terms of the "content" of the early Buddhist monastery is quite limited.[9] For instance, some have argued that the stupa, which was the most important symbolic structure of early Chinese Buddhism but which originated outside of China, posed challenges to the Chinese tradition of architecture because of its height and shape.[10] In this view, early Chinese monastic architecture made critical changes in the stupa to answer these challenges: the foreign-style building was gradually adapted to conform more to China's own multistoried architecture of the period and eventually became the tower-like pagoda known today; its centrally located position inside the monastery was, moreover, gradually superseded by the Buddha hall. Some regard the change in the focus of monastic layout, from the stupa that held the relics to the Buddha hall that housed the icons, as resulting from a doctrinal shift in ritual focus, from relics to icons.[11] The evidence, however, seems to suggest otherwise. Beginning very early on in China, both relics and icons were primary objects of veneration, and both were equally fundamental in their role as religious agents.[12] The veneration of relics continued to be a key element in monastic practice well into the Tang dynasty (618–907), long after the main Buddha hall began to take the central position in a typical Chinese monastery. In addition, although Buddhist monastic architecture eventually developed in accordance with Chinese building conventions, its historical trajectory was most likely also determined by other important factors, in particular, issues related to creating or marking a sacred precinct where the Buddhist divine presence could be observed and worshiped.

Originally, the word "stupa" referred to a funeral mound built over cremated bodily remains, or relics (*śarīra*), a practice already existing in Vedic tradition before the Buddha's time.[13] In Buddhism, the most venerated stupas were those containing relics of Śākyamuni Buddha, preserved after his death, which was understood as his entrance into nirvana, a state of enlightenment transcending the world of cyclic reincarnation.[14] The enshrined relics were therefore a physical testimony to his spiritual transformation. As such, the stupa was never a sign of death, and veneration of the stupa (*śarīra-pūjā*) was performed as if the Buddha were still alive. Through ritual and worship, the stupa was "a symbol of divine presence" as manifestly powerful as an image of the Buddha.[15] The stupa, insofar as it possessed in its physical form the same iconic economy as the sacred presence without depicting it directly, could be viewed as "an iconography without an icon," one that evoked, as a statue or painting might, the presence of the Buddha here and now and stipulated the ritualistic actions of the practitioner around the Buddha's presence.[16]

Not surprisingly, the earliest monasteries in China were built around relic legends. In addition to the relics said to perform miracles, the alleged discoveries of "relics of Aśoka" (some of the 84,000 relics that according to legend were distributed by the Indian king Aśoka) were also reported in several urban centers, leading to the building of pagodas at the many "Aśoka monasteries" (Ayuwangsi). These relic legends might have been the result of an urge on the part of the Chinese to validate the position of the "Central Kingdom" (China) in the map of the Buddhist continent (i.e., Jambudvīpa), over which the relics were distributed.[17] More important, the marvelous appearance of the Buddha's relics on Chinese soil also confirmed that a ritual practitioner could come into Buddha's presence, as Kang Senghui did so many years before. The consequent building project at the site of the miracle served to unite the presence with the locality and to connect the architecture to the site, so the practitioner might partake in the presence of the Buddha in the here and now. The application of the Chinese term, *si*, for Buddhist monasteries captures this point precisely. Used as early as the third century CE, *si* designated specifically "the very place where a foreign deity was present," in contrast to *ci*, which referred to temples for local deities.[18] Making this presence perceivable is at the heart of the early development of Buddhist monasticism and architecture, working in tandem with each other and with monastic disciplines in the built environment.

As Buddhism developed in China, indeed, divine presence was no longer limited to relics. Alongside the miraculous stories of found relics, there grew up stories of found images, as in the so-called Aśoka images (*Ayuwang xiang*), often described in early Buddhist texts as golden statues in the Indian style, extrapolated as originating from the devout Indian king's dissemination of the belief.[19] Other images included steles with Sanskrit inscriptions, or parts of Indian stupas—finials or golden discs, for example—that were found by chance; their dislocation and appearance in China attracted native patrons and eventually led to the building of monasteries.[20] This "sacred archaeology" placed the sacrality of the foreign religion firmly in China and thus established the country as the land of the Buddha.[21] More specifically, each monastery, marking the locus of the Buddha's presence, not only functioned as an efficacious place for spiritual pursuit but itself partook in the spiritual quality of the divine presence as sacred place. It is not unusual to read about radiant statues glowing through the night inside the image hall and icons arriving of their own volition to reside at specific monasteries. In the monasteries of this early period, agencies (i.e., relics and icons), story, ritual, and place of the divinity could not be clearly separated.

The early development of Buddhist monastic architecture in China is intricately connected to the content of monastic practice and spirituality evolving around the issue of divine presence. This emphasis on presence highlights not only the religious function of presence but also the anxiety of Chinese Buddhists about living in a time and place without the Buddha. Seeing the Buddha here and now, or any other deities in the enlarged Mahayana pantheon after Buddhism became transmitted eastward, compensated for the spatiotemporal distance from the original sources, lent authority to particular monastic orders, or *saṅghas*, and sanctioned their spiritual disciplines and practice. Monastic architecture that developed in tandem with the evolving Chinese Buddhist monasticism would necessarily in some way be indicative of the monastic spirituality and expressive of its religious ideology—as is suggested in the definition of a monastery that appears in the epigraph to this chapter, from the scholar-monk Daoshi in his encyclopedic work *Jade Grove of the Dharma Garden,* compiled in 668. Unfortunately, the dearth of surviving evidence has prevented us from substantiating in detail the direct connection between monasticism and the monastic architecture that was designed at this early stage to promote and facilitate it. What can be claimed, however, is that the early monastic architecture did not evolve along a simple trajectory (i.e., from the pagoda to image hall), but reflected the ways in which the legend, ritual, and place were correlated to help the practitioner comprehend the sacred presence. It is through this correlation that we may investigate how monastic architecture structured monasticism spatially and symbolically within its built environment.

Monastery: The "Sacred Presence" in Devotional and Liturgical Buddhism

The third through the sixth centuries were a transformative period in China, and critical in the development of Buddhist monasticism.[22] After the fall of the Han dynasty and before the Sui-Tang unification—the period of the Wei, Jin, and Northern and Southern dynasties (220–581)—China was divided among short-lived political regimes engaged in constant military conflict and warfare, and none of the regimes conquered more than half of China's territory.[23] This social and political instability likely would have encouraged people to seek spiritual refuge; Buddhism, which offered universal salvation, seemed to have attracted Chinese followers and garnered support from regional rulers under these circumstances. Monastic communities were established in several urban centers in both the north and south and so began to change the religious landscape in China.[24] Although the textual evidence about early monastic communities is less than clear, an emphasis on spiritual praxis in both ritual and devotional forms seems to have been a major part of monastic life. The style of monastic discipline, characterized as "liturgical" and "devotional," suggests a growing engagement with a host of different rituals that had a strong devotional purpose.[25] Monastic spirituality was cultivated through prescribed liturgical procedures and meditative instructions—for example, the veneration of Buddhas and bodhisattvas, incantations, offerings, praise, vows, and confession—that engaged iconic images for the visionary experience of the divine presence. By the sixth century, monastic praxis had developed in response to the needs and circumstances of Chinese practitioners, and visionary experience with the sacred was paramount in transforming Buddhism in early medieval China.[26]

Throughout the various Buddhist traditions, devotional acts developed from the earliest forms of veneration of the historical Śākyamuni Buddha, as practiced in his lifetime and continued after his death. In the Theravāda tradition of Southeast Asia, rituals of veneration were conducted primarily through relics (as well as texts and images in later periods) to mediate the Buddha's continual and symbolic presence. This tradition maintained that the historical founder had passed out of this world and could best be accessed through "physical proximity to the remains of the Buddha."[27] In contrast, the Mahayana tradition that took root in East Asia affirmed the simultaneous existence of countless Buddhas and bodhisattvas who could interact directly with devotees, and were thus not subject to particular locations. In both traditions, the Buddha's presence received through devotional acts was held as the chief spiritual aspiration, but it is a distinctive characteristic of Mahayana Buddhism that liturgical performance was conducted as well to evoke the sacred presence of one or a host of deities, and, depending on the nature of the liturgy and its purpose, to bring about a vision of transcendent reality. The attainment of this vision in a monastic environment rests on this notion of "presence," which was essential to devotional activities of the early Buddhist period in China. Before moving ahead with the discussion of monastic practice, therefore, let us consider how the notion developed.

During the early medieval period, marvels such as the radiant and rattling relics in the legend of Jianchu Monastery were not unheard of in China. In early Chinese literature, there were fantastic fables, strange tales, and reports of supernatural occurrences, heralding a literary genre known as "recording the strange" (*zhiguai*) that was popular in the early post-Han era.[28] Working in a similar literary language and narrative structure were Buddhist miracle tales about an occult presence in instances of timely divine intervention or karmic retribution.[29] For instance, the widely celebrated Bodhisattva Avalokiteśvara (Guanyin), was often characterized as a savior because of his unfailing and immediate response (*ying*) to the urgent prayers of the devout believer. The religious economy and power of divine presence in the form of marvelous wonders or holy apparitions derived from the fact that the presence could be seen in ordinary life and not in "some specially demarcated 'sacred' realm."[30] These qualities no doubt contributed to the popularity of the bodhisattva cult during the early period.

The very same qualities, however, could undermine the authenticity of sacred presence. For not only could tales of the supernatural elicit skepticism, but too many alleged encounters with deities could dilute the efficacy (*ling*) of this presence. The rise of organized monasticism revolving around the sacred presence during this period hence can be seen as an ecclesiastic action to institutionalize the economy of presence and the issues surrounding it. This is not to say that there was a clerical strategy to subdue superstitious or cultic practices, because the learned monks in this early period were often also the experts in evoking and receiving those miracles.[31] Instead, as the monastic communities were formed and developed, monastics were meant to observe the sacred presence in a sanctioned practice and space. Indeed, because the "ideology of presence"[32] rested on both the efficacy of the presence and the karmic wholesomeness of the beholder to perceive it, monastic discipline was instituted to ensure that the presence be realized as desired. Furthermore, when properly invoked in a correct practice following ritual observance and procedure, the intended visionary experience with the divine would have an important salvific significance that other forms of divine manifestation did not.

Seeing the presence thus was not only potentially beneficial to the practitioner in his or her spiritual pursuit, but also essential to justifying the religious program and legitimizing the monastery as the place that could bring about spiritual fulfillment. The *Gaṇḍavyūha Sutra* repeatedly stresses the importance of seeing a Buddha:

> All obstructions are removed when a Buddha is seen,
> Increasing the immeasurable virtue whereby enlightenment will be attained.
> The sight of a Buddha severs all the doubts of sentient beings,
> And fulfills all purposes, mundane and transcendent.[33]

The scholar-monk Daoshi, quoted earlier in this chapter, said of the monastery that "upon seeing [*du*] it, one is inspired to take vows to become a Buddhist; [and] looking [*jian*] at it, one no longer thinks of returning."[34] The value of seeing is explicitly stated, but what is implied is that the vision of the sacred presence is attainable, once one enters the monastery. Indeed, because the monastery was built to facilitate the structured liturgical and devotional praxis that would assist the practitioner in seeing the divine, its architecture also symbolically embodied the manifestation of the divine presence and spatialized the vision of a transcendent reality.

Entering the Monastery: Spatializing the Sacred Presence

The veneration of stupas is a practice that originated in India, where it always involved material offerings and physical gestures. The most ubiquitous offerings were garlands and incense, which were dedicated along with mental or verbal recitations. A flower-offering ritual based on an early Indian tradition went as follows: The devotee first removed both shoes before entering the area of greater purity; then she or he would approach the stupa, assuming a formal posture of reverence, usually the *añjali* gesture—placing the palms of the hands together with extended fingers pointing upward. The devotee could then circumambulate the stupa clockwise three times, keeping the right arm facing the stupa as a sign of respect. She or he would pause at the four cardinal directions and perform a gesture of respect such as standing with hands in *añjali,* stooping, kneeling, or fully prostrating the body. The ritual of relic veneration, as has been pointed out, may have been modeled after acts of obeisance and material offering directed toward the Buddha during his lifetime.[35] In other words, the ritual confirms that the Buddha, after entering nirvana, could still manifest through his relics enshrined in that very stupa, but it was also the devotional act itself performed by the practitioner that made the sacred reality present. Between the presence and ritual performed to enact the presence, the sacred space around the object of veneration became perceptible.

To a surprising extent, the devotional ritual directed toward a pagoda in medieval China is consistent with that found in the roots of Theravāda tradition in India. A fifth-century sutra stipulated flowers, incense, and lamps in the devotional offering (*gongyang*) to a pagoda.[36] With concentration, it continues, the devotee

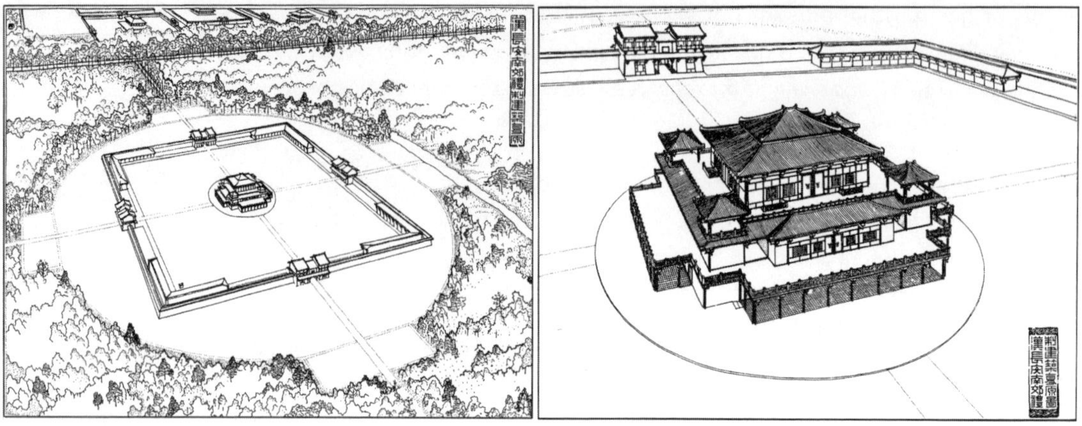

FIGURE 1.2. A reconstruction of Wang Mang's (45 BCE–23 CE) Bright Hall (Mingtang), Chang'an. Xin dynasty. 4 CE. From Wang Shiren, "Han Chang'an cheng nanjiao lizhi jianzhu," figs. 20–21.

should walk clockwise starting from the west, with the right shoulder respectfully toward the Buddha (i.e., the pagoda), for three, seven, ten, or one hundred circumambulations. This ritual performance was dedicated to the transcendent presence of the Buddha, manifested through the pagoda, by repeating and reenacting the symbolic gestural and bodily movements peculiar to the typological ritual of relics. Ritual circumambulation around a building (Sanskrit: *pradakśiṇā;* Chinese: *raoxing* or *xingdao*) was not a Chinese tradition. The plan of a pagoda, however, finds a precedent in the Bright Hall (Mingtang) in the capital city of Chang'an during Wang Mang's interregnum (9–23 CE) (fig. 1.2), an important building of state ritual constructed to symbolically embody and govern the universe. Consisting of a series of twelve rooms in a concentric plan, the Bright Hall symbolically mapped the cyclic rotation of twelve months; moving through the sequence of rooms clockwise, the ruler was able to keep the celestial time harmoniously.[37] Unlike the interior movement inside the Bright Hall, which had a greater, exterior cosmological implication, Buddhist circumambulation was primarily exterior, practiced to confirm and partake in the divine presence at the sacred center. The pagoda, marking the sacred locus of the relic depository, in turn, fixed the direction and orientation of the ritual (walking clockwise starting from the west) toward the center of the divine presence, thus turning the initially undefined space of the site into a sacred place.

The early Buddhist monastery, centered on the pagoda, differed in its spatial conception and symbolism from other architectural spaces in China. A centrally positioned pagoda creates its space by stipulating a walking circuit around the center, one that complicates the axial and symmetrical pattern. Because most early pagodas were four-sided (*sifang shi*), corresponding to the four cardinal directions,[38] a walk around the pagoda in real time—for example, three circumambulations with venerations made at the four cardinal points—brings to the sacred center a spatiotemporal dimension that bears a range of symbolic meanings. In addition to the threefold temporal order of past, present, and future, a threefold circumambulation around a pagoda invokes several other sets of three in traditional Buddhist thinking: it symbolizes and acts out one's reverence to the Three Jewels—Buddha, Dharma, and Saṅgha (Sanbao)—and brings about the eradication of the three evil afflictions, removal of the three karmic obstructions, and elimination of the three evil destinies.[39] The ritualistic and cyclical walk in circumambulation arouses one's mental and karmic state so that it may activate the symbolism implicated in the space and perceive the sacred presence upon entering the monastic precinct. The walking circuit makes the pagoda the architectural center of the monastic precinct, but it is also the spiritual path for attaining favorable karma and an act of monastic endeavor in the presence of the Buddha.

The early monasteries in China were built under varying circumstances, and many of them may have been converted from nonreligious structures and complexes.[40] The development of early monastic architecture and its expansion in subsequent centuries is hence quite difficult to chart with any accuracy. Four enclosing walls and pagoda that was centrally positioned (at least in religious terms), however, seem to have been the basic vocabulary that defined the monastic precinct and its sacred space. The spatial differentiation of inside from outside made the entry into the monastery a particular spiritual threshold. In his commentary on the *Nirvana Sutra,* Daoshi explicates: "What we call entering the monastery requires one to abandon swords, staffs, and other sundry items before making entry into the monastery. To abandon weapons is to eradicate [the three evil afflictions of] anger, malice, and hatred toward the Three Jewels; to casting away sundry items humbles one's mind for the Three Jewels. Only when these two faults are removed can one enter the monastery."[41] Entry into the monastery was then followed by a threefold circumambulation around the Buddha's presence (i.e., pagoda). The commitment to take the arduous path to spiritual liberation was further affirmed by a formal act of taking the Threefold Refuge (S: Triśaraṇa; C: Sanzigui) in the Three Jewels of Buddha, Dharma, and Saṅgha, because one was to devote oneself to becoming a Buddhist disciple, figuratively entering the monastery (*rumen*). It is from here that the sacred center at the pagoda became the point of departure for monastics to learn and to see the sacred presence.

Monasticism: Monastic Practice in the Sacred Presence

Although there is little available material evidence for monastic architecture in the earliest periods, beyond a central pagoda surrounded by four walls, the life and practice in the monastic community, the saṅgha, would have required more than just those structures. As it developed, the saṅgha was not just an assembly of world renouncers, but a religious community regulated by codified rules that would not only confer a proper or legitimate monastic identity upon those who followed them but also aid the monastic in her or his spiritual achievements. The monastic rules (i.e., discipline and behavioral codes), or *vinaya,*[42] were thus fundamental to the development of the early Buddhist monastic community. Although no "complete *vinaya*" (*guanglü*) was fully translated in Chinese until the fifth century, these religious communities were concerned from very early on with proper monastic conduct and performance, observance of the precepts, repentance, and other religious aspirations as part of the ritual and liturgical devotion observed daily in the early monastery.

A text of particular significance in this regard is a set of monastic guidelines titled *Regulations for Monastics* (Sengni guifan), compiled by Daoan (312–85). An eminent monk influential in Buddhist communities of both northern and southern China, Daoan, famously stressing the precepts as the foundation of the faith, was one of the first Buddhist masters to have undertaken translations of saṅgha regulations.[43] Daoan participated in the translation of several Sanskrit *vinaya* texts, an endeavor that lead him to realize that pragmatic guidelines specifically for the monastic community of his time were also needed. *Regulations for Monastics* thus was compiled as a supplement of the *vinaya* tailored to the experience and needs of monasteries in China; during and after Daoan's time, these guidelines were "adopted by monasteries throughout the entire country."[44] The complete text itself is no longer extant, but parts of it survive in later monastic codes, in particular, those compiled by the *vinaya* master Daoxuan (596–667), of the Tang dynasty.[45] The *Regulations for Monastics* is perhaps too early to be representative of the monastic tradition, and the fact that so little survives of it hinders any extensive application or interpretation of the text. But if examined along with other texts of later monastic codes and rules, what remains can, nevertheless, still elucidate some essential forms and structures of the monastic disciplines in early Buddhism and help identify a sacred field of spiritual cultivation definable inside the monastery.[46]

The *Regulations for Monastics* specified three different procedures for the monks to follow. First, the procedure for offering incense while circumambulating the hall, taking one's seat, and preaching the sutra; second, the procedure for daily practices to be performed at six periods of the day, including circumambulating the image, taking meals, and chanting at mealtimes; and third, the procedure for fortnightly confession and the ritual of repentance.[47] That studying and preaching the sutra precede other practices should suggest the importance of learning and wisdom in the monastic training. The second procedure concerns routine activities that regularize monastic life and ritual on a fixed schedule, whereas the confession and repentance of the last procedure are primarily for purposes of purification and recommitment to the faith on special occasions. These three aspects of the monastic discipline, though different in nature and purpose, together structured the monastery into a ritual field of time and space, in which the key intentions are communal, habitual, and performative.

The three procedures set up a ritual field in which practitioners could practice in and before the divine presence. All three presumed that the Buddha or other deities presided at the very site of the monastery. The doctrinal learning specified in the first procedure commonly included the invocation of the name of the deities and recital of scriptures prior to the lecture. Daoan is credited for the use of incense as a liturgical prelude to the procedure, called "offering incense" (*xingxiang*), which might include offering and scattering flowers and incensing the hall while circumambulating it and engaging in ritual prostrations and chanting. Incensing was a symbolic act to invite or summon the presence of deities to the assembly.[48] After the monks or nuns had circumambulated the hall to enact the sacredness, and the bell was struck to start the lecture, they would take their seats, chanting praise verses and reciting sutras. The priest (*fashi*) and the reciter (*dujiang*) would then ascend to high seats, bow to the statues, seat themselves on each side of the main images, and begin the lecture.[49] The deity, the priest, and the attendants were united in a liturgical relationship ensured by the prescribed procedure and performance. The Buddha was present to oversee and lend his authority to the words being preached, recited, and chanted, which all together activated the scriptures throughout the entire procedure.[50]

In the confessional ritual (S: *posadha;* C: *busa*) of the third procedure, a similar relationship between the practitioner and the Buddha was created.[51] Before the ritual, the selected site in the monastery would be cleansed, incensed, and adorned, and thus be turned into a delimited place for a liturgical purpose. Monks and nuns performed the ritual separately. To begin, the precept master (*lüshi*) was called after participants were convened; then, the master would ascend to the high seat, and monks on duty would sprinkle water and scatter flowers for purification. The rector (*weinuo*) then offered incense while reciting scriptural verses (S: *gāthā;* C: *ji*) devoted to and invoking "Innumerable Buddhas of the Ten Directions."[52] At this point, novices not yet fully ordained were requested to leave; those who remained would then recite the precepts and make confession. This was followed by the return of novices to chant the verses of praise to conclude the ritual. The ritual was of paramount importance because offenses could result in unfavorable karmic retribution or obstructions to spiritual advancement. Although transgressions were not necessarily against particular Buddhist deities, confession and repentance could be effectively and ritually confirmed only in the presence of the Buddha(s), invoked as witness, guarantor, and expediter to amend one's karma. Simultaneously the distinctions of gender, seniority, and monastic status were also affirmed, such that the "monastic body" of each practitioner through the liturgical process literally embodied the institutional discipline and spiritual hierarchy in relation to the divine presence.[53]

As important as the other two procedures were in assisting the monastic to perceive the sacred presence in the monastic space, it was the second procedure, of daily worship at six designated intervals of day and night, on which the monastery was centered and by which it was temporally regulated. Every liturgical day was divided into three daytime periods (dawn, noon, and sunset), and three nighttime periods (early night, midnight, and late night).[54] Each period, at least during the time of Daoan, would begin with a rite of worship, entailing circumambulation around images of the Buddha and probably other deities. By the sixth century, the liturgical routine, which had become unmistakably devotional, would include such stock ritual components as offerings, taking refuge in the Three Jewels, hymns, invocations, venerations, confession, and vows, each of which might vary according to scheduled periods. Before each of the communal meals, which were served twice a day, monastics would follow a simplified procedure—incensing, circumambulating, and chanting. These and other scheduled disciplines routinized the daily liturgical cycle, which inculcated the frame of mind and habit of body that were subjected to a transcendent order and aspiring to a higher spiritual realm.[55] In particular, the repetition of the daily ritual necessarily imparted a temporal rhythm, a cyclic infinity that was timeless. It was precisely through the cycle of liturgical routine that one was able to do away with the endless continuation of worldly impermanence that was bound in the secular time of day and night.

This temporal implication also has a spatial dimension. The focal point of the daily liturgy was the veneration of the Buddhist deities. Depending on the texts in use, at each designated ritual period the monastics would intone the names of different sets and ranks of Buddhas, either six, seven, eight, ten, thirty-five, or fifty-three in number, as well as those of various bodhisattvas.[56] These Buddhas and bodhisattvas were regarded in Mahayana Buddhism as celestial deities residing in different times and universes, yet correlating to the ritual site at the cardinal directions. By eliciting their presence from the ten directions (the four cardinal ones, those between them, and the directions up and down), the ritual site was perceived as constructing a dharma field (S: *bodhimaṇḍa;* C: *daochang*)—literally a site of enlightenment or ritual enactment that operated in its own (celestial) temporal and spatial order. It was in such "sacral spatiotemporality," at once outside and beyond regular time and space, that the monastic was able to reorient himself or herself and practice in the divine presence.

Without a particular frame of reference, cultural, religious, or political, ritual acts are meaningless in themselves. When enacted in context, ritual performance becomes expressive and efficacious, mediating meaning and power through bodily movement, symbols, or other implementations. As far as monastic learning and discipline are concerned, the ritual or ritualized lifestyle provided "body techniques," that is, bodily protocols sanctioned by the monastic authority to shape the identity of the practitioner and to prepare her or him for higher spiritual attainment.[57] On the other hand, it is also the practitioner's body that enters, circumambulates, prostrates, recites, chants, repents, and so on; that is, by virtue of devotional performance, the practitioner literally embodies the relation with sacrality and enacts its manifestation inside the monastery. A monastery was built not just to provide a space for different regimental disciplines and liturgical activities but to create a sort of "spatial liminality" that took the built environment as its physical realization and yet negotiated this world with the transcendent by making the divine presence perceivable within the four walls of the monastery.

Seeing the Sacred Presence: Meditative Visualization

Examining Daoan's guidelines closely, one may be surprised by the absence of some components often associated with Buddhist monastic practices. For one, there is no explicit instruction in regard to icons, although the use of Buddhist images is implied. For another, there is no mention of meditation (S: *dhyāna;* C: *chan*), a mental (spiritual) discipline that had most likely been practiced since Buddhism was first transmitted to China. The textual evidence, however, indicates that early in his career Daoan was interested in scriptures and treatises that introduced Buddhist meditation; and according to his biography, he would also have been familiar with the use of icons in a monastic setting.[58] Their exclusion from the monastic guidelines thus seems to suggest that practices with icons and meditation were separated from other monastic routines because they had different religious purposes. The two missing components in Daoan's guidelines would merge in the next centuries, since the practice of meditation was increasingly involved with the use of icons, to give monastics an important access to the sight and insight of the divine presence. In particular, meditative visualization became an indispensable element of the more advanced practices devised to assist the monastic in taking the bodhisattva path, as expounded in some newly translated Mahayana scriptures.[59]

Daoan established his monastic community in the metropolis Xiangyang (in present-day Hubei), and lived there from approximately 365 to 379; it was here that he compiled his monastic guidelines. A local magistrate donated his mansion to be converted into what was later named Tanxi Monastery (Tanxisi), to which was added a five-story pagoda and accommodation for four hundred monastics. In this same period, accounts of miraculous icons related to Tanxi Monastery began to circulate.[60] Another donation of ten thousand catties of bronze was, by Daoan's request, used to cast a sixteen-*chi* statue of the Buddha that correctly showed the Buddha's perfect and minor body marks. It was said that every night the statue emitted light that completely illuminated the hall; one night the statue even moved out of the hall under its own power and had to be brought back to the monastery. The statue was widely recognized for its marvelous acts, but it was the divinity manifested through the statue (by its automation and levitation) that was vital to the monastic spirituality. Daoan's most celebrated pupil, Huiyuan (334–416), later wrote a eulogy about the statue: "To represent a supernatural model prepares the heart for its final crossing [into salvation]. An iconographically-correct form divinely imitated opens the way to an understanding of all wisdom."[61] Similarly, in another account, an archaic and foreign-looking statue was found to contain a radiant relic when the rounded protuberance or topknot that is traditionally represented on top of the Buddha's head (*uṣṇīṣa*) was removed at Daoan's instruction; the statue was thus sanctified by the presence of the hidden relic. Even without the miracles or a special origin, the divine presence that could be mediated through a statue gave the icon a lasting legacy as the primary agent of divinity. Indeed, if the stupa/pagoda in the foregoing discussion can be seen as a metaphysical body, or an "architectural body,"[62] of the Buddha activated by the enshrined relics, an icon turns this bodily connotation of the presence into a primacy of vision. And it was by the practice of meditative visualization through the liturgical veneration of icons in a monastic setting during the fifth and sixth centuries that Chinese Buddhists began to learn to "see" the divine presence.

One of the earliest sources for this meditative practice is from the record of Huiyuan's veneration of another statue, that of Amitābha Buddha, documented in his biography.[63] In 402 CE, Huiyuan assembled 123 monks and laymen at Mount

Lu (Lushan, in today's Jiujiang, Jiangxi); after a ceremonial fasting and recitation of liturgy, Huiyuan and the assembly collectively made a vow in front of an image of Amitābha Buddha to strive for rebirth in his Pure Land (Sukhāvatī), the blissful world located in the extreme west of the universe, where this Buddha resides. This emphasis on vow taking and the ultimate aim of being reborn in Amitābha's Pure Land most likely were inspired by one of the three main scriptures in the Pure Land tradition, the *Amitābha Sutra* (Amituo jing), that had just been translated into Chinese at this time.[64] To vow and veneration, a new element was added in Huiyuan's practice: an intense meditative concentration on the iconic image as an efficacious technique for coming into the actual presence of the Buddha in vision.

This meditative visualization most likely originated in a practice that helped the practitioner recollect the attributes of the Buddha and call to mind his presence, a meditation known as *buddhānusmṛti* (C: *nianfo*).[65] The practice of *buddhānusmṛti* can be traced back to pre-Mahayana Buddhist history in India, but already in its early form, it was performed to see the Buddha in one's mind and be constantly in his presence even after he was no longer available to his followers. To acquire this "mental seeing," the practitioner is instructed to recite the ten epithets of the Buddha, a list of titles and qualities of the Enlightened One as a means to concentrate the mind on the attributes of the Buddha, until the practitioner "comes to feel as if he were living in the Master's presence . . . as though he were face to face with the Master."[66] It was on this vision of the presence that the style of Huiyuan's meditative practice was based.

The meditative practice of *buddhānusmṛti* is derived from the *Pratyutpanna Samādhi Sutra* (Banzhou sanmei jing), translated by Lokakṣema (fl. 168–88) in 179 CE.[67] According to this sutra, the practitioner entering a secluded place should become fully mindful of Amitābha Buddha by concentrating on the ten epithets of the Buddha and, additionally, by visually recollecting thirty-two major marks and eighty minor excellences of the Buddha's body. To effectively visualize the Buddha's physical form, the sutra instructs the practitioner to use a statue or an image of the Buddha. How the actual mental recollection is aided by the image is not detailed in this sutra, but it is explicated in some other contemporaneous works, including a short meditation manual, *Abridged Method of Meditation* (Siwei lueyao fa). In this manual, the visualization process is described as follows:

> When you see a beautiful image that looks like a real Buddha, carefully note every sign—from the topknot on the Buddha's head [*uṣṇīṣa*] and curls between his eyebrows [*ūrṇā*] to the feet and back from the feet to the topknot on his head—and then go to a quiet place, close your eyes, and fix your mind on the image, with no other thoughts. . . . When you have thus meditated until you can see the image whenever you wish, this is to attain to *samādhi* by meditation on an image. . . . Only after this will you be able to see the living body of the Buddha, no different from being face to face with him.[68]

A Buddhist term related to meditation, *samādhi* (C: *sanmei*), refers more specifically to a state of mental concentration, or ecstasy, and/or the spiritual discipline designed to cultivate and experience such a mental state. A meditator, in other words, could begin the practice with a mental concentration on abstract and nonfigural or aniconic attributes of the Buddha, and follow this by visualizing the physical or iconographic form of his perfect body, until an image of the Buddha's living body would arise in an ecstatic vision. Practicing meditation in this form leads to *samādhi,* in which the practitioner feels as if he or she is standing presently face to face with the Buddha. In the meditative process, the "tactility" of the iconic image gained through intensive concentration on the physical qualities of the body form gradually gives way to the visuality of the divine presence. The physical icon (the statue or image) that mediates this face-to-face encounter with the Buddha also gives primacy to the eidetic image of the divinity.

The term *buddhānusmṛti* is most often rendered as "mindful recollection of the Buddha" (*nianfo*) in Chinese, a usage also applied in Huiyuan's meditative practice, called "Samādhi in Mindful Recollection of the Buddha" (*nianfo sanmei*).[69] "Mindful recollection" (*nian*) had a double emphasis, on both the mental and the eidetic or calling-to-mind aspects of the meditative act of contemplating and recalling the image of the Buddha. In the case of Huiyuan's vow before a statue of Amitābha in 402, however, although the splendor of the Buddha's Pure Land was contemplated and imagined, it is unclear how the icon was meditated upon by Huiyuan and his followers to evoke the vision and ensure a collective rebirth there. When another scripture of the Pure Land tradition, the *Sutra on the Visualization of Amitāyus* (Guan wuliangshou fo jing), was translated into Chinese by Kālayaśas between 424 and 442, the visualization of the Buddha practiced in front of the icon was evidently a subject of instruction.[70] The immediate goal of the practice was more than a favorable rebirth in the future as in Huiyuan's practice; it was to induce a theophany, a direct revelation of the divine in an unmediated vision, where one comes face to face with the divinity: "Those who practice *samādhi* will be able to see [*jian*] in the present life Buddha Amitāyus [i.e., Amitābha] and the two great Bodhisattvas."[71] The reception of the sacred vision was thus not only a crucial sign for a successful meditative practice, but also necessarily salvific in terms of monastic spirituality, that is, it would lead to both the present cultivation and the future salvation of the practitioner.

Seeing the Buddha and being in his presence in early medieval China would no doubt be tremendously significant however they occurred. Yet, although seeing the Buddha is certainly a visionary experience, it may not necessarily be a consequence of systematized visualization.[72] The vision could appear as a divine intervention according to karmic law or manifest as a result of the Buddha's miraculous power to benefit the practitioner's spiritual progress. In either case, the occult vision acting on the religious practitioner is "gratuitous, unsought, given."[73] In comparison, the divine presence activated or enacted in visualization could be sought out to make sacred reality present for salvific or other spiritual goals. In a monastic context, the sight of the divine is closely related to "insight." The word *guan* for meditation could also imply "contemplating" or "discerning," a mental comprehension leading to awareness, knowledge, and ultimately a discerning vision.[74] In this sense, seeing the Buddha is equated with seeing the Dharma, a result also of the process of visualization that proceeds from observing first the physical form of the Buddha (*rūpakāya*), then the eidetic or recollected image in vision, and eventually the Buddha's formless body of transcendent reality—the dharma-body (*dharmakāya*). Rather than seek the presence that manifests voluntarily, the quest of sacred vision for a monastic is to acquire a capacity for seeing, an ability to correctly visualize and perceive the sacrality in order to gain ultimate truth and awakening.

Although not included in the earliest records of monastic routines and disciplines, meditative practice, and meditative visualization in particular, developed into the mainstream of monastic spirituality during the fifth and sixth centuries. Meditation, though it may have involved additional sutra recitations or bodily movements, was integrated in an extended ritual procedure, comprising such activities as offering of incense, veneration of the Buddhas, confession, dedication of merits, and profession of the bodhisattva vow. The liturgical and devotional components provided purification and catharsis that served to purge the gross forms of bondage such as craving, hatred, and jealousy—mental afflictions often described in Buddhist discourse as diseases of the eye. The clarity and substantiality of the vision determined whether the meditative visualization could be performed correctly and successfully. As another important meditation text, the *Ocean-Like Samādhi of Buddha Visualization Sutra* (Guanfo sanmei hai jing), has it: "If one keeps in mind polluted, evil, and bad thoughts, or if one has broken the Buddha's precepts, one sees an image [of the Buddha] as pure black, like a man of charcoal. . . . When [one] repents to the Buddha, [one's] spiritual eyes open, and see the Buddha's magnificent and refined physical body, like light from [Mount] Sumeru illuminating the ocean."[75] In turn, effective visualization would remove karmic obstructions, remit sins, and improve spiritual vision so that the monastic could come into relation with the Buddha face to face in the monastery.

In the next centuries, as we have seen, the monastery developed along with the emerging practice of icon veneration and a complex program of meditative visualization was devised to solicit the divine presence, marking an increasing emphasis on the visual, vision, and visionary experience. This visual emphasis, though not diminishing the role of the body, had significant implications for the ways the early monastery was perceived. We have also seen how devotional monasticism in early medieval China lent itself to a number of symbolic equivalences among pagoda (with its relics), icon, and scriptures in terms of divine presence in a liturgical context. Attempts to make that presence perceivable, however, also implied that the Buddha was actually absent. The primacy of seeing was thus not unrelated to an intention to negotiate this absence and the desire to acquire a spontaneous vision face to face with the divine, which became more important over time in the religious career of the monastic. By locating the divine presence and seeing him face to face in ritual circumambulation or meditative visualization, the practitioner transformed the Buddha from the "one who has thus gone," or *tathāgata* (C: *rulai*, one of the traditional epithets of the Buddha) to truly the "one who has thus come." This sacred vision of the divine presence would thus confirm a "monastic utopia" in the monastery, ideal for both spiritual and salvific ends. As a sacred, utopian realm, the monastery could be built anywhere; it was not fixed at any particular locus, but it would have to be actualized both spatially in an architectural layout and temporally in the ritual structure of *the* monastery. This monastic utopia eventually led the elite sponsors and the ever-growing number of Buddhist believers of the Northern Dynasties to envision a city of the Buddha that could be realized in this world through material dedications and monastic undertakings. Beginning with the pagoda and its ritual choreography, Chinese architecture for the first time in history was conceived, built, and acted upon as a place of the foreign divine.

Monastic Architecture: The Sacred Presence at the Center of a Structured Space

The stage set for this development was the northern dynasty Northern Wei (386–534), founded by the Tuoba (Tabgach), who originated from a tribal branch of the Xianbei. After taking control of present-day Shanxi and Hebei, this new, non-Chinese regime established its capital at Pingcheng (today's Datong), just inside the Great Wall in northern Shanxi. In 439, the Tuoba swept into the Gansu area, then ruled by the Northern Liang (398–439), and completed its unification of north China, providing a much-needed period of stability that led to its cultural and religious prosperity. Except for a brief setback of nationwide persecution against Buddhism during 446 to 452, the Buddhist community developed steadily and extensively under the favorable policy and royal patronage of the Northern Wei regime. In this history, the watershed event of northern Buddhism was the conquest of the region in today's Gansu.[76] A stronghold of Buddhism since the early third century, the Gansu area controlled much of the traffic of Buddhist teachings and missionaries going through the Hexi corridor that linked China with the Western Region (as the regions beyond the border were called) and boasted some of the earliest Buddhist cave temples along its route. During the Northern Liang, the area around its capital at Guzang (present-day Wuwei), known as Liangzhou, was built into a center of scripture translation, housing several foreign ecclesiastics of Indian and Central Asian origin. These ecclesiastics introduced tales of the Buddha's previous lives (*jātaka*), the concept of nirvana, the Mahayana pantheon, and bodhisattva precepts, some of which were subsequently widely spread and practiced in China. The pivotal activities advocated in the region were those related to stupa worship and meditation, developing a style of Buddhism, as well as architectural and iconographic features, that has been termed "Liangzhou style."[77] After the annexation of the Gansu region in 439, a massive deportation of the Northern Liang population brought artisans and Buddhist religious zeal to Pingcheng, where "the teaching by images spread far and wide."[78]

With the arrival of Liangzhou Buddhism and the ending of persecution began a flowering of Buddhist piety in both teaching and images among all levels of society.

Tanyao (fl. 450–90), a well-versed master from Liangzhou, was especially instrumental in implementing the Buddhist revival.[79] Appointed the controller of clergy (*shamen tong*), supervising national Buddhist affairs and communities, Tanyao established a system of Buddhist households (*sengzhi hu*), recruiting anyone who could make yearly donations of grains to the monastery for helping the poor and needy. This was instituted to provide a "merit field" of compassion, by which Buddhist householders were able to become affiliated with the monastic community and thus participate in their own future salvation.[80] The monastic clergy, in turn, played a contributory role in organizing and initiating common-class believers into the Buddhist charitable society (*yiyi*), in which monks served as monastic advisors or preceptors. In the north of the fifth and sixth centuries, lay patrons and clerical members of the charitable societies were responsible for a proliferation of cave temples, steles, and votive images as part of the collective meritorious acts and undertakings. It was this material devotion and visual piety of both (wealthy) laity and clergy that helped substantiate a Buddhist vision in the Northern Wei.[81]

The ambition to bring the vision into practice, however, could not have been carried out without imperial support. By the end of the 470s, about one hundred monasteries were built inside the capital city alone, many of which were officially sponsored monasteries said to have been constructed with multistory pagodas.[82] Although none of the monasteries has survived, we can still learn much about how a monastic space was structured architecturally from other indirect but related evidence. A primary source is the cluster of cave temples at Yungang, formerly known as Mount Wuzhou (Wuzhoushan), sixteen kilometers west of Pingcheng. According to *History of the Northern Wei* (Weishu), the building of the earliest caves, Caves 16–20, in Yungang began during the 460s at Tanyao's petition to dedicate five caves to each of the five previous Northern Wei emperors (fig. 1.3).[83] More relevant to this discussion are the major cave temples built over the next twenty years until 494, when the Northern Wei capital was relocated southward to Luoyang. The caves temples were decorated abundantly with motifs, carved in the rock, of timber-frame architecture, evidently following the model of the monasteries being built in this same period in the capital.[84]

Most of these caves, Caves 1–13, came in pairs or sets and were built on comparable plans (fig. 1.4). Compared with the initial five caves, each accommodating a group of colossal images (14–16.5 m high), the later caves are smaller in scale, yet feature a more complicated iconographic program and better-articulated architectural space. Most of them are either single or double chambers, with either a central pillar (Caves 1, 2, 6, 11) or a large Buddha (Caves 5, 9, 10) centrally located for circumambulation; Caves 7, 8, and 13, however, have neither.[85] The iconographic images and motifs in these caves do not form a schematic whole (fig. 1.5). In addition to the primary icons and carvings of lotuses and flying celestial beings (S: *apsaras;* C: *feitian*) on the coffered ceiling, many dedicatory images offered by lesser clerics and local residents fill the available wall surface, and are only tenuously related to the overall image program in the cave. The dazzling profusion of imagery nonetheless is delimited by its architectural setting.

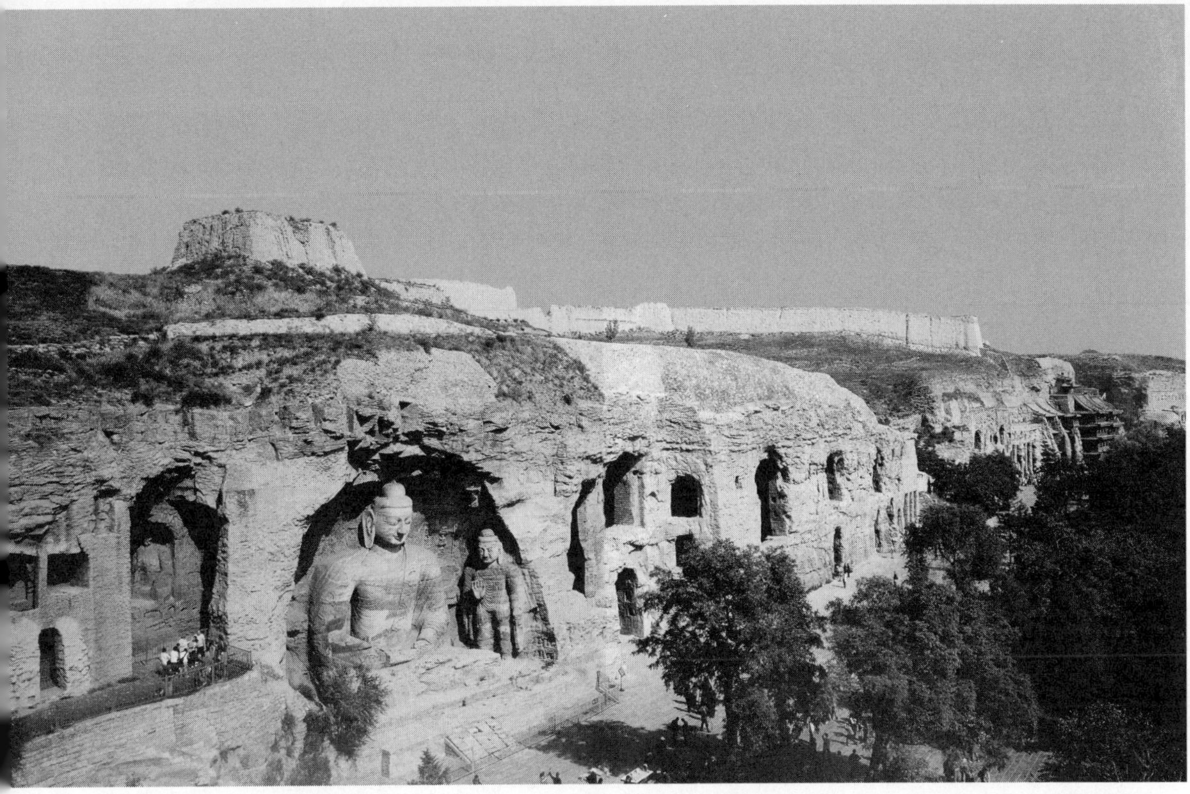

FIGURE 1.3. Bird's-eye view of the caves at Yungang, Shanxi, with the colossal Buddha of Cave 20 in the foreground. 460s–480s CE. From Yungang Shiku Yanjiuyuan, *Yungang shiku*, 87–88. Photograph by permission of Wenwu Press.

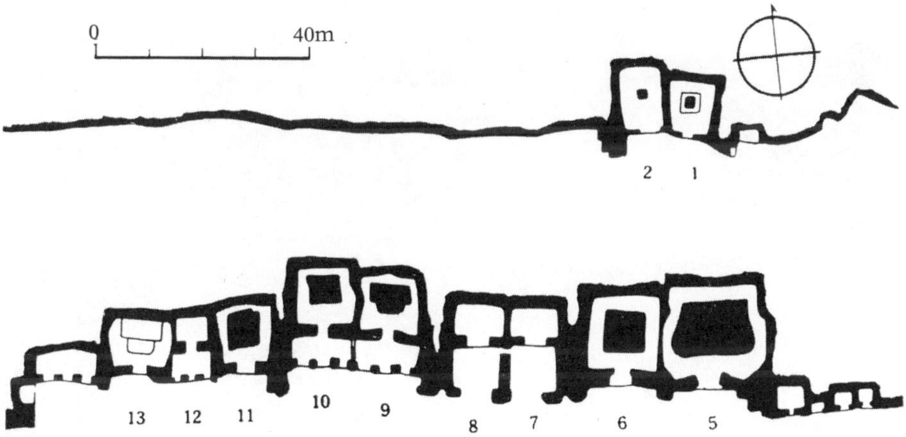

FIGURE 1.4. Plans of Yungang Caves 1–13, including four paired caves. 470s–480s CE. Two unfinished caves, Caves 3 and 4, are not shown in the diagram. From Soper, "Imperial Cave-Chapels of the Northern Dynasties," 249. Diagram courtesy of *Artibus Asiae*.

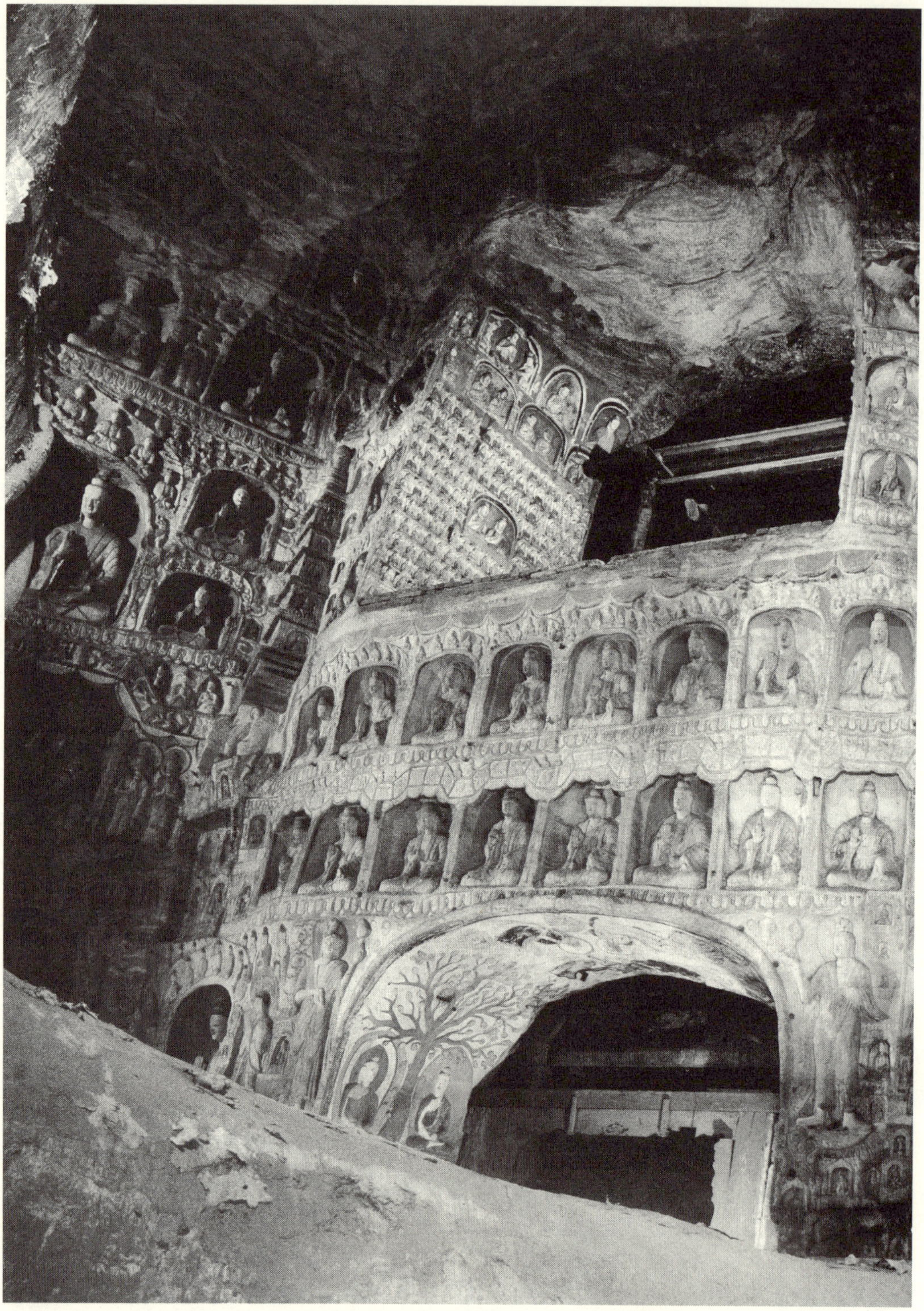

FIGURE 1.5. South interior wall of Cave 5, Yungang. 486–495 CE. The twin Buddhas, Śākyamuni and Prabhūtaratna, can be seen in a small niche in the sidewall of the window above the arched entryway, and the two monks meditating under a tree are just below, on the sidewall of the entryway. From Yungang Shiku Wenwu Baoguansuo, *Yungang shiku*, vol. 1, pl. 42. Photograph by permission of Wenwu Press.

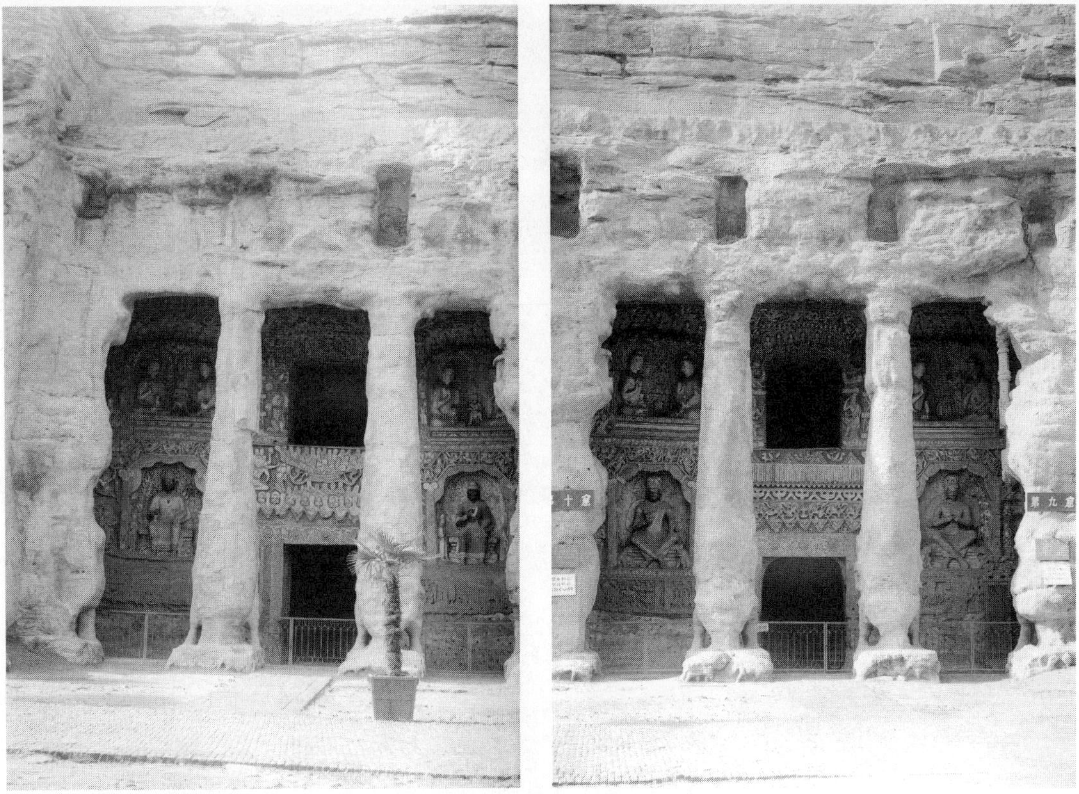

FIGURE 1.6. Exterior of Caves 9 (right) and 10 (left), Yungang. 470s–480s CE. The cliff facade of the twin caves was originally carved in the form of wooden columns and brackets, with additional wooden eaves fixed into the sockets above the columns. From Yungang Shiku Wenwu Baoguansuo, *Yungang shiku*, vol. 2, pl. 2. Photograph by permission of Wenwu Press.

Most of the thirteen caves in Yungang had a proper facade of original rock carved to resemble wooden architectural features, a feature not seen in the first five imperial caves (Caves 16–20). Although most of these cave facades are now corroded or altered, the single facade shared by Caves 9 and 10 (fig. 1.6) still retains its initial form, indicative of the layered architectural view and spatial depth that one would have encountered (and still encounters) when approaching the caves.[86] The entryway into the chamber of each of the thirteen caves is accessed from the antechamber behind the facade, as in Caves 9 and 10, each entryway having a window above it to allow more light into the cave. Accordingly, to arrive at the cave interior, whether it was a single- or double-chamber cave, one needs to pass through the facade and antechamber, and then through the entryway, before reaching the centrally located icon or pillar. One's movement through space is structured by the architectural features, which in turn add a symbolic significance to the cave temple. Of the architectural features, the entryway with the aperture above it would have been the most critical.

The importance of the entryway is signaled not only by its position in the ar-

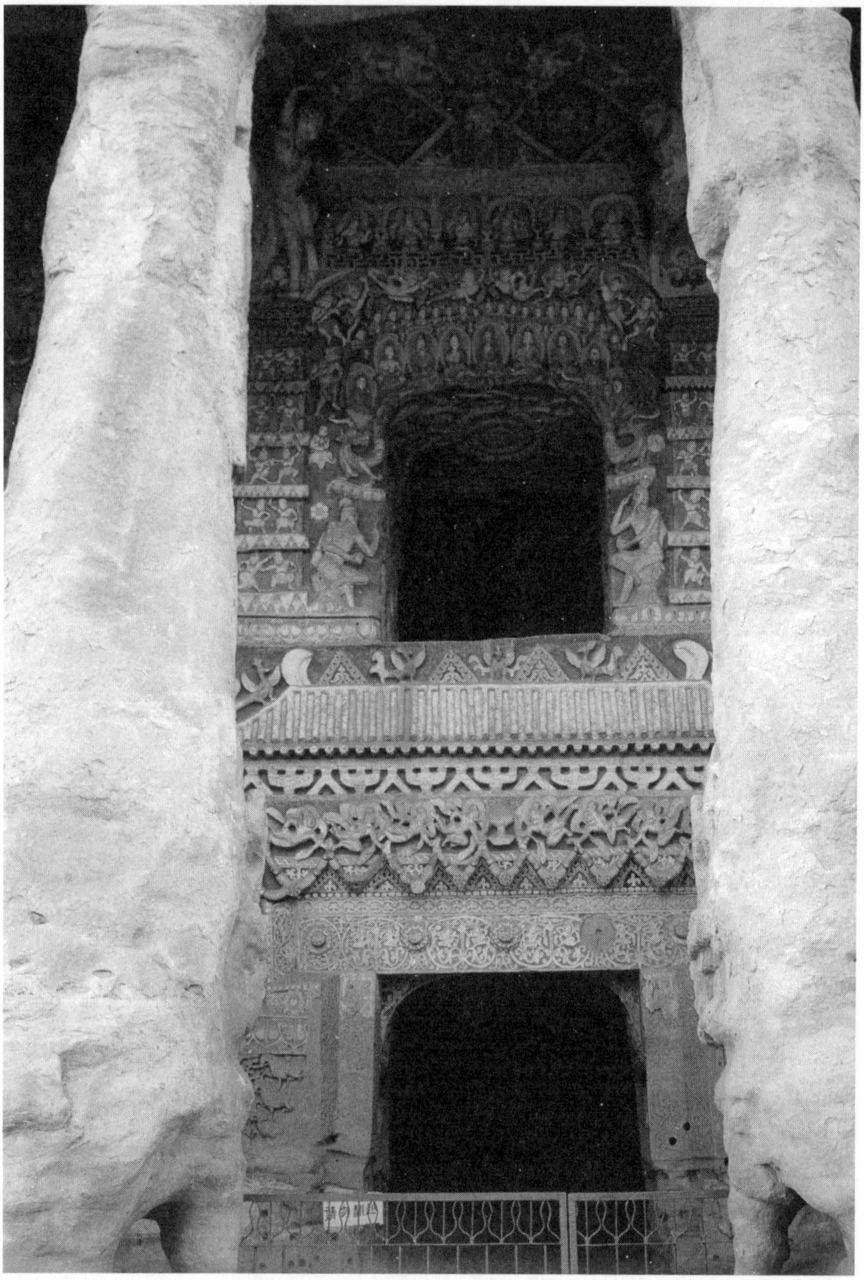

FIGURE 1.7. Detail of the entryway to Cave 9, Yungang. 470s–480s CE. Decorative patterns border the door frame and a small tiled roof supported by brackets projects over the lintel. From Yungang Shiku Wenwu Baoguansuo, *Yungang shiku*, vol. 2, pl. 3. Photograph by permission of Wenwu Press.

chitectural layout but also by the decorative and iconographic images arranged around it. In Cave 9 (fig. 1.7), the palmette patterns bordering the door frame and architectural elements such as the small projecting tiled roof supported by brackets over the lintel formally acknowledge the entry as important. Inside the entrance, instead of architectural elements, there are figures carved in high relief: the portal is decorated with modeled figures of Buddhas, most prominently the Buddhas of the three times (past, present, and future) and the Seven Buddhas (Śākyamuni and his six predecessors) (fig. 1.8), iconography signifying specifically

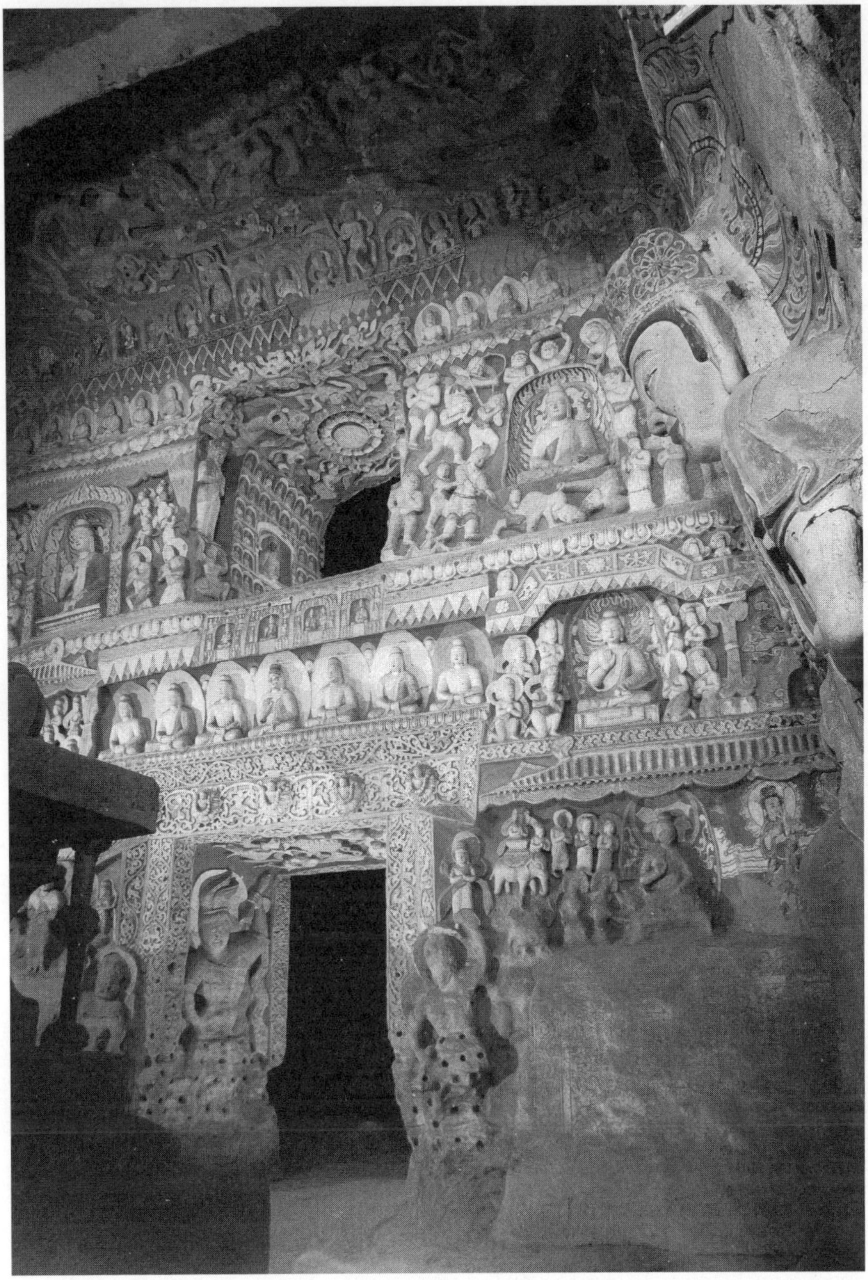

FIGURE 1.8. South interior wall of Cave 10, showing the motif of the Seven Buddhas above the entryway. 470s–480s CE. From Yungang Shiku Wenwu Baoguansuo, *Yungang shiku*, vol. 2, pl. 65. By permission of Wenwu Press.

a world of transtemporality beyond the entrance.[87] Entering the cave through the gateway is therefore both transitional and transformative. One iconography that may have served to articulate this threshold is the motif of the twin Buddhas Śākyamuni and Prabhūtaratna.[88] Cave 5 provides an example (see fig. 1.5) in the two Buddha figures visible in a small niche in the sidewall of the window, which is surrounded by carved images of a thousand Buddhas; these images signal the success of the devotee's meditative practice as instructed in the *Lotus Sutra*.[89] The sight of the twin-Buddha image is the result of the meditation indicated by the two meditating monks depicted under a tree on the sidewall of the entryway just below, a scene that symbolically indicates a transitional point of spiritual progression. The physical process of entering the cave was thus analogous to the process that prepares one for a vision of the divinity. Passing over the threshold, indeed, one enters to the ritual circumambulation, around either a main icon or a pillar located centrally in the cavern, demarcated as a transcendental and sacred realm, for an opportunity to meet the divine face to face. The cave temple, in short, was an architecturally defined ritual field with a centralized divine presence that could be perceived and experienced through both the iconographic program and symbolically organized space.

No traces of the monastic architecture have survived from Pingcheng, the first Northern Wei capital, but archaeologists have uncovered and, since 1976, investigated the precinct of a royal monastery at Mount Fang (present-day Mount Siliang) about twenty-five kilometers north of Pingcheng. It was the Buddhist Monastery of Contemplating the Past (Siyuan Fosi), commissioned in 479 by Empress Wenming (442–90), also known as Lady Feng. A devout Buddhist, the empress was also the chief force behind the construction of the Yungang cave temples.[90] Facing south, the monastery occupied a large rectangular area, consisting of two tiers of terraces with the upper level close to the north end of the lower one (fig. 1.9).[91] Each terrace could be accessed from a south-facing ramp aligned along a central axis; at the top of the second ramp was a freestanding entrance gate (*shanmen*), inside which lay the main monastic ground. A large centrally located pagoda (see fig. 1.9, at point 1), whose base was constructed on a square pounded-earth core, would have dominated the monastery. The elevation of the pagoda cannot be estimated, but rows of column plinths around the earthen core indicate an interior walkway built at ground level that could have been used for circumambulation. Fragments of sculptural images uncovered around the foundation, moreover, suggest that Buddhist statues would have been installed inside the pagoda. The archaeological report of the site also reveals the foundation of a seven-bay-by-two-bay Buddha hall (*fodian;* in fig. 1.9, point 2; "bay" refers to the space between two columns) immediately to the north of the pagoda and constructed on the same central axis and some building remnants farther to the north, possibly for lodgings.[92] It is unclear whether the monastery was built for specific Buddhist or monastic practices, but the walkway inside the pagoda would have provided a further entry into the sacred center to observe its iconography. The central pagoda and the Buddha hall behind it, the two fundamental monastic buildings, aligned on the same axis with the main entrance are also an early example of the major monastic plan in the next centuries. Yet this layout of Siyuan Monastery, with its centrally located pagoda, strongly recalls the layout of the Yungang caves of the same period just discussed, which were also centered on an icon or pillar, which stood for the stupa in the cave.[93] One's entry into the monastery was, as in the cave temples, structured by the architecture, with the entrance gate as the point of transition, beyond which one could arrive at the pagoda, enter the sacred center, and proceed to the ritual circumambulation.

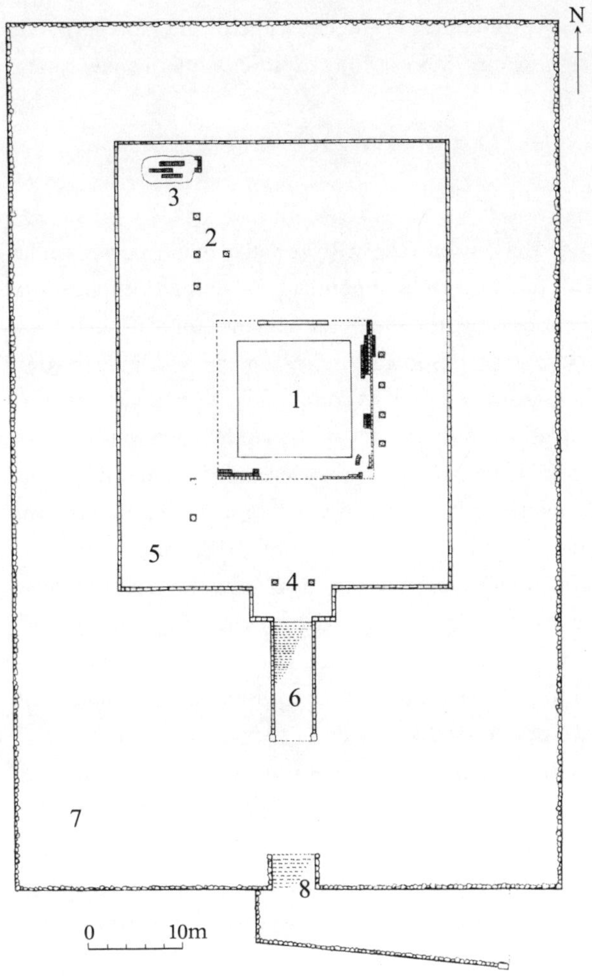

FIGURE 1.9. Site plan of the Buddhist Monastery of Contemplating the Past (Siyuan Fosi), Datong, Shanxi. Commissioned in 479 CE. (1) Pagoda; (2) Buddha Hall; (3) dormitories; (4) entrance gate; (5) upper terrace; (6) ramp leading down from the higher terrace; (7) lower terrace; (8) ramp leading down from the lower terrace. After Datongshi Bowuguan, "Datong Beiwei Fangshan Siyuan Fosi," fig. 5. Diagram by permission of Wenwu Press.

On the other hand, unlike the central pillars or icons in the cave interiors at Yungang, the soaring structure of the pagoda at the Siyuan Monastery would have functioned as a visual marker of the divinity that could be seen from afar. The same could be said about the pagodas of the many grand monasteries built in the Northern Wei capital, Pincheng. Li Daoyuan (ca. 470–527), the author of the *Commentary on the Waterways Classic* (Shuijing zhu), remarked on the Buddhist monuments of Pingcheng during the 480s: "The way of Buddhism in the capital had greatly flourished. The magnificent pagodas [were decorated] with numinous imagery, their towering profiles echoing each other. They are the superior sign for the turning of the dharma wheel [*dharmacakra*] in the eastern land [i.e., China]."[94] As though vertical measurement indexed religious devotion, pagodas were built for height: the higher the pagoda, the greater the implied devotion. Already in 467, the largest imperial monastery, the Monastery of Eternal Peace (Yongningsi), was built on the south side of the city; it boasted a seven-story pagoda, "more than three hundred *chi* high [approx. 82 m], with a wide foundation and spacious structure, ranked the grandest in the land under heaven."[95] This verticality provided a new vocabulary for monastic architecture in the cityscape of the Northern Wei capital, but its multivalent significance was not fully explored until the new capital was moved to Luoyang after 494.

City of the Buddha: Remaking the Capital

The relocation of the capital to the central Yellow River Valley that occurred under Emperor Xiaowen (r. 471–99) had far-reaching political and cultural implications and consequences. Moving to Luoyang, the site of the ancient capital of such great dynasties as the Zhou (770–256 BCE), Eastern Han (25–220 CE), and Jin (265–316), the Tuoba Wei symbolically refashioned itself as comparable with, if not equal to, the Chinese dynasties that ruled from the center of the land.[96] Different reforms in areas such as administration, ritual, and customs were initiated and new state architectural projects implemented, placing the non-Chinese Tuoba Wei regime in the position that traditionally defined a Chinese empire. In art and architecture, a more Sinicized style replaced the Central Asian mode of expression and supplied the Northern Wei with a new symbolic language to represent its political power. To this project of reshaping the central authority, the Northern Wei added a few new elements—a retooled monasticism and a religious vision on a national scale that had developed over the past decades.

The rebuilding of the capital city in Luoyang was itself an elaborate task that took almost twenty years to complete.[97] Unlike the former Luoyang, the new plan included one palace-city (*gongcheng*) inside an inner city (*neicheng*), while a second city wall was built to enclose a much larger area, the outer city (*waicheng*) (map 3). The expanded city range was then divided by four east-west and north-south arteries, with the forty-two-meter-wide Imperial Avenue (Yujie), also known as Bronze Camel Avenue (Tongtuo Jie), running along the major north-south axis, through the three south gates of the palace, inner city, and outer city. In brief, the new Luoyang was structured by lateral expansion, a prescribed axiality, and an imperial center, reinforced by the triple-wall system—a layout that later became typical for Chinese imperial cities.

In a different respect, Luoyang of the Northern Wei was ultimately a Buddhist city. A former resident, Yang Xuanzhi (d. 555), compiled accounts of Buddhist monasteries, devotions, and popular tales and legends of the city from 494 until 534 in a work titled *Record of the Monasteries of Luoyang* (Luoyang qielan ji), dated 547. According to Yang, Luoyang during the Jin dynasty, between 307 and 313, had only forty-two temples inside its city perimeter, but the number swelled dramatically to 1,367 under the Northern Wei. The city limits were much expanded by the time of the Northern Wei, and the space was rapidly filled with religious structures. Yang stated, "Buddhist temples were built side by side; pagodas rose up in row after row. People competed among themselves in making or copying the sacred images. Golden pagodas matched the imperial observatory in height, and Buddhist lecture halls were as magnificent as the Ebang Palace [of the Qin Empire]."[98] The huge growth of Buddhist buildings was accompanied, as Yang notes,

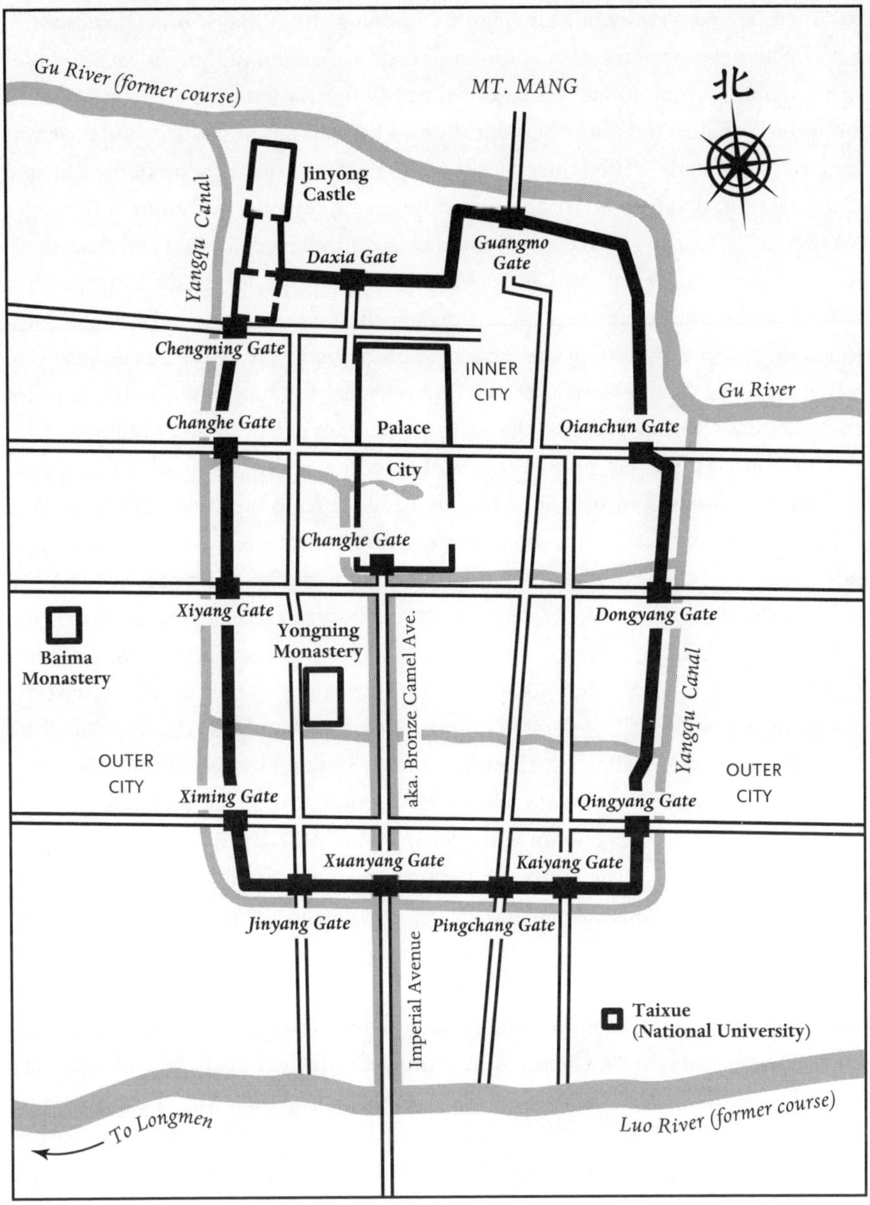

MAP 3. Luoyang during the Northern Wei era, based on an archaeological report of the city site conducted in 1973. Adapted from Tsiang, "Antiquarianism and Re-envisioning Empire," 132. Reproduced courtesy of Katherine R. Tsiang.

by a proliferation of Buddhist images, most of which were donated by residents of the city for gaining karmic rewards. Yet this very urban piety was also necessarily material (expressed through buildings and images), turning the new capital and its monasteries into the main stage of tangible devotion and a locus of spiritual vision and transformation.[99]

In fact, the rebuilding of the city was on a par with the measures undertaken to materialize its Buddhist vision. After Emperor Xiaowen's death in 499, Emperor

Xuanwu (r. 499–515) began his reign by building three major official monasteries.[100] The new emperor also continued to sponsor the building of cave temples at Longmen, a major cave site about thirty-two kilometers to the southwest of Luoyang, constructed after the relocation of the capital. In 505, the emperor was said to have already visited the cave site to oversee the construction of the Binyang Central Cave, dedicated to his parents, Emperor Xiaowen and Empress Dowager Wenzhao.[101] He also received the Indian monks Bodhiruci (d. 527) and Ratnamati (d. ca. 513) when they arrived at Luoyang in 508 and sponsored their sutra translations in the palace. Among their works is the *Commentary on Ten Stages Sutra* (Shidi jing lun), expounding the ten stages of the bodhisattva path as discussed in a chapter of the *Flower Garland Sutra* (Dafangguang fo Huayan jing), the scripture that identified Mount Wutai as the sacred mountain of Bodhisattva Mañjuśrī.[102]

The most ambitious project was still to come, after the death of Emperor Xuanwu, and was commissioned by one of his concubines, Lady Hu. Raised in a Buddhist family, Lady Hu, who later became the empress dowager, was a pious follower of the religion.[103] Soon after taking power as the de facto ruler, she launched more large architectural projects, including erecting pagodas in existing monasteries, building extravagant new monasteries, sponsoring the construction of the Longmen caves, and, above all, commissioning the imperial monastery, Yongning Monastery.[104] In 516, the empress dowager handpicked a location close to the center of the entire city, about five hundred meters south of the palace-city and two hundred meters west of Imperial Avenue, as the site of the monastery (see map 3). In a public ceremony, she led a host of officials to lay the foundation, and later, it is told, in the course of excavation, thirty golden statues turned up deep underground, a discovery that was taken as an auspicious sign.[105] The result of this endeavor was a spectacular nine-story, four-sided pagoda. In the *Record of the Monasteries of Luoyang,* it is described as a towering structure decorated with precious stones, jeweled inlays, and golden plates for collecting dew, rising to an unprecedented height.[106] The account continues: "[Its architecture] embodied the best of masonry and carpentry, and its design reached the limit of ingenuity. Its excellence as Buddhist architecture was almost unimaginable. Its carved pillars and gold doorknockers fascinated the eye. When the bells chimed in harmony deep in a windy night, they could be heard over ten *li* away."[107]

The Yongning Monastery took its name from the imperial monastery of the former capital in Pingcheng, but its architectural plan was much more ambitious. According to the report of the excavation, which began in 1979,[108] the Yongning Monastery of Luoyang occupied a rectangular lot with a longer north-south axis, enclosed by four walls, each presumably having a gate at its center (fig. 1.10); the northern gate has not yet been located. Within its four walls, there was a Buddha hall to the north, and a high-rising pagoda prominently located at the center. This "centrality" was also symbolically built into the temple's architectural program, both inside and outside. Inside the pagoda, at its center, was an underground crypt (*digong*) used as the relic depository that would physically and religiously mark the very center of the monastic complex. Outside the pagoda, four exterior ramps at

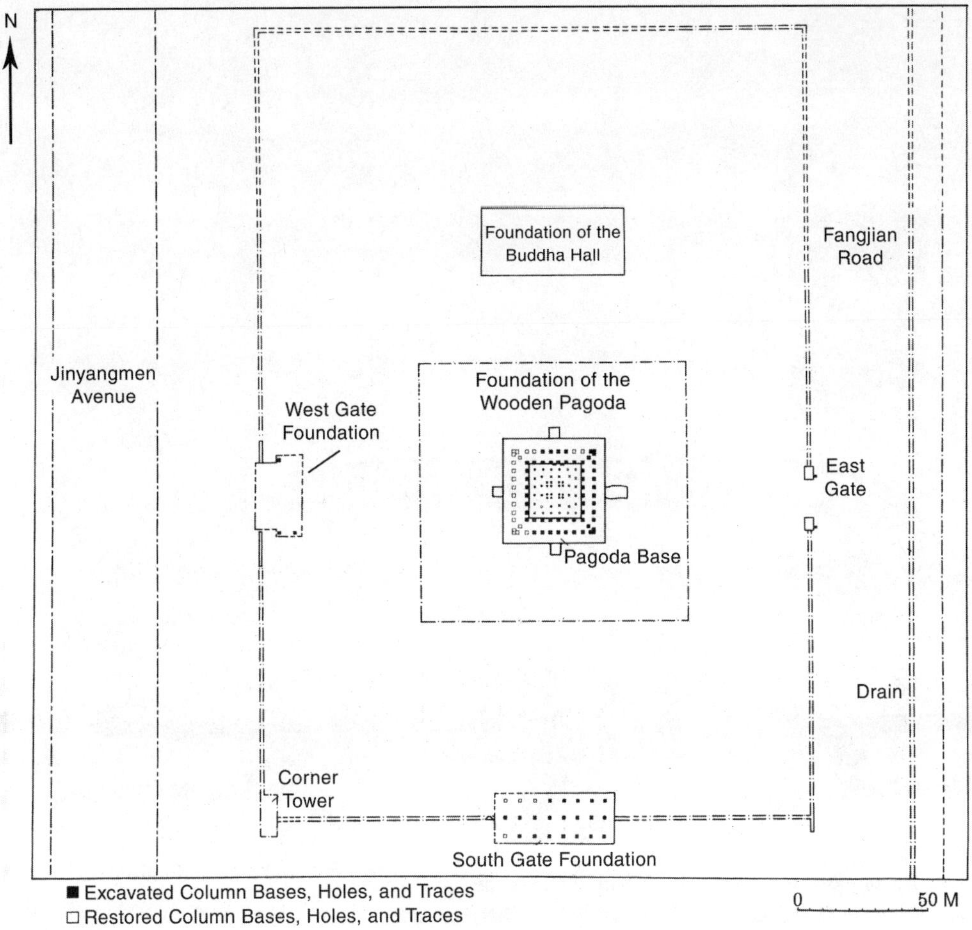

FIGURE 1.10. Site plan of the excavation of Yongning Monastery, Luoyang, Henan. 516 CE. The foundation of the pagoda is located at the center of the site. From Zhongguo Shehui Kexue Yanjiuyuan, *Beiwei Luoyang Yongninsi*, fig. 4. Diagram courtesy of the Institute of Archaeology, Chinese Academy of Social Sciences.

the four cardinal directions were constructed for accessing the interior, which was built around the earthen core, leaving a one-bay interior space around the core decorated with carved niches and clay sculptures. This centralized scheme with its circumambulatory interior recalls the similar plan of the Yungang caves. The spatial arrangement of the pagoda and Buddha hall, aligned on the same axis with the main gate, also follows the model in the Siyuan Monastery.[109] At Yongning Monastery, however, the scheme of centrality seems to have been devised with a larger context in mind.

During the archaeological excavation at Yongning Monastery, more than two thousand fragments of polychrome clay sculpture were found around the foundation of the pagoda, suggesting that an elaborate image program had once been installed. The largest figures would have been as much as three meters in height, and others were either near life-size or smaller, indicating some hierar-

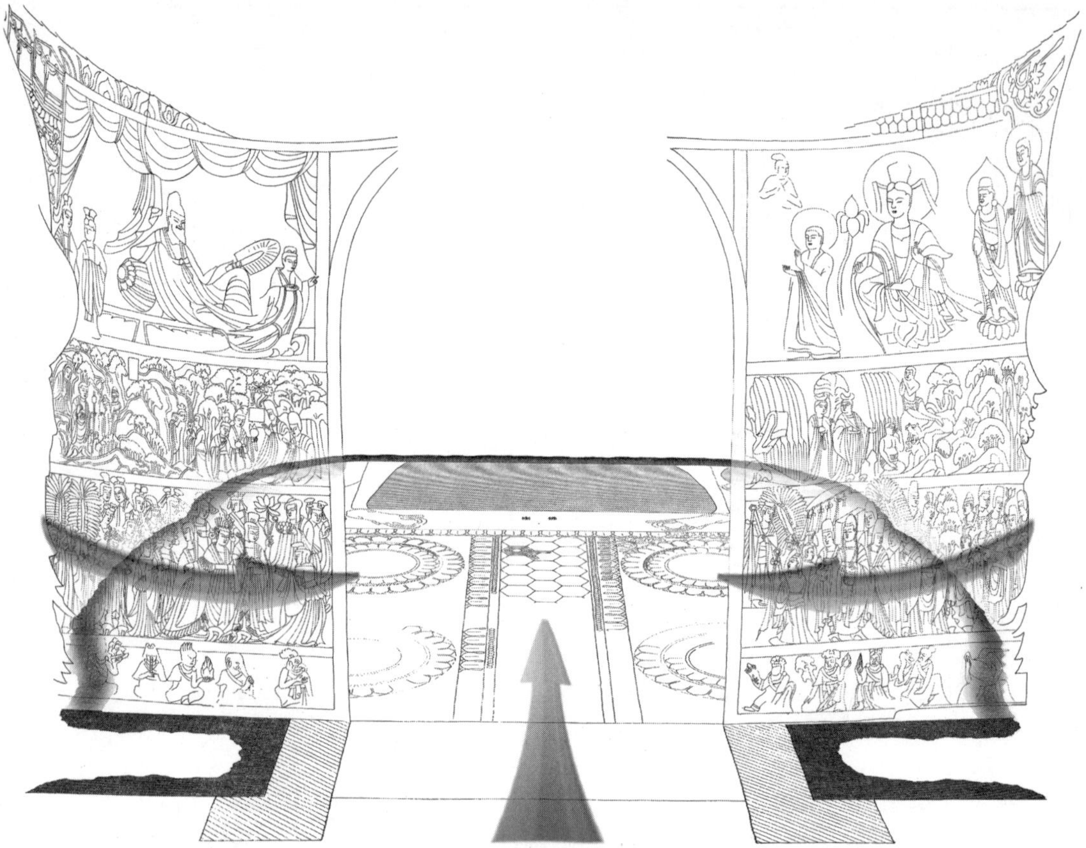

FIGURE 1.11. Reconstruction of the east wall reliefs from the viewpoint of the entering visitor, Binyang Central Cave, Longmen, Henan. 523 CE. The relief depicting the imperial procession of the emperor is located in the second register from the bottom to the right side of the cave entrance; the relief of the procession of the empress is in the same register on the other side of the entrance. The two processions face each other in opposite directions (indicated by the arrows), as if marching into the viewer's space when one enters the cave. After Mizuono and Nagahiro, *Kanan Ryūmon sekkutsu no kenkyū,* figs. 13, 18, 19.

chical arrangement of the iconography.[110] Sculptural fragments were also found that may have been part of the narrative scenes about the life of Śākyamuni and other miracle stories; other images include reliefs of an imperial procession led by members of the royal family. While most of the finds were typical for a Buddhist monastery, the last group of images was specific to the Yongning Monastery and emblematic of its imperial sponsorship.[111] Given their appearance in the same space as other sacred icons, they not only testify to imperial patronage but also indicate that members of the imperial household took part in devotional and ceremonial processions here. The original scene of the imperial procession that took place at Yongning pagoda cannot be recreated, but the same subject was also represented in devotional cave temples elsewhere, including Binyang Central Cave and Huangfu Cave in Longmen, and Caves 1, 3, and 4 in Gongxian, Henan, all constructed around this time under imperial patronage.[112] The procession would have consisted of richly dressed aristocratic figures with courtiers, Buddhist clerics, and servants bringing offerings, all arranged in a line and facing the same direction, as though moving from one end to the other. It has been argued that the composition of the imperial processions modeled in Binyang Central Cave, as well as their positions in the cave, creates multiple optical illusions that give "the impression they are moving forward into the viewer's space" (fig. 1.11).[113] Although each of these caves has a different spatial arrangement for the display, the procession seems to also lend an important performative thrust to the image program that would participate in the visitor's veneration of the Buddha figures.

Located at the center of the new Luoyang, the Yongning pagoda was intended to be beheld, entered, circumambulated, and used for worship. Entering the city from the south, one would follow the ceremonial Imperial Avenue and pass through gates of both outer and inner city walls to finally reach the Yongning Monastery (see map 3). In a larger spatial scheme of the city, the journey, punctuated by gates, or thresholds, would turn the cityscape into a "sacred topography," at the center of which soared the Yongning pagoda. One's walk into the monastery and entering the pagoda would be anticipated by the sculptural relief of the imperial procession that would accompany one inside the sacred center to complete the journey. Arriving from Central Asia, the Persian monk Bodhidharma (ca. 461–534) was said to have been amazed by the "divine work" (*shengong*) of Yongning pagoda after "seeing the golden plates making dazzling reflections of the sunlight and shining into the clouds, and having heard the ringing of bejeweled bells lofted into the sky by the wind." The foreign monk concluded that though he had visited every corner of the world, "[he] had never seen anything like the monastery [in China]."[114] Built when urban piety in Luoyang was at its height, the Yongning pagoda was the ultimate symbol of divine presence, and the imperial procession, though only in representation, set in motion the act of offering worship around the sacred center of the city.

It is interesting to note that in *Record of the Monasteries of Luoyang*, Yang Xuanzhi begins his account by mapping out all the city gates in its four walls, thus demarcating the boundary of the city within. This is then followed by the main narrative, which recounts anecdotes or histories of various monasteries of particular interest. As it continues, the narrative appears to follow an itinerary that takes its readers through the city in a certain sequence; not surprisingly, the tour begins from Yongning Monastery in the inner city and proceeds to the suburbs of the outer city in a clockwise route—east, south, west, and north. This "itinerary" clearly prioritizes the inner city, but it no less explicitly indicates that the rest of the journey was designed to circumambulate the center, which, in a sense, assimilates the city to a monastery built as the locus of the sacred presence. Writing fourteen years after the demise of the dynasty, Yang could produce his account only from memory; but this effort to recall the sight of the city once replete with architectural wonders and miraculous icons enabled him to reconstruct the image, or imagination, of an idealized city. In religion, a utopia such as nirvana or heaven is often conveyed through the image of a city—not a material-historical city, but an imaginary and unconditioned realm to which a human city can aspire.[115] Not to discount other political and cultural factors, Luoyang under the Northern Wei was built through its imperial support and monastic endeavors to create a utopian city of the Buddha on earth.

Urban piety and popular devotion were not enough to sustain the dynasty through political turmoil in its last years after the death of Empress Dowager Hu in 528. Luoyang fell to its rival in 534; in the same year, the Yongning pagoda was struck by lightning and burnt to ashes. Pagodas continued to be built, but never again on the same scale. Despite the intention and ambition to build the city into a Buddhist utopia, the divine presence envisioned was not fixed in the city and, with the fall of the dynasty, the divinity began to be perceived in different forms and manifestations. Replacing Luoyang, Ye in present-day Linzhang, Hebei, became the next political center as the capital of the Eastern Wei (534–49) and Northern Qi (550–77) that succeeded the Northern Wei in northeastern China. Like Luoyang, the new capital also developed into a hub of Buddhist activities; however, the spiritual pursuit was restaged, not only in the urban center, but in mountain areas, remapping the Buddhist sacred geography in a very different manner. Mount Wutai, located in the vicinity adjacent to Pingcheng (see map 5 in chapter 2), would likely have been a site for monasteries during the Northern Wei, though it was not yet an important one.[116] In the reduced territory of the Eastern Wei and Northern Qi, Mount Wutai was also close to the central region of the restructured sacred geography. While many eminent monks left the cities for mountains to practice meditative concentration in seclusion, Mount Wutai began to draw dedicated practitioners not only for its natural beauty and serenity, but also for a potential encounter with the presence of a particular Buddhist deity, the bodhisattva Mañjuśrī, offering a localized utopia and unfailing hope for salvation within the native Chinese terrain.

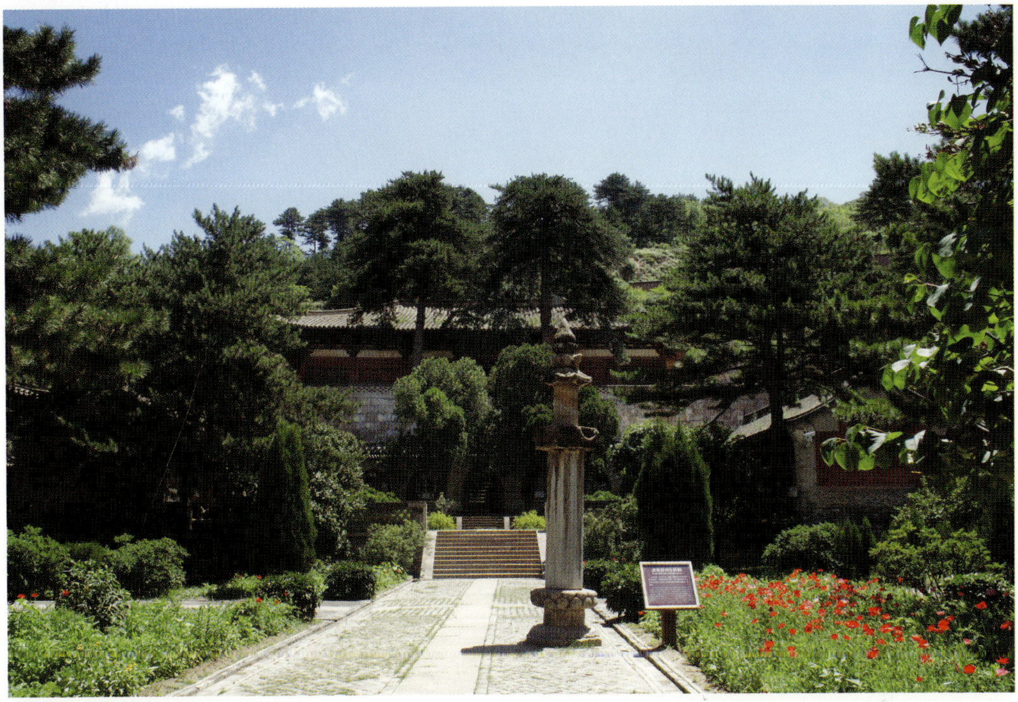

PLATE 1. The Great Buddha Hall, built on the highest level of Foguang Monastery, Mount Wutai, Shanxi. 857 CE. Photograph by author.

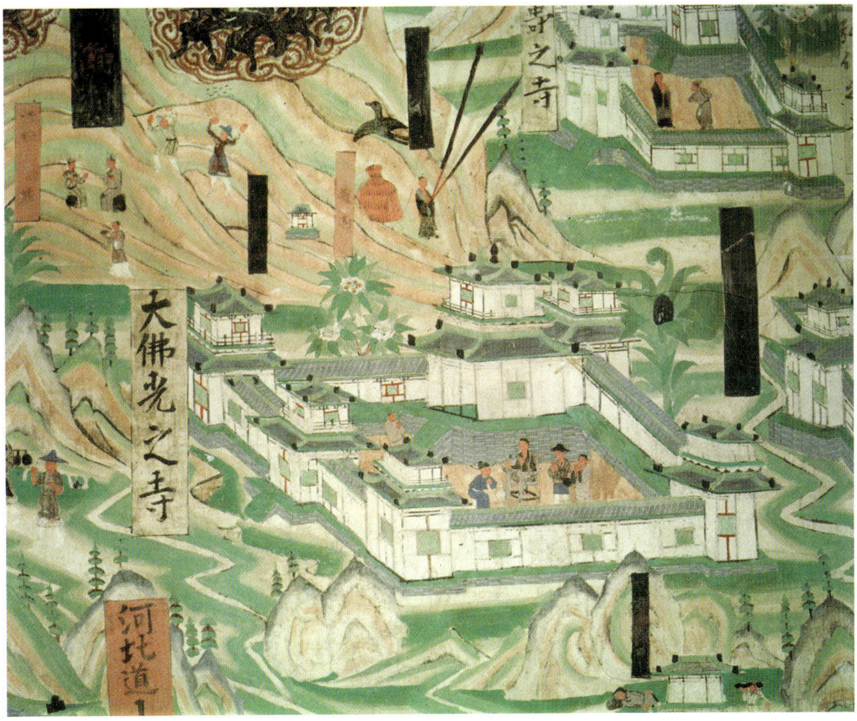

PLATE 2. Detail of Foguang Monastery in the mural depicting the panorama of Mount Wutai on the west wall of Mogao Cave 61, Dunhuang, Gansu. Mid-10th century CE. From Dunhuang Wenwu Yanjiusuo, *Dunhuang Mogaoku,* vol. 5, pl. 52. Photograph by permission of Wenwu Press.

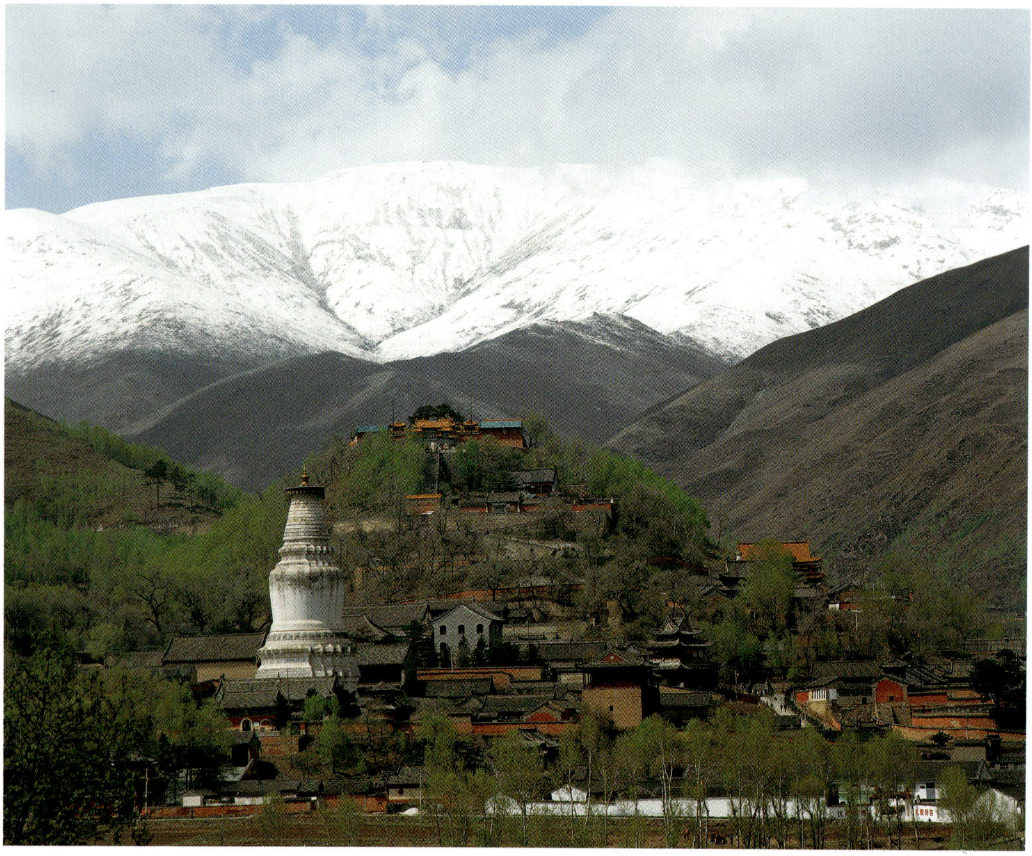

PLATE 3. Site of the former Monastery of Great Faith in Vulture Peak (Dafu Lingjiusi), named after the hill Vulture Peak, on which the monastery was built. The monastery was renamed Great Huayan Monastery (Da Huayansi) in the early 700s CE. During the Ming dynasty, its components were separated into several individual monasteries, which continue into modern times. Photograph courtesy of Guo Zhicheng.

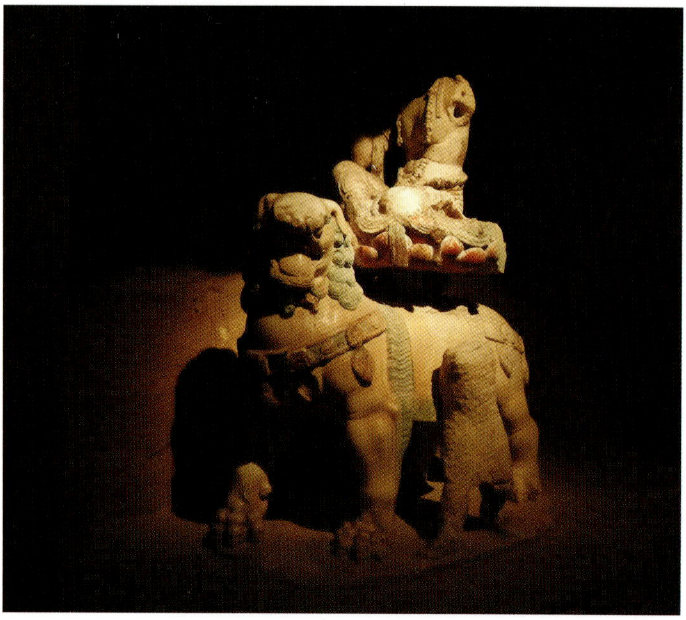

PLATE 4. The "true-presence" (*zhenrong*) icon of Mañjuśrī riding a lion. Painted white marble. Mid-8th century. Shanxi Provincial Museum. Photograph by author.

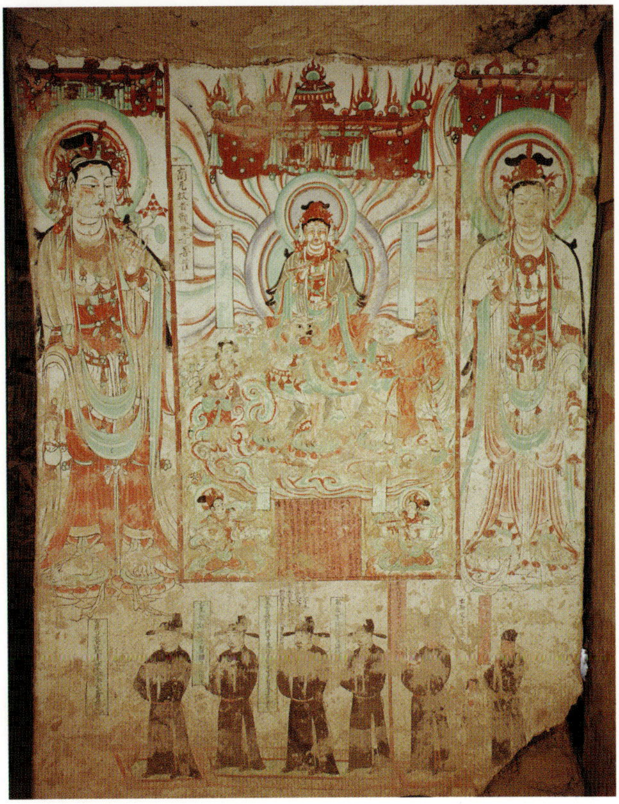

PLATE 5. Mural on the north wall of the corridor leading to Mogao Cave 220, Dunhuang. 925 CE. At the center is the "new-mode" Mañjuśrī (Xinyang Wenshu). Dunhuang wenwu yanjiusuo, *Dunhuang Mogaoku,* vol. 5, pl. 20. Photograph by permission of Wenwu Press.

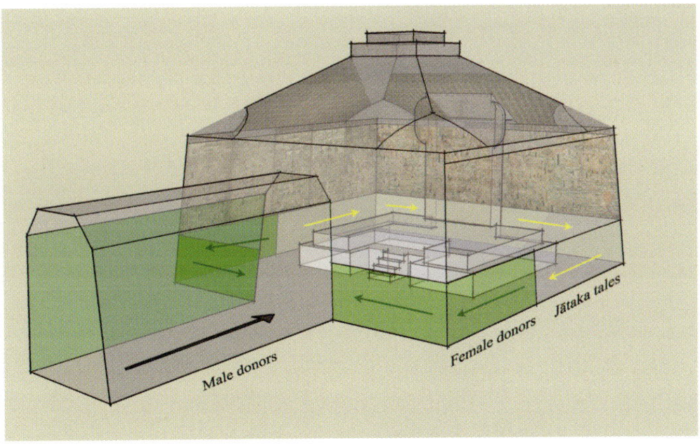

PLATE 6. Perspective view of Mogao Cave 61, Dunhuang. 947–951 CE, showing the image program and viewing direction. On the lower register, women donors are depicted in the green area facing the eastern entrance, as indicated by green arrows. Thirty-three mural panels depicting the *jātaka* tales occupy the space on the lower register that wraps around the rear part of the cave, in a chronological sequence indicated by yellow arrows. Images of men donors originally covered the walls of the corridor. Drawing by author.

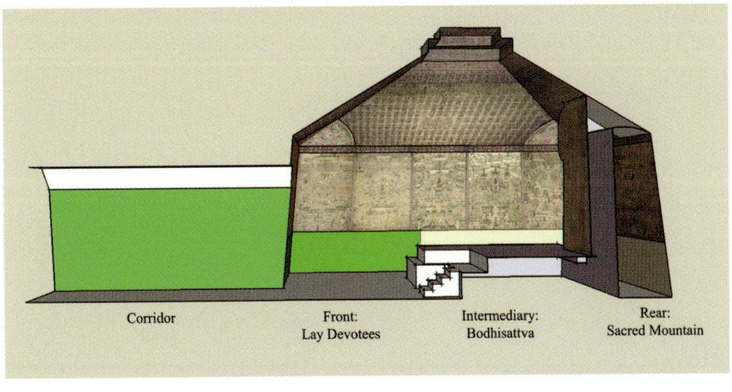

PLATE 7. Cutaway view of the south half of Mogao Cave 61. The cave space can be divided into three zones: the front zone of the lay devotees; the intermediary zone of the bodhisattva; and the rear zone of the sacred mountain. Drawing by author.

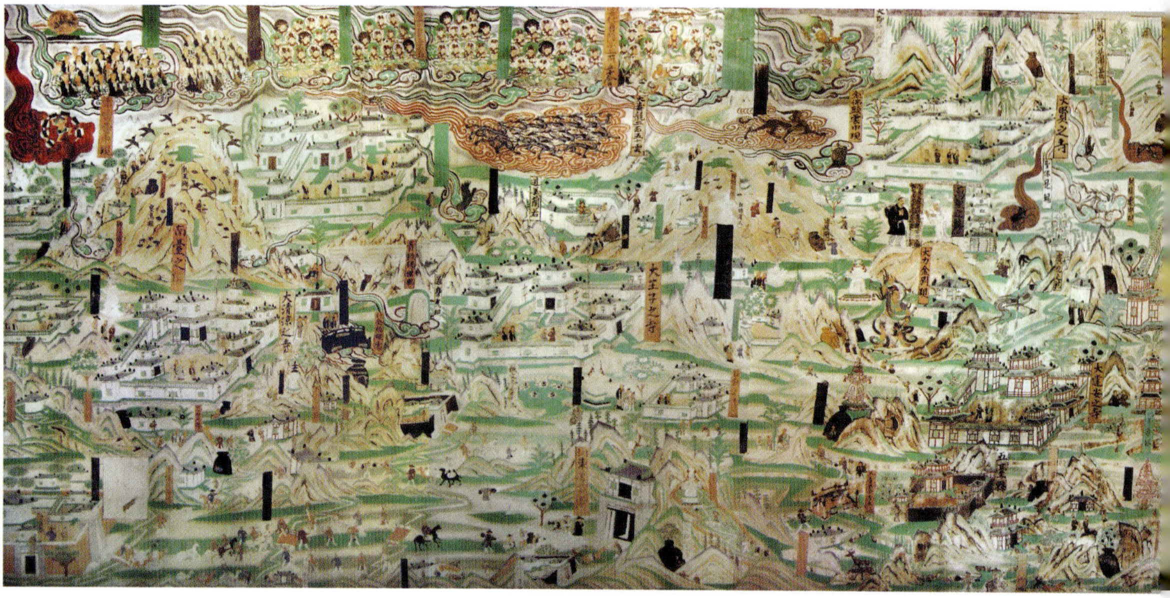

PLATE 8. Mural of Mount Wutai, west wall, Mogao Cave 61, 13.45 by 3.42 m. Composite digital image by author.

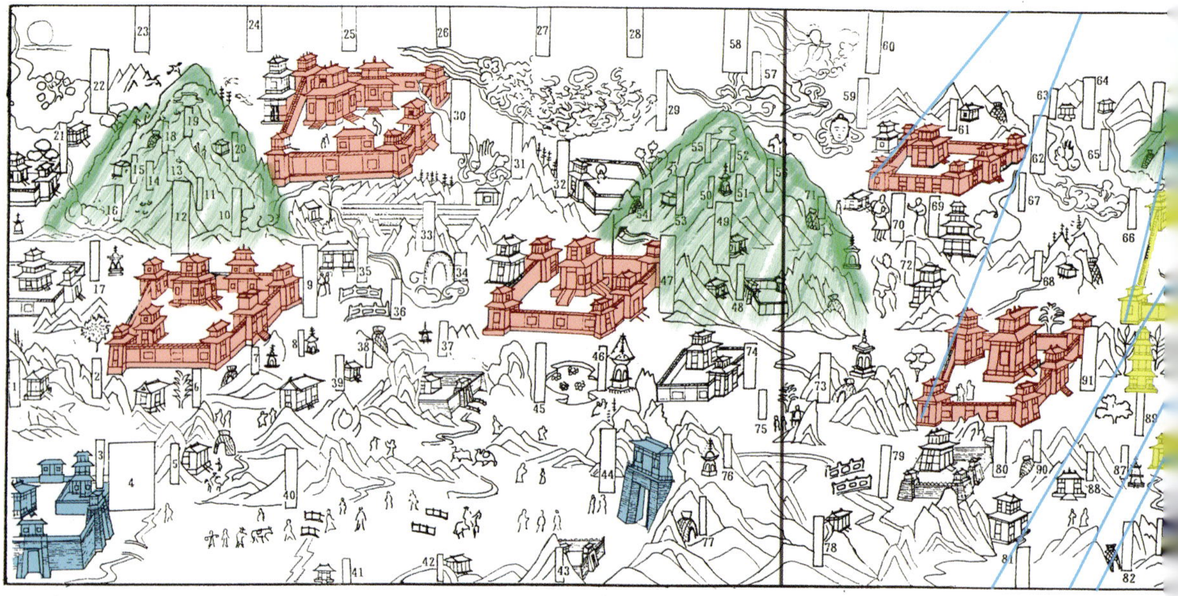

A B

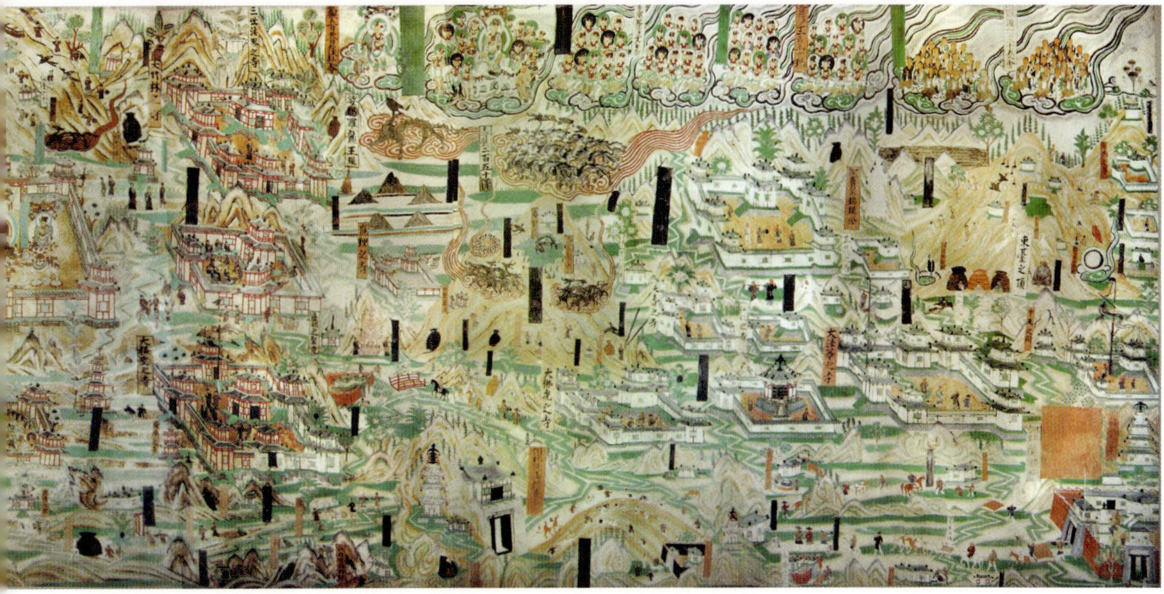

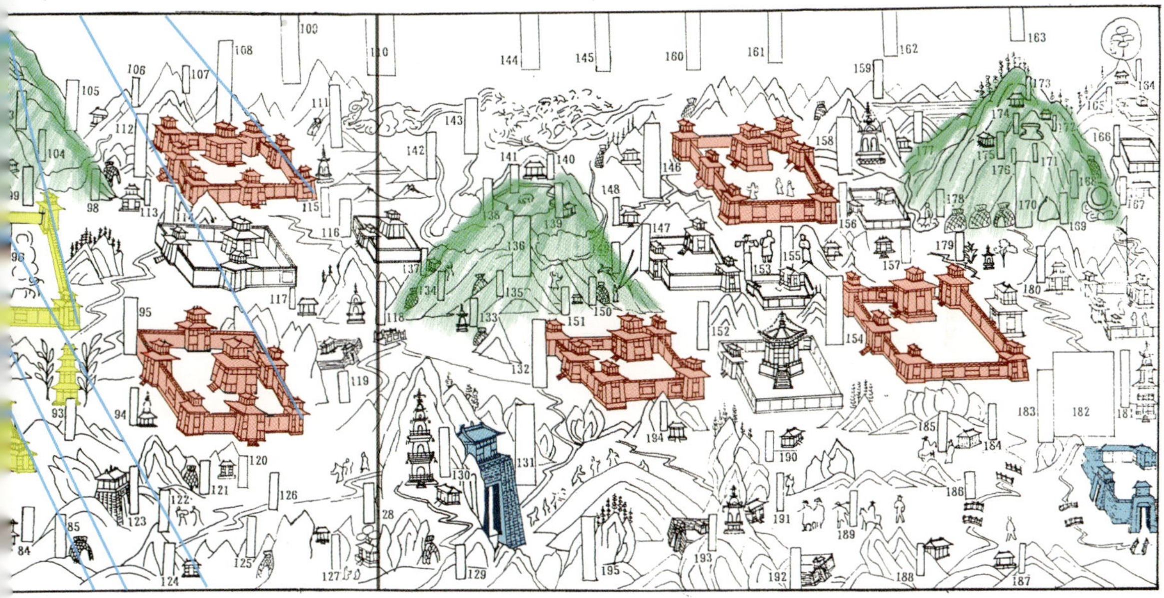

PLATE 9. The Mount Wutai mural, Mogao Cave 61, showing the major components of the mural: the Five Sacred Peaks, the ten great monasteries, and the visionary monastery at the center (the perspectival lines drawn to indicate a "herringbone perspective"; see fig. 6.14), and the four gateways along the pilgrimage routes into Mount Wutai: (A) Taiyuan in the Hedong Circuit; (B) Mountain Gate of the Southwest Route in the Hedong Circuit; (C) Mountain Gate of the Southeast Route in the Hebei Circuit; (D) Zhenzhou in the Hebei Circuit. After Zhao Shengliang, *Dunhuang shiku yishu: Mogao ku di 61 ku*, 18–19. Line drawing courtesy of Zhao Shengliang.

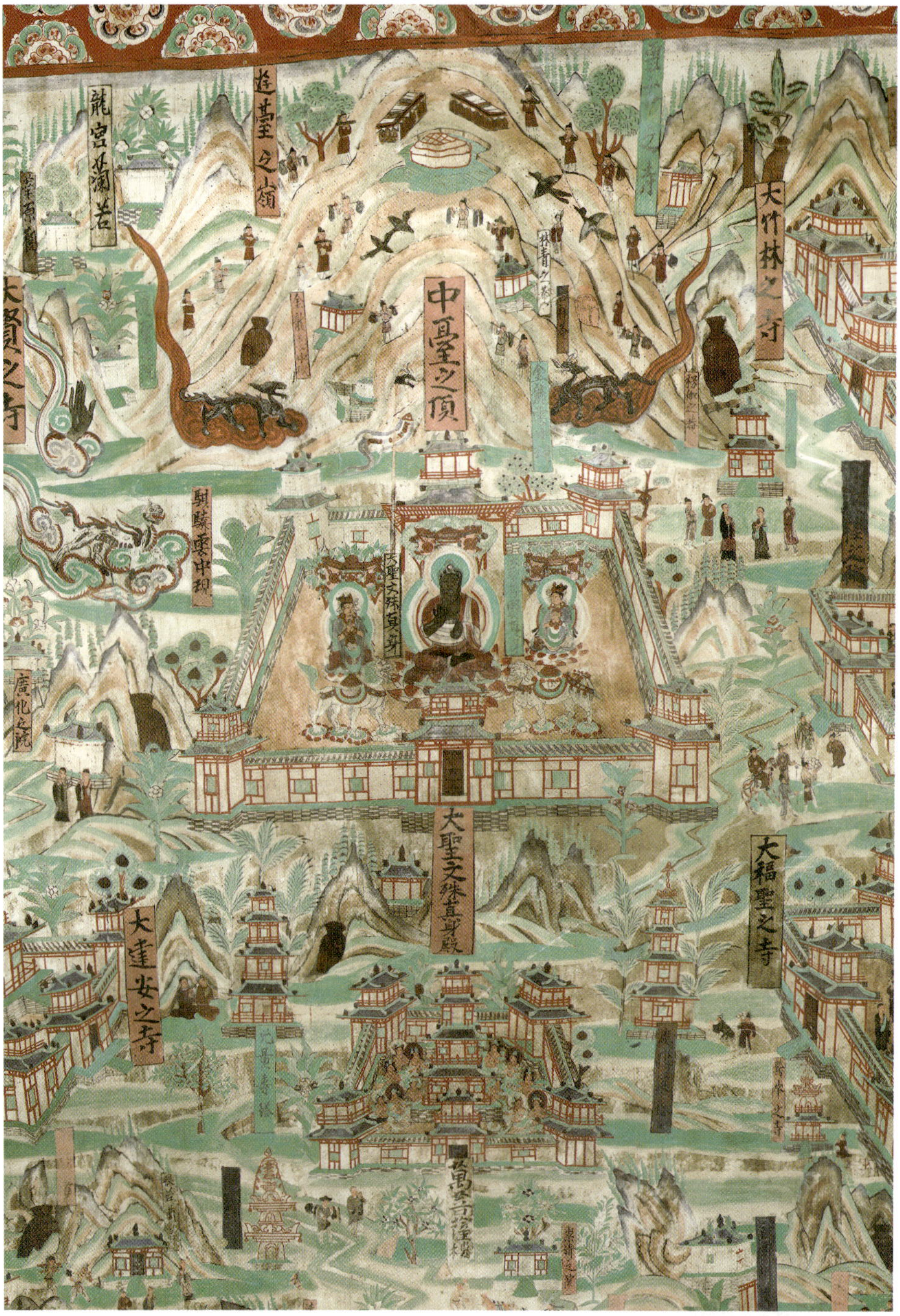

PLATE 10. The central area of the Mount Wutai west wall mural, Mogao Cave 61. The Hall of the True Body of the Great Sage Mañjuśrī, featuring the iconic triad of the Buddha and two bodhisattvas, is at the center of the mural. The hall is aligned on the same central axis as the Central Peak above and the Pavilion of Ten Thousand Fellow Bodhisattvas below. Photograph permission by Dunhuang Academy.

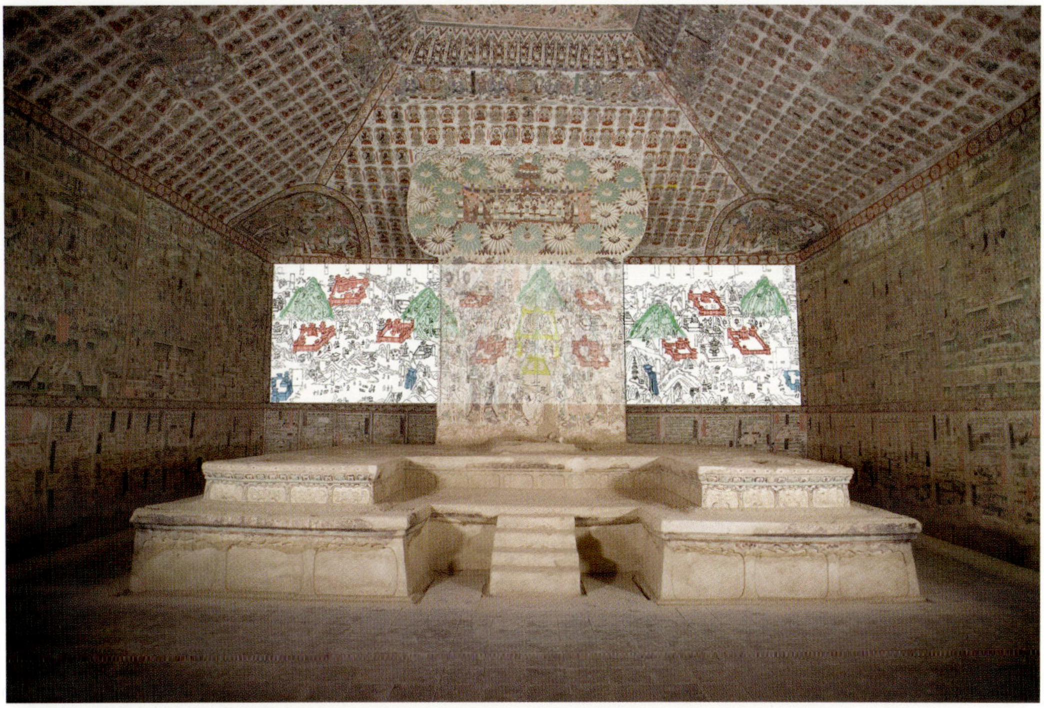

PLATE 11. The major components of the Mount Wutai mural and their positions in relation to the screen behind the altar, as seen from the eastern entrance of the cave. Composite digital image by author.

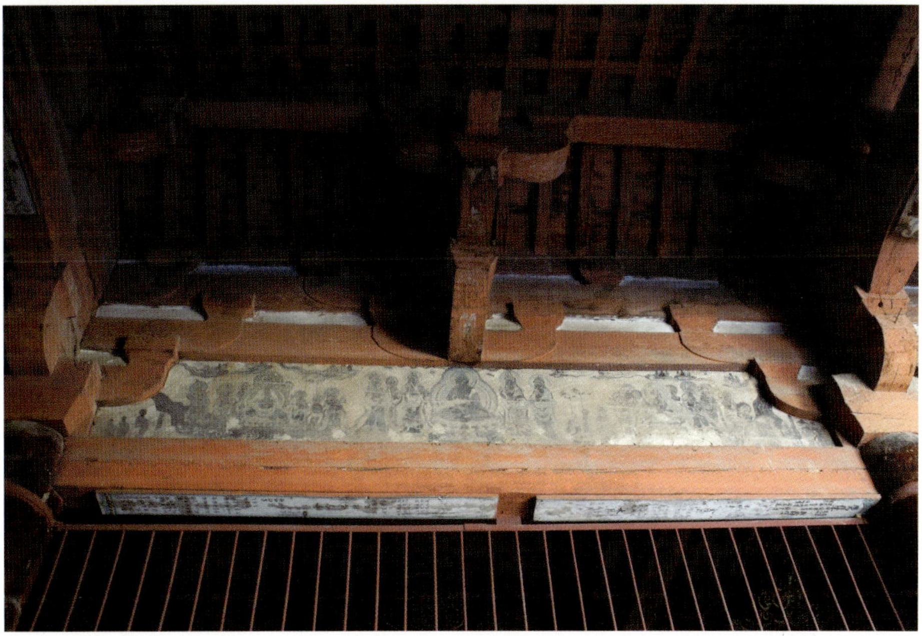

PLATE 12. Mural on the board above the architrave (*gongyan bi*) of the second north bay above the front row of interior columns, Great Buddha Hall, Foguang Monastery, Mount Wutai. 857 CE. It depicts the Amitābha Buddha preaching, surrounded by his bodhisattva attendants. Photograph by author.

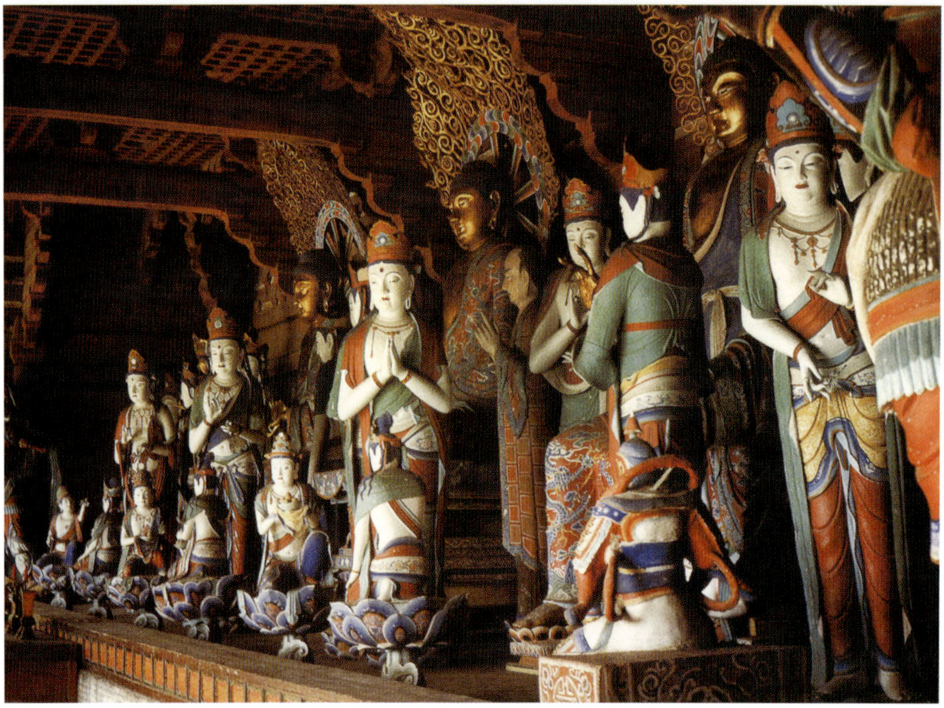

PLATE 13. Color reproduction of Figure 1.3. Main icons enshrined in the Great Buddha Hall, Foguang Monastery. 857 CE. From Chai and Chai, *Shanxi gudai caisu*, 37. Photograph by permission of Wenwu Press.

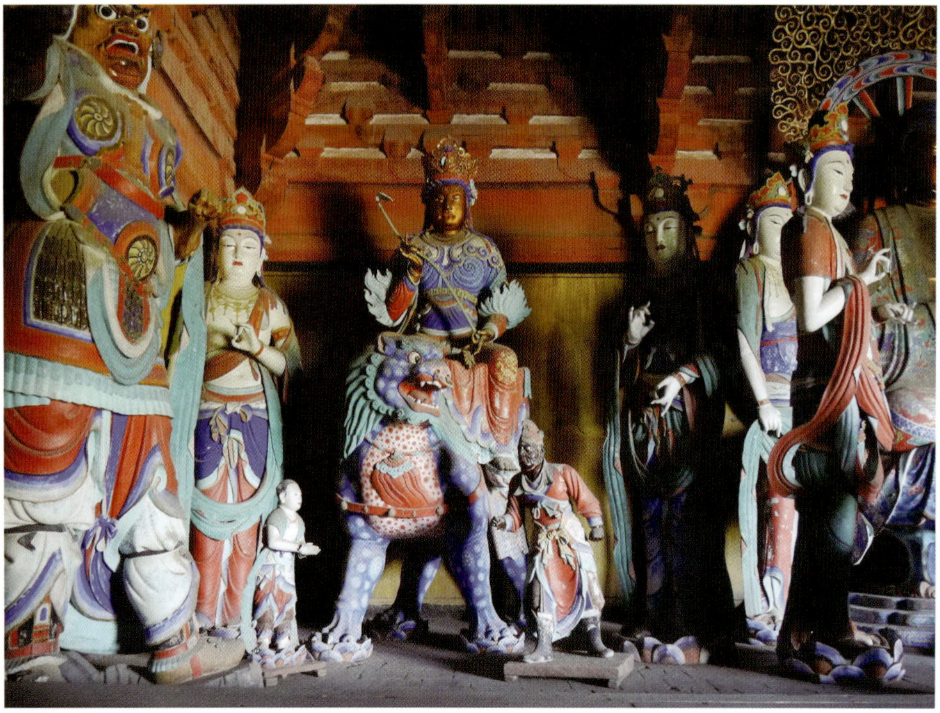

PLATE 14. Color reproduction of Figure C.4. Statue of the "true-presence" icon of Mañjuśrī riding a lion, enshrined inside the Great Buddha Hall, Foguang Monastery. 857 CE. Photograph by author.

CHAPTER TWO

Entering the Mountains, Localizing the Sacred Presence

It must be noted that the strong association between Buddhist monasteries and mountains—especially "sacred" mountains—is a typically Chinese phenomenon.

—E. Zürcher, *The Buddhist Conquest of China*

In 645, in a dedicatory prayer to Mount Heng (Hengshan), the Northern Sacred Peak, Emperor Taizong (r. 626–49) wrote:

> The dignified peak of the sacred mountain [*lingshan*] that extends across the northern wilderness marks the most extraordinary [landscape]. Beasts roar and dragons ascend where wind and rain breathe; the rainbow is its dress, and cranes are its canopies [at the place] where immortals travel to and fro. Its hills overlap one another haphazardly, and icy-cold mist wraps around their vegetation; layers of ridges crisscross randomly, all tinged here and there by rays of sunlight. . . . Soaring grandly, it is solid enough to last forever with Heaven and Earth; subtly potent, its energy has never been exhausted since antiquity.[1]

Although brief, and composed long after the sacred mountain cult was established in China, the prayer exhibits several basic characteristics of Chinese attitudes toward mountains. In ancient China, mountains were places of power, full of potencies and occult potentialities, and throughout China's history, it was a fundamental belief that mountains were breathing and moving, possessing animated and living forces accorded to none but the spiritual. Mountains were not only the domiciles of immortals in early China but, to use a term from Edouard Chavannes, they were themselves "les divinités."[2] In concluding his prayer, Emperor Taizong made a supplication to the sacred peak for protection of the northern territory, for which he promised to perform the most elaborate sacrifice, "for only the divinities [of the sacred mountain] to partake of."[3]

As much as mountains were deeply rooted in Chinese culture, the term "sacred mountain" has no precise Chinese equivalent. In Western religious tradition, the sacred is often associated with transcendent reality of a wholly different order, opposite to that of the profane.[4] In Chinese, for the terms that are translated as "sacred mountain" in English, the roots "numinous and efficacious" (*ling*) or "divine" (*shen*) were most often applied, to form the compound words *lingshan* and *shenshan* (*shan:* mountain).[5] In English, "sacred," "numinous," and "divine" all similarly refer to the category of ideas or things related to spiritual qualities, but concepts of *ling* and *shen* were quite different in ancient China, on two counts. First, they emphasized more specifically a sense of marvelous or extraordinary power, derived from the rarefied, potent, and dynamic energy (*qi*) that imbued an object or a site with a sacred quality or presence.[6] In its etymological origin, *shan*, or mountain, means "diffusion, what is able to diffuse and disperse vital energy, giving life to myriad things."[7] The same vital energy that constitutes the entire universe is what gives mountains their critical role in the cosmological scheme as the very life-nurturing source of the world. All mountains in this regard could potentially be divine (and sacred) and an object of worship in their own right.[8] Second, as seen in Taizong's prayer, a mountain was considered *ling* and *shen* because it was efficacious: it could respond not only to the supplication of men but also to human affairs (e.g., protect the nation, ensure the virtue of the ruler). In addition, located as they were often found at the extremities of the empire, great mountains demarcated and guarded the boundary of the known terrestrial land. In other words, instead of lying outside of the human realm, mountains were an inseparable part of it in the conception of reality and worldview of ancient China. Seeing the numinous and divine in a mountain was thus to recognize its productivity and fecundity in its prominent form, towering height, and inner energy, as well as its divine resonance in the larger cosmological context that qualified it as a sacred mountain.

With these fundamental understandings one can begin to observe the development of native traditions of the sacred mountain in China. For example, the cult of the Five Sacred Peaks (Wuyue) was instituted as an important state ritual dedicated to the chosen mountains located at the center and in each quadrant of the empire (see map 1, in introduction). Thus highly charged with spatial symbolism and geographic identity, the five peaks were the far points of the emperor's inspection tours around the imperium and the sites of important state sacrificial rituals dedicated to Heaven and Earth.[9] Impregnated with political and religious significance, sacred mountains were the recipients of sacrificial offerings throughout dynastic history; they were also inhabited by powerful (regional) deities and were known to have concealed the most sacred sources and treasures in their vast interior regions. Ge Hong's *The Master Who Embraces Simplicity* (Baopuzi), citing the now-lost *Scriptures of Immortals* (Xianjing), includes a list of twenty-seven "efficacious" mountains within the territory of China, the first-listed being the Five Sacred Peaks. All these mountains had their own deities, as well as earthbound "transcendents" (*dixian*), a kind of divine human who, rather than occupying heavenly realms, lived in the upper reaches of the mountains, where rare flowers and potent herbs grew.[10] Later, Daoists were trained to find and enter the sacred terrain to forage for herbal ingredients for medications and elixirs, to summon and subdue mountain spirits by talismanic exorcism, and to acquire from the interior of the mountain terrain the most profound knowledge of its sacred geography. Most important, sacred mountains were believed to be immune to the horrors of war, flood, and pestilence, and thus could be cultivated as the ideal place for

Daoist practitioners, who built religious structures there to pursue longevity or even immortality.[11]

When Buddhism made its way into China, it encountered this rich and long-standing tradition of the sacred mountain. In India, Buddhist sacred geography was conceived primarily around the sites associated with the life and work of Śākyamuni Buddha, and later with the distribution of his relics, as marked by stupas.[12] There is no comparable Indian example in which monasteries were built at a particular sacred mountain in order to partake of its spiritual quality. Instead, the relation between Buddhist monasteries and sacred mountains seems to derive from indigenous Chinese practice and understanding of religious geography.[13] The Buddhist sacred mountain cult in China can thus be regarded as part of the general Sinicization of Buddhism with its spread into China.[14] The first of the four great Buddhist mountains to be established in the fifth and sixth centuries, Mount Wutai, therefore represents the earliest attempt by Buddhists to take a native mountain and use it in the formation of a tradition of Buddhist sacred geography in China. But why were Buddhist practitioners drawn to mountains, why Mount Wutai in particular, and how was architecture deployed as part of the process?

Buddhism and the Indigenous Mountain Culture

Long before Mount Wutai was made into the premier Buddhist sacred site, Buddhists had already found their way into the mountains. Textual records of Buddhist practitioners taking residence in mountains can be traced back as early as the mid-third century.[15] At least twenty-four mountains played major roles as either Buddhist religious centers or places of mountain hermitage during the third through the sixth centuries (map 4).[16] Some of these mountains were close to urban centers, but most of them were in isolated areas.

Like Daoists, Buddhists were attracted to the loftiness and magnificence of great mountains, but the Buddhists aspired to different mysteries and religious goals. For Buddhists, mountains were for seclusion and the austere, monastic life and the ideal environment for self-discipline and religious devotion. Mountains set Buddhist ascetics apart from the ordinary, placing them on the fringes of secular life and on the threshold of spiritual and otherworldly attainment. The purity and tranquility of the mountain were regarded by many Buddhist masters as key to calming oneself through meditative practice and liberating the mind that was shackled to worldly things.[17] Early Buddhist monks showed little anxiety when entering native mountains and confronting local deities; rather, they are said to have subjugated the mountain spirits and demons and lived in peace with practitioners of local cults.

A prime example of this peaceable relation between mountain culture and Buddhism occurs in the biography of the eminent monk Huiyuan (334–416), whom we met briefly in chapter 1 making his vow before the image of the Amitābha Buddha. Originating from Yanmen in present-day northern Shanxi, Huiyuan first became acquainted with Buddhism at the monastery where Daoan resided, then

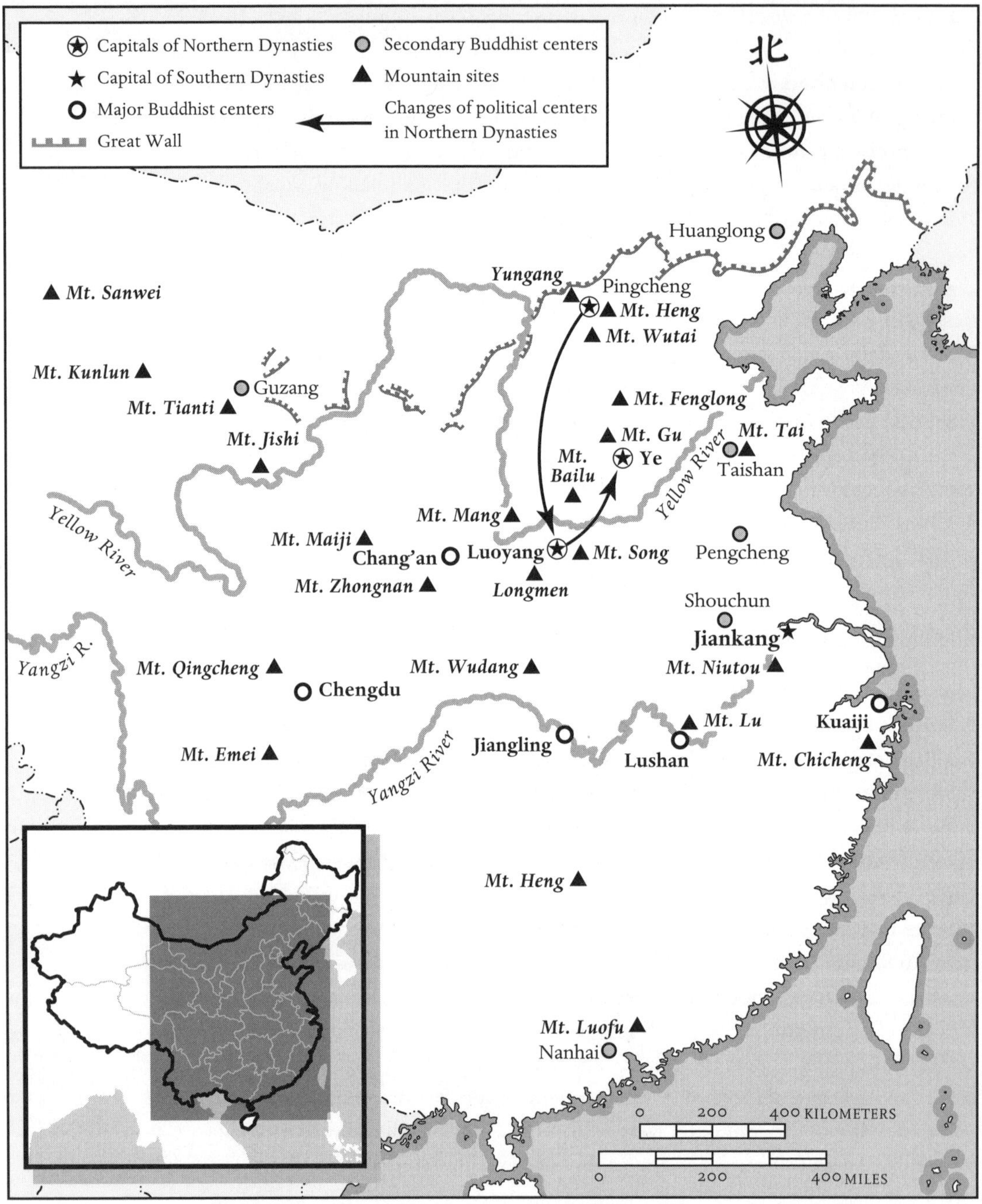

MAP 4. Early Buddhist urban centers and mountain sites in China from the third to sixth centuries. Adapted from Yan Gengwang, *Wei Jin Nanbeichao fojia*, 41. Reproduced with permission of the Academia Sinica.

located at Mount Heng (see map 4), the Northern Sacred Peak mentioned in Emperor Taizong's prayer. In 365, along with Daoan and his disciples, Huiyuan fled to Xiangyang in the south. Later, seeing that it "was pure and tranquil and a place worthy to appease the mind," Huiyuan decided to retire from the city and settle on Mount Lu (Lushan; see map 4), a mountain colorful with local tales of mountain lords and spirits, in today's Jiujiang, Jiangxi.[18] In building his monastic community, Huiyuan was said to have cracked open the ground, from which water then sprang out, creating a creek that supplied water to his followers. Later he summoned a giant snake to conjure rains that saved his followers from a drought. Inside the monastery, he set up a separate location for meditative practice, "where among the trees of the forest the mists gathered and the stony paths were covered with moss. Every spot seen by the eye or trodden by the foot was full of spiritual purity and majesty of atmosphere."[19]

Huiyuan's engagement with the mountain was clearly tinged with indigenous mountain culture, but he quickly understood the mountain's characteristics (its vital form, the resources to be found there) in different terms.[20] In a eulogy of Mount Lu, for instance, he said that the shape of the mountain peak "aspires to that of Vulture Peak" (Gṛdhrakūṭa), near Rājagṛha in central India, reputed to be the site where Śākyamuni Buddha delivered many teachings.[21] His revisioning of the mountain thus recast Mount Lu in a Buddhist conception of sacred geography. This conception was further justified by the divine presence of the Buddha, brought in to imbue Mount Lu with a particular Buddhist ambience: Huiyuan made a painting of the "Buddha's shadow," originally cast on the wall of a cave in Nagarahāra, after a visiting monk from India described to him the remarkable sight of that holy image.[22] Later, Huiyuan is said to have guided a statue of King Aśoka, reportedly found in the sea, to his monastery. After all, Mount Lu was not only the site where Huiyuan and his followers made a vow before the statue of the Amitābha Buddha to be reborn together in the paradise of the Pure Land, but also the place where they practiced *samādhi* in mindful recollection of the Buddha (*nianfo sanmei*), in the hope of seeing the Buddha face to face.[23]

Mount Lu under Huiyuan can be viewed as a prototypical example of how a native mountain was constructed as a Buddhist sacred site in early medieval China (though not a Buddhist *sacred mountain,* a status earned first and foremost by Mount Wutai). The natural constituents of mountains were considered numinous but were reconceived not so much for their own intrinsic qualities as by virtue of the sacramental presence. Two strategies for establishing mountains as Buddhist sacred sites can be recognized: converting the meaning of a mountain's natural features and bringing in sacred objects (miraculous images, scriptures, and relics, for example) from outside.[24] These two strategies align with the general argument made by many recent scholars that a sacred site is not a preconceived cosmic center but a sociocultural construct, subjected to revision and rewriting, and circumscribed by different historical trajectories in a "geohistorical synthesis."[25] Building Mount Wutai into the first Buddhist sacred mountain would have involved no less than such a construction; but curiously, the reconception and revision alone did not make it happen. Moreover, considering that many "mountains of renown" (*mingshan*) were charted in early Chinese territories, it is puzzling why Mount Wutai was chosen as *the* mountain to receive such unexpected and unprecedented recognition as the first Buddhist sacred mountain in China.

The natural wonders of Mount Wutai may be comparable to those of many great mountains, but its name was not as well known in early China. In fact, it was not even recognized in any early taxonomies of cultural and religious geography. One finds no Mount Wutai in the twenty-seven numinous mountains listed in *The Master Who Embraces Simplicity.* Some of the mountains in that list had early associations with Buddhism, in particular, Mount Heng—the renowned Northern Sacred Peak where Huiyuan joined Daoan's monastic order—which was in such close proximity to Mount Wutai that one wonders why the early records of the former never included the latter (see map 4).[26] In another system, after Daoism became a widespread religion during the second and third centuries CE, the network of Daoist sacred sites was gradually formulated into ten major and thirty-six minor "grotto heavens" (*dongtian*) and seventy-two "auspicious terrains" (*fudi*). Although the network was not systematized until after the dissemination of the canonical works by Sima Chengzhen (647–735) and Du Guangting (850–933), it bore some ancient sets and hierarchies of sacred sites.[27] In the now-lost *Scripture of Immortals,* Mount Wutai was recorded to have been named Purple Palace (Zifu), for "it constantly emanates purple vital energy [*qi*], and transcendents reside in it."[28] And yet, in the Daoist sacred geography, one still finds no Mount Wutai. This absence of Mount Wutai in the early documentation is probably most pointed in dynastic history, which includes no records of the mountain until 564 CE.[29] Considering its absence from the historical records of sacred mountains, Mount Wutai during the fifth and sixth centuries probably became a Buddhist sacred site under different terms and in a different context from those of other mountains, such as Mount Lu, in early China.

Leaving the City, Entering the Mountains

Exactly when Mount Wutai became a Buddhist mountain is unclear, although it is widely known that its recognition is based on specific passages from the *Flower Garland Sutra* (Huayan jing) translated into Chinese around 420 CE.[30] Mount Wutai was identified in the scripture as the mountain domicile of the bodhisattva Mañjuśrī, who figures prominently in several important early Mahayana sutras as one of the chief exponents of Śākyamuni's teachings.[31] This identification of bodhisattva with mountain, however, is most certainly an extrapolation that validated the numinous quality of the mountain and promoted the Buddhist practice there. Yet the most intriguing aspects of this identification are that it required the transportation of a foreign deity to a Chinese native mountain and had lasting consequences in the formation of a Buddhist sacred mountain tradition in China.

Identifying a Buddhist deity in China's territory, scholars argue, helped the clergy disseminate Buddhism strategically, in that they could build on the indigenous mountain culture and pursue their practice while domesticating the foreign religion in China's territory.[32] More specifically, establishing Mount Wutai as the sacred abode of an important bodhisattva helped reorient China in the hitherto Indocentric geography, subverting its peripheral status and making it a Buddhist center. Since the third and fourth centuries, many Chinese Buddhist monks had made pilgrimages to India to both visit the holy places related to the Buddha and gain a more complete understanding of his teachings. Around 400, when Faxian (337–422) arrived at Jetavana, one of the most important monasteries in India, the local monks exclaimed: "Wonderful! To think that men from the frontier of the earth should come so far as this from a desire to search for the Law."[33] With the alleged presence of Mañjuśrī at Mount Wutai, the creation of the sacred mountain as the domicile of the bodhisattva in China thus narrowed the gap between China and India and helped restructure Buddhist sacred geography, dispelling "the borderland complex that had tormented the Chinese clergy since the third and fourth centuries."[34] In this light, Mount Wutai can be viewed as part of the continual endeavor of Chinese Buddhists to seek and experience, right here at home, the divine presence that could authenticate their paths of spiritual pursuit.

All this, however, still does not fully explain why a mountain that was hitherto unknown became the particular sacred locus of the new divinity. Furthermore, to look at the formation of a Buddhist sacred mountain only in the larger historical and geographical context does not take into account the regional circumstances and Buddhist practices in north China that may have informed or shaped how Mount Wutai was built into a sacred mountain.

Located in the vicinity of Pingcheng to its north and Jinyang (near present-day Taiyuan) to its south, Mount Wutai was close to the military strife and political unrest that followed the disintegration of the Northern Wei in 534. In the dynasties that subsequently took control of northeastern China—the Eastern Wei (534–49) and Northern Qi (550–77)—the political center was relocated from Luoyang to a new capital in Ye, in modern Linzhang, Hebei (see maps 4, 5).[35] Members of the Gao family, the de facto power of the Eastern Wei and founders of the Northern Qi, were devout Buddhist patrons, and with their support the capital Ye was briefly the center of Buddhist learning and activities such as scripture translations. At one point, the city of Ye was said to have contained four thousand monasteries—including several large, imperially sponsored ones—and accommodated eighty thousand monastics.[36] A recent archaeological excavation at the site of Ye uncovered a large monastic complex to the south of the city's southern gate that may have been one of the official monasteries.[37] It comprises several walled compounds and has a large pagoda at its center, which is comparable to the Yongning pagoda in the former Northern Wei capital of Luoyang. The urban piety and popular devotion of the new capital also resembled those of the previous capital, but in Ye, the importance of the urban monasteries was complemented by the rise of monastic establishments in the mountains, where more intensive meditative and

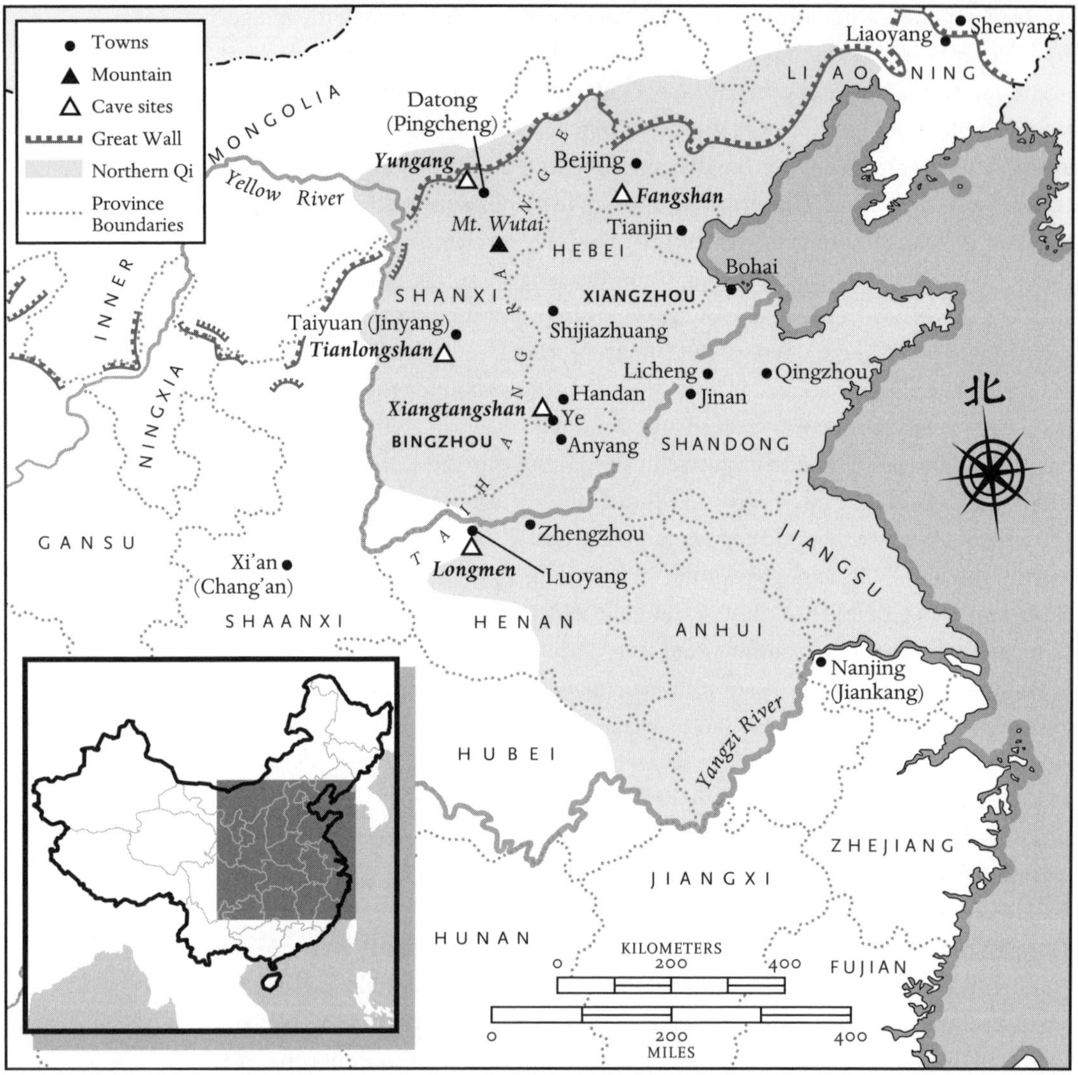

MAP 5. Territory held by the Northern Qi dynasty (550–577).

ascetic disciplines were practiced. Several masters were actively involved in exegetic studies and lectures in the capital, while also deeply engaged in regimented and spiritual practices at the mountain monasteries they established.[38]

From the last decade of the Northern Wei onward, political upheavals and the subsequent succession of short-lived dynasties necessarily reshaped both doctrinal emphasis and monastic praxis. Already before the fall of the Northern Wei, Yang Xuanzhi reported in *Record of the Monasteries of Luoyang* that meditative practices had become more important than scriptural studies at many monasteries in the city.[39] In the following decades, meditation, repentance, and intensive rituals increasingly became indispensable, even in the schools that traditionally prioritized exegetic and doctrinal learning. A great number of monasteries were established around Ye and Jinyang along the Taihang mountain range (today's Hebei and Shanxi), which reaches north to Mount Heng and Mount Wutai, attracting both meditative masters and austere ascetics (see map 5).[40] Most of the monasteries established in the mountain areas no longer exist, but some meditation caves and their icons, statues, and textual carvings survive at sites of former monasteries and reveal a strong eschatological concern with the anticipated demise of the Dharma.

The notion of the dissolution of the Dharma (*mofa,* or as it is known in Japanese, *meppo*) refers to the time of the "destruction of the true teachings" (S: *saddharma-vipralopa;* C: *famie*).[41] It is based on the periodic theory of Buddhist cosmological time, allegedly expounded by the Buddha on his deathbed, predicting the decline and final extinction of all things, including his teachings. The concept itself was transmitted to China through early Indian scriptures, such as the *Nirvana Sutra* (Niepan jing), as well as through Liangzhou-style Buddhism after the region was occupied by the Northern Wei, although it was not systematized into the scheme of the well-known "three periods of teachings" until the sixth century. The tripartite temporality describes this fear-inducing decline as proceeding from the beginning period of the Buddha's true teaching (*zhengfa*), through a period where the semblance of the true teaching is still retained (*xiangfa*), to a period in which the true teaching is no longer attainable (*mofa*). Although there were different thoughts about when the decline would have begun, it was believed that the epoch had already commenced, a conviction further reinforced by earlier suppression of Buddhism during the Northern Wei and recent warfare in northern China.[42] If "the whole of later Buddhism proceeds under the shadow of this sense of decline,"[43] this shadow also demanded a new system of exegesis and practice to counter the anxiety and look for possible ways into the light. The need was pressing and personal for monks to be diligent now and to search for methods of prolonging spiritual pursuit in the current period until they were rewarded with salvation.

To the master Huisi (515–77), who helped define the first tripartite scheme, going to the mountains may have offered a viable means to cope with the decline. He was drawn to Mount Heng (Hengshan), the Southern Sacred Peak, as documented in his *Tract on the Vow Made by the Great Master [Hui]si of the Southern Sacred Peak* (Nanyue si dachanshi lishi yuanwen), composed in 558. In his vow, Huisi pledged to retreat to the mountains: "I am now entering the mountains to practice asceticism [and to] confess and repent for breaking the *vinaya,* hindering the Way, and any cumbersome sins," as he intended to "meet Maitreya [the Future Buddha] in this very body in a future period." To gain such a vision, he continues, "[I] vow to enter the mountains to search for [the way] of transcendents [and to] seek longevity in order to attain the final enlightenment."[44] Although personal, Huisi's desire to find numinous and efficacious mountains and his belief that his experience of the divine presence there might bring about timely salvation here and now in the advent of the decline are explicitly declared.

This eschatological concern may reflect the awareness that the Chinese had of their physical and temporal distance from the Buddha and may have reinforced the perception that the chaotic social and political circumstances of the time indicated an imminent demise of the Dharma. Before his arrival at Mount Heng in the south in 568, Huisi was active in the Eastern Wei and Northern Qi as part of the northern

Buddhist community.[45] Like Huisi, many members of this community left cities and relocated to the mountains as the ideal venue in the preparation for the final age. The surviving monastic structures at mountain sites along the Taihang range with their images and scripture engravings can therefore be investigated as both a rhetorical apparatus and a material solution in this *mofa* discourse. The material evidence in turn provides a broader and circumstantial context to examine how Mount Wutai, in this particular area and period, was built into the mountain domicile of the bodhisattva Mañjuśrī.

Mount Wutai in Regional Perspectives

Aside from sporadic mentions in the official history, the most reliable texts concerning Mount Wutai came from a few monk-scholars during the early Tang. The most comprehensive and earliest extant work is *Ancient Records of [Mount] Qingliang* (Gu Qingliang zhuan), compiled by the monk Huixiang (fl. mid- to late seventh century) during 680–83 after a visit to the mountain in 667.[46] The *Ancient Records* introduce the origin, history, miraculous tales, numinous sites, and renowned people of Mount Wutai—a format later developed into the literary genre known as mountain gazetteer (*shanzhi*).[47] The name Mount Qingliang, literally "Mount Clear and Cool," a name not corroborated in any pre-Tang official records, is used by Huixiang as a synonym for Mount Wutai. According to Huixiang, the name was taken from a scriptural passage that had been used to identify Mount Wutai as a sacred abode. In the chapter "Dwelling Domiciles of the Bodhisattvas" (Pusa zhuchu pin) of the *Flower Garland Sutra* is a list of locations alleged to host a particular bodhisattva, Mount Qingliang among them: "In the northeast there is a bodhisattva domicile, named Mount Qingliang. In the past, various bodhisattvas dwelt in it. At present there is the bodhisattva named Mañjuśrī with his fellow ten thousand bodhisattvas, to whom [Mañjuśrī] frequently preaches the Dharma."[48]

This often-quoted passage contains no obvious indication as to where Mount Qingliang could be, exactly, not to mention which mountains in China might be called such. Early Indian sutras yielded no direct linkage between the bodhisattva and China, and did not name Mount Wutai,[49] although the passage just quoted could be interpreted in favor of the identification. Mount Wutai is indeed located in the northeast (of China), and its five snow-covered peaks would be cold all year round, befitting the name Mount Clear and Cool. Yet, as the *Flower Garland Sutra* was mostly composed in India without any apparent reference to China, the connection was more likely interpolated retrospectively, after Buddhism had already been established at Mount Wutai.[50] Still, why and how was Mount Wutai recognized as the mountain where Mañjuśrī presides?

We know very little about the early history of Mount Wutai, or what kind of place it was when the "canonical evidence" from the *Flower Garland Sutra* was translated circa 420. Huixiang cites an otherwise lost passage from *Commentary on the Waterways Classic* (Shuijing zhu, ca. 515–24), as a reference to the pre-Buddhist Mount Wutai:

> The mountains whose five crests rise majestically above others are called Five Peaks [Wufeng]. In the third year of the Yongjia reign of the [Western] Jin [309 CE], over one hundred households from Suoren County of the Yanmen Commandery entered the mountains to avoid turmoil. They followed the mountain inhabitants they came upon, and subsequently lived amid the rocks and wild [of the mountains], never to return. People who passed by from time to time saw the dwellers from afar but could not find their whereabouts when visiting [the mountains]. Consequently, people regarded the mountain as the domain of transcendents.[51]

The "turmoil" refers to the invasion of the non-Chinese Huns who caused continuous warfare and eventually felled the Western Jin (265–316) in 316.[52] During that chaotic period, Mount Wutai was a hideout for residents of neighboring regions, but its inaccessibility and striking natural features also cast the mountains in a mysterious veil of immortality.

The Daoist tenor of the description recalls another early name for Mount Wutai, "Purple Palace" (Zifu), as noted by Huixiang, and that continued to be used into the sixth and seventh centuries.[53] Located just inside the northern border of China, the remote mountain fastness of Mount Wutai appeared suited to mental concentration, the preparation of elixirs, and even achieving what was for some Daoists the ultimate goal, immortality. A Daoist practitioner, Lu Taiyi, known for his almanac and techniques of prognostication, traveled to Mount Wutai around 600 to look for the potent medicinal herbs growing in the mountains. While he was there, it is recorded that "with many of his followers, [Taiyi] built thatched huts under some mountain rocks, believing that immortality could be attained [there]."[54] In the early Tang, the official gazetteer of geography, *Gazetteer Encompassing the Earth* (Kuodizhi, ca. 640), was quoted by Huixiang as saying of Mount Wutai: "Its hills rise magnificently in layers and its winding paths coil and spiral. [With] its numinous peaks and divine streams, [the mountain is] not the place for the mundane to dwell. All those who stay are masters of meditation and cultivators of profound knowledge."[55] As late as the sixth and early seventh centuries, Mount Wutai was still perceived in the terms and conventions of the traditional Chinese mountain culture.

Yet the mountain's perceived qualities, numinous (*ling*) and divine (*shen*), were equally enticing to Buddhist masters, although these qualities inspired different religious practices and visions from those of their precursors. An example comes from the Pure Land master Tanluan (ca. 476–ca. 542), who was from Yanmen, in the vicinity of Mount Wutai. According to his biography, before making up his mind about his spiritual path, Tanluan was attracted to Mount Wutai for its "divine traces and numinous marvels that were popularly known among people." He was then determined to "go [to the mountains] and search [for the traces and marvels] in order to observe all the sacred vestiges left by the divine."[56] Inspired by his experience at the mountains, he decided to become ordained, and he later devoted himself to practices of meditative visualization for a rebirth in the Amitābha's Pure Land of Sukhāvatī. Similarly, Tanqian (542–607), the renowned monk of the Ten

Stages school (Dilun), also paid homage at Mount Wutai early in his career. "The mountain," his biography records, "is replete with numinous traces," and he was able to "observe [there] all the divine marvels."[57] Tanqian later moved from Mount Wutai and stayed in Ye before finally taking up residence in the nearby Mount Linlü (Linlüshan). Records such as these of eminent monks who visited Mount Wutai increased after the first half of the sixth century, and rather than exegetes, those who made their way to the mountains were mostly masters engaged in meditative practices or seeking "spiritual resonance" (*gantong*) at the mountains.[58] The numinous and divine qualities and (natural) marvels of Mount Wutai, for Buddhists, were taken as "traces" and "vestiges" that certified the presence of the divinity at the mountains, making the site conducive to more intensive meditative concentration and spiritual aspirations.

Interestingly, neither Tanluan's nor Tanqian's account specifies exactly who left the traces and vestiges or to what these traces and vestiges refer. In other words, although suggestive of the divine presence, Mount Wutai had not yet been connected to the bodhisattva Mañjuśrī. The localization of the bodhisattva's presence at this mountain site seems to have occurred only gradually over the second half of the sixth century and continued into the early seventh century. Yet once the connection was made—that is, the claim that the unmediated presence of the bodhisattva could not be observed elsewhere but at this very site—Mount Wutai was deemed the most sacred among mountains. This shift represents a critical transition in the ontology of Mount Wutai. In order to investigate how a desire to localize the sacred presence came about in this broader region and why this particular bodhisattva, and no other Buddhist deity, was bound to Mount Wutai, we must first take into account two aspects of this regional context: the Buddhist communities that evolved with a cluster of canonical texts in this region, and the geographic relations of Mount Wutai with other sites of the region.

Although lasting only briefly, from 534 to 577, the capital Ye of the Eastern Wei and Northern Qi, which replaced Luoyang as the seat of empire, was the new epicenter of the northern Buddhism. Yang Xuanzhi reports in *Record of the Monasteries of Luoyang* that during the last years of the Northern Wei, "the imperial seat moved to Ye, accompanied by monks and nuns of different monasteries."[59] To a significant extent, Ye inherited the style and canonical emphases of Buddhism from the previous capital. A cluster of texts translated during the first decades in the earlier capital Luoyang continued to be influential in shaping religious aspirations in northeastern China (including Mount Wutai). In particular, the Ten Stages school developed, based on the *Commentary on Ten Stages Sutra,* which addressed the requirements of the bodhisattva path. Several monks figuring prominently during the period, among them Huiguang (468–537), Sengchou (480–560), Daoping (488–559), and Lingyu (518–605), were involved in the learning of the bodhisattva path. Other scriptural references interwoven into these studies include the *Nirvana, Lotus, Perfection of Wisdom* (Prajñāpāramitā), and *Vimalakīrti Sutras* and most important, the *Flower Garland Sutra.*

Treading the path, however, was more than doctrinal study and had to be implemented in ritual and meditative practice. For most monks in the Ten Stages tradition, both exegesis and doctrine were driven by praxis.[60] Indeed, it is within this frame, of a praxis that complemented the doctrinal texts, that we can begin to sketch a fuller picture of the Buddhist scene during this period from a regional perspective. A variety of meditative practices were devised, many of which involved visualization and repentance and had an emphatic salvific import, evoking the vision of the Pure Land for not only a rebirth in the blissful world but also attainment of Buddhahood. These practices also reveal people's anxiety and desire for ultimate liberation from the darkening days of the decline. Evidence comes from the religious content of the meditation caves, images, scripture engravings, and devotional inscriptions that have survived in the mountain areas of this region. The region of northeastern China can thus be viewed as a large community linked by texts and practices, whose members shared similar religious goals and spiritual aspirations, of which the localization of Mañjuśrī's presence at Mount Wutai would have been an integral part.[61]

To see this, we need to turn to the second of the two regional considerations mentioned above, Mount Wutai's geographic position in northeastern China. After the founding of the Eastern Wei, the shift of the political center from Luoyang to Ye changed the Buddhist map in northern China. Not only did Ye assume the central position, but Jinyang—the base of the Gao family and an important garrison city—to the south of Mount Wutai, became ever more important (see map 5). In particular, mountain passes (*xingdao*) linking the two jurisdictional provinces Xiangzhou and Bingzhou, generally corresponding to today's Hebei and Shanxi provinces, served to expedite travel between the two cities otherwise separated by the Taihang mountain range.[62] After the start of the Northern Qi, Jinyang was designated the lower capital (*xiadu*), as opposed to the superior capital (*shangdu*), a designation given to Ye.[63] Through the sponsorship of the reigning Gao family, Buddhism flourished in both capitals and the mountain areas in their vicinities; several monastic establishments were built along the mountain passes between the two capitals, as the imperial court frequently traveled to and fro. Some were individual pagodas and caves, while others were major monasteries, receiving lavish support from the imperial patronage. By the second half of the sixth century, there is little doubt that the area from Ye to Jinyang on both sides of the Taihang range was considered a sacred area inhabited by a large Buddhist community.

Although there are still missing pieces in the early history of Mount Wutai, in all likelihood it is during this brief but transitional period of the Eastern Wei and Northern Qi that the mountain began to receive significant attention. Located to the south of Pingcheng, Mount Wutai may already have seen the construction of Buddhist monastic establishments under imperial auspices of the Northern Wei. The evidence becomes more certain after the beginning of the Northern Qi. In the *Ancient Records*, Huixiang reports: "The Gao family of the Northern Qi fervently promoted the teachings. The [number of] pagodas and monasteries in the nation was close to forty thousand; over two hundred monasteries were here at [Mount Wutai]. Moreover, [a percentage of] taxes from eight prefectures was subtracted to provide funds for clothes and food to be used by [clergy and laity] at the mountains."[64] This passage can be read together with another record from the biography of Sengchou, the leading figure in the northern Buddhist community of this period. According to his account, Emperor Wenxuan (r. 550–59) once declared to Sengchou that the court was committed to set aside one-third of the annual state revenue to support the Three Jewels.[65] Exactly how this commitment was realized is unclear, but there is sufficient evidence to suggest that Buddhism regained its former prominence during the Northern Qi and that traces of its practice were widespread not only in the urban centers but, more important, in mountain areas that, as indicated in Huixiang's account, likely would also include Mount Wutai.

Recent research has revealed the geographic distribution of surviving sutra engravings, meditation caves, and devotional images produced during the Northern Qi period.[66] The evidence indicates four distinctive regions of Buddhist activities: the vicinity around the capital Ye, the Bingzhou area around Jinyang, the Dingzhou area in today's Hebei, and the Qingzhou area in Shandong (map 6). All four regions can also be compared based on the type of artifacts they contain, which further suggests a "center-and-periphery pattern" among them.[67] The vicinity of Ye, containing both sutra engravings and Buddhist images, forms the overall center; the area to the west of the Taihang range and the central Shandong region in the east that flank the Ye region compose the first peripheral zone, which has only sutra engravings; and a larger area stretching from Bingzhou around Jinyang, Dingzhou, and Qingzhou in Shandong forms the second peripheral zone, which has only images. Until more evidence is found, it can only be speculated why some areas produced only images and others only textual engravings. It is certain, however, that under the Northern Qi the Buddhist communities in the broader northeastern China shared the same religious sentiments about the decline of the Dharma, and similar aspirations to create icons and sutra carvings to address this abiding concern. The sacred mountain cult at Mount Wutai established during this same period, though it was not known for any surviving icons or textual carvings, seems to have offered yet another solution, namely the immanent presence of the presiding bodhisattva Mañjuśrī. Or more precisely, the sacred presence was assiduously sought after by Buddhists of the religious communities in this large area; with its "numinous traces" and "divine marvels," Mount Wutai was slowly developed into the ideal site not only for "perfecting various meditative concentrations,"[68] but more important, for the potential encounter with the divinity. Surviving images, carved scriptures, and monastic structures provide clues about how the desire for a divine vision of a timely salvation was expressed and substantiated.

Monumental Desire: Buddhist Structures in Stone

The Northern Qi was prolific in constructing Buddhist monuments during its short-lived dynasty, yielding a style of art that is at once dynamic and delicate. Its achievement can largely be attributed to the generous sponsorship of the court

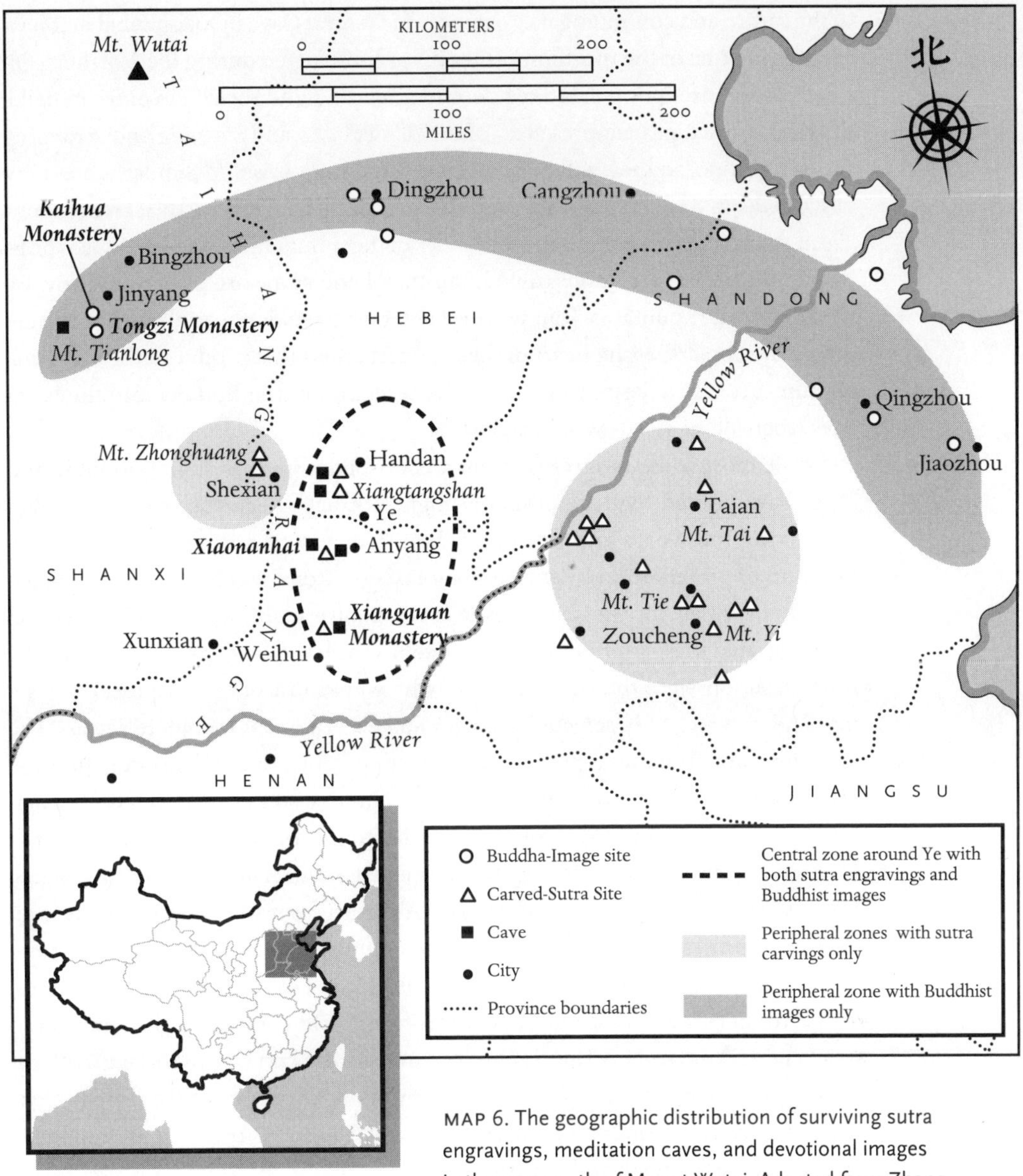

MAP 6. The geographic distribution of surviving sutra engravings, meditation caves, and devotional images in the area south of Mount Wutai. Adapted from Zhang Zong, "Northern Qi," 286. Reproduced with permission of the Academia Sinica.

and local elites, but more significantly, to the anxiety about the decline of the Dharma that led to construction activities addressing eschatological concerns. The last point can be observed in the scriptures—from a few passages, to excerpts of sutras, to complete sutras—carved directly on the surface of cliffs or engraved on the walls of caves hewn into mountainsides. Transcribed onto the surface of such imperishable material, Buddhist teachings, along with Buddha images, were made permanent, to be passed down to later generations, thus transmitting Dharma to the future and continuing its existence. At Central Cave in Xiaonanhai in the vicinity of Ye, one of the most important caves constructed during the Northern Qi, a dedicatory inscription dated 560 describes "cutting into the cliff in order to make the cave and sculpt true presence [of the deities] . . . [and] carving and arranging sutras on stone, so they will be transmitted and not perish."[69] Similarly, a eulogy of 579 dedicated to the scripture carved in oversize characters on the cliff of Mount Tie in Shandong emphasizes the durability of the mountain surface in these words: "Silk and bamboo are easily ruined, but metal and stone are hard to destroy. By virtue of high mountains, [the writing] will be passed down endlessly."[70] As suggested by scholars, at the heart of these undertakings that produced the surviving monuments was a desire to preserve the teachings of the Buddha into the latter days when all his words would be lost.[71]

While most scholars agree that this anxiety of decline was an important factor, some have argued that preservation might not have been the only motivation for carving the words and images of the Buddha in permanent materials. The program of preservation by transcribing texts on stone was by no means unique to sutra carvings, for the same desire to keep alive words and memories is also demonstrated in inscriptions of tomb epitaphs from the same period.[72] Moreover, if preservation were the consideration, why were most of the scriptural engravings and carvings only selected passages and excerpts, not complete sutras? The ambitious undertaking to preserve the entire Buddhist canon did occur, after the Sui dynasty (581–617), when the monk Jingwan (d. 639) began a project that systematically carved sutras on stone slabs gathered in hand-hewn caves at the Yunju Monastery (Yunjusi) near Beijing. It was the first attempt in history to completely preserve the entire collection of sutras.[73] A record from the caves explicitly indicates Jingwan's intention: "This set of stone scriptures has been prepared for a time in the future when calamity will befall the Buddhist Law. As long as there are still scriptures in this world, do not open [this cave]."[74] In contrast to this decision to store and seal the stone scriptures in caves, most sutra carvings of this period were exposed to natural hazards on mountain slopes or cave surfaces, and their physical presence and visibility endowed them with the status of public monuments, meant to be seen, read, and worshiped.

The prime motivation for patronizing Buddhist monuments in medieval China was not so much to preserve the Dharma as to acquire worldly prestige and religious merits. According to several popular Mahayana texts, the transcription of a sutra in any form that causes anyone to read, recite, or write the scripture would bring to the donor many spiritual benefits. Like image, text (i.e., Dharma) in its physical form was also an object of worship, and preserving it in stone made both its existence and its presence monumental. Making copies of the teachings in imperishable material would create permanent shrines and concurrently provide durable evidence of the power and wealth of the Buddhist establishment and its patrons.[75] In this regard, these carved texts, sculpted images, and hand-hewn caves were monuments, capable of recalling and reenacting in the future the social, political, and religious significance of their making.

While this monumental aspect is important, there is yet a different but more exigent and personal aspect of these undertakings. Aiming not only for perpetuity, these texts, images, and caves were created with an effort to turn preservation for the future into an embodied practice now. The pressing issue of the decline of the Dharma ignited the idea of preserving the teachings in stone until the latter time, but it also brought about a more pragmatic mindset concerning the present, looking for ways in which karmic destiny could be interrupted or at least delayed. One can recall Huisi's vow to "enter the mountain" to search for the way of transcendents and to seek longevity in order to attain final enlightenment in this life. Hand-hewn caves, stone scriptures, and sculpted images had all existed before this time, but their sudden popularity and spread in mountain areas during the Northern Qi, coinciding with the growing awareness about the advent of the final days among the same Buddhist communities, was not merely by chance. The pronounced use of stone, a medium that did not have a long history in Chinese monuments or architecture, cannot be overlooked.[76] Its durability served to not only preserve the moment of the ritual for the future but also make that moment repeatable, therefore prolonging its duration to at least delay, if not counteract, the eventual demise and deterioration. These caves were not just stone structures but ones carved with texts and images that could evoke specific rituals through an embedded reading and viewing logic that could be practiced repeatedly over time for spiritual and salvific purposes. It is by way of this practice, to preserve the moment of ritual enactment in these stone structures at the mountain site, that we can begin to see the desire for localizing the divine presence here and now.

One of the earliest examples of cave temples is at Xiaonanhai near today's Anyang, Henan. Located close to the major mountain pass between Ye and Jinyang (see maps 5, 6), the Xiaonanhai site has three caves, all cut into rock (East, Central, and West), and was associated with the leading Buddhist scholar-master Sengchou. According to the dedicatory inscription engraved above the entrance to the Central Cave, initiated in 550 by a master Sengfang from the Lingshan Monastery (Lingshansi), the caves and sculpted images were completed by Sengchou and his disciples, then residing in nearby Yunmen Monastery (Yunmensi), and the textual engravings were added after Sengchou died in 560. Because of extensive quarrying, the three caves now look like free-standing structures, but originally they were all carved into the same slope, each with its own small entrance. Of the three caves, the Central Cave (fig. 2.1a) retains the most complete ritual program and can be used as a representative of the group for this analysis.[77]

Unlike caves from the Northern Wei period, Central Cave at Xiaonanhai is relatively small, with a floor measuring 1.34 by 1.19 meters wide and 1.78 meters high. Everything inside the cave is carved or engraved in the solid rock from which the cave itself is made: a low, raised platform runs round the left (west), rear (north), and right (east) walls in a horseshoe shape, each wall containing a set of iconic figures. On the west and east walls are, respectively, the Amitābha Buddha with his two attending bodhisattvas, and Maitreya with his (figs. 2.2a, 2.2b); each set is backed by engraved images that facilitate visualization of its associated Pure

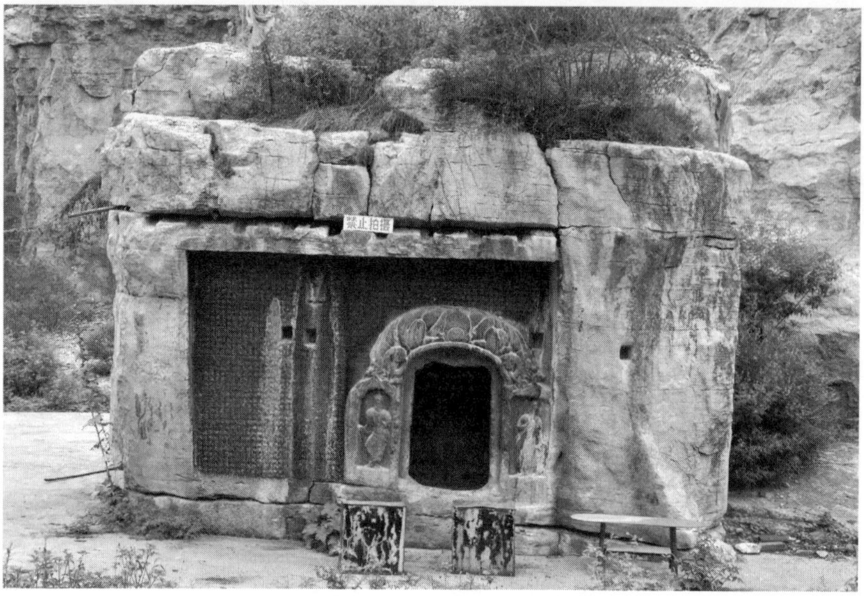

FIGURE 2.1a. Front facade of Xiaonanhai Central Cave, Anyang, Henan. 550–560 CE. Its surrounding rock has been quarried in past years, leaving the cave an isolated structure. Photograph courtesy of Jungmin Ha.

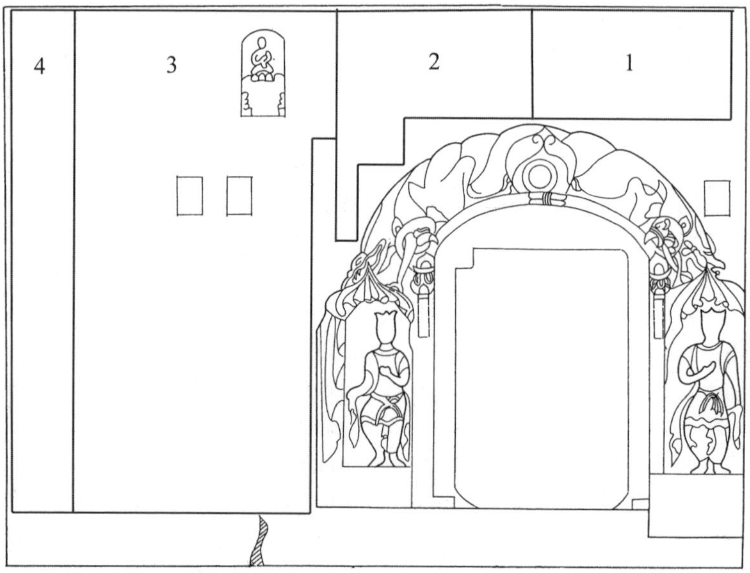

FIGURE 2.1b. Front facade of Xiaonanhai Central Cave. The numbered areas contain inscriptions: (1) dedication; (2) hymn redacted from the *Flower Garland Sutra;* (3) excerpt from the "Sagely Practice" chapter of the *Nirvana Sutra;* (4) hymn excerpted from the "Sagely Practice" chapter of the *Nirvana Sutra.* Line-drawing after Yen, "Beiqi changuan ku de tuxiang kao," fig. 36. Diagram courtesy of Yen Chüan-ying.

Land—Sukhāvatī for the former, and Tuṣita for the latter. On the north wall is a sitting Buddha flanked by two disciples, at the corners. Used for meditative purposes, the iconic program inside the cave is preceded by scripture engraved on the facade of the cave (fig. 2.1b), which states the meditational content and result of the meditative practice.

The chief meditative aspiration at Xiaonanhai is revealed in the inscription (see fig. 2.1b, at point 3), a passage from the "Sagely Practice" chapter (Shengxing pin) of the *Nirvana Sutra,* the scriptural basis for Sengchou's practice of Four Foundations of Mindfulness (*Si nianchu*).[78] The meditation is a fourfold visualization procedure, in which the practitioner concentrates on the impurity of body, feeling, and mind,

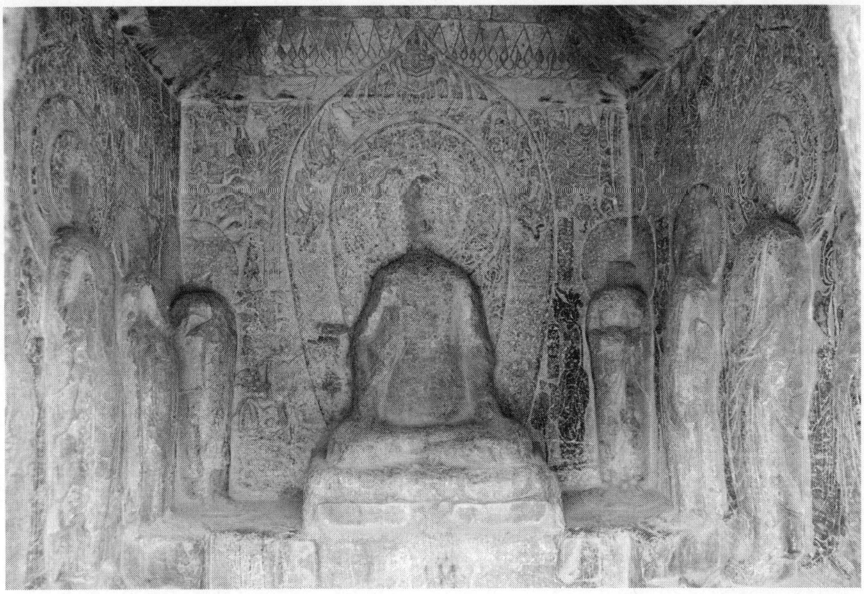

FIGURE 2.2a. Interior of Xiaonanhai Central Cave. All heads of the statues have been chiseled away. Photograph courtesy of Jungmin Ha.

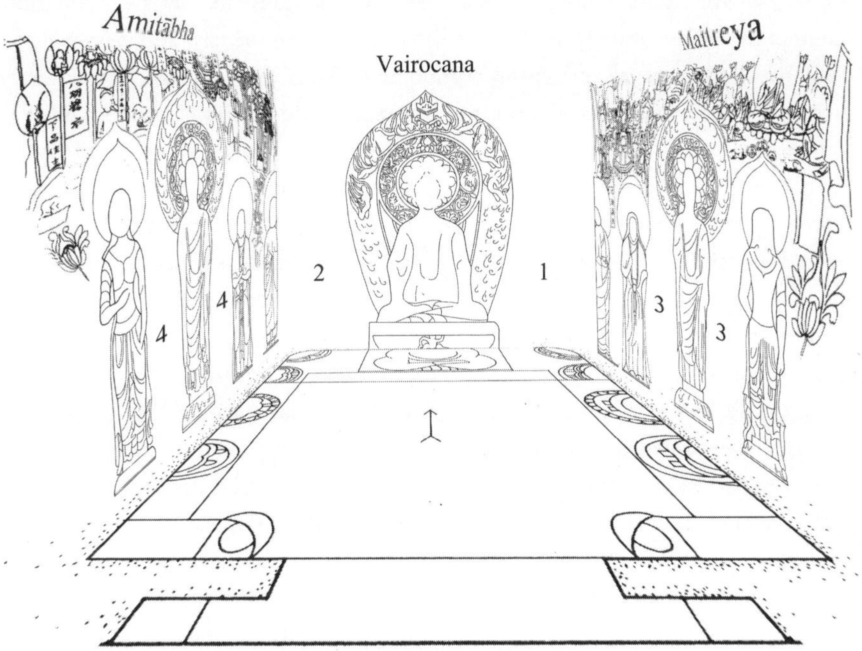

FIGURE 2.2b. Reconstruction of the image program inside Xiaonanhai Central Cave. In addition to the Pure Land of Amitābha and that of Maitreya represented on the west and east walls above the two sets of iconic triads, the remaining engraved images are: (1) Sengchou; (2) Brāhmana *Jātaka;* (3) Monks holding incensing burners; (4) Donors offering flowers. Drawing by author.

and in the final stage contemplates the concept that all things are devoid of inherent existence. Being fully aware of impurities and nonexistence leads to the notion of nirvana, represented in the Buddha in the center of the rear wall, identified as the cosmic Vairocana Buddha, whose transcendent body offers the clearest image of the true body of the Dharma (*dharmakāya*). Vairocana is named in the four four-line verses inscribed above the entrance (see fig. 2.1b, point 2). While the first three verses are taken verbatim from chapters of the *Flower Garland Sutra*, Sengchou was most likely responsible for the last verse, which reads:

> The grace of the Buddha Vairocana is omnipresent,
> Supreme among the auspicious;
> The Buddha has once entered this chamber,
> Therefore this place is the most auspicious.[79]

Arriving at the cave, one would begin by reading these texts on the exterior, then enter the cave with one's mind guided by the image of Vairocana Buddha (see figs. 2.2a, 2.2b). The scene engraved on the back wall to the left of the central Buddha depicts a tale of the Buddha's previous lives (see fig. 2.2b, point 2) that reinforces the doctrinal message of nonexistence,[80] while to the right is an image of Sengchou (see fig. 2.2b, point 1), identified by the accompanying cartouche, which represents incense and flowers. One's meditation inside the cave is further assisted by images, next to the iconic triad of Maitreya and two accompanying bodhisattvas, of two monks engraved on the east wall incensing the field (see fig. 2.2b, point 3), and the corresponding images of two donors on the west wall offering flowers (see fig. 2.2b, point 4). As suggested in the last text engraved on the exterior, after meditative visualization, repentance, and vowing to take the right path, one is prepared to see the Buddha (*jianfo*),[81] an attainment complemented by the meditation vision of the Pure Land represented in the imageries on the east and west walls.

Many of the textual and visual components from Xiaonanhai Central Cave, such as the dedicatory inscription, donor images, and offerings, were shared by contemporary pictorial steles (*zaoxiang bei*).[82] In this regard, the cave may be seen as an attempt to transform a freestanding public monument (i.e., stele) into a space of practice by integrating the inscribed texts and pictorial imageries in a three-dimensional structure. Each entry into the cave space is to reenact the ritual and vision in meditation. The efficaciousness of the meditative practice is further solidified by the fact that this very place had, according to the lines quoted above, been visited by the Vairocana Buddha. Not a direct quote from the *Flower Garland Sutra,* the verse was likely added to suggest a particular spiritual quality that distinguishes the place from others.[83] The use of the phrase "the most auspicious" to characterize the place may be related to a much older Indian usage that designated particular signs as auspicious (*maṅgala*) by virtue of their association with the Buddha's life or teachings. These auspicious signs could be used as amulets for protection or as markers that helped establish places as auspicious sites associated with the Buddha's presence.[84] In the early history of Buddhism, the emphasis on the presence of the Buddha through the auspicious signs "was a direct continuation and intensification of the auspiciousness that characterized Buddhist cultic sites."[85] In this light, Xiaonanhai Central Cave was "supreme among the auspicious," for its auspicious sign was none other than the Vairocana Buddha who once graced the chamber.

Most of the caves from the Northern Qi period were constructed near the precinct of a regular monastery. In the example of Xiaonanhai, the three caves were closely related to Lingshan Monastery and might be considered part of the nearby Yunmen Monastery, founded by Sengchou in 552.[86] Isolated today, these caves were in fact not originally alone but were monastic structures set apart for particular meditative or ritual practices. Yet in contrast to other monastic buildings made of timbers, these caves were meant to materialize in rock the practice that could enliven and thus preserve the teachings by means of the prescribed ritual that benefited one's spiritual pursuit. Their difference from wooden buildings is expressed not only by the imperishable material but also through the imagery and texts inscribed on them. Embodying the words of Dharma and true presence of the deities, the hewn-rock caves provided no less than a sacred space. To emphasize the sacral nature of their architecture, many caves around the Ye region had facades constructed in the form of a stupa.

In fact, the motifs and forms of a classic stupa are the most discernible characteristics among many caves constructed around Ye during the Northern Qi period.[87] These stupa caves include two groups at Xiangtangshan near today's Handan in southern Hebei province—three caves (North, Central, and South) in the northern group and seven caves (nos. 1–7) in the southern group—and a third nearby group located in the former location of the monastery known as Shuiyu Monastery (Shuiyusi).[88] The stupa can be seen in these caves in the decoration of many of the lintels above cave entrances, in the ornamental frames setting off individual niches, and in the cave facade through which one enters the cave, as if entering a stupa (figs. 2.3a, 2.3b). The stupa facade of these caves can be either single- or two-story in appearance, with an inverted-bowl-shaped roof. Most of the stupa caves have a four-sided central pillar, around which circumambulation inside the cave is possible.[89]

The reasons for forming the cave into a stupa could be manifold, related to both the meditation ritual and the additional sacrality associated with the meaning of stupa. Some visualization sutras instruct practitioners to enter a stupa to concentrate on Buddha images when their meditational practice has not been producing intended results.[90] For example, the chapter "Pure Practices" (Jingxing pin) from the *Flower Garland Sutra*, engraved on the side wall of Cave 1 in Southern Xiangtangshan, instructs practitioners who wish to take the bodhisattva path to, among other things, venerate Buddhas and pay homage to stupas. According to the text, upon seeing the stupa one should "behold the stupa wholeheartedly," "prostrate to venerate the stupa," "circumambulate the stupa clockwise," and "praise excellent marks of Buddha images."[91] Inside many of the caves at the Xiangtangshan sites, the scriptures were engraved on the walls in horizontal bands or registers, which would facilitate ritual reading of the scriptures; the devotional images, set at eye level, would meet the practitioner's meditative gaze while he or she circumambulated around the central pillar.[92] Yet, if engaging practitioners in liturgical veneration of the stupa was the primary purpose, why not just build a true freestanding stupa, such as the Four-Entry Stupa (Simenta), built in 611 in Shandong, which also has a central-pillar plan with four image niches on the pillar facing the four cardinal directions (fig. 2.4)?[93]

Shaping caves as stupas appears to have enabled the Buddhist texts incised inside and outside the caves to be regarded as "dharma relics" and objects of

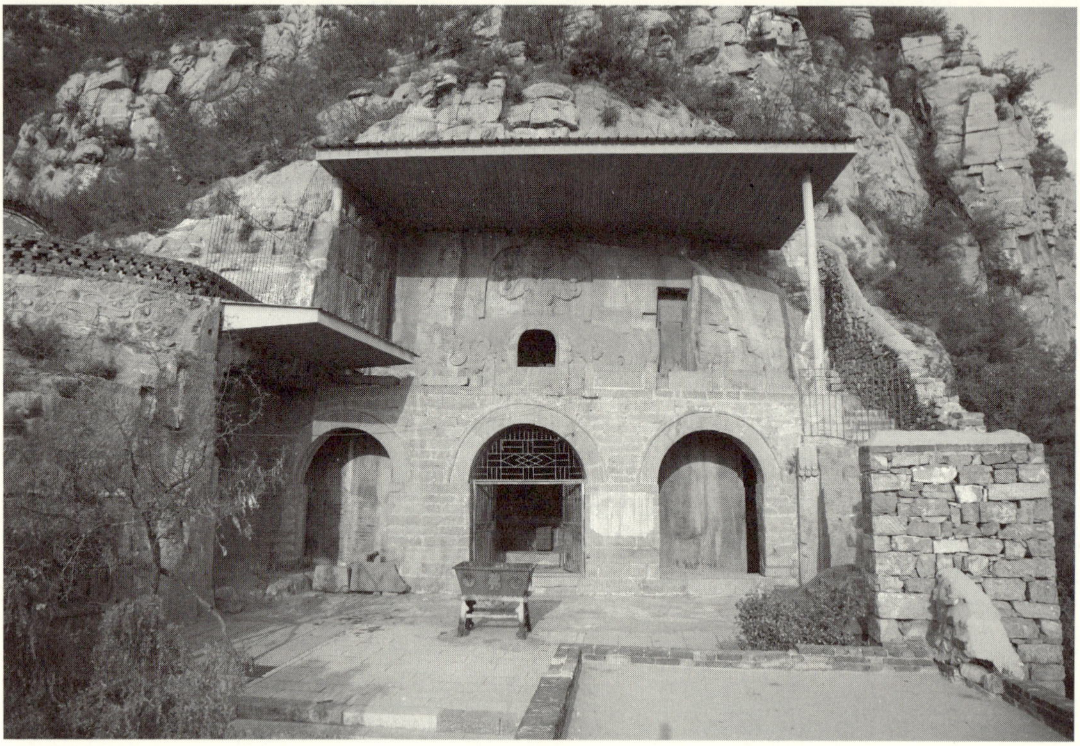

FIGURE 2.3a. Stupa facade, Southern Cave, Northern Xiangtangshan, near Handan, Hebei. 562–72 CE. From Tsiang, *Echoes of the Past*, fig. 17. Photograph courtesy of Katherine R. Tsiang.

FIGURE 2.3b. Details of the "stupa facade" before the modern protective structure was installed, Southern Cave, Northern Xiangtangshan. Photograph courtesy of Katherine R. Tsiang.

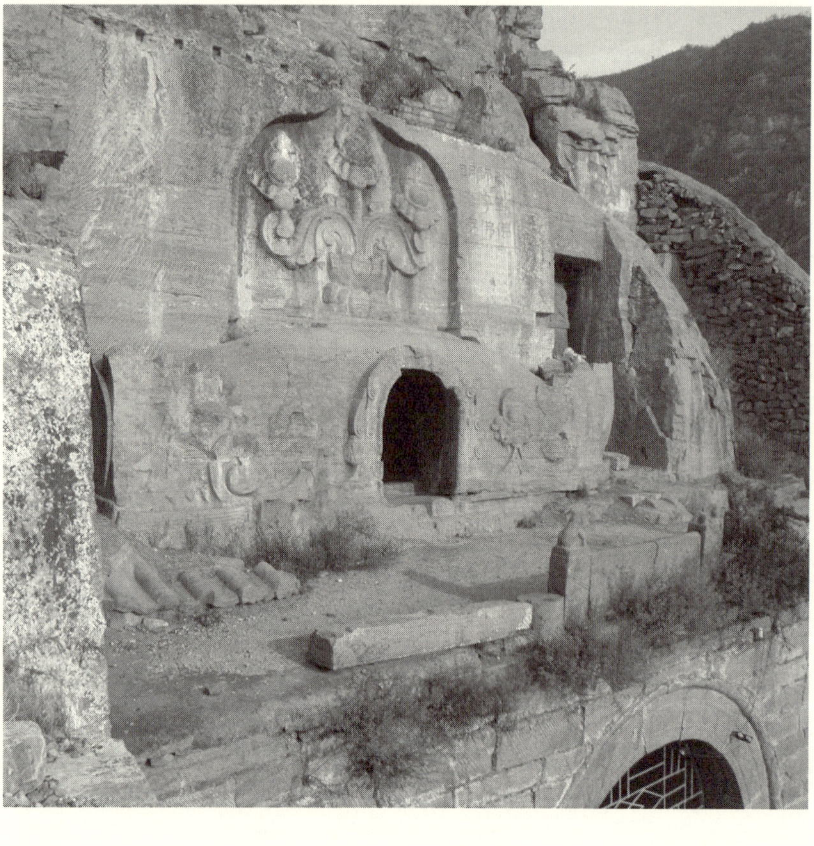

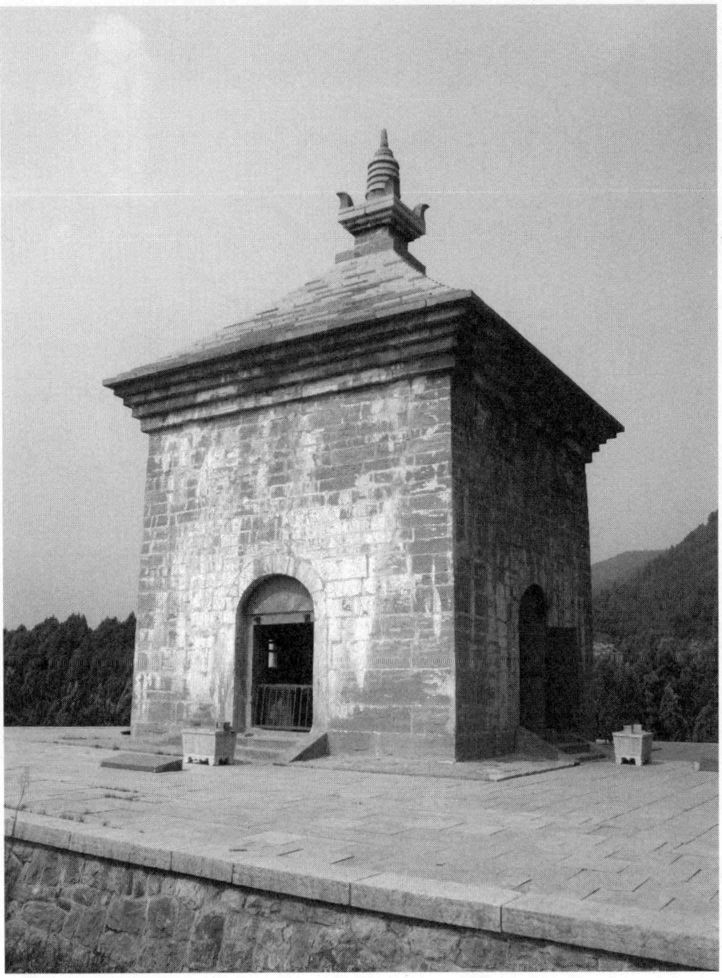

FIGURE 2.4. The Four-Entry Stupa (Simenta), Shentong Monastery, Licheng, Shandong. Ca. 611 CE. Photograph courtesy of Jungmin Ha.

veneration. The precedents of this association between sutra and stupa can be found in the fifth-century miniature stupas carved with scriptures for votive purposes from the Northern Liang region,[94] or the practice in China and in Japan and Korea in which stupa reliquaries either contain or bear scriptures.[95] An important implication of this association between sutra and stupa is what has been called the "cult of the book" in early Mahayana Buddhism, which ascribed sacrality to places where texts were recited, written, or kept.[96] The inscription of texts at the caves, in other words, "brings to the caves the blessing of the Buddha's teachings and enhances their numinosity."[97] Constructing these caves with a stupa exterior carved out of the rock surface was to permanently mark the numinosity of the site and to receive the presence of the Buddha in the ritual veneration of the stupa and the dharma relics enshrined therein.

Unlike miniature stupa pillars or stupa reliquaries, however, the stupa cave in its monumental form also necessarily reshaped part of the mountain surface and physically transformed the natural terrain into a sacred place. While each of the three caves at Northern Xiangtangshan has its own single-story stupa facade, caves

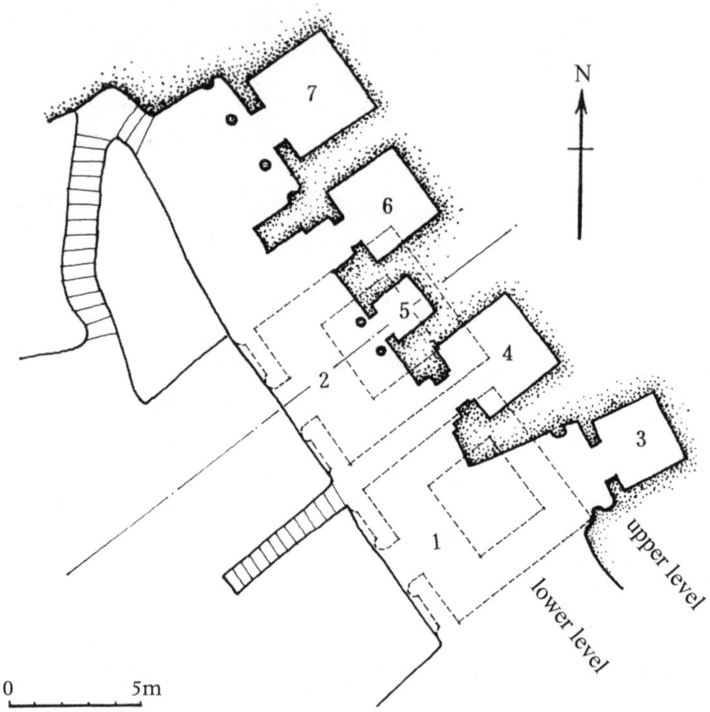

FIGURE 2.5. Site plan of the Southern Xiangtangshan Caves, near Handan, Hebei. Ca. 565–75 CE. Caves 1–7 are arranged on two levels: Caves 1 and 2 are on the lower level; Cave 3 above Cave 1 and Caves 4, 5, 6 above Cave 2 (only Cave 7 has no cave below it). After Zhong Xiaoqing, "Xiangtangshan shiku jianzhu lüexi," fig. 2. Diagram by permission of Wenwu Press.

at Southern Xiangtangshan have been conceived as two double-storied stupas (fig. 2.5): Caves 2, 4, 5, and 6 comprising one, and Caves 1 and 3 comprising another (figs. 2.6a, 2.6b).[98] While Caves 1 and 2 on the lower level were set up as the interior of a stupa with a central pillar, Cave 3 (above Cave 1) and Caves 4, 5, and 6 (above Cave 2) on the upper level were originally topped with decorative railing, domed roof, and flaming jewels, much like the roof of Cave 7, which retains most of its original form (figs. 2.7a, 2.7b). Rising upward from leveled ground on the hill, the two "stupas" appear to lean against the slope of the mountainside. On both levels, the facade is divided into three bays by columns decorated with bands of lotus petals that may have originated far to the west of China (see fig. 2.6b), as well as "wooden" brackets in traditional Chinese timber-frame-style, carved out of rock, that support the roof rafters (fig. 2.6c).[99] The hybrid style is a point of interest, but more relevant to the current discussion was an emphatic effort to carve the stupa facade entirely in rock and by so doing, turning part of the mountainside itself into a stupa. The stupa cave—regarded as a distinctively sacred structure, sanctifying the site and transforming the natural mountain into a "virtual stupa"—thus had a topographic significance that a freestanding stupa could not have.[100]

Moving out of the central region around the capital Ye, one finds comparable examples, albeit not in architectural structures, reflecting the desire of Buddhists to locate or create the sacred locus here and now in the advent of the final age. In Shandong, as noted earlier, instead of building meditation caves, Buddhists carved sutra texts directly onto mountain surfaces. The power of text to sacralize the very place where it is seen, read, or venerated is illustrated in the passages from the

Clockwise from top:

FIGURE 2.6a. Facade of Caves 1, 2, and 3, Southern Xiangtangshan. Caves 1 and 3 together comprise a two-story stupa. From Handanshi Fengfeng Kuangqu Wenguansuo, "Nan Xiangtang shiku," fig. 3. Drawing courtesy of Li Yuqun.

FIGURE 2.6b. Reconstruction of the stupa facade of Cave 1, Southern Xiangtangshan. From Zhong Xiaoqing, "Xiangtangshan shiku jianzhu lüexi," fig. 6. Drawing by permission of Wenwu Press.

FIGURE 2.6c. Detail of brackets carved out of rock, Cave 1 facade, Southern Xiangtangshan. Photograph by author.

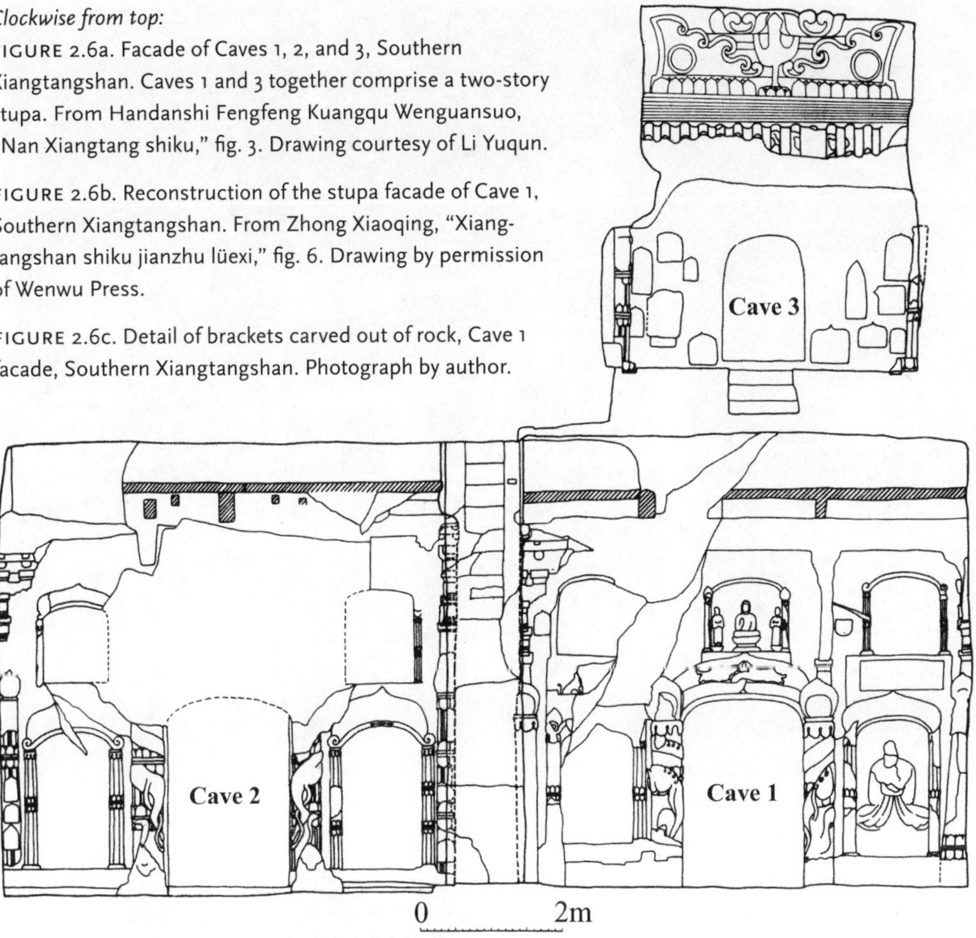

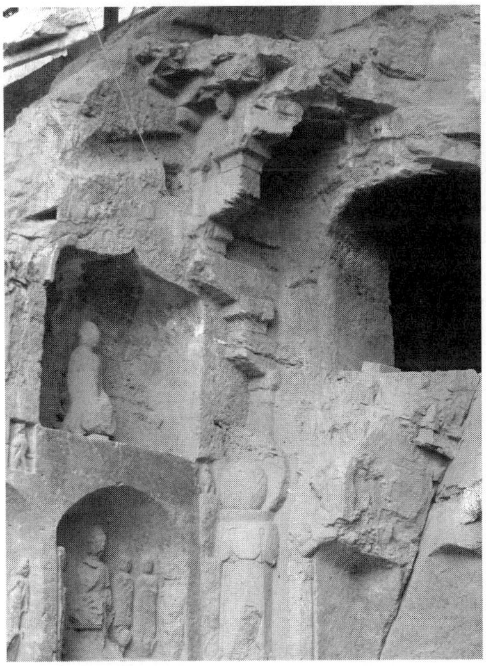

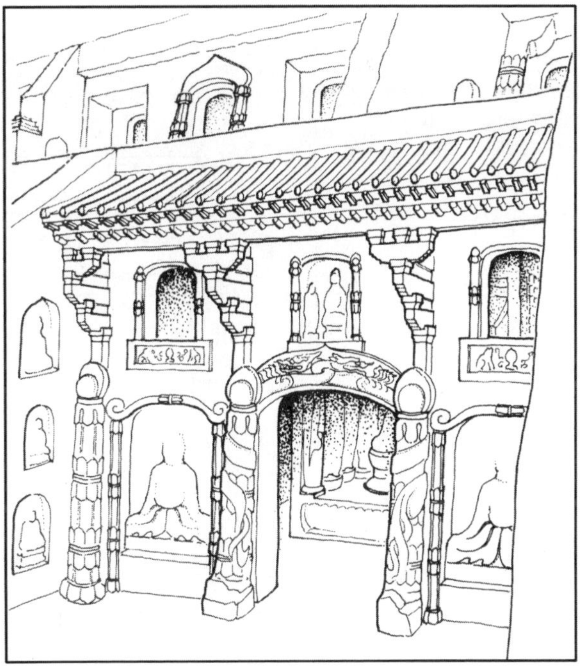

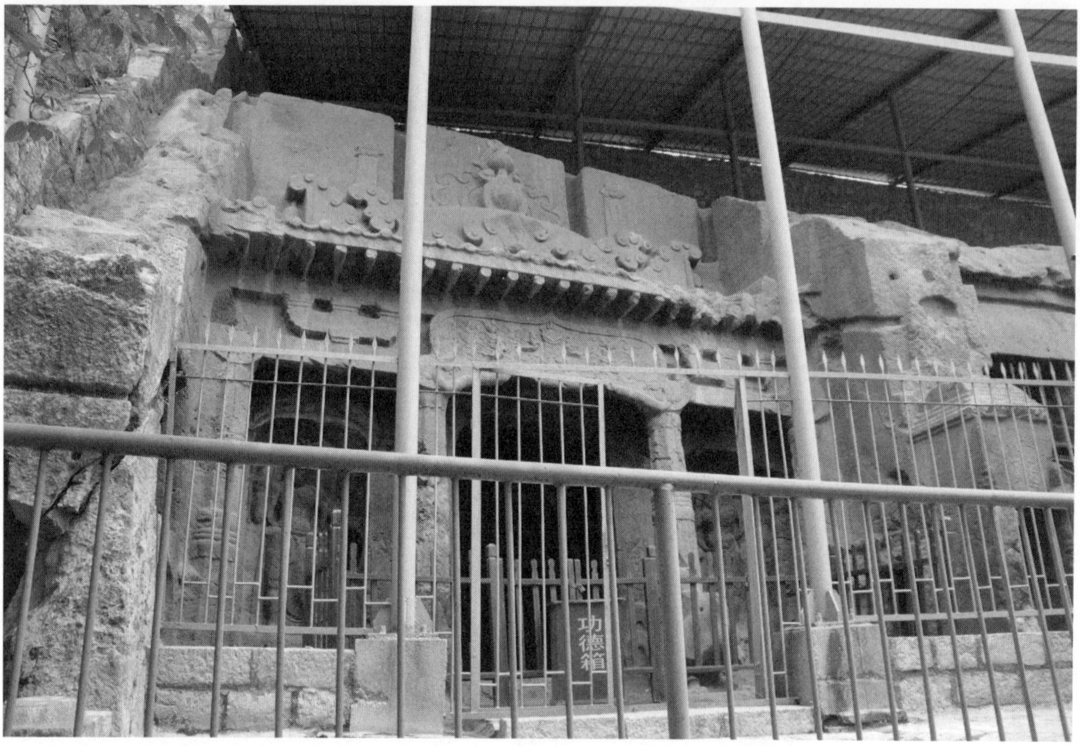

FIGURE 2.7a. Stupa facade of Cave 7, Southern Xiangtangshan. Ca. 565–75 CE. Of the Southern Xiangtangshan caves, Cave 7 retains most completely the original shape and ornaments of the facade that make it a stupa. Photograph courtesy of Jungmin Ha.

FIGURE 2.7b. Stupa facade of Cave 7, Southern Xiangtangshan. From Zhong Xiaoqing, "Xiangtangshan shiku jianzhu lüexi," fig. 3. Drawing by permission of Wenwu Press.

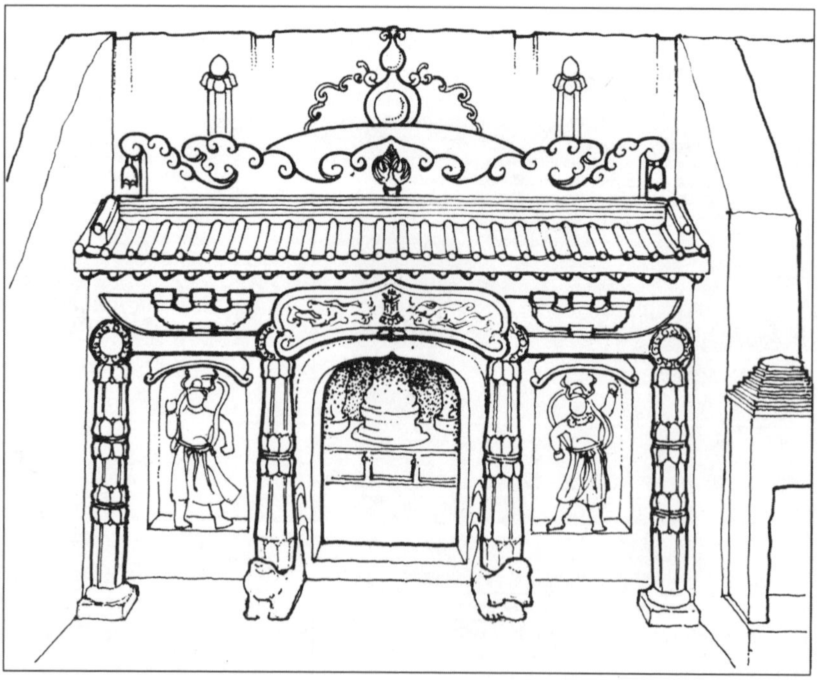

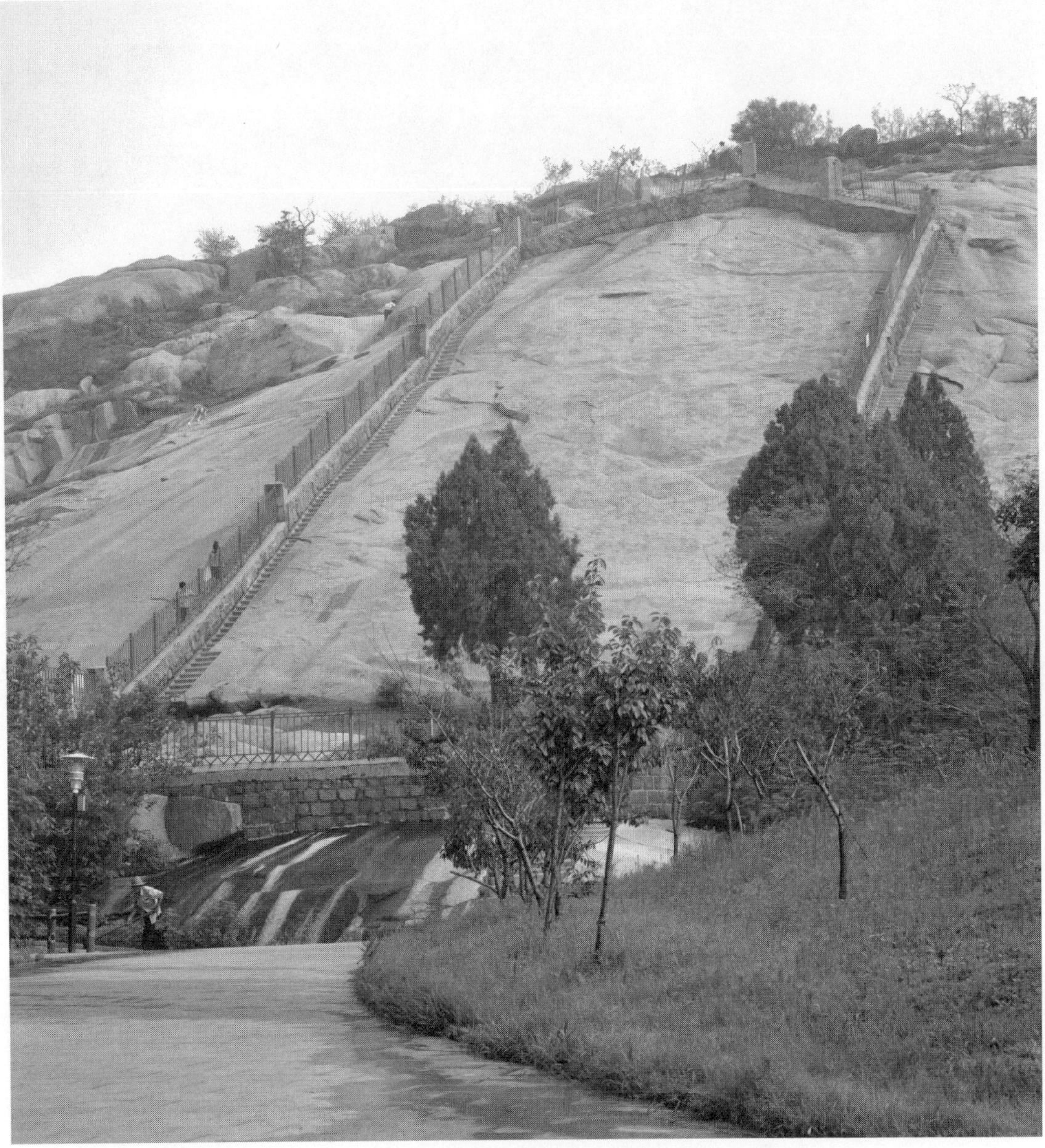

FIGURE 2.8. Sutra carving on the cliff surface of Mount Tie, Zou County, Shandong. 579 CE. The inscriptions, 946 characters in all, were carved in the slope surrounded by modern fencing. Each character is approx. 50 cm high. Photograph courtesy of Jungmin Ha.

Diamond Sutra carved on Mount Tie: "Wherever this sutra is kept, the place is to be regarded as if Buddha or a venerable disciple of his were present there. . . . That spot of earth where this sutra will be revealed, that spot of earth will be worthy of worship by the whole world with its gods, men, ashuras, worthy of being saluted respectfully, worthy of being honored by circumambulation. That spot of earth will be [like a] pagoda."[101] This emphasis on "that spot of earth" (*cichu*), which can be read as referring to the mountain site on which the sutra was actually carved,

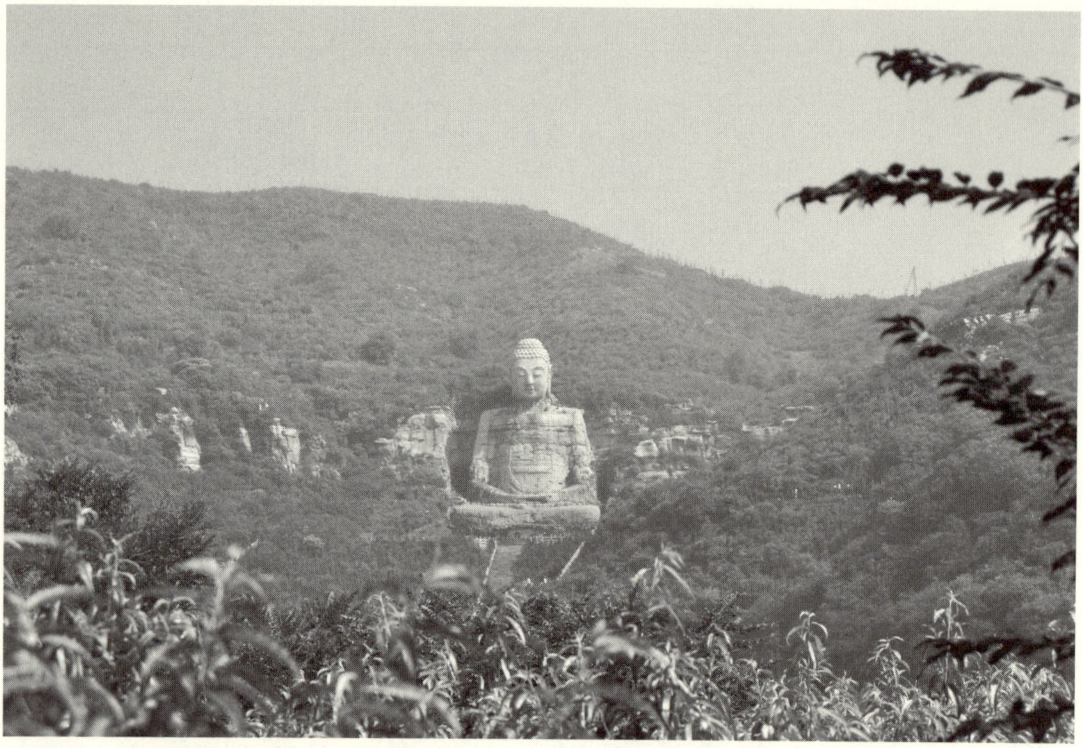

FIGURE 2.9. Sitting colossal Buddha carved out of rock at the former Kaihua Monastery, Mount Meng, Taiyuan, Shanxi. After 551 CE. The height of the sitting body of the Buddha measures approximately 30 meters. The original head had long been missing and was replaced in 2008 with a concrete one, 12 meters high. Photograph courtesy of Jungmin Ha.

echoes the designation of Xiaonanhai Central Cave as "the place" (*cidi*) that is the most auspicious. As in the case of many other large-scale sutra carvings in Shandong, the dimension of the carving at Mount Tie is monumental. The text covers an area of 2,064 square meters, and each character measures fifty centimeters in diameter (fig. 2.8). Being physically written on the mountain itself, the words of the Buddha transform the natural terrain into the literal bearer of his teachings. The monumental scale of the text provides no easy way of reading it, but entails one's physically walking or climbing to "that spot of earth" that turns the written text into an embodied place of religious practice "as if the Buddha were present."

A similar sense of scale and dimension in the search for the "very presence" can also be found in the area around Jinyang, near today's Taiyuan, Shanxi (see map 6). In addition to the nearby caves at Mount Tianlong (Tianlongshan),[102] during the Northern Qi the two most important Buddhist monasteries outside of Jinyang were both located in mountain areas and built with colossal images: the Kaihua Monastery (Kaihuasi) at Mount Meng (Mengshan) and the Tongzi Monastery (Tongzisi) at Mount Long (Longshan). Founded in 551, the Kaihua Monastery undertook the construction of a colossal Buddha before the end of the decade, likely with imperial support.[103] The statue was a sitting Buddha, said to have been as tall as 200 *chi* (approx. 59 meters), although currently only the Buddha's body

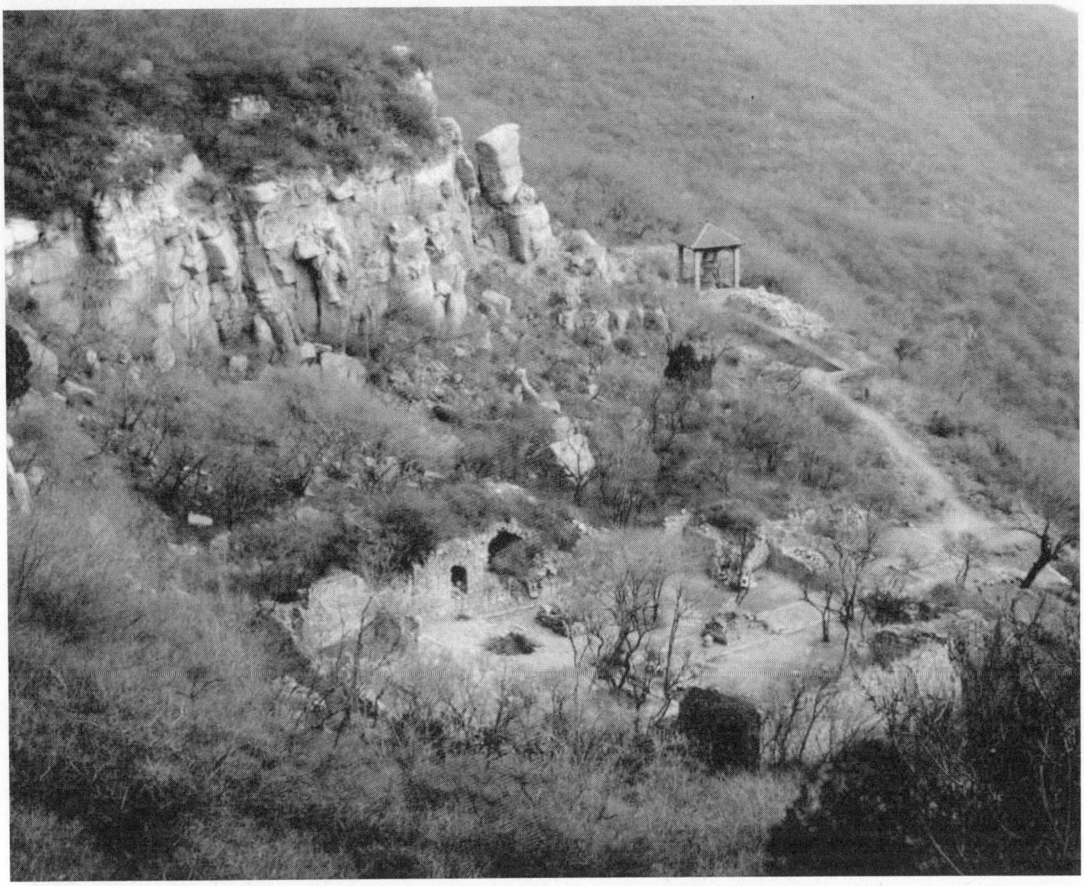

FIGURE 2.10. Site of Tongzi Monastery, Mount Long, Taiyuan, Shanxi. 556 CE. In the foreground are the excavated foundations of the main hall. The traces of the original colossal statues carved out of the rock are visible in the background. From Li and Yan, "Taiyuanshi Longshan Tongzisi," pl. 10.1. Photograph courtesy Li Yuqun.

remains of the original (approx. 30 meters); a head was recently added (fig. 2.9). Established in 556, in comparison, the Tongzi Monastery featured a sitting Amitābha recorded at 170 *chi* (approx. 57 meters) and his two principal bodhisattva attendants, Avalokiteśvara and Mahāsthāmaprāpta, each 120 *chi* (approx. 41 meters). Archaeological excavation has located the site of Tongzi Monastery and identified partial remains of the statues and the foundation of the structure built to shelter these iconic triads (fig. 2.10).[104]

The colossal statues carved out of rocky mountainsides at these two monasteries turned the natural topography into gigantic stages for Buddhist figures.[105] Although sculpting colossal images had been done before, the two monumental projects near Jinyang during the Northern Qi were different, in motivation and purpose. According to a tenth-century stele at the Kaihua Monastery, the creators of this project "hewed the rock and channeled the paths, sculpting the [Buddha] statue by following the mountain contour. . . . [Sculpting the colossal statue] accrues favorable causes for the monastery and captures the true form of the Śākyamuni [Buddha]."[106] Seeing the sacred form in the physical profile of the mountain also played a role in prompting the building of the mighty figures at the Tongzi Monastery. An early record says that the meditation master Hongli arrived at Mount Long in 556. One day, a multicolored radiance appeared suddenly and lit up the air, and in it Hongli saw four children (*tongzi*) on green lotus seats playing, causing the earth to tremble and subsequently cracking open the mountain. From the fractured mountainside miraculously appeared an image of Amitābha, accompanied by many other marvelous occurrences. Later, the Tongzi Monastery was built and named after the numinous vision of the playful children, and the colossal figures of Amitābha and his attendants were carved to retain permanently the visionary image that emerged from the mountain.[107] Constructed during the period when Buddhism was revived under the devout rulers of the Northern Qi, both undertakings were intended to penetrate the numinosity of the site and reveal its divine presence in the colossal image. In both cases, the natural topography of the mountain was the primary substance that materialized the divine, sculpted into the gigantic imagery that localized the sacrality at the very place.

The religious artifacts discussed here, including caves created for meditation, sutra carvings, and colossal statues from the Northern Qi period, are highly diverse. They were from different regions and supported by different monastic communities and lay sponsors; yet they also shared many features. In contrast to the urban constructions in Luoyang and Ye, all the major sites in this discussion of the brief period of the Eastern Wei and Northern Qi were located on mountains. The great number and superb quality of the surviving artifacts indicate the flourishing of Buddhism under the support of the court, while their contents are informed by the abiding anxiety about the demise of the teachings. Although realized in different ways, each object of veneration—stupa, text, and icon—was created in rock to permanently localize the divine presence by marking, altering, or transforming the natural mountain into the sacred place. In particular, the hewn-rock caves as part of the monastic establishment at the mountain did not just preserve the teachings, but permanently embedded in them the methods by which the teachings could be reenacted repeatedly in meditative practice. Given all these common features, the regional preferences of sutra carvings and/or iconic images should be reconsidered as different undertakings that collaboratively reinvented a sacred geography mapped over the Northern Qi's territory by creating the many loci at various mountain sites where the sacred presence could be localized and experienced.

Mount Wutai as *the* Very Place

Recent studies have elucidated the major trends of popular devotion and spiritual aspiration among Buddhist communities, based on dedicatory inscriptions from the fifth and sixth centuries.[108] In this period, the role of Mañjuśrī seems to have been relatively minor, and only a few records cite Mañjuśrī as a primary object of veneration before the sixth century. So why did this particular bodhisattva emerge at this historical moment as the chief mountain lord of the first Buddhist sacred mountain in China?

As a "tenth-stage" bodhisattva—that is, a bodhisattva who has passed through all ten stages needed to gain full enlightenment and become a Buddha—Mañjuśrī, to fulfill his vow as a bodhisattva, stays in this current world to aid all beings taking the spiritual path. Like Avalokiteśvara, another tenth stage bodhisattva, who incarnates compassion (*karuṇā*), Mañjuśrī also embodies a virtue, in his case, wisdom (*prajñā*); together these two virtues are keys to enlightenment. In the early history of Chinese Buddhism, Mañjuśrī was best known as the bodhisattva who illuminated issues concerning ultimate truth in such popular sutras as the *Vimalakīrti Sutra*—one of the sutras inscribed in the Southern Cave in Northern Xiangtangshan, which narrates the debate between Mañjuśrī and Vimalakīrti that was also engraved above the entrance inside the Xiaonanhai Central Cave. Mañjuśrī also figures prominently in *Sutra of Prajñāpāramitā Preached by Bodhisattva Mañjuśrī* (Wenshu shili suoshuo mohe banruo boluomi jing), which focuses on the doctrine of emptiness and perfect wisdom.[109] Excerpts of this sutra can be found in caves in Southern Xiangtangshan and Mount Zhonghuang, as well as several locations of sutra carvings in Shandong.[110] Most important, Mañjuśrī is paired with Samantabhadra, the two being the leading exponents of the Buddha's teaching as detailed in the *Flower Garland Sutra,* which was closely studied in the Buddhist communities of northern China during the sixth century. As already noted, the Ten Stages school, based on exegesis and practice of the commentary on the "Ten Stages" chapter of the *Flower Garland Sutra,* flourished around Ye in this period. The meditative practice for entering the bodhisattva path as instructed in this same sutra is represented in the cave at Xiaonanhai Central Cave and in Cave 1 in Southern Xiangtangshan, as well as in the nearby Dazhusheng Cave at Mount Bao (Baoshan). Seen in the light of all these textual associations, Mañjuśrī, although not among the best-known Buddhist deities in popular devotion, would have been one of the bodhisattvas most relevant to the canonical studies and liturgical practices of this particular region.

The early history of Mount Wutai during the sixth century was, indeed, inextricably tied to the *Flower Garland Sutra,* and yet it did not follow the practice of monasteries in and around Ye and place emphasis on doctrinal, exegetic studies of the sutra. At Mount Wutai, they had different aspirations. Huixiang records in his *Ancient Records* two illuminating examples. In the first, a monk named Lingbian, from the Jinyang region, devoted himself to the study of the *Flower Garland Sutra.* In 516 he entered Mount Wutai, where, seeking inspiration at the sacred site, he carried the sutra above his head while performing ritual circumambulation until his feet began to bleed. Lingbian's faith and diligent search for the divine response were answered, for by this act he attained full comprehension of the sutra.[111] In a similar vein is the story about a eunuch from the Northern Qi court named Liu Qianzhi. Feeling ashamed of his castrated body, Liu was drawn to Mount Wutai for its numinous power and decided to visit there. At the mountain, he performed a twenty-one-day ritual of constant recitation of the *Flower Garland Sutra,* at the end of which, he received a profound response (*mingying*), not only regaining his castrated organ but also becoming enlightened and writing an extensive commentary on the sutra.[112] The accounts of these miraculous events were compiled after Mount Wutai was already firmly recognized as the sacred abode of Mañjuśrī, and thus it is difficult to verify how much of them might be true. The inspiration that each experienced at the site, following ritual practice with the *Flower Garland Sutra*, was nonetheless what prompted many monks specializing in this particular sutra, such as Jietuo (561–642) and Mingyao (b. 556), to take residence at Mount Wutai.[113] In another account, a monk, Tanyun (563–642), from the area south of Jinyang, was devoted to reciting the *Lotus Sutra* at an early age. According to his biography, after turning nineteen during the 580s, he joined a monastery near Mount Heng, the Northern Sacred Peak. Tanyun left his monastery when he "learned that Mount Wutai was the Mount Qingliang [Clear and Cool] in the *Flower Garland Sutra*, regarded as the domicile of Mañjuśrī. Many monks since ancient times have gone [to Mount Wutai] to offer prayers, and many whose prayers were answered received his teachings."[114] The fact that Tanyun left Mount Heng for Mount Wutai is noteworthy, because before the sixth century Mount Wutai had been overshadowed by the Northern Sacred Peak. Also noteworthy, if we can trust the account, is the implication that after the 580s it was not just the *Flower Garland Sutra* but also Mañjuśrī, tied to Mount Wutai, that became the main reason for devout monastics to visit, reside, or practice at the mountain.

The decade of the 580s is significant on another count. Under the Eastern Wei and Northern Qi, Buddhism enjoyed uninterrupted prosperity for more than forty years. This came to an abrupt end in 577, when the Northern Qi fell to the Northern Zhou under the reign of Emperor Wu (r. 561–78). By 574, Emperor Wu had already launched in his empire the violent persecution of Buddhism, which continued into the Northern Qi territory after 577, causing the destruction of monasteries, images, and scriptures of its Buddhist communities. Emperor Wu died the following year, putting an end to the oppression, and Buddhism was quickly restored. The Northern Zhou dynasty did not last much longer; a few years later, its territories fell to Emperor Wen (r. 581–604), who founded the Sui dynasty and eventually unified China in 589. Emperor Wen proved to be a generous new patron. Despite this revival, however, the brief suppression of Buddhism was serious enough to be viewed as an ominous sign of the advent of the darkening age.[115] This fear was presaged by the translation of the *Candragarbha Sutra* (Yuezang fen jing) in 566 by Narendrayaśas (516–89) in Ye.[116] The sutra prophesies the arrival of the *mofa*—that is, dissolution of the Dharma—but presents a different account of the timing of this dissolution and states that the final age would be accompanied by misconduct of monastics, persecutions of saṅgha, and the destruction of images and stupas. It is likely that the concern already felt in China about the *mofa* triggered intense interest in the *Candragarbha Sutra*,[117] and, indeed, after 577 and into the 580s, the different discourses of *mofa* and practices shaped by it accelerated, among both the Three Stages (Sanjie) and Pure Land (Jingtu) movements. When he moved to Mount Wutai during the 580s, the monk Tanyun may have made his decision in hopes of receiving the immanent presence of the bodhisattva—a spiritual experience not available anywhere but at this specific mountain site—bringing about his enlightenment before it was too late. This urge was clearly widely shared, and can be explicated more fully through an examination of the iconic and textual program at Dazhusheng Cave.

The Dazhusheng ("Great Abiding Holiness") Cave was built in 589 at Mount Bao near the Xiaonanhai site to the southwest of Ye as part of the Baoshan Monastery (Baoshansi), founded by the influential master of the Ten Stages school, Daoping, in 546 and renamed Lingquan Monastery (Lingquansi) in 591.[118] The cave was attributed to Lingyu, the most eminent disciple of Daoping. Learning from his master, Lingyu also belonged to the Ten Stages lineage, specializing in main scriptures of the school, such as the *Ten Stages, Flower Garland,* and *Nirvana Sutras,* as well as in monastic codes (*vinaya*) and meditation.[119] During the persecution, the monastery suffered grave damage, while Lingyu survived by hiding out in villages and telling fortunes. After the 580s, he returned and began to restore the monastery at the foot of Mount Bao, and he built Dazhusheng Cave approximately a half kilometer west of the monastery on a south-side hill of the same mountain.

Built about thirty years after the Xiaonanhai Caves, Dazhusheng Cave (fig. 2.11a) retains several characteristics of its nearby precedent, but with many important innovations. Like Xiaonanhai Central Cave, it is a single-chamber cave, with a square floor measuring 3.4 by 3.4 meters and a ceiling 2.6 meters high. Also as the Xiaonanhai Central Cave, veneration of the images inside the cave is prompted by selected texts inscribed on the exterior and interior wall on either side of the entrance; the texts were likely recited and observed while one entered the cave. Most of the texts have an explicit concern with the *mofa,* including two excerpts from the *Candragarbha Sutra,* providing a detailed timetable for the end of the Dharma.[120]

Also part of the textual and visual program that structures ritual veneration inside and outside the cave is an emphasis on hearing and reciting names of various Buddhas. A liturgy of repentance inscribed on the exterior instructs the practitioner to invoke seven different ranks of Buddhas and in front of them to repent all wrongdoings.[121] Following the Buddha names inscribed on the walls, one would start from outside the cave, proceed to the interior, and circumambulate around the cave, while calling out the name of each individual Buddha and performing repentance (fig. 2.11b).[122] Unlike the Central Cave at Xiaonanhai, whose restrained space is specifically for sitting meditative visualization, that of Dazhusheng Cave facilitates ambulatory worship. One performs the liturgy both outside and inside the cave, conjuring a vision of different hosts of Buddhas by reciting their names. Following this ritual, as the text of the liturgy concludes, "Now all the Buddhas, the World Honored Ones, should bear witness to know me; should recall and hold me in mind."[123] To counter the coming *mofa,* the ambulatory meditation ritually transforms the physical cave into a place of permanent practice and eventual salvation.

As we have seen, Dazhusheng Cave at Lingquan Monastery, through liturgy,

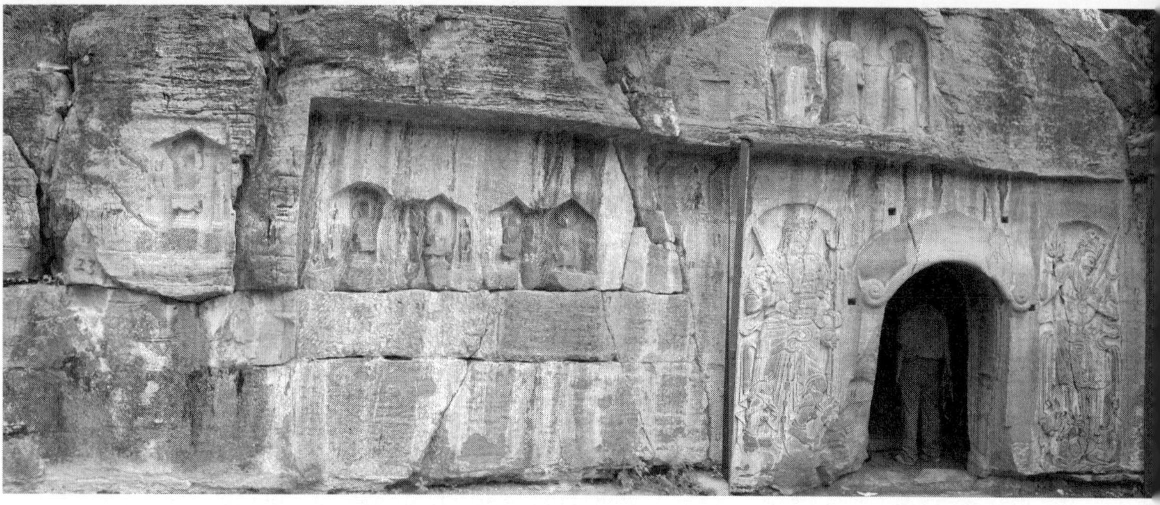

FIGURE 2.11a. Exterior of Dazhusheng Cave, Lingquan Monastery, Mount Bao, Henan. 589 CE. The engraved texts are to the left of the cave entrance. From Sonya S. Lee, "Transmitting Buddhism to a Future Age," fig. 15. Photograph courtesy of Sonya S. Lee.

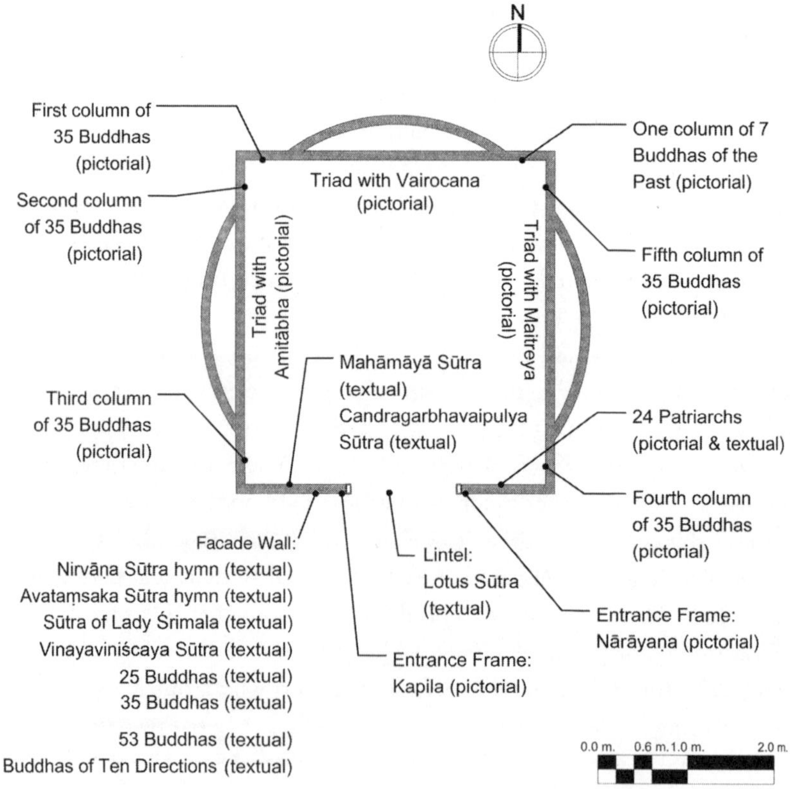

FIGURE 2.11b. Distribution of pictorial motifs and engraved texts inside and outside the cave. After Sonya S. Lee, "Transmitting Buddhism to a Future Age," fig. 17. Diagram courtesy of Sonya S. Lee.

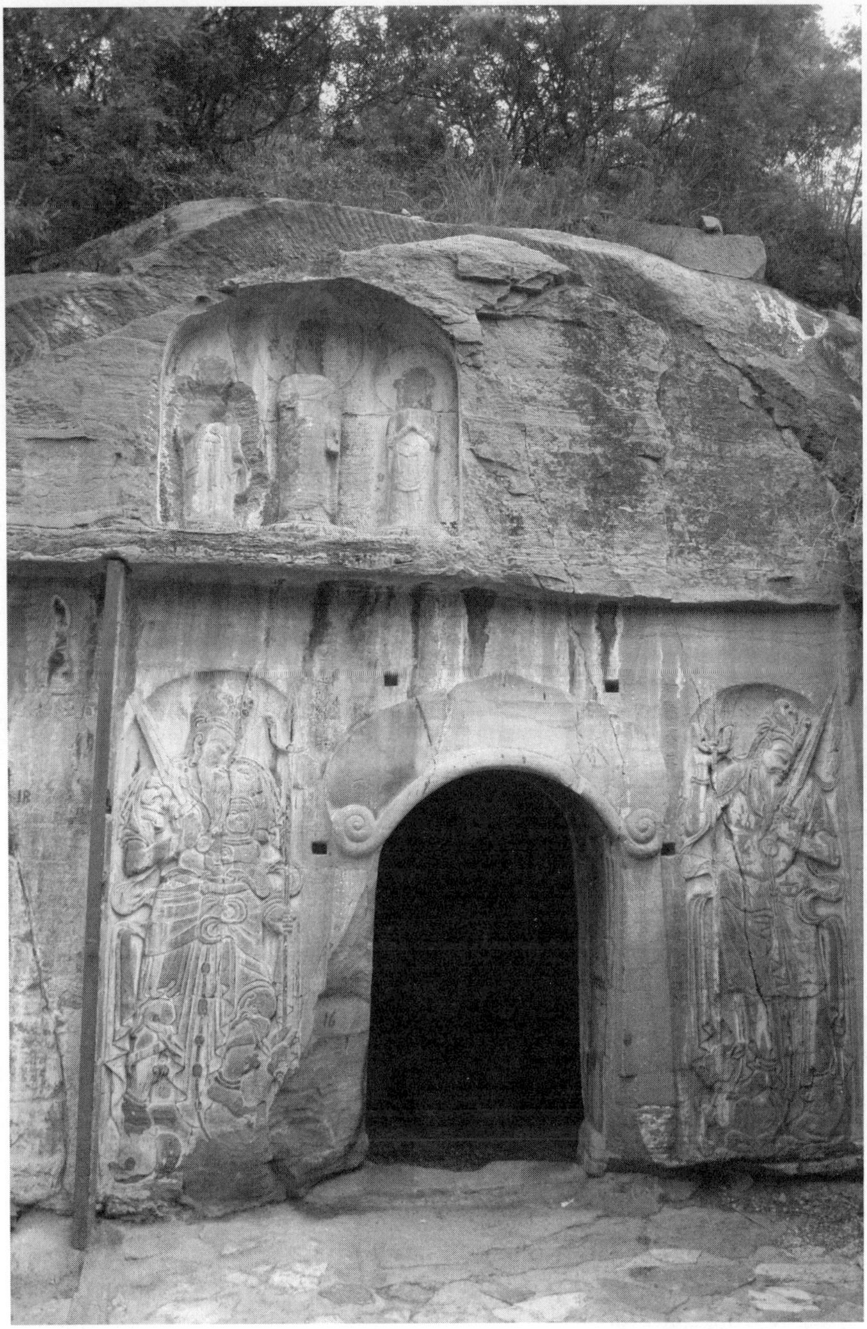

FIGURE 2.11C. Two guardian kings, Nārāyaṇa and Kapila, carved next to the cave entrance. Photograph courtesy of Jungmin Ha.

was meant to be a sacred place of aspiration for salvation. In particular, this "marriage of a ritually and/or geographically bounded place with a soteriological motivation" creates a place of practice and enlightenment (*bodhimaṇḍa*).[124] This cave, although not large enough to physically alter the landscape, would have ontologically changed the nature of the mountain site (fig. 2.11d). This fact is asserted by the two forcefully portrayed deva kings, Nārāyaṇa and Kapila, guarding the entrance (fig. 2.11c). According to the *Candragarbha Sutra* and a related work, the

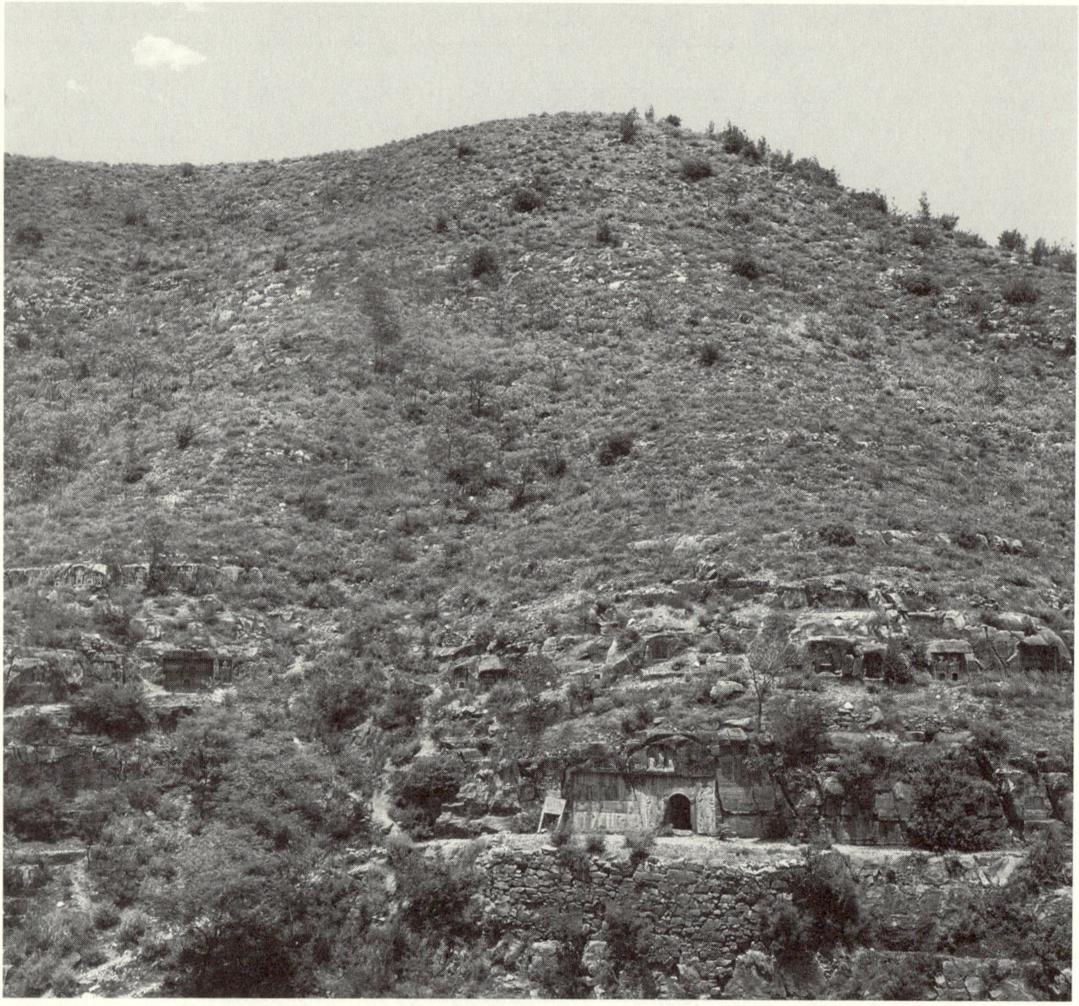

FIGURE 2.11d. Dazhusheng Cave in its mountain landscape setting. From Chen Mingda, *Gongxian, Tianlongshan, Xiangtangshan, Anyang shiku diaoke*, pl. 205. Photograph by permission of Wenwu Press.

Sūryagarbha Sutra (Rizang fen jing), Kapila and Nārāyaṇa were both protectors of China.[125] Nārāyaṇa, in addition to being a fearful subjugator of evildoers, was said to have dwelled in Zhendan, a transliterated name used in ancient India for China. By virtue of this association, Dazhusheng Cave was recorded in Lingyu's biography as the "Cave of Nārāyaṇa, Upholder of the Power of the Adamantine Nature" (Jin'gangxing Li Zhuchi Naluoyan Ku).[126] The implication is that the cave was guarded by the indestructible divine power of the Indian deva, and more important, that the mountain site had a specific affiliation and position in the Buddhist sacred geography.

I have shown in this chapter that, although the early association between Buddhist monasteries and mountains was largely informed by Chinese mountain culture, during the sixth century the urge to enter mountains was more specifically motivated by a growing emphasis on liturgical and meditative practices, for which mountains provided an ideal venue. We know very little about Mount Wutai during this period, but its geographic position would have put it among the important loci in the sacred geography developed and mapped over the Northern Qi territory. Many meditation caves were built, images made, and sutras carved in stone, which in various ways asserted that the divinity was indeed present to sanctify and transform the mountain site as the very place of practice and salvation, in the advent of the *mofa*. It is in this regional context and religious impetus that Mount Wutai emerged as a sacred site around this period.

The desire to localize the presence and thus mark the very place by means of architecture is well illustrated in the case of Dazhusheng Cave. Its permanent material, incised scriptures, iconic images, and space for veneration all made it a sacred place, and made the mountain a sacred site, further safeguarded by two deva kings identified as the protectors of China. A geographic connection between the cave and particular Buddhist deities is not surprising, considering the case of Mount Wutai with Bodhisattva Mañjuśrī. It cannot be a coincidence that the name Nārāyaṇa, one of the devas depicted at Dazhusheng Cave, also appears in the "Dwelling Domiciles of the Bodhisattvas" chapter of the *Flower Garland Sutra,* which speaks of Mañjuśrī's connection to a mountain (Mount Qingliang) identified in China as Mount Wutai. According to the chapter, "There is a bodhisattva domicile in the territory of Zhendan [i.e., China] named Mount Nārāyaṇa, in which many bodhisattvas of the past resided."[127] This evidence, from the cave as well as from Mount Wutai, reflects the intense desire of the time to find or found a sacred locus that could be mapped on the broader sacred geography of Buddhism. Mount Wutai in fact continued to develop into the seventh century to become *the* very place among places, the sacred site where the "sight" of the divine presence—that of its presiding bodhisattva—was attainable.

CHAPTER THREE

The Sacred Presence in Place and in Vision

The mountain top is a revelatory landscape, its height offering both the vision of heaven and a broad perspective on earth.

—Diana L. Eck, "Mountains"

Vision was critical in Mount Wutai's conversion into a Buddhist sacred site. Traditionally in China, great mountains were admired foremost for their towering height. The renowned Sacred Peaks (Yue) were eulogized in a poem from the *Book of Odes* (Shijing), beginning with the lines: "Grand and lofty are the Sacred Peaks, / their magnificence reaching to the heavens."[1] Close to Heaven's view, the landscape of the high mountains evokes otherworldly and revelatory visions in China, as well as in many other cultures. But in Chinese premodern history, the sight of the mountains and the visions that people saw or hoped to see there were inseparable from the cultural and religious significance of the mountains.

Early visitors at Mount Wutai, however, were looking for a more specific vision, namely that of the presiding bodhisattva Mañjuśrī, to whom Mount Wutai was gradually tied over the course of the sixth century. To have sight of the bodhisattva's divine presence there became the chief aspiration for the religious practitioners visiting the site. A "tenth-stage" bodhisattva, Mañjuśrī was described in several canonical texts as possessing extraordinary divine power (S: *abhijñā;* C: *shentong*) and thus able to perform supernatural acts in order to save and enlighten all beings. Most specifically, according to the *Mañjuśrī Parinirvāṇa Sūtra* (Wenshu shili ban niepan jing), he could manifest in various transformations (S: *nirmāṇa;* C: *huaxian*); moreover, the sutra continues, now that the Buddha has entered nirvana, whoever hears the name of Mañjuśrī and sees, meditates, and worships his image could receive bountiful benefits and wisdom that would assist the pious in treading the path.[2] The salvific or redemptive reward that came with "seeing" Mañjuśrī must have been one of the factors that contributed to the rise of the sacred mountain cult at Mount Wutai, especially given the anxiety over the demise of the Dharma that then pervaded Buddhist communities.[3] By the time the *Ancient Records of [Mount] Qingliang* was compiled circa 680, the manifestation of the bodhisattva at the mountains was something people could count on. As Huixiang remarks, "If you believe in [Mañjuśrī's] divine power [*shentong*], [his holy presence] is near!"[4] Mount Wutai was not only a mountain of towering peaks but the place where the revelatory vision and immanent presence of the bodhisattva could be experienced.

This place-specificity, however, is not unproblematic. Theoretically, early Buddhism did not recognize places as spiritually distinct, and any place on earth could be "sacred" or, at least, be treated with some respect. But as time passed, Buddhist practitioners were able to establish and sanctify the *place* of practice and salvation by various means—in China, as we have seen, by virtue of sutra carvings, stupa caves, or colossal statues, which literally altered, marked, and transformed mountains into a sacred site. The early cult of Bodhisattva Avalokiteśvara (known as Guanyin, in Chinese) raises questions regarding a "demarcated 'sacred' realm," in which the divine manifests. As many miraculous tales circulated during the fifth and sixth centuries indicate, the divine interventions of Guanyin did not occur at specific sites but in response to immediate need anywhere in this world. The "real" presence of the bodhisattva was marked "by a characteristic [temporal] precision, clarity, and effect."[5] In other words, Guanyin's presence was not localized but universal; "unlocalized conceptions of Buddhism as universal doctrine"[6] in fact deny that there can be a specific sacred locus to which a Buddhist deity is exclusively bound. As such, turning Mount Wutai into a sacred abode of the bodhisattva Mañjuśrī not only subverts the Buddhist notion of the possibility of salvation in any place in the universe, but also begs the questions, how the utopian vision of Buddhism could be "emplaced,"[7] and how it could be replaced by such a different vision and conception as we see in Mount Wutai.

In Chan Buddhism, a site can become sacred, but sacredness is not a quality reserved only for sites with specific features or for certain specific sites.[8] In this sense, the Chan view is utopian, and its notions of place and space include no distinguishing physical particularities. In contrast, some kind of "locative specificity and thick associative content" underlay the presence of Mañjuśrī at Mount Wutai and made this natural terrain the sacred abode of the bodhisattva.[9] The specificity and content were the particular ways in which the vision was manifested and localized: through a powerful icon in the context of monastic architecture, which together reconfigured and reconceived the topography of the site and fundamentally changed the ontology of Mount Wutai.[10]

Mount Wutai Spatialized in (Terms of) Numinous Signs and Traces

Like most renowned mountains in China, Mount Wutai was said to be a site once inhabited by immortals; vital energy (*qi*), it was believed, constantly emanated from its peaks. Early religious practitioners, including Buddhists, were attracted to its mysterious ambience and extraordinary secret treasures. Even during Huixiang's time, in the later half of the seventh century, Mount Wutai continued to have this affinity with local traditions of sacred mountains. And it should be noted that in Huixiang's *Ancient Records,* the division between local cults and Buddhist practices was not always clearly drawn. The numinous marvels and natural anomalies observed at the mountains thus should not be considered non-Buddhist, but

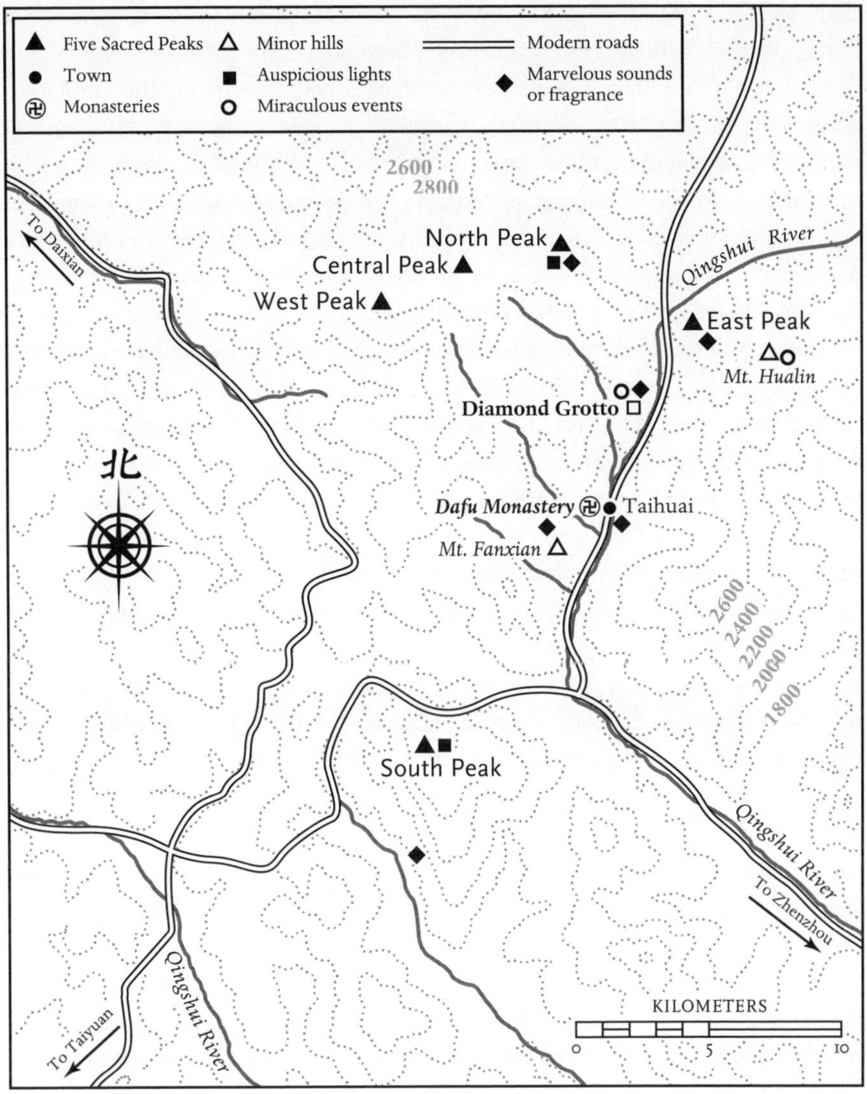

MAP 7. Locations of unusual events and other marvels at Mount Wutai, as recorded in Huixiang's *Ancient Records of [Mount] Qingliang* (Gu Qingliang zhuan).

as providing a vocabulary and language to decipher Mount Wutai as a Buddhist sacred site.

In the *Ancient Records,* Huixiang explains the divine qualities of the Mount Wutai area as manifesting in two ways: first, in the numinous places, where, for instance, wild medicinal herbs grew or other potent ingredients effective for cultivating immortality, and second, in the mountain deities and immortal beings who dwelled at the mountains. Mount of Buddhist Immortals (Fanxianshan), for example, in the center of the Mount Wutai complex, to the southwest of present-day Taihuai (map 7), grew pines and chrysanthemums and little else; it was initially known as Mount of Immortal Flowers (Xianhuashan), for "once in the past someone ate chrysanthemums [there] and attained immortality."[11] Huixiang tells of a monk of the Northern Zhou (557–81) who arrived at Mount Wutai, hoping for an encounter with the numinous. On reaching Mount of Flowery Woods (Hualinshan) located to the east of East Peak, he saw a stone mortar containing some freshly ground medicine. Out of curiosity, he waited there and, after a while, two people with unusually long eyebrows and hair appeared, who led the monk into a visionary world of the immortals.[12] In both accounts, Mount Wutai possesses the numinous energy and divinity characteristic of mountains and assists a pious person to reach his goal of immortality. These and several other examples of extraordinary places and meetings with immortals included in Huixiang's work demonstrate the pluralistic characteristics of Mount Wutai as a sacred site, creating dense, heterogeneous realms of spirituality.

These qualities are exemplified most suggestively in the Diamond Grotto (Jin'gang ku), located south of the Central, North, and East Peaks (see map 7).[13] We are told in the *Ancient Records* of the monk Xiangyun of the Northern Qi (550–77), who, drawn by the numinous potency of Mount Wutai, went to the mountain and joined the Dafu Monastery (Dafusi), located in today's Taihuai. One day, he was unexpectedly greeted just outside the monastery by a group of people headed by a man of extraordinary appearance. Identifying himself as the mountain lord (*shanshen*), the man respectfully requested Xiangyun to perform a seven-day ritual at the Diamond Grotto. Xiangyun was then led inside the grotto into a palatial complex decorated with paintings to recite scriptures. After the ritual was concluded, the mountain lord offered Xiangyun some spirit-power herbs (*shenling zhi yao*), and upon taking them, Huixiang attained immortality.[14] A paradisiacal place where powerful deities dwelled, reachable only by a secret route in a cave or grotto, was a common motif in the Chinese conception of sacred mountains. What is noteworthy in this account is the nature of the spiritual gift bestowed by the mountain lord: Xiangyun attained immortality, not the Buddhist ultimate goal of enlightenment. Buddhism, this tale implies, was only one among many cults that shared the site.

Interestingly, in the *Ancient Records,* Huixiang includes a second account of the same Diamond Grotto, one that contradicts its earlier characterization. In this second account the Diamond Grotto is recognized as an important place of storage for "all the worship offerings to the Buddhas of the triple times,"[15] including a heavenly musical instrument, texts of monastic rules, and sacred scriptures written in silver on gold paper, all prepared for the age after the extinction of the Dharma. When that time arrived, the account concludes, Mañjuśrī would go to Mount Qingliang, that is, Mount Wutai, and enter the Diamond Grotto.[16] Both accounts of the Diamond Grotto in the *Ancient Records* depict the grotto as a place inhabited by deities, but each associates it with a different understanding of the sacred space: whereas the first account established the grotto as a particular locus on the numinous mountain, the second account places the grotto in the broader spatiotemporal conception of Buddhism. In the changing nature of the grotto, from a place revered by a local cult to a place revered as a site where sacred Buddhist treasures were stored, the role of the mountain lord was explicitly overtaken by Mañjuśrī.[17] This reconception of the Diamond Grotto in Buddhist terms illustrates an effective strategy of removing the location-specific affinity and reconsecrating the space with the presence of Buddhist icons and a Buddhist divinity.

Because the primary goal of the devout practitioner visiting Mount Wutai was to gain a revelatory vision of Mañjuśrī (a vision attainable only at Mount Wutai), many meditation masters in the *Flower Garland Sutra* (Huayan jing) tradition were drawn to the sacred mountain. According to the *Ancient Records,* a form of meditative concentration, known as Visualizing the Buddha's Radiance (*Foguang guan*), was practiced specifically at Mount Wutai by two meditation masters, Jietuo (561–642) and Mingyao (b. 556).[18] The meditation practice was based on the chapter "Awakening by Light" (Guangming jue pin) of the *Flower Garland Sutra,* which instructs the practitioner to visualize spiritual radiances emitting from different parts of Vairocana Buddha's body, until eventually they experienced a transcendent vision of the cosmological universe that merges with this current world.[19] To take on such concentrated meditation, both Jietuo and Mingyao were recorded to have devoted themselves to attaining the vision of Mañjuśrī, for the opportunity to behold the bodhisattva's true presence was believed to bring with it the wisdom to obtain through meditation the ultimate vision of Vairocana. It is not clear if the two masters accomplished this goal; Huixiang's *Ancient Records* does not record what vision of the bodhisattva they actually experienced.[20]

What the *Ancient Records* does include are many site-specific accounts of the bodhisattva's transformative manifestations, known as "auspicious signs" (*ruixiang*).[21] For instance, during the Longshuo reign (661–63) of the Tang dynasty, the monk Huize of the Huichang Monastery (Huichangsi) in Chang'an was dispatched by the court to Mount Wutai to observe the many miraculous occurrences for which the sacred mountain was increasingly becoming known.[22] Along with a painter and other officials, Huize arrived first at Central Peak. Before reaching the top, they saw from afar a Buddhist statue waving its hands and feet, which they took to be the "true presence" (*zhenrong*) of the bodhisattva.[23] The moving statue, however, disappeared suddenly when Huize was only five paces away. Though sorry to miss the chance to come much closer to the divine presence, Huize's search was not in vain. After reaching the summit of Central Peak, he and other officials were greeted by "sounds of great resounding chimes" (*hongzhong zhi xiang*) while they were venerating a pagoda. Huize and his group then descended to Dafu Monastery and moved on to Mount of Buddhist Immortals, the mountain hill that grew only pines and chrysanthemums; there Huize reported encountering the "smell of an unusual fragrance" (*yixiang zhi qi*).[24] Thus, one by one, Mount Wutai was mapped with traces of miraculous events. In the *Ancient Records,* these events were not limited to auditory and olfactory phenomena, but included other visual marvels—such as divine radiance (*shenguang*), five-color "celebratory" clouds (*wuse qingyun*), and a multicolor "auspicious" blaze (*zese ruiguang*)—each recorded with the specific site of its happening (see map 7). After his visit, Huize compiled the accounts of all the marvels that he encountered, along with a painting of the mountains, likely in the form of a small screen (*shantu xiaozhang*), into an *Abridged Records* (Lüezhuan) of Mount Wutai (now lost) that was said to have widely circulated around the capital.[25]

The illustration of Mount Wutai included in Huize's *Abridged Records* is the earliest image or a representation of the sacred mountain on record. Neither the painting nor the text has survived, but the painting may well have indicated the locations of each "auspicious sign" and "sacred trace" (*shengji*) that Huize observed, perhaps much like my map 7.[26] Mapped over the sacred domain, the many site-specific tales and legends of the bodhisattva's transformative manifestations (replacing prior affinities of place and pluralities of cults) weave the threads of history and geography into one cohesive entirety. Far from presenting the sacred site as an abstract space, these traces and signs were events to be heard, smelled, and observed at specific locations, through which the divine presence could be bodily experienced and thus localized. In *Ancient Records*, these traces and signs, although most were transitory, comprise the spatial syntax of Mount Wutai, embodied in the vision seeker and practitioner of the way, who see, hear, and smell.[27] It is through this spatial syntax that the five peaks, sacredness, and potency of Mount Wutai become decipherable. On the other hand, as signs always refer to something other than themselves and because traces are markers of a passing existence, they also act to reinforce the absence of the ineffable "true presence" of the bodhisattva.

Topographic Appropriation: Making a New Center

As the natural landscape of Mount Wutai was gradually associated with sacred traces and numinous sightings, the revelation of the divine presence also had topographic significance. In the *Ancient Records,* Huixiang sets out to describe the mountain range as defined by the five peaks in the sequence, Central, East, West, North, and South Peaks, corresponding to their positions in the four cardinal directions radiating from the center (in reality, the first four of those five peaks cluster together in the north, and South Peak rises far to the south of them) (map 8).[28] Regarding the definition of the five peaks, Huixiang states, "The heights [given for the five peaks] and distances between each peak are often contradictory, perhaps as a result of different measuring routes or peak designations. Now, I wish to [conclude the debate and] propose one designation that would keep the general range of the five peaks [as it has been understood]."[29] Huixiang did not document the competing designations, but at least one older description exists in the *Extended Records of [Mount] Qingliang* (Guang Qingliang zhuan), compiled by Yanyi (b. 999) in 1060.[30] According to Yanyi, East and West Peaks were the same in the older designations as in his day; the North, Central, and South Peaks differed, however: the peak designated Central had been renamed North Peak, the peak designated South had been renamed Central Peak, and the old North Peak had the name Mount Da Huangjian (Da Huangjianshan) and was located further north, out of the contemporary area (map 9).[31] These earlier "five peaks" were thus clustered in a smaller group, with the highest peak at its center. In comparison, the range of the new "five peaks," that is, the current designation, was greatly expanded and thus included many more monasteries and provided a much different dynamic. This restructuring of the sacred topography of Mount Wutai around Huixiang's

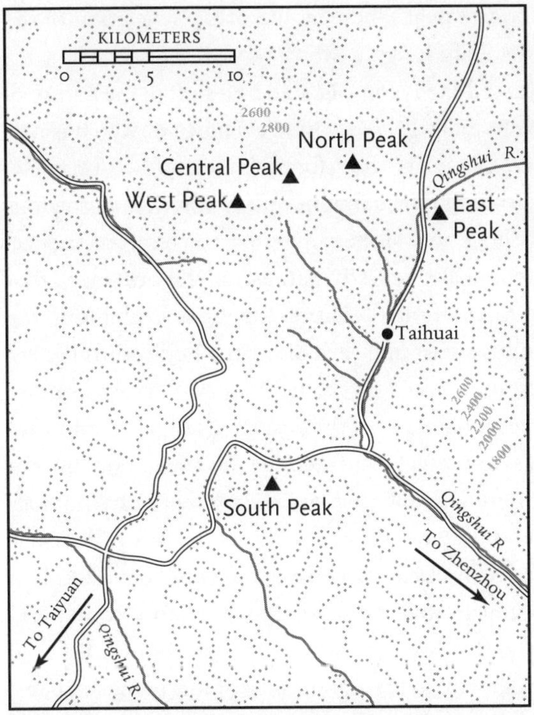

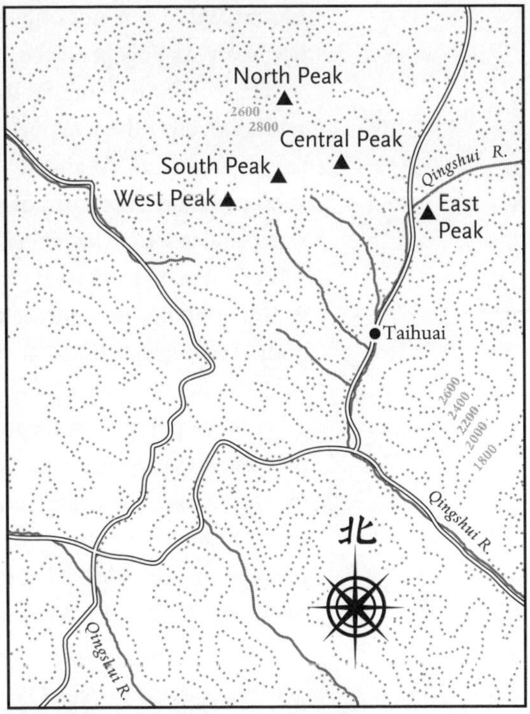

MAP 8 *(left)*. The designation of the Five Sacred Peaks of Mount Wutai according to Huixiang, *Ancient Records* (Gu Qingliang zhuan), early 680s.

MAP 9 *(right)*. An earlier designation of the Five Sacred Peaks of Mount Wutai made before the 680s, as reported in Yanyi's *Extended Records of [Mount] Qingliang* (Guang Qingliang zhuan).

time had profound consequences, especially, in terms of how the presence of the bodhisattva in visions gradually became the central characteristic of the site.

Any transposition and alteration of a sacred site is the result of circumstantial considerations or consequences.[32] The change in designations almost certainly came about because a new center required a new definition. The earlier peak designation, as mentioned, centered on the middle peak (Central Peak), but the reassigned five peaks created a new center—in the valley of today's Taihuai, where the largest monastery at Mount Wutai was located (plate 3). This monastery was the Dafu Monastery in *Ancient Records,* later also known as Monastery of Great Faith in Vulture Peak (Dafu Lingjiusi), so named after the rising summit behind the monastery, which resembled a vulture.[33] The name alludes also to Vulture Peak (Gṛdhrakūṭa), the hill in India where Śākyamuni Buddha is said to have delivered several important teachings, later recorded in Mahayana sutras. But, the monastery's name and its allusions were not what made it the center of the Mount Wutai region. "Above [this summit]," Yanyi reports, "auspicious clouds arise, [in which] the holy presence [*shengrong*] manifests recurrently. [This is why the place was] called the Terrace of Mañjuśrī's Transformation [Hua Wenshu Tai] in ancient times."[34] In other words, the five peaks were redesignated such that the center of

Mount Wutai was not one of the five peaks, but the site of the revelation of the bodhisattva's holy presence, at the Dafu Lingqiu Monastery.

This change of center at the sacred site is consolidated by a shift in the nature of revelation after the five peaks were redesignated, visual evidence of which is narrated in the texts. As already seen, Mañjuśrī's transformative manifestations (*huaxian*) could take the form of an array of unusual signs or symbols (i.e., auspicious signs) indicative of the divine presence and, at the same time, traces of its absence. A transformative manifestation could also refer to Mañjuśrī's "real presence," that is, to the bodhisattva himself, a form of manifestation known as "exhibiting the body" (*xianshen*).[35] Both "auspicious signs" and "exhibiting the body" thus belong to the same category of manifestation based on the bodhisattva's transformative power. The contemporary sources took many of the auspicious signs as indicative of Mañjuśrī's presence, and thus as sanctifying and defining the sacred domain, but the moments in which the bodhisattva manifested his "real presence" are not narrated in these accounts.[36] The bodhisattva's elusive presence did not materialize until the first decades of the eighth century. It was during this time that the cult of Mañjuśri flourished at Mount Wutai around the new center of Dafu Lingjiu Monastery, which was renamed early in that century Monastery of the Flower Garland [Sutra] (Huayansi); I shall return shortly to the significance of this name change.

According to *Extended Records,* during the Jingyun reign (710–11), a monk by the name of Fayun, at Huayan Monastery, decided to commission a statue of Mañjuśrī.[37] This new icon was intended to be different from all other statues of the bodhisattva: an image that would capture the spiritual quality of the divinity as manifested at Vulture Peak, in order to benefit pilgrims who came to experience the bodhisattva's holy presence. A skilled artisan named An Sheng was summoned and promised a lucrative reward for the task. Sheng, however, hesitated and stated, "[I] cannot accomplish this [task] faultlessly if I am not able to observe the [bodhisattva's] true image [*zhenxiang*]."[38] He then burned incense and performed appropriate abstinences, at the conclusion of which, Mañjuśrī appeared at once on the back of a lion, right in front of the artisan. Overjoyed, Sheng finished the work faultlessly after beholding and transcribing the bodhisattva's seventy-two magic transformations into the statue. The statue was then enshrined in the Cloister of the True Presence (Zhenrong Yuan), built on the summit of Vulture Peak.[39] When the Japanese monk Ennin (794–864) traveled to Mount Wutai and reached the cloister in 840, he was told that "today, when Mañjuśrī's sacred image is commissioned for monasteries at Mount Wutai, this is the image that will be modeled."[40]

Like the redesignation of Mount Wutai's five peaks, the origin of this iconic image of Mañjuśrī is a watershed in the history of the bodhisattva cult and its significance is manifold. This first true-presence icon at Mount Wutai has been lost, but two eighth-century examples survive. One is inside the Main Hall of Nanchan Monastery (Nanchansi), dating to 782, as part of an iconic set with Śākyamuni flanked by Samantabhadra and Mañjuśrī, among others (fig. 3.1); the other example is a marble statue, undated but, based on its iconography, likely to be from the mid-eighth century, unfortunately already damaged when uncovered in the

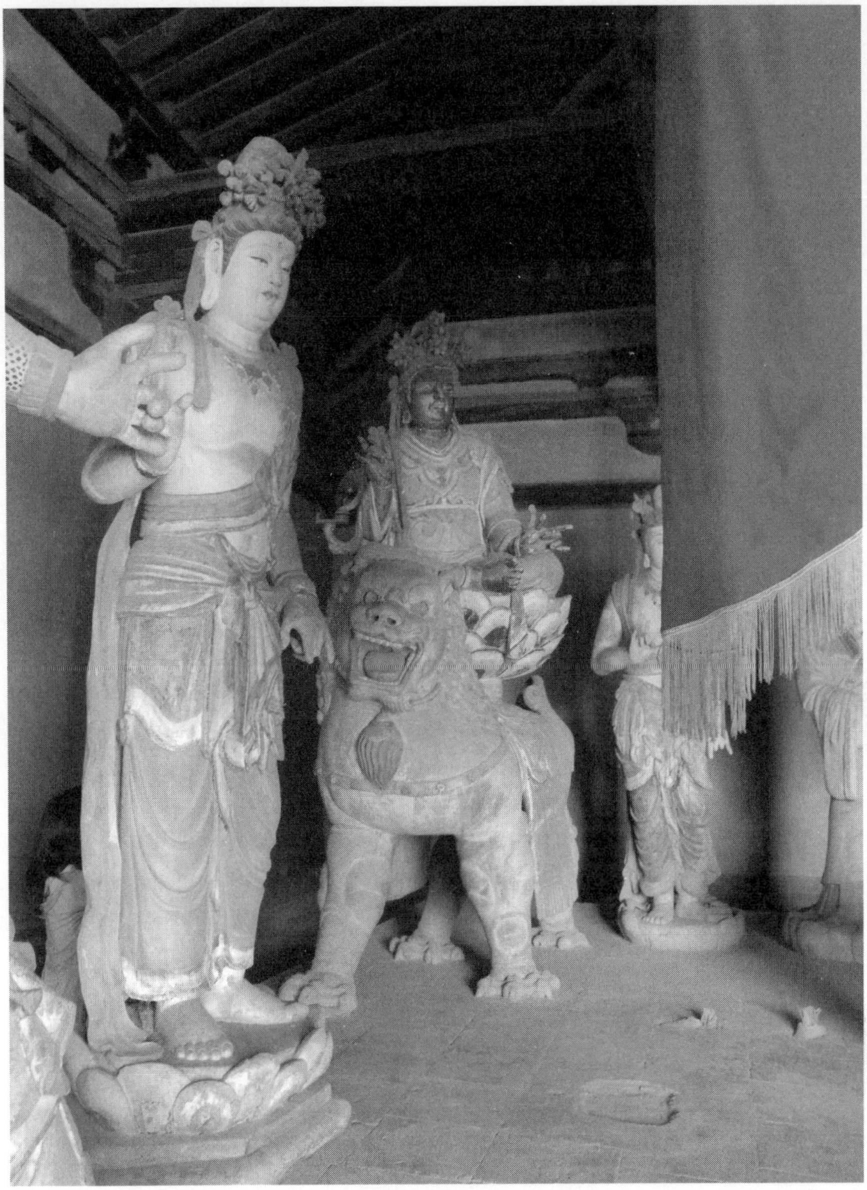

FIGURE 3.1. "True-presence" (*zhenrong*) icon of Mañjuśrī riding a lion, Nanchan Monastery, Mount Wutai. 782 CE. A standing bodhisattva is seen to the left of Mañjuśrī. Photograph by author.

twentieth century (plate 4).[41] In both examples, Mañjuśrī is depicted in his bodhisattva attire, sitting on a lotus seat mounted on the back of a lion and accompanied by a lion tamer or groom. The lion is powerfully depicted: proportionally larger than Mañjuśrī, and with its head turned to the side, its mouth open in a roar. The importance of the true-presence icon, however, did not lie in its particular representational form, which had already been seen outside Mount Wutai, but in its nature and power.[42] The statue, according to the story of its creation, was wrought by way of divine intervention, which distinguished it from other icons of Mañjuśrī and endorsed its authenticity. And as this intervention was made by none other than the bodhisattva himself, the image was believed to partake or participate in the true presence of what it was made to represent, as suggested in the term "real presence" (*zhenrong*). In medieval China, one of the goals of Buddhist practice was to bridge, if not completely eliminate, the distance between manifest and divine essence, and it seems that the icon, made in the presence of the divine, was believed to be able to mediate between the secular and sacred and to enact and reveal the essence through the manifest.[43] The icon thus made visible the as yet elusive bodhisattva that made the particular place sacred. The monastic building, Cloister of the True Presence, was built not only to enshrine the icon but to bring together the divine presence, the sacred icon, and topography at the new center of Mount Wutai.[44]

To a great extent, building the Cloister of the True Presence around 710–11 was the culmination of many attempts since the sixth century to search for the unmediated vision of Mañjuśrī at Mount Wutai. In the account of the official monk Huize, who led the court delegation to visit Mount Wutai in the 660s, the monk came close to capturing a glimpse of the "true presence" of the bodhisattva at Central Peak, only to see it disappear before his eyes. With Huayan Monastery (the former Dafu Lingjiu Monastery) built to replace Central Peak as the new center of the sacred site, the phantom statue in Huize's vision was substantiated and materialized in the icon of Mañjuśrī riding a lion. The icon, as the term "true presence" implies, could transfigure from an image to the real presence, thus offering the most imminent and potent manifestation. In the account in the *Extended Records,* after the iconic image was finally made and enshrined, it was described as "efficacious in divine resonance, [so much that devotees] from near and afar all came to venerate it faithfully."[45] The holy manifestation of Mañjuśrī, previously observed only above the summit of Vulture Peak, was now reframed in the monastic context and architecture.

Sacral Architecture at the Sacred Mountain: The Case of Huayan Monastery

Mount Wutai, in all likelihood, began to draw practitioners no later than the second half of the sixth century, although it is difficult to ascertain from the textual evidence the size of the community and number of monasteries in that early period. We do know, however, that those that were there were devastated during the years of repression, when the Northern Qi fell to the Northern Zhou in 577. In the *Ancient Records,* Huixiang wrote, "[Mount Wutai] suffered from the persecution of the Dharma [initiated] under Emperor Wu of the Northern Zhou. Buddhist scriptures were disrespected and scattered; splendid monasteries and grand rituals were destroyed and abolished. If not for the blessing of the divine, nothing would have survived."[46] In the early seventh century, Mount Wutai would have been still rebuilding, attracting monastics or individual practitioners largely from the neighboring regions.

Even when Huixiang visited Mount Wutai in 667, the architecture of the major monasteries was still modest. In contrast to the highly decorated palatial complex that Xiangyun saw in a vision inside the Diamond Grotto, even the largest monastery described in Huixiang's *Ancient Records,* Dafu Lingjiu Monastery, located in the central valley, comprised only two image halls, a garden, corridors, and other building foundations in disrepair.[47] Huixiang reports an aged statue of Mañjuśrī in one of the image halls, but provides no details. He mentions also some stone structures on the mountaintop of Central Peak, which enshrined a standing statue of Mañjuśrī in an east chamber and a sitting statue of Maitreya in the west, and, on the road south from Central Peak another stone chamber, inside of which was an iconic triad of Śākyamuni flanked by Mañjuśrī and Samantabhadra.[48] It seems that around Huixiang's time not only was there a lack of major architectural undertakings at Mount Wutai, but a chief iconic image of Mañjuśrī as the primary focus of worship was also absent at the sacred abode of the bodhisattva.

The Mañjuśrī cult began to garner more attention, most likely as a result of the promotion by Huize after his visits in the early 660s. The textual evidence also suggests that the number of pilgrims increased in the second half of the seventh century, the majority of them traveling to the sacred site for short-term visits in the hope of attaining the vision of the bodhisattva there.[49] Most pilgrimage activities took place at the Central Peak and the central valley area, and according to the *Ancient Records,* Central Peak was the most numinous site of all, where sacred signs or traces were expected. During the last decades of the seventh century, more elaborate descriptions about monastic establishments at Mount Wutai became available, in particular, those regarding Dafu Lingjiu Monastery (Dafu Lingjiusi). Already in 664, Daoxuan (596–667), the prolific scholar-monk, included accounts of the monastery in his writings about Mount Wutai.[50] Located in the central valley, Dafu Lingjiu Monastery was the usual stopping point for pilgrims, and by the 680s, it had been built into a multicloistered complex.[51] Most significantly, the imperial court renamed the monastery Huayan Monastery—in Chinese, Huayansi (it was also called Da Huayansi, with the prefix meaning "great"). Only five monasteries in the nation were granted this name, to celebrate the new translation of the *Flower Garland Sutra* (669), and only one was so honored at Mount Wutai.[52] In the 700s, there was little doubt that Huayan Monastery was the center of the sacred site, and that the summit behind the monastery, Vulture Peak, was the place where Mañjuśrī manifested his "true presence."

Huayan Monastery, formerly Dafu Lingjiu Monastery, was one of the earliest monasteries built at Mount Wutai, aside from Monastery of Buddha's Radiance (Foguangsi) and Monastery Clear and Cold (Qingliangsi), but the precise date of its founding is not known. All three monasteries played a significant role in the early history of the sacred mountain, but geographically they were quite far apart from each other in the larger area of Mount Wutai (see map 2, in introduction).[53] Approaching Mount Wutai from the southwest, one passes first Foguang Monastery, in the plain, followed, as one moves to the higher elevations, by Qingliang Monastery, until one reaches Huayan Monastery at the head of a valley, surrounded by prominent peaks (see plate 3). The current set of "five peaks" may have been so designated to encompass all three monasteries, as well as the histories and legends

FIGURE 3.2a. Site plan of monasteries built on the rising hill of the former Huayan Monastery. A central axis that aligns the three major monastery complexes—White Pagoda, Xiantong Temple, and Pusading Cloister—can still be discerned. After Pei, *Yanbei wenwu kanchatuan baogao*, 183.

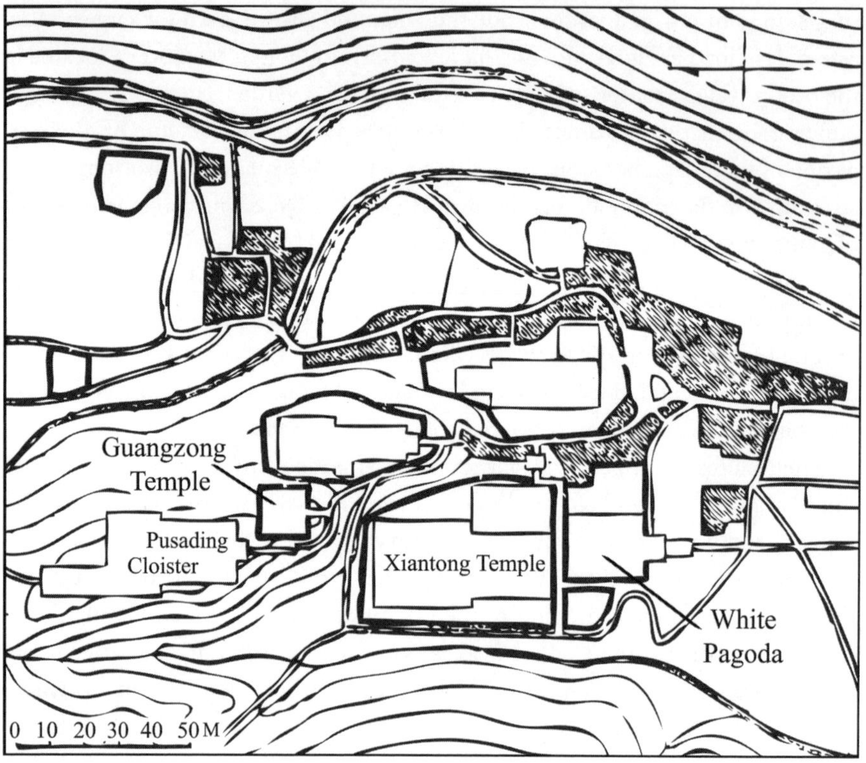

associated with them, within the extended parameter of the sacred site, which, simultaneously, placed Huayan Monastery at the geographic and religious center.

Huayan Monastery continued to expand through the Tang era. Arriving at the monastery in 840, Ennin described it in his diary as a large complex of twelve cloisters built over a rising hill, with the Cloister of the True Presence at its top.[54] Inside the monastery, the largest cloister was the Cloister of the Well-Abiding Pavilion (Shanzhuge Yuan), built close to the entrance; in front of this cloister, a two-story octagonal pagoda was erected, which, according to Ennin, marked the underground crypt that enshrined "relics of Aśoka."[55] In the centuries that followed after the Tang, the history of Huayan Monastery fluctuated, and by the early Ming (1368–644), when major restorations were undertaken with imperial support, it was divided into several separate temples. By 1579, three monastic complexes existed along the central axis of the site (figs. 3.2a, 3.2b): White Pagoda Temple (Tayuansi), centered on a grand white pagoda that may have been built at the former spot of the relic depository;[56] the Temple of Manifested Penetration (Xiantongsi), most likely rebuilt from the former Cloister of the Well-Abiding Pavilion; and the Cloister of the True Presence of Bodhisattva's Crown (Pusading Zhenrong Yuan),[57] on the former Vulture Peak. Rebuilding projects at the site continued into the Qing dynasty (1644–1911), a period that saw the last revival of the bodhisattva cult at Mount Wutai before modern times.[58]

At least by the Ming dynasty, Mount Wutai had transformed into a different kind of sacred site with a strong sectarian inclination toward Tibetan Buddhism,[59]

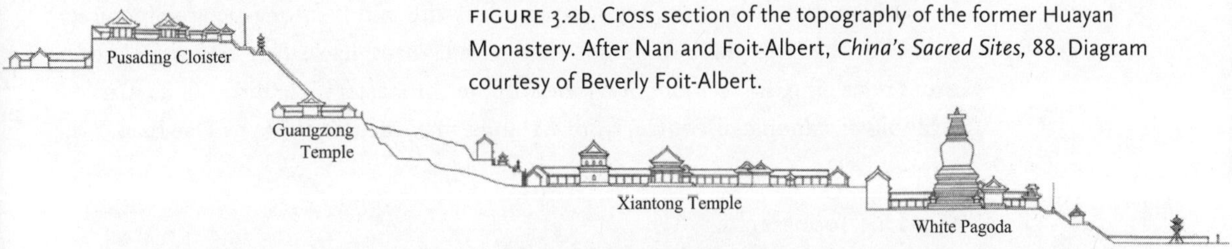

FIGURE 3.2b. Cross section of the topography of the former Huayan Monastery. After Nan and Foit-Albert, *China's Sacred Sites*, 88. Diagram courtesy of Beverly Foit-Albert.

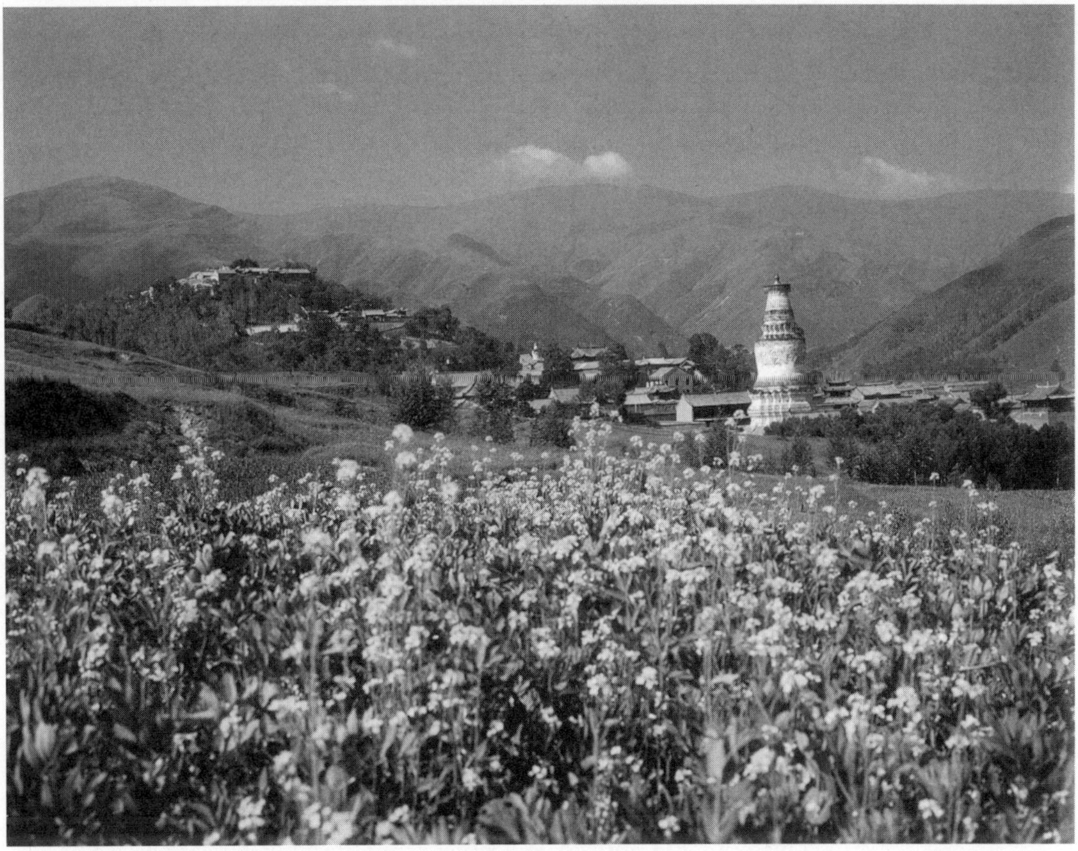

FIGURE 3.2c. The current monastic buildings at the site of the former Huayan Monastery on the rising hill. From Guo Zhicheng, "Wutai Shan," fig. 1. Photograph courtesy of Guo Zhicheng.

and a different architectural style from its medieval counterpart. None of the surviving structures at the site of the former Huayan Monastery dates from the Tang; we can only make conjectures, based on the current structures on the site. Fortunately, their southward orientation, alignment along a central axis, and relational positions on a rising hill do indicate how the Tang monastic complex might have been experienced (fig. 3.2c). In particular, the gradual rise of the site might have conditioned the way the true-presence icon was experienced and thus given it a greater religious or ritual import. Or, to look at it another way, the icon, enshrined as it was at the highest point of the monastery, may have changed the structure of the space and the user's conception of the monastery's sacral architecture. Huan Monastery, located at the (new) geographic center of Mount Wutai, may have become also its spiritual center by virtue not only of the vision conferred by its sacred icon, but also of the topography of its site and its monastic architecture built over the rising hill. To pursue these conjectures, let us first explore related issues regarding the contemporary view of the "monastery" (in terms of its space, symbolism, canonic discourse) from writings, in particular, those by Daoxuan.

Monastic Topography

Daoxuan is well known for his works on monastic rules (*vinaya*), such as his commentaries on the *Four-Part Vinaya.*[60] It was through his efforts that Buddhist monastic practice in China synthesized the several previously divergent and inconsistent monastic regulations. Daoxuan also produced other writings, including biographies of eminent monks, catalogues of canonical scriptures, and works related to sectarian lineages. The wide spectrum of his output established Daoxuan's fame as a scholar-monk in the early Tang Buddhist community, but his emphasis on monastic discipline, scriptural learning, and transmission of dharma also points to the widespread laxity of the clerical orders of his times, which Daoxuan criticized sternly in his writings.

Daoxuan's dissatisfaction with the state of the monasteries was further exacerbated by the state policy to keep Buddhist communities at bay. In a decree of 637, for instance, Emperor Taizong (r. 626–49) favored Daoist clergy over Buddhist monks and nuns. In the same year, he also promulgated "Regulations for Daoist and Buddhist Clerics" (Daosengge) in a new Code of the Zhenguan Reign (Zhenguan Lü). The new regulations, meant to bring the clergy under the official system of secular laws, took Buddhist communities into the state's legal jurisdiction.[61] Buddhist monastic institutions reacted to this control, as well as attacks by Confucian scholars, by condemning corrupt clerics and promoting *vinaya.* As Daoxuan states, "*Vinaya* is the life of the Dharma. If one propagates it, the life [of the Dharma] is complete; now, if one doesn't have the intention to promote [*vinaya*], the True Dharma will be extinguished."[62] The anxiety over the decline of the Dharma implied in the passage was still a concern during the seventh century. His contemporary Daoshi (d. 683) writes about the monasteries of his days:

> A long period has elapsed [since the Buddha's time] and Dharma has [since] gradually declined. Monasteries and images continue to be erected, but none live up to the ideal. . . . Consequently, one sees the traces [of the Buddha] but does not know the meaning; one attends daily rituals, yet knows nothing about why one is doing so. [Consequently] those who participate in the liturgy do not know where their mind should abide. The unproselytized thus show no respect for Dharma, bringing about contempt and arousing assaults [against Buddhism].[63]

Daoshi speaks critically, but also distinguishes the Buddhist from the unconverted other and underlines the role of monasteries as strongholds of the religion, a belief that would have also been in Daoxuan's mind when he composed his visionary texts regarding the ideal model of the earthly monastery.

Daoxuan also collected miracle tales, under the heading "resonant [or sympathetic] response" (*gantong*), referring to miraculous intervention of the divine in response to particular people, places, or objects. He includes tales of miracles or magic, extraordinary visions, numinous sites, and different types of relics.[64] Mount Wutai was not overlooked, and Daoxuan recounted important details about the sacred mountain, including its numinous sightings and marvels, a hagiography of the meditation master Jietuo during the first half of the seventh century, and Huize's visit at Dafu Lingjiu Monastery in the early 660s.[65] The events that constituted "resonant response" at Mount Wutai were offered as proof of the efficacy of the sacred site. For Daoxuan, the mystique of the revelatory vision was apparently just as valid as doctrinal learning and compliance with clerical rules as part of monastic aspirations. In fact, encountering divine presence may even have been the most powerful experience in shaping the monastic's world, contributing to a revisioning of the faith in the final age of the Dharma. It is likely in such political and religious circumstances that Daoxuan, in order to revitalize the monastery, wrote a text in accordance with a vision he experienced of the Jetavana Monastery in Śravāstī, India (present-day Sahet Mahet), a monastery where Śākyamuni Buddha resided and preached for many years.[66]

Daoxuan wrote the *Illustrated Scripture of Jetavana Monastery of Śrāvastī in Central India* (Zhong tianzhu sheweiguo Qiyuansi tujing) in 667, shortly before he died.[67] The monastery was well known in Buddhist communities through the story of Anāthapiṇḍada's purchase of Jetavana Garden as the ground of the new monastery; it appears in several Buddhist texts from as early as the fifth century and is also illustrated in murals of many image caves.[68] As Daoxuan had never set foot in India, he would have had to rely on relevant textual records for his knowledge of Jetavana Monastery. In his preface to the text, Daoxuan states that at first he was unable to resolve many contradictory accounts of the place, but then "all of a sudden, I awoke and felt the stimuli of the divine. Years of my accumulated and heavy grief [disappeared], and suddenly I was writing like torrents of rain, and [what was] obscure in darkness then became somewhat manifest."[69] The monastery, however, was described largely with reference to general principles of Chinese architecture, rather than Indian models. It is thus plausible that the *Illustrated Scripture,* by fusing the historical and the visionary, was composed for Chinese readers of Daoxuan's times to evoke a vision of an idealized monastery, in which the sacred presence of the Buddha was the center of the monastery. Not intended as a true account of the historical Jetavana Monastery, the *Illustrated Scripture* is instead a vehicle for comments and thoughts critical of the ways in which monasteries were conceived during the early Tang.

According to the *Illustrated Scripture,* the Jetavana Monastery was built over an extensive area; it contained 120 cloisters divided by six great avenues that ran in north-south and east-west directions and intersected each other (fig. 3.3a). These avenues connected nine great gates, three each on the east, south, and west, and a north wall that enclosed the entire monastic precinct. The cloisters were defined by the functions they served. All cloisters were more or less similar in architec-

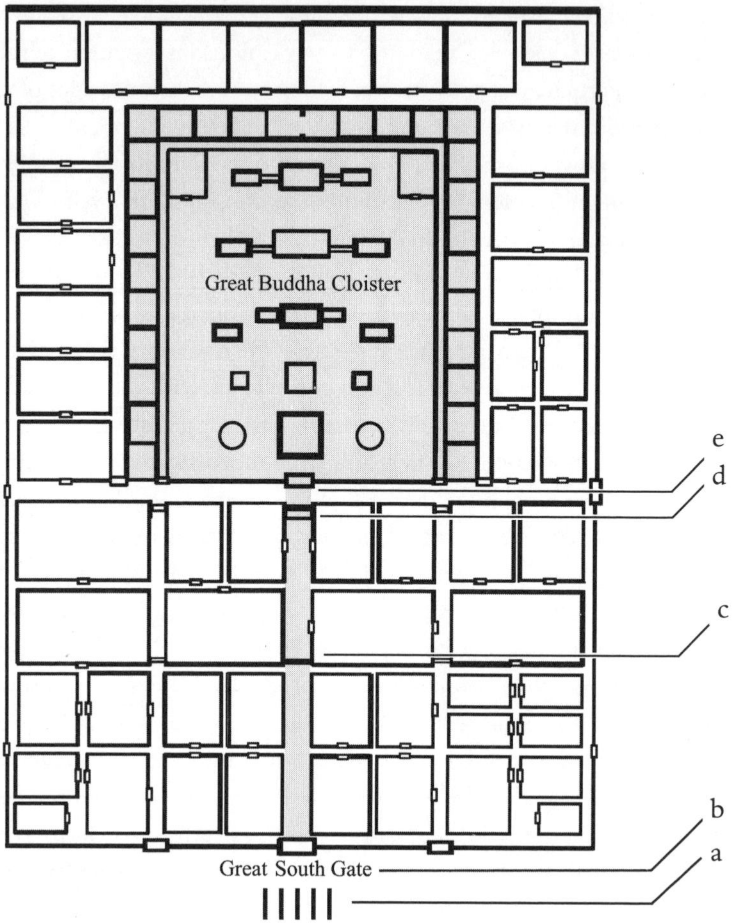

FIGURE 3.3a. Reconstruction of Jetavana Monastery based on the *Illustrated Scripture.* The monastic ground is divided by six major avenues that connect nine main gates. The major markers along the central south-north avenue before one enters the Great Buddha Cloister are (a) five bridges; (b) three-story Great South Gate; (c) five-passageway Crow-Head Gate (Wutoumen); (d) seven-story Median Gate; (e) south gate of the Great Buddha Cloister. After Fu Xinian, *Liangjin, Nanbeichao, Sui-Tang, Wudai jianzhu*, fig. 3.7.3. Diagram courtesy of Fu Xinian.

tural details—a walled courtyard built with one or two main structures and an entrance—except for the central Great Buddha Cloister. The largest and the most grandiose, the Great Buddha Cloister was the center of the entire monastery, and contained a series of structures located along a central axis: a square lotus pond, the seven-story Great Buddha Pagoda, a Great Buddha Hall, the Second Great Hall, and a multistory pavilion; each was grander and higher than the one before it (fig. 3.3b). The Great Buddha Cloister opened to the south with a great gate, which faced the central avenue that connected to the Great South Gate of the monastery.

The layout, division, axiality, and symmetry of the Jetavana Monastery all speak in an architectural language that recalls not any Indian prototypes but the ward-and-street system of the urban planning of major cities in Tang China, for example, its capital, Chang'an. During the Tang, Chang'an underwent an intensive building period unprecedented in history,[70] and the magnificent cityscape of the capital might have been in Daoxuan's mind when he was envisioning Jetavana Monastery. In particular, the palatial city-within-the-city structure of Chang'an corresponds to the Great Buddha Cloister at the center of the Jetavana Monastery.

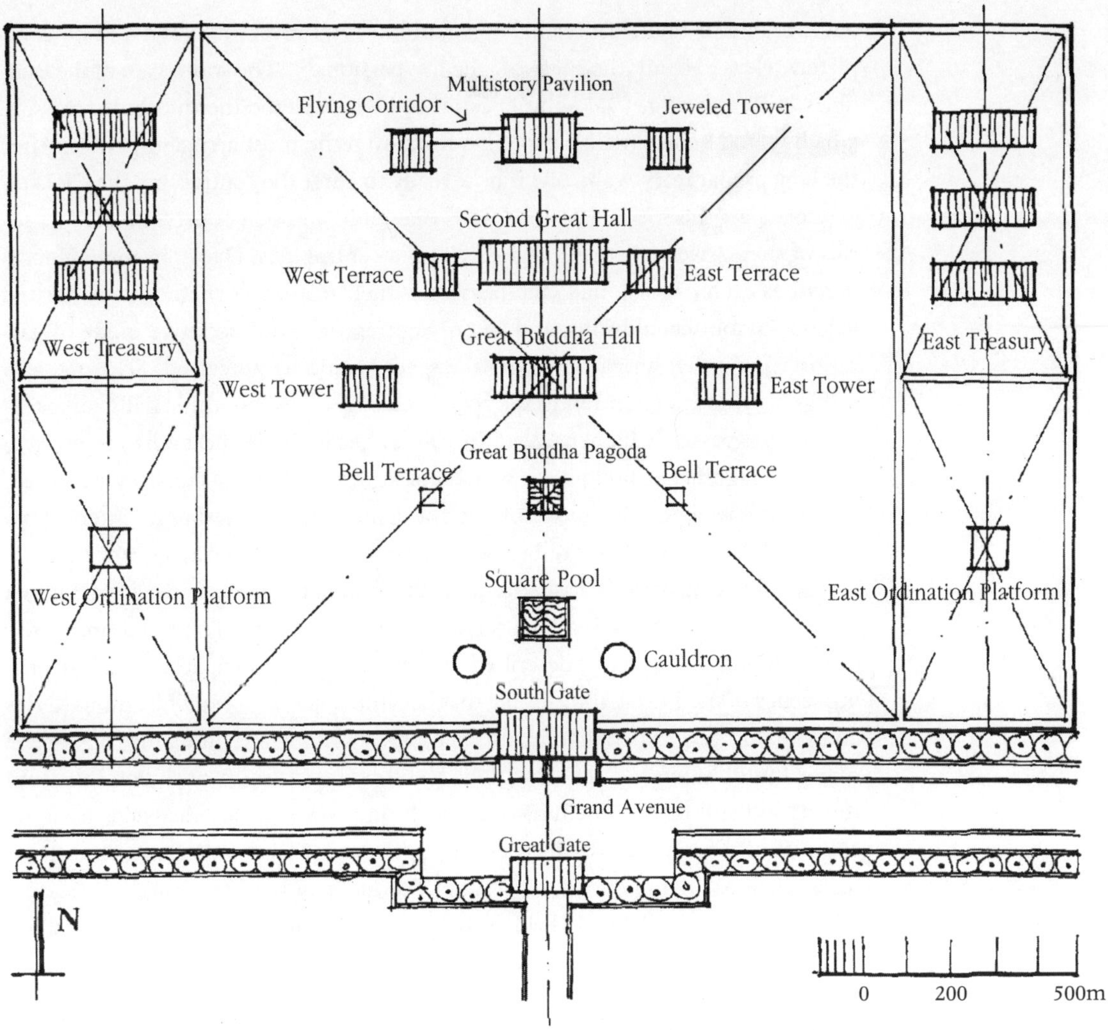

FIGURE 3.3b. Detail of the Great Buddha Cloister, Jetavana Monastery. After Puay-peng Ho, "The Ideal Monastery," fig. 7. Diagram courtesy of Puay-peng Ho.

The parallel makes sense, since "one was the seat of the earthly monarch, and the other that of the Universal Monarch."[71]

Despite the fact that the model, Chang'an, is a worldly city, the views and vision inspired by the architecture of the Jetavana Monastery in Daoxuan's text are described in distinctly Buddhist terms. In the ceremonial approach along the central avenue from the south (see fig. 3.3a), for example, one arrives first at a set of five bridges leading to the Great South Gate; crossing the bridge, Daoxuan tells his reader, connotes one's departure from the shore of the mundane world into the paradisaical precinct of the Buddha. Next, one would enter the Great South Gate, whose three stories symbolize the three emptinesses (*sankong*),[72] a state of mind necessary for making one's entry into Buddhism. One then proceeds along the long axial avenue, passing through a crow-head gate[73] with five passageways and another grand, seven-story gate, before arriving at the south gate of the central Buddha Cloister. Daoxuan writes, "Going north, the visitor thus beholds the layers [of ornate and magisterial gates] repeated in succession, and one's spirit will startle and tremble. If one cleanses his eyes and looks up reverently, one will be completely released from [the snare of] the five passions."[74] The south gate of the Buddha Cloister (see fig. 3.3a, point e) can thus be considered the threshold, crossing which would banish malign thoughts from even the most arrogant person. After the long preparatory walk, one is now ready to enter the central Buddha Cloister.

Once past the south gate, one finds oneself in an open courtyard facing a series of successive structures aligned along a central axis. Daoxuan meticulously describes each pagoda, hall, and pavilion—their features, ornaments, associated legends, symbolic allusions, and so on. Shifting from a descriptive mode of narration to one that anticipates how the space would be perceived, Daoxuan also brings his reader's attention to the spectacular view: "These three halls and pavilion are progressively higher. What the eye can see in the farthest north is [nothing but the magnificent buildings], which could not have been humanly executed, and must have been the abode of ancient divinities."[75] Accordingly, entering the central cloister, the pious are provided with a spectacular view, an otherworldly and transcendent vision, arising as a result of one's preparatory walk, taken as a spiritual journey, through a long section of the monastery. The vision inside the central Buddha Cloister as described by Daoxuan thus anticipates murals depicting scenes of the Pure Land, a topic that became popular in Buddhist monasteries and worship caves, including many examples surviving at Dunhuang, one of the major Buddhist sites of the time, which still preserves most of the murals from this period still extant in China. One such mural depicts an idealized monastic complex of the kind Daoxuan is describing (fig. 3.4).[76] Daoxuan used architectural terms such as "flying corridor" (*feilang*), "connecting hall" (*jiadian*), "storied pavilion" (*chongge*), and "flying bridge" (*feiqiao*) to describe his visionary monastery, and all appear in the fantastic monastic complex depicted in this mural.[77] The architectural ensemble of the Pure Land is arranged symmetrically, with buildings of an increasing degree of grandeur along the central axis, as if the topography were rising gradually in order to allow one to see the complex in greater spatial depth and visual majesty. The vision that one attains on entering the central Buddha Cloister, in this light, is a transformed and transcendent view of the monastery, in which, though the ground is level, the topography is conceived as elevation, a kind of "monastic topography."

As a religious site, the monastery was not only understood physically, but also symbolically or metaphorically. In another text, entitled *Exhortation on Manners and Etiquette for Novices in Training* (Jiaojie xinxue biqiu xinghu lüyi), Daoxuan compiled 466 rules of conduct grouped in twenty-three sections for newly ordained monks.[78] He specifies the appropriate deportment of the monk according to the location inside the monastery, for each place had a different sacred nature and potential. Starting with "Norms for Entering the Monastery" (Rusi Fa), the monastic, for instance, must prostrate himself before entering, avoid stepping on the shadow of any monastic buildings, and circumambulate the pagoda or Buddha hall only clockwise.[79] The newly entering monk is then led through the monastery with specific instructions for how he is to act at each particular place. Going

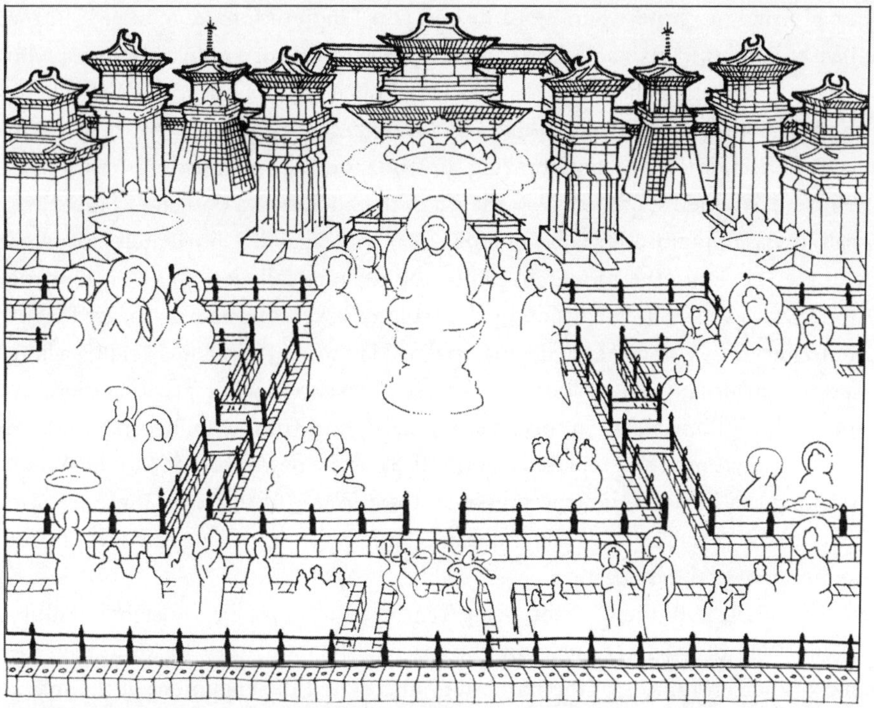

FIGURE 3.4. Mural depicting a scene from the *Sutra on Visualizing the Amitāyus Buddha* (*Amitāyurdhyāna Sūtra*), north wall, Mogao Cave 217, Dunhuang, Gansu. Early Tang. The drawing shows how a monastic complex could be perceived symmetrically with a clear central axis as if built over a rising topography. From Xiao Mo, *Dunhuang jianzhu yanjiu*, 66. Drawing by permission of Wenwu Press.

through the monastery could accordingly be regarded as a spiritual process of ascent, a mental reorientation that allowed one to attain monastic spirituality. The two texts, the guide for monastics and the account of Jetavana Monastery, together add a layer of religious significance to the physical space of the built monastery: the "monastic topography," that is, the physical terrain of the monastery reconceived in terms of the approach to the presence of the Buddha, may also be understood as a "religious terrain," which the practitioner would enter for spiritual aspiration and visions. The later appellation of "mountain gate" (*shanmen*) for the main entrance gate of a monastery almost certainly reflects this notion of a spiritual ascent, as does the ever-rising "mountain topography" inside the monastery.[80]

Visualizing Mañjuśrī at Mount Wutai

At Huayan Monastery (see plate 3, fig. 3.2c), our immediate attention would be drawn to the monastic complex that takes the rising hill as the primary foundation of its monastic topography. Initially, there was little there to connect the site specifically to visions of Mañjuśrī. Daoxuan, writing in the 660s, included Mount Wutai in his collection of "resonant responses," but Huayan Monastery (still known as Dafu Lingjiu Monastery) was still relatively undeveloped, just as there was little for Huixiang to note when he came to Dafu Lingjiu Monastery in 667. In the *Ancient Records,* Huixiang tells of an early seventh-century monk Mingyao, who routinely practiced the form of meditative concentration known as Visualizing the Buddha's Radiance, often joined by Monk Jietuo; he reports that they "went to Dafu [Lingjiu] Monastery, praying for [the vision of] Mañjuśrī."[81] Yet no texts tell of an experience of the true presence of the bodhisattva until after Huixiang's visit. It was not until after Huayan Monastery was expanded into a multicloistered complex covering the mountain hill in the decades following his visit that the bodhisattva was seen in a vision by the sculptor asked to create an image for the monastery. His vision eventually materialized in the icon of Mañjuśrī riding a lion, and was enshrined in the Cloister of the True Presence, built in 710–11 at the summit of the Vulture Peak. In this process, the sighting of the bodhisattva became the defining center, and replaced Central Peak as the new center of Mount Wutai. Marking the locus of the true presence, the Cloister of the True Presence also marked the culmination of the monastic topography, imparting spiritual import to the space of the monastery.

The addition of the Cloister of the True Presence in the early eighth century would relandscape and restructure the space of the monastery. Its location at the end of the central axis of the monastery articulated the alignment of the major buildings in succession, each higher than the one before, suggesting a greater spatial depth. It also extended the monastic precinct longitudinally, so that "walking up" was the basic way the body moved across the length of the monastery. Walking through the monastery up the rise that ended with the sight of Mañjuśrī riding a lion (a vision of the bodhisattva's true presence) inside the cloister would have had several important implications. It conveyed the idea that one's spiritual advancement—symbolized in the movement through the monastery—would, if successful, be affirmed at the end with a revelatory vision of the bodhisattva's divine manifestation. The vision might also be a spiritual reward for the correct practice of the Visualizing the Buddha's Radiance meditation, leading to the wisdom one needs for comprehending the Buddhist cosmological universe, as described in the *Flower Garland Sutra.*[82] Indeed, after the true-presence icon was made, almost every time a manifestation of the bodhisattva at Mount Wutai was recorded, it was as Mañjuśrī riding a lion, hovering in midair. Every sighting of the bodhisattva riding his lion—both the vision and the icon—affirmed a spiritual resonance with the divine, attainable by walking up the monastic topography at Mount Wutai (fig. 3.5).

There is yet another implication. The ascending movement through the monastery was undertaken and practiced to reproduce the "sacred topography" of Mount Wutai. As discussed previously, Huayan Monastery in the central valley became the new center of the sacred site, replacing Central Peak with the building of the Cloister of the True Presence. Arriving at the monastery and reaching Vulture Peak, in this regard, *was* to reach the center of the sacred mountain. In other words, all of Mount Wutai was concentrated in the monastic space of Huayan Monastery, which, in turn, crystallized the very *siteness* of the bodhisattva's sacred

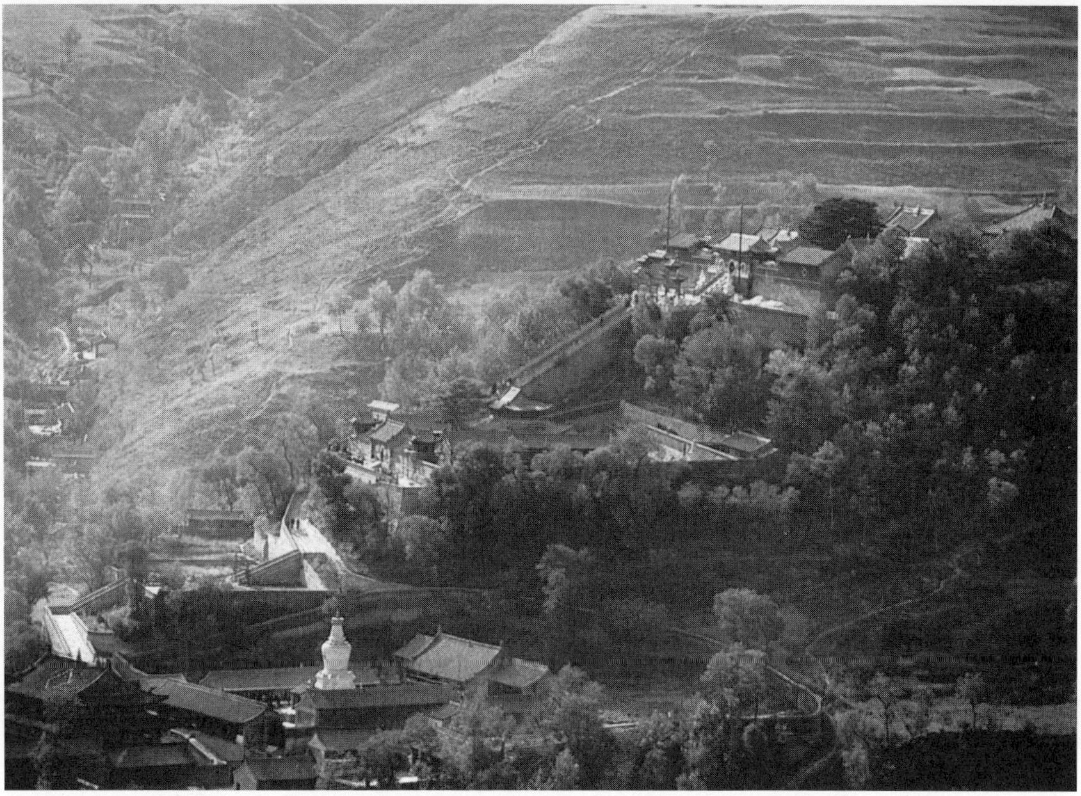

FIGURE 3.5. Aerial view of the monastic complex built on the highest point of the former Huayan Monastery of the Tang dynasty. Guo Zhicheng, "Wutai Shan," fig. 4. Photograph courtesy of Guo Zhicheng.

abode: its topography, elevation, centrality, and most important of all, the sacred place where Mañjuśrī could be beheld manifesting his true presence. Traveling to Mount Wutai in 840, the Japanese pilgrim Ennin, having arrived at Huayan Monastery, was eager to venerate the sacred image of Mañjuśrī. The next day, after touring through the several cloisters of the grandest monastery of the time, he reached the Cloister of the True Presence, and opened the door of the image hall. Ennin wrote in his diary: "The statue of bodhisattva Mañjuśrī of the Great Sage appears in awesome spirit, and its dignified appearance is without comparison. Riding a lion, the statue [of Mañjuśrī] seems to take up the entire five-bay hall. The lion looked animated and nimble, seemingly ready to move. Vapor came out of his [open] mouth; for a while as I was beholding the view, it felt as if the lion were going to take off."[83] The spatial organization and monastic topography of the monastery thus structured both its physical and religious context in which the vision of the bodhisattva could be perceived and understood there and then; attaining the vision of Mañjuśrī riding a lion was the same as being at the center of the bodhisattva's sacred realm at Mount Wutai.

This chapter has shown that the divine presence of bodhisattvas in the early history of Chinese Buddhism was supposed to be universal and unbounded by location, as in the cases of Guanyin's supernatural rescues. Mount Wutai during the early

Tang, as we have seen, offers a different paradigm. The five peaks of Mount Wutai underwent a critical redesignation and topographic appropriation that localized the holy manifestation of the bodhisattva's "true presence" (*zhenrong*) at the very center of the sacred domain. The creation of the true-presence icon not only gave material and visual form to the initially ineffable presence of the bodhisattva, but also initiated a new vision and conception of Mount Wutai that shifted the most essential element of the sacred mountain from site to sight, delegating the five peaks to the background of the revelatory vision of Mañjuśrī. Yet, as Diane Eck says, "[m]ountain ascent is associated with vision and the acquisition of power,"[84] and the seemingly disembodied vision of the bodhisattva required the practitioner or vision seeker to physically move through the sacred topography. This ascent was also replicated and reproduced inside Huayan Monastery, at the highest point of which the sacred icon could be venerated and the vision attained. Mañjuśrī riding the lion, as described in Ennin's diary, was often envisioned as capable of taking off and flying above his sacred mountain. Even when the bodhisattva cult spread outside of Mount Wutai during the ninth and tenth centuries, as evidenced in the iconic image depicted inside many of the Mogao caves in Dunhuang (see fig. 6.2b), the universal reach of Mañjuśrī's supreme power and wisdom was still recognized, not in terms of his celestial identity, but the terrestrial location of his sacred abode.[85]

Built on a rising hill in the central valley of Mount Wutai, Huayan Monastery and the view it provided call to mind the imaginary architecture of the Jetavana Monastery as described in Daoxuan's *Illustrated Scripture.* Inside the central Buddha Cloister of the latter, a seven-story pagoda was the first building in the series of magnificent halls and pavilions (see fig. 3.3b). The primary position of the pagoda on the central axis has been taken as evidence for a pre-Tang style of monastic architecture, after which Daoxuan's description of Jetavana Monastery was modeled.[86] In the Tang dynasty, pagodas in monasteries gradually gave way to image halls as the prime focus of the monastery and were more often than not allocated to positions not on the central axis.[87] At Huayan Monastery, however, a pagoda (built on the spot of today's White Pagoda) was located on the central axis close to the front of the monastery; it was built sometime during the eighth century, according to Ennin, to mark the underground depository of the relics of Aśoka. In this light, the addition of the pagoda at Huayan Monastery was not so much a matter of architectural style or building tradition as a miraculous or spiritual component that added yet another layer of sacrality to the site of the monastery. Both the idealized monastery in Daoxuan's vision and the earthly monastery of Huayan Monastery at Mount Wutai were meant to be a place of practice and enlightenment (*bodhimaṇḍa*) in the sacred presence of the divine. Furthermore, the spectacle of both these architectural complexes built on gradually rising elevations also evoked the image of the Pure Land paradise. Indeed, as the sacred abode of a bodhisattva of the tenth stage, Mount Wutai was built to aspire to a greater transcendent status, as a realm of the Pure Land, or Mañjuśrī's buddha field (S: *buddhakṣetra;* C: *fotu*), presided over by Mañjuśrī flying high above it on the back of his lion.[88]

CHAPTER FOUR

Mediating the Distance to Mount Wutai

Offerings are made at each of the peaks; [pilgrims] come to venerate from all directions. Many even arrive from other countries or distant lands to join [the pilgrimage]. [Here] monasteries that have name [plaques] number about one hundred; smaller monasteries and hermitages number about a thousand. Each year more than ten thousand clerical and lay pilgrims [come to] venerate at all peaks. The Pure Land of the West would not be different from [Mount Wutai].

—Zhang Chuzhen, *A Record of Mount Wutai and the [Stone] Lantern* (Wutaishan ji dengtai ji)

Around the end of the seventh century, Mount Wutai underwent a critical transition: the occult vision of the divine, icons, topography, and architecture all changed, decisively shifting the focus from the mountains to the bodhisattva. As its unique characteristics were construed as "traces" and "signs" of the divine presence associated with the bodhisattva cult, and as its architecture was constructed to spatialize the bodhisattva's presence at the site and reconfigure and reconceive its topography, Mount Wutai was converted over time, as we have seen, into a Buddhist sacred site. Eventually, the manifestation of Mañjuśrī's true presence fundamentally altered the ontology of Mount Wutai.

The primary textual sources of Mount Wutai also testify to the changing character of the sacred site: Huixiang's *Ancient Records of [Mount] Qingliang*, compiled around 680, and Yanyi's *Extended Records of [Mount] Qingliang*, which documents the history of Mount Wutai from the time after Huixiang's text was completed until the time Yanyi was writing, in 1060.[1] The two texts differ in important respects. For instance, unlike *Ancient Records*, which begins with explications of the name, geographic range, topography, and canonical origins of Mount Wutai, Yanyi began his account by introducing the presiding bodhisattva—his divine powers and karmic affinities with Mount Wutai as expounded in several scriptures—before bringing Mount Wutai into discussion. His *Extended Record* does not concern itself with early definitions of the five sacred peaks. Yanyi says, simply, that the existing designation was divinely reaffirmed in the 670s by five-colored clouds that suddenly covered the five designated peaks when a saintly monk was looking across the mountain site.[2] Indeed, in Yanyi's text the voices of non-Buddhist practitioners that could be heard in Huixiang's *Ancient Records* have been muted, a consequence of Buddhism's establishment on the mountain.[3] Yanyi lists seventy-two major monasteries at Mount Wutai during the Tang, some of which were already built by the end of the eighth century, while more were constructed through-

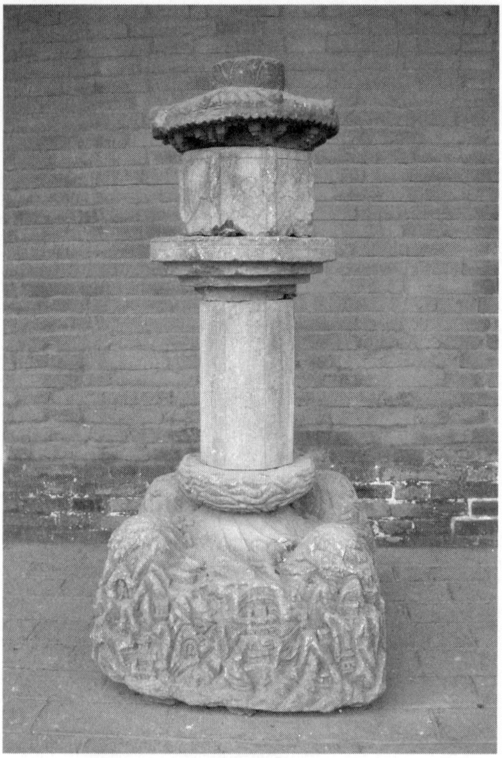

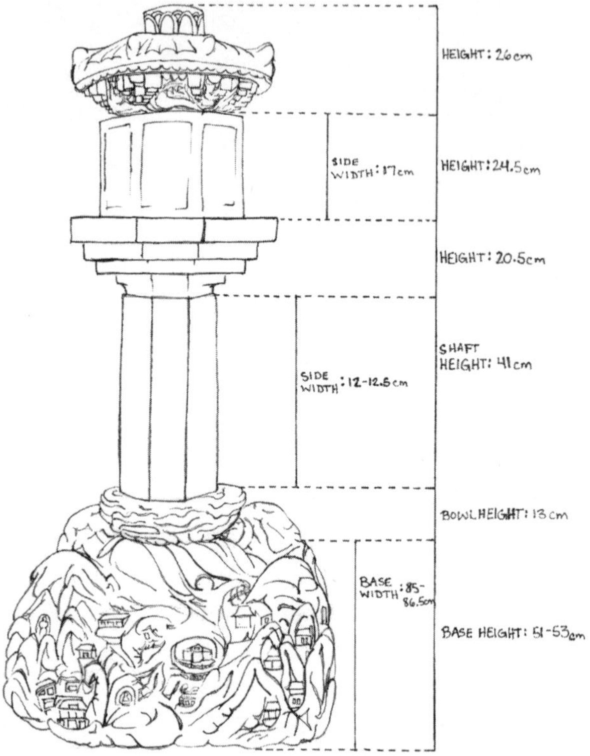

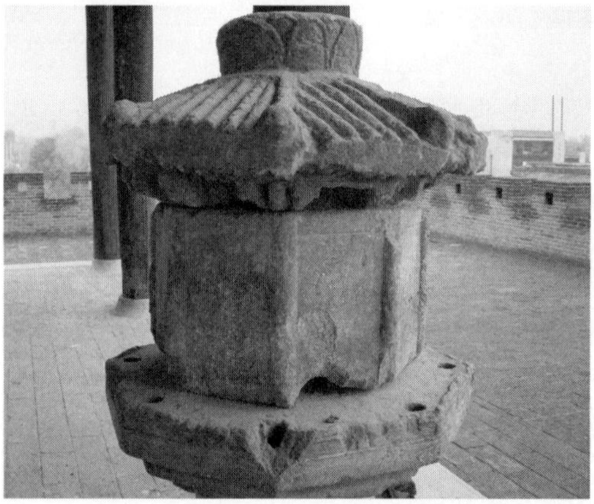

FIGURE 4.1a. Stone lantern (*dengtai*) with octagonal shaft and a base carved in the shape of Mount Wutai, approx. 190 cm. Dongzhang, Shanxi. 713–39 CE. Currently at the Drum Tower, Daixian, Shanxi. Photograph by author.

FIGURE 4.1b. Line-drawing of the Dongzhang stone lantern. Drawing by Amanda Newton.

FIGURE 4.2. Upper structure of the Dongzhang stone lantern in the shape of an eight-sided wooden structure, described as a "heavenly palace" (*tiangong*) in the inscription carved on the shaft. Photograph by author.

out the next centuries.[4] The increased number of monasteries was indicative of Mount Wutai's growing popularity outside its sacred precinct as the earthly domicile of Mañjuśrī. By this time, Mount Wutai was no longer defined from within its mountain range but from without, by its position in the larger context of Tang Buddhism.

It is in this context that a stone lantern surviving from the early eighth century can provide rare visual evidence of the new conception of Mount Wutai in this transition (figs. 4.1a, 4.1b). Although translated as "lantern" (*dengtai*), it is more of a large candle stand or rack that holds candles around its main structure. Although currently in rather poor condition—the wooden parts originally attached to it

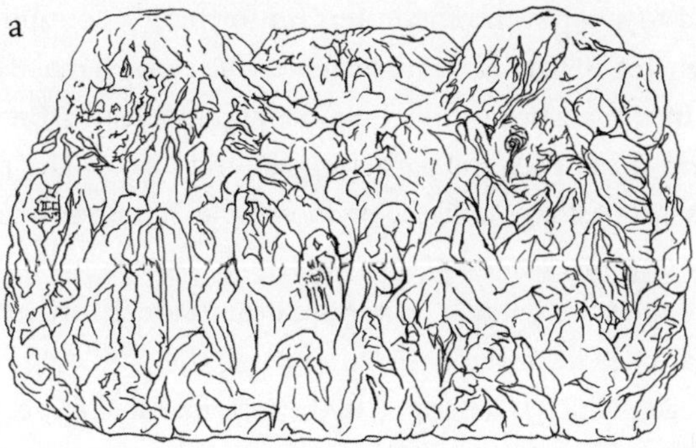

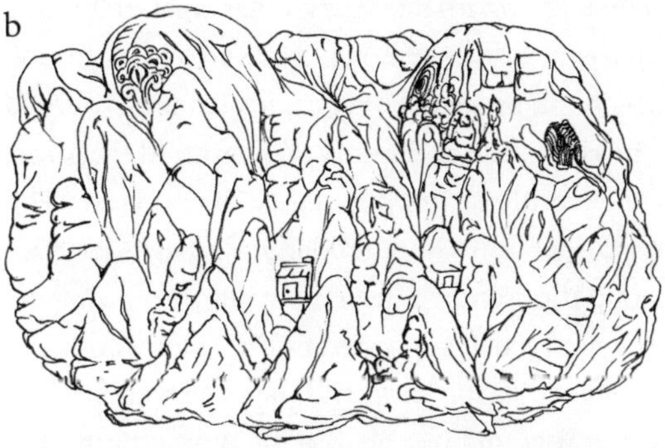

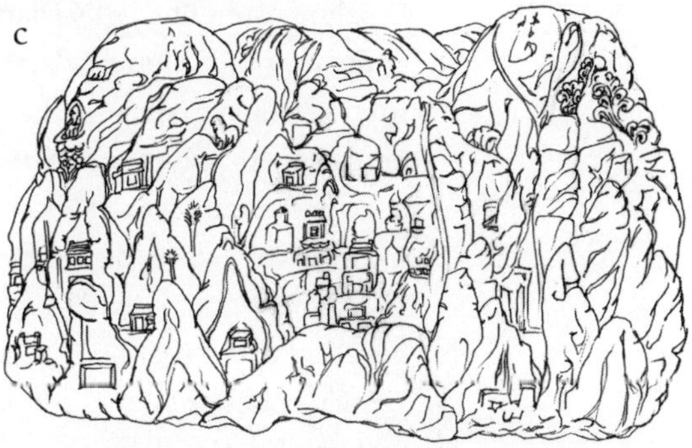

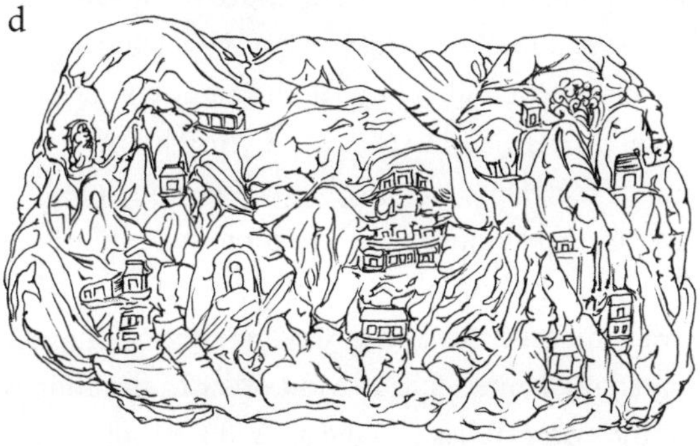

FIGURE 4.3. The four sides of the Dongzhang stone lantern base: (a) back, (b) left, (c) right, (d) front. Drawings by Amanda Newton.

have been lost and its carved imagery has eroded over time—the lantern's form and inscription are still useful and suggestive for our purpose. Nearly 190 centimeters in height, the lantern as it is now consists of a base, an octagonal shaft, and an upper structure shaped like an eight-sided timber-frame building (fig. 4.2). Although the tripartite structure is common for a stone lantern of this time, or its close variant, the pagoda-shaped burner (*randeng ta*),[5] this example is unique in both its visual form and content. The oversized base is a roughly square block, each corner of which is topped with a rounded bulge; another rounded bulge, in the center of the block, supports a bowl-shaped piece carved with wavy lines, which in turn supports the shaft. The base itself is carved with irregular patterns of grooves and ridges. According to the inscription engraved on the shaft, the base depicts the five peaks of Mount Wutai, with the central peak rising up from the Jade Floral Pond (Yuhua Chi, located at Central Peak).[6] Each side of the stone base is carved to suggest mountain terrain forming a continuous landscape (fig. 4.3). Although not all details are discernible, one can still make out figures and beasts of burden moving over the hills, pagodas and monastic structures dotting the mountains, and cloud patterns gathering around peaks. The religious elements (e.g., pilgrims, monasteries, and the divine) in the mountain landscape, vividly captured in the inscription quoted in the epigraph to this chapter, were meant to convey an image of the Pure Land. The paradisaical vision is further indicated in the central peak that rises from the base, supporting the "building" (the uppermost part of the lantern), which is described in the inscription as a "heavenly palace" (*tiangong*).

The lantern was dedicated between 713 and 739 in a town named Dongzhang, in Daizhou (present-day Daixian), Shanxi, approximately sixty miles west of Taihuai at the center of Mount Wutai.[7] The town, located on one of the two northbound routes leading to the mountains (which can be seen in map 11, in chapter 6), would have been in a position to witness the rise of the bodhisattva cult around this time, and the lantern was likely made as a result of the popularity of the cult.[8] The spirited scene described in the inscription—one hundred large monasteries built at Mount Wutai, visited yearly by one thousand cleric and lay pilgrims—may be hyperbolic, but the thriving pilgrimage practice suggested in the record, the conceptual cohesion of the five peaks depicted at the base, and the "heavenly palace" that gives rise to the transcendent vision would not be. Mount Wutai during the seventh and eighth centuries had developed from a regional sacred site to a national pilgrimage center, the historical context in which the stone lantern was made.

This development is illustrated in the name conferred on the former Dafu Lingjiu Monastery, renamed Huayan Monastery by the imperial court after the new translation of the *Flower Garland Sutra* was completed in 699. The name attested to the increasing prominence of the monastery, but it also signified the imperial validation of Mount Wutai, asserting the court's prerogative over the site. The renaming was proposed by Fazang (643–713), the chief Buddhist advisor at the court, who assigned the name Huayan Monastery to five monasteries in the nation: one at each of the two capitals (Chang'an and Luoyang), one in each of the southern frontier states of Wu and Yue, and one at Mount Wutai.[9] The name thus located Mount Wutai no longer in an isolated area inside the northern border but in the larger political territory of the Tang Empire. Fazang was also the major supervisor of the new translation of the *Flower Garland Sutra,* a project that could not have been undertaken without the support of Empress Wu Zetian (624–705).[10] Since the 660s the empress had planned a series of Buddhist projects aimed to fulfill her aspiration to be both a pious Buddhist and an ideal (female) ruler. Concurrently, the court became increasingly aware of Mount Wutai's religious import and sent a delegation led by the monk Huize to the sacred mountain during the Longshuo reign (661–63).[11] It is unclear to what extent the empress was involved in the decision to send Huize to Mount Wutai, but her sponsorship for the bodhisattva cult at Mount Wutai is explicitly recorded in Huixiang's *Ancient Records.*[12] Supporting Mount Wutai was one of the many initiatives taken under Empress Wu's auspices to establish Buddhism as the primary religion of the dynasty.[13] If Huayan Monastery developed into the grandest and most centrally located monastery, it was not just because of the vision of the bodhisattva but also because of the intervention of the empress.

By the first decades of the eighth century, Mount Wutai was on its way to becoming the most important pilgrimage site in Tang China even though it was in a relatively remote location. The distance to Mount Wutai would need to be overcome if the pious believer was to access the sacrality of the site and the vision of the divine.[14] Hence developed the practice of pilgrimage to the site; paths and stops along the way were established. Once Mount Wutai was reached, monasteries played a significant role in mediating access. By and large, monasteries at Mount Wutai were destinations of pilgrimage, where the faithful could venerate particular icons or attend particular rituals in order to attain certain spiritual experiences. Many devout Buddhists who came to Mount Wutai to seek the sacred traces of the bodhisattva reported that they entered what we may call a "virtual" monastery, one seen in a vision, where they encountered the holy presence of the bodhisattva. Although merely visionary and disembodied, the monasteries these pilgrims describe do provide evidence of how monasteries were conceptualized as an integral part of the sacred experience, vision, and imagination in the landscape of Mount Wutai. In this sense, this "virtual monastery" (*huasi*)[15] is not unlike the imagery of monasteries depicted on the base of the stone lantern, or the building structure rising over the sacred landscape, evoking a utopian view of the Pure Land, to which the actual monastery could aspire.

Mount Wutai within Reach: Imperial Sponsorship under Empress Wu

The greater attention paid to Mount Wutai after the visit of the court delegation in the early 660s coincided with Empress Wu Zetian's rise to power. The fact that the empress's family originated in the Taiyuan area just to the south of Mount Wutai may have spurred her to heed the increasing popularity of the sacred site. Her interest in the *Flower Garland Sutra,* which prompted her to sponsor the new translation of the sutra in 699, may have also prompted her support for the bodhisattva cult at Mount Wutai throughout her reign. Most important, Buddhism served the empress well as a means to legitimize her assumption of power after the illness and death of her husband, the emperor.[16] She commissioned stupas, translations of sutras, and installations of relics, all to solidify her mandate as the "universal monarch" (*cakravartin*) in accordance with Buddhist prophecy. Mount Wutai, with its miraculous tales and numinous sightings, would have been a valuable spiritual asset for Empress Wu Zetian. The process by which she became the female monarch is well documented, but the part Mount Wutai played in this process has not been noted until recently.[17] And it is Mount Wutai's becoming an extension, as it were, of the political center both religiously and spatially that turned it into a pilgrimage center readily accessible for the religious.

Empress Wu took over political power after her husband, Emperor Gaozong (r. 649–83), fell ill in 660. Early in 664 she assumed the role of the emperor's political partner, "with power and authority no different from that of the emperor."[18] After Gaozong died in 683, Empress Wu became the de facto ruler, claiming authority through her son and adopting the title Holy Mother and Divine Sovereign (Shengmu Shenhuang), one who communicated with the divine. In 690, Wu Zetian declared the founding of the Great Zhou dynasty and gave herself the male title of Holy and Divine Emperor (Shengshen Huangdi).[19] She then designated her capital in Luoyang with the name "divine capital" (Shendu), where she started several architectural projects, including both orthodox state buildings and Buddhist structures, expressive of her intent to legitimate her sovereignty.[20] Even in this brief review, one notes that Wu Zetian's dominance largely operated in the existing imperial and male dominant framework but with a "gender reversal" on her part, not by asserting a new paradigm.[21] Wu Zetian's reign in the name of the new dynasty was short-lived, ending with her death in 705, but left indelible marks in Tang political and religious history.

In particular, most of the religious projects initiated by Wu Zetian had important implications for the conception of a religious space in Tang China. During the 660s, Empress Wu was involved in three concurrent but separate events—including an official delegation to Mount Wutai—that had decisive ramifications later in her ascendance to the throne. The first is the transportation of the relics enshrined at Famen Monastery (Famensi) outside of Chang'an into the court for public veneration during the period 659–62. This created a precedent for bringing the relics of Famen Monastery to the court, and the practice was repeated five more times later in the Tang dynasty.[22] The origin of Famen Monastery is obscure, but its relics have been linked to the campaign that took place some fifty years earlier, during the Sui dynasty, under the orders of Emperor Wen (r. 581–604) to distribute relics to 112 monasteries nationwide.[23] Empress Wu was evidently enthusiastic about the relics from the Famen Monastery, as she made several donations for the enshrinement of the relics, including a set of nested reliquaries made of gold and silver.[24] In 677, ten thousand relics were miraculously uncovered in the Guangzhai Ward in Chang'an; in the following year, the Guangzhai relics were distributed nationally by order of Empress Wu, following the campaign of relic distribution by Emperor Wen before her.[25] The discovery and distribution of the relics transformed the geographic space of Tang China into a political and religious territory under the empress's reign. Indeed, its significance was revealed just before Empress Wu's proclamation of the new dynasty: in the commentary of the *Great Cloud Sutra* (Dayun jing), a text that played a tremendous role in legitimating Wu Zetian's reign, the discovery of the relics in 667 was recorded as the divine proof that the empress was the chosen one.[26]

While the first event, bringing the relics of Famen Monastery to the court, was about spatial range, the second event was related to the spatial locus. In 665, under Emperor Gaozong (husband of Empress Wu), a state rite, *fengshan,* was conducted at Mount Tai (East Sacred Peak). It was last performed there in the Eastern Han dynasty more than five hundred years earlier, and its purpose was to receive the heavenly mandate.[27] Initially reluctant, the emperor was persuaded by his ministers to conduct this most symbolic state ritual as political testimony to his sovereignty. By 665, Empress Wu already enjoyed an equal share of imperial authority, and consequently, she was recorded to have not only secretly supported the plan but also performed a significant part of the ritual, a manner of participation hitherto unprecedented for any female royal members.[28] Thirty years later, in 695, Wu Zetian, then the emperor of the Zhou dynasty, again performed the *fengshan* rite, only this time as the chief conductor. Rather than at the traditional site, Mount Tai, the rite was performed at Mount Song (Songshan), Central Sacred Peak, which was renamed Divine Peak (Shenyue), for it now had the significance of "Heaven's Center" (Tianzhong).[29] This relocation of the state ritual to Central Sacred Peak repeated a familiar theme of Wu Zetian's reign: her centrality in the reconceived political and religious territory of the dynasty.[30] The change of the sacred locus reoriented and recentered the imperial territory, thus distinguishing her reign from those of the past in spatial terms.

The third important event of the 660s was the official delegation dispatched to Mount Wutai for the period 661–63, and it is clearly related to the others in its purpose and ramifications. For, although different from relics or the *fengshan* rite, the sacred domicile of a bodhisattva would have provided Empress Wu with another avenue to consolidate her power. In fact, she did not just sponsor the bodhisattva cult at Mount Wutai, but took great interest in the auspicious signs (*ruixiang*) that made the mountains a Buddhist sacred site within the territory of Tang China. Writing in about 700, in a work entitled *Biographies and Record [of Those Who Promote] the* Flower Garland Sutra, Fazang characterized those signs at Mount Wutai in the following way: "[At the mountains] one may meet divine monks or holy assemblies. Fairy pavilions [appear] over the peaks of treasures; spiritual light shines, [while] wonderful fragrance scents [the air]. Bells without clappers sound by themselves, [while the chanting of] precious verses can be heard from afar. In a matter of a second, thousands of transformations occur, [all of which] are exactly like what has been recorded in [Huixiang's *Ancient*] *Records of Mount Qingliang*."[31] The delegation led by Huize, indeed, brought back to the capital Huize's compilation of the *Abridged Records* of Mount Wutai (now lost), accompanied by a painting that may have recorded the divine traces left by the bodhisattva.[32] Yet, in terms of the court's relation with Mount Wutai, this delegation was just the beginning.

About thirteen years later, Mount Wutai was again linked to the imperial court, but this time in a rather different context. A monk by the name of Zhijing reported in a preface to a translation of the *Sutra of the Superlative Dhāraṇi of the Buddha's Crown,* that in 676 an Indian monk named Buddhapālita traveled to Mount Wutai.[33] As he arrived, he prostrated himself before the sacred peaks, stating that since the Buddha's death, all other spiritual sages were hidden, and only Mañjuśrī continued to assist assiduous practitioners in their spiritual pursuits at the mountains. He prayed, tearfully wishing to observe the bodhisattva's "sacred presence" (*shengrong*). An elderly man (a disguise of Mañjuśrī) then appeared and approached him to praise the hardship that he had endured to arrive here. For Buddhapālita, to be able to see Mañjuśrī, however, would require one specific condition, as the old man continued: "Many are the beings of the Han lands who commit sinful acts, and many are those among renunciates, as well, who break precepts and rules. Only the *Sutra of the Superlative Dhāraṇi of the Buddha's Crown* can destroy all the evil deeds of being. I wonder if you have brought it with you?"[34] Buddhapālita confessed regretfully that he did not have a copy of the sutra. The old man instructed him to return to India and said that when he returned to Mount Wutai with the sutra, the way to see the bodhisattva would be revealed to him. In 683, writes Zhijing, Buddhapālita traveled once more to China, and this time he reported to the throne with the sutra. The emperor, however, ordered the Sanskrit text translated by Du Xingyi and Divākara.[35] Buddhapālita, then, requested to have the original text returned to him and produced another translation with the assistance of a Chinese monk. After his translation was completed, Buddhapālita took the original Sanskrit sutra and entered the sacred area of Mount Wutai. He was never seen again.

The content of the *Sutra of the Superlative Dhāraṇi of the Buddha's Crown* has no obvious connection with Mount Wutai, but its text and legend were inextricably tied to the medieval history of the sacred mountain.[36] The text instructs the practitioner to recite the *dhāraṇi* (incantation) to eliminate defilements, remove bad karma, and attain salvation from being reborn in hells. The legend of Buddhapālita is recorded in the preface to the translation attributed to him.[37] But this legend was not mentioned at all in Huixiang's *Ancient Records,* which was completed no earlier than 680, so the story must have originated after then. In addition, Zhijing's account of Buddhapālita's translation of the sutra as occurring in the 683 preface also raise questions. If Buddhapālita returned to China in 683 with the Sanskrit sutra, for instance, two separate versions of the *Sutra of the Superlative Dhāraṇi* were already available, translated by Du Xingyi and Divākara in 679 and 682 respectively.[38] The "Buddhapālita version" thus should be a third and different version from the previous two. By 683, furthermore, Emperor Gaozong was bedridden and not likely able to receive Buddhapālita and order the translation of an original brought from India. Instead of the ailing emperor, it was more likely Empress Wu who ordered the new translation, which was completed close to 689 on the eve of her declaration of the Great Zhou dynasty in the following year.[39] Most significant, the new translation was recorded to have been disseminated in the capital by two monks, Xinggan and Bolun, close supporters of Empress Wu's reign.[40]

In all likelihood, the legend of Buddhapālita is fictitious, taking advantage of the rising popularity of the bodhisattva cult at Mount Wutai to facilitate the empress's political moves at this critical time. Yet the legend may have a more profound significance, upon which Wu Zetian wished to draw. By the last decades of the seventh century, Buddhist communities in India were aware of Mañjuśrī's presence at Mount Wutai.[41] Huixiang also included in the *Ancient Records* an account of the Indian pilgrim Śākyamitra, who visited Mount Wutai in 667.[42] However, the legend of Buddhapālita—how he endured the assiduous journey to reach Mount Wutai and, upon arrival, how he wept and prostrated before the sacred peaks—pointedly reversed the Sino-Indian relation in terms of Buddhist geography.[43] Reconceiving

China as the center of Buddhism would have resonated with Wu Zetian's goal to reorient and recenter the religious and political territory of the Tang. We see the same appropriation of space in 693, in Wu Zetian's declaration of herself as the Holy Emperor of the Golden Wheel (Jinlun Shengshen Huangdi) of the Great Zhou China, like the devout Indian king Aśoka, who had once ruled over his land as the wheel-turning sage king (*cakravartin-raja*), that is, as an idealized universal monarch who turns the wheel of the Dharma.[44]

Considered in this context, Wu Zetian's interest in the *Flower Garland Sutra* is likely related to her recognition of Mount Wutai and of its important position in the reconceived Buddhist geography. In 695, she asked a Khotanese monk, Śikṣānanda (652–710), to retranslate the *Flower Garland Sutra,* an eighty-fascicle version completed in 699. It was in celebration of the new edition that the five most important monasteries in the nation were renamed Huayansi, or Monastery of the *Flower Garland [Sutra],* including the Dafu Lingjiu Monastery located at the central valley of Mount Wutai. The sacred mountain was now brought into much closer political proximity with the seat of central power, and the sacred site in turn became the source of the empress's self-claimed divine power. In 702, the monk Degan (ca. 640–ca. 705)[45] was dispatched by Wu Zetian from the capital to Mount Wutai to supervise a repair project at Qingliang Monastery. While fulfilling his duty, Degan did not miss the opportunity to observe the auspicious signs for which Mount Wutai was famous. Yanyi recorded in his *Extended Records:*

> On the twentieth day of the seventh month, [Degan] reached [Central] Peak, [together with] one thousand clerics and laypeople, beholding the image of the Buddha's hand manifesting within the five-colored clouds, [with] the docile white fox and white deer in front. Sounds of sutra recitation flowed in the wind echoing in the mountains and valleys. Rare sweet fragrance permeated [the air] around people near and far. [They] also saw the Great Monk in purple-gold dress standing before them, and then, the bodhisattva who wore pearls and tassels appearing [in the direction of] West Peak.[46]

Degan depicted all the marvels in a painting and presented it to Wu Zetian. She was greatly gratified by the good omens, seeing them as a divine response to her support of the sacred site and the religion, and by extension, to her newly established political authority.

Wu Zetian herself, however, never set foot on the sacred mountain, perhaps due to her declining health after 700 or to the remote location of the site. As Fazang stated, "[Mount Wutai] is located at the border of Daizhou, [about] 1,600 *li* from the capital. It is located in the outlying land and extremely cold."[47] To travel the "distance" to Mount Wutai entails pilgrimage, the arduous experience of which "activates a yearning for intimate closeness," readying one for the sacred site, as no short journey can.[48] From a political standpoint, however, this distance between the imperial center and the sacred site at the border also implied a sense of control and supremacy. After Degan's visit, Wu Zetian ordered a jade statue fashioned in her likeness (*yü yürong*) to be installed at Mount Wutai. On this unprecedented gesture, Yanyi commented in his *Extended Records,* "The emperor [i.e., Wu Zetian], recognizing [Mount Wutai] to be the true domain inhabited by the bodhisattva, though she had myriad things to manage daily, still [ordered] the making of [her] jade body to venerate the Great Sage."[49] Although the jade statue was later moved to Chongfu Monastery (Chongfusi) in Taiyuan, the token of the emperor traveling to Mount Wutai not only validated the site as the "true domain" (*zhenjing*) of the bodhisattva, but more important, asserted Wu Zetian's transcendent presence, symbolized in the use of precious jade, at the sacred mountain.[50] This symbolic gesture eclipsed the distance and brought Mount Wutai under imperial power and patronage.

A great builder who initiated many ambitious architectural projects in the two capitals, Chang'an and Luoyang, Wu Zetian, however, did not order the construction of any new monasteries at the sacred mountain. Rather, she chose to patronize Qingliang Monastery, the oldest monastery at Mount Wutai, and she conferred the name of Huayan Monastery on Dafu Lingjiu Monastery, the most centrally located monastery. Instead of building anew, her patronage strategically served to superimpose the imperial vision on the sacred site that was initially defined only from within, thus making Mount Wutai contingent on the broader political and religious space of the new dynasty. This pattern of imperial patronage at Mount Wutai would be the norm throughout most of the medieval period.[51] Yet through the empress's patronage, the distance was bridged and Mount Wutai became reachable physically, as well as imaginatively in the vision of devout practitioners in the centuries to come.

Mount Wutai through the Virtual Monastery

There is then little doubt that during the eighth century, Mount Wutai enjoyed its first prosperity as a pilgrimage site. In addition to the continuous sponsorship from the imperial court that contributed to the prominence it attained, the new icon of Mañjuśrī riding a lion sculpted around the 710s also attracted vision seekers to Mount Wutai from not only China but also neighboring countries. The rapid spread of the *Sutra of Superlative Dhāraṇi* immediately after the 690s was another factor that enhanced the presence of Mañjuśrī at Mount Wutai and promoted the bodhisattva cult.

As early as 702, a devotional pillar—known as sutra pillar or *dhāraṇi* pillar (*jingchuang*)—engraved with the *Sutra of Superlative Dhāraṇi* was made.[52] According to the sutra, one could benefit spiritually from the pillar by reciting or copying the *dhāraṇi* engraved on it, and one's bad karma would be removed even if one was only in the shadow of the pillar or touched by the very least particle of dust blown from it.[53] The redemptive nature of the sutra was consistent with how Mount Wutai was perceived by practitioners around this time, and created an environment in which the pillar could be carved, making the practice of the *dhāraṇi* widely accessible.[54]

The sutra appeared also on another artifact. Dating to the years between 758 and 777, a now-lost stone column, originally part of the outer gate of the Kai-

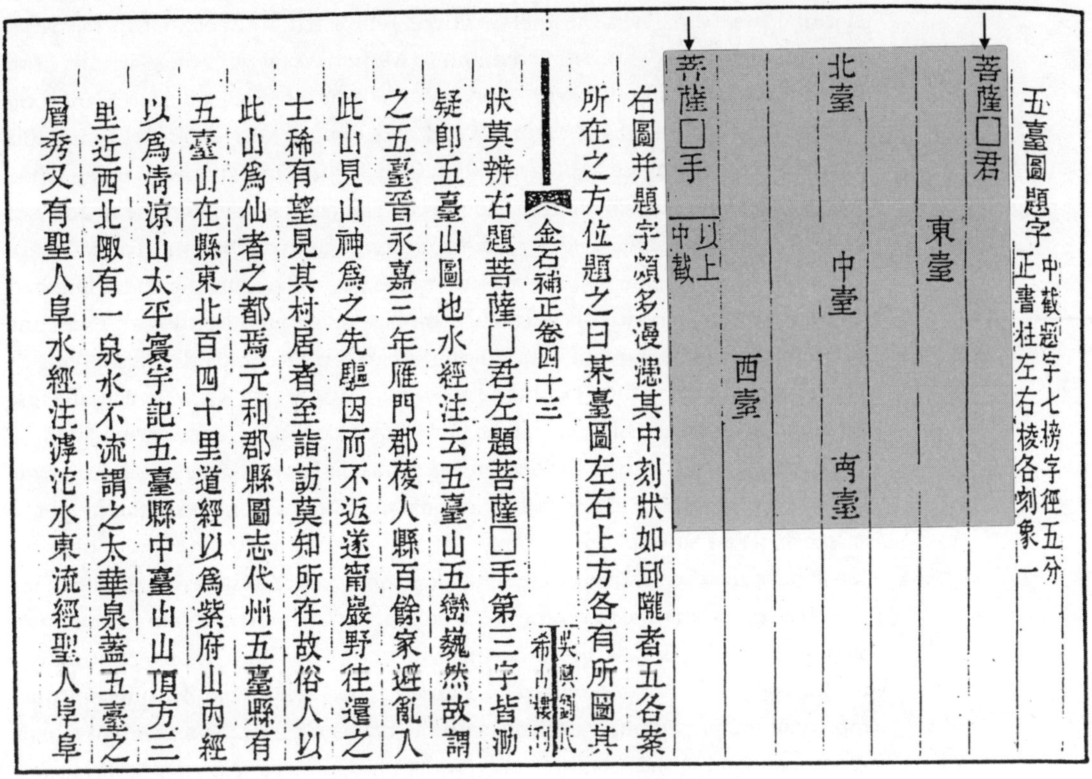

FIGURE 4.4. "Picture of Mount Wutai" documented by Lu Zengxiang (1816–82), based on a stone engraving, made between 758 and 777 CE, on the outer gate of Kaiyuan Monastery in Zhengding, Hebei. The drawing, as deciphered by Lu, shows the five sacred peaks (indicated by the characters) in the gray area. The five sacred peaks were originally flanked by two other images, identified by cartouches marked with arrows; the left cartouche reads, "the [manifestation of] bodhisattva's hand," and the right, "the [manifestation of] bodhisattva's presence." From Lu Zengxiang, *Baqiongshi jinshi buzheng, juan* 43.

yuan Monastery (Kaiyuansi) in Zhenzhou (present-day Zhengding, Hebei, about two hundred kilometers southeast of Mount Wutai) was engraved with the *Sutra of Superlative Dhāraṇi* and its preface (see map 11).[55] According to Lu Zengxiang (1816–82), who documented the column and recorded the titles of the engraved texts before it was lost, the sutra was surmounted by an engraved "picture of [Mount] Wutai" (*Wutai tu*), of which he made a sketch indicating the major visual components (fig. 4.4).[56] The picture, according to Lu's description, consisted of five ridged hills at the four cardinal directions and the center, all labeled with their respective cardinal directions. Two cartouches on either side of the space where the image of the five peaks was indicate that two additional images, no longer decipherable, depicted Bodhisattva Mañjuśrī's transformative manifestations.[57] In other words, from the last decades of the eighth century, as the *Sutra of Superlative Dhāraṇi* was disseminated, so was the bodhisattva cult at Mount Wutai.

In the early 710s, a monk named Shenying trained in the Tiantai tradition left his home base in Hebei for Mount Heng, South Sacred Peak, to deepen his spiritual practice. There he met with the renowned Southern Chan patriarch Shenhui (668–760), who redirected him to Mount Wutai with these words: "You have great karmic affinities with Mount Wutai. You should travel northward soon to venerate the Great Sage Mañjuśrī and seek out his vestiges."[58] Following this advice, Shenying arrived at Huayan Monastery in 716. One day after a meal, while wandering alone outside Huayan Monastery, Shenying suddenly came to another monastery, whose name plaque read "Cloister of Dharma Blossom" (Fahua Yuan). Entering, he saw a marvelous structure called Many Treasures Pagoda (Duobao Ta), followed by a series of spectacular monastic buildings housing sacred icons of Mañjuśrī and Samantabhadra among others. After completing his circuit of veneration, Shenying then exited the monastery wondering if it were actually just a vision. As he turned his head, all he had just vividly experienced disappeared.

At first glance, the story of Shenying, recorded in Yanyi's *Extended Records*, reads like a tale of marvels and anomalies, resonating with the numinous quality of the sacred site. As Daoxuan once wrote, "[At Mount Wutai] extraordinary monks often appear and then suddenly are difficult to find. Sacred vestiges and divine temples manifest from time to time and then disappear."[59] Looked at more closely, the story of Shenying is seen also to fit the category of "spiritual resonance" (*gantong* or *ganying*) known from medieval Chinese hagiography. That is, some spiritual quality of the practitioner resonant with the divine triggers the marvelous occurrence, confirming the vibrant reality of the practitioner's religious experience.[60] The "visionary experience" in Shenying's account, however, is also different and peculiar to this time at Mount Wutai. In fact, it is only one of many visionary experiences recorded to have happened at the sacred site, and all have important things to say about the divine qualities of the site. A review of these visionary experiences should thus shed light on the mediating role of the monastery in the expanding influence of Mount Wutai in eighth-century China.

The story of Shenying is one of the four accounts grouped together in Yanyi's *Extended Records* that tell of a named monk—a historical personage, not a fictional character—who entered a transformed or transformative monastery (*huasi*).[61] The term *huasi* has been rendered "manifestation of a monastery" and "architectural revelation," with reference to the epiphanic vision of architecture as the main theme in these accounts, but neither translation reflects the historical use of the term or the particularity of the visionary experience to Mount Wutai.[62]

In medieval China, *huasi* appears quite early, preceded by two other comparable forms of manifestation, namely, "heavenly monastery" (*tiansi*) and "transcendent monastery" (*xiansi*). Occurring in episodes reported before the Tang, both terms refer to the apparition of a monastery in the sky or simultaneously at multiple locations.[63] According to Yanyi, a now-lost text titled *Ancient Records of Monasteries* (Gu qielan zhuan) defined *huasi* as "[a monastery] not fixed on the ground but manifesting [itself] in midair,"[64] a meaning close to that of the two earlier terms. In addition to the four grouped *huasi* accounts, Yanyi recorded two other *huasi* episodes at Mount Wutai, both similarly carrying the early meaning of the term, but providing no details of the monastery. Yet, on seeing the visionary monastery, as Yanyi puts it, "[one's] mundane impulses would dissipate at once."[65] In fact, records of the apparition from the Tang period were not limited to Mount Wutai, although the term *huasi* is not always applied.[66] In all cases, the opportunity to see the *huasi* was considered a spiritual reward for the faith and assiduous practice of the vision seeker. And the appearance of these terms in medieval texts—*tiansi, xiansi,* or *huasi*—indicates that the idea, or even a tradition, of "visionary monastery" in Buddhism was taking shape around this time during the seventh and eighth centuries in China. In this tradition, seeing itself was more important than what was seen and how it was seen.

The four *huasi* accounts singled out by Yanyi in the *Extended Records,* however, are different. Rather than an emphasis on seeing, all four accounts stress what is seen by someone entering, "virtually," into the visionary monastery. In addition to Shenying, whom Yanyi records having entered the Cloister of Dharma Blossom in 716, there is Daoyi, who entered the Monastery of the Golden Pavilion (Jin'gesi) in 736; Wuzhu, who entered the Monastery of Prajñā (Banruosi) in 767; and Fazhao, who entered the Monastery of the Bamboo Grove (Zhulinsi) in 770. All these accounts tell of a monk who was either already at the site and was moved by the numinous presence of Mañjuśrī, or had a vision of the sacred domain of Mount Wutai and consequently made a trip to the sacred mountain.[67] All four monks believed that, living in the world without the Buddha, they could only experience the true presence of the divinity at Mount Wutai in order to achieve their specific religious goals.[68] After arriving at the mountain, they all wandered into a magnificent monastic complex inhabited by extraordinary monks. Upon entering, they were received and taken to tour the divinely revealed architecture, which aspired to the inconceivable realm or Pure Land of Bodhisattva Mañjuśrī. All protagonists, except Shenying, conversed with Mañjuśrī, receiving words of encouragement about their particular forms of spiritual pursuit or practice, before leaving the monastery. As soon as they exited, reality returned, and they were left in deep sorrow at being unable to retain the vision, and yet the fulfillment they felt through interacting with the divine inside a monastery, even merely in a vision, proved to be the turning point of each of their spiritual careers at Mount Wutai.

Equally significant is the time period during which the four monks were reported to have encountered the *huasi* vision. In Yanyi's *Extended Accounts,* all four events are said to have occurred during the eighth century, from the 710s to 770s, a period that coincides with the rise of Mount Wutai as a pilgrimage center. Three of the monks were from southern China, and their travels to the site indicate the increasing national popularity of Mount Wutai as a sacred site. In addition, three out of the four monks had distinct lineage associations—Shenying with Tiantai, Wuzhu with Chan, and Fazhao with Pure Land—and their arrivals also brought with them the presence and practice of their respective lineages to a site thus far dominated primarily by the Huayan school. We can see, then, that it was through the mediation of the vision, or more specifically, the vision of the monastery, that practitioners from outside built their new associations and establishments at Mount Wutai. As such, although on the surface the visionary monastery was no more than an apparition or revelation, it was nevertheless a peculiar but effective way of addressing personal spiritual issues and demonstrating divine responses at Mount Wutai.

The monastery in vision, the "virtual monastery" that could be entered, toured, and exited, merits further investigation. "Virtual" applies here in two different senses. First, deriving from the Latin *virtus* ("excellence," "potency," or "efficacy") and the Middle English *virtuall* ("effective" or "powerful"), "virtual" suggests that the monastery in vision was meant to be a powerful semblance that not only redeems the real but imparts a utopian ideology of the monastery as the place where seeing the divine presence could be attained. Second, "virtual" as applied to a visionary monastery suggests a space that is malleable and ineffable (unlike a physical building). The two meanings, combined, allow the virtual space of the monastery, the components of monastic architecture—its buildings, structures, ornaments, space, and so on—to became the primary vocabulary and language in the discourse of the religious or monastic ideology. The virtual monastery is effective in provoking thoughts and mediating between the abstract ideology and material buildings.[69] Indeed, as three of the four *huasi* accounts led to the actual building of new monasteries (Fahua Monastery, Jin'ge Monastery, and Zhulin Monastery), it is all the more important to observe how the "virtual monastery" participated in the reconception of the monastery, as exemplars were built at Mount Wutai during the period when the sacrality of the site was also under redefinition.

Bridging Reality: Entering Zhulin Monastery

Of the four *huasi* accounts in Yanyi's *Extended Records*, the most elaborate is the last, about the Pure Land master Fazhao (fl. eighth century) and his vision of a monastery named Zhulinsi.[70] A monk whose early career was rather obscure, Fazhao traveled to Mount Lu and Mount Heng to learn to practice intensive meditative visualizations during the 760s.[71] One day in 767, according to Yanyi, Fazhao suddenly saw in his alms bowl a vision of a monastery located at Mount Wutai with a name plaque that read "Bamboo Grove Monastery of the Great Sage" (Dasheng Zhulin Zhi Si). Two weeks later, he experienced the same vision but this time in greater detail. As Yanyi reports: "[Fazhao saw] Mount Wutai in its entirety, with Huayan Monastery and other monasteries all clearly discernible. Everywhere the ground was a shimmering gold. Unimpeded by mountain or forest, [every landmark] inside and outside was fully visible. Pools, terraces, storied buildings, and towers, all were adorned resplendently with myriad precious gems. The Great Sage Mañjuśrī, accompanied by his retinue of ten thousand bodhisattvas, [could be seen] dwelling in its midst."[72] Fazhao was suspicious about the vision but did not feel pressed to take action until three years later. In 769 he experienced a third vision of Mount Wutai, which ultimately led him there. The last vision was more specifically about monasteries at Mount Wutai, and Yanyi's description recalls the *huasi* already discussed: "Five-color auspicious clouds spread over the entire [grounds of] the monasteries [at the mountains]; within the clouds multistoried towers and roofed pavilions appeared."[73] Seemingly not fixed to the ground, the visionary monasteries were never completely revealed, accessible only by the divine, while Fazhao, who "dropped, weeping, to the ground in prostration" when he saw the vision, could only behold it. This denial of entry into the visionary monastery would be reversed once Fazhao reached Mount Wutai.

After an eight-month journey from Mount Heng, according to Yanyi, Fazhao finally arrived at Foguang Monastery at the sacred mountain in 770. He saw shafts of bright light outside the monastery, following which Fazhao went north until he was greeted at a hill by two youths, who identified themselves as attendants of Bodhisattva Mañjuśrī. Escorted by them, Fazhao was jubilant, anticipating not just beholding the holy presence but actually meeting with the bodhisattva. Indeed, proceeding further north, they came to a towering golden gate, through which a magnificent monastery could be seen with the plaque inscribed "Bamboo Grove Monastery of the Great Sage." Crossing a great golden bridge (*da jinqiao*) into the monastery, Fazhao was mindful of a different reality into which he was now entering. The text reads:

> [The monastery] was all just as it had appeared in [Fazhao's] bowl. The precincts of the monastery covered an area of nearly twenty *li* in circumference. Within its grounds were 120 cloisters, each magnificently adorned with jeweled pagodas. The ground was of pure gold. Clear brooks and flowering fruit trees filled their midst. Entering the monastery, Fazhao went [directly] into the lecture hall, where he saw the Great Sage Mañjuśrī to the west and Samantabhadra to the east. Each was seated on a lion throne, engaged in preaching the Dharma, and the seat and body together towered nearly one hundred *chi* tall. To either side of Mañjuśrī were ten thousand bodhisattvas, while similarly Samantabhadra was surrounded by countless bodhisattvas.[74]

The depiction of the monastery—its gold pavement, jeweled pagodas, and 120 cloisters—harks back to the idealized Jetavana Monastery described in Daoxuan's text.[75] However, unlike the Jetavana Monastery, a site centered on the presence of the absent Buddha, the virtual monastery was the place where the manifestation of the bodhisattvas could be experienced. The two bodhisattvas, while described as two icons for veneration, were the divinities themselves, face to face with the practitioner in the vision. In the presence of the bodhisattvas, Fazhao was assured that in the age of dissolution of the Dharma (*mofa*), it was of utmost importance to practice Buddha-mindfulness (*nianfo*) and attentively visualize the blissful land of the Amitābha. The two bodhisattvas then extended their hands to rub the head of Fazhao as a sign of his future Buddhahood.[76] After receiving the teaching, Fazhao was instructed by Mañjuśrī to venerate all other bodhisattva cloisters in the monastery, after which Fazhao was sent off by the attendants, and as he exited, the virtual monastery disappeared behind him.

Fazhao's visionary experience is strikingly similar to that of meditative visualization, in which one comes face to face with the divine.[77] The difference is that whereas in meditation in a built meditation hall the image of the deity arises in the vision of the meditator, in Fazhao's narrative, he enters a visionary monastery and receives the teachings virtually. In a sense, the internal attainment through meditative vision of the former is translated into the external architectural space of the latter. The virtual monastery thus constitutes a space in which the sacred presence could be realized and religious experience heightened.

The visionary Zhulin Monastery shares the numinous qualities peculiar to Mount Wutai. Fazhao was, for instance, guided to the virtual monastery by shafts of bright light, like "the inconceivable auroras" of the bodhisattva frequently witnessed around Foguang Monastery.[78] Light, in this regard, serves to spiritually reorient Fazhao and assist his entry into the virtual monastery; in a complementary sense, the events that follow his vision help integrate the virtual monastery into the historical fabric and hagiography of Mount Wutai. Two days after the visionary experience, Fazhao went on a tour to venerate the famous Diamond Grotto (Jin'gang Ku), where he performed ritual prostration while reciting the names of thirty-five Buddhas ten times over. At the conclusion of the ritual, Fazhao suddenly had a vision of a palatial complex made of precious jewels, inside which were Mañjuśrī and Samantabhadra, ten thousand bodhisattvas, and Buddhapālita, the Indian monk who, as we recall, was never seen again in the flesh after he brought the *Sutra of Superlative Dhāraṇi* with him into Mount Wutai in 683. As if seeing this vision was insufficient, Fazhao returned to the same location after midnight, and this time, after performing the same ritual and recitation, Buddhapālita appeared again before him and showed him the hidden way into the Diamond Grotto, wherein Fazhao experienced a second virtual monastery. Fazhao's visit to the Diamond Grotto—formerly associated with a mountain lord who lived in a fantastic building complex inside the cave—not long after his experience with the visionary Zhulin Monastery is surprising, though the Diamond Grotto had already been reappropriated by the bodhisattva cult at Mount Wutai.[79] Yet the sequence of these two and other subsequent visionary events, taken together, appears to intentionally provide a context that legitimized and associated the virtual monastery of Zhulin Monastery both spatially and historically (temporally) with the sacred site. "Vision" was the critical means by which one could access and enter a Mount Wutai of different temporalities. In this spatiotemporal matrix of Mount Wutai, the virtual monastery was firmly built into the mountain's entire sacred topography, and its virtuality evoked a reality that could transcend normal time and space—a reality to which the physical monastic architecture could aspire.

There is one extra layer of significance to the virtual monastery. The *huasi* narrative of Zhulin Monastery was not written about or publicized by Fazhao until four years after his visionary experience, in 774.[80] His account was circulated alongside a treatise that he had compiled on a chant form called the five-tempo Buddha recitation (*wuhui nianfo*). The treatise explained the method of ritual intonation that Fazhao allegedly received directly from Amitābha in the vision in which he was transported to the Pure Land of Sukhāvatī during his meditation at Mount Heng in 766.[81] The same five-tempo Buddha recitation was validated before the bodhisattvas in his visionary Zhulin Monastery. These two different but related accounts of the two visionary experiences, and their circulation together, indicate the importance and function of the virtual monastery.[82] First, the *huasi* vision that could be attained only at Mount Wutai was paired with the vision of Sukhāvatī, the Pure Land; not only this, but the account of the vision served as the spiritual authority that validated the particular practice devised by Fazhao and his interest in building Pure Land associations with the sacred site. Second, although the two accounts were about two different visionary locations, Zhulin Monastery at Mount Wutai and Amitābha's Pure Land, they nonetheless share many motifs. For example, in the treatise on the five-tempo Buddha recitation, Fazhao writes that the vision of the Pure Land arose while he was in a deep meditative ecstasy: "All of a sudden, I could no longer see the meditation hall, but saw only a cloud-like terrace of five-color light that filled the entire Dharma field [around me]. Within it a golden bridge [*jinqiao*] appeared, which stretched out before me directly toward the ultimate blissful world [Sukhāvatī] in the west. In a flash I arrived [across the bridge] into the presence of the Buddha Amitābha."[83] Canonically speaking, Amitābha's Pure Land is located nowhere in this world, but in the farthest western end of the universe, reachable only in one's next favorable rebirth.[84] The golden bridge thus symbolically bridges this and the other worlds. Similarly, in Fazhao's narrative of Zhulin Monastery, the golden bridge served to join reality and virtuality, thus making the virtual monastery much more accessible (or perceivable) as a means through which the bodhisattva could be encountered.

During the eighth century, the *huasi* vision also functioned to bridge the distance between Mount Wutai as *the* sacred site and the world outside. Before Fazhao decided to take the journey to Mount Wutai, he was urged to do just that, and it was the vision of monasteries in the "Golden World" (Jinse Shijie), a term referring to Mañjuśrī's Pure Land,[85] that eventually brought Fazhao there. At Mount Wutai, his visionary experience—crossing the golden bridge into the virtual Zhulin Monastery—became an important motif of imagination, or visualization, of entering Mount Wutai, so much so that Fazhao's crossing of the bridge was later used as a literary trope to describe one finding one's way into the reality of the sacred site. Preserved in manuscripts from Dunhuang in the borderland of the far northwest, an early tenth-century poem that eulogizes Mount Wutai contains the following lines:

> In the five-color clouds appears a visionary golden bridge,
> [Across the bridge] the monk of great compassion weaves his banner.
> The disciples who have karmic affinity pass over the bridge;
> The disciples who do not, whirl away in the contrary wind.[86]

From Virtuality to Reality

In 777 when worshiping at East Peak of Mount Wutai with a group of monks, Fazhao had a vision in which "Mañjuśrī riding a blue lion" appeared in midair from a radiant globe of crimson light.[87] This is the last revelatory vision recorded in Fazhao's account. It was, however, after seeing the "true presence" of the bodhisattva that Fazhao commissioned a monastery, named Zhulin Monastery, at the very location where he had experienced the virtual one of the same name. There are no records of its completion, but when Ennin visited the monastery in 840, it had become one of the major monasteries at Mount Wutai, comprising six large cloisters and an official ordination platform, one of two such ritual structures in the nation.[88] In addition, inside a meditation hall, a portrait of Fazhao was enshrined alongside a picture of Buddhapālita meeting Mañjuśrī in the disguise of an elder. The times had changed, but the founding legends were kept alive, taking the monastery as "three-dimensional, inhabitable narratives of memory."[89] Moving from the virtual to the actual, the conception and significance of the monastery would have also been mediated through the "virtuality" of the visionary monastery—its idealism, numinosity, and totality as *the* monastery of Bodhisattva Mañjuśrī's sacred mountain.

The narrative of Fazhao's visionary experience was circulated as an independent volume, which was among the texts brought to Japan by Ennin. This text did not survive but it might have been comparable to the account of Zhulin Monastery included in Yanyi's *Extended Records.* Curiously, whereas in *Extended Records,* the account was simply titled "Monk Fazhao Entering Virtual Zulin Monastery" (Fazhao heshang ru hua Zhulinsi), the text acquired by Ennin had the elaborate title *Records of Monk Fazhao from the Great Sage Zhulin Monastery at Mount Wutai Receiving the Vision of the [Sacred] Realm of Mount [Wu]tai.*[90] This elaboration seems to have been deliberate. In fact, the use of the phrase "the [sacred] realm of Mount [Wu]tai" (*Taishan jingjie*) appears also in Fazhao's account in *Extended Records,* referring to Fazhao's vision of the transcendent reality of Mount Wutai.[91] The phrase implies that, in a metonymic sense, the virtual monastery could be perceived as the essence of the sacrality of Mount Wutai in its entirety. There is a parallel here with the monastic structure on top of the stone lantern from Dongzhang, introduced in the beginning of the chapter (see fig. 4.1a and b, fig. 4.2). Taking the form of a base representing Mount Wutai's five peaks, a shaft and, on top, a lamp holder in the form of a building, the lantern reflects the visionary monastery and its significance. Its inscription reads: "Mount Wutai forms its base, and [the distribution of its five peaks] resembles that of the five Sacred Peaks. Located at [the top of] Central Peak is a pond called Yuhua (Jade Flora), inside which grows a trunk. On [and above] the trunk are cloud patterns. Five-colored [wooden] canopies, layer by layer, open four windows over the eight-sided heavenly palace."[92] The wooden canopy that would have been mounted in the socket on top of the lantern no longer exists. Regardless, the "heavenly palace" held aloft by the shaft growing out of Yuhua Pond at Central Peak can be seen to render in miniature the fantastic visionary monastery rising above the sacred realm of Mount Wutai.

On the base of the stone lantern (see fig. 4.3), monasteries can be seen dotting the rolling mountains, some hidden while others are revealed, as if taking on the spiritual qualities of the site. Chengguan (738–839), also known as the national master of [Mount] Qingliang (*Qingliang guoshi*) and regarded as the fourth patriarch of the Huayan lineage, took up residence in Huayan Monastery at Mount Wutai during the years 776–95.[93] In his commentaries on the *Flower Garland Sutra*, composed in 804, Chengguan wrote an extensive section elaborating the origin and history of Mount Wutai as the sacred abode of Bodhisattva Mañjuśrī. Near the end of the section, Chengguan states: "In regard to the current majesty, Emperor Dezong [r. 779–804], who enthusiastically admires the sacred mountain, has issued an edict to make offerings of divine garments at the five sacred peaks and supply fragrance and medicines without fail at the seasonal junctures of the year. Jin'ge Monastery emerges from surrounding clouds as if coming into being through divine transmutation; Zhulin Monastery towers above the outcroppings as if arriving from heaven. [Mount Wutai] as such has thus received hundredfold venerations and offerings throughout the Nine States of China."[94] In the mountain landscape, the visionary quality and divine origin became crucial attributes of the *built* monasteries as an integral part of the sacred topography.

Of the four virtual monasteries, three were realized in material form. The first, Zhulin Monastery, was built on a hilly area to the northeast of Foguang Monastery and close to the center within the range enclosed by the five peaks (see map 2). Jin'ge Monastery, built in 767, was due south of Zhulin Monastery. The third monastery in the *huasi* accounts, Fahua Monastery was located further south, on the southwest flank of South Peak.[95] All three monasteries were among the monasteries documented in Yanyi's *Extended Records* as new additions to Mount Wutai since the beginning of the Tang dynasty.[96] As we saw earlier, Huayan Monastery was the uncontested center of Mount Wutai under Empress Wu's sponsorship, which continued to be the case into the first decades of the eighth century. Imperial patronage was directed to the existing monasteries, which thereby enjoyed the prestige of support from the political center. But they were not the only monasteries on Mount Wutai. Religious masters attracted by the fame of Mount Wutai as a rising pilgrimage center arrived and built new monasteries. We do not know the exact histories or precise locations of all the newly added monasteries listed by Yanyi, but just like the three monasteries discussed here—Zhulin, Jin'ge, and Fahua—the new monasteries effectively expanded the range of Mount Wutai and changed the configuration of the sacred topography of the site. Each of the new monasteries did not just add a new piece to the complexity of the sacred site but also provided a potential competing viewpoint to construct and construe the sacrality of Mount Wutai. The contest could be so drastic that it altered the reading of Mount Wutai, as exemplified in the case of Jin'gesi, explored in the next chapter.

CHAPTER FIVE

Reconfiguring the Center

The language of "center" is preeminently political and only secondarily cosmological.

—Jonathan Z. Smith, *To Take Place*

In 766, Amoghavajra (705–74), the master of the Esoteric Buddhism (Mijiao) school at court, petitioned the emperor Daizong (r. 762–79) in a memorandum to support the building of a monastery, called Monastery of the Golden Pavilion (Jin'gesi), at Mount Wutai:

> On the twenty-fourth year of the Kaiyuan reign [736], a monk Daoyi from Quzhou went to Mount Wutai and observed a [virtual] monastery of Mañjuśrī's holy traces, named Cloister of the Golden Pavilion [Jin'ge Yuan]. It had thirteen halls to accommodate monks, the number of which was said to have been about ten thousand. Its towers and halls and gates and pavilions were all made of gold. Daoyi then submitted a copy of the plan [of the monastery] to the court. Everyone under Heaven [had since] wished to see Jin'ge Monastery completed—for who would not wish this? [Suzong (r. 756–62), the late emperor, thus] ordered Daohuan, a monk from Zezhou, to send supplies daily to the mountains. [As I] admire [the marvel] the Chan master Daoyi experienced, I vowed to build Jin'ge Monastery accordingly for the sake of the nation. The number of buildings in the monastery will be the same as was seen [in Daoyi's vision]. . . . [Now] there are five official plaques at Mount Wutai, [granted to] Qingliang, Huayan, Foguang, and Yuhua—four [monasteries] that have been completed—and Jin'ge, the only one that has not. As [Jin'ge Monastery] was built after holy traces, who would not regard [this project] with great reverence?[1]

This official record is important on several counts, and complicates the history of Mount Wutai during the second half of the eighth century. First, like Zhulin Monastery, Jin'ge Monastery was built after a vision—that is, it was first a "virtual monastery" (*huasi*) and was subsequently built in reality. But unlike Zhulin Monastery, commissioned by Fazhao, Jin'ge Monastery was sponsored by the powerful master Amoghavajra, who, accorded a series of high ranks and honors including the title "master of the state" (*guoshi*), served the emperor directly as the most influential Buddhist figure of his times at court.[2] Jin'ge Monastery was thus the first to have been built entirely with imperial funds. During the Tang, the imperial patronage of Mount Wutai had taken either of two forms—devotional offerings or conferrals of status—but had stopped short of constructing a whole monastery. Even when limited to offerings and recognition by the state, two ends were accomplished: the spiritual practice and religious reputation of a given monastery were endorsed and privileged by the imperial authority, while the monastery in return provided the court with a point of access to the sacred site.[3] The direct involvement of the state in constructing Jin'ge Monastery thus no doubt guaranteed the monastery national prominence, which was also testified in the magnificently constructed main image hall described in the dynastic history as follows: "Its roof tiles were made of copper and covered with gold leaf that shone over the hills and valleys [of Mount Wutai]."[4] More important, however, this rather unusual form of imperial sponsorship of Jin'ge Monastery was also meant to alter the conception of Mount Wutai by instituting a new center.

Among the five monasteries that received an official name plaque (*si'e*) recorded in the memorandum were Qingliang Monastery, Huayan Monastery, and Foguang Monastery—the best known and reputable monasteries that had a long-standing history at the sacred site. The remaining two, Jin'ge Monastery, discussed here, and Yuhua Monastery, whose building projects were approved by the throne in 758, were new constructions.[5] The number of monasteries selected to receive the imperial patronage is not without significance, for five carried symbolic meaning in the esoteric, tantric practice promoted by Amoghavajra. The numerology was also expressed topographically at the sacred site. One year after the earlier memorial in 767, Amoghavajra requested the ordination of twenty-one monks, who would constantly recite sutras at each of the five designated monasteries to ensure the prosperity and protection of the nation.[6] The five designated monasteries were the ones named in Amoghavajra's 766 memorandum, with one exception: Dali Fahua Monastery, also founded after a *huasi* account, replaced Foguang Monastery.[7] This seemingly minor substitution was of paramount significance in the reconception of the sacred site as a whole. As illustrated in map 10, now four of the designated monasteries were approximately at the four cardinal directions enclosing an area with Jin'ge Monastery, the fifth, at its center. Seen in this light, the designation of the five specific monasteries must have been a deliberate decision, and so was the imperial patronage lavished on the building project of Jin'ge Monastery that anchored the new center.

The language of center is necessarily political and competitive, as the epigraph to this chapter tells us. Mount Wutai is fixed in space but certainly not fixed in significance, constantly shaped and reconceived as it was, as a result of competing discourses regarding its spiritual power and the notion of sacrality. Before the 760s, Huayan Monastery had been the center—a position decided by the five peaks, by the name change granted under Empress Wu, and by a locale marked by the "true presence" of Mañjuśrī. In the new pentad of monasteries, Huayan Monastery continued to be prominent as one of the five designated monasteries, but no longer held central position. A shift of the center of Mount Wutai from Huayan Monastery to Jin'ge Monastery also meant a changing conception of the sacred site.

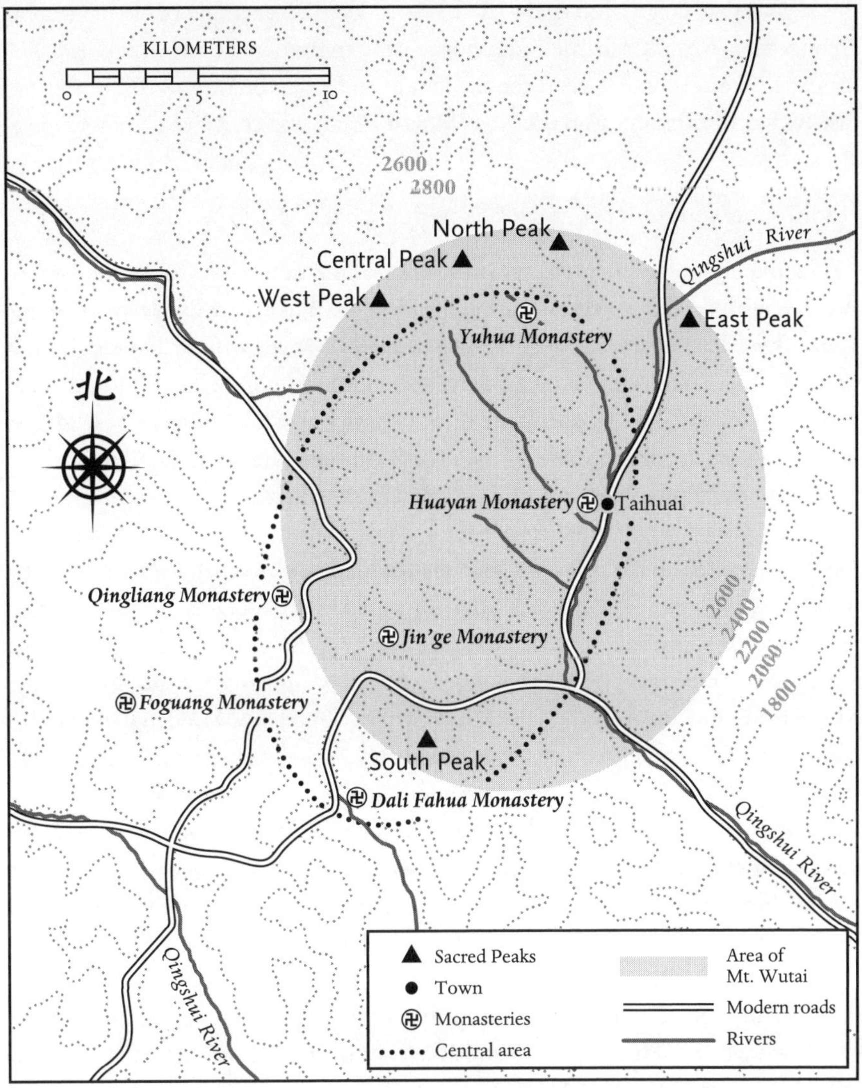

MAP 10. Locations of the five monasteries established by Amoghavajra: four located approximately at the four cardinal directions, with the fifth, Jin'ge Monastery, in the center (in the area marked by the dotted line). The boundaries of Mount Wutai enclosed by the five peaks are marked by the gray circle.

Instead of the five sacred mountains defining the sacred topography, it was now the five monasteries together that provided a different and more diagrammatic perspective to view the sacred mountain, a perspective related to the esoteric doctrine taking shape in Tang China during the second half of the eighth century. It is in this context that the system of monasteries took on a greater iconographic significance in reconceiving of Mount Wutai as a powerful sacred site. Scholars have long noted the key role of Jin'ge Monastery in Amoghavajra's esoteric program, particularly as a connective point that linked Mount Wutai to the court, but they have not taken into account its central position in the newly established pentad of monasteries and in the sacred mountain reconceived by the new arrangement.[8] The main image hall at Jin'ge Monastery contained a complicated set of icons, and this iconographic program was correlated with the fivefold complex of monasteries to suggest a maṇḍala based on the esoteric teachings of Amoghavajra. It is in this regard that Jin'ge Monastery can be considered an example of "iconographic architecture" that transformed the entire sacred mountain into its ritual field. The dialectic relationship between the mountain and the monastery around this period had a critical impact on the ways Mount Wutai was conceived as a whole.

From Topography to Iconography: Esoteric Turns at Mount Wutai

Before the eighth century, the scripture most often drawn on to identify Mount Wutai as the sacred abode of the bodhisattva Mañjuśrī was the *Flower Garland Sutra,* the sixty-fascicle version translated into Chinese around 420 CE. Mount Wutai in northeastern China was identified with Mount Qingliang, Mount Clear and Cool, located in the northeast of the continent—Jambudvīpa, in Buddhist geography. In the first decade of the eighth century, the identification was corroborated by a new scripture of a rather different nature. Translated in 710 by Bodhiruci (672–727), a Buddhist master of south Indian origin, the text was titled the *Scripture of Mañjuśrī's Dharma Treasure-Store Dhāraṇī* (Wenshu shili fa baozang tuoluoni jing); it contains passages that suggest Mount Wutai is not just a sacred place, but *the* sacred place.[9] The scripture, quoting the words of Śākyamuni in a meditative trance, prophesies the appearance of Mañjuśrī after the Buddha has passed from this world: "When my Dharma has all but disappeared in Jambudvīpa, in that wretched time, Mañjuśrī with broad abilities will benefit innumerable sentient beings and will do the work of a Buddha." Upon being asked when and where the bodhisattva could be found, Śākyamuni replies: "After I have passed away, in this Jambudvīpa in the northeast quarter, there is a country named Mahācīna [i.e., Great China]. In the country there is a mountain named Five Peaks [Wuding], in which the youth Mañjuśrī will roam about and dwell, expounding the Dharma at the mountain for sake of sentient beings."[10] The scripture, as scholars have pointed out, has an eschatological function in that it instructs practitioners to perform rituals with *dhāraṇī* (incantations) and images of the bodhisattva in order to access directly the divine power of Mañjuśrī.[11] But another of its significant functions was to assert that the place where the bodhisattva manifests his sacred presence was a mountain area known for its five peaks, in the northeast of China.

The cluster of five soaring peaks is Mount Wutai's most prominent topographic feature, inseparable from the history of how the mountain was constructed as a sacred site. It is not surprising that the five peaks appear in the translation of this sutra, but the name Wuding, devised to refer to the peaks was nonetheless unprecedented. After arriving in China in 693, Bodhiruci was quickly involved in several important projects of sutra translation in Luoyang, including a new version of the *Flower Garland Sutra* (eighty fascicles), led by Śikṣānanda in 695–99.[12] The new translation of the *Scripture of Mañjuśrī's Dharma Treasure-Store Dhāraṇī* coincided with the renewed enthusiasm of Empress Wu toward the sacred site and the cult of Mañjuśrī. Mount Wutai was widely known, as was the empress's interest in it. In other words, when translating the *Scripture of Mañjuśrī's Dharma Treasure-Store Dhāraṇī,* Bodhiruci must have known the readily available names for Mount Wutai such as Wutai (Five Terraces), Qingliang (Clear and Cool), or an earlier but equally appropriate name Wufeng (also, Five Peaks).[13] The application of "Wuding" was thus not only surely intentional but signaled the "esoteric turn" that occurred at Mount Wutai in the eighth century.

As a Buddhist term in seventh and eighth century China, *ding,* or more often *foding,* is the translation of the technical term *uṣṇīṣa,* referring to what is most accurately rendered in the language of physiology as "cranial protuberance." It is one of the "perfect bodily marks" of the Buddha, that is, one of the distinctive features that embody his perfection. In practice, this term is often rendered as "peak" or "topknot," and the related word "crown," as in "Buddha's crown" (*buddhoṣṇīṣa*).[14] As the "peak" or "crown" of the Buddha, *uṣṇīṣa* also suggests the most sacred and secret part of his perfect body, from which bright radiance emanates, indicative of his superior wisdom. The concept of the *uṣṇīṣa* came to China in early esoteric practice, and the buddhas in the expanding esoteric pantheon all possessed this feature. In the *Collection of Coded Instructions* (Tuoluoni ji jing), translated in 653, the *uṣṇīṣas* of various buddhas are, as emblems of wisdom and perfection, personified and invoked, as, for example, in the liturgies based on the *Wheel-Turning King of the One-Syllable Buddha's Crown* (Yizi foding lunwang).[15] Not coincidentally, Bodhiruci also translated one of the earliest liturgies in the *Wheel-Turning King of the One-Syllable Buddha's Crown,* incorporating oblations or offerings (*homa*), incantations (*mantra*), and visualization in the rituals.[16] His usage of *Wuding* for the five peaks of Mount Wutai, therefore, would have alluded to the notion of *uṣṇīṣa.* In addition, related to the meaning of "topknot," *Wuding* has another more specific reference. It could also refer to the five tufts of hair (*pañcaśikhin*) on the head of the young Mañjuśrī, a feature of the iconographic representations of the bodhisattva described in esoteric scriptures.[17] The term *Wuding* thus provides a visual and spiritual relation between the young Mañjuśrī with his five topknots who roams and dwells in the mountain of five peaks.

In fact, Mañjuśrī at Mount Wutai is predominantly associated with the number five, which may have prompted yet another esoteric reading of its five peaks. One of the most typical manifestations of Mañjuśrī in esoteric teachings is the Five-Syllable Mañjuśrī (Wuzi Wenshu), referring to the fivefold wisdom of Mañjuśrī and represented by the five-syllable mantra: *A-ra-pa-ca-na,* rendered either in Siddham script or Chinese transliteration. The five syllables represent one of the primary mystic formulae of Mañjuśrī's divine power and eventually became associated with the five peaks of Mount Wutai.[18] In a woodblock print of the tenth century (fig. 5.1), Mañjuśrī riding a lion and flanked by two attendants manifests his presence in midair;[19] above the iconic group is a cluster of seven clouds, the five top clouds each carrying one of the five syllables in Siddham script. The text at the lower register lists the five syllables in Chinese transliteration, expounding both the secular and spiritual benefits if one recites the mythic mantra.[20] In a related but later print (fig. 5.2), currently in the collection of the Daigoji in Kyoto, a similar Mañjuśrī riding his lion and flanked by four attendants is shown in midair, and the five sacred peaks of Mount Wutai in the background seem to have

FIGURE 5.1. Mañjuśrī riding a lion with two attendants. Woodcut print, 57 x 29.7 cm. Ca. 984. It was found inside a cavity on the back of an Udāyana Śākyamuni statue brought by Chōnen from China to Seiryōji in Kyoto in 988. Above Mañjuśrī are clouds that carry the five-syllable mantra written in Siddham script. From Nara Kokuritsu Hakubutsukan, *Higashi Ajia no hotoke tachi,* 127. Reproduction courtesy of Seiryōji.

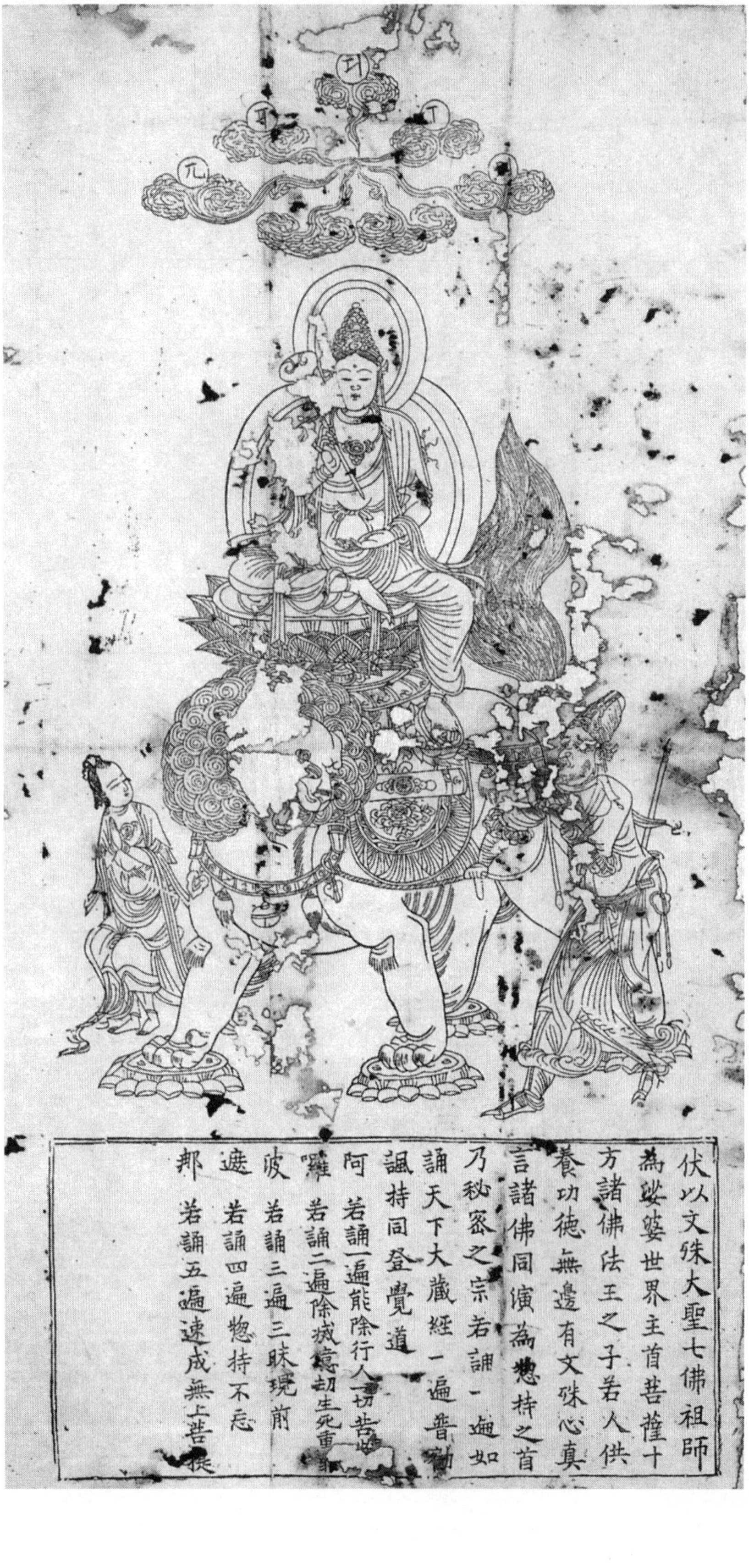

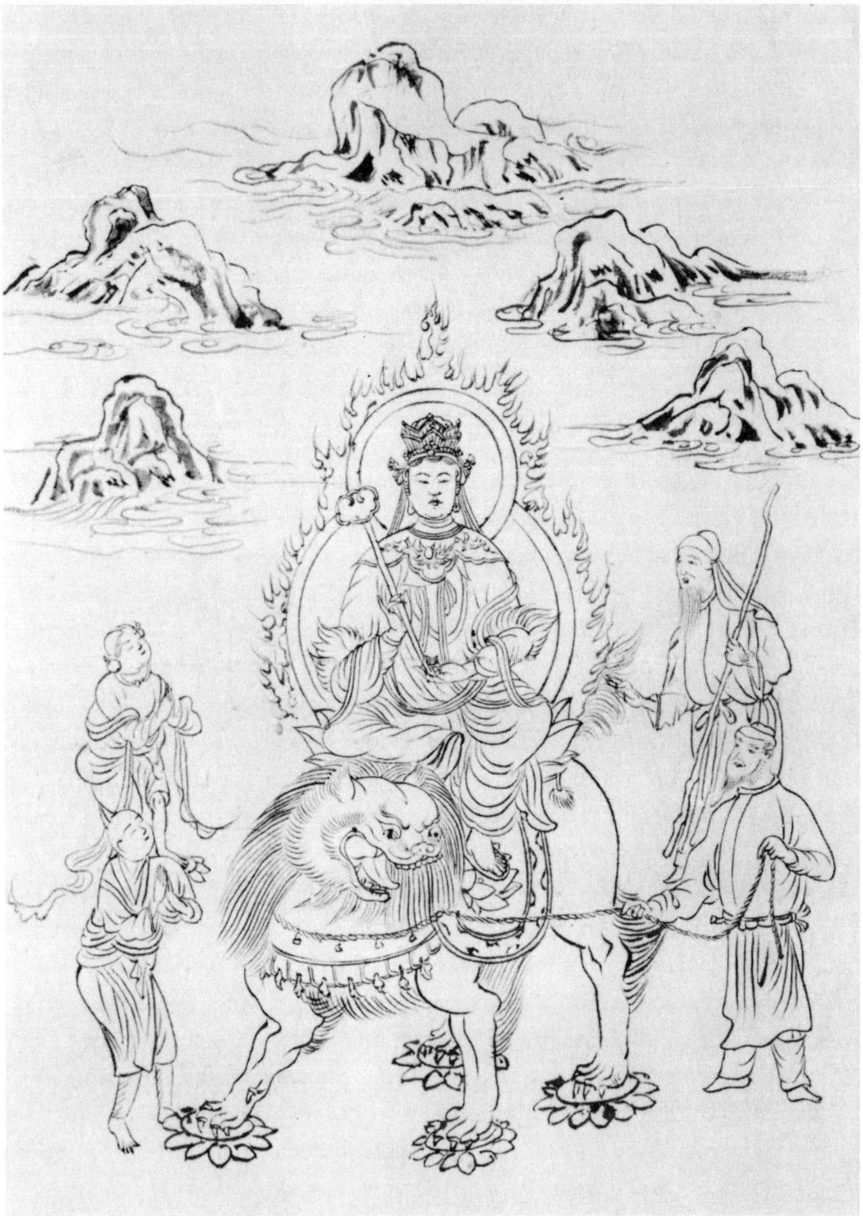

FIGURE 5.2. Mañjuśrī riding a lion surrounded by four attendants with Five Sacred Peaks of Mount Wutai in the background. Woodcut print, 12th century. From Nishikawa et al., *Daigoji taikan,* vol. 2, 113. Reproduction courtesy of Daigoji.

substituted for the five syllables in figure 5.1.[21] These interrelated associations of the five peaks with Mañjuśrī's five topknots, the five wisdoms, and the five-syllable mantra are perhaps captured most comprehensively in Yanyi's *Extended Records* (ca. 1060). Quoting from the *Gate for Visualization of the Five-Syllable Yoga* (Wuzi yuqie guanmen),[22] Yanyi writes:

> *A* illuminates the gate of nonexistence, that is, all Dharma is nonexistent, manifesting the wisdom of the great round mirror of Akṣobhya of the East Vajra Family, referring to the east topknot on the bodhisattva's head. *Ra* illuminates the gate of no defilements, that is, all Dharma is without defilements,

> manifesting the wisdom, which regards all things equally, of Ratnasaṃbhava of the South Ratna Family, referring to the south topknot on the bodhisattva's head. *Pa* illuminates the gate of nonreality, manifesting the wisdom of profound insight of Amitābha of the West Lotus Family, referring to the west topknot on the bodhisattva's head. *Ca* illuminates the gate of nonaction, manifesting the wisdom for perfecting oneself and others of Amoghasiddhi of the North Karma Family, referring to the north topknot on the bodhisattva's head. *Na* illuminates the gate of nonsubstance without languages and words, manifesting the wisdom of the embodied nature of the *dharmadhātu* of Vairocana of the Lord Tathāgata, referring to the central topknot on the bodhisattva's head. It is thus not without reason why the bodhisattva's head is distinguished with five topknots and the mountain with five peaks, isn't it?[23]

The original scripture from which the quotation was made has not been found, but nonetheless, the passage deomonstrates complex correlations within the fivefold symbolism that extrapolated the basic unit of the Five Peaks (Wuding) into a grand system in the centuries after the translation of the *Scripture of Mañjuśrī's Dharma Treasure-Store Dhāraṇī* by Bodhiruci. Indeed, as explained in the quoted passage, the five peaks of Mount Wutai and five topknots of the bodhisattva were matched with and mapped onto the fivefold mandalic structure of esoteric cosmology, consisting of the five central buddhas—Vairocana at the center, and four other buddhas at four directions: Akṣobhya in the east, Ratnasaṃbhava in the south, Amitābha in the west, and Amoghasiddhi in the north. This fivefold structure, in turn, represents the Five Wisdoms of Vairocana as envisioned in the teaching of the Vajra Crown (S: *vajra-uṣṇīṣas*, or *vajroṣṇīṣa;* C: *jin'gang ding*) tradition promulgated by Amoghavajra and his teacher Vajrabodhi (671–741).[24] The conflation of the multiple systems nested in the five peaks of Mount Wutai as such might not have one specific canonical or scriptural basis, but it was in the esoteric turn during the eighth century, with the building of Jin'ge Monastery, that Mount Wutai began to be conceived from a more conceptual perspective, making possible the extrapolation of the symbolism as recorded in Yanyi's text of 1060.

In this conceptual perspective, the five sacred peaks of Mount Wutai were more than outstanding topographic features; they were also necessarily iconographic, by virtue of the term *wuding*. From topography to iconography, the conceptual change took not only a new nomenclature and its related symbolism, but also a new ritual praxis that provided different sets of terms and references for experiencing and envisioning the sacred topography of Mount Wutai. Interestingly, this was not achieved by performing rituals, or any other religious acts, among the five peaks, but through the pentad of monasteries and the imperial patronage that recognized Bodhisattva Mañjuśrī as the official tutelary deity of the nation. And the reason for the sponsorship of Mount Wutai as the site of the national cult primarily from the 760s to the 780s is tied to the legend of the Indian monk Buddhapālita, whom we met in chapter 4, who disappeared on Mount Wutai in 676, taking with him the *Sutra of the Superlative Dhāraṇī of the Buddha's Crown*.[25]

Amoghavajra: From the *Sutra of the Superlative Dhāraṇī of the Buddha's Crown* to the Cult of Mañjuśrī

As suggested by its full name, the *Sutra of the Superlative Dhāraṇī* falls into the category of esoteric scriptures rooted in the notion of *uṣṇīṣa* (*foding*), and it is one of the earlier *dhāraṇī* texts translated in the period of what has been termed "proto-esoteric" Buddhism.[26] The *dhāraṇī* portion of the text is framed within a story that introduces the power of the incantations and the various ways to evoke that power. The story concerns a son of a god named Shanzhu, who, in the midst of a good life, enjoying the gardens of the Heavens of the Thirty-Three Gods (Trāyastriṃśas), suddenly hears a voice that foretells his impending death in seven days and his subsequent miserable rebirths and suffering in hell. Deeply distressed, Shanzhu calls upon Indra, the great god of all deities, for help. Indra, however, is unable to provide a solution for the situation, and turns to the Buddha for remedy. After learning of Shanzhu's plight, the Buddha emanates from the top of his head (i.e., *uṣṇīṣa*) rays of light that spread across the ten directions, circle the Buddha three times, and enter his mouth.[27] The Buddha then begins to extol the benefits of the *Sutra of the Superlative Dhāraṇī of the Buddha's Crown*—such as eradicating all negative karma, destroying the suffering from unfavorable rebirths, and deliverance from all hells—which could reverse Shanzhu's dreadful karmic destiny. The Buddha further elucidates that one may receive the spiritual rewards if one hears, recalls, or recites the *dhāraṇī*, or inscribes it on pillars or inserts it into stupas.[28]

The *Sutra of the Superlative Dhāraṇī* was among the most popular *dhāraṇī* texts in Tang China, testified by the great number of *dhāraṇī* pillars either surviving or recorded in texts from this period.[29] Because of its esoteric components and ritual techniques, the scripture also appealed to translators of early esoteric texts. Already in 685, Divākara (612–87) translated the earliest esoteric version with elaborate ritual instructions for actualizing its spiritual power.[30] This was followed by a version translated in 710 by another important translator of esoteric texts, Yijing (635–713).[31] Further into the eighth century, with more canonical teachings of new ritual systems transmitted to China that introduced the panoply of mantric texts, deities, and practices, the redaction of the *Sutra of the Superlative Dhāraṇī* also became more complex. These new systems were primarily brought to Tang China from India through the effort of the three great masters: Śubhākarasiṃha (637–735), Vajrabodhi, and Amoghavajra.[32] Śubhākarasiṃha adapted and translated the *Sutra of the Superlative Dhāraṇī* into the first ritual manual (*yigui*) of the scripture in 722, and in 764 Amoghavajra produced a second, simplified, but more influential redaction, entitled *The Rite for the Recitation of the Superlative Dhāraṇī of the Buddha's Crown* (Foding zunsheng tuoluoni niansong yigui fa).[33]

Of the esoteric masters, Amoghavajra was the most enthusiastic advocate for the practice and benefits of *dhāraṇī*. Arriving in the capital Chang'an with his teacher Vajrabodhi in 721, Amoghavajra spent most of his early career translating esoteric teachings and adapting them to Chinese concerns and circumstances. After his master's death in 741, Amoghavajra was summoned to serve Emperor Xuanzong

(r. 712–56). After the emperor's death he stayed in the capital through the rebellion in 756 of An Lushan (703–57) and the ensuing chaos of the next eight years, performing rituals at the court to help defeat rebels and setting up altars to avert disasters and subjugate evils.[34] Through the turbulent years of political upheaval and social unrest, Amoghavajra attained more prominence than his predecessors, solidifying his position as the chief religious advisor of the next two emperors, Suzong (r. 756–62) and Daizong. In 762, Amoghavajra presented a gift to Daizong on his birthday of the Sanskrit version of an incantation, titled the *Great Dhāraṇī of the Buddha's Crown* (Da foding zhenyan);[35] three years later in 765, under the threat of Tibetan and Uighur invasion to the west and north, Daizong ordered Amoghavajra to select fourteen monks to chant the Incantation of the Buddha's Crown (*Foding zhou*) at the court for the sake of the nation.[36] Neither of the mantric scriptures can be precisely identified, but judging from their titles, both were likely closely related to the *Sutra of the Superlative Dhāraṇī;* they may in fact be the sutra under other titles.[37] By the time Amoghavajra died in 774, the *Sutra of the Superlative Dhāraṇī* had become one of the most important *dhāraṇī* texts in use among Buddhists. In 776, two years after the master's death, Daizong issued an edict that ordered "monks and nuns of the country to chant the *Superlative Dhāraṇī of the Buddha's Crown* and to memorize it by heart within one month. From then on it is to be recited twenty-one times daily, and on the first day of each year a delegate should be sent to report to the throne how many times it has been recited [in the past year]."[38]

From its first translation by Divākara in 685 until its inclusion in the monastic routines made mandatory in the 776 imperial edict, the *Sutra of the Superlative Dhāraṇī* went from being a scripture of apotropaic and salvific efficacy for the individuals who used it, to being one of national import. This trajectory took off especially under Amoghavajra, who saw the esoteric teaching as the most effective method for the pursuit of both personal salvation and enlightenment and national defense and protection. In 771, Amoghavajra presented to Daizong a list of seventy-seven scriptures to be included in the official catalogue. Notable among them were texts of the *Yoga of the Vajra Crown* (Jin'gang ding yuqie), concerning practices derived from the sutras and doctrines of the Vajra Crown tradition, with which the esoteric master was most associated. In his memorandum Amoghavajra states:

> Of those [works I have] translated, [the texts of] the *Yoga of the Vajra Crown* are the teachings for swiftly becoming a Buddha. Those who cultivate them will perforce suddenly transcend all limitations and reach the other shore. As for the remaining classes of mantra teachings and all the Buddha's skillful means—their disciples are legion. All these translations are canonical scriptures of the Mahayana. I present [them] to the state for the pacification of disasters, to keep the stars on their regular courses, and to ensure that the wind and rain are timely, assisting the nation by resorting to the power of the Buddha.[39]

The system of teachings newly coalescing during Amoghavajra's tenure, later known as Esoteric Buddhism, should thus be understood through this lens. Most significantly for my purpose, it was also during the 760s and 770s that Amoghavajra turned to the cult of Mañjuśrī at Mount Wutai as this new school's most eloquent advocate, starting from the petition in 766 that requested that Daizong sponsor the building of Jin'ge Monastery.

Although Amoghavajra's patronage of Mount Wutai did not occur until late in his career, his interest in the *Sutra of the Superlative Dhāraṇī* may have been key to this decision.[40] The Buddhapālita legend that associated the *dhāraṇī* text with Mount Wutai continued to be circulated around this time and likely inspired Amoghavajra's interest. More critically, the Vajra Crown tradition that defines Amoghavajra's esoteric vision and practice shares the conceptual notion of Buddha's crown with the *Sutra of the Superlative Dhāraṇī* and the five peaks of Mount Wutai. The sutra falls into the group of esoteric scriptures rooted in *uṣṇīṣa,* which was later incorporated into the Vajra Crown or Vajroṣṇīṣa tradition introduced through both Vajrabodhi and Amoghavajra. It is evident in ways in which the sutra was "updated" in Amoghavajra's ritual manual of the scripture with expanded esoteric iconography.[41] Moreover, the Vajroṣṇīṣa is important in Amoghavajra's teachings of the Five Wisdoms and the fivefold mandalic structure that became the template for new rituals for his imperial and aristocratic patrons.[42] Mount Wutai, with its five sacred peaks (or more appropriately, *wuding,* in this context) matching the fivefold system of Vajroṣṇīṣa, would therefore provide a physical and at the same time ideal and iconographic site whose sacrality and power could be accessed through its presiding deity, the bodhisattva Mañjuśrī.

In this matrix of historical circumstances, Amoghavajra's patronage of the cult of Mañjuśrī in the last years of his career from 766 to 774 should be regarded as an endeavor that dovetailed with his larger project to transform the esoteric religion into a more cohesive system. If the way in which the *Sutra of the Superlative Dhāraṇī* was appropriated and updated into a more complex ritual manual of state liturgy was indicative of the style of esoteric practice around this time, the promotion of the cult of Mañjuśrī would also involve no less than new esoteric texts, rituals, iconography, and even architecture to put the new form of the cult into practice. However, unlike the rite of the *Sutra of the Superlative Dhāraṇī,* which was not tied to a particular site and could be performed at any selected liturgical space or constructed *maṇḍala,* those related to the cult of Mañjuśrī always alluded to a spatial relation symbolically or ritualistically to Mount Wutai. It is nevertheless in this particular relation that the cult of Mañjuśrī at Mount Wutai was incorporated into the esoteric practice and religion developed under Amoghavajra.

Amoghavajra continued to translate texts related to esoteric liturgies (e.g., mantras, *maṇḍalas,* etc.) dedicated to Mañjuśrī before his death in 774. Among the translations are several scriptures of the five-syllable mantra associated with the *vajra* crown, important to exploring the power of Mañjuśrī in esoteric terms.[43] The development of Mañjuśrī into the national tutelary deity continued meanwhile, and can be divided into two phases at two different locations: the first few years after Amoghavajra made the petition to support the building of Jin'ge Monastery in 766 at Mount Wutai, and the years after 769 in the capital Chang'an.[44] The building of Jin'ge Monastery into the new center at the sacred mountain bears examination in light of new scriptures and related practices in the two different phases of development. Three related events that followed its building reveal the ultimate goal of Amoghavajra's patronage of the sacred site and thus provide a useful context.

The first event came in 769 when Amoghavajra requested an imperial edict that would require monasteries in the empire to install the image of Mañjuśrī as the main deity (*zhuzuo*) in the refectory, above the usual statue of Piṇḍola.[45] One of the main arhats (holy ascetics), Piṇḍola was known for helping devotees attain enlightenment by accepting their food offerings. The practice of placing a statue of Piṇḍola in the refectory can be traced back to the earliest monastic communities in China, and yet, his Indian origin was never lost.[46] The installing of Mañjuśrī above Piṇḍola at the refectory thus not only indicated Mañjuśrī's power to bring similar spiritual assistance to monastics, but also demonstrated that his identity and divinity had already been unequivocally localized in China. To justify his proposal, Amoghavajra writes, "The Great Sage Bodhisattva Mañjuśrī expounds both Mahayana and esoteric teachings. Now [he] stands guard at Mount [Wu]tai to benefit everyone in the nation."[47] Mañjuśrī, the bodhisattva associated with wisdom, now entered every monastery in the nation as a teacher for monks of both Mahayana and esoteric doctrines.

To take this doctrinal importance of Mañjuśrī one step further, in 772 Amoghavajra solicited another imperial edict that ordered every monastery in the empire to establish a Cloister of the Great Sage Bodhisattva Mañjuśrī (Dasheng Wenshu Shili Pusa Yuan).[48] Inside the cloister, an uncolored image of Mañjuśrī adorned in a dignified manner would be enshrined and worshiped. The request recalls the previous campaigns of Emperor Wendi of the Sui and Empress Wu of the Tang to distribute relics and rename new monasteries throughout the nation that in a sense mapped a Buddhist sacred geography over the territory of China.[49] By so doing, the ruler was able to claim his or her reign of the nation supported by the religion. Indeed, after his request was granted, Amoghavajra gratefully praised the emperor for his rule in accordance with the new doctrines by evoking the idea of "wheel-turning ruler" (*cakravartin*). One year later in 773, Amoghavajra translated and presented to the throne the *Sutra [That Numerates] the Virtue and Magnificence of the Pure Land of the Great Sage Bodhisattva Mañjuśrī* (Dasheng Wenshu shili pusa fosha gongde zhuangyan jing), which describes the paradisaical scene of Mañjuśrī's Pure Land (*buddhakṣetra*). It was made mandatory that every large monastery select seven monks and every smaller monastery select three monks to recite the sutra and give lectures on it at the newly established cloisters throughout the empire for the cause of the nation.[50] The simultaneous chanting of the sutra would thus give rise to the vision of the Pure Land presided over by Bodhisattva Mañjuśrī, the deity now standing guard over the empire.

The third event was related to a building project that also began in 773. In that year, the emperor ordered the construction of a pavilion of Mañjuśrī inside the Great Xingshan Monastery (Da Xingshansi), the home monastery of Amoghavajra and the "headquarters" of the esoteric practice.[51] With the emperor being its main patron (*gezhu*), the building was recorded as having been constructed as a magnificent two-story structure: the upper level as a sutra repository and the lower level for ritual consecration, installed with a painted set of nine images of the "Six-Syllable Mañjuśrī" (Liuzi Wenshu) accompanied by 104 fellow bodhisattvas painted on the remaining interior walls.[52] Amoghavajra did not live to see the completion of the pavilion. But he made a final request in his will: "After the pavilion is completed, twenty-one monks should be selected for the nation to continually recite all sutras in order to increase the longevity of the emperor, and this will fulfill my will."[53] Upon its completion in 775, the will of the deceased master was granted and the building was bestowed with an official plaque bearing its name inscribed in gold: Pavilion of the Great Holy Mañjuśrī for the Protection of the Nation (Dasheng Wenshu Zhenguo Zhi Ge).[54]

Mañjuśrī reached a more elevated status than any other esoteric deities in a span of only a few years. A network of monastic edifices dedicated to the bodhisattva was established throughout the empire, and the lengthy chanting of his mantra and the sutra of his Pure Land were meant to bring about a utopian vision to which this secular empire could aspire. This seemingly universal status of Mañjuśrī as a national tutelary deity, however, cannot be separated from his sacred mountain as the origin and source of his divine power. The building of Jin'ge Monastery surrounded by four other designated monasteries that reconfigured the centrality of Mount Wutai was the critical step taken by Amoghavajra before the three events just summarized. The name of the Mañjuśrī pavilion in Great Xingshan Monastery, conferred after the death of the master, indeed, recalls none other than the official name plaque of Jin'ge Monastery at Mount Wutai: Monastery of the Great Sage's Golden Pavilion That Responds to the [Calls to] Protect the Nation (Dasheng Jin'ge Baoying Zhenguo Si).[55] Thus we see two distinct phases: in the first, the building of Jin'ge Monastery at Mount Wutai; in the second, the building of the Pavilion of the Great Holy Mañjuśrī in Chang'an. Whereas the pavilion was built as the center of the new national cult of Mañjuśrī, Jin'ge Monastery was constructed to materialize and embody the iconography of the Mañjuśrī cult, and with an architecture that transformed Mount Wutai into a ritual field (*maṇḍala*) of the cult.

Jin'ge Monastery: Iconographic Architecture

In Amoghavajra's 766 petition, quoted at the beginning of the chapter, Jin'ge Monastery was to constructed after a building plan presented by the monk Daoyi, who reported to have encountered a monastery by this name in a vision while visiting Mount Wutai in 736. Describing Daoyi's experience in the virtual monastery, Yanyi writes, "The grand [Golden] Pavilion is three stories tall, with the nine-bay facade through the three levels. Amazed by the sight, [Daoyi] venerated the building earnestly. He then entered [further] into the monastic complex, seeing halls and corridors all decorated with golden jewels."[56] The story continues with his being brought to Mañjuśrī and conversing briefly with the bodhisattva, and then resuming his tour through another twelve cloisters before the vision vanished.[57]

Not until almost thirty years after Daoyi's initial vision did the construction of the monastery begin. Yet, the building project did not just certify Daoyi's marvelous visionary experience or add a new monastery to Mount Wutai; it also provided Amoghavajra a means to explore the power of the sacred site. In his memorandum, the master reported to the emperor that Jin'ge Monastery was built exactly after the virtual monastery Daoyi had entered, thus faithfully actualizing the divinely revealed architectural plan in material form. Built with copper- and gold-plated roof tiles, the main image hall, the Golden Pavilion (Jin'ge), was intended as a simulacrum of the architectural grandeur in the idealized vision.

The religious tour de force of the pavilion, however, lay beyond its impressive facade and differed from Daoyi's revelatory vision in its complex iconographic ensemble, structured and spatialized inside its architecture. An Indian monk named Chuntuo (d. 767) from Nālandā Monastery was said to have been the architect responsible for the construction of Jin'ge Monastery and for the iconographic program inside the Golden Pavilion based on the model of the monastery.[58] The entire project was supervised by Hanguang (d. after 774), one of Amoghavajra's most competent disciples, who received full consecration and accompanied the master to South Asia during his four-year mission from 742 to 746 to collect esoteric scriptures and complete his training in ritual. After the completion of Jin'ge Monastery, Hanguang was also assigned as its first abbot.[59] In short, there is little doubt that Jin'ge Monastery was closely associated with its most prominent supporter, Amoghavajra. More important, the religious function and icons of the monastery seem to have also been related to the master's esoteric teachings, recently available in India and transmitted to China through his effort in collecting and translating crucial scriptures and ritual manuals.

No detail of the monastery, however, is included in documents that concern Amoghavajra. The most valuable record of Jin'ge Monastery comes from the Japanese pilgrim Ennin (794–864), who arrived at the monastery in 840, visiting a sutra repository, a ritual arena for *dhāraṇī*-chanting *maṇḍala* practice (the Chinian Mantuluo Daochang), and a hall of Samantabhadra, in addition to the Golden Pavilion. Ennin described the pavilion in greater detail—the single building whose iconographic program received his most attentive observation during his entire pilgrimage at Mount Wutai—quoted in full here:

> [Together with several monks of the monastery] we opened the Golden Pavilion to venerate the Great Sage. Bodhisattva Mañjuśrī, who rides a blue lion, is gilded and his countenance and presence is unmatchably serene. We also saw the Buddha image painted on the skin from Venerable Ryōzen's arm [enshrined inside] a gilded copper stupa;[60] we further saw the tooth of Pratyeka-buddha and other body relics. Above the bodhisattva's head is a seven-jewel canopy, bestowed by imperial order. The pavilion is nine bays wide and three stories tall, and over one hundred *chi* high. No place on its walls and eaves and columns and

beams is unpainted. Its exterior and interior are adorned in a dignified manner with all the rarities of the world. [The pavilion] stands out alone majestically above the groves. The white clouds roll below it [such that] the green [roofs of its upper] levels appear to soar even higher above them.

Next [we] ascended to the second level to worship the statues of the Five Buddhas of the Yoga of the Vajra Crown [Jin'gang Ding Yuqie], which was commissioned by Amoghavajra on behalf of the nation and made after the model provided by Nālandā Monastery. Each Buddha has two flanking bodhisattvas and all statues are installed in a row on the platform of planks.

Next [we] ascended to the third level to worship the golden images of the Five Buddhas of the Yoga Assembly of the Wheel-Turning King of [the Buddha's] Crown [Ding Lunwang Yuqiehui Wufo]. Each Buddha has one attending bodhisattva. Two other bodhisattvas, with their hands joined together, stand in front of the Buddha facing south. The *mudras* and facial features of the Buddhas and bodhisattvas are all distinguished from those of the statues on the second level. On the surface of whitewashed interior walls are drawn *maṇḍalas* of various deities and the colors are filled incompletely. These, too, were commissioned by Amoghavajra on behalf of the nation.[61]

A few scholars, primarily Japanese, have identified texts translated by Amoghavajra that were most likely the scriptural bases for the iconography inside the pavilion.[62] Equally important is the role of architecture in creating the ritual experience, in that it spatializes the iconographic ensemble vertically through its three floors. The diagram in figure 5.3 provides a guide to the iconography of each of the three levels inside the Golden Pavilion.

On the first level, the most important icon is the statue of the gilded Mañjuśrī riding a blue lion. Ennin did not say whether the statue resembled the true-presence icon that he had already seen at the Cloister of True Presence at Huayan Monastery;[63] however, considering Amoghavajra's role in building Jin'ge Monastery, it is likely that the statue of Mañjuśrī would have appeared here in a different, esoteric style. As the number five figures largely in the Vajra Crown that dominates Amoghavajra's teachings, scholars suggest, the sculpture of Mañjuśrī on the first level of the pavilion may have been the "Five-Syllable Mañjuśrī," and its iconography may have been based on the *Rite of Bodhisattva Mañjuśrī According to the Vajraśekhara Sūtra* (Jin'gang ding jing yuqie Wenshu shili pusa fa), translated by Amoghavajra.[64] In this sutra, the Vairocana Buddha explains that the wisdom of Mañjuśrī would be imparted to the practitioner through the chanting of the five-syllable mantra, *a-ra-pa-ca-na*. To perform the chant, a *maṇḍala* would be set up with an image of Mañjuśrī: "At the center of the *maṇḍala* paint an image of the youth Mañjuśrī with five topknots, with its torso saturated in golden color and adorned with necklaces of different treasures. [The bodhisattva carries] in his right hand a sword with a *vajra* blade and [he holds] in his left a palm-leaf scripture, sitting inside a lunar disc."[65] If the statue were indeed to look like this, however, a question arises. Whereas Ennin's diary records the statue, no scriptures about the

FIGURE 5.3. Diagram showing the iconographic program in each of the three levels inside the Golden Pavilion (Jin'ge) at Jin'ge Monastery, based on the description in Ennin's travel diary, *Nittō guhō junrei gyōki*. Circles indicate icons enshrined on each of the three levels. Diagram by author.

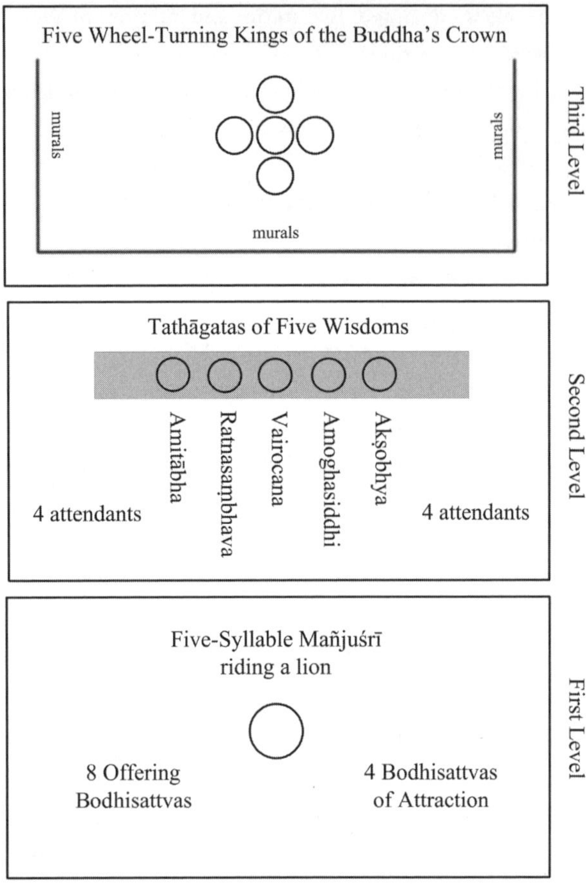

Five-Syllable Mañjuśrī describe an image of the bodhisattva with five topknots "riding a lion."[66] Is it possible, then, that the iconographic program inside the Pavilion was based on something other than the scripture?

Jin'ge Monastery, as we have seen, was intended to bring about a new conception of Mount Wutai's topography and the iconography of its residing bodhisattva. If the main icon on the first level of the pavilion was, indeed, a statue of the Five-Syllable Mañjuśrī on a lion, the familiar "true-presence" icon developed in the earlier history of Mount Wutai—the bodhisattva riding his lion—might have been modified so that a new embodiment of it would be the first icon the practitioner would face on entering the pavilion; it would be this version of the icon that introduced the practitioner to the panoply of esoteric iconography inside the pavilion's architectural space. In the *Rite of Bodhisattva Mañjuśrī,* the instruction further specifies that inside the *maṇḍala,* the characters of the five-syllable mantra *a-ra-pa-ca-na* should be written around the image of Mañjuśrī; additionally, images of the eight "offering bodhisattvas" (*gongyang pusa*) and four "bodhisattvas of attraction" (*sishe pusa*) should be painted at its four sides.[67] The mandalic field thus created was to help the practitioner conceive and evoke the protective power of Mañjuśrī as promised in the sutra. The main icon of Mañjuśrī, modified to assume the "true presence" of the bodhisattva specifically at his sacred mountain, would not only increase the efficacy of the ritual but also draw on its iconic economy in the new esoteric system.

This hypothesis, that the main statue on the first level is the Five-Syllable Mañjuśrī riding a lion, can be further corroborated by its relation with other icons enshrined in the building. First, let us note that the eight offering bodhisattvas and four bodhisattvas of attraction that mark the four sides of the *maṇḍala* just discussed are the same bodhisattvas who comprise the deities on the outer periphery of the *Vajradhātu maṇḍala*, as elaborated in the *Vajraśekhara Sūtra*.[68] There is a major difference between the two *maṇḍalas*, however. Whereas the *Rite of Bodhisattva Mañjuśrī maṇḍala* is centered on the Five-Syllable Mañjuśrī, the *Vajradhātu maṇḍala* is centered on the "Tathāgatas of Five Wisdoms"—the Vairocana Buddha with the buddhas of the four directions: Akṣobhya in the east, Ratnasaṃbhava in the south, Amitābha in the west, and Amoghasiddhi in the north—that is, the "Five Buddhas of the Yoga of Vajra Crown" described by Ennin as the main deities enshrined on the second level. Ascending from the first level to the second, one would seem to have entered the *Vajradhātu maṇḍala* from its periphery and moved into the center. This ascendance, or entry, was thus not a casual action but would have been facilitated in ritual through the icon of Mañjuśrī on the first floor. In the *Rite of Bodhisattva Mañjuśrī*, after the *maṇḍala* is set up with the Five-Syllable Mañjuśrī, the practitioner is instructed to start the ritual by invoking and worshiping none other than the buddhas of the four directions before inviting and contemplating the presence of the bodhisattva at the center.[69] In this light, moving upward from one level to another, from one *maṇḍala* into another, would have both elevated and drawn one into the source of power and enlightenment.

This spatial, vertical reading of the iconography would have also encouraged the association of the Five-Syllable Mañjuśrī with the Tathāgatas of Five Wisdoms. The five topknots of the Five-Syllable Mañjuśrī are, as noted earlier, usually understood as symbolizing the fivefold wisdom of the bodhisattva.[70] The vertical movement from the fivefold wisdom of Mañjuśrī to the Tathāgatas of Five Wisdoms thus prompts the notion of Buddha's crown (*buddhoṣṇīṣa*): as if from the five topknots of Mañjuśrī's crown (*uṣṇīṣa*) emanate the five dimensions of the wisdom synonymous with ultimate reality, embodied in the tathāgatas on the pavilion's second level. In other words, the relations and movements between levels are not only architectural but also ritual and iconographic, turning abstract religious notion and correlation into something that could be visually meditated upon, spatially imagined, and spiritually revealed through the building.

The meaning of the icons on the third level may be unpacked and deciphered in a similar way. Continuing the fivefold structure, on the top level is a pentad described by Ennin as the "Five Buddhas of the Yoga Assembly of the Wheel-Turning King of the Buddha's Crown." These five buddhas, personifying Śākyamuni Buddha's five forms of wisdom, are the main deities invoked in the *Scripture Spoken at the Bodhimaṇḍa on the One-Syllable Wheel-Turning King of [the Buddha's] Crown* (Putichang suoshuo yizi ding lunwang jing), also translated by Amoghavajra.[71] The scripture is a *dhāraṇī* text supposedly given by Śākyamuni for invoking the fivefold wisdom of the Buddha, personified as the Five Wheel-Turning Kings. All five kings are described as having golden bodies emanating different marvelous radiances; they are individualized by the different mudras (hand positions) they adopt and symbolic objects that they hold. According to the sutra, a Vajradhātu *maṇḍala* or altar of the five kings would be set up for the several different rituals that integrate rites for conferring the precepts (*abhiṣeka*), offering oblations (*homa*), and practicing visualization for such worldly benefits as protection and prosperity. These benefits—which could also be directed to the cause of the empire—would have been one of the major reasons why this pentad was worshiped at the monastery that stood guard over the nation at the sacred mountain.

Moving thus from the second level to the third, one also finds correlations between the tathāgatas and the five kings. The second level of the pavilion may have represented the inner court of the Vajradhātu *maṇḍala* with the five buddhas at the center, corresponding to the fivefold wisdom of Vairocana. As a systematic unity, the Vajradhātu *maṇḍala* consists of five celestial groups, altogether thirty-seven divinities, conceptually and spatially arranged from the center outward: the Tathāgatas of Five Wisdoms, four "perfection bodhisattvas," sixteen "great bodhisattvas," eight offering bodhisattvas, and four bodhisattvas of attractions.[72] At least three texts attributed to Amoghavajra explicate the reciprocal interrelations of the five groups and the attributes of each of the groups, together suggesting the unconditioned and self-produced reality of the universe.[73] One text in particular, likely the latest of the three, the *Casual Revelations of the Thirty-Seven Divinities of the Yoga of the Vajra Crown* (Jin'gang ding yuqie sanshiqi zun chusheng yi) makes an analogy between the fivefold system of the thirty-seven divinities and the structure of a four-sided stupa, at the center of which is Vairocana surrounded by the four directional Buddhas. Drawing attention to the center, the text states: "[Vairocana] enters the Samādhi That Arises from the Buddha's Crown, manifesting [different] bodies arising from his topknot [*uṣṇīṣa*]. Now [the reason] why there is nothing but the assembly of the Five Wheel-Turning Kings on top of the stupa is that the topknot [of Vairocana] gives rise to [five] bodily forms [of Wheel-Turning Kings] acting for his superior fivefold wisdom."[74] In other words, it is the power of Vairocana that causes the Five Wheel-Turning Kings to rise from and represent his *uṣṇīṣa*. With this power, the text continues: "The Five [Wheel-Turning Kings] of the Buddha's Crown, for they are the commanders of all superlative mantras, are thus called kings."[75] As such, Vairocana—the center of the iconic assemblage on the second level of the pavilion—literally from the top of his head gives rise to the Five Wheel-Turning Kings, whose images could be seen and worshiped on the next level.

All three levels inside the Golden Pavilion at Jin'ge Monastery enshrined a different set of esoteric icons (fig. 5.3): the Five-Syllable Mañjuśrī riding a lion on the first level, the Tathāgatas of Five Wisdoms on the second, and the Five Wheel-Turning Kings of the Buddha's Crown on the third. The icons on each of the three levels all had their specific ritual functions and significance, and yet they most likely also had been planned and arranged to orchestrate a grander and more powerful iconographic ensemble throughout the three levels. Two critical themes helped create the religious-architectural matrix. First, time and again the number five served as language and template in presenting and structuring the icons of each level; and second, the notion of *uṣṇīṣa* (*ding*)—the invisible source of ineffable and superior wisdom—conjured a sense of the mythic center and power rising from the top of the deity's head, literally connecting the three vertical levels. Moreover, the *vajra* crown (*vajroṣṇīṣa; jin'gang ding*) system, to which the iconic group on the second level belongs, appears to have encompassed the Buddha's Crown (*buddhoṣṇīṣa; foding*) tradition that emphasized both the Five-Syllable Mañjuśrī riding a lion and the Five Wheel-Turning Kings of the Buddha's Crown. Accordingly, taken as a whole, it may be suggested that the Golden Pavilion was built to be conceived as a three-dimensional Vajradhātu *maṇḍala* that had at its core five buddhas on the second level, preceded by the Mañjuśrī icon peculiar to Mount Wutai as the bodhisattva's sacred domicile, and capped by the five deities of particular mantric powers for the protection of the empire.

This conclusion may be speculative, but building the sacred mountain into a ritual field centered on the Golden Pavilion that simulated the Vajradhātu *maṇḍala* must have been in the mind of Amoghavajra. Recall that in 767 when the construction of the monastery was close to completion, Amoghavajra asked for twenty-one monks who, for the cause of the nation, would chant esoteric scriptures and perform rituals at five designated monasteries at Mount Wutai, among them Jin'ge Monastery (see map 10); he asked for the same number of monks in his will to "continually chant all sutras" at the Pavilion of Mañjuśrī inside the Great Xingshan Monastery at Chang'an. Yet his request for the five monasteries at Mount Wutai gave more particular details: it specified that "each [of the five monasteries] separately ordain two times seven monks, while one times seven ritual-performing monks be selected from all prefectures. Together each monastery has three times seven monks performing rituals on the behalf of the nation."[76] The particular expression "three times seven" in Chinese could also be read as thirty-seven, the number of the deities of the Vajradhātu *maṇḍala*,[77] which together with the five schematically disposed monasteries at the sacred mountain, are again suggestive of a larger mandalic field built into the sacred topography of Mount Wutai.

The above reconstruction of the iconic program and associations inside and outside the Golden Pavilion, to a great extent, is prompted by the architecture of the three-story building. As one moved from floor to floor, the iconography seems to have been the constitutive, rather than coincidental, part of the architecture, and together, they transform the building. Because the Golden Pavilion of Jin'ge Monastery predates the earliest surviving Buddhist image hall—the much smaller and more moderate main hall of Nanchan Monastery, built in 782 also at Mount Wutai—Ennin's record of the pavilion provides a rare glimpse into the interrelation of architecture and iconography in Chinese building tradition around this time.

Rather than being regarded as objects standing in isolation from their surroundings, icons of different media installed inside the building were perceived cohesively, dynamically, and performatively. In the case of the Golden Pavilion (see fig. 5.3), on the first level, the Five-Syllable Mañjuśrī would have animated its space during the ritual with additional images—those of the eight offering bodhisattvas and four bodhisattvas of attraction, represented either in *siddham* script or *samaya* (emblematic) form—temporarily demarcating a sacred zone of liturgy within the timber-framed floor space. Ascending to the second level, one goes from beholding one principal icon to venerating a set of five buddhas, each accompanied by two attending bodhisattvas, all together "installed in a row on the platform of planks," described by Ennin. The larger number of icons was indicative of more complexity in both iconography and visuality.[78] Ascending further to the top level, the spatial arrangement was yet again different from those of the previous levels. To form a *maṇḍala* or altar of the Five Wheel-Turning Kings of the Buddha's Crown, these five statues would have been arranged in a circle, with four at four cardinal directions and the chief wheel-turning king at the center facing south.[79] The circular and centralized assembly would thus have prompted circumambulation among surrounding walls that had drawn on them "*maṇḍalas* of various deities, and the colors [were] filled incompletely." The incomplete coloring may refer to the ritual function of these murals; that is, the practitioner would visually fill in the color to petition the deities to descend to the ritual space.[80] Unlike the icons of the first two levels, therefore, the iconic ensemble of statues and murals here entails an ambulatory religious experience, both visually and bodily enacting the presence of the divinity.

Chinese wooden architecture is usually believed to have evolved over time in structural, not in functional, terms. Its non-weight-bearing timber-frame structure provides greater flexibility in the interior, and by the Tang period, the network of interior columns was distributed according to a well-developed grid-like floor plan that regulated the interior space in a modular system.[81] For monastic purposes, before the extensive destruction and persecution against Buddhism in 845, it has been suggested, there must have been at least two types of interior (fig. 5.4) built in China for different kinds of ritual purposes.[82] The first type has the interior divided by the pillars across both width and depth to form an inner space enclosed by aisles on its four sides; in comparison, the second type, with a square floor plan, is divided into inner and outer spaces. While the suggestion is plausible, the building of the Golden Pavilion demonstrates that even though the three stories might have been built with a similar style of timber-frame structure, disposition of interior columns, and floor space, each level was arranged and perceived in a unique way so that its iconography could perform and interact with the practitioner in the architectural space. In other words, Chinese religious architecture may not be defined by a particular iconography (e.g., symbolic details), building typology, or interior type as much as by how its religious program (i.e., iconography) is integrated with the architecture that determines the ways in which its structure and space should be understood and experienced.[83]

Though certainly not unprecedented, the multilevel structure of the Golden Pavilion should not be overlooked. Its importance lies not so much in its technical or structural aspect as in the manner in which its iconographic program was able

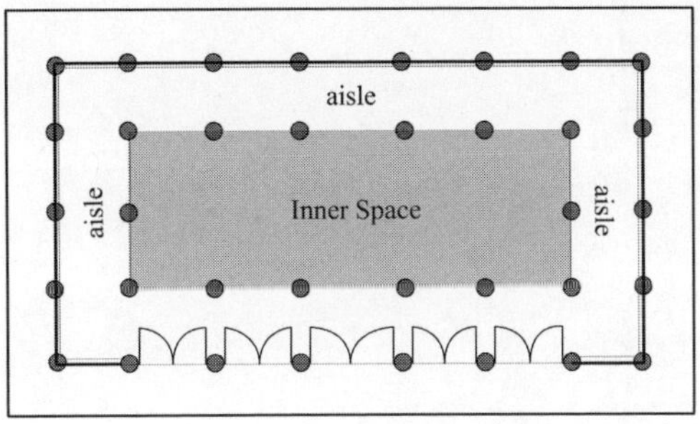

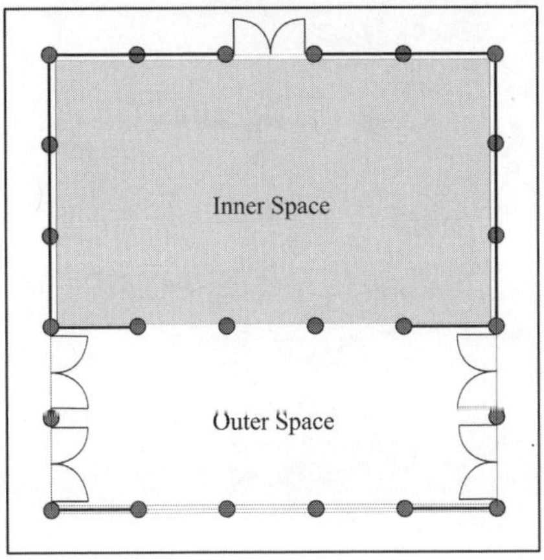

FIGURE 5.4. Two major types of wooden hall interior built during the mid-Tang: (a) an inner interior space separated from the aisles on its four sides by a network of pillars; (b) a square interior divided by columns into front and back areas. Diagram by author.

FIGURE 5.5. Section of the Guanyin Pavilion of Dule Monastery, Jixian, Hebei. Liao dynasty, 984 CE. Three interior levels are integrated by a larger iconographic program centered on the colossal Guanyin figure. From Liang, "Jixian Dulesi Guanyin ge," pl. 5.

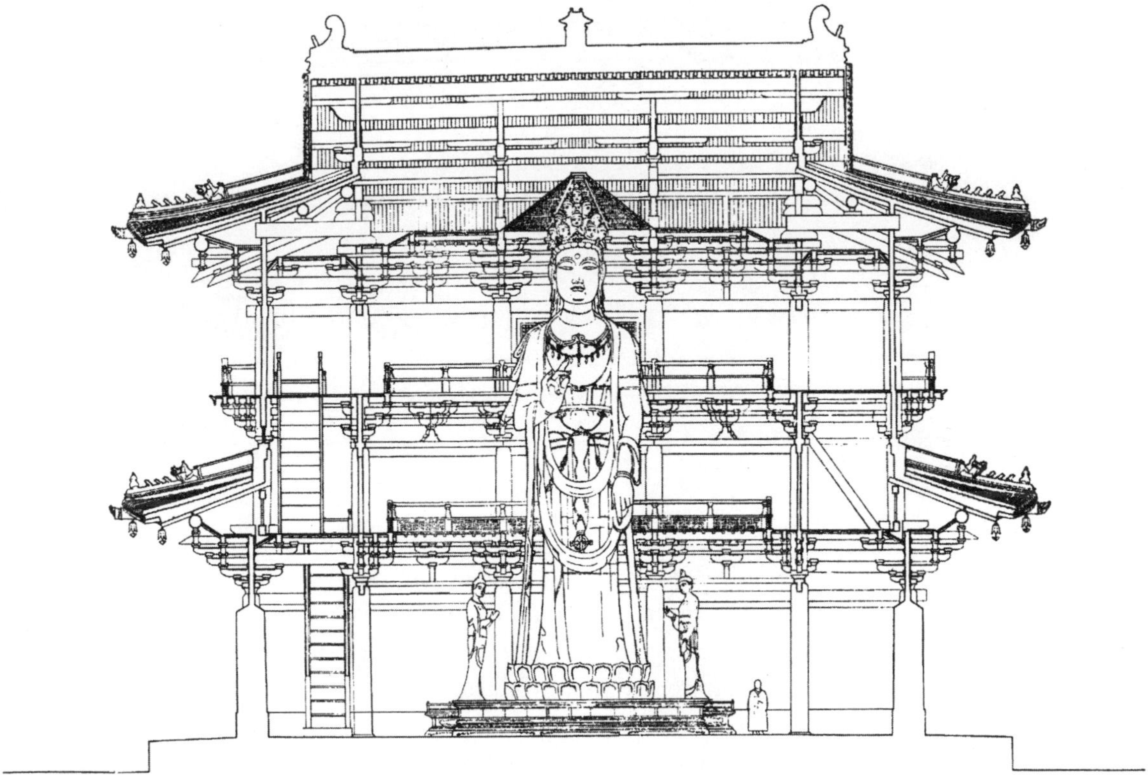

FIGURE 5.6. Section of the Wooden Pagoda, Fogong Monastery, Yingxian, Shanxi. Liao dynasty, 1056 CE. Five interior levels each featuring a particular iconic set are integrated into a larger iconographic ensemble experienced in sequence, rising from the first level and gradually ascending to the higher levels. After Liang, *A Pictorial History of Chinese Architecture,* fig. 31d. Drawing courtesy of Lin Zhu.

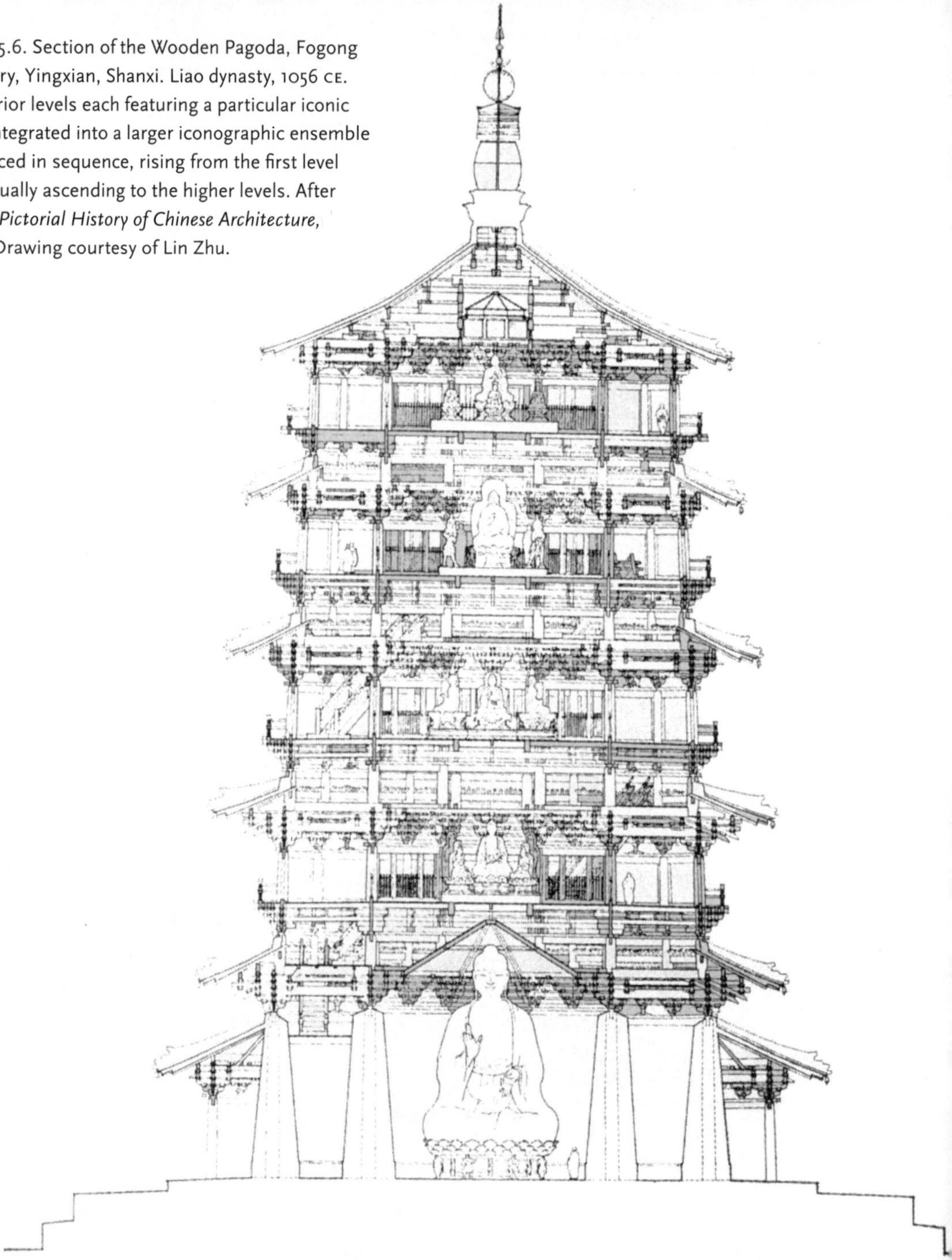

to unfold vertically throughout the building. Since early on, the tradition of the monastic complex had been organized horizontally around two principles: the central axis and lateral symmetry. Even by the eighth century, it was still unusual to encounter a multistoried wooden structure.[84] Height by itself thus would have taken on extra or symbolic meaning amid the otherwise horizontal sprawl of monastic buildings. In the case of the Golden Pavilion, its vertical structure would elevate one through levels in succession and enable a religious experience that transcended the limits of height, until one literally reached the crown of the head (*uṣṇīṣa*) of the central Vairocana, personified as the five Wheel-Turning Kings on the top floor. In this regard, the Golden Pavilion at Jin'ge Monastery should be considered an important precedent for the Guanyin Pavilion of Dule Monastery (Dulesi), dated 984, in Jixian, Hebei (fig. 5.5), as well as the Timber Pagoda of Fogong Monastery (Fogongsi), dated 1056, in Yingxian, Shanxi (fig. 5.6).[85] All three examples testify to the dual principles of concentricity and elevation that may categorize the three structures as a particular kind of "iconographic architecture"—architecture constructed with an intention of integrating and spatializing its iconographic program. The iconographic import of the Golden Pavilion is unique in that it was not limited to the building's interior but correlated with and extrapolated from the central position it occupied in the pentadic monastic system, enclosed by the five peaks, the five topknots of Mount Wutai.

Building *Is* Contesting: From Mountain to Monastery

A sacred site, as many have argued, is among many other things also a social arena of competing discourses.[86] Its significance is never static, nor is its center predetermined. In fact, the very act of relocating or recreating a sacred center is necessarily political, because the idea of center is not bound in place, but contested and subjected to circumstantial factors. At Mount Wutai, the most effective means of "contesting the center" was through building. Early in its history, the five towering peaks, to which the name Wutai refers, were the uncontested referents of the sacred site, serving as the geographic anchors of its sacred precincts within which the "center" could be located. The history of Mount Wutai is also often presented as the story of the five sacred summits, as documented in Huixiang's *Ancient Records.* During the eighth century, however, with the effort of Amoghavajra to develop Mount Wutai as a center of tantric practice, the building project of Jin'ge Monastery was commissioned to contest the traditional center of the sacred site and to reconceive its five peaks.

There is little doubt that the iconographic program of Jin'ge Monastery, in particular, that installed inside its main image hall, the Golden Pavilion, was intimately related to the Esoteric Buddhism advocated by Amoghavajra. Of particular importance is the dialectic relation between the monastic building and the sacred mountain. Two main devices were used concurrently to structure the religious and architectural matrix inside the pavilion, namely, the number five and the notion of the Buddha's crown (*uṣṇīṣa*), which together would have evoked the image of the five sacred peaks outside the building. The concentric design of the building further articulated its centrality within the five peaks, while its multiple stories paralleled the soaring peaks. If the pavilion was indeed built to simulate a Vajradhātu *maṇḍala* at the sacred mountain, Jin'ge Monastery would be at the center of the mandalic field, which, however, would be circumscribed not by the five peaks but by the four other monasteries at the four cardinal directions (see map 10). In other words, the two fivefold systems—five monasteries and five peaks—overlapped, yet each defined the sacred precinct with a rather different, and competing ideology. Whereas the designation of the five sacred peaks took shape over time in association with the earlier emphasis on the "true presence" of the bodhisattva, the five monasteries were built to create a ritual field that would transform the sacred site into the universal realm of the Buddha. While the power of the first system lies in the sacred topography of which the five towering peaks were the most essential, the second derives its power from the geometric pattern of the five monasteries (four directions and the center) that reshaped the sacred topography into both a conceptual and cohesive unit. The building of Jin'ge Monastery thus not only contested the center but also precipitated the transition from one system to the other, from mountain to monastery, in the conception of Mount Wutai. The pentadic monastic system nevertheless did not eclipse the previous dominance of the five peaks so much as present the dispositions of the peaks in a new way, in a more idealized symbolic formation.

After the death of Amoghavajra in 774, Hanguang continued to manage Jin'ge Monastery as the abbot, although records about the monastery became less frequent. Two specific accounts have been found dating from 777 and 779 and both relate to another of Amoghavajra's disciples, Huixiao of Ximing Monastery (Ximingsi) in Chang'an. In the first account, Huixiao was sent to Jin'ge Monastery by Emperor Daizong to examine the physical form, mudra, and *samaya* of each icon installed in the monastery; in the second, Huixiao was again assigned by the throne to perform the oblation (*homa*) rite at Jin'ge Monastery to ensure the peace and prosperity of the empire.[87] Both of Huixiao's trips attest to the political function that Jin'ge Monastery continued to serve at the time and to Mount Wutai as a ritual field for the esoteric practice. Emperor Daizong died in the same year of the second account, in 779, and the emperor's order is the last on record for the cult of Mañjuśrī that had been promoted by the court since the early 760s. The lack of records thereafter about the fivefold system of monasteries seems to suggest the cult's declining influence, although, entering the next century Jin'ge Monastery remained one of the principal monasteries for Esoteric Buddhism in Tang China. Through the building of Jin'ge Monastery during the last decades of the eighth century, nevertheless, the five peaks of Mount Wutai could no longer be seen without conjuring the multiple iconographic symbolisms, as indicated in Yanyi's *Extended Records*—the five mantric syllables, five topknots, fivefold wisdom, and five buddhas—organizing the topography of Mount Wutai into a greater schematic and representative cohesion.

CHAPTER SIX

Narrative, Visualization, and Transposition of Mount Wutai

There is, however, one mode of transposition that is most difficult for ritual praxis and thought—the transposition of space marked as sacred.

—Jonathan Z. Smith, "Constructing a Small Place"

In the years after the death of Amoghavajra, the dominance of Esoteric Buddhism at Mount Wutai began to wane,[1] but this did not reduce Mount Wutai's importance as a national pilgrimage site. From the last year of Emperor Daizong's reign in 779 to the persecution initiated by Emperor Wuzong (r. 840–46) in 845, the number of eminent monks visiting Mount Wutai increased steadily.[2] The popularity of the bodhisattva cult, moreover, went hand in hand with its transmission outside of Mount Wutai through textual and visual representations of the sacred site. In 824, for example, it was recorded that the Tibetan king, who then ruled an extensive area west of China, including the Mogao cave site near Dunhuang, Gansu, sent envoys to Tang China to request a copy of the "Picture of Mount Wutai" (Wutaishan tu).[3] This is not the first recorded visual image (*tu*) of Mount Wutai, but unlike its precedents, which were made as records of miraculous occurrences at the sacred site,[4] the picture requested by the Tibetan king was much more significant. It suggests not only the spread of the bodhisattva cult into the western region, but also the possible religious import of the image that depicted the sacred mountain. No later descriptions of this picture or its whereabouts exist, but the earliest murals of Mount Wutai in Mogao meditation caves did appear around this period. As such, two questions arise: What was depicted in the picture of Mount Wutai, and why were textual and visual depictions of the sacred site not produced in greater numbers until this period?

Until more evidence is found, it would be difficult to properly address the first question, but we may approach it indirectly, by answering the second. To represent Mount Wutai in its entirety requires first conceptualizing on a smaller scale its five soaring peaks and extensive spatial range. Two examples from the eighth century, the base of the stone lantern (see fig. 4.3), from 713–39, and a stone engraving with the title "Picture of [Mount] Wutai" (Wutai tu) (see fig. 4.4), from 758–77, are early attempts to do just this. In them, Mount Wutai was represented schematically, with four peaks at the four cardinal directions and one in the center. In the later eighth and early ninth centuries, in comparison, it was the monastery that played a more notable role in the presentation of Mount Wutai in its totality, the religious import of which may have consequently prompted more demands for and creations of both visual and textual representation. This rising importance of the monastery can be explained by the nature of the monastery system and the growth of pilgrimage to Mount Wutai.

The fivefold monastic system promoted by Amoghavajra was eclipsed by a new, tenfold system, the ten great monasteries of Mount Wutai (*Wutaishan shisi*).[5] This term is first recorded as part of an official title, that of the chief officer of the ten great monasteries at Mount Wutai (*Wutaishan shisi dujianjiao*); the first monk assigned to the post was Zhijun (d. 853), an eminent monk affiliated with the Huayan Monastery during the first half of the ninth century.[6] The appearance of this post in charge of the administrative branch of the monastic community suggests that a much more institutionalized Mount Wutai was taking shape then, and also that its center had, again, returned to Huayan Monastery. As far as which monasteries were included among the ten, however, there are no records until much later.[7] This evident lack of emphasis on which monasteries were the most important may have been due to the fact that the tenfold system was not initially a fixed designation, but a more flexible notion, representing and epitomizing the complete monastic establishment and community as a whole. Ten not only doubles five but is also the number of greatest fullness in the numerology of the *Flower Garland Sutra*.[8] The phrase "ten great monasteries of Mount Wutai," in this view, did not merely function as a shorthand expression, but more important, referred to the holistic, coherent entirety of the sacred mountain and all its content. This entirety made Mount Wutai as a whole more perceivable on the one hand, but it also required a change of viewpoint.

A close look at the list of monasteries at Mount Wutai provided in Yanyi's *Extended Records* (ca. 1060) will elucidate this changed viewpoint.[9] Although close to two centuries later than the period of our discussion, Yanyi's list—consisting of seventy-two monasteries in all, built in both pre-Tang and Tang periods—is nonetheless the most comprehensive among extant texts and thus the best representation of the ways in which monasteries at Mount Wutai were grouped. But, it is also the most puzzling, particularly, in terms of the geographic locations of the monasteries with respect to the five sacred peaks. For instance, among the monasteries grouped with Central Peak is a short list of monasteries in more or less close proximity to the peak: Huayan Monastery, Zhulin Monastery, and Yuhua Monastery; yet it also includes other monasteries—Jin'ge Monastery, Qingliang Monastery, and Foguang Monastery—that are closer to South Peak (see map 2, in Introduction). All these monasteries are among the most renowned in the history of the sacred site, and they could be all associated with Central Peak only if this association was viewed in terms of their "central positions" in the history of Mount Wutai, rather than in strict geographic terms. This mismatch of monasteries with their actual geographic locations in the *Extended Records* suggests a more fluid and conceptualized relation between monasteries and the five peaks. Indeed, if the natural geography is a "form of representing the world as real,"[10] the "ten monasteries of Mount Wutai" as a whole represents a very different landscape of the sacred site, one that was created, enlivened, and substantiated by pilgrimage.

While the tenfold monastic system was more of a conceptual notion, it was pilgrimage that provided an embodied viewpoint that perceived the sacred site on foot, turning the system into a peripatetic practice. A long poem eulogizing the pilgrimage at Mount Wutai has survived in several manuscripts from Dunhuang, all dated to the tenth century. Entitled *Eulogy on Mount Wutai* (Wutaishan zan), the poem begins by calling the attention of Buddhist disciples (e.g., pilgrims) to the Five Sacred Peaks of Mount Wutai, in which the Great Sage Mañjuśrī dwells. This section concludes with the stanza:

> Disciples,
> The holy lamps blaze and blaze, arrayed before us,
> Illuminating the divine mountain so that it is bright everywhere.
> The mountain abounds with numinous and extraordinary birds,
> The music at the ten monasteries of [Mount] Wutai resounds and resounds.[11]

The phrase "ten monasteries of [Mount] Wutai" (Wutai *shisi*) in this stanza, though not referring to specific monasteries, maps the monasteries over the sacred site as part of the itinerary and narrative of the pilgrimage. Either itinerary or narrative provides an overarching structure that connects individual components of the sacred topography into a greater coherent landscape, which consequently lends itself to representation.[12]

The growing number of representations of Mount Wutai in various media and scale, from the ninth century onward correlates with the emergence of a more holistic unity to the sacred site, shaped by both the institutional system and the thriving pilgrimage scene. These depictions in turn essentialized the site's sacrality, a full experience of which could not otherwise be acquired. The representation of Mount Wutai, more than simply re-presenting the mountains, could conjure a vision of the sacred site with iconic economy, ritualistic import, and salvific purpose. In this regard, it was "visualization," rather than representation, that made Mount Wutai transferable.[13] The depiction therefore attempts a kind of transposition, whether to a woodcut print or lantern base or cave chapel. Although the transposition of a sacred site is difficult to achieve—as pointed out in the epigraph to this chapter—such an effort was undertaken at the Mogao caves near Dunhuang, Gansu, during the mid-tenth century. Mogao Cave 61, built between 947 and 951 and dedicated to Bodhisattva Mañjuśrī and his sacred abode, was designed to recreate Mount Wutai and enact the divine presence of the bodhisattva in a cave located thousands of miles west of the actual mountain site (see map 1). The recreation, in turn, mediated the sacrality of the sacred site right in the cave,[14] and sheds light on the interrelation between mountain and monastery in the last phase of Mount Wutai's history in medieval China. By transporting Mount Wutai inside its space, the cave constitutes a materialized discourse of the monastery at the sacred mountain, in short, a "metamonastery," revealing the qualities that made Mount Wutai into a Buddhist sacred mountain.

Spatial Practice: Pilgrimage and Monastic System

The most important and complete pilgrimage account of Mount Wutai during this period is that of Ennin, who traveled in China from 838 to 847 and recorded in detail the Buddhist practice in Tang China in his travel journal *The Record of a Pilgrimage to China in Search of the Law* (Nittō guhō junrei gyōki).[15] Ennin visited Mount Wutai for about three months in 840, and the record that he kept during his sojourn is the most important firsthand source for ninth-century Mount Wutai. Following Ennin's footsteps moves us to see the ways in which Mount Wutai was structured holistically for him as a sacred site.

Pilgrimage on foot connects and appropriates into a continuous itinerary and spatial narrative what appears disjunctive on a map: routes, locales, topography, and architecture. A sacred site can be thought of as being created by the steps of pilgrims along an itinerary, regardless of how transitory and traceless those steps are.[16] For an itinerary is also necessarily prescriptive, in that a pilgrimage through the space of a sacred site necessarily brings about, or enacts, certain religious results and spiritual experiences particular to the site. This is not to discount individual versions of the spatial narrative, such as the one by Ennin—a master of the Japanese Tendai (C: Tiantai) school, who undertook his pilgrimage at Mount Wutai with certain sectarian purposes in mind.[17] Ennin, moreover, appeared to have been well informed in the history, tales, and legends of Mount Wutai, and was also aware of the major monasteries that were the most popular pilgrimage destinations before his arrival in China. Reading between the prescribed itinerary and individual enunciation of the space, one will find in Ennin's journal of Mount Wutai a structured narrative and a coherent site.

Traveling to Mount Wutai from the east, Ennin appeared to follow the most developed route to the sacred site during his time. Entering, he took the major route going northwest from Zhenzhou, present-day Zhengding, in Hebei; exiting, he took the main southbound route that ended in Taiyuan, in Shanxi (map 11).[18] Along the way, leading to and leaving from the mountain range, he mentioned altogether twenty-two pilgrim way stations (*putong yuan*), lodges or rest stops that provided meals and accommodations free to all pilgrims.[19] No details about these places were recorded, yet these way stations could be found along both of the routes. On his way through the region, Ennin recorded hundreds of monks and nuns, both Chinese and foreign, that he met at several of those stops, as well as official envoys and beasts of burden carrying items for monastic use. The activities documented in Ennin's journal before he reached the mountain range are evidence of the thriving practice of pilgrimage in the region peripheral to the sacred site, which, though still not Mount Wutai, was a prelude to one's arrival at the sacred mountain.

Six days after passing Zhenzhou, Ennin finally reached Tingdian way station, the last stop before entering Mount Wutai, and from there he could see Central Peak rising high in the distance. With Mount Wutai in sight, Ennin, in tears, dropped to his knees in worship; he wrote, "This is Mount Qingliang [i.e., Mount Wutai], the Golden World [i.e., Pure Land] [of Bodhisattva Mañjuśrī], who mani-

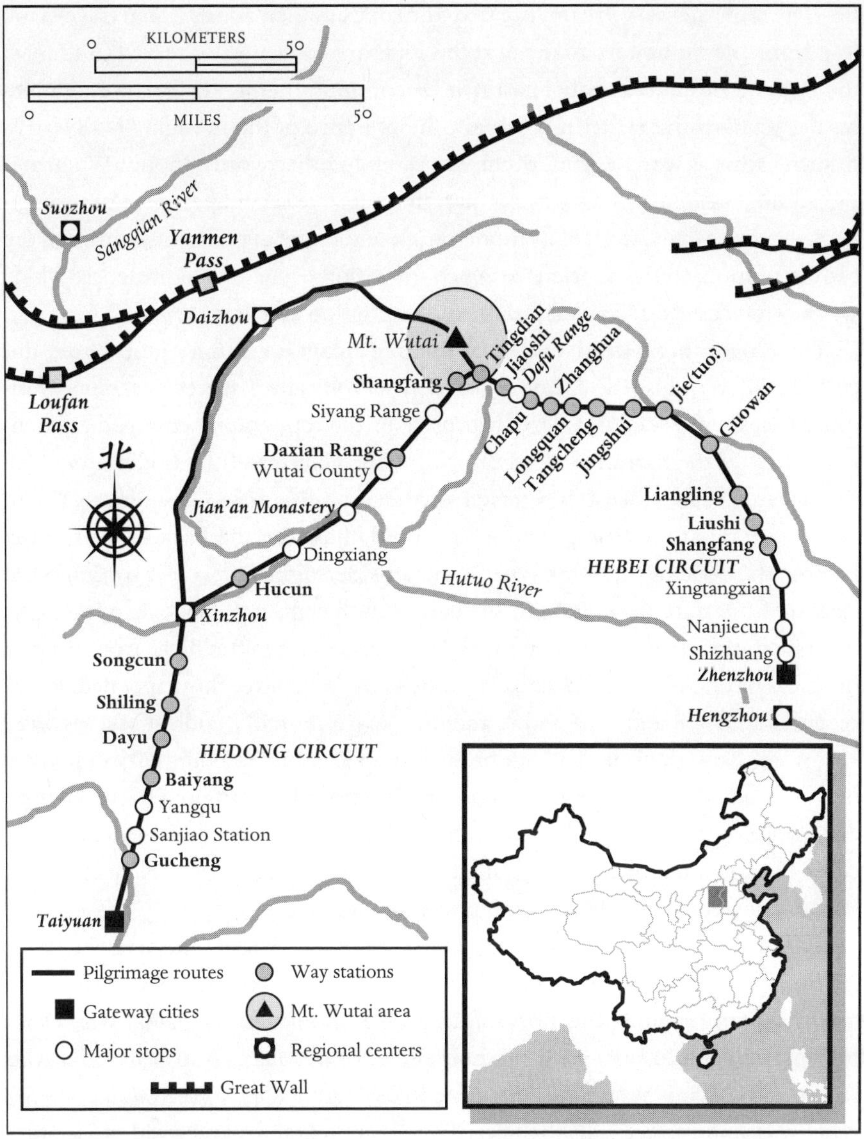

MAP 11. The major stops and pilgrim way stations along two major pilgrimage routes, as described by Ennin, *The Record of a Pilgrimage to China* (Nittō guhō junrei gyōki), mid-ninth century.

fests himself right here for our benefit."[20] After his long travels, the distance was finally overcome, and the sacred landscape with its soaring peaks confirmed Ennin's understanding that he had arrived. The sight of the mountains and his prostration and tears served to mark the point of transition from the outer mountain range into the most sacred center.

Indeed, after he entered the sacred domain, anchored by its five peaks, Ennin's diary became longer and more substantive, almost all about the monasteries. He lodged at three of the major ones, Zhulin Monastery, Huayan Monastery, and Jin'ge Monastery, and visited several others, such as Yuhua Monastery, Qingliang Monastery, Dali Fahua Monastery, and Foguang Monastery. At these monasteries, Ennin paid particular attention to different rituals and lectures and provided descriptions of several image halls—both their iconic programs and building interiors. The monasteries were not isolated from one another, and as Ennin traveled on foot from one monastery to the next, his itinerary conveniently served to connect the monasteries into a spatial narrative. A common theme, furthermore, unifies his diary's narrative structure, namely, the presence of the presiding bodhisattva in such forms as icon, legend, ritual, or vision. In other words, Mount Wutai as a sacred site in Ennin's diary was not just about its five sacred peaks, but more important, about the system of its monasteries; and it was in pilgrimage through the system of monasteries that one attained the vision of the divine presence, which was key to acquiring spiritual insight and inspiration at Mount Wutai.

This diachronic narrative time of the pilgrimage in Ennin's journal did not exclude different historical times evoked synchronically. Layered meanings from other times embedded in a particular place or the topography emerged as an integral part of the narrative. For example, at the Cloister of the Bodhisattva Hall (Pusa Tang Yuan), formerly Cloister of the True Presence (Zhengrong Yuan), Ennin venerated the true-presence icon of Mañjuśrī on the back of his spirited lion. At the conclusion of his veneration, an elder monk explained to Ennin the legend of the statue's creation in the early eighth century.[21] Since its miraculous beginning, the elder monk continued, "the statue has emitted light from time to time and frequently manifested auspicious signs. Whenever this happened, it was recorded in detail and reported to the throne; [in return] Buddhist scarves were bestowed. Now the one that can be seen draped over the bodhisattva's body is one of these."[22] The divine trace, icon, and legend, all contributed to the identity and meaning of this particular place, where the divine presence of the bodhisattva could be worshiped and offerings made. In narrative, the sense of *place* at Mount Wutai is necessarily made up of multiple temporalities.

Similarly, when Ennin paid a visit to the Diamond Grotto (Jin'gang Ku), both its history and legends were called to mind. After describing his arrival at the grotto, Ennin recounts the story of the Indian monk Buddhapālita, who came to Mount Wutai to search for the holy presence of Mañjuśrī in 676,[23] and who returned to Mount Wutai a second time in 683 with a copy of the *Sutra of the Superlative Dhāraṇī of the Buddha's Crown*. "Whereupon Mañjuśrī received and led him into this grotto," Ennin continued. "As soon as Buddhapālita entered, the entrance of the grotto closed of itself, and it has not opened to this day."[24] In his narrative, he stands in front of the grotto entrance, mediating what is known from the past but is silent about the present.

This is the second mention of Buddhapālita in Ennin's diary. Already at Zhulin Monastery, the first monastery at which he lodged at Mount Wutai, Ennin described seeing an image depicting the Indian monk meeting Mañjuśrī in the disguise of an elder next to the portrait of the Pure Land master Fazhao, who was reported to have met with Buddhapālita in 770 at the grotto. His second mention of Fazhao comes after he concludes his veneration at the grotto entrance. Ennin describes climbing a slope to reach two image halls that may have been built after Fazhao; "It was here," Ennin wrote, that the "Monk of Great Awakening [i.e., Fazhao] observed the [vision of the bodhisattva's] Golden World."[25] Through

Ennin's footsteps—as he arrived, moved, walked up—and in his peripatetic view, different segments of history and legends, initially disjunct and fragmented in time and space, were evoked and reenacted in the coherent spatial narrative of the place.

Ennin also mentioned Buddhapālita once more when he was leaving Mount Wutai. Traveling southward, Ennin first left the area of monasteries connected by the pilgrimage circuit (see map 11). From there, he wrote:

> Walking further southwest for about seven *li,* [we] arrived at Siyang Range [Siyang Ling]. In the first year of the Yifeng reign [676] the Indian monk of the Western Lands, Buddhapālita, reached here. His tears rained down, when he worshiped Mount [Wu]tai from a distance, [which] moved the Great Sage to appear in the disguise of an elder. Here is the place where [Buddhapālita] was ordered to return to India and obtain a copy of the *Buddha Crown [Dhāraṇī Sutra*]. A [sutra] pillar erected then still can be seen today inscribed with the *Buddha Crown Dhāraṇī* [*Sutra*] and its preface, in which the story of Buddhapālita meeting with the elder is mentioned.[26]

This account, no doubt, harks back to Ennin's report of the Diamond Grotto, thus linking together two important moments and places in the Buddhapālita legend: his encounter of Mañjuśrī disguised as an elder here at Siyang Range and his disappearance after following Mañjuśrī into the grotto. In addition to the historical narrative, this account was also self-referential, referring to the earlier two occasions in which the name of Buddhapālita was brought up in the narrative of Ennin's pilgrimage. Taken together, the three occasions marked Ennin's pilgrimage in such a way that he seems to have relived the spiritual journey of the Indian monk, who visited Mount Wutai about one hundred years before him, in a reversed temporal sequence. Now at Siyang Range near the end of his journey, reading the inscription on the sutra pillar about the tears that Buddhapālita shed upon arriving and seeing Mount Wutai—echoing his own when he first sighted the sacred site—Ennin's pilgrimage had come full circle. In this fullness, the textual narrative in Ennin's diary reveals vicariously to his readers one truer religious experience and a higher reality of completeness—multiple temporalities and localities of the sacred site in a structured and integrated whole.

Traveling on foot is more than a gymnastic exercise, and in the case of a pilgrimage such as this one at a mountain site, it entails a "walking up" that takes on the meaning of "spiritual ascension" with a particular purpose and implication.[27] It appropriates and transforms individual geographic particularities of the natural terrain into a continuous itinerary, or narrative, of the religious topography and landscape, marked literally by a series of footnotes. In Ennin's diary, the pilgrimage to Mount Wutai shapes the landscape in a unique way, such that it can be conceived as consisting of three concentric areas: the larger region of Mount Wutai (from Zhenzhou to Taiyuan), the mountain area, and the sacred center defined by the monastery system. Each major monastery in the system, furthermore, is a particular locus, wherein specific events are observed, signs searched, and history and memory recalled, together creating layers of past and present evocations peculiar to the monastery. But the experience at each monastery is also contextualized in the new narrative time and space of pilgrimage, making each locus incomplete without others.

At the center of the pilgrimage, and the climax of its narrative, was the vision or visionary experience of divine manifestation. As indicated in Ennin's account, the statue of Mañjuśrī riding the lion continued to be the most powerful icon of the bodhisattva at Mount Wutai during the ninth century, and in all likelihood, into the tenth century. Another of the manuscripts found at Dunhuang is a travel diary from 926–36, by an Indian pilgrim named Puhua. In the diary, Puhua, after reaching Huayan Monastery, writes:

> [We] asked to venerate the [icon of the] true presence, and were able to finally fulfill the wish. We earnestly worshiped [the icon] until the night and lodged in the monastery, while our devotion became deeper. Holy lanterns suddenly appeared; we all observed [the marvels] and not one did not feel the joy. [The next day] on the twentieth, renewing our sincere dedication, we revisited the sacred hall. At night, we beheld the true image [of the statue], which suddenly emitted radiance from its forehead between the eyebrows, lighting up the holy visage like the hanging bright moon. After seeing the divine omen, [our hearts] became even more earnest.[28]

An intensified desire to obtain the true vision of Mañjuśrī, indeed, is a recurrent theme in the pilgrimage literature of Mount Wutai during the ninth and tenth centuries. It endowes the narrative with purpose, as well as supplying a climactic moment, when the vision is manifested before the faithful pilgrim. In this long period, the vision of the bodhisattva and the transcendent reality of the sacred site could not be separated from the increasingly totalized and conceptualized Mount Wutai portrayed in the pilgrimage literature. The representation of the vision made the revelatory vision more perceivable, tangible, believable, and transmittable, giving rise to a more imaginable religious experience—and helping the spread of the bodhisattva cult.[29]

Vision and Visualization

Leaving Siyang Range, Ennin passed through the South Mountain Gate of Mount Wutai (Wutai Nan Shanmen)[30] on the way to Taiyuan, the regional urban center, then also serving as the southern gateway to Mount Wutai. In the city, he continued his pilgrimage to several monasteries, while also stopping to transcribe several "steles and records related to the various divine manifestations of Mount Wutai."[31] Separately, a Chinese monk, Yiyuan, who accompanied Ennin during the last part of his pilgrimage at Mount Wutai, commissioned an artist to make a painting, titled "Picture of Transformative Manifestations at Mount Wutai" (Wutaishan huaxian tu).[32] Neither the transcriptions nor the painting have survived, but the use of the term "transformative manifestation" (C: *huaxian;* S: *nirmāṇa*) in the title is suggestive. If the term refers to the transformative power of Bodhisattva

Mañjuśrī to manifest in different forms, either as an auspicious sign or in his true presence, the visual image most likely would have comprised the vision of the divine manifestation over the sacred mountain.[33] The absence of the painting as visual evidence may be compensated for by Yiyuan's comments on the religious function of the representation when he presented it to Ennin: "I am pleased to have met with you, and have venerated the [sacred] peaks and beheld the bodhisattva's transformation manifestations together. Now I present to you the 'Picture of Transformative Manifestations' [Huaxian tu]. Please bring it back to Japan and venerate it with offerings, so it may enable the viewer to have an earnest intention for enlightenment and to advance those who possess favorable karma to be reborn together in the Assembly where Mañjuśrī preaches."[34] To a great extent, the fundamental benefit for a pilgrim who observes and venerates the bodhisattva's holy presence at Mount Wutai was acquiring the spiritual aspiration for enlightenment and a favorable karma that would lead to a rebirth in Mañjuśrī's Assembly. In this regard, the painting (*tu*) was not merely a pictorial form that re-presents the mountain, but a sacred image that could both simulate the pilgrimage through Mount Wutai and consequently stimulate the vision of the divine manifestation (*huaxian*) attainable only at the sacred mountain. As to how these purposes were translated in visual form, however, we can only speculate from later examples.

A vision in the context of pilgrimage is a supernatural manifestation, observed by a viewer in a direct and unmediated encounter as a transcendent reality. It could be experienced as a dream, in a trance, or at a numinous or sacred site, where normal order and empirical logic are no longer relevant.[35] A vision thus entails the divine manifestation and a recipient who observes the vision at a favorable place and time. Items like the painting Yiyuan gave to Ennin have the purpose and function of transmitting this vision. Transmission, in this context, is not merely the *representation* of what and how the divinity manifests, but the *visualization*, that is, the making visual, of the ethereal presence of the divinity and its spiritual potency as received by the recipient. The paradigm of this "visualization" would be the true-presence (*zhenrong*) icon of Mañjuśrī riding his lion, which, according to its creation legend, not only materialized the divine presence, but also visually constituted part of the sacred essence. Therefore, the icon was not just an image of the bodhisattva but something that could help the viewer visualize his "true presence." Moreover, once the true-presence icon became popular in the early eighth century, visions at Mount Wutai began to show the five peaks as a cohesive realm centered on the true-presence icon. Religious vision and visualization thus functioned dialectically, involving ways of both seeing and understanding the otherwise ineffable and transitory.[36] In this light, visualization (e.g., "representation" of vision)[37]—iconic or narrative—would have to involve mediating the belief visually according to specific religious praxis and doctrines, as well as visual conventions. In other words, vision is not static, and different ways of visualizing, such as in different contexts or media, suggest shifting ideas about the vision as to how it should be interpreted and constructed. The fact that the imagery of Mount Wutai transmuted over time after it was transmitted outside of its mountain site also indicates

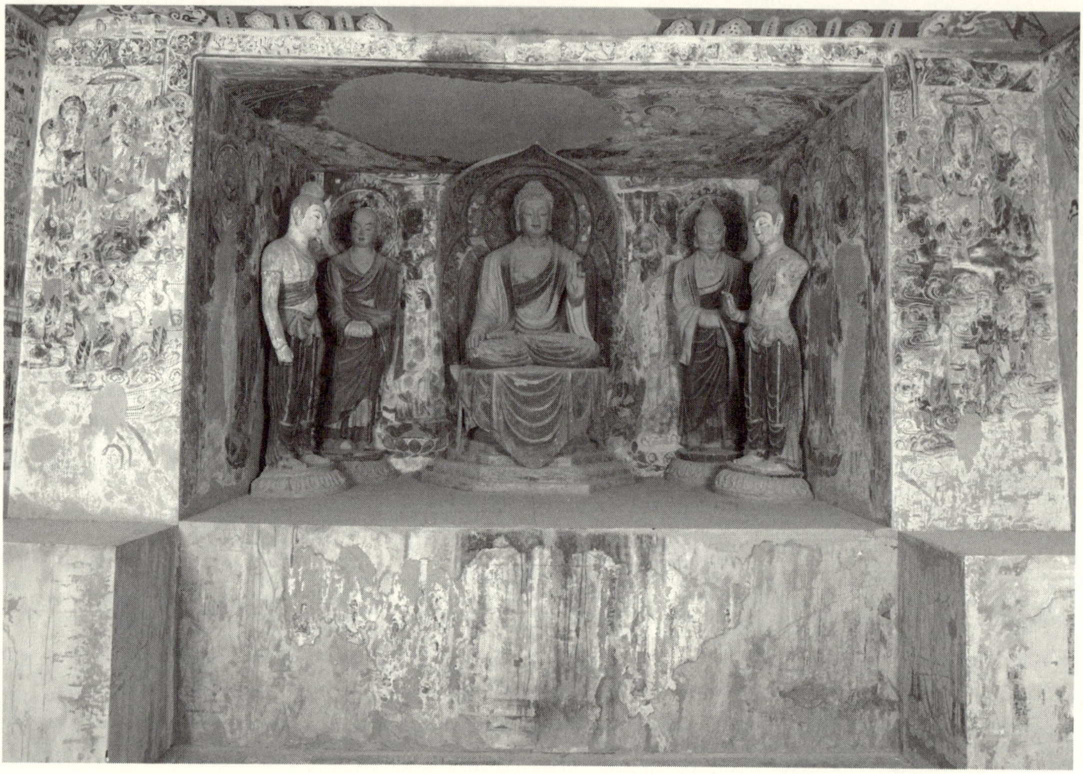

FIGURE 6.1a. Main niche on the west wall of Mogao Cave 220, flanked by two murals outside the niche: Mañjuśrī riding a lion on the right (north) and Samantabhadra riding an elephant on the left (south), Dunhuang. 642 CE. Photograph courtesy of Sun Xiaogang.

the different ways of construing and appropriating the vision of the divinity and his sacred site by those who viewed and put it to work. In this transmission, nevertheless, the different visualizations made explicit the most essential components of the sacrality that made Mount Wutai, illuminating the ways in which Mount Wutai and its monasteries were conceptualized during the ninth and tenth centuries.

Mount Wutai in Transmission and Transposition

Around the time of Ennin's travel in China, murals depicting Mount Wutai began to be painted in the Mogao caves near Dunhuang, in the outlying area close to the western border of Tang China, about three thousand kilometers from Mount Wutai. Ennin's travels coincided with the period of Tibetan occupation in Dunhuang from 781 until 848,[38] and the transmission of the imagery of Mount Wutai may have begun in 824 when the Tibetan king solicited the Tang court for a copy of the representation of Mount Wutai. Long before 824, however, the iconography of the bodhisattva, including Mañjuśrī riding a lion, was already developed in the Mogao caves, and this would have been the iconographic tradition to which the transmitted imagery of Mount Wutai needed to adapt. The new imagery, the picture of Mount Wutai, was necessarily part of the overall iconographic program of the cave, a religious setting in which it would have been interpreted. In other words, transmitted to the Dunhuang region, the vision of Mount Wutai was no longer an isolated image but had to be reoriented in the new visual field and religious context, both different from its origin in China. Still, the essential concern of this transmission was how the divine presence of the bodhisattva was to be reenvisioned in and through the architectural space of the cave.

The bodhisattva Mañjuśrī, in Mahayana Buddhist iconography, is depicted in various forms, based on the bodhisattva's role described in sutras; the most prominent and also most relevant to this present discussion is that of Mañjuśrī mounted on the lion's back. It was already in the Mogao caves as early as the seventh century during the early Tang, where Mañjuśrī riding a lion was paired with the bodhisattva Samantabhadra riding an elephant.[39] The pair of bodhisattvas most often appears in the caves on either side of the east-facing central niche on the rear wall. As in Cave 220 (figs. 6.1a, 6.1b), dated to 642, the two bodhisattvas are accompanied by their heavenly attendants and the clouds on which they stand are floating toward the central niche, which resembles a celestial stage on which the central Buddha is delivering the sutra sermon.[40] Entering the eighth and ninth centuries, the pair of bodhisattvas became more elaborate, with the use of intricately patterned aureoles and mandorlas that define the bodhisattvas' hieratic positions. The heavenly entourage of the bodhisattvas also grew, including, in the case of a mural in Cave 159 from the early ninth century, a dark-skinned animal tamer, angelic musicians and dancers, and ferocious guardians (figs. 6.2a, 6.2c). In the background of this expanded celestial group is a mountain landscape, rendered simply and in a rather generic style, suggesting an aerial space through which the band of celestials is traveling.[41] Mount Wutai is not identified in this mural, and neither is the mountain depicted behind Samantabhadra on the opposite panel, although this bodhisattva's sacred site at Mount Emei had just become known around this same period.[42] The appearance of mountainscapes in both scenes, nonetheless, suggests an existing knowledge and perhaps worship of Bodhisattva Mañjuśrī in Dunhuang.

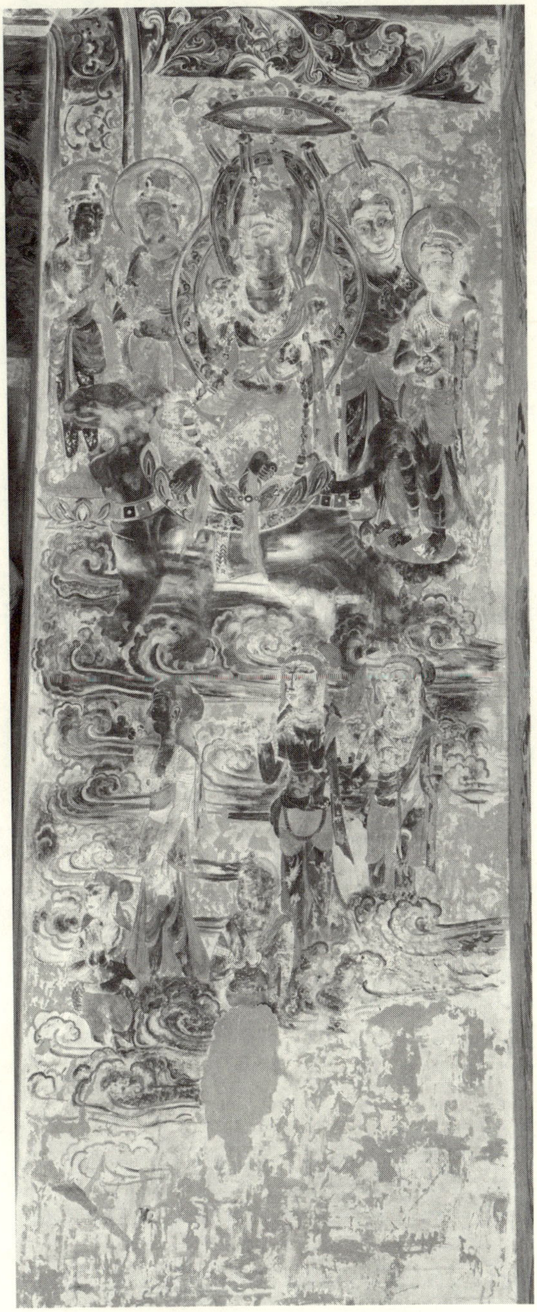

FIGURE 6.1b. Mural to the right (north) of the main niche, depicting Mañjuśrī on a lion's back, along with other celestial deities, transported by clouds toward the central niche. From Sun Xiaogang, *Wenshu pusa tuxiang*, pl. 21. Photograph courtesy of Sun Xiaogang.

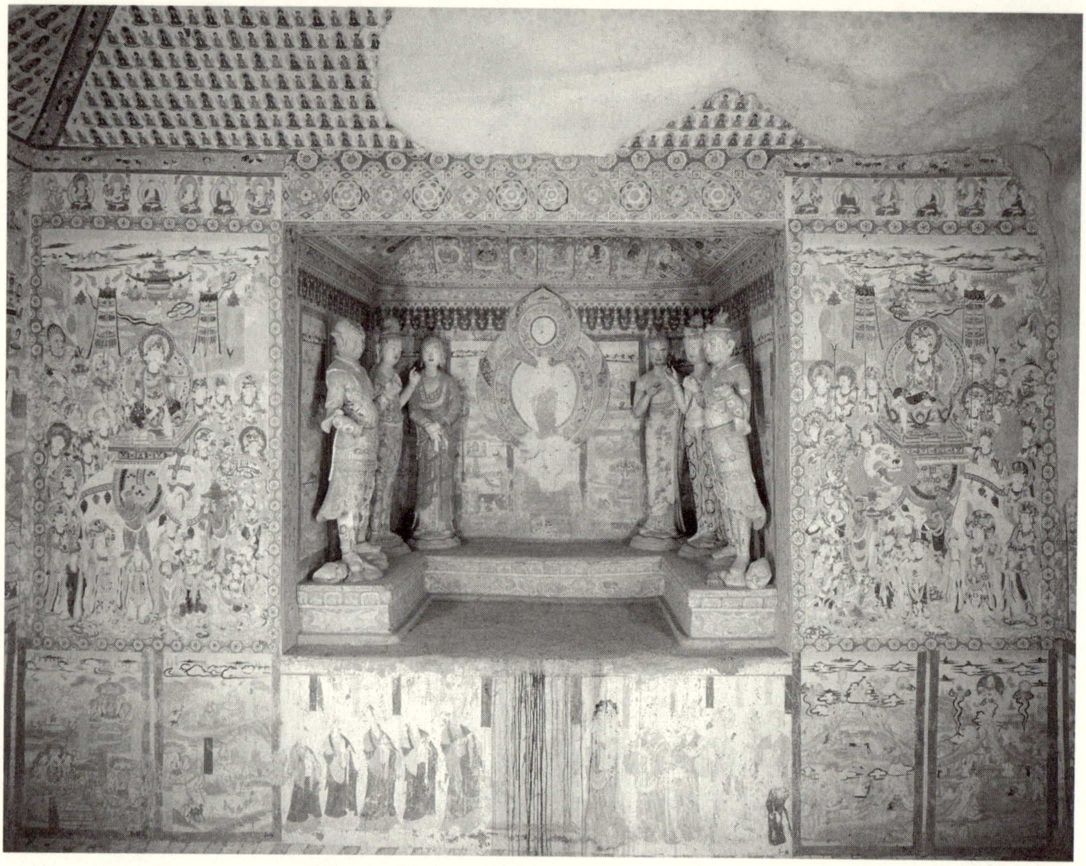

FIGURE 6.2a. West wall of Mogao Cave 159, Dunhuang. Early 9th century CE. Dunhuang Wenwu Yanjiusuo, *Dunhuang Mogaoku,* vol. 4, pl. 75. Photograph permission by Wenwu Press.

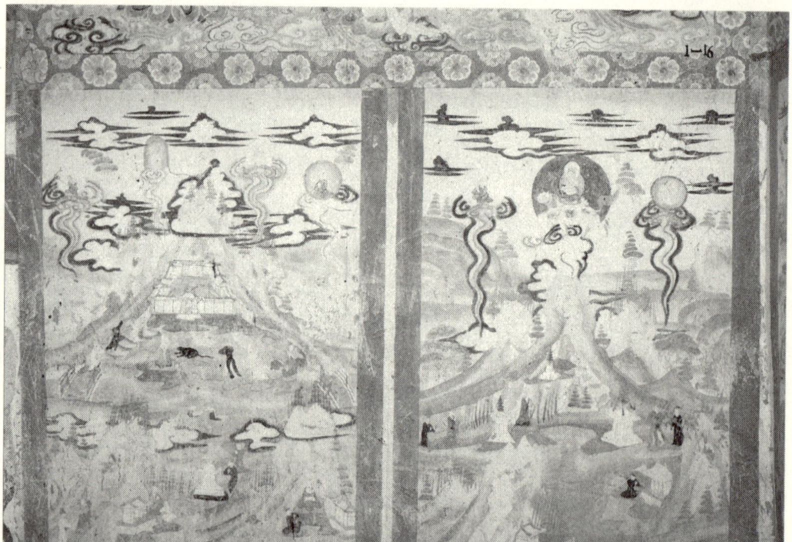

FIGURE 6.2b. Mural in the lower section to the right (north) of the main niche, Mogao Cave 159, depicting Mount Wutai with the Five Sacred Peaks, monastic structures, and religious activities. Mañjuśrī riding a lion flying in midair appears in the right panel above one sacred peak. Dunhuang Wenwu Yanjiusuo, *Dunhuang Mogaoku,* vol. 4, pl. 76. Photograph by permission of Wenwu Press.

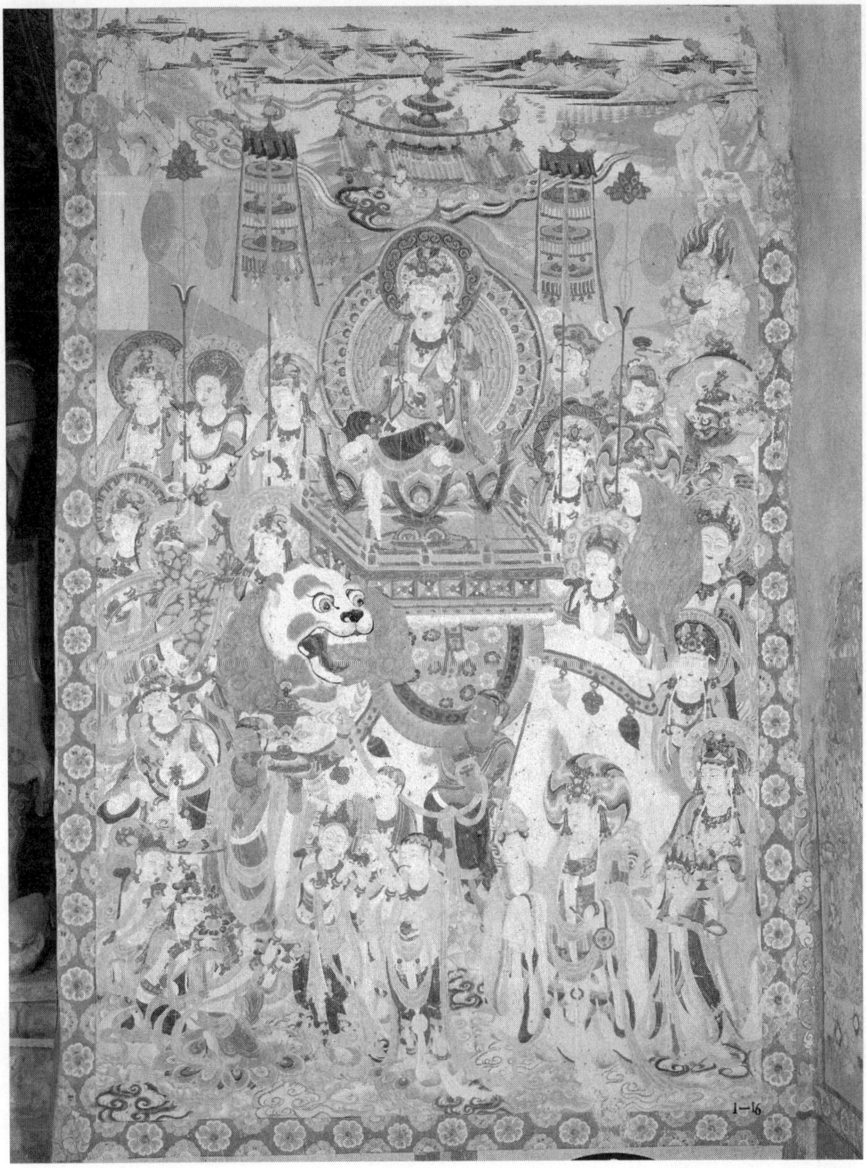

FIGURE 6.2c. Mural to the right (north) of the main niche, Mogao Cave 159, depicting Mañjuśrī riding a lion with his entourage transported by clouds toward the central niche. Mountain landscape can be discerned in the top of the background. Dunhuang Wenwu Yanjiusuo, *Dunhuang Mogaoku*, vol. 4, pl. 81. Photograph by permission of Wenwu Press.

From the outset the transmitted imagery of Mount Wutai was adopted to work in tandem with depictions of the bodhisattva.[43] In Cave 159, again, one finds the earliest complete view of Mount Wutai, depicted in a diptych, located on the lower right, just below the mural of Mañjuśrī surrounded by his entourage (fig. 6.2b). The sacred peaks are disposed across the two panels, leaving room below and above for the lower terrain and the sky; on the left panel a major monastic complex is linked via bridges and routes to other monastic structures, around which several figures are engaged in different religious activities; more such figures and structures are visible on the right panel. Above the summits, various miraculous manifestations appear, including, on the right panel, the bodhisattva riding a lion; the two are in profile and surrounded by a nimbus, as if flying across the sky.

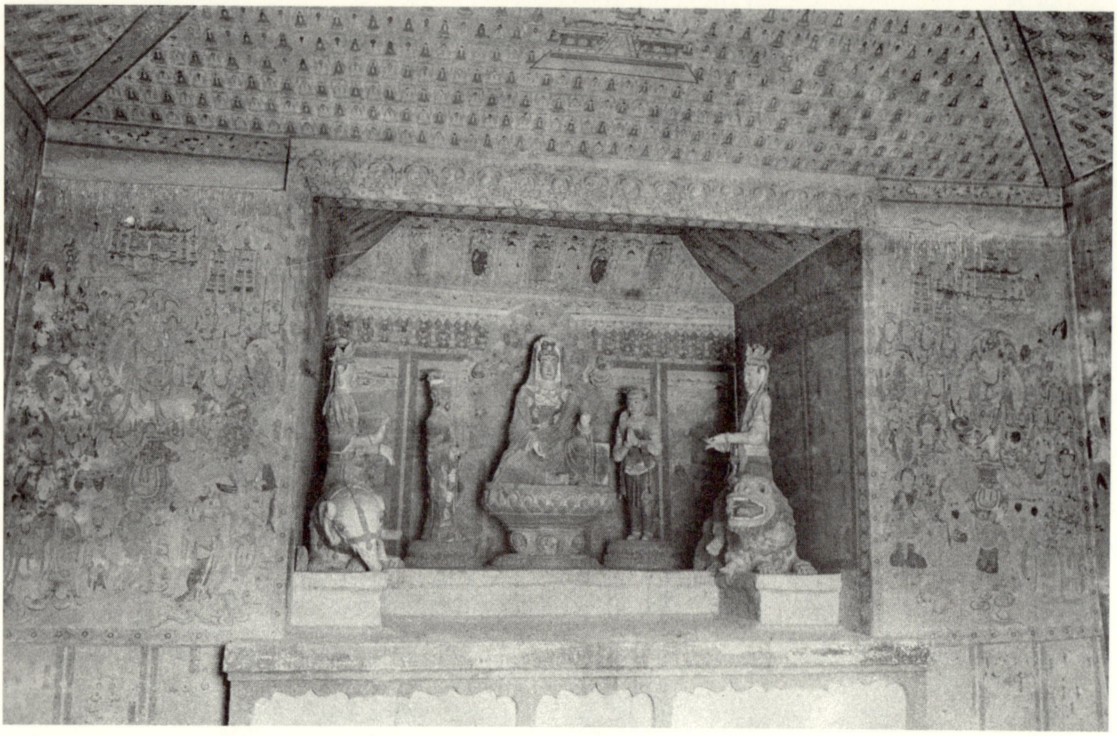

FIGURE 6.3a. West wall of Mogao Cave 237, Dunhuang. Early 9th century CE. The mural of Mount Wutai is depicted in the triptych in the lower section to the right (north) of the main niche. Photograph by permission of the Lo Archive.

The scene—the five sacred peaks, monastic buildings, zealous pilgrims, and above all, the vision of the divinity—epitomizes the totalized Mount Wutai, consistent with the sacred site portrayed in Ennin's narrative. Other pictorial elements, for instance, the floating clouds painted in horizontal calligraphic strokes that taper at both ends, enhance the sense of movement and simultaneity of the apparitions in midair. Viewed together with the mural above, the lion-riding Mañjuśrī flying over Mount Wutai corresponds to the same movement of Mañjuśrī and his entourage transported on clouds toward the central niche in the larger mural above. The parallel between the two murals is suggestive, in terms of not only their iconography but also their function and meaning in the religious program inside the cave: the Mañjuśrī in the upper mural that flanks the central niche can now visually derive its authority and authenticity from the "true presence" of the bodhisattva manifested at his sacred mountain, visualized in the lower mural.

This scene of Mount Wutai is necessarily framed in its particular iconographic ensemble, but the imagery appears also in other caves at Mogao, and becomes even more expansive. In Cave 237, also built in the first decades of the ninth century, the mural of Mount Wutai is located in the same position with respect to a central niche as in Cave 159, on the lower right (in both caves, these are on the north side of the niche), but the depiction is spread across three panels, instead of two (figs. 6.3a, 6.3b). The image has deteriorated, but the full view of the sacred site presented in panorama is still visible, showing West and South Peaks in the left panel, Central Peak in the center, and East and North Peaks in the right, identified by the inscriptions in cartouches that accompany them.[44] The number of

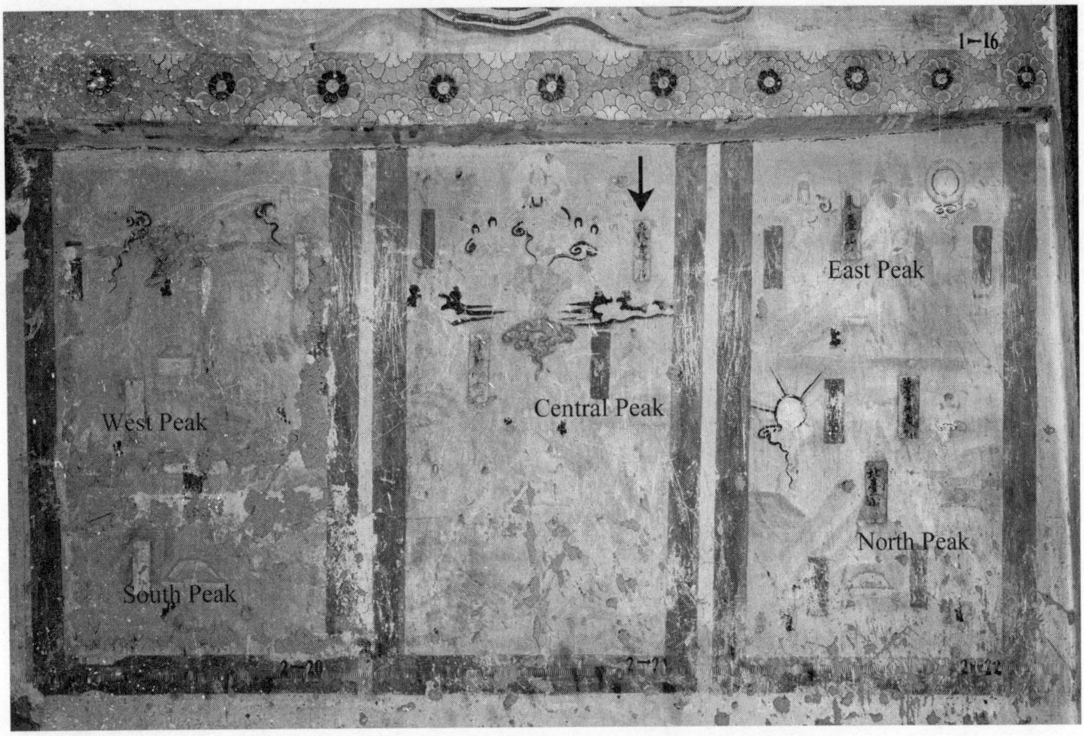

FIGURE 6.3b. Mural in the lower section to the right (north) of the main niche of Mogao Cave 237, showing the panorama of Mount Wutai. The inscription inside the cartouche (marked by an arrow), next to the image of Mañjuśrī riding a lion at the top center of the entire composition, reads: "The moment in which Bodhisattva Mañjuśrī manifests." Photograph by permission of Dunhuang Academy.

monastic structures and miraculous sightings that fill the mountain landscape has also increased. Mañjuśrī on his lion inside a nimbus is escorted by a large group of figures, representing the ten thousand fellow bodhisattvas attending him at Mount Wutai, and with his entourage dominates the sky right above Central Peak. The inscription in the cartouche to the right of the divine assembly underlines the commanding presence of the bodhisattva: "The moment in which Bodhisattva Mañjuśrī manifests" (*Wenshu pusa xian shi*). Here *xian* is likely a shorthanded rendering for *huaxian* (i.e., manifestation). The character *shi* (i.e., the moment) is a suffix frequently seen in cartouche inscriptions in Mogao murals to describe or emphasize the temporal aspect of devotional acts or miraculous events.[45] The *shi* in this case also serves to highlight the moment "right here and now" in the otherwise elusive manifestation of the bodhisattva. This moment of apparition corresponds to the motion depicted in the mural above, in which Mañjuśrī with his entourage are shown moving in time toward the central niche where the Buddha is preaching, as though about to arrive.

Considering their iconographic relation and function in the cave, it is not surprising that the initially separate subjects in Caves 159 and 237 were eventually merged into a single representation toward the end of this period. Cave 144 contains a single mural which conflates the two Mañjuśrīs—the one arriving at the Buddha's lecture and the other arriving at Mount Wutai (fig. 6.4).[46] Accompanied by the ten thousand bodhisattvas who crowd in midair, Mañjuśrī and his striding lion move majestically across the clouds above a mountain landscape dotted by monastic buildings. In another variation, from Cave 361, which has a niche within

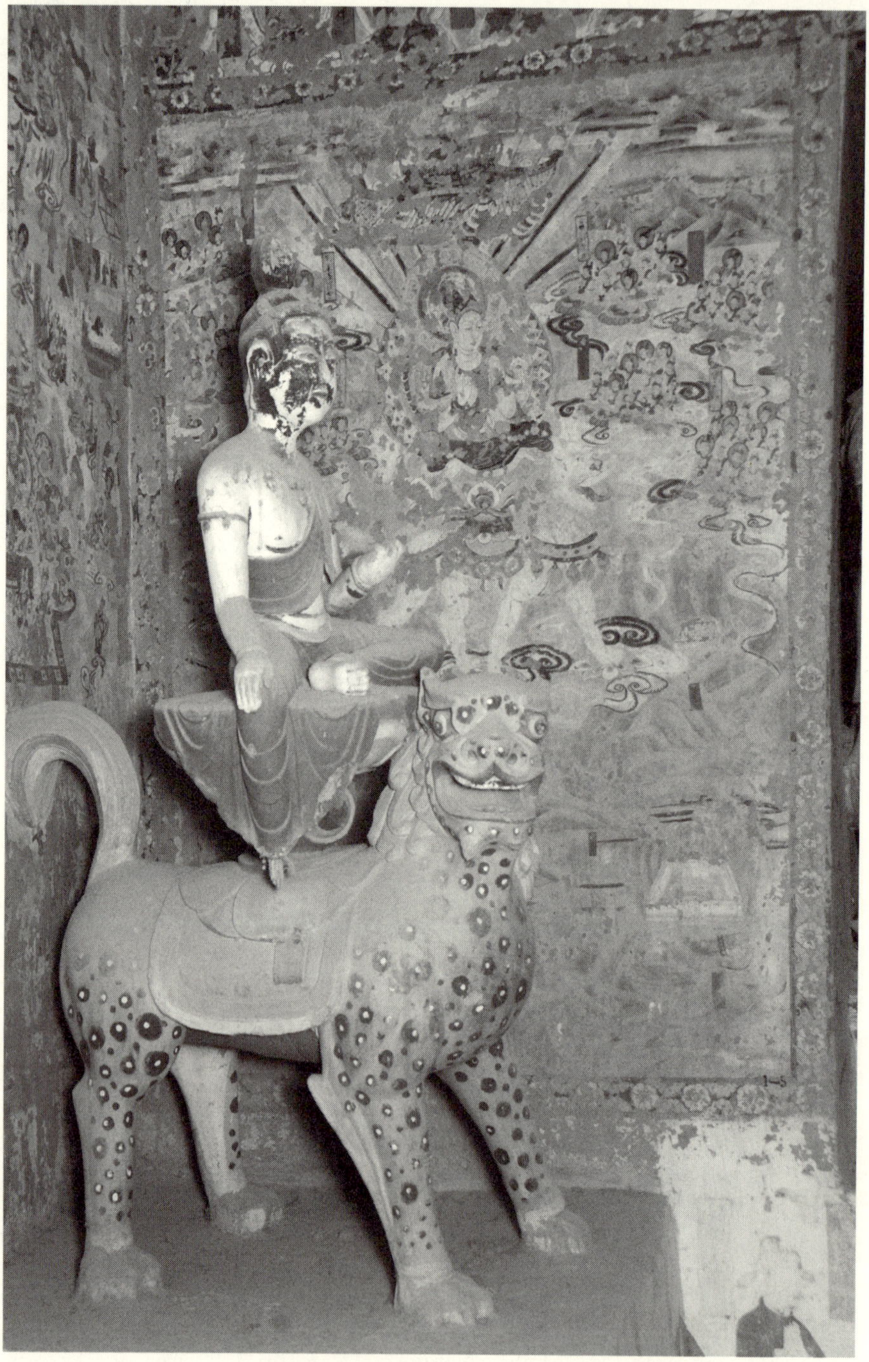

FIGURE 6.4. Mural to the left (south) on the west wall of Mogao Cave 144, Dunhuang, next to the main niche recessed into the same wall (visible on far right). 9th century CE. The mural depicts Mañjuśrī riding a lion, with his entourage, carried by clouds flying over Mount Wutai. In the foreground, a statue of Mañjuśrī and lion of a later date on a raised platform. Photograph by permission of Dunhuang Academy.

a niche, the mural is located on the right, in the right angle formed by the back and right (west and north) walls of the outer niche (fig. 6.5a); to accommodate the restricted space in the angle, the mural occupies two panels, like the panels of a screen joined at right angles. The full view of Mount Wutai is therefore not seen at once, but entails a viewing sequence, from the panel on the north wall, continuing into the next on the west, that is, from right to left (fig. 6.5b). One's

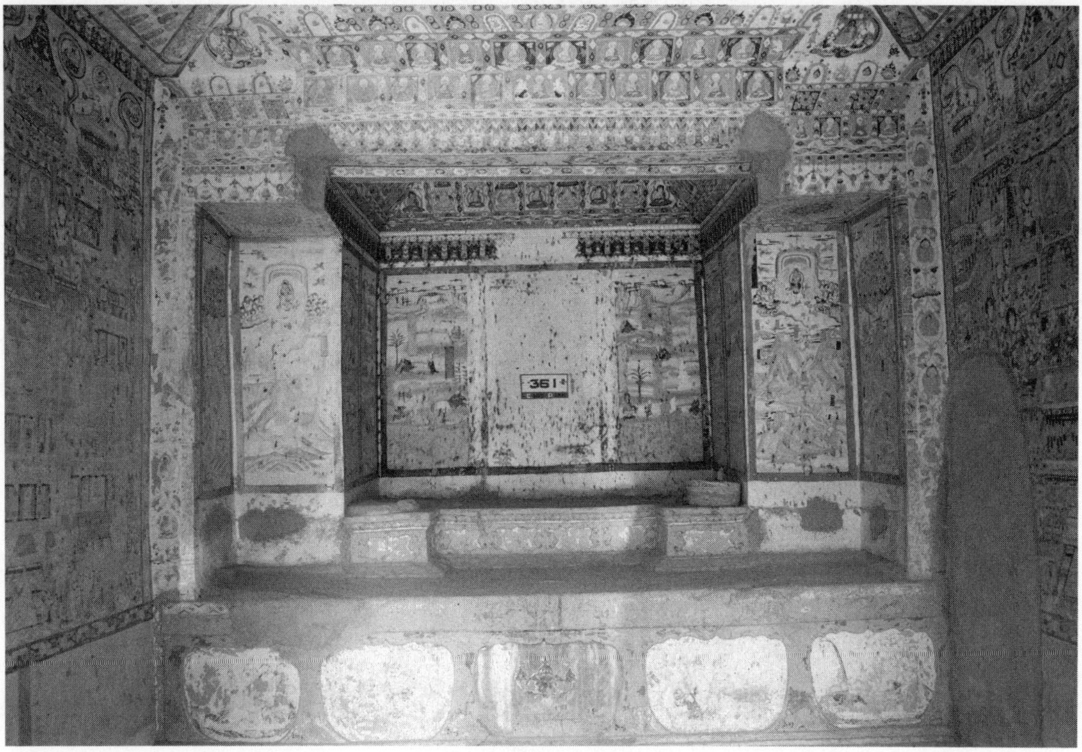

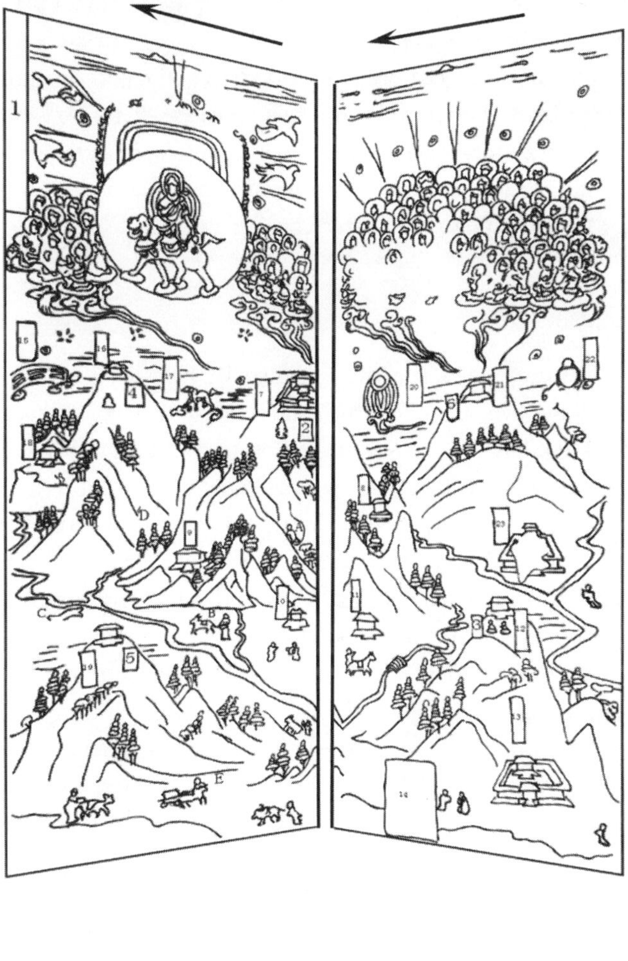

FIGURE 6.5a. West wall of Mogao Cave 361, Dunhuang. 9th century CE. This is a "double-niche" cave: a smaller niche cut into the main niche on the west wall; the picture of Mount Wutai is located on the two adjacent panels to the right (north) of the smaller niche. Dunhuang Wenwu Yanjiusuo, *Dunhuang Mogaoku,* vol. 4, pl. 117. Photograph by permission of Wenwu Press.

FIGURE 6.5b. Two adjacent mural panels to the right (north) of the smaller niche. The two panels together form a unified composition that depicts the flying motion of Mañjuśrī in midair from the right (north) panel to the left (west) panel. After Zhao Xiaoxing "Tufan tongzhi shiqi," 122. Drawing courtesy of Zhao Xiaoxing.

scan of the view is facilitated by the pilgrimage routes, traceable from one panel to the next, and by the mountainous topography, rolling continuously over two panels. On Central Peak, located on the right panel, is a monastic structure, from which a large formation of clouds arises supporting the assembly of bodhisattvas, identified by a cartouche as "the ten thousand bodhisattvas" (*wan pusa*).[47] Mañjuśrī on his lion along with other bodhisattvas are seen on the left panel, ferried across the space on clouds, whose trails point back to the monastic structure, as if the holy assembly were moving from one panel to the other in real time. The implied temporality brings about both the moment and momentum, in which Mañjuśrī arrives from his sacred domain to manifest his holy presence inside the religious space of this cave, to extol and glorify the Buddhist icons in the central niche; Samantabhadra, on the other side of the outer niche, is portrayed in symmetric parallel, also moving inward, toward the central scene.

The consensus that the imagery of Mount Wutai was transmitted to the Dunhuang region during the Tibetan occupation is supported by textual records. The Mogao caves conserved all the essentials of Mount Wutai—its sacred peaks, monasteries, pilgrims, and the vision of the bodhisattva—albeit following a different iconographic program and visual conventions specific to the local practice. In these images, Central Peak plays an increasingly prestigious role as the most favored peak for the bodhisattva's revelation, thus aligning both topographic and spiritual centrality at the same sacred peak. Most significant, the iconic ensemble and visual presentation inside the cave cultivate the sense of motion in Mañjuśrī's travel in midair, making his divine presence immanent in both time and space, as though the physical distance between the cave and Mount Wutai could be transcended through visualization. And it seems to have been the case that this vision of Mañjuśrī's true presence transferable through visualization inspired the local governors in the Dunhuang region to not only promote the bodhisattva cult but also strive to transpose Mount Wutai to the western borderland.

New Emanation of Mañjuśrī

After the Chinese general Zhang Yichao (799–872) expelled the Tibetans in 848, the border area west of the Yellow River was under the control of the regional military governor, who held the title military governor of the Return to Allegiance Army (Guiyijun *jiedushi*). The position was first held by the Zhang family and passed into the Cao family in 921. Although both pledged loyalty to the central authority in China, the Zhang and Cao families were the de facto rulers of the larger area known as Shazhou, including Dunhuang.[48] China was plagued by warfare in the last decades of the Tang period before the dynasty collapsed in 907, and during this period the Dunhuang region was gradually built into the regional center of both politics and religion, in particular, during and after the tenure of Cao Yijin (d. 935), who ruled between 914 and 935. Traffic between the Dunhuang region and the rest of China was interrupted by the fall of the Tang dynasty and not restored until the 920s, when there were again records of pilgrims making trips to Mount Wutai, as well as the many eulogies and songs of Mount Wutai transmitted into the border region, which celebrated the numinous qualities of the sacred mountain and the power of the bodhisattva in his various magical manifestations.[49] It is likely this renewed impetus that brought about a new iconography of Mañjuśrī, which would elucidate the ways in which the bodhisattva's sacred presence was reenvisioned and Mount Wutai was "transposed" to the region.

This new iconography, like the iconography from the Tang period, is found at Mogao, Dunhuang. A notable example is in a mural on the north wall of the corridor leading to Cave 220, initially built in 642, known as Cave of the Family Zhai (Zhai Jiaku).[50] The mural (plate 5), dated 925 by its inscription, depicts Mañjuśrī in bodhisattva attire mounted on his lion, accompanied by a youthful figure, identified as Sudhana (a young pilgrim from the *Flower Garland Sutra*), on his left, and the king of Khotan as a lion tamer, on his right; the figures are riding together above clouds and under a hanging canopy. The central scene is clearly outlined, separating the central group from the two flanking bodhisattvas and the donors' images that form a border below. Cartouches were used to identify each donor in the mural. The devotional purpose, rather than the iconographic context inside the cave, explains its rather unusual location and composition, as the inscription at the lower center states:

> Zhai Fengda [883–961?] [who] disposed of his [entire?] meager assets to respectfully commission one image of the new-mode Great Sage Mañjuśrī with attendants, and an attending bodhisattva [Mañjuśrī] and a bodhisattva Avalokiteśvara. The meritorious rewards received from it [will be transferred] firstly to the spirits of the deceased [ancestors] who constructed the cave to enable for them a divine rebirth in the Pure Land. . . . Before resting the pen, [I] also write the following eulogy: The Great Sage Mañjuśrī, [whose] auspicious image [*ruixiang*] appears magnificently, shining in the world and manifesting in response [to the faithful his] thousandfold power.[51]

This mural has attracted much scholarly attention since 1978, when a later mural layer made in the twelfth century was removed to reveal it, and the discussion has focused on the "new-mode Mañjuśrī" (Xinyang Wenshu), identified in the inscription. Although scholars agree that this "new mode" refers to the central image of Mañjuśrī riding a lion, what exactly is new about this image, or what constitutes the newness, is still largely under debate.[52] Most of these discussions, however, concentrate chiefly on the figure's iconographic characteristics and constituents—such as, its full frontal pose, the number and identities of the attendants, its not being paired with Samantabhadra—but pay less attention to the ways in which the "new-mode Mañjuśrī" could have engaged its viewers visually and religiously. It may be that this Mañjuśrī should be understood less in terms of style or iconography and more in the manner the bodhisattva himself manifests. The "new mode," in this regard, may be the "new emanation" of the bodhisattva.

The most notable characteristic of the new Mañjuśrī is his centrally articulated position: he is shown directly facing the viewer, asserting himself as the icon and the visual focus of the entire composition. This is achieved in two different ways. On the one hand, the posture of Mañjuśrī, perfectly encircled in double halos (one encircling his head, the other his body), and perfectly still and attentive, suggests a religious icon that requires a viewer to meet its gaze. On the other hand, the roaring lion, contrasting to the motionless Mañjuśrī, is shown in full motion, responding more naturally to the billowing clouds that carry the deity and his attendants in a continual motion over the surface of the mural, as indicated in the trailing tails of cloud that stretch and undulate along the right side of the frame until they disappear out of the frame.[53] While the iconic presence of the bodhisattva suggests no time or the timeless, the moving clouds and their tails imply both the path of movement and the lapse of time. The movement in this image reminds us of the lion-riding Mañjuśrī in earlier caves, hovering over and traveling from his sacred mountain, even though the mountain is not depicted, and what fills the background is not scenery but the multicolored radiance emanating from the bodhisattva's halos.

Clouds are common in the religious imagery of China and are often used to identify a superhuman figure and its apparitional manifestation. In the case of this image from Cave 220, the "cloud vehicle" used to transport the celestials or deities serves yet another function: it guides the viewer's gaze across the pictorial surface by means of the trailing tails, suggesting the tremendous momentum from which the divine manifests. This motif would have been quite familiar to Buddhists in Dunhuang, as it was also employed in several banners produced in the late ninth and tenth centuries, such as *Tejaprabhā Buddha and the Five Planets,* dated 897 (fig. 6.6).[54] The new-mode "emanation" of Mañjuśrī, however, is different in at least one critical sense from the banner illustrated: while Tejaprabhā and his five attendants are traveling in one direction across the pictorial space, Mañjuśrī is facing the viewer, himself still while all around him is in movement, as if in an "iconic moment" suspended within the temporal movement, in which the bodhisattva is turned into an icon and object of veneration.

The iconicity of the new Mañjuśrī may have been related to a particular category of sacred images, known as auspicious images (*ruixiang*), which became popular in the Dunhuang region during the ninth and tenth centuries.[55] In the early history of Mount Wutai, this term *ruixiang* was also used, referring to "auspicious signs" indicative of Mañjuśrī's holy presence. In the new context described here, *ruixiang* as auspicious images was applied more specifically to an array of Buddhist icons characterized by their unusual genesis.[56] Each of these icons was associated with a specific locale somewhere outside the area where the icon was first installed, and had elaborate legends of origin or creation that justified its authenticity—which in turn, proved the supernatural power of the icon to move and act miraculously. Because they had supernatural power, these icons had "'come flying,' *feilai,* from India, across Asia to Khotan, Kucha, or other sites further along the Silk Road to China," and eventually their images were found in the Dunhuang region.[57] In paintings, the auspicious images could be presented in two different ways: one is in the style of an icon, that is, it appears in a static, formal frontal pose, and either

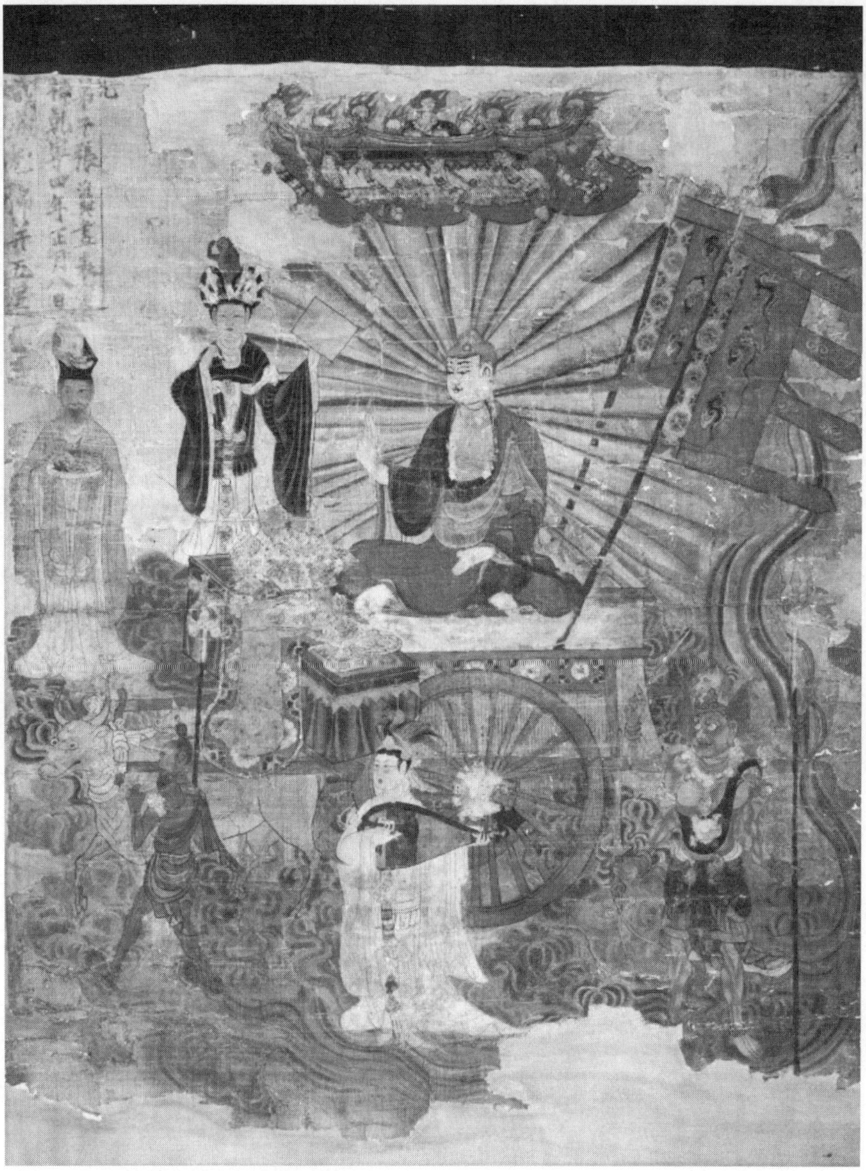

FIGURE 6.6. *Tejaprabhā Buddha and the Five Planets,* ink and colors on silk, 80.4 x 55.4 cm, from Mogao Cave 17. 897 CE. Photograph © Trustees of the British Museum.

stands or sits, with the hands held in specific positions (mudras); the other style is narrative, and depicts the creation legend of the icon or the miraculous story of its origin. Although different in approach, they are related to each other. The narrative provides the raison d'être for the iconic "auspicious images" to represent and act like the deity itself. For example, an icon known as the "auspicious image from Fanhe" (Fanhe *ruixiang*), from Cave 231 in Dunhuang, representing a colossal statue located in Fanhe, in Liangzhou (in today's Gansu province), which, according to a legend in the sixth century, emerged out of rock by itself (fig. 6.7).[58] As with most *ruixiang* icons, the "auspicious image from Fanhe" is identified by its name, place of origin, and legend in an inscription accompanying it; the term "holy presence" (*shengrong*) also occurs in its description. In similar icons, the term

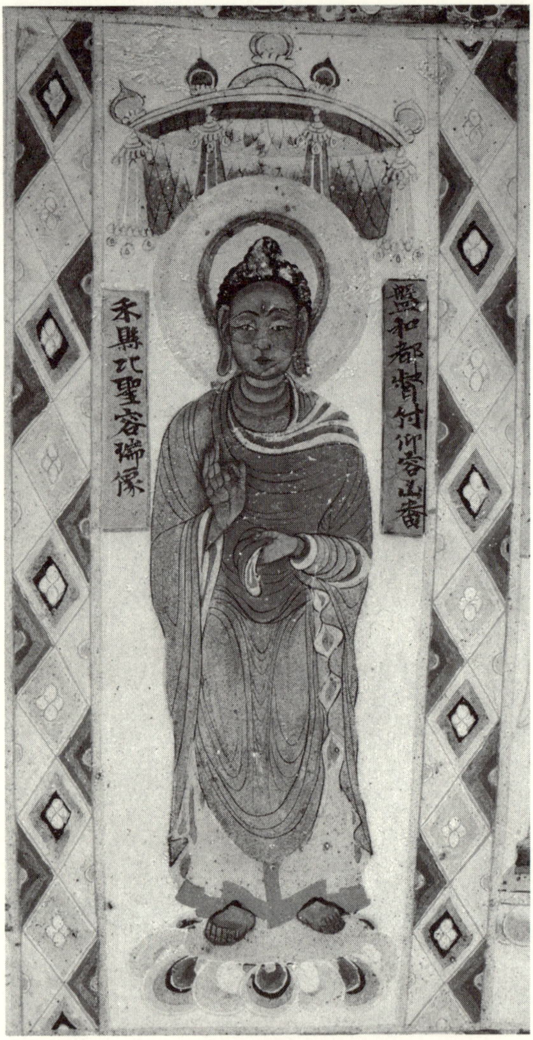

FIGURE 6.7. The "auspicious image" (*ruixiang*) from Fanhe, ceiling of the west niche, Mogao Cave 231, Dunhuang. 9th century CE. Photograph by permission of Dunhuang Academy.

"true presence" (*zhenrong*) is used of the deity, suggesting that *ruixiang* icons are more than simple representations; these images partake in the true sanctity of the divine. Together with its inscription, an iconic *ruixiang* is a sacred image for veneration, and with extreme visual economy calls to mind the narrative (the legend of creation or origin) that guarantees its divinity, even though the narrative itself is not depicted.

The Mañjuśrī from Cave 220 can be seen as a new icon of the bodhisattva, whose apparitional manifestation was revisualized in the visual language and conventions associated with the "auspicious images." The clearest evidence for this is the eulogy at the end of the inscription quoted earlier: "The Great Sage Mañjuśrī, [whose] auspicious image [*ruixiang*] appears magnificently, shining in the world and manifesting in response [to the faithful his] thousandfold power."[59] As described in several Dunhuang manuscripts that contain legends of auspicious images, these icons could "come flying" or "come through the air" (*tengkong er lai*), or they might "travel on the clouds" (*qixia chengyun*) and "emit lights" (*fangguang*).[60] The glowing image, or icon, of Mañjuśrī riding his lion (see plate 5), identified in the cartouche to the right as "the true presence of the Great Sage Mañjuśrī,"[61] conjures up precisely the transformative power of the bodhisattva as recorded in the creation legend, in which Mañjuśrī riding a lion manifested his true presence before the sculptor who went on to make the sacred statue at Mount Wutai. Indeed, not only was the same creation legend transmitted in writing to the Dunhuang region, the same term, "true presence" (*zhenrong*), was also used.[62] In this revisualized image in Cave 220, Mañjuśrī mounted on his lion, traveling with two attendants across the sky in trailing clouds, literally "comes flying" to the border region of China in Dunhuang from his sacred mountain.

The bodhisattva's traveling through air from Mount Wutai is addressed even more explicitly in a number of surviving woodblock prints from Mogao; an example is shown in figure 6.8.[63] The prints date from the period 944–74, when Dunhuang was governed by Cao Yuanzhong (d. 974), under whose reign Cave 61, discussed in the next section, was constructed. The print illustrated here, from Cave 17, consists of a devotional image with dedicatory verses and instruction for

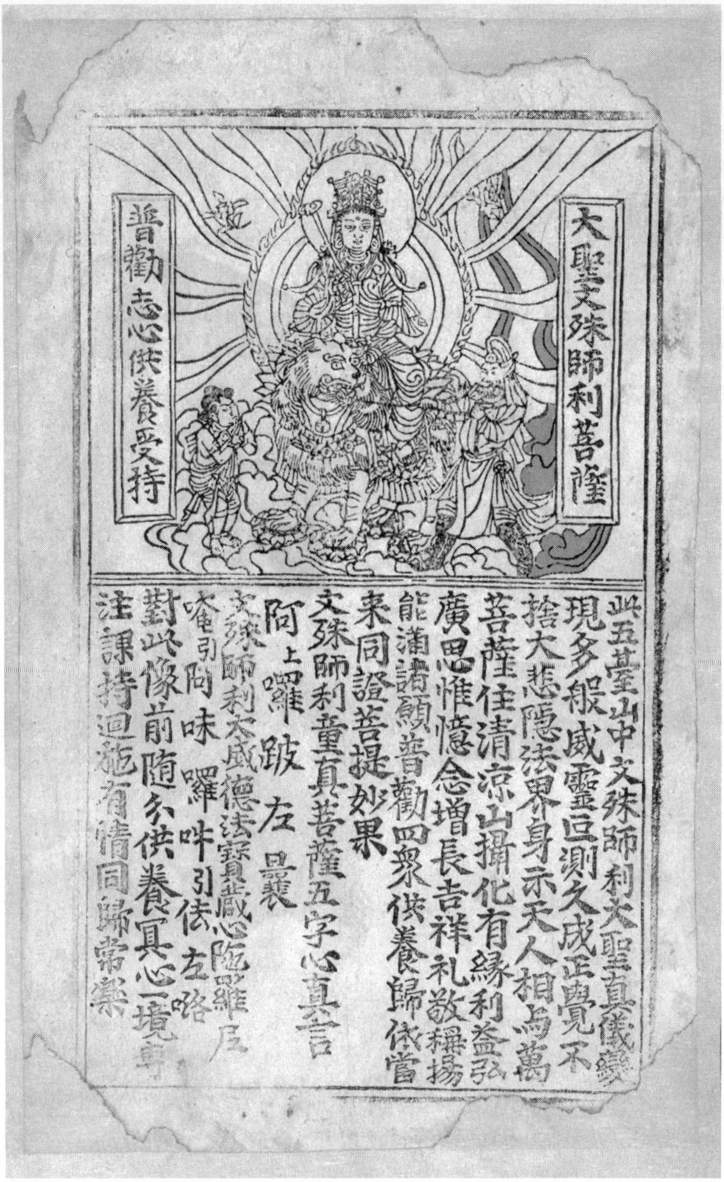

FIGURE 6.8. "New-Mode Mañjuśrī," woodcut print, 27.9 x 16.8 cm, from Mogao Cave 17. First half of the 10th century CE. The cloud trail (marked in gray) that swirls into the background and eventually out of the frame indicates the flying path of Mañjuśrī on the lion and his attendants. Photograph © Trustees of the British Museum.

ritual observance of the image below it. The image is the new emanation of Mañjuśrī, identifiable by the front-facing icon of the bodhisattva riding a lion and the trailing clouds suggesting a moving path and movement in time. The inscription reads: "This is the true appearance [*zhenyi*] of the Great Sage Mañjuśrī at Mount Wutai, who manifests in many diverse forms and whose might and magic are unfathomable."[64] The inscription continues, with instructions for invoking the bodhisattva (by reciting Mañjuśrī's five-syllable and eight-syllable mantras) in order to truly observe the bodhisattva as he appears in the iconic image.[65] Because the text requires the invocation to be performed before the image, the icon has to be the Mañjuśrī who appears to not only "come flying" but, as indicated in the inscription, to come specifically from Mount Wutai.

Adopting the visual economy of auspicious images, the creation of the new-mode Mañjuśrī may have reflected an intention to transpose the bodhisattva and actualize his sacred presence in Dunhuang. In particular, because he is represented in the visual language of moving, flying, and arriving, Mañjuśrī manifests his true presence over his sacred mountain precisely in Dunhuang in a much more readily perceivable way than in distant Mount Wutai. Although in the new visualization, exemplified in the mural from Cave 220 and the woodcut print from Cave 17, Mañjuśrī riding his lion became the sole iconographic element, the visual economy of the new icon was able to evoke the vision of the sacred topography and monasteries of Mount Wutai. In this regard, Mañjuśrī riding his lion, as an iconic image, not only reenacts the true presence of the bodhisattva but also mediates the sacrality of Mount Wutai with those who seek to see and experience its sacred landscape. This is particularly the case when this vision and visualization are expanded into a three-dimensional cave.

Constructing a Small Place: Mogao Cave 61

Although replicating a sacred space tied to a specific locale is difficult, recreating the sacred space ritualistically in miniature can be successful in evoking its sacrality. The notion of *praesentia,* the holy presence that marks a specific locale and space as sacred, is of central importance in this recreation.[66] In regard to the transposition of Mount Wutai to Dunhuang, how could the "true presence" be conjured through the icon of Mañjuśrī inside the cave space?

Mogao Cave 61, identified by a document of 1011 as the Hall of Mañjuśrī (Wenshu Tang), seems to have been built with this particular intention.[67] Constructed between 947 and 951, Cave 61 was one of the largest caves in Mogao; it was sponsored by the governor, Cao Yuanzhong, and his wife, Lady Zhai, a daughter of the Zhai family that constructed Cave 220.[68] It comprises a sizable and roughly square interior space (13.1 x 14.3 wide x 9.75 m high) with a ceiling shaped in a truncated pyramid, a lengthy corridor (9.25 m), and an east-facing cave entrance, which, originally was sheltered by a timber antechamber that no longer exists (figs. 6.9a, 6.9b, 6.9c).[69] It also contains one of the grandest iconic programs in Mogao, combining murals and sculpture in the cave space, of which the most important would have been the central icon and the mural on the west wall (fig. 6.10). Like many other large cave temples from this period, Cave 61 was built with a central raised altar or platform close to the rear wall but not attached to it and backed by a screen of the original rock that rises behind the altar to the ceiling. On top of the altar was a now missing group of statues, which, based on the traces on the altar and marks on the back screen, would have centered on a large statue of Mañjuśrī riding a lion.[70] This identification is further verified by the enormous mural (13.45 x 3.42 m) that stretches the full length of the west wall behind the central altar, depicting the entire range of Mount Wutai (see plate 8). Entering the cave, one would have been received by the imposing image of the bodhisattva standing before an extensive representation of his sacred mountain. Accordingly,

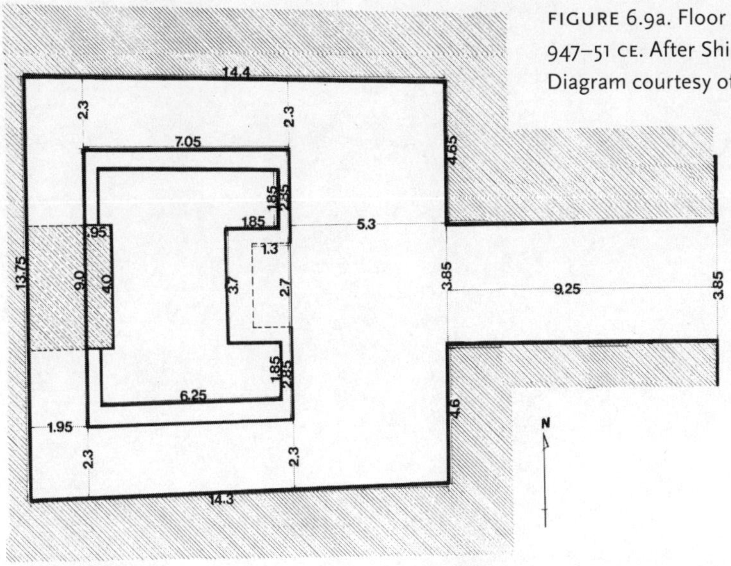

FIGURE 6.9a. Floor plan of Mogao Cave 61, Dunhuang. 947–51 CE. After Shi Zhangru, *Mogao ku xing*, vol. 2, 64. Diagram courtesy of Academia Sinica.

FIGURE 6.9b. Cross section of Mogao Cave 61. After Shi Zhangru, *Mogao ku xing*, vol. 2, 65. Diagram courtesy of Academia Sinica.

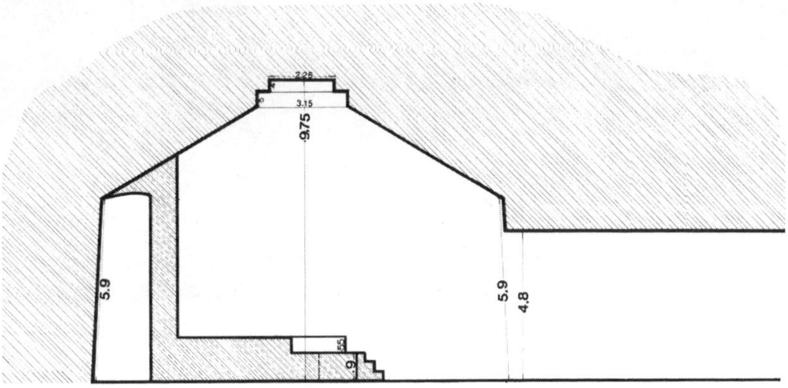

FIGURE 6.9c. Perspective drawing of Mogao Cave 61. Drawing by author.

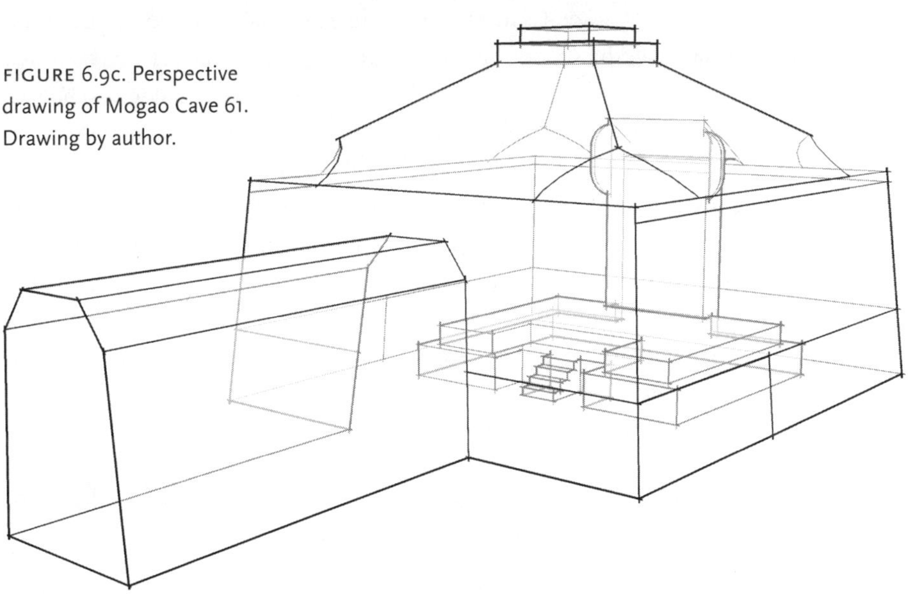

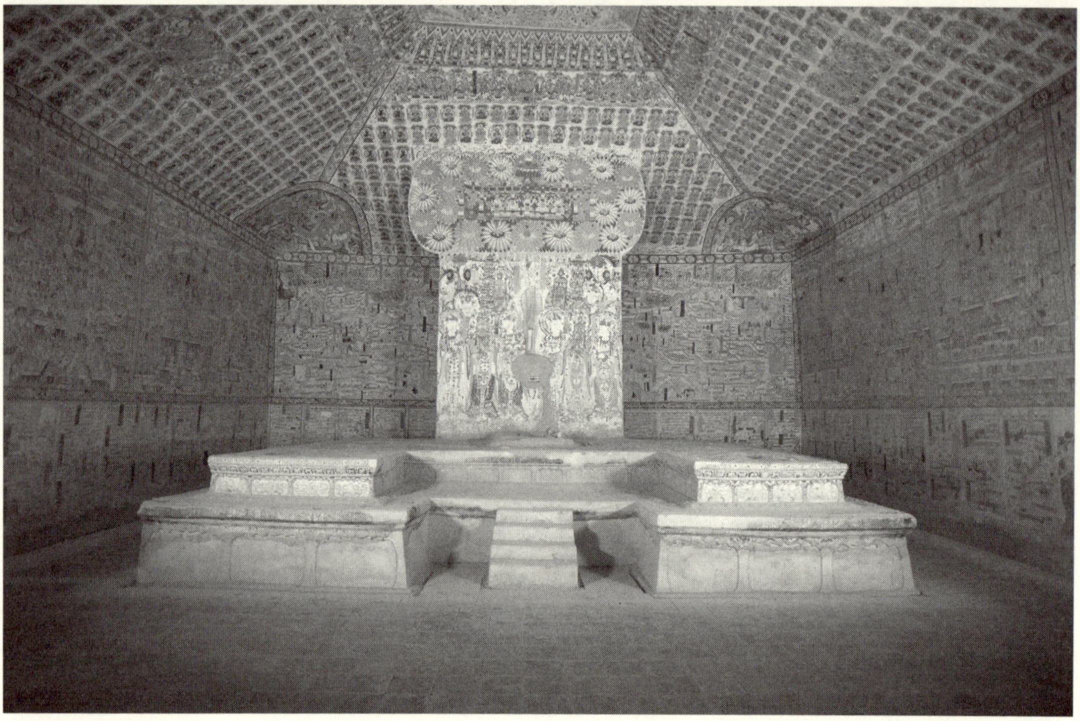

FIGURE 6.10. Interior view of Mogao Cave 61, seen from the eastern entrance, Dunhuang. 947–951 CE. The floor-to-ceiling screen at the rear of the altar partially blocks from view the central one-third of the mural on the west wall. Photograph by permission of Dunhuang Academy.

many scholars accept the view that Cave 61 is a replica of the sacred mountain.[71] Questions remain, however, not so much about the iconography or its interpretation as about the particular religious visuality of the cave[72]—that is, how could the sacredness of the mountain be visualized inside the cave and what was the nature of the revelatory vision?

To a large extent, the Mogao caves from the tenth century inherited many of the characteristics in layout and iconographic content established in the period of Tibetan occupation.[73] Inside Cave 61, above the central altar are the painted images of a thousand buddhas covering the four sloping sides of the ceiling, anchored at the four corners by images of the four heavenly kings. To the side and behind the central altar are five large panels of sutra paintings, each approximately 3.4 by 2.8 meters, on each of the north and south walls, bordered below by a series of thirty-three smaller screened panels (each approximately 1.6 x 0.87 m) depicting the Buddha's past and present lives (*jātaka*), which wrap around the cave in the lower registers on the south, west, and north walls (fig. 6.11). Above the panels on the west wall is the mural of Mount Wutai, and on the corresponding east wall, above the donor images, an equally large mural painting of *Vimalakīrti Sutra,* depicting the debate scene between Vimalakīrti and Mañjuśrī. The location of the sutra painting on the east wall is typical, as are the placements and positional relations among the ten other sutra paintings on the north and south walls, which follow the conventions already established in the Mogao caves during the ninth century.[74]

In addition to the religious images, those of lay devotees (donors) also figure

FIGURE 6.11. The iconographic program inside Mogao Cave 61: (1) mural of Mount Wutai; (2) statue of Mañjuśrī on a lion, with twelve other statues; sutra paintings of (3) *Vimalakīrti Sutra* ; (4) *Laṅkāvātara Sutra*; (5) *Maitreya Sutra*; (6) *Sukhāvatī Sutra*; (7) *Lotus Sutra*; (8) *Bao'en Sutra*; (9) *Ghanavyūha Sutra*; (10) *Devatā Sutra*; (11) *Bhaiṣajya-guru Sutra*; (12) *Flower Garland Sutra*; (13) *Viśeṣacinta-brahma-paripṛcchā Sutra*; (14) thirty-three mural panels depicting *jātaka* tales; (15) female donor images. Diagram by author.

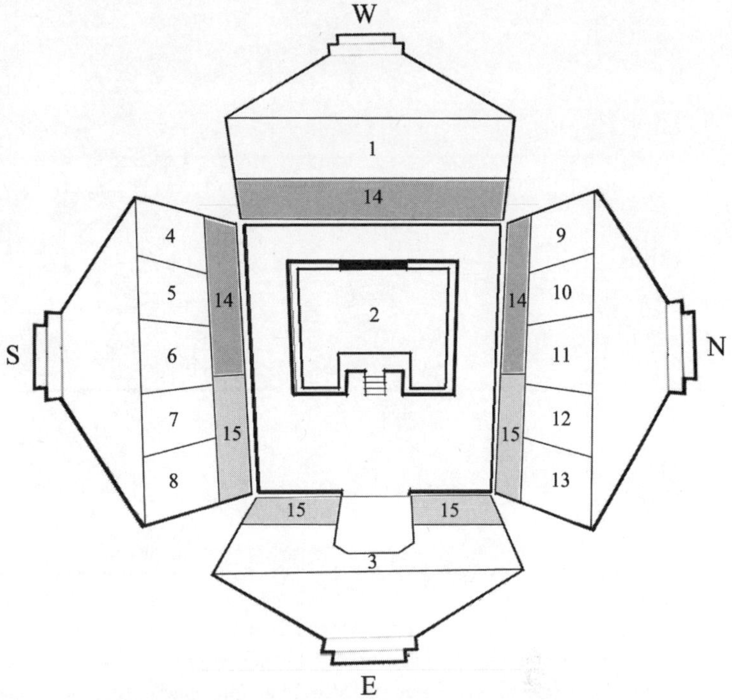

prominently inside the cave, starting where the *jātaka* images end, roughly level with the front of the altar. The panels of donors continue around the lower registers of the walls and end at the entrance on the east wall. All the donors, on both sides of the cave, are women members of the Cao family, and all are shown facing toward the entrance. The figures of men donors were also painted, also facing toward the entrance, but their figures were on the walls of the corridor leading into the cave, now covered by the mural made later during the eleventh and twelfth centuries (plate 6). All the donor figures are life-size, and their placements and orientations provide clues about how practitioners were to move around the cave, suggesting that a full view of the entire cave space could be observed from the entrance on the east wall.[75] There is one problem, however: Cave 61 is so large that the viewer will not get a comprehensive view of the cave all at once. The massive screen behind the central altar makes any attempt to obtain an unobstructed view into the cave space impossible; instead, it requires one to move, to enter and pass through space, while adjusting one's viewing perspective. In other words, the visuality and even visibility inside the space of the cave space became new factors that structured and constructed the religious meaning of the cave.

Taking into account the iconographic program, the donor images, and this necessary movement of the body, the interior of Cave 61 may be considered as consisting of three zones: the front zone of the lay devotees, nearest the entrance; the intermediary zone of Mañjuśrī riding his lion on the altar; and the rear zone of Mount Wutai depicted on the mural beyond and behind the altar and its screen (plate 7). Perceiving the cave as such emphasizes the spatial relationships among

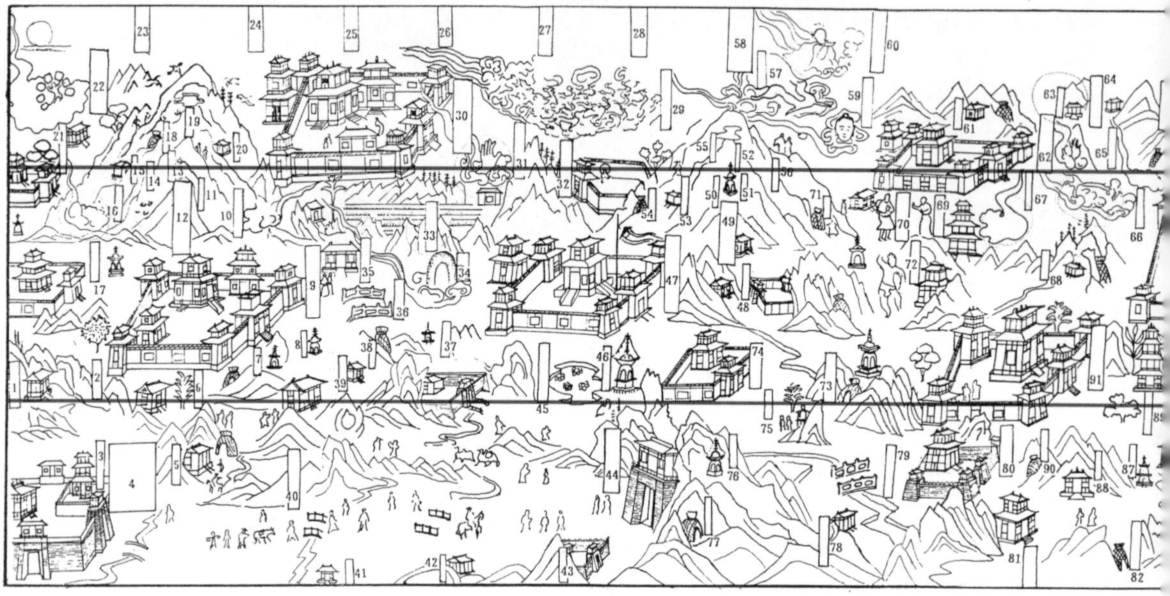

FIGURE 6.12. The Mount Wutai mural in Mogao Cave 61, showing the three horizontal sections of the mural: pilgrims in the lower, mountains and monasteries in the middle, and celestials in the upper. After Zhao Shengliang, *Dunhuang shiku yishu: Mogao ku di 61 ku,* 18–19. Drawing courtesy of Zhao Shengliang.

iconographic components and explores the complexity of the religious program inside the cave as a whole. A movement through the three zones would not have been a casual walk, but necessarily at once visual, physical, experiential, and ritualistic. The prominent presence of Mañjuśrī on the altar would have been the visual focus of devotion as well as the mediation in the spatial structure of the cave between the faithful and the bodhisattva's sacred mountain. Any examination of the mural on the west wall has to keep in mind this spatial structure.

Occupying one of the most expansive murals in all of the Mogao caves, the panorama of Mount Wutai (plate 8) inside Cave 61 is among the best-known and researched mural paintings from the cave site.[76] It merits its fame, for the incredible amount of detail depicted and labeled over the extensive mural surface is arranged masterfully in a structure that encompasses and intertwines geographic, religious, and supernatural aspects of the sacred site seamlessly in one composition. Many scholars see a tripartite world in the depiction of Mount Wutai (fig. 6.12):[77] in the lower section is the human realm of pilgrims who travel through major routes leading to the mountain range; the middle section belongs to the sacred mountain, including the five peaks disposed prominently and evenly across the section, and monasteries and other religious edifices distributed to fill the mountain territory; and the celestial realm consists of bodhisattvas, *nāga*-dragons, arhats, and other apparitions carried by the clouds, together occupying the upper section. It is a comprehensive record of Mount Wutai presented in a visual panorama.

Two different viewpoints inform two interrelated realities of Mount Wutai: the

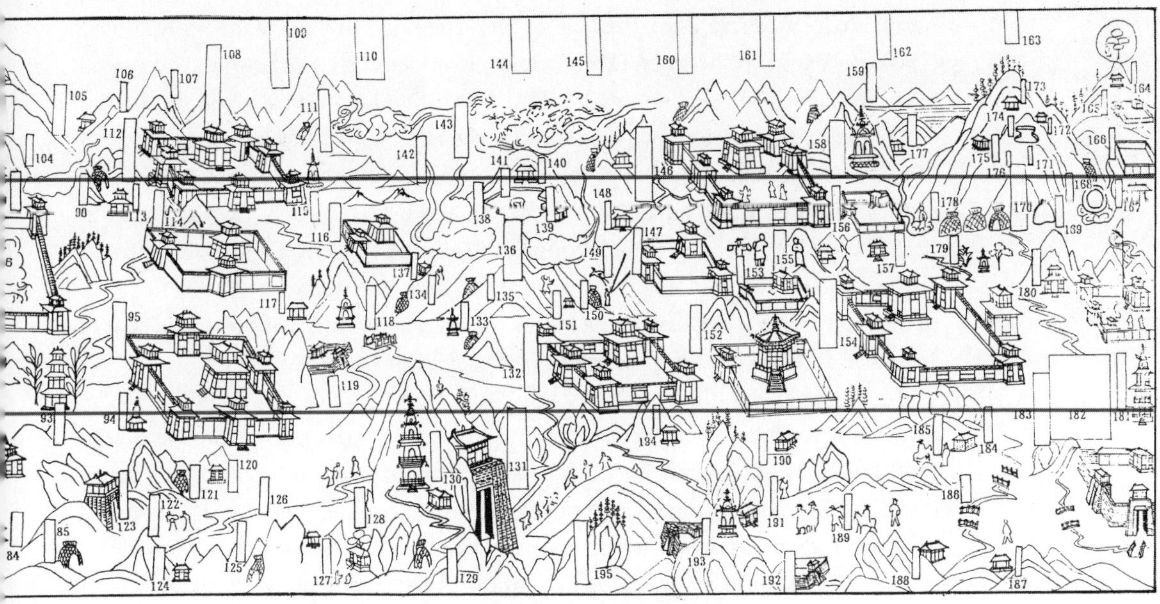

cognitive or experiential and the transcendent. The first viewpoint is that of the pilgrim, who enters the pictorial realm of Mount Wutai through one of two walled compounds, one at the lower left corner of the mural (plate 9), labeled "Taiyuan in the Hedong Circuit" (Hedong dao Taiyuan), and the other at the lower right corner, "Zhenzhou in the Hebei Circuit" (Hebei dao Zhenzhou). Taiyuan and Zhenzhou, located respectively in the Hedong and Hebei administrative circuits, or *dao* (generally corresponding to present-day Shanxi and Hebei provinces) were the two major cities at either ends of the pilgrimage route recorded in Ennin's travel diary (see map 11). Along the pilgrimage routes starting at both corners of the mural, one sees groups of pilgrims, troops of loadbearing animals, and official envoys bringing offerings to the sacred site, as described by Ennin in his journal. Many of the buildings along the routes leading to and leaving from Mount Wutai have been identified as depictions of actual pilgrim way stations (*putong yuan*).[78] Moving into the middle section, one enters the mountain area where the monasteries take the central stage. A great number of monastic buildings—grand monasteries, cloisters, pavilions, pagodas, and shrines—dot the landscape, providing the spatial markers, in and around which monastics and laypeople go about different activities or engage in Buddhist events. Intervening in the religious landscape of the middle section are images of transformative manifestation (*huaxian*) appearing in midair—from auspicious signs (multicolored light, glowing mandorlas, precious bells, and auspicious birds) and the Buddha's body parts (head, hand, and foot), to the revelatory vision of Mount Wutai and the Pure Land in the form of the Golden World—all together symbolically transforming the natural terrain into the sacred domicile of the bodhisattva Mañjuśrī. Moving further into the mountain area and reaching the central part of the mural, one arrives at the center of the sacred mountain, where the most important pictorial and iconographic elements of the mural are located (plate 10): the Hall of the True Body of the Great Sage Mañjuśrī (Dasheng Wenshu Zhenshen Dian), which enshrines in its courtyard the holy triad of the Buddha and two flanking bodhisattvas—Mañjuśrī riding a lion on the left and Samantabhadra riding an elephant on the right; and below it, the Pavilion of Ten Thousand Fellow Bodhisattvas (Wan Pusa Lou), housing a group of bodhisattvas who sit around a pagoda in worship. These are the only two buildings in the entire composition depicted frontally, aligned with Central Peak above them in the same central axis. The centrality of this area also marks the climactic point of the pilgrimage, after which one leaves the sacred mountain in a reversed spatial sequence and a step-by-step return to everyday life.

To a great extent, the visual tour into Mount Wutai on the mural unfolds in its pictorial space the textual narrative in Ennin's diary. Both present Mount Wutai in a structured totality consisting of its topography and monasteries linked together through a narrative or itinerary of pilgrimage that has as its climax at the very center of the sacred mountain, where the main icon can be observed and vision of the divine manifestation attained. On the mural, each labeled place, event, building, and vision serves the "plot" in the narrative and each is given a meaning by being included as an integral part of the whole.[79] From one end of the mural to the other end, the itinerary progresses in time, as well as in space over the mural surface. The temporal linearity of the narrative, however, is not fixed on the mural, as multiple temporalities could be simultaneously juxtaposed in space—as in the figure of Buddhapālita, who appears twice on the mural, marking the two moments of his visit at Mount Wutai. From this viewpoint, the Mount Wutai depicted on the mural is a visualized "chronotope," that is, a sacred topography with a spatio-temporal matrix that is at once experiential and revelatory.[80]

Related to this itinerary narrative from a pilgrim's viewpoint is a more conceptual but omnipresent vision that sees Mount Wutai in its totality. In this totality, Mount Wutai is presented methodologically and ritualistically to reveal the sacrality of the site. The sacred realm is foremost defined by the five anchoring peaks, from left to right: South, West, Central, North, and East Peaks.[81] Arranged over the mountain range and divided evenly by the five peaks in the middle section are ten monastic complexes labeled "great" (*da*) monasteries (see plate 9),[82] most certainly referring to the ten-monastery system that epitomized the holistic and coherent entirety of the sacred site. All the great monasteries are depicted similarly and generically; all are walled compounds enclosing one or two buildings, along with a few figures engaged in unspecified religious activities. All ten, furthermore, are shown at an angle, distributed at regular intervals from both ends of the mural moving toward the center, one after another. The rhythmic repetition is also replicated in the upper section (figs. 6.13a and 6.13b). Here, celestials are arrayed on either side of the mural and carried on a series of trailing clouds in order, one after the other, toward the center; if one counts the number of celestials as indicated in each of the cartouches, there are ten thousand bodhisattvas, five hundred arhats, and five hundred poisonous dragons. Clearly, the mural is meant to show everything schematically, to be comprehensive rather than realistic, symbolic rather than representational, transcending therefore any particular geography and temporality. It is Mount Wutai visualized in its ritualistic completeness, which, as elucidated in the *Flower Garland Sutra,* gives rise to a world of perfection and perfect vision.[83]

If we think of the mural as simply a three-tiered structure, it would be tempting to conclude that the two viewpoints just discussed converge at the center of the entire composition, making the central peak and the two centrally presented monastic buildings the visual and spiritual, as well as experiential and conceptual, focus. Their central position in the mural, however, poses questions about ways of reading this mural. As noted earlier, the central third of the mural is located right behind the rear screen of the altar, not only keeping the central area from view as one enters the cave but also undermining the panoramic presentation of the mural. As the mural was not to be viewed all at once in the cave, the three-tiered structure has to be understood conceptually rather than as something to experience empirically all at once. The placement of the altar and its screen right in front of the most centrally positioned area of the mural also forces us to consider the mural in relation to the statue of Mañjuśrī riding his lion on the altar.[84] In fact, judging from the pictorial convention of Mount Wutai depicted in other Mogao caves, the statue of Mañjuśrī has to be part of the vision of the sacred mountain depicted on the mural, but the spatial arrangements in Cave 61 makes the relation between the icon and the mural much more complex.

If we take into account the statue of Mañjuśrī and the screen, we see that the central part of the mural is best observed in its vertical divisions, rather than as part of a single horizontal panorama (fig. 6.12). From one's point of entry into the cave (plates 9, 11), one sees first the statue of Mañjuśrī riding his lion majestically on the altar; one then circumambulates clockwise from the front of the cave into the zone at the side of the altar, then around the back of the altar into the zone of the sacred mountain and round back toward the entrance again. This movement is facilitated by the ample space on the three sides of the altar and behind it, and is also invited by the arrangement of the murals at eye level. After passing the images of the women donors, one comes to the panels depicting the past lives of the Buddha on the south wall, continuing into his birth and worldly life as a prince on the west wall, and ending with his career as a Buddha through his enlightenment, nirvana, cremation, and the distribution of his relics on the east.[85] The panels are organized sequentially to represent past, present, and future times in the life of the Buddha, making them concurrently spatial and temporal. This spatiotemporal progression around the altar parallels the visual tour of pilgrimage implied in the mural of Mount Wutai. Beginning from the lower left corner of the Mount Wutai mural, one's walk along the west wall embodies the viewpoint of the pilgrim, entering the mountains from the left, reaching the climax in the central area behind the screen, and leaving the sacred site from the right.

The correlation between the visual tour of pilgrimage in the mural and parallel

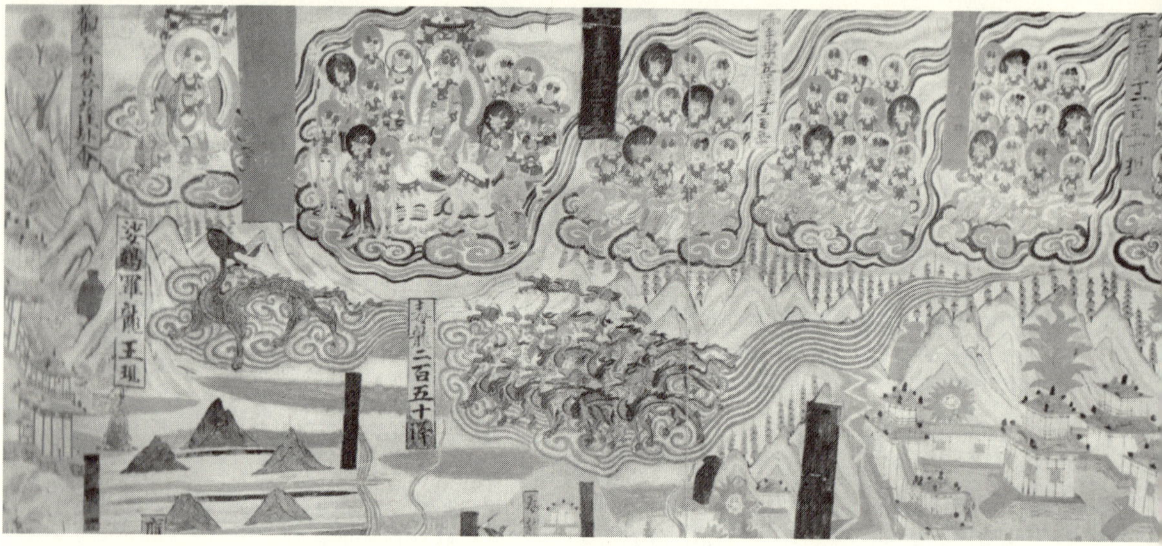

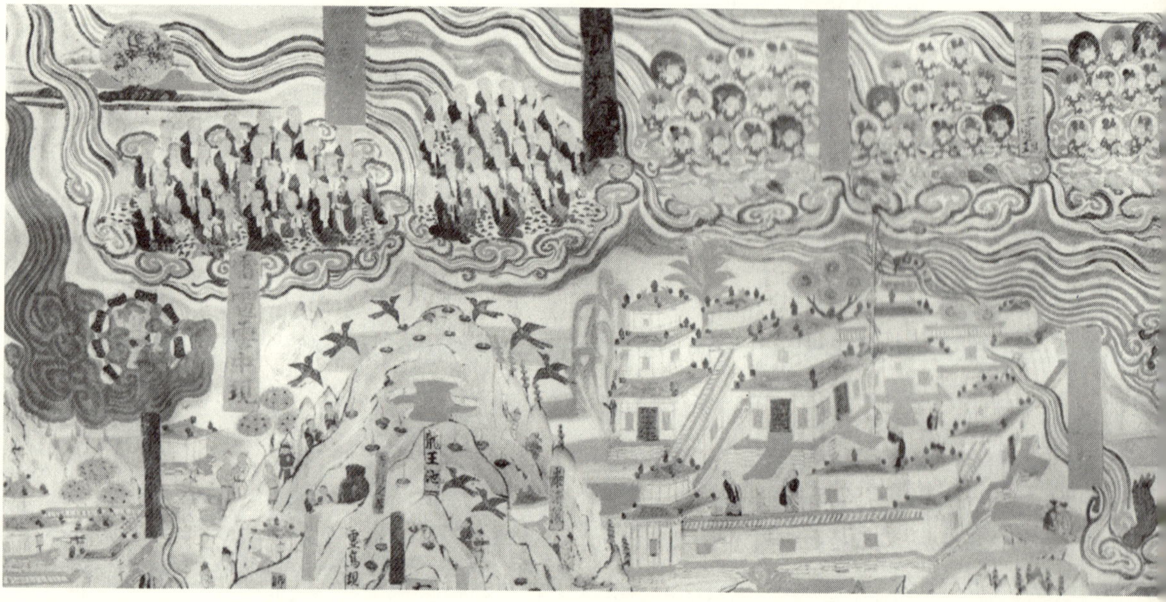

tour on foot along the mural is further prompted and unified by two pictorial elements. On the mural along the pilgrimage route near the central area are two "mountain gates" (see plate 9, points B and C): on the left is the "Mountain Gate of the Southwest Route in the Hedong Circuit" (Hedong dao Shanmen Xinan[lu]) and on the right, "Mountain Gate of the Southeast Route in the Hebei Circuit" (Hebei dao Shanmen Dongnanlu). Unlike the cities of Taiyuan and Zhenzhou at the two lower corners of the mural (plate 9, points A and D), these two mountain gates, not verified in texts, most likely were not actual sites.[86] Yet, as they are the last two prominent structures that can be seen outside the central area behind the screen, they appear to be pictorial markers, intended to serve as the threshold into the center of Mount Wutai in the mural and to demarcate the boundary of one's

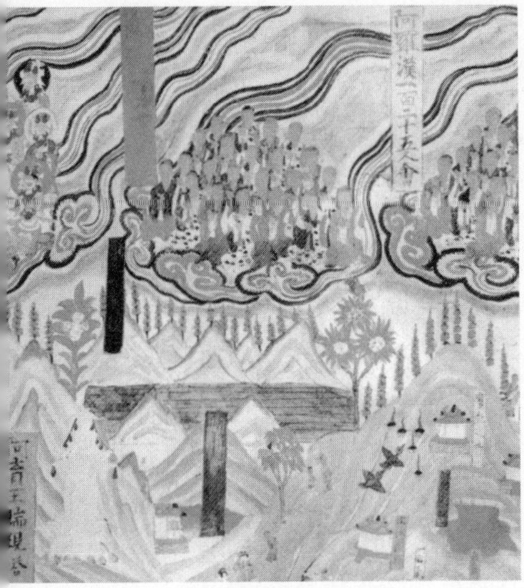

FIGURE 6.13a. Top right corner of the Mount Wutai mural, Mogao Cave 61. It shows celestials carried by clouds, led by Avalokiteśvara. Composite digital image by author.

FIGURE 6.13b. Top left corner of the Mount Wutai mural, Mogao Cave 61. The celestials carried by clouds are being led by Vaiśravaṇa. Composite digital image by author.

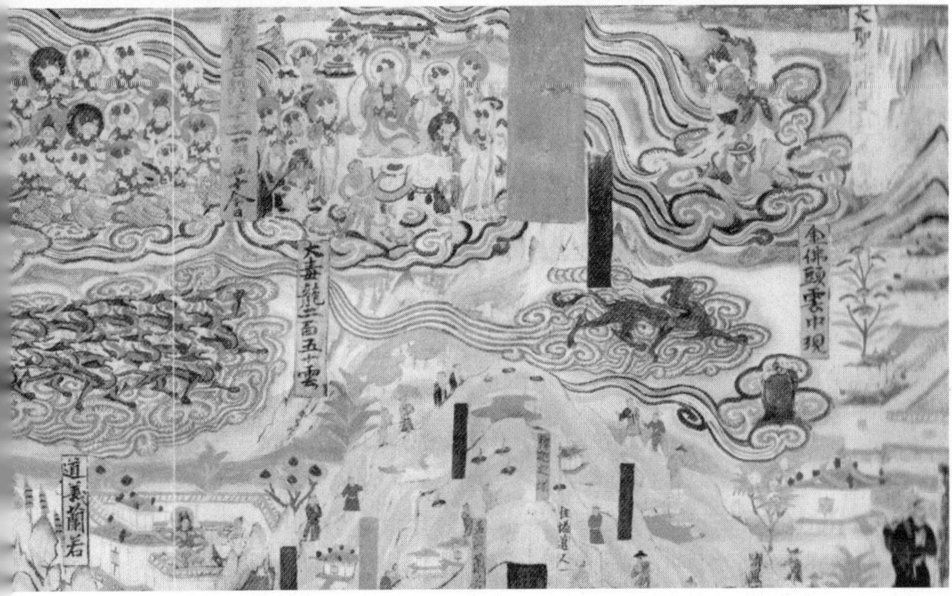

walk in and out of the central area. In resonance with the visual walk across the sacred landscape on the mural, the ambulatory movement around the altar also suggests a travel on foot into the climactic yet hidden area behind the back screen.

Most scholars are of the opinion that the main monastic structure, the "Hall of the True Body of the Great Sage Mañjuśrī" depicted in the central area of the mural (plate 10), is the Cloister of the True Presence at Mount Wutai, where the statue of Mañjuśrī riding a lion was reputedly first made after the bodhisattva manifested his true presence.[87] This matching is primarily based on the centrality they occupy in their individual contexts, the mural for the former and the sacred site for the latter. The travel diaries by the Japanese monks Chōnen (938–1016), who visited Mount Wutai in 985, and Jōjin (1011–81), who visited in 1072, have been cited to prove that the Cloister of the True Presence indeed thrived as the center of the bodhisattva cult at Mount Wutai after the Tang dynasty. However, as both diaries are later than the construction of Cave 61, their records are not likely to be the sources for the mural. In the two Japanese accounts, the cloister in question was named the Cloister of the Bodhisattva's True Presence at the Great Huayan Monastery (Da Huayansi Pusa Zhenrong Yuan), that is, it was not an independent monastery but one of the cloisters inside this most important monastery at Mount Wutai.[88] On the mural, the main hall at the center is completely detached from the Great Huayan Monastery, depicted in the far right of the mural. Another difficulty in identifying the main monastic structure is that when Chōnen and Jōjin visited the monastery, the Cloister of the True Presence had developed into a larger cloistral complex of several buildings, with a focus on the hall that housed the icon of Mañjuśrī riding his lion. The multiplicity of monastic structures at Great Huayan Monastery further contrasts with the depiction of the Hall of the True Body on the mural as a simple monastic structure with the holy triad in its courtyard.[89] The mural depiction, indeed, might have been meant to be a shorthand and symbolic in name, rather than realistic in form. This consideration, however, still cannot justify why the central building on the mural is labeled "Hall of True Body of the Great Sage Mañjuśrī," not "Cloister of the Bodhisattva's True Presence at the Great Huayan Monastery," as recorded in the Japanese diaries, while names of all other well-known monasteries were accurately matched on the mural. Was the name discrepancy between "true body" (*zhenshen*) and "true presence" (*zhenrong*) an error made in transcription? In exploring such questions, we will find that the differences between the central building in the mural and the cloister at Mount Wutai provide clues to the ways in which Mount Wutai was transposed into the cave and how its essentials were visualized through the iconographic ensemble made for the cave space.

Considering the central area of the mural of Mount Wutai from the point of view of its interior composition and its location in the cave, rather than in terms of identifying the Hall of True Body of the Great Sage Mañjuśrī, may explain better how it presents or reveals a transcendent vision of the sacred mountain. Flanked on both sides by the ten great monasteries, the central monastic structure—the eleventh great monastery—is simultaneously outside the tenfold system and superior to it. If one focuses only on the central area (see plate 9), the central structure is precisely framed by four of the great monasteries in the directions of its four corners. The composition thus is arranged by the converging of multiple-point perspectives, the so-called herringbone perspective, suggesting a moving viewpoint along the central axis. Together with the smaller cloister (Wan Pusa Lou) housing the ten thousand fellow bodhisattvas below and the two four-story pagodas symmetrically positioned above it, the composition of the central area is not unlike that of the Pure Land image often seen in the Mogao caves after the eighth century (fig. 6.14).[90] As in a Pure Land scene, the central structure serves as the Buddha's preaching stage in a setting consisting of multiple architectural complexes, decorated by pagodas and in front of an assembly of bodhisattvas.

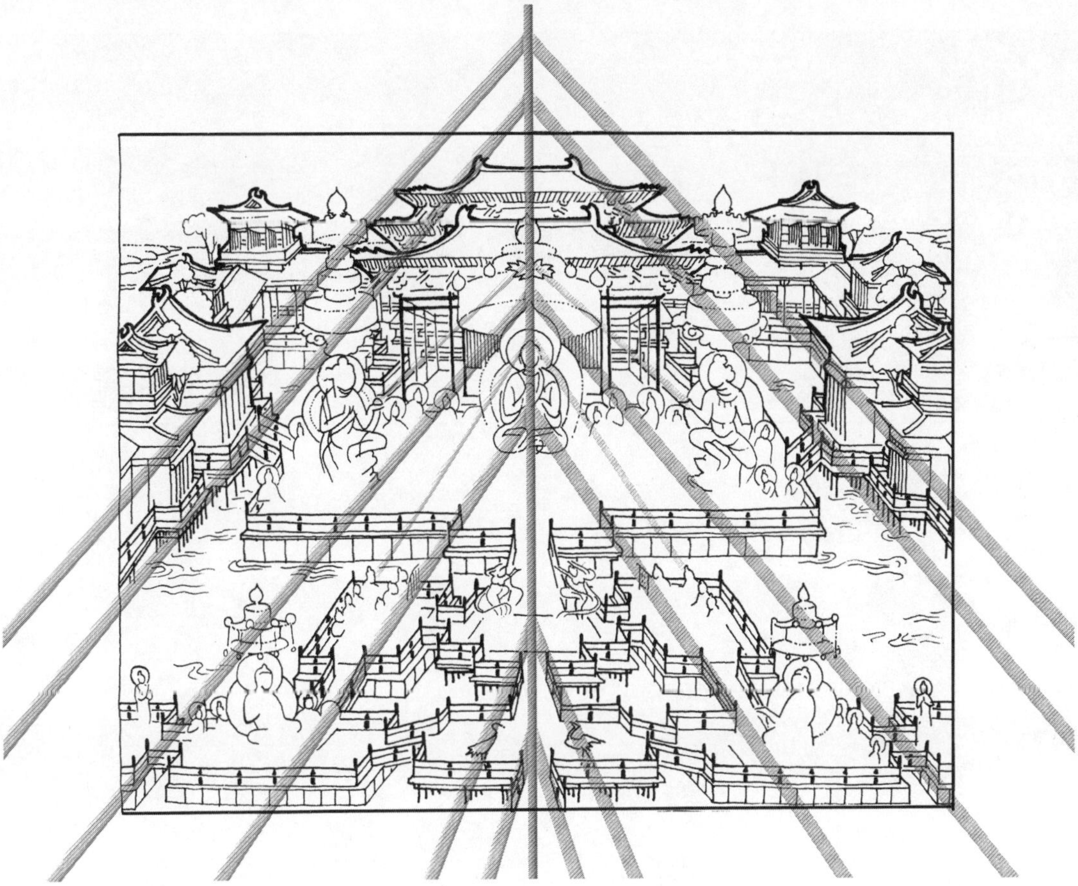

FIGURE 6.14. Painting of a scene from the *Sutra on Visualizing the Amitāyus Buddha* (Amitāyurdhyāna Sūtra), north wall, Mogao Cave 172, Dunhuang, Gansu. The added lines indicate the so-called herringbone perspective, the perspectival lines that converge at several points along the central axis, suggesting several moving viewpoints rather than a fixed one. After Xiao Mo, *Dunhuang jianzhu yanjiu,* fig. 1.21. Drawing by permission of Wenwu Press.

Above are two apparitional dragons, and further away are celestials arriving at the central area from both sides, convening to hear the Buddha's sermon; both leading bodhisattvas, Avalokiteśvara on the right (fig. 6.13a) and Vaiśravaṇa on the left (fig. 6.13b) leading the two troops of celestials, are labeled as "arriving to attend the [sermon] Assembly" (*fuhui*). Seen as such, the central area is also comparable to many of the sutra paintings (*jingbian*) in the Mogao caves, including the ones on the northern and southern walls inside Cave 61. It is notably similar to the composition of the sutra painting of the *Lotus Sutra* (Fahua jingbian) on the south wall of the cave, in that both preaching scenes are depicted with sacred mountains in the background, celestials in the sky, and surrounding monastic complexes (fig. 6.15). Thus, like the legendary mountain at which the historical Buddha preached the *Lotus Sutra*, Mount Gṛdhrakūṭa, Central Peak of Mount Wutai anchors the sacred realm identified by the central figure of the Buddha delivering his sermon. Unlike Mount Gṛdhrakūṭa, a sacred site more mythical than factual, Mount Wutai

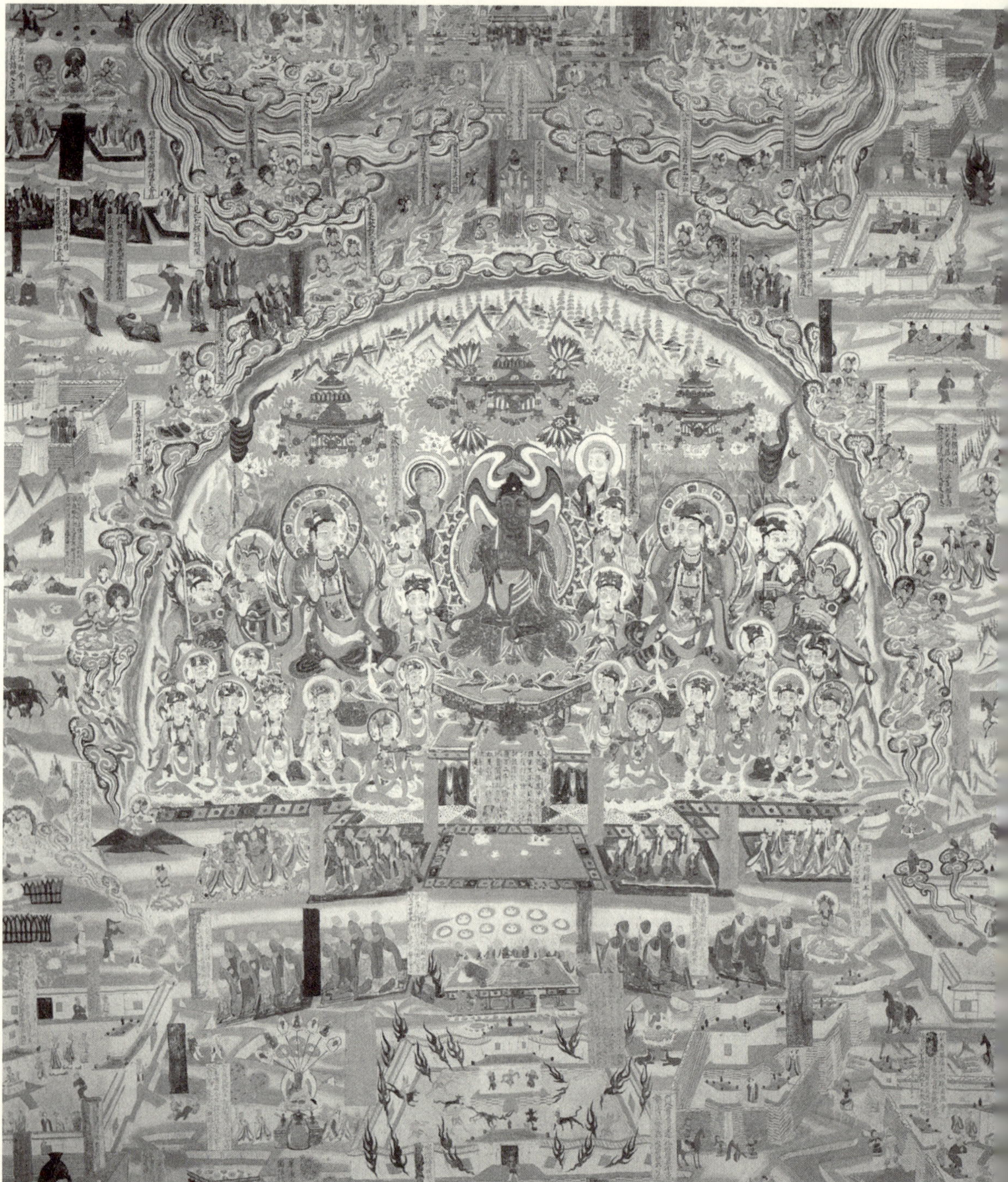

FIGURE 6.15. Sutra painting of the *Lotus Sutra* (Fahua jingbian), south wall, Mogao Cave 61. In the mural, the Buddha is shown preaching the *Lotus Sutra* at Mount Gṛdhrakūṭa, represented by series of hills in the background. Photograph by permission of Dunhuang Academy.

was a true mountain site. But it could nevertheless aspire to be, through vision, a transcendent realm of the entire holy assembly, manifesting in the very mundane world (*sahā*).

The holy triad in the courtyard of the central structure is most likely a reference to the supreme role of the three holy ones featured in the *Flower Garland Sutra*.[91] Their images on the mural, however, are not just symbolic, but revelatory, for the benefit of religious seekers. In the *Extended Records,* Yanyi pairs the image or statue of Mañjuśrī at Mount Wutai most frequently with that of Samantabhadra, both enshrined as icons for veneration; but as illustrated in the accounts he gives of the virtual monastery (*huasi*), the two great bodhisattvas could also be encountered in vision not as images but in their true presence.[92] On the mural, the two bodhisattvas inside the central structure are each labeled as the "true body" (*zhenshen*), a term that could mean either a powerful icon capable of acting as the deity it represents or the true presence of the deity.[93] The term "true body" prevailed in the Buddhism of medieval China, and its prevalence may have everything to do with this potential metamorphosis of an image into the real presence. There was, however, also an exegetic intent to separate the representation from the presence of the deity because of the different ontologies in which the two different meanings of "true body" may function. The distinction also underlines the visual economy of the icon of "auspicious image" (*ruixiang*) discussed previously; as "holy presence" (*shengrong*) or "true presence" (*zhenrong*), an icon of auspicious image calls to mind the power and authority of the real presence, yet is different from it. In the example of the "auspicious image from Fanhe" (Fanhe *ruixiang*) (see fig. 6.7), the icon represents a colossal statue that was thought to be the "holy presence" of a heavenly deity in material form. In the narrative of the legend, the deity in his true body was described on several occasions as descending in clouds from heaven. In a detail of the narrative depicted on the southern mural of Mogao Cave 72 (fig. 6.16), a cartouche that accompanies a cloud-riding deity reads: "The moment when the true body of the statue's holy presence arrives on clouds."[94] Although both are related to the divine (and to the same deity in this case), this differentiation between the mediated appearance (i.e., holy presence) and the unmediated true body stresses the role of the auspicious image as the tangible and reliable agent through which the divine becomes more perceivable. The same differentiation seems applicable to Cave 61.[95]

Unlike previous examples of murals or woodcuts, the now-missing statue of Mañjuśrī riding a lion would have been more than an invocative image but a physical presence on the altar located at the center of the cave interior—literally, the icon that ushers the faithful toward and into the mountain's precincts, so that these pilgrims may attain the transcendent vision of the sacred site behind the screen. The statue of Mañjuśrī on the altar emphasizes the moment in which the bodhisattva arrives as if in apparition (comes flying) before the beholder right here and now. The mural depicting the bodhisattva's sacred domain, in contrast, is schematic, conceptual, and beyond normal temporality, centered at the true body of the holy triad that includes the Buddha and his two attending bodhisatt-

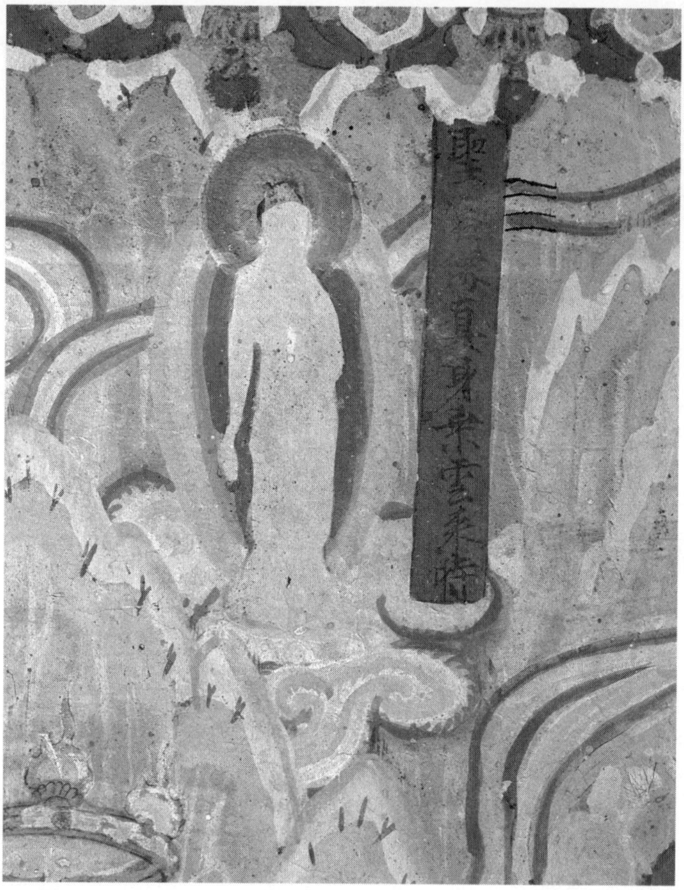

FIGURE 6.16. Detail of the mural depicting the legend of the "auspicious image" (*rui-xiang*) from Fanhe, south wall, Mogao Cave 72, Dunhuang. Mid-9th–10th century. The inscription in the cartouche reads: "The moment when the true body of the statue's holy presence arrives on clouds." Photograph by permission of Dunhuang Academy.

vas, Mañjuśrī and Samantabhadra. The statue engages the viewer frontally and visually, whereas the central triad behind the back screen entails a walk around the altar and a visual pilgrimage to find it in the complete view of Mount Wutai in the mural. The walk around the altar to see the initially unseen through the mediation of the true-presence icon becomes a metaphorical move from the secular (i.e., the zone of the laity) to the sacred (i.e., Mount Wutai) for the eternal truth that is visualized in the sacred landscape of the mural and conceptualized in the centrality of the Buddha in that landscape.

Mount Wutai: A Metamonastery

Inside Cave 61 the veneration of Mañjuśrī involves walking, seeing, and recollecting, united in a ritualistic process. Entering the cave, one walks along the corridor lined with images of men donors, while Mañjuśrī on the lion's back gradually enters one's view. One then stops at the point of entry into the cave interior where the figures of men and women donors meet to behold the bodhisattva on the altar against the background of Mount Wutai in perspective. Continuing into the cave, one takes the circumambulatory walk around the altar, past the donors and the tales of Buddha's lives and the sutra paintings above them, and embodying the pilgrim's steps into the sacred area of Mount Wutai on the back wall mural, culminating at the very center behind the back screen. Leaving, one follows more panels of the Buddha's lives and more donors, until one returns to the entrance, rejoining the men donors in the corridor. The walk is laden with multiple layers of meanings, not least in arousing a visionary experience as if traveling through the sacred site.

As much as seeing, religious vision in medieval China involved walking, that is, the vision arises via the steps taken by the practitioner, a "peripatetic vision."[96] This conception is well demonstrated in Cave 61, for one of its goals was to recreate a vision of the sacred site as experienced on foot. The constantly shifting viewpoints of the walking process through Cave 61 as just described, giving no primacy to any singular commanding view, suggest not only an ambulatory experience but also a physical negotiation between subjectivity and the visual environment. It is in this complex embodied religious visuality that the true presence of Mañjuśrī can be enacted in vision—a process that not only erases the distance between the cave and Mount Wutai but also mediates between the faithful and the transcendent realm—all in the "small place" created inside the cave. In this regard, Cave 61 is not so much a replica as a transported Mount Wutai, and its miniature scale conjures a utopian vision of the mountain's sacrality and recreates the spiritual experience supposedly attainable only at Mount Wutai.

It is not surprising that the imagery of Mount Wutai after it was transmitted to the Dunhuang region during the tenth century was not the same as in its place of origin in northern China. The visual language and economy in which they were reframed and envisioned were regional, resulting in an imagination of the sacred site that answered to the religious needs and mentality of the outlying region.[97] Through the transmission and transmutation of the imagery inside such a small place as Cave 61, however, we begin to see more explicitly the ways in which Mount Wutai was increasingly perceived and conceived as a whole during the ninth and tenth centuries, the last phase of its medieval history. The true presence of the bodhisattva, the monastic system, and the sacred topography were all sustained in transmission as the most essential elements of Mount Wutai, the ones that defined its sacrality. To reenact and make that sacrality accessible, Cave 61 is structured to simultaneously reveal a visual, physical, and empirical reality, on the one hand, and a spiritual, conceptual, and transcendent reality on the other. One's physical movement in one reality would have evoked corresponding significance in the other. Inside the cave, though the ground is level, the ensemble of the religious program recreates the "monastic topography." The deeper one goes into the cave, the higher the ground, figuratively speaking, rendering a feeling of continuous ascendance until one reaches the "virtual monastery" behind the screen, beholding the true body of the bodhisattva.

The sacred mountain thus created in the cave is an embodied discourse of the monastery at Mount Wutai. It is not just because the cave provides an architectural interior that spatializes and organizes the pilgrimage experience into a structured cohesion that suggests a monastery,[98] but more important, it seems to have rebuilt in its religious program the functions and qualities that had over time shaped and defined the monastery as the most critical means of building Mount Wutai into a sacred mountain. This mountain/monastery inside the cave locates, reveals, and accesses the initially elusive and intangible sacred presence; it solicits vision and imagination in which the true presence of bodhisattva could be encountered; it serves as a locale into which the site's legends and history was deposited; and it contains the iconography and offers a place around which the sacred topography could be restructured conceptually, yet holistically. In this regard, by the end of our period, Mount Wutai could no longer be thought of in terms of a sacred mountain but would have to be reimagined and reconceived as a monastery, or a "metamonastery" of the bodhisattva Mañjuśrī.[99]

Revisiting Foguang Monastery

[It has been said] for generations that Mount Wutai in Daizhou is where Mañjuśrī resides. Those who visit [there] often see in a radiant circle of billowing multicolored clouds the presence of the bodhisattva and the lion. It is said that long ago there was a statue of Mañjuśrī at [Mount Lu]. In recent years since the Huangyou [1049–54] and Zhiping [1064–67] reign periods, [the sighting of Mañjuśrī] has been no less frequent [here] than at [Mount] Wutai.

—Chen Shunyu, *The Record of Mount Lu* (Lushan ji)

Monastic architecture in early Chinese Buddhism was not a readily defined category of architecture, nor was its discussion and understanding limited to structural aspects. Serving an initially foreign religion as a place of divinity, monastic architecture in China developed as the belief and its practice evolved and became integrated in the religious landscape of medieval China. Mount Wutai, whose early history was inseparable from the development of early Chinese Buddhism, provides an ideal context in which to analyze monastic architecture. In the dialectic relation between the monastery and mountain, monastic architecture was not only the most crucial and substantive factor in the rise of the bodhisattva cult at Mount Wutai, but while the cult grew, flourished, and spread, it also underwent corresponding shifts and changes. Monastic architecture at Mount Wutai in this regard is necessarily both historical and historiographical.

Built at the sacred site to mark the holy traces of the bodhisattva, the monastery provided a sanctioned place for monastic routines and ritual performances, enacting and spatializing the sacred presence in its architecture and transforming the natural terrain on which the monastery stood into the sacred (monastic) topography. As the monastic ground was reperceived as such, architecture served to structure and enlarge its space, giving the uphill gradient a spiritual import, as in the case of Huayan Monastery, which climaxed with the building where the "true presence" of the bodhisattva manifested in its iconic form to the faithful. This early history of monastic architecture at Mount Wutai was later enriched and idealized in the legends of the "virtual monastery," in which buildings appeared to be divinely planned and engineered to evoke (and instantiate) a vision of transcendent reality, to which a regular monastery could aspire. The utopian vision was further elaborated in the reconception of Mount Wutai catalyzed by the building of the "iconographic architecture" of Jin'ge Monastery as the new center of the sacred mountain, turned into a mandala of esoteric practice. A pentad of monasteries—four monasteries at the four cardinal directions surrounding Jin'ge Monastery at the center—was established, schematically representing the ineffable sacred ground and the five peaks of Mount Wutai as a cohesive conception. This cohesion continued to take shape during the ninth and tenth centuries through pilgrimage, the experience of which, literally step by step, came to structure the sacred site in a narrative entirety, across the so-called ten major monasteries of Mount Wutai. Yet as the tenfold system of monasteries developed gradually into an overarching notion that essentialized Mount Wutai as a whole, the sacred site became a place that could be represented, or "visualized." By the end of our period, Mount Wutai as a sacred site of Bodhisattva Mañjuśrī could not be experienced completely without the mediation of this totalized imagery of Mount Wutai. Once transferable into imagery, on the other hand, Mount Wutai, no longer the only site where the holy presence of Mañjuśrī could be localized and observed—as suggested in the passage quoted in the epigraph—entered a different period of its history.

To a great extent, monastic architecture embodied the "perceived, conceived, and lived" spatial aspects of Mount Wutai in a trajectory parallel to the increasingly complex and conceptually sophisticated history of Mount Wutai as the first Buddhist sacred mountain in China.[1] Eventually the mountain site could be symbolically reconceived in the "image" of a monastery—as in the case of the Mogao Cave 61—as something that "the imagination seeks to change and appropriate."[2] Any discussion of monastic architecture at Mount Wutai must take into account both the history of the monastery at the mountain and its role in the way Mount Wutai was perceived, conceived, and lived as a Buddhist sacred site. With this premise, let us briefly revisit the Great Buddha Hall of Foguang Monastery (Monastery of Buddha's Radiance) (see plate 1), one of the two buildings surviving from Tang-era Mount Wutai, to conclude this book.

Located to the southwest of present-day Taihuai, Foguang Monastery is one of the few monasteries whose names were already known in Mount Wutai's earliest history (see map 2). Perhaps because of its location just outside the mountain range enclosed by the five peaks, Foguang Monastery was not at the center of discussion for the better part of the site's history during the Tang period, except for the legend of the master Jietuo (561–642) and his meditative practice at the monastery.[3] When the Japanese monk Ennin visited the mountain in 840, he did not record any details about Foguang Monastery, mentioning its name only in passing.[4] The surviving building of the Great Buddha Hall at Foguang Monastery, which still remains on its original site, however, provides us a starting point into the history of the monastery at the sacred mountain.

As suggested by its name, Foguang Monastery (Monastery of Buddha's Radiance) was famous for the light divinely emanating around it, which provided the monastery an undisputed affiliation to the numinous quality of Mount Wutai. In 770, the Pure Land master Fazhao was recorded to have been led by the radiant lights outside Foguang Monastery to his encounter of the "virtual monastery" called Zhulin Monastery.[5] In 820, Pei Du (765–839), then the regional military governor (*jiedushi*) of the greater Shanxi area, reported to the emperor that, while visiting Foguang Monastery, he had observed the sight of radiant and auspicious clouds (*qingyun*) and Mañjuśrī riding a lion in midair, accompanied by ten thousand fellow bodhisattvas.[6] Although it did not attract much of Ennin's attention during his pilgrimage, Foguang Monastery nevertheless developed into one of the ten major monasteries at Mount Wutai, first under a master named Faxing (d. 828), in the decades following the military governor's report.

A monk from the capital Chang'an, Faxing came to Mount Wutai for its numinous sightings and eventually took up residence at Foguang Monastery.[7] During his tenure, he was recorded to have commissioned a Grand Maitreya Pavilion (Mile Dage), no longer standing, nine bays wide and three stories high; it measured ninety-five *chi* in height, slightly shorter than the Golden Pavilion at Jin'ge Monastery, which is recorded as over one hundred *chi*. About its interior, Yanyi writes in the *Extended Records*, "All [main] icons were adorned in a dignified and comprehensive manner. Others, such as the Seventy-Two Worthies and Eight Dragon Kings, as well as the [many] holy images [made after those] at all monasteries at Mount Wutai, altogether more than ten thousand, were all painted or sculpted [at the pavilion]."[8] Yanyi does not describe the interior layout, but it must have been equally grand, and Faxing was not only praised for his building of the pavilion but also consequently elected chief officer, or rector, of Mount Wutai.[9]

During the persecution of Buddhism under Emperor Wuzong (r. 840–46), the extent to which Foguang Monastery was damaged is unclear, though the rebuilding of the monastery began immediately after Buddhism was reinstated in 847. The next year, Emperor Xuanzong (r. 846–59) had five monasteries rebuilt at Mount Wutai.[10] Again, no records are available about which five monasteries were selected, but with its rising influence Foguang Monastery, under another abbot, Yuancheng (d. 887), was most likely one of them. Yuancheng became an ordained monk at Foguang Monastery in 831 before the proscription; when monastic communities were persecuted, Yanyi writes, "The master [Yuancheng] persisted in his pursuit without change. [After] Xuanzong ascended to the throne, monasteries were restored. [The monastic leader] of the mountain was reselected, and [Yuancheng] was called upon to be the head, and [consequently] granted with special permission to repair Foguang Monastery."[11] After its completion, Yuancheng was further rewarded with the title "chief officer of the Mountain Gate" (Sanmen *dujianjiao*).[12] The Great Buddha hall of Foguang Monastery would have been built around this time, in 857, when the fame of the monastery was on the rise amid the Buddhist revival at Mount Wutai. The grand scale, elaborate bracket styles,[13] and quality of carpentry of the hall bespeak the prominent status of Foguang Monastery (fig. C.1), testified also by the names of patrons, including the surveillance and supervisory commissioner (*guancha chuzhi shi*) of the regional government of the greater Shanxi area, inscribed on the undersides of the four main roof beams.[14]

On the Foguang Monastery after the persecution, two manuscripts from Dunhuang, though surviving only in part, provide rare eyewitness accounts by two pilgrims who traveled to Mount Wutai in the early tenth century. One of the two accounts (translated in the introduction), by an unnamed pilgrim, describes a Great Buddha Hall, whose scale and main icons, indeed, match those of the main image hall built in 857, and a Maitreya Pavilion that would be the same building

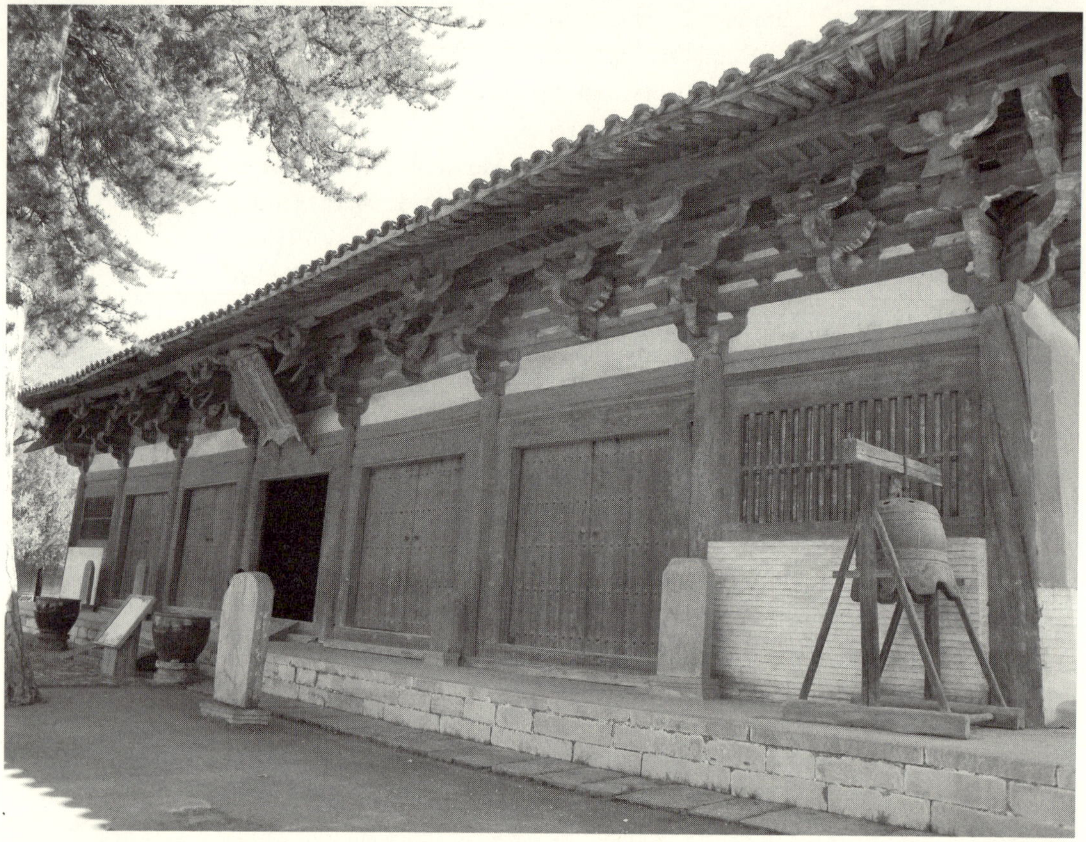

FIGURE C.1. Front facade of the Great Buddha Hall, Foguang Monastery, Mount Wutai, Shanxi. 857 CE. A grand, seven-tier bracket set is used at the top of the columns; it includes two downward-pointing cantilevered brackets, an indication of the building's status. Photograph by author.

commissioned earlier under Faxing.[15] The account also mentions dormitories, a sutra repository, and two relics pagodas among other buildings. Some of the same buildings were also observed by the Indian monk Puhua, author of the second manuscript: "I [then] rushed to Foguang Monastery, where music filled the air and banners and flowers covered the ground. [I] venerated a large statue of Maitreya and toured the great monastery of Nirvana. [I] burned incense before the [relics pagoda] of Master Jietuo and prayed at the Sage's floor. [I] lodged at the [Cloister of] Constant Abiding [Changzhu]."[16] In both accounts, the spiritual aspirations of pilgrims coming to Foguang Monastery are expressed in the recorded names of the buildings—Maitreya (the future Buddha), Nirvana (signifying enlightenment), Jietuo (liberation), and Changzhu (constant abiding)—aspirations to be embodied by pilgrims passing through the buildings.

Unfortunately, only one of the buildings depicted by the two tenth-century pilgrims survives: the main Buddha Hall, which sits on the highest ground at the end of the central axis of the architectural compound (fig. C.2; see also fig. I.4). The monastery grounds are now divided into three levels, with the lowest, open ground close to the entrance, a division that appears to be have been in the original monastery, for two Tang sutra pillars (*jingchuang*) are still standing intact, one (dated 857) on the highest level right outside the main image hall and the other (dated 877) on the lowest level. A large stone column base (1.05 x 0.96 m) carved with lotus

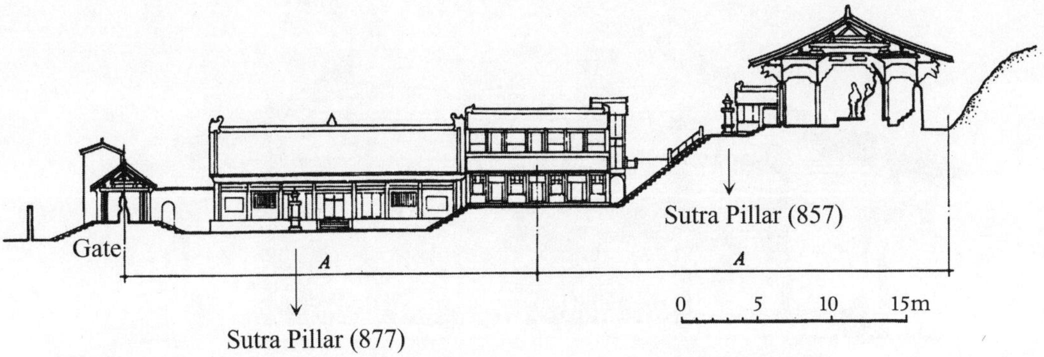

FIGURE C.2. Cross section of the topography of Foguang Monastery. The monastic site consists of three ground levels, with the Great Buddha Hall built on the highest level. Two original sutra pillars, whose dates are indicated in the figure, are still standing in their original locations. After Fu Xinian, *Liangjin, Nanbeichao, Sui-Tang, Wudai jianzhu*, fig. 3.7.14. Drawing courtesy of Fu Xinian.

leaves was reported to have been found on the middle level, which belonged to the Maitreya Pavilion.[17] Given the size and location of the column, the pavilion would have been erected on the central axis of the monastery (see fig. I.4, area marked in light gray), serving as the median between the lower front court and the Great Buddha Hall. The iconography inside the pavilion, described in Yanyi's account quoted earlier, would also have attested to its central and intermediating position.

According to Yanyi, the pavilion contained the statues of the Seventy-Two Worthies (Xiansheng)—an unusual set of deities, but characteristic for Mount Wutai around this time—which would have been key to the relation between architecture and iconography at Foguang Monastery. A set of paintings of the same seventy-two deities was also observed by Ennin during an assembly of worship (*fahui*) held at Zhulin Monastery.[18] For the liturgy, the images of all seventy-two worthies were arranged around the hall, marking the position and presence of each individual deity when its name was called to descend to the ritual field. After all worthies were ritually invited, five more deities were summoned: Śākyamuni, Maitreya, Bhaiṣajyaguru, Mañjuśrī, and Samantabhadra, followed by the chant invoking the Amitābha or Pure Land Buddha, which ended the rite.[19] At Foguang Monastery, it is likely that the Seventy-Two Worthies would have been worshiped in a similar manner inside the pavilion, and have guided the visitor's religious experience from the pavilion on the middle level to the Great Buddha Hall on the top.

Worshiping at the pavilion and entering the Great Buddha Hall, one would be ready to behold a similar host of statues—a central triad of Śākyamuni, Maitreya, and Amitābha flanked by Mañjuśrī and Samantabhadra—arranged on the altar placed centrally inside the hall, which was seven bays across and four bays deep (fig. C.3; see also fig. I.4). Bhaiṣajyaguru, who was among the five deities invoked in the pavilion, is, in the Great Buddha Hall, replaced by Amitābha, and this may have something to do with an emphasis on the vision of the Pure Land or Paradise inside the hall. The interior walls were initially covered with murals;

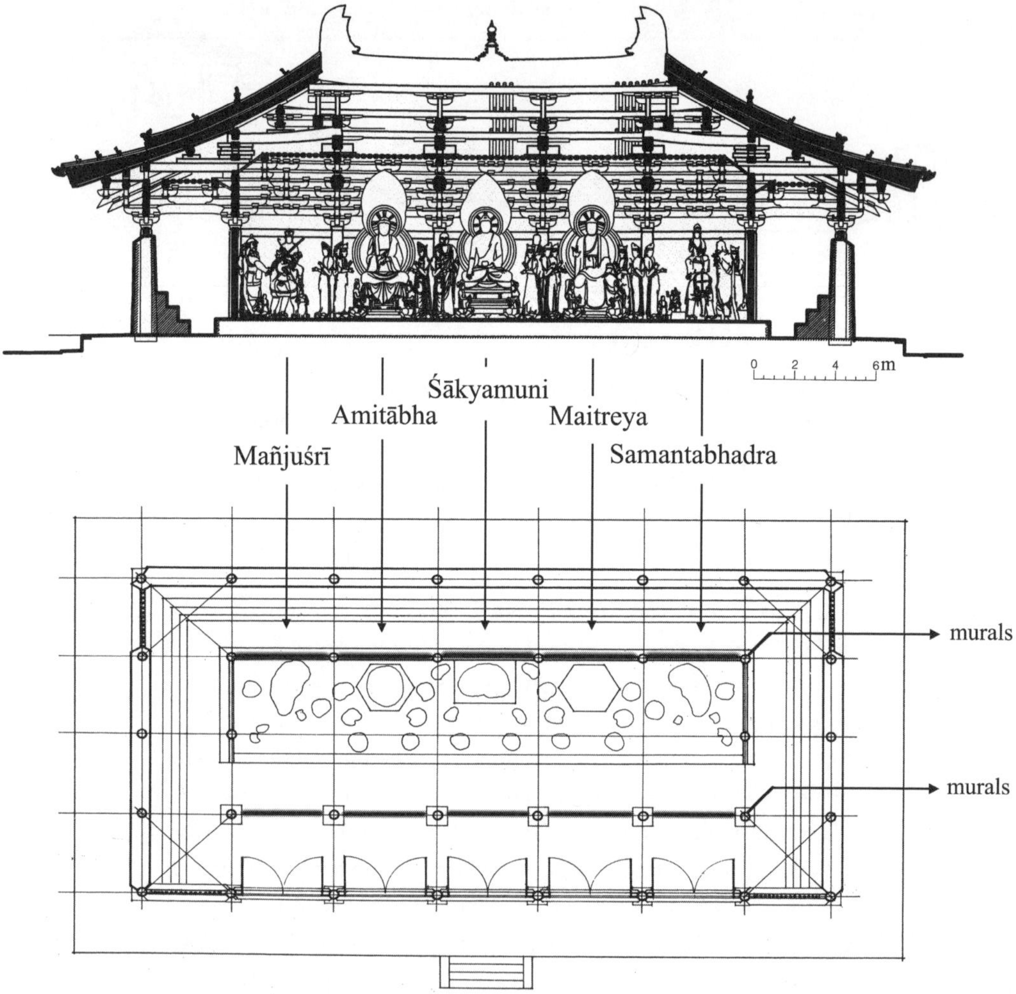

FIGURE C.3. Section and floor plan of the Great Buddha Hall, Foguang Monastery, indicating the five major enshrined icons. Murals are visible on the board above architrave (*gongyan bi*), between brackets on the first row of interior columns and above the back screen of the altar. After Fu Xinian, *Liangjin, Nanbeichao, Sui-Tang, Wudai jianzhu,* fig. 3.7.21 (section); Fu Xinian, "Wutaishan Foguangsi jianzhu," fig. 2 (floor plan). Drawings courtesy of Fu Xinian.

though most have long since been damaged, among the remaining ones, primarily on boards above the architrave (*gongyan bi*), are the scene of Amitābha preaching and his bodhisattva attendants (plate 12) and others of assemblies of bodhisattvas.[20] Appearing as they did at the center of the main hall and surrounded by the celestial assemblies and buddhas in murals, the five main deities, including the true-presence (*zhenrong*) icon of Mañjuśrī (fig. C.4), would have asserted their presence majestically to those who, through much monastic space and architecture, reached the last building on the highest ground of the monastery.

The perceived and conceived—or real and symbolic/transcendent—aspects of space in Foguang Monastery were informed by topography, ritual, icons, and

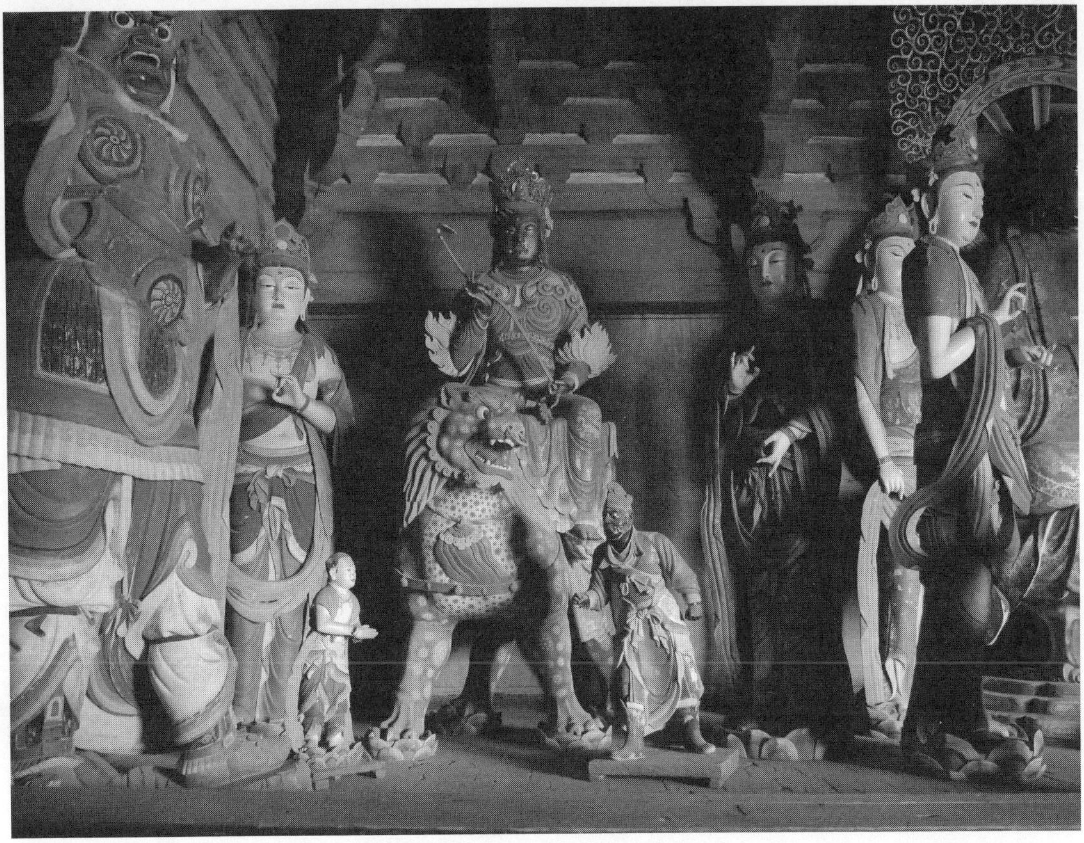

FIGURE C.4. Statue of the "true-presence" icon of Mañjuśrī riding a lion, enshrined inside the Great Buddha Hall, Foguang Monastery. 857 CE. Photograph by author.

architecture as one walked through the monastery, enacting its spatial/religious meaning and efficacy. Inside the monastery, pilgrims would recognize where to go, what to see, how to approach, and when to react within the built environment in order to attain the otherwise unattainable and see the otherwise invisible. In the first travel account discussed earlier, the unnamed pilgrim reported, "At night of the twenty-seventh day of the fifth lunar month, I witnessed [at Foguan Monastery] luminous lanterns in a cloud form [flying] in the dark [sky] eighteen times."[21] This seemingly "expected miracle," negotiating between the real and transcendent, corroborated the religious ensemble and practice inside the monastery.[22] After all, Foguang Monastery was the place where many observed a marvelous radiance, before they had advanced northeastward to the sacred mountain range enclosed by the five peaks. The monastery was a precursor of what lay ahead, a preparation. The complete view of Mount Wutai in the Mogao Cave 61 presents a coherent and holistic image of Mount Wutai unified by the tenfold system of monasteries, which came to mediate the way in which the sacred site was experienced and understood. It is in this regard that Foguang Monastery was neither a single monastery couched at the hill of the mountain site nor an isolated destination in the pilgrimage narrative, but one that served as the "mountain gate" (*shanmen*) leading the faithful into the "Monastery of Mount Wutai."

The Creation Legend of the True-Presence Icon of Bodhisattva Mañjuśrī at Huayan Monastery

This appendix includes the Chinese texts and my translations of all three extant versions of the creation legend of the icon of Mañjuśrī riding a lion, the most important iconic representation of the bodhisattva in the medieval history of Mount Wutai. The terms "true presence" (*zhenrong*) and "true body" (*zhenshen*), and closely related terms, are underlined in both the original text and translation.

1. Ennin, *Nittō guhō junrei gyōki* 入唐求法巡禮行記, ca. 847–858

初造此菩薩時，作了便裂，六遍捏作，六遍頹裂。其博士惆悵而云：「吾此一才，天下共知，而皆許孤秀矣，一生來捏作佛像，不曾見裂損之。今時作此像，齋戒至心，盡自共巧之妙，欲使天下人瞻禮，特為發心之境。今既六遍造，六遍皆催裂，的應不稱大聖之心。若實然者，伏願大聖文殊菩薩為我親現真容，親睹金顏，即仿而造」。才發願了，開眼見文殊菩薩騎金色獅子，現其人前。良久，乘五色雲騰空飛去。博士得見真容，歡喜悲泣，方知先前所造不是也。便改本樣，長短大小容貌仿取所現之像，第七遍捏作此像，更不損裂。每事易為，所要者皆應矣。其人造此像了，安置此殿，露光，眼中注汨。乃云；大奇！曾來未曾見者，今得見也。願劫劫生生常為文殊師利弟子，言竟身亡。向後，此像時時放光，頻現靈瑞。

When the [statue] of the bodhisattva was made, it cracked every time before it was completed. It was molded six times, and the statue cracked badly six times. The artisan was frustrated and said, "My skill is well known throughout the land and everyone praises my unmatchable talent. I have made Buddhist statues all my life and they have never cracked. Today in order to make this statue, [I] performed ritual abstinence with the most sincere mind and exhausted the wonder of my art, so everyone in the land could venerate it, aspiring to the most earnest mind for enlightenment. Now I have attempted to make it six times and yet it cracked six times, and so it must have not pleased the Great Sage. If that were truly the case, I would humbly plead to the Great Sage Mañjuśrī to manifest his true presence for me. [If I could] see the golden face, [I would] sculpt it by copying [the appearance]." As soon as the vow was said, he saw Bodhisattva Mañjuśrī riding a golden lion manifesting before him. Not for a while did [the bodhisattva] fly away into the sky. Seeing the true presence, the artisan was overjoyed and in tears. He also realized that what he made was incorrect and thus changed the earlier mold, based on the measurements and look of the manifested appearance. In the seventh attempt to mold this statue, it did not crack again. Every time [when changes were needed?], the request [of the artisan] was answered. After, he completed the statue and placed it in the hall. [The statue] emanated radiance and tears were shed from its eyes. [The artisan] thus said:

"It is marvelous. I just saw today what I had never seen before. I wish to be born as the disciple of the bodhisattva Mañjuśrī in the countless cycles of the world." He then died after finishing his words. Afterward, the statue often radiated and manifested auspicious miracles.

2. Dunhuang Manuscript, S529v, ca. Early Tenth Century

後至大唐睿宗皇帝時，數現真身，盡一萬眷屬。時花嚴寺僧法雲召得一匠人，姓安名生。曰：「興寺遂教，塑菩薩真身」。安生曰：「不睹聖容，疑傳不定」。遂乃焚香啟告，願見真身。俄爾之間，文殊親降，巍巍相好，色類金山。屈大聖之降靈，令蒼生之有望。請祝食頃，貌下真儀。前後七十二度現身，方遂如法。自天下僧俗，海內英賢，巡禮瞻依，盡真容者已。其真身至今見在。

Later, during the reign of Emperor Ruizong [r. 710–12], [Mañjuśrī] manifested his true body several times, [along with] all the ten thousand attendants. Then Monk Fayun at Huayan Monastery acquired an artisan, whose family name was An and given name Sheng. [To him, Fayun] said, "That the monastery may prosper and realize the teaching, [it is necessary] to sculpt a true body of the bodhisattva." An Sheng replied: "if I do not see the holy presence, I am hesitant and uncertain [about the bodhisattva's appearance]." Subsequently, [Sheng?] burned incense and supplicated in the hope of seeing the true body. In a short time, Mañjuśrī descended in person, his grandeur in perfect form and his color resembling that of Gold Mountains. [One] submitted [oneself] to the descending spirit of the Great Sage, which gave rise to hope for all sentient beings. Pleading with [the bodhisattva] to stay on for about the time for a meal, [An Sheng] was able to sculpt the true appearance. It took all together seventy-two manifestations of him to complete the task as instructed. Since then both monks and laity in the land and the able and virtuous from the world, all came to venerate and worship nothing but the true presence. Now, the true body is still there.

3. Yanyi, *The Extended Records of [Mount] Qingliang*, T.51: 2099, 1110a16–26, 1060 CE

唐景雲中，有僧法雲者，未詳姓氏，住大華嚴寺。每惟大聖示化，方無尊像，俾四方遊者，何所瞻仰？乃繕治堂宇，募工儀形。有處士安生者，不知從何而至。一日，應召為雲塑像。雲將厚酬其直，欲速疾工。生謂雲曰：「若不目覩真像。終不能無疑」。乃焚香懇啟。移時，大聖忽現於庭。生乃欣踊躄地，祝曰：「願留食頃，得盡模相好」。因即塑之。厥後，心有所疑，每一迴顧，未嘗不見文殊之在傍也。再期功畢，經七十二現，真儀方備。自是靈應肹蠁，遐邇歸依，故以真容目院焉。

During the Jingyun reign [710–11] of the Tang, there was a monk named Fayun, whose original name was unknown. He took residence at the Great Huayan Monastery, often pondering that although the Great Sage manifests to enlighten [the beholder], there was no image to benefit the itinerant pilgrims coming from afar, and as such what could they venerate? [Fayun] therefore commissioned a building and recruited artisans to portray the [bodhisattva's] image. There was a layman named An Sheng, and no one knew where he came from. One day [An Sheng] responded to the call [for artisans] to sculpt the image for [Fa]yun. [Fa]yun would reward [An Sheng's] work lucratively but urged [An Sheng] to hasten the work. Sheng told [Fa]yun, "[I] cannot accomplish this without fault if not able to observe the [bodhisattva's] true image." Subsequently [Sheng] burned incense and supplicated for answers, at which moment the Great Sage appeared swiftly at the court. Sheng was overjoyed and jumped up and down, pleading [the bodhisattva]: "Please stay on for just about the time for a meal, so [I] can completely sculpt your perfect form." [Sheng] was therefore able to sculpt the image, and after then, whenever feeling hesitant in his mind, he would turn around and look, and he never failed to see Mañjuśrī right there. In order to finish the work, [Sheng] again supplicated [to the bodhisattva], and [only] through seventy-two manifestations was the true appearance finally completed. [The completed statue] was surely efficacious in divine resonance, [so much that devotees] from near and afar all came to venerate it faithfully, and thus [the hall that housed the statue] was named True Presence.

Transcription and Translation of the Inscription on the Dongzhang Stone Lantern

The shaft on which the inscription was carved is supported by a square base (sculpted in a shape that resembles Mount Wutai) and topped by a candle rack in the form of a building (see figs. 4.1–3). According to the inscription, the stone lantern was originally made in Dongzhang village, located in present-day Daixian, Shanxi, to the east of Mount Wutai (see map 11). The inscription, twenty-six lines in all, was carved on four contiguous sides of the eight-sided shaft, while the remaining four sides are carved with names of patrons. Illegible characters in this transcription are indicated by a square □. Punctuation has been added.

[Side 1] 五臺山及燈臺記

A Record of Mount Wutai and the Lantern

柱國張處貞 匠常泰貞 聶孝忠

Pillar of State Zhang Chuzhen, Artisan Chang Taizhen, Nie Xiaozhong

上為開元神武 皇帝、師僧父母、太子諸王、文武百僚、州牧縣宰。

[This is dedicated to benefit] the Origin-Beginning Divine-Prowess Emperor, teachers and masters, princes and all state governors, all officials and marshals, and governors of all regions, and counties.

蓋聞能仁不測，宏開八政之門；真相無邊，廣闢二乘之路。雖復日宮煥爛，尚假慈燈；月殿玲瓏，猶資慧炬。欲使騰輝法界，有冥皆明；散彩恆沙，無幽不燭。故知像之不滅，燈乃常明，照耀諸塵，不生不滅。

It is heard that [the greatness of] Mighty-in-Lovingkindness [i.e., Śākyamuni] cannot be measured, as he broadens eight aspects of governance; the true presence is without limit, as it opens wide the path for both Mahayana and Theravada. No matter how gloriously magnificent the palatial halls are, the light of compassion is still needed; no matter how exquisite the moon palaces are, the torch of wisdom is still required. If one wishes to illuminate the Dharma Field, to enlighten all who have Buddha nature, to spread color over all grains of sand in the Ganges River, and to light up all darkness with candles, then [one should know that] the image [of the Buddha] will not perish and light will forever glow, shining over all dust without beginning or end.

眾生蠢蠢，五濁俱懷，三毒四蛇，競相催逼。又乃貪居惡室，恆日荒迷，久在泥黎，[Side 2] 蹤橫被縛。近者方知自悟，虛度終朝，各發善緣，擬茲來路。

All ignorant beings possess five defilements, and in them three unwholesome roots fight with four evils. They indulge in evil places for a long time, losing themselves day after day. [They have] long been sunk in mud, being bound from all sides. Only recently have people become aware that they have wasted all their days. [They thus] made vows to accrue good causes in order to secure the road to come.

導引禪師，釋名無碍，住寺僧文爰及合村宿老、優婆夷等，人人勵己，各各用心。抽減淨財，將充舍施。亦能衣中減縷，食內抽飧。同發善因，敬造燈光明臺一所。

The leading Chan master, whose monk name is Wuai, the monk in residence named Wen'ai, and all the reputable male elders and female lay believers of the village, each encourages the other, from their hearts, to take from their pure belongs for donation: [they] save by using fewer threads when making clothes, or save by omitting dinner from their daily meals. [By so doing,] all [in the village] together are able to plant favorable causes by respectfully making a bright-light lantern.

其臺也，置五臺山為座，昉五岳而立其形。中臺池有玉華，池裹演生其幹，幹上雲花，五色散蓋，疊疊重重。四窗猶在，天宮八闥，不離其內，兼加八柱，遞代相承。燈盞汪汪，中心汎曜。

Regarding the lantern, Mount Wutai forms its base, and [the distribution of its five peaks] resembles that of the five Sacred Peaks. Located at [the top of] Central Peak is a pond called Yuhua (Jade Flora), inside which grows a trunk. On [and above] the trunk are cloud patterns. Five-colored [wooden] canopies, layer by layer, open four windows over the eight-sided heavenly palace. In addition, there is an octagonal shaft, [symbolizing] the transmission one generation after another. Candles shine from the center [of the lantern].

其散蓋也，蘭（欄）簷 紫柏，椽 [Side 3] 用沉香，升拱飛仙，純金帖作。雲花曖曖，雜彩鮮明，舞風吹笙，百禽皆足。

About the canopies, the eaves are made of fragrant cedar and rafters are made of eaglewood; the flying brackets are covered with gold leaves and cloud-like flowers, delicate and bright in their mixed colors. The wind dances, blowing the *sheng*-pipe; all fowl are here, not missing one.

其五臺山也，五百毒龍居此，一萬菩薩同臻，兼加密跡金剛，頗亦不知其數。臺臺供養，累道來巡；他國遠方，皆來奔湊。置寺名當一百，蘭若約有數千。每年禮謁，諸臺道俗，強過一萬，西方淨土，與此無殊。

Mount Wutai [is the place] where five hundred venomous snakes live, together with ten thousand bodhisattvas, as well as the Guardian of Secret Trace Vajra, all these cannot be numbered. Offerings are made at each of the peaks; [pilgrims] come to venerate from all directions. Many arrive even from other countries or distant lands to join [the pilgrimage]. [Here] monasteries that have name [plaques] number about one hundred; smaller monasteries and hermitages number about a thousand. Each year more than ten thousand clerical and lay pilgrims [come to] venerate at all peaks. The Pure Land of the West would not be different from [Mount Wutai].

邀様鐫形，非加不妙。至如般若妙詞，已闡燃燈之義；法花奧旨，復載燈光之文。灌頂章表於延齡，阿那律得其天眼。燈之為福，其若是乎！

[We therefore] acquired a model and sculpted its form, and made it until we could not perfect it more. The verses in the *Prajñā Sutra* have expounded the significance of lighting candles; the profound words of the *Lotus Sutra* have moreover recorded enlightening meanings of light. [As] the ritual *abhiṣeka* grants one's prolonged lifespan and Aniruddha acquired the divine eye, the blessings from the light are equal to just such!

欲報合村 [Side 4] 之恩，須憑法王之力。於是共申洪愿，各舍微資，雕鐫光焰之帘，建立長明之炬。

To repay the merits received by the whole village still depends on the power of the Dharma Lord. We thus together take a vow, each donating a few resources, for sculpting the window of the flaming light and building the torch of the eternal glow.

其臺也，府臨雁塞，方偎風游之儀；北接滹沱，以吐青蓮之秀。明如法鏡，足豪相之神光；皎若意珠，助金容之妙色。庶使彼岸之際，壯瑞彩於□樓；禪林之中，散祥殊於火樹。

Mount Wutai of the base, looking over the far border, in close proximity to the landscape of the [northern] steppes; connecting in the north to the Hutuo River, it exhales the delicacy of the blue lotus. It is clear like the dharma mirror, reflective of the light of the divine presence; [it is] bright as pearls, enhancing the indescribable appearance of [the bodhisattva's] golden presence. It is thus like the shore of the other side, magnificently colorful as [?] pavilions, and as in the dharma field, scattering auspicious signs as the night scene is dotted by lights.

其詞曰：風游山旁，名望東張。伽藍妙寺，亞次西方。釋僧文爱，端坐禪房。精心供養，灑掃是常。悲敬二福，不乏米糧。他方一僧，釋名無碍。又引諸子，皆無向背。法水流布， 滅除其罪。兼造燈臺，真成可愛。遍布觀望，世界□□。□國無封，東張一村。奇異幾精，心練行總。

The verses read: nesting next to the mount [Wutai], it is named Dongzhang [village]. Grand monasteries and wonderful temples are next to only the West [Pure Land]. Master Wen'ai sits in the meditative chamber, making offerings wholeheartedly and purifying and cleansing [the field] regularly. Compassion and veneration are two of the meritorious deeds and food is never lacking. An itinerant master whose name is Wu'ai leads all disciples [onto the right path] and none has gone astray. [His teachings are like] dharma water, flowing widely and rescinding all wickedness. In addition, [he also] commissioned the lantern, truly liked and admired. All would look up to it, and the world [?]. [?] is no enclosure, in which there is the village of Dongzhang. The marvelous creation [of the lantern] is almost perfect, reflecting the devout heart that led to the deed.

Transcriptions of Key Passages from Chinese Texts Used in This Study

The six Chinese passages transcribed here are translated and discussed in the text. Each passage comes from a contemporary account or document concerning Mount Wutai. Punctuation has been added.

SECTION 1

Travel diary of an unnamed pilgrim to Mount Wutai, ca. early tenth century, Dunhuang Manuscript S397. See book introduction.

又到佛光寺，四十里。二十七日夜，見雲燈十八遍現；兼有大佛殿七間，
中間二尊，兩面文殊普賢菩薩。彌勒閣三層七間，七十二賢，萬菩薩，十六羅漢。
解脫和尚真身塔，鏁子骨和尚塔，云是文殊普賢化現。常住院大樓五間，
上層是經藏，於下安眾，日供僧五百余人。房廊殿宇更有數院，功德佛事極多，
難可具載。

SECTION 2

Fazhao's description of the "virtual monastery" named "Bamboo Grove Monastery of the Great Sage" at Mount Wutai; recorded in *Guang Qingliang zhuan* (Extended records of [Mount] Qingliang), T. 51: 2099.1114b16–21, by Yanyi, ca. 1060. See chapter 4.

一如缽中所見，周圓可二十里，中有一百二十院，院中皆有寶塔莊嚴。其地純是
黃金，渠流花果充滿其中。法照入寺至講堂內，見大聖文殊在西，普賢在東，
各處師子之座說法，次其身及座，高可百尺。文殊左右菩薩萬餘，普賢亦有無數
菩薩前後圍繞。

SECTION 3

Amoghavajra's petition to build the Monastery of Golden Pavilion (Jin'gesi), dated 766, recorded in *Daizong chao zeng Sikong da bianzheng guangzhi sanzang heshang biaozhi ji* (Collection of the memoranda on regulations bestowed by the court of Daizong to the minister of works, the greatly skillful and upright Guangzhi, the venerable Tripiṭaka master), T.52: 2120.834a9–a20, compiled by Yuanzhao. See chapter 5.

開元二十四年，衢州僧道義至臺山，所見文殊聖跡寺，號金閣院，有十三間，
居僧眾云有萬人。臺殿門樓，茲金所作。登時，圖畫一本，進入在內。天下百姓咸
欲金閣寺成，人誰不願，令澤州僧道環日送供至山。景慕道義禪師所見之事，
發心奉為國家依圖造金閣寺，院宇都少一如所見 . . . 五臺靈山，寺額有五：
清涼、華嚴、佛光、玉花，四寺先成；獨唯金閣一所未就，既是聖跡，誰不具瞻。

SECTION 4

The *Gate for Visualization of the Five-Syllable Yoga* (Wuzi yuqie guanmen), quoted in *Guang Qingliang zhuan*, T.51: 2099.1104b24–c7, by Yanyi. See chapter 5.

阿者，無生門，詮一切法無生，表大圓鏡智。東方金剛部主阿閦如来，即菩薩頂上東邊一髻之象也。囉者，無垢門，詮一切法無垢，表平等性智。南方寶部主寶生如來，即菩薩頂上南邊一髻之象也。跛者，無第一義諦門，表妙觀察智。西方蓮花部主無量壽如來，即菩薩頂上西邊一髻之象也。左者，諸法無行門，表成所作智。北方羯磨部主不空成就如來，即菩薩頂上北邊一髻之象也。娜者，諸法無性相離語言文字門，表清淨法界。中方如來部主毘盧遮那如來，即菩薩頂上中方一髻之象也。故菩薩頂分五髻，山派五峰，豈徒然哉。

SECTION 5

Description by the Japanese pilgrim Ennin, 840 CE, of Buddhist statues and murals in the Golden Pavilion of the Monastery of the Golden Pavilion, as recorded in his *Nittō guhō junrei gyōki* (Record of a Pilgrimage to China in Search of the Law); see *NGJG*, vol. 3, 89.

開金閣，禮大聖。文殊菩薩騎青毛獅子，聖像金色，顏貌端嚴，不可比喻。又見靈仙聖人手皮佛像及金銅塔。又見辟支佛牙、佛肉身舍利。當菩薩頂懸七寶傘蓋，是敕施之物。閣九間，三層，高百尺餘，壁檐椽柱，無處不畫，內外莊嚴，盡世珍異。顒然獨出樹林之表，白雲自在下而靉靆，閣層超然而高顯。次上第二層，禮金剛頂瑜伽五佛像。斯乃不空三藏為國所造，依天竺那蘭陀寺樣作，每佛各有二脇士，並于板牆上列置。次登第三層，禮頂輪王瑜伽會五佛金像。每佛各一脇士菩薩，二菩薩作合掌像，在佛前面向南立。佛菩薩手印容貌，與第二層像各異。粉壁內面，畫諸重曼荼羅，填色未了，是亦不空三藏為國所造。

SECTION 6

Description by the Indian pilgrim Puhua of a visit to observe the true-presence icon of Mañjuśrī riding a lion at Huayan Monastery, ca. 926–36; Dunhuang Manuscript P3931. See chapter 6.

尋禮真容，果諧夙願，瞻虔至夜，宿在殿中，持念更深。聖灯忽現，舉眾皆睹，無不忻然 。二十日再啟虔誠，重趨聖殿。夜觀真相，忽現毫光，晃輝尊顏，如懸明月。睹其聖瑞。轉切殷勤。

CONVENTIONS AND ABBREVIATIONS

All names of monasteries (*si*) are rendered in English as "Monastery" followed by the transliteration of their Chinese names, for example, Foguang Monastery (Foguangsi). The literal meanings of the names of major monasteries—for example, Monastery of Buddha's Radiance, for Foguangsi—are given in the text when they are first mentioned; they are also listed in the glossary.

NGJG Ono Katsutoshi 小野勝年, *Nittō guhō junrei gyōki no kenkyū* 入唐求法巡禮行記の研究 (A study of the *Record of a Pilgrimage to China in Search of the Law*). 4 vols. Tokyo: Suzuki gakujutsu zaidan, 1964–69.

P Numbered Pelliot manuscripts from Dunhuang in the Bibliothèque Nationale, Paris.

S Numbered Stein manuscripts from Dunhuang in the British Library, London.

T. *Taishō shinshū daizōkyō* 大正新修大蔵経 (The *Tripiṭaka* in Chinese), 100 vols., ed. Takakusu Junjirō 高楠順次郎 et al. (Tokyo: Taishō issaikyō kankōkai, 1924–32). All citations from the Taishō Canon are given as follows: T. set number (followed by colon and space), volume number (followed by period), and page number, followed immediately by register (a, b, or c) and line number(s). For example: T.51: 2122.591a18–19.

NOTES

INTRODUCTION

The epigraph is from Ge Hong, *Master Who Embraces Simplicity* (Baopuzi), *juan* 17.

1 Mountains were among the topics dealt with in the earliest surviving texts, and since then mountains had been imagined in the construction of such notions as space, power, and universe. See He Pingli, *Chongshan linian yu Zhongguo wenhua,* 1–82; Lewis, *Construction of Space in Early China,* 284–303.

2 For a discussion on the intermediary position of mountains between heaven and earth, see Munakata, *Sacred Mountains in Chinese Art,* 1–12.

3 For a discussion of how mountains were important as territorial marks and sites of state rituals in early China, see Tsai, "In the Steps of Emperors and Immortals."

4 See Zheng, *Shan wenhua.*

5 The identity and canonical role of Mañjuśrī as a bodhisattva in Mahayana Buddhism is discussed in chapter 3. It should be noted that although mountains have long been venerated in China, the term "sacred mountain" in English has no precise Chinese equivalent. On the Chinese terms used for the concept of sacred mountains, see chapter 2.

6 The bodhisattva Mañjuśrī undoubtedly originated in India, but the sacred mountain cult associated with the bodhisattva did not start there. The cult that developed at Mount Wutai was a particularly Chinese phenomenon and should be considered an effort to domesticate the foreign deity during a period when Buddhism was localized in China.

7 See Sen, *Buddhism, Diplomacy, and Trade,* esp. chap. 2, 55–101.

8 The four Buddhist sacred mountains associated with different bodhisattvas are Mount Emei (Emeishan), associated with Samantabhadra (Puxian), in present-day Sichuan; Mount Putuo (Putuoshan), associated with Avalokiteśvara (Guanyin), in Zhejiang; and Mount Jiuhua (Jiuhuashan), associated with Kṣitigarbha (Dizang), in Anhui; in addition to Mount Wutai, associated with Mañjuśrī, in Shanxi. Of the four, Mount Wutai was the first established as a Buddhist sacred mountain, followed by Mount Emei in the ninth and tenth centuries, and the last two mountains most likely after the fifteenth century. The collective term, "four great famous mountains" (*sida mingshan*), referring to these four Buddhist mountains, was not in use until the seventeenth century. While the emergence of the four Buddhist mountains as a cluster in China's religious geography had a long, slow development, Mount Wutai was clearly a model for each of the later three mountains, either in its founding legend or in the pattern of its historical development. For a discussion on the four mountains in terms of sacred mountain cults, see Qin, *Sida mingshan.* For an analysis of each of the three later sacred mountains, see Yü, "P'u-t'o Shan"; Ng, *The Making of a Savior Bodhisattva;* and Hargett, *Stairway to Heaven.*

9 For how "medieval" can be applied to China's historical periodization, see Knapp, "Did the Middle Kingdom Have a Middle Period?"

10 See, for example, Naquin and Yü, *Pilgrims and Sacred Sites;* Eade and Sallnow, *Contesting the Sacred.*

11 See Van Gennep, *The Rites of Passage;* Turner, "Betwixt and Between." *Communitas* is a term referring to an unstructured/liminal state of a community.

12 Shanxi lüyou, *Wutaishan zhi,* 14–15.

13 *NGJG,* vol. 2, 419; the translation is adapted from Reischauer, *Ennin's Diary,* 214. Ennin traveled to China in 838 and stayed until 847.

14 *NGJG,* vol. 2, 419. Mount Qingliang (Qingliangshan) is the mountain identified in the *Flower Garland Sutra* as Bodhisattva Mañjuśrī's sacred mountain, and has thus been used interchangeably with Mount Wutai throughout its history. This scriptural origin for the name Mount Qingliang is discussed in chapter 2.

15 See De Certeau, "Hagiographie"; Peter Brown, *The Cult of the Saints.*

16 This emphasis on extrinsic determinants may have been the most important characteristic of a Buddhist mountain, compared to a native one. In his research on indigenous mountain traditions in China from pre-Daoist to Daoist practice, Julius Tsai argues in slightly different terms: "We should view the Chinese mountain not in its exteriority, as a mass of terrestrial material, but rather as an interiority, a generative matrix, a receptacle of life, in short as a womb"; see Tsai, "In the Steps of Emperors," 20.

17 This separation is found in works such as Durkheim, *The Elementary Forms;* Eliade, *The Sacred and Profane.*

18 See, for example, De Certeau, *The Practice of Everyday Life;* Lefebvre, *The Production of Space;* Harvey, *Justice, Nature, and the Geography;* Casey, *The Fate of Place.*

19 The term "spatial turn" comes from Edward S. Casey's introduction to the second edition of *Getting Back into Space,* xxi. The notion *longue durée,* emphasizing a long-term historical structure over particular events, is introduced in Braudel, "History and the Social Sciences," in Braudel, *On History,* 25–54.

20 See Robson, *Power of Place,* for the Southern Sacred Peak; Dott, *Identity Reflections,* for the Eastern Sacred Peak; Hargett, *Stairway to Heaven,* for Mount Emei. All these works are in turn inspired by two important earlier works: Chavannes, *Le T'ai chan,* and Schafer, *Mao Shan in T'ang Times.*

21 For examples of material culture in medieval China, see Watt et al., *China.*

22 For studies on Buddhist material culture, see Kieschnick, *The Impact of Buddhism;* Rambelli, *Buddhist Materiality.* Some of the terms of analysis in this regard can also be found in scholarship on Western religions; for example, see Patricia Cox Miller, *The Corporeal Imagination;* Bynum, *Christian Materiality.*

23 More scholars have paid attention to the material aspect of the sacred, which, in addition to material objects, would also include architecture, space, built environment, and landscape, in which the spiritual could be revealed, expressed, and understood. On architecture, see Wescoat and Ousterhout, *Architecture of the Sacred.* In regard to how built environment and landscape can be studied in terms of material culture, see Hicks and Beaudry, eds., *The Oxford Handbook,* 427–517.

24 This is the title of the book *Architecture of the Sacred,* edited by Wescoat and Ousterhout.

25 For example, for the idea of architecture as dwelling, see Heidegger, "Building Dwelling Thinking," in Heidegger, *Poetry, Language, Thought,* 143–59.

26 This is observed in Robson, "Monastic Spaces and Sacred Traces," 44.

27 The suffix *si* in the name of the monastery is translated variably as "temple" or "monastery." In medieval Chinese Buddhism, the ways *si* was used was not always consistent; for a discussion of the use of the term, see Robson, "Monastic Spaces and Sacred Traces," 45–46.

28 The fragmentary text (S397) is among the scrolls of manuscripts and paintings stored in Mogao Cave 17, the so-called Library Cave, near Dunhuang, sealed up sometime after 1000 CE. The cave was not opened again until it was discovered in 1907. The uncovered scrolls have since then been removed and collected in various places, most prominently, in the United Kingdom, France, and Russia, in addition to China. The quoted text is transcribed and annotated in Du Doucheng, *Dunhuang Wutaishan wenxian*, 143–46. It is translated in Rhie, *The Fo-kuang ssu*, 49–60. My translation is after Rhie's, with revisions. The Chinese text is given in appendix 3, sec. 1.

29 The "Great Buddha Hall," a name recorded in one of the inscriptions found in the hall, however, has been called Great Eastern Hall (Dong Dadian) in modern scholarship because of its east-facing orientation. See Chai, "Wutai Foguangsi" and "Foguangsi Dongdadian"; Fu Xinian, "Wutaishan Foguangsi jianzhu." The first monograph on Foguang Monastery with a focus on its Buddhist statues is Rhie's *The Fo-kuang ssu;* more comprehensive studies of this important monument, including its history and architecture, and the research undertaken on it, were not available until the two recent publications: Rujivacharakul and Luo, *Liang Sicheng and the Temple of the Buddha's Light;* Shanxisheng gu jianzhu, *Wutaishan Foguangsi.*

30 It was first reported in Liang, "Ji Wutaishan Foguangsi jianzhu." About Liang Sicheng (also spelled Liang Ssu-ch'eng), the most comprehensive discussion in English is still Wilma Fairbank, *Liang and Lin.*

31 For an introduction to *Yingzao fashi,* the earliest building treatise in China, see Glahn, "On the Transmission"; Qinghua Guo, "Yingzao Fashi." Most recently, the manual is more thoroughly discussed in Feng, *Chinese Architecture and Metaphor.*

32 See Steinhardt, "The Tang Architectural Icon."

33 On Liang's modernist approach to the history of Chinese architecture, see Wei-Cheng Lin, "Preserving China" and "Untranslatable Iconicity."

34 Zhang Rong et al., "Foguangsi Dongdadian shice shuju jiedu." A more recent publication based on the investigation is Lü Zhou, *Foguangsi Dongdadian jianzhu kancha.*

35 For the measurements of the Great Buddha Hall, see Fu Xinian, "Wutaishan Foguangsi jianzhu."

36 On the sutra pillar, see Liang, "Ji Wutaishan Foguangsi jianzhu," 21–23; the particular *dhāraṇī* sutra (i.e., a canonical text that contains magic spells for ritual incantations) and its relation to the history of Mount Wutai is discussed in chapter 4.

37 The plaque gives the date of the forty-second year in the Wanli reign of the Ming dynasty (1614 CE), but no surviving texts record when exactly Foguang Monastery took "True Presence" (*zhenrong*) as part of its official name or when it was turned into a Chan monastery.

38 Zhencheng, *Qingliangshan zhi, juan* 2, 35.

39 The mural is among many that depict Mount Wutai in the Mogao caves. Their appearance in a location so far from the mountain site should raise questions about the spread of the sacred mountain cult, a topic that will be discussed in chapter 6.

40 Robson, "Monastic Spaces and Sacred Traces," 47–48.

41 See Ono Genmyō, "Godaisan dai Bukkōji." According to Ono and Hibino, Ono Genmyō also later published photos taken from Mount Wutai in *Godaisan shashinshū* (The photo album of Mount Wutai) in 1923, and Itō Chūta, an architectural historian, published two general articles, both with the title "Godaisan" (citations in Ono and Hibino, *Godaisan*; see ibid., 356 and 358). The most important contribution in this early stage of research on Mount Wutai came from Inoue Ichii, who published a series of four articles on the history of Mount Wutai, "Godaisan shi no issetsu"; and another four-part article on the history of Mount Wutai during the Tang, "Tōdai ni okeru Godaisan no bukkyō." The best-known contribution is Sekino Tadashi and Tokiwa Daijō's multivolume publication, *Shina bukkyō shiseki*, volume 5 of which includes a lengthy section on major monasteries at Mount Wutai.

42 Ono and Hibino, *Godaisan*.

43 Ibid., preface, 3–7.

44 A recent survey of Mount Wutai's history is Debreczeny, "Wutaishan: Pilgrimage to Five Peak Mountain," which appears in a special issue of *Journal of the International Association of Tibetan Studies* dedicated to the history of Mount Wutai during the Qing period; see Tuttle and Elverskog, *Wutai Shan and Qing Culture*. For its history after the Tang, see Gimello, "Chang Shang-ying on Wu-t'ai Shan" and "Wu-t'ai Shan during the Early Chin Dynasty." For the imperial patronage from the Qing court, see Farquhar, "Emperor as Bodhisattva"; Wen-shing Chou, "Ineffable Paths"; Köhle, "Why Did the Kangxi Emperor Go to Wutai Shan?" The relation of Mount Wutai with the Qing court is also discussed in Berger, *Empire of Emptiness*.

45 The first notable attempt at a contextual study of monasteries at Mount Wutai in this regard is Rhie's *The Fo-kuang ssu*, published in 1977, based on her dissertation of the same title, completed in 1970. It is, however, primarily a study of the surviving Tang Buddhist statues enshrined in the Great Buddha Hall of Foguang Monastery (see fig. I.3). The group of icons was analyzed in the tradition of icon veneration of the period by exploring the textual records, both transmitted and uncovered, relating to Mount Wutai in the Tang era. Foguang Monastery in Rhie's study was not just a surviving structure from the past but a critical context to investigate the Buddhist statues in the larger cultic practice at the sacred site. From a different approach, Birnbaum's seminal work of 1983, entitled *Studies on the Mysteries of Mañjuśrī*, though it does not address issues directly related to monasteries, greatly enhances our understanding of Mount Wutai by introducing how the bodhisattva cult developed during the Tang dynasty through the legends, hagiographic tales, and monastic practice at Mount Wutai.

46 In the past decade, there has been much new research on Western medieval concepts and practices of space; see, for example, Hanawalt and Kobialka, *Medieval Practices of Space*; Davies et al., *People and Space in the Middle Ages*; Goodson et al., *Cities, Texts, and Social Networks*.

47 A recent collection of essays that account for these factors in establishing a sacred site is Benn, Chen, and Robson, *Images, Relics, and Legends*.

48 Smith, *To Take Place*, 104.

ONE. Building the Monastery, Locating the Sacred Presence

The epigraph is taken from Daoshi (d. 683), *Jade Grove of the Dharma Garden* (Fayuan zhulin), *juan* 39, T.53: 2122.591a18–19.

1 *Chu sanzang ji ji*, T.55: 2145.96b7. My discussion of this particular account is based on the biography of Kang Senghui in Sengyou (445–518), *Chu sanzang ji ji, juan* 13, T.55: 2145.96a29–97a17; a different version of Kang's biography is in *Gaoseng zhuan, juan* 1, T.50: 2059.325a13–326b13.

2 *Rulai*, or *tathāgata* in Sanskrit, literally "thus come," is one of the ten epithets of the Buddha.

3 *Chu sanzang ji ji*, T.55: 2145.96b11–13.

4 See Strong, *The Legend of King Aśoka.*

5 See also Zürcher, *The Buddhist Conquest of China*, 51–55.

6 For Buddhism as a "practice religion," see Lopez, "Introduction" to *Religions of China in Practice.*

7 See, for example, Puay-Peng Ho, "Chinese Buddhist Monastic Architecture"; Steinhardt, "Early Chinese Buddhist Architecture"; Fu Xinian, *Liangjin*, 155–203.

8 Fu Xinian briefly discusses the three-stage development in his "The Three Kingdoms," 85. Several important articles look at the early history of Chinese monasteries in terms of their function, spatial layout, and style; see, for example, Su, "Donghan Wei Jin Nanbeichao" and "Suidai fosi buju"; Fan Peisong, "Zhongguo siyuan xingzhi"; and most recently, Li Yuqun, "Sui Tang yiqian Zhongguo fojiao siyuan"; Wang Guixiang, "Dongjin ji Nanchao shiqi"; and "Fojiao chuchuan zhi Xijin mo."

9 My comment about the limitations of viewing early Buddhist monasteries in terms of their content is echoed, from a different standpoint, in the observation made by James Robson: "In general studies of monasteries there has been a perduring tendency to discuss them as mere 'containers' for the actions of a religious community"; see Robson, "Monastic Spaces and Sacred Traces," 47.

10 Steinhardt, "Early Chinese Buddhist Architecture," 41; Sickman and Soper, *The Art and Architecture of China*, 230–31.

11 See, for instance, Kajiyama, "Stūpa." Another explanation for this shift from pagoda to image hall has been proposed by Fu Xinian: "As long as the pagoda remained the focus of Buddhist worship, worship space was limited. . . . The lack of a central image may have detracted from the desired solemn and focused mood and may be the reason the pagoda was eventually superseded by large halls that could both house sculpture and provide additional devotional space"; Fu, "The Three Kingdoms," 80.

12 Zürcher lists several factors that may have contributed to the acceptance and spread of Buddhism in early medieval China, and in most of them, both relics and images were crucial; see Zürcher, *The Buddhist Conquest of China*, 269–80.

13 For the origin and history of the stupa before its transmission to China from India, see Pant, *The Origin and Development of Stupa Architecture.* Two books dealing with the stupa from different viewpoints are Dallapiccola and Lallemant, *The Stūpa*, and Snodgrass, *The Symbolism of the Stupa.*

14 For a discussion about the meaning and different implications of the term *nirvana*, see Williams, *Mahāyāna Buddhism*, 52–54 and 181–84.

15 Dutt, *Buddhist Monks and Monasteries*, 185.

16 See Coomaraswamy, "The Origin of the Buddha Image," 293.

17 Zürcher, *The Buddhist Conquest of China,* 277.

18 Fukui, "Butsuji no jigi." Although it was still being used for funeral shrines, the suffix *ci* was later used primarily for Daoist temples; see Steinhardt, "Taoist Architecture," 57–59. See also Zürcher, *The Buddhist Conquest of China,* 38–39; Robson, "Monastic Spaces and Sacred Traces," 45–46.

19 For an example, see the biography of a fourth-century monk, Huida, recorded in Huijiao's *Gaoseng zhuan* (Biographies of eminent monks) in T.50: 2059.409b13–410a7.

20 See Shinohara, "Changing Roles for Miraculous Images."

21 Barrett, "Stūpa, Sūtra and Śarīra," 14. See also Shinohara, "Story of the Buddha's Begging Bowl."

22 For an overview of Buddhist monasticism, see Nietupski, "Monasticism." More related to my study here of early Buddhist monasticism in China is Huaiyu Chen, *The Revival of Buddhist Monasticism;* Benn, Meeks, and Robson, *Buddhist Monasticism in East Asia.* A related study on Daoist monasticism is Kohn, *Monastic Life in Medieval Daoism.*

23 This period is also known as the Six Dynasties, derived from the number of dynasties during this period, all of which designated their capitals in today's Nanjing. For the cultural history of this period, see Dien, *Six Dynasties Civilization.*

24 The best studies of the early Buddhist activities are still Zürcher, *The Buddhist Conquest of China;* and Soper, *Literary Evidence for Early Buddhist Art in China.*

25 See Stevenson, "The T'ien-T'ai Four Forms of Samādhi," 11–12.

26 See two works by Bruce Charles Williams: "Mea Maxima Vikalpa," 71–80 and 125–216; and "Seeing through Images."

27 Trainor, *Relics, Ritual, and Representation,* 151. For more general information on the Theravāda tradition as distinct from Mahayana Buddhism, see King, "Theravāda in Southeast Asia." For the issue of the divine presence of various Buddhas and bodhisattvas in the Mahayana tradition, see Paul Williams, *Mahāyāna Buddhism,* 29–33.

28 See, for example, Campany, *Strange Writing.*

29 See Gjertson, *Miraculous Retribution.*

30 Campany, "The Real Presence," 236.

31 See Kieschnick, *The Eminent Monk,* chap. 2.

32 See Faure, *Visions of Power,* 275.

33 Vaidya, *Gandavyūhasūtra,* 23.

34 See the epigraph to this chapter. Regarding the importance and implication of "seeing," David L. McMahan argues that "the language of seeing provides a great deal of the metaphorical vocabulary of knowing in the Mahayana"; McMahan, *Empty Vision,* 5.

35 Trainor, *Relics, Ritual, and Representation,* 154; see also Hallisey, "Devotion in the Buddhist Literature," chap. 2, esp., 121–30.

36 That is, "scattering flowers, burning incense, lighting candles, and worship are what [one does] for the devotional offering" (*Fayuan zhulin, juan* 37, T.53: 2122.582c6–7). The text from which the procedure was derived is the *Sutra of Trapuṣa and Bhallika* (Tiwei boli jing), an indigenous Chinese scripture compiled in the fifth century, one of the so-called apocrypha (*weijing*). There are two existing texts of the scripture in Dunhuang manuscripts S.2051 and P.3732; however, the exact description of the procedure referred to in *Fayuan zhulin* cannot be found in either of these texts.

37 See Wu, *Monumentality,* 182–86.

38 See Su, "Donghan Wei Jin Nanbeichao," 32. The four-sided plan may have been a Chinese adaptation of a similar plan that has been called "corridor style" (*huilang-shi*), which developed in Central Asia around the same period; see Chen Xiaolu, "Xiyu huizixing fosi."

39 *Fayuan zhulin, juan* 37, T.53: 2122.593b.

40 For example, the donation of mansions (*shezhai*) was a common meritorious practice among wealthy patrons during this early period; see Kieschnick, *The Impact of Buddhism,* 185–88.

41 See *Fayuan zhulin, juan* 39, T.53: 2122.593b1–3.

42 The term *vinaya,* literally "extinction of evil," refers to a collective body of monastic rules or precepts by which one could "restrain oneself from doing wrong or evil"; see Yifa, *The Origins of Buddhist Monastic Codes,* 221, n. 2.

43 For Daoan, see Ui, *Shaku Dōan kenkyū;* Daoan's biography in *Gaoseng zhuan, juan* 4 (T.50: 2059.351c3–354a29), is translated in Link, "Biography of Shi Tao-an." See also Zürcher, *The Buddhist Conquest of China,* 184–204.

44 *Gaoseng zhuan, juan* 5, T.50: 2059.353b27.

45 Daoxuan adopted the rules into his *Notes Adding and Amending* Four-Part Vinaya (Sifen lü shanfan buque xingshichao), T.40: 1804. I discuss Daoxuan's prolific writings, including those on *vinaya,* in chapter 3.

46 Zürcher has suggested that "Xiangyang [where Daoan led a large monastic community] is the earliest case where we can form a notion, however vague, of the daily life and activities in a Chinese Buddhist community" (Zürcher, *The Buddhist Conquest of China,* 189). A brief discussion of Daoan's contribution to the formation of Buddhist monastic disciplines in China and the historical position of his monastic rules can be found in Foulk, "Daily Life in the Assembly."

47 *Gaoseng zhuan, juan* 5, T.50: 2059.353b24–26. My discussion of the three procedures is based on the following works: Ui, *Shaku Dōan,* 24–27; Tang Yongtong, *Han Wei Liangjin Nanbeichao,* vol. 1, 152–55; Shioiri, "Shaku Dōan no Sōni"; and in particular, Yifa, *The Origins of Buddhist Monastic Codes,* 3–52.

48 See Mizuo, "Gyō-kō ni tsuide."

49 See Aramaki, "Jōyō jidai no Dōan kyōdan," 398–413.

50 A comparable procedure in medieval Daoist monasteries can be found in Kohn, *Monastic Life in Medieval Daoism,* 178–81.

51 For the fortnightly confession (*busa*), see Kanazawa, "Shoki Chūgoku bukkyō no sai."

52 This description is based on Daoxuan's similar procedure in *Notes Adding and Amending* Four-Part Vinaya. Daoxuan records the verse to be recited at this point: "Incense of precepts, meditation, and liberation, like radiating clouds permeating the dharma-field, is being offered to the Innumerable Buddhas of the ten directions, and its fragrance permeates the vision and the hearing to realize calm" (T.40: 1804.36c9–11). The procedure was also recorded in several Dunhuang manuscripts related to the confessional ritual; see Wang Huimin, "Mogaoku di 276 ku"; Chenru, "Dunhuang busa wen."

53 See Reinders, "Ritual Topography."

54 Pas, "Six Daily Periods of Worship."

55 This daily procedure was exemplified in monastic rules set up by Zhiyi (538–97) for the Guoqin Monastery (Guoqingsi) at Mount Tiantai. Included in *One Hundred*

Records of the Guoqin [Monastery] (Guoqing bailu), dating to ca. 595, there are "Rules in Ten Clauses" (Lizhi fa shitiao), regulating the daily cycle of monastic life arranged around worship at six designated periods (*liushi lifo*) and sitting meditations at four designated periods (*sishi zuochan*); see T.45: 1934.793c3–20. The ten clauses are translated in Yifa, *The Origins of Buddhist Monastic Codes,* 20–21. A text that contains the vow to be recited at the six designated worship times, titled "Vows Taken at the Six Periods of Day and Night" (Zhouye liushi fayuan wen), is included in Zhisheng, *Ji zhujing lichan yi* (730 CE), T.47: 1982.465b10–c13.

56 For example, two different types of daily liturgies, the Procedure for Offering Veneration (*Jingli fa*) and the Procedure for Offering Universal Veneration (*Puli fa*), are preserved in *One Hundred Records of the Guoqin [Monastery],* T.46: 1934.794a18–795b15. A similar liturgy can also be seen in the ritual devised by Xinxing (540–94) for the Three Stages sect (Sanjie jiao); see Yabuki, *Sangaikyō no kenkyū,* 523–24.

57 See Mauss, *Sociology and Psychology,* 97–105; Coakley, *Religion and the Body.*

58 For instance, during the time Daoan was in Xiangyang (present-day Hubei), ca. 365–79, where he compiled the monastic guidelines, it was recorded that "whenever a lecture or assembly occurred, the holy images would be set out; banners and canopies would be hung up; festoons of beads would swing; everywhere would be incense, smoke, and flowers; so that those who mounted the steps and crossed the threshold [to the hall] were awestruck and gave their utmost devotion" (*Gaozeng zhuan, juan* 5, T.50: 2059.352b15–17); the translation is after Soper, *Literary Evidence for Early Buddhist Art,* 15–16. For the early history of the meditative practice in Daoan's monastic community, as well as others around his time, see Greene, "Meditation, Repentance, and Visionary Experience," chap. 1.

59 For instance, the scripture *Commentaries on the Ten Stages Sutra* (Shizhu piposha lun, T.26: 1521) was translated by Kumārajīva (344–413). This important commentary on the *Ten Stages Sutra* (Daśabhūmika-sūtra), compiled in the first decade of the fifth century, may have been the most important teaching at that time about the bodhisattva path. The idea of the bodhisattva path hinges on the rising of *bodhicitta,* a thought or intention to achieve enlightenment, as described in the *Ten Stages Sutra.* Once the practitioner can arouse the thought, she or he firmly enters the first stage (*bhūmi*) on the path to Buddhahood. Two points relevant to our discussion are as follows: first, the metaphor of path (*mārga*) in this program of spiritual attainment implies a structured way that is materialized in the monastery; and second, meditation is of great importance in the cultivation of a practitioner taking on the bodhisattva path, in that the capability to see is crucial. For more information on these two points, see Bielefeldt, "Practice," 236–40, and Paul Williams, *Mahāyāna Buddhism,* 204–14.

60 See *Gaoseng zhuan, juan* 5, T.52: 2059.352b.

61 The eulogy is included in *Guang hongming ji, juan* 15, T.52: 2103.198b14–c16, trans. Soper, *Literary Evidence for Early Buddhist Art,* 16.

62 The term is borrowed from Faure, *Visions of Power,* 268.

63 For Huiyuan's biography, see *Gaoseng zhuan, juan* 6, T.50: 2059.357c23–361b13, and *Chu sanzang ji ji, juan* 15, T.55: 2145.109b10–110c9. See also Zürcher, *The Buddhist Conquest of China,* 204–39.

64 The *Amitābha Sutra* is also known as *Shorter Sukhāvatīvyūha-Sūtra,* trans. Kumārajīva, T.12: 366.

65 See Paul Williams, *Mahāyāna Buddhism*, 217–20; Karlsson, *Face to Face with the Absent Buddha*, chap. 3; Stevenson, "Pure Land Buddhist Worship"; Greene, "Meditation, Repentance, and Visionary Experience," chap. 3.

66 This is a passage from a fifth-century Theravadin Buddhist text, *Visuddhimagga*, by Buddhaghosa, trans. in *The Path of Purification* by Ñyanamoli, quoted in Karlsson, *Face to Face with the Absent Buddha*, 64; also see Trainor, *Relics, Ritual, and Representation*, 185; Rotman, *Thus Have I Seen*.

67 The title of the sutra is based on the name of the meditation in a longer Sanskrit phrase, *Pratyutpanna-buddhasaṃmukhā-vasthita-samādhi*, literally meaning "a meditative practice in which one is brought face to face with the Buddhas of the present" or "the meditation of direct encounter with the Buddhas of the present"; see Harrison, *The Pratyutpanna Samādhi Sutra*, 2.

68 *Abridged Method of Meditation* (Siwei lüeyao fa), T.15: 617.299a9–15; the translation is adapted from Beyer, "Notes on the Vision Quest," 337. A similar procedure can also be found in another fifth-century meditative manual, *The Essence of the Meditation Manual Consisting of Five Gates of Chan* (Wumen chanjing yaoyong fa), in T.15: 619; see Yamabe, "The Sūtra on the Ocean-Like Samādhi," 9–11, 84–100.

69 Stevenson, "Pure Land Buddhist Worship," 361.

70 *Guan Wuliangshou fo jing*, T.12: 365; trans. in Müller, *The Sacred Books of the East*. For the visualization instructed in the text, see Soper, *Literary Evidence for Early Buddhist Art*, 144–45; Pas, *Visions of Sukhāvatī*, 35–64. The sutra is one of the six existing sutras containing a core meditative practice that entails visualization. All six sutras became available during the fifth century, and each of the six titles contains the word *guan*, generally translated in the meditative context as "visualizing" or "visualization"; the sutras in this group have accordingly been termed "visualization sutra" (*guanjing*); see Soper, *Literary Evidence for Early Buddhist Art*, 144–45.

71 *Sutra on the Visualization of Amitāyus* (Guan wuliangshou fo jing), T.12: 365.346b9–10.

72 See Yamabe, "The Sūtra on the Ocean-Like Samādhi," 162.

73 Beyer, "Notes on the Vision Quest," 330.

74 See a useful discussion in Bogel, *With a Single Glance*, 191–96.

75 *Ocean-Like Samādhi of Buddha Visualization Sutra* (Guanfo sanmei hai jing), T.15: 643.660a28–c26, trans. in Yamabe, "Visionary Repentance and Visionary Ordination," 34–35; in his article, Yamabe points out, "The idea that karmic obstructions hinder vision is found in many kindred visualization texts and clearly presupposes visionary practice," 34.

76 For the history and Buddhist art of this region, see Juliano, "Buddhist Art in Northwest China"; Howard, "Liang Patronage of Buddhist Art."

77 The term "Liangzhou style" (*Liangzhou moshi*) was coined by Su Bai in his "Liangzhou shiku."

78 *Weishu*, *juan* 114, 3032; Soper, "Northern Liang and Northern Wei in Kansu," 141.

79 For the biography of Tanyao, see *Xu Gaoseng zhuan*, *juan* 1, T.50: 2060.427c21–428a21.

80 The saṅgha household system was recorded in *Weishu*, *juan* 114, 3037, trans. and discussed in Gernet, *Buddhism in Chinese Society*, 99–105. Also see Tsukamoto, *Hokuchō bukkyōshi kenkyū*, 97–140.

81 For instance, in Yungang Cave 11, an inscription dated from 483, during the Northern Wei, reads: "To elicit blessings for the nation, we reverently made a stone temple with ninety-five images and many bodhisattvas, wishing by this means, first that the

virtue of the Emperor, the Empress Dowager, and the Prince shall be resonant with heaven and earth . . . and that they shall bring all peoples of the ten directions into submission and make glorious the Three Jewels which shall not disappear forever." The transcription of the text is based on the rubbing (no. 18408) in the collection at Academia Sinica, Taipei; the translation is after Abe, *Ordinary Images,* 213.

82 *Weishu, juan* 114, 3039. See also Su, "Pingcheng shili de jiju," 133–34.

83 *Weishu, juan* 114, 3037. No existing inscriptions in situ from around this time can help us secure the dates of the caves' construction, but scholars generally date them to the 460s and the early 470s, about a decade after the period of persecution; see Soper, "Imperial Cave Chapels," 242–43; Su, "Yungang shiku fenqi shilun."

84 The rise of the building trade during this period in the Northern Wei can also be observed in other areas. A similar application of architectural motifs in a different context, for example, can be found in the house-shaped sarcophagus excavated from a Northern Wei tomb just outside present-day Datong, built no later than 477 for Song Shaozu, a former official of Youzhou (present-day Shanxi and Hebei); see Shanxisheng kaogu yanjiusuo and Datongshi kaogu yanjiusuo, "Datongshi Beiwei Song Shaozu mu."

85 Nancy S. Steinhardt divides these caves in four different arrangements based on single or double chambers and the location of the central pillar or colossal Buddha; see Steinhardt, "The Sixth Century in East Asian Architecture," 32–33. For the construction of Caves 7 and 8 as different from the rest of the caves from this period, see Tsiang, "Reconsidering Early Buddhist Cave-Making."

86 See Yang Xiaoneng, *New Perspectives on China's Past,* vol. 2, 353–55; Nagahiro, "Unkō sekkutsu."

87 The Buddhas of the three times are explicated in *Weishu:* "Before Śākyamuni there were six Buddhas, and Śākyamuni, succeeding the six Buddhas, achieved his enlightenment during his time in this present age. It is written that in the time to come there will be Maitreya Buddha, who will succeed Śākyamuni and come down to this world"; *Weishu, juan* 114, 3027.

88 The twin-Buddha motif is based on the *Lotus Sutra,* one of the first Mahayana sutras (translated into Chinese ca. 406 CE), which explicitly proclaims the Buddha as a deity transcending current temporality. This theme is expressed most pointedly in a scene where Śākyamuni appears side by side with the Buddha Prabhūtaratna, a Buddha of the timeless past, sitting in a seven-jeweled stupa, often called the "many treasures" stupa (Duobao Ta). For the importance of the *Lotus Sutra* in Mahayana doctrines, see Suguro, *Hokekyō no seiritsu to shisō;* for the representation of this particular motif, see Davidson, *The Lotus Sutra in Chinese Art,* 24–25. The twin-Buddha motif is frequently placed with Maitreya in the later image compositional scheme at Yungang, and this arrangement likely suggests the triple worlds of past, present, and future; see Caswell, *Written and Unwritten,* 67. The twin-Buddha motif can also be seen by itself above the entrance portal, as in Cave 12, or surrounded by the thousand Buddhas around the entrance, as in Cave 5.

89 The combination of these motifs is discussed in Eugene Wang, *Shaping the Lotus Sutra,* 23.

90 The empress was given the title of empress dowager when her husband, Emperor Wencheng, died in 465. Afterward, Lady Feng gained her equal right to reign by deftly manipulating the two succeeding emperors; see Li Ping, *Beiwei Pingcheng shiqi.*

91 Datongshi Bowuguan, "Datong Beiwei Fangshan Siyuan fosi."

92 Ibid., 9.

93 The central-column cave finds its precedents in the Northern Liang in the Gansu corridor; see Li Chongfeng, *Zhong Yin fojiao shikusi*, 242–54. For a discussion of the central pillar viewed as a stupa/pagoda inside the cave, see Puay-Peng Ho, "The Symbolism of the Central Pillars."

94 Li Daoyuan, *Shuijing zhu* (ca. 515–24), *juan* 13.

95 *Weishu, juan* 114, 3037; one Northern Wei *chi* equals 27.3 centimeters.

96 Regarding the choice of Luoyang as the nation's new capital, Emperor Xiaowen was recorded as saying, "Yiluo [Luoyang] is in the center of North and South, and pivotal point of contact between heaven and earth, the juncture of yin and yang, of wind and rain, and of [man's] accordance with natural principles. It is not to be attained by [a ruler] lacking in virtue"; in *Weishu, juan* 21, 537, trans. in Tsiang, "Changing Patterns of Divinity," 230. See also Lu Yaodong, *Cong Pingcheng dao Luoyang.*

97 See Steinhardt, *Chinese Imperial City Planning,* 82–92; Pingti Ho, "Lo-yang, A.D. 495–534"; He Yeju, *Zhongguo gudai chengshi guihuashi;* Du and Qian, *Han Wei Luoyang cheng.*

98 Yang Xuanzhi, *Luoyang qielan ji*, preface; see Fan, *Luoyang qielan ji jiaozhu*, 1. The English translation is based on Yi-t'ung Wang, *A Record of Buddhist Monasteries,* 5–6.

99 In his analysis of *Record of the Monasteries of Luoyang,* Whalen Lai argues that Buddhism in Luoyang was in effect a form of urban piety, which "was by its very nature untutored, emotional and obsessed with karmic Heavens and Hells"; see Lai, "Society and the Sacred," 257.

100 The three major monasteries were Jingming Monastery (Jingmingsi), Baode Monastery (Baodesi), and Yaoguang Monastery (Yaoguangsi).

101 See McNair, *Donors of Longmen,* 33 and 184, n. 15. See also Su, "Luoyang diqu beichao shiku."

102 See the preface written by Cui Guang (449–522) to the *Commentary on Ten Stages Sutra* (Shidi jing lun), T.26: 1522.123b1–5; also Tang Yongtong, *Han Wei Liangjin Nanbeichao,* vol. 2, 610–12.

103 For Empress Dowager Hu's biography, see *Weishu, juan* 13, 337–40, trans. in Holmgren, "Empress Dowager Ling," 160–70.

104 The chief undertakings to support Buddhism made by Empress Dowager Hu are discussed in McNair, *Donors of Longmen,* chap. 3.

105 *Weishu, juan* 114, 3043; Yang, *Luoyang qielan ji, juan* 1; Yi-t'ung Wang, *A Record of Buddhist Monasteries,* 16.

106 There have been at least two different proposals regarding the height of the Yongning pagoda: Yang Hongxun, "Guanyu Beiwei Luoyang Yongningsi ta," and Zhong, "Beiwei Luoyang Yongningsi ta."

107 Yang Xuanzhi, *Luoyang qielan ji, juan* 1; the translation is after Yi-t'ung Wang, *A Record of Buddhist Monasteries,* 16.

108 Zhongguo Shehui Kexueyuan, *Beiwei Luoyang Yongningsi.*

109 See the discussion in Steinhardt, "The Sixth Century in East Asian Architecture," 37–38.

110 Zhongguo Shehui Kexueyuan, *Beiwei Luoyang Yongningsi,* chap. 2.

111 Ibid., 144. See the more detailed discussion in Qian, "Beiwei Luoyang Yongningsi suxiang"; Li Li, "The Artistic and Period Characteristics of Sculptures."

112 The imperial procession scenes in Binyang Central Cave and Huangfu Cave are discussed in McNair, *Donors of Longmen,* 41–44, 67–71; for the Gongxian caves, see Henansheng Wenwu Yanjiusuo, *Gongxian shiku si.*

113 McNair, *Donors of Longmen,* 48.

114 Yang Xuanzhi, *Luoyang qielan ji, juan* 1; Yi-t'ung Wang, *A Record of Buddhist Monasteries,* 20.

115 See Collins, *Nirvana and Other Buddhist Felicities,* 291–92.

116 Most early accounts of Mount Wutai link the beginning of its development as a sacred Buddhist site to imperial support from the Northern Wei; see Yun-jo Lin, "Wutaishan yu Wenshu daochang," 50–54; Cui Zhengsen, *Wutaishan fojiao shi,* vol. 1, 111–26.

TWO. Entering the Mountains

The epigraph is from E. Zürcher, *The Buddhist Conquest of China: The Spread and Adaptation of Buddhism in Early Medieval China* (Leiden: E. J. Brill, 1959), 207. Reproduced with permission by Koninklijke Brill NV, Leiden, Netherlands.

1 "Worship Prayer to Mount Heng of the Northern Peak" (Si Beiyue Hengshan Wen), collected in *Quan Tangwen, juan* 100, 130.

2 Chavannes, *Le T'ai chan,* 8.

3 *Quan Tangwen, juan* 100, 130.

4 See, for example, Eliade, *The Sacred and the Profane.*

5 There was also a broader category, of "famous mountains" (*mingshan*), which was only loosely defined but which included all the mountains of renown; see a similar discussion in Hargett, *Stairway to Heaven,* 4–5.

6 See, for example, the definitions for *ling* and *shen* discussed in Major et al., *The Huainanzi,* 880–81 and 885–87.

7 Xu Shen, *Shuowen jiezi,* compiled ca. 100 CE.

8 See Kleeman, "Mountain Deities in China."

9 See Tsai, "In the Steps of Emperors and Immortals"; Lewis, "The *Feng* and *Shan* Sacrifices"; Lewis, *The Construction of Space,* 284–303.

10 The related passage reads: "All these [listed mountains] have auspicious deities; in them there may be earthbound transcendents. These mountains [are where] funguses and herbs grow and [people can] escape from wars and calamities. There [one] can mix [efficacious ingredients] to make medicines. If there are people who seek the Dao entering [the mountains], the deities of the mountains will definitely assist [them and bring about] blessings" (in the chapter "Golden Elixir" [Jindan], *Baopuzi,* by Ge Hong); see Wang Ming, *Baopuzi neipian jiaoshi,* 85. See also Robson, *Power of Place,* 44. For a brief discussion on the transcendents, or immortals, and their close ties to sacred peaks, see Little, *Taoism,* 147–61.

11 See Tsuzuki, "Rokuchō kōhanki ni okeru dōkan." Also, as Thomas H. Hahn points out, "In Daoist belief, the macro-structure, and the best place to work toward the realization of perfection is the mountain" (Hahn, "Daoist Sacred Sites," 684). The Daoist conceptions of mountains as visualized in pictorial forms are discussed in Huang, *Picturing the True Form,* chap. 3.

12 See Trainor, *Relics, Ritual, and Representation,* chap. 2; Ray, "The Stūpa."

13 Quoted in the epigraph to this chapter.

14 This view is echoed by Susan Naquin and Chün-fang Yü in their discussion of Buddhist sacred sites in China: "As Buddhism became domesticated, in a process parallel to that of Christianity in medieval Europe, believers began to create a sacred geography on their native soil, marked here by relics, the miraculously preserved bodies of monks, famous temples, and finally the four great Buddhist mountains (and many lesser ones)" (Naquin and Yü, *Pilgrims and Sacred Sites in China,* 15).

15 Zürcher, *The Buddhist Conquest of China,* 207.

16 Yan Gengwang (1916–96), a well-known Chinese historian of cultural and religious geography, drawing mainly on biographies of Buddhist monks, documented the geographic spread of Buddhist activities during this period. See Yan Gengwang, *Wei Jin Nanbeichao fojiao,* chap. 5.

17 For example, identifying mountains as the perfect setting for meditation, the *Lotus Sutra* states: "The one who practices meditation [according to the scripture] will see himself in the midst of mountains and forests practicing the good law, understanding the true form of all phenomena, entering deeply meditation and seeing the Buddhas of the ten directions" (T.9: 262.39c4–5); the translation is after Hurvitz, *Scripture of the Lotus Blossom,* 223.

18 *Gaoseng zhuan, juan* 6, T.50: 2059.358a22–23.

19 Ibid., 358b6–7; the English translation is adapted from Zürcher, *The Buddhist Conquest of China,* 241.

20 See Inoue Ichii, "Rosan bunka to Eon"; Tamaki, "Rosan Eon no shizen kannen"; Miyakawa, "Shindai oyobi sore ikō no Rosan."

21 See Xie Lingyun (385–433), *The Eulogy for Dhyāna Master Huiyuan at Mount Lu* (Lushan Huiyuan fashi lei), in *Guang hongming ji, juan* 23, T.52: 2103.267a12–b21.

22 *Gaoseng zhuan, juan* 6, T.50: 2059.358c4–6. Huiyuan's conversation with the Indian visitor about the "cave of the Buddha's shadow" in Nagarahāra, is summarized in his *Inscription on the Shadow of the Buddha* (Foying ming), in *Guang hongming ji, juan* 15, T.52: 2103.197c7–198b13. For more discussion about Huiyuan's painting of the "shadow of the Buddha," see Zürcher, *The Buddhist Conquest of China,* 223–4; Soper, *Literary Evidence for Early Buddhist Art,* 32–33.

23 The meditative practice is discussed in chapter 1.

24 See Shinohara, "Literary Construction of Buddhist Sacred Places."

25 See the collection of essays in Eade and Sallnow, *Contesting the Sacred.* For the concept of "geohistorical synthesis," see Dodgshon, *Society in Time and Space.*

26 See Tang Xiaofeng, "Wuyue dili shuo." The earliest text to include both Mount Heng and Mount Wutai is Li Daoyuan's *Commentary on the Waterways Classic* (Shuijing zhu), dated ca. 515–24.

27 This network eventually coalesced into the system summarized in Du Guangting's *Records of Grotto Heavens, Auspicious Terrains, Sacred Peaks, Rivers, and Famous Mountains* (Dongtian fudi yuedu mingshan ji), of ca. 901, collected in *Daozang,* 599. See Miura, "Dōten fukuchi shōron"; Li Sheng, *Xianjing xinyang yanjiu,* 147–51; Hahn, "Daoist Sacred Sites," 695–698; Weiss, "Rectifying the Deep Structures of the Earth"; Verellen, "The Beyond Within."

28 *Gu Qingliang zhuan,* T.51: 2098.1093a13–14. This is recorded in Huixiang's *Ancient Records,* a text that is discussed in more detail in a later section of this chapter.

29 See "Biography of Bai Jian" ("Bai Jian zhuan"), in *Beiqi shu, juan* 40, 532–33.

30 *Flower Garland Sutra,* T.29: 278.

31 On the bodhisattva Mañjuśrī, see Lamotte, "Mañjuśrī"; Birnbaum, "Mañjuśrī"; Paul Williams, *Mahāyāna Buddhism,* 238–41.

32 For an example, see Sen, *Buddhism, Diplomacy, and Trade,* 76–86.

33 Quoted and translated in Coleman and Elsner, *Pilgrimage,* 176.

34 Sen, *Buddhism, Diplomacy, and Trade,* 56. In his chapter 2, Tansen Sen argues that the worship of relics, Maitreya cults, and the rise of Mount Wutai as Mañjuśrī's sacred mountain were all steps taken to dispel the borderland complex. The notion of a "borderland complex," referring to a sentiment commonly felt among Chinese Buddhist communities during and before the Tang dynasty, that they inhabited a borderland, was proposed by Antonio Forte in Forte, "Hui-chih."

35 Ye, also known as Yedu, became the dynastic capital for the first time in the Wei Kingdom (220–65) during the Three Kingdoms period. See Murata, *Chūgoku no teito,* 181–255; Steinhardt, *Chinese Imperial City Planning,* 88–89; Dien, "The Historical Background."

36 *Xu gaoseng zhuan* records that "the [Northern] Qi dynasty under the Gao family fervently revived Buddhism. The larger monasteries in the capital alone were approximately four thousand, lodging about eighty thousand monks and nuns" (T.50: 2060.501b13–14).

37 See Zhongguo Shehui Kexueyuan, "Hebei Linzhang xian Yecheng yizhi"; this point is briefly mentioned in Steinhardt, "The Sixth Century in East Asian Architecture," 34–35.

38 Suwa, *Chūgoku chūsei bukkyōshi kenkyū,* 203–323.

39 Yang Xuanzhi stated, "Thereupon, monks in the capital were devoted to meditating and chanting sutras, rather than lecturing on them" (*Luoyang qielan ji, juan* 2); the translation is after Yi-t'ung Wang, *A Record of Buddhist Monasteries,* 76.

40 Yan, *Wei Jin Nanbeichao,* 217–28. For austere ascetics who practiced rigorous regimens known as *toutuo,* see Kieschnick, *The Eminent Monk,* 33–35.

41 The term *mofa* was also rendered variously in Chinese as *mohou* (ending) and *moshi* (latter time or final age). Bibliographical references for *mofa* are extensive; for example, see Chappell, "Early Forebodings of the Death of Buddhism"; Nattier, *Once upon a Future Time;* Hubbard, *Absolute Delusion;* Kumoi, "Hōmetsu shisō no genryū."

42 See Hubbard, *Absolute Delusion,* chap. 3; Yin, "Shilun mofa sixiang yu Beiliang fojiao." For the tripartite scheme, see Wakae, "Chūgoku ni okeru shōzōmatsu sanji."

43 Conze, *Buddhism,* 114–17, quoted in Weidner, *Latter Days of the Law,* 37.

44 *Nanyue si dachanshi lishi yuanwen,* T.46: 1933.791c11; T.46: 1933.789b3–4; T46: 1933.791c22.

45 This is indicated in both Huisi's biography in *Xu gaoseng zhuan, juan* 17, T.50: 2060.562c6–564a17, and *Nanyue si dachanshi lishi yuanwen,* T.46: 1933.

46 Two Japanese articles dedicated to this obscure monk are Ogasawara, "Rankoku shamon Eshō ni tsuite" and Ibuki, "Tōsō Eshō ni tsuite." In addition to the *Ancient Records,* Huixiang left only one other work, *Eulogizing the Anthology of the Lotus Sutra* (Hongzan fahua zhuan), T.51: 2067. Also see Lian, "Huixiang 'Langu shamen' yiduan."

47 For a general discussion on this genre of geographical writings, see Brook, *Geographical Sources of Ming-Qing History.*

48 From the *Flower Garland Sutra* (Avataṃsaka Sūtra), translated by Buddhabhadra ca. 420 CE, in T.9: 278.590a3–5. Huixiang cites this passage in the opening section of *the Ancient Records;* see *Gu Qingliang zhuan,* T.51: 2098.1092c27–29.

49 Lamotte, "Mañjuśrī," 73–84.

50 This is pointed out in Sen, *Buddhism, Diplomacy, and Trade,* 77–78.

51 *Gu Qingliang zhuan, juan* 1, T.51: 2098.1093a8–13. The passage is in Li Daoyuan, *Shuijing zhu, juan* 11; the same passage, with minor differences, is also cited in *Taiping yulan, juan* 45, 344.

52 See *Jinshu, juan* 5, 132.

53 On Daoists at Mount Wutai in the early history of the area, see Sōma, "Godaisan kinpen no dōkyō teki huniki."

54 *Beishi, juan* 89, 2950.

55 This is an otherwise lost passage, quoted in Huixiang's *Gu Qingliang zhuan, juan* 1, T.51: 2098.1093a16–18.

56 *Xu gaoseng zhuan, juan* 6, T.50: 2060.470a14–15. For Tanluan and Pure Land Buddhism, see Tanaka, *The Dawn of Chinese Pure Land,* 17–19, 61–64.

57 *Xu gaoseng zhuan, juan* 18, T.50: 2060.571c22. For Tanqian, see Jinhua Chen, *Monks and Monarchs.*

58 Yan Gengwang, *Wei Jin Nanbeichao,* 251–54.

59 Yang Xuanzhi, *Luoyang qielan ji,* preface, trans. in Yi-t'ung Wang, *A Record of Buddhist Monasteries,* 6.

60 Bruce C. Williams, "Seeing through Images," 38.

61 The concept of "textual community" in the context of, for example, Buddhist learning or millennial movements, has been studied in Blackburn, *Buddhist Learning and Textual Practice,* and O'Leary, *Arguing the Apocalypse.*

62 The mountain passes crossing the Taihang range were called collectively the "Eight [Mountain] Passes of the Taihang" (Taihang Ba Xing). Of the eight passes, the traffic between Ye and Jinyang went through the Fukou Pass (Fukou xing) and Jingxing Pass (Jingxing xing); see Yan Gengwang, *Tangdai jiaotong tu kao,* vol. 5, 1421–24.

63 *Beiqi shu, juan* 40, 533.

64 *Gu Qingliang zhuan,* T.51: 2098.1094a1–3.

65 The passage reads: "Today, [I] divide the nation's holdings into three parts, for the nation, the imperial household, and the Three Jewels" (*Xu gaoseng zhuan, juan* 16, T.50: 2060.554b25–26).

66 The new research is primarily by Zhang Zong; for example, see Zhang Zong "Northern Qi Inscribed Sutras."

67 Ibid., 292.

68 *Xu gaoseng zhuan, juan* 20, T.50: 2060.591.b19–20. A monk named Huibin (574–645) left the city for Mount Wutai because its tranquility was perfect for focused meditative practices.

69 See Henansheng Gudai Jianzhu Baohu Yanjiusuo, "Henan Anyang Lingquansi," 12.

70 Translation after Harrist, *The Landscape of Words,* 180.

71 See, for example, Ma Zhongli, "Yedu jinyi Beiqi fojiao kejing chutan," 171–75.

72 Harrist, *The Landscape of Words,* 180–82.

73 On the stone sutras at Mount Fang, see Lü Tiegang, *Fangshan shijing yanjiu;* Ledderose, "Thunder Sound Cave"; Sonya S. Lee, "Transmitting Buddhism to a Future Age."

74 Translated in Sonya S. Lee, "Transmitting Buddhism to a Future Age," 48.

75 Tsiang, "Monumentalization of Buddhist Texts," 259.

76 The use of stone for architecture was limited in early China, and when applied from the Han period onward, stone was mostly used for funerary purposes or particular public monuments, such as stone steles. See Wu, *Monumentality,* 121–42; for the history of steles, see Dorothy C. Wong, *Chinese Steles.*

77 The archaeological report by the Henan Province Research Institute of all three caves can be found in Henansheng Gudai Jianzhu Baohu Yanjiusuo, "Henan Anyang Lingquansi." For the secondary research, see Yen, "Beiqi Xiaonanhai shiku"; Hsu, "The Xiaonanhai Cave-Chapel"; Inada, "Shōnankai chūkutsu to Sōchū zenshi."

78 *Niepan jing,* T.12: 374.433c–434b. On the meditative practice Four Foundations of Mindfulness (*Catvari-mrty-upasthanani*), see Ha, *Si nianchu yanjiu.*

79 The scriptural significance of these lines, as well as the chapters in the *Flower Garland Sutra* from which the first three verses—all quatrains like this one—come, are explained in Yen, "Beiqi Xiaonanhai shiku," 584–87; Hsu provides a complete translation of all four stanzas in "The Xiaonanhai Cave-Chapel," 37–38.

80 The story carved in relief is based on the *Brāhmana jātaka,* one of the ancient Indian tales of the Buddha's previous incarnations. The message of this tale is primarily about renunciation of the corporeal body in order to attain the truth of nonexistence.

81 This is recorded in the last engraved inscription on the exterior, also taken from the "Sagely Practice" chapter of the *Nirvana Sutra.* It tells the story of Ajātaśatru's meeting with the Buddha and his conversion to Buddhism, when he expresses the wish for all living beings to have their *bodhi* mind awaken and meet with their own Buddha nature. Because he had this wish, Ajātaśatru was able "to see the Buddha"; see Yen, "Beiqi changuan ku," 402.

82 Yen, "Beiqi Xiaonanhai shiku," 581; Yen, "Beiqi changuan ku," 392. Zhang Zong uses the term *beixing ku,* or "stele-shaped caves," to describe the cave style of the Xiaonanhai caves; Zhang Zong, "Shandong Sculpture Tradition."

83 Eileen Hsiang-ling Hsu, in her analysis of the cave, suggests that the poem might refer to "the vision of Buddha Vairocana [that] was attained by Sengchou while practicing meditation in the cave"; see Hsu, "The Xiaonanhai Cave-Chapel," 39.

84 Karlsson, *Face to Face,* 188.

85 Ibid., 190.

86 The Yunmen Monastery, sponsored by Emperor Wenxuan, was founded by Sengchou in the third year of the Tianbao reign, in 552 (*Xu gaoseng zhuan,* T.50: 2060.554b14–16).

87 For example, Sofugawa, "Kyōdōsan sekkutsu kō."

88 For the Xiangtangshan caves, see Mizuno and Nagahiro, *Kyōdōsan sekkutsu;* Handanshi Wenwu Baoguansuo, "Hebei Handan Gushan Changlesi yizhi"; a recent exhibition catalogue on these caves is Tsiang, *Echoes of the Past.* On caves at Shuiyu Monastery, see Handanshi Wenwu Baoguansuo, "Handan Gushan Shuiyusi shiku."

89 A notable exception is South Cave at the Northern Xiangtangshan site, which has recessed niches on three walls, leaving the central area of the cave chamber to be used for worship.

90 For example, "One visualizes the sitting image of Tathāgata [until] it is as if one sees the [real] body of the Buddha without difference, [upon which, one's] hundreds and thousands of accumulated sins can be absolved. If one cannot [do as such], one

should enter a stupa and meditate on all sitting buddhas, after the completion of which, [one should] repent for sins that obstruct one's mind" (*Guanfo sanmei hai jing, juan* 7, T.15: 643.681c2–4).

91 *Huayan jing,* T.9: 278.432c02–09.

92 Nancy Steinhardt has made a similar observation: "At Xiangtangshan, the horizontal organization and integrated design focus the worshipper's eyes on the deities in deep-set niches in the central pillars and along the cave walls" (Steinhardt, "Xiangtangshan and Northern Qi Architecture," 64).

93 Ibid., 66.

94 Yin, *Beiliang shita;* Abe, *Ordinary Images,* chap. 3

95 See Tsiang, "Monumentalization of Buddhist Texts," 255–57; Eung-chon Choi, "Early Korean and Japanese Reliquaries."

96 Schopen, "The Phrase 'sa pṛthivīpradeśaś caityabhūto bhavet.'"

97 Tsiang, "Monumentalization of Buddhist Texts," 257.

98 For more details regarding the stupa facade and its architectural details, see Zhao Lichun, "Xiangtangshan Beiqi taxing ku lunshu," and Zhong Xiaoqing, "Xiangtangshan shiku jianzhu lüexi."

99 Steinhardt briefly discusses decorative motifs such as lotus petals that appear on Xiangtangshan Caves in "Xiangtangshan and Northern Qi Architecture," 73–74.

100 Carving the rock-cut cave facade into forms that imitate wooden details or structures is peculiar to this period, and most examples date to the sixth century. A similar practice can be found among the caves at Mount Tianlong (Caves 1, 10, and 16) outside present-day Taiyuan and at Mount Maiji in eastern Gansu. For caves at Mount Maiji, see Fu Xinian, "Maijishan shiku." For caves at Mount Tianlong, see Yen, "Tianlongshan shiku de zai xingsi," and Li Yuqun and Li Gang, *Tianlongshan shiku.*

101 Quoted and translated in Harrist, *The Landscape of Words,* 187. In his chapter 3, "The Virtual Stele on Mount Tie and the Merits of Scale," Harrist proposes that the mountainside carved with sutra passages in a monumental scale be seen as a "virtual stele." The scriptures carved on Mount Tie are from *Jin'gang banruo boluomi jing* (Vajracchedikā prajñāpāramitā sūtra), T.8: 235.748c20–750c23; see Jiang, "Taishan Jingshigu moya kejing kao."

102 For caves at Mount Tianlong, see Yen, "Tianlongshan shiku de zai xingsi," and Li Yuqun and Li Gang, *Tianlongshan shiku.*

103 When the project of sculpting the colossal Buddha began is still under debate; see Li Yuqun, "Jinyang Xishan dafo," 19–21.

104 See Li Yuqun and Yan Yaojin, "Taiyuanshi Longshan Tongzisi."

105 Two colossal Buddhas, constructed during the Southern Dynasties at Qixia Monastery (Qixiasi) near Nanjing and Baoxiang Monastery (Baoxiangsi) in today's Xinchang, Zhejiang, are dated to about the late fifth and early sixth centuries. See Su Bai, "Nanchao kanxiang yiji chutan."

106 The passage is from an inscription titled *A Record on the Rebuilding of the Zhuangyan Pavilion at Kaihua[si]* (*Chongxiu Mengshan Kaihua zhuangyange ji*), dated 945, by Su Yugui (894–956) on a now-missing stele.

107 See Li Yuqun, "Jinyang Xishan dafo," 22.

108 The most comprehensive research on dedicatory inscriptions from this period is Hou Xudong, *Wu liu shiji beifang minzhong fojiao xinyang.*

109 *Sutra of Prajñāpāramitā Preached by Bodhisattva Mañjuśrī,* T.8: 233.

110 For the sutra carvings at Mount Zhonghuang, see Ma Zhongli et al., "Shexian Zhonghuangshan."

111 *Gu Qingliang zhuan, juan* 1, T.51: 2098.1094c23–24.

112 Ibid., T.51: 2098.1094c14–20.

113 Both Jietuo and Mingyao are included in *Huayanjing zhuanji* (T.51: 2073), in the section on biographies of eminent monks in the Huayan (i.e., *Flower Garland Sutra*) lineage, compiled by Fazang (643–712); for Jietuo, see T.51: 2073.169a15–c10; for Mingyao, T.51: 2073.169c11–22.

114 *Xu gaoseng zhuan, juan* 20, in T.50: 2060.592c27–29.

115 For example, Fei Changfang in *Lidai sanbao ji* (ca. 597) made a direct connection between the persecution under Emperor Wu of the Northern Zhou and the end of Dharma; see T.49: 2034.107b17–20.

116 See T.13: 397.298a5–381c11. The title of the *Candragarbha sūtra* can be literally translated as *Sutra of the Extensive Discourse of the Bodhisattva Moon-Embryo;* it is included as a section of *Daji jing* (Mahāsaṃnipāta-sūtra). See Chappell, "Early Forebodings of the Death of Buddhism," 145–45; Nattier, *Once upon a Future Time,* 170–88; Fujiyoshi, "Meppōka toshite no Narendaireiyasha."

117 Nattier, *Once upon a Future Time,* 110–18.

118 See Henansheng Gudai Jianzhu Baohu Yanjiusuo, *Baoshan Lingquansi;* Lee Yü-ming, "Baoshan Dazhusheng ku chutan."

119 Lingyu's biography is included in *Xu gaoseng zuan,* T.50: 2060.495b05–498a22. For discussion on Lingyu in relation to Dazhusheng Cave, see Bruce Charles Williams, "Mea Maxima Vikalpa," 112–18; Makita, "Hōzanji Ryōyū ni tsuite."

120 The first excerpt appears on the exterior, urging practitioners to safeguard the Dharma, while the other, situated inside the cave next to the entrance, explicates the timetable of the decline.

121 *Text of the Abridged Repentance for Venerating the Buddha Names of the Seven Registers* (Lüe li qijie foming chanhui deng wen). The text is discussed and translated in Adamek, "Dimensions of Endtime." I thank Wendi Adamek for sharing her manuscript with me.

122 The ambulatory liturgy from outside to inside the cave is discussed in Lee Yü-ming, "Baoshan Dazhusheng ku," 24–29, and Adamek, "Dimensions of Endtime."

123 The text is transcribed in Lee Yü-ming, "Baoshan Dazhusheng ku," 39.

124 Adamek, "Dimensions of Endtime."

125 This is discussed in Lee Yü-ming, "Baoshan Dazhusheng ku," 8–9. Like the *Candragarbha Sūtra,* the *Sūryagarbha Sūtra* was translated by Narendrayaśas and later included as a section in *Daji jing* (Mahāsaṃnipāta-sūtra). See Nattier, *Once upon a Future Time,* 171–72.

126 *Xu gaoseng zhuan, juan* 50, T.50: 2060.497b11–12.

127 *Huayan jing,* T.9: 278.590a27–28.

THREE. The Sacred Presence in Place and in Vision

The epigraph is from Diana L. Eck, "Mountains," in *Encyclopedia of Religion,* 2nd ed., ed. Lindsay Jones (Detroit: Macmillan Reference, 2005), vol. 9, 6213. © 2005 Gale, a part of Cengage Learning, Inc. Reproduced by permission.

1 *Shijing*, "Songgao" chapter, in Ruan, *Shisan jing zhushu*, vol. 1, 297.

2 See the relevant section in *Mañjuśrī-parinirvāṇa-sūtra*, in T.14: 463.481a13–b10. In the section, *huaxian* is interchangeable with *bianxian*, both referring to the concept of miraculous transformation (*nirmāṇa*). A Chinese translation of the sutra, attributed to Nie Daozhen, was completed at the end of the third century CE. The text is translated into English in Cartelli, *The Five-Colored Clouds of Mount Wutai*, 40–46. On the sutra, see also Hattori, "Monju shūri hatsu nehangyō"; Quinter, "Visualizing the *Mañjuśrī Parinirvāṇa Sutra*."

3 In *Gu Qinglian zhuan*, Huixiang used the term *moshi* (lit. end of the world) to describe the situation regarding the end of the Dharma in his times; see T.51: 2098.1100c22.

4 Ibid., 1096c14.

5 Campany, "The Real Presence," 245.

6 Faure, "Space and Place," 338. Faure proposes that the differences between Buddhism and popular religions may be understood in terms of "utopian" and "locative" visions of the world. According to Faure, whereas the universal teachings of Buddhism would void the spatial meanings tied to the disruptive power of local spirits, the supposedly unlocalized practice of Buddhism would in turn require a territorial concession from the spirits to resacralize the place.

7 Here "emplaced" is used to emphasize that it was the localizing of the utopian vision at the specific mountain site that turned the initially unqualified space of Mount Wutai into the place of the localized divinity. For the use of the term "emplacement," see Ambros, *Emplacing a Pilgrimage*. For a more general discussion on the engendering of place, see Casey, *Getting Back into Place*, esp. chap. 1, "Implacement."

8 Faure, "Space and Place," 354–55.

9 The phrase and related idea are borrowed from Smith, *To Take Place*, 86.

10 For comparable studies on issues of localizing the sacred, see Grapard, *Protocol of the Gods;* Moerman, *Localizing Paradise;* Huber, *The Holy Land Reborn*.

11 *Gu Qingliang zhuan*, T.51: 2098.1094c9.

12 Ibid., 1097a6–a26.

13 The Diamond Grotto is discussed in detail in Birnbaum, "Secret Halls of the Mountain Lords."

14 *Gu Qingliang zhuan*, T.51: 2098.1095a12–a27.

15 Ibid., 1095a1–a2.

16 Ibid., 1094c29–1095a11. This second story about the Diamond Grotto, as explained in Birnbaum's article, is based on a longer account from Daoxuan's *Zhong tianzhu sheweiguo Qiyuansi tujing* (Illustrated scripture of Jetavana Monastery of Śrāvastī in Central India), T.45: 1899; see Birnbaum, "Secret Halls of the Mountain Lords," 125, n. 32. Daoxuan's text is discussed later in this chapter.

17 On this point, Birnbaum argues: "When Buddhists took over the Mount Wu-t'ai territory as their own, they transformed this native Chinese phenomenon into a Buddhist one: the Diamond Grotto was recognized as the home of Wen-shu [i.e., Mañjuśrī] (who replaced the mountain-lord)" (Birnbaum, "Secret Halls of the Mountain Lords," 125).

18 Jietuo's biography can be found in the following texts: *Gu Qingliang zhuan*, T.51: 2098.1095c11–1096b2; *Huayan jing zhuanji*, T.51: 2073.169a12–169b19; *Xu gaoseng zhuan*, T.50: 2060.603b11–603c3. For Mingyao, see *Huayan jing zhuanji*, T.51: 2073.169.c11–c22, and *Gu Qingliang zhuan*, T.51: 2098.1098a26–b9.

19 This meditative practice is rather obscure, and except for the accounts of Jietuo and Mingyao from *Huayan jing zhuanji,* most of what we know is based on the work of a lay Buddhist scholar, Li Tongxuan (635–730 or 646–740), especially *New Commentaries on the Flower Garland Sutra* (Xin Huayan jing lun), T.36: 1739. See Gimello, "Li T'ung Hsüan"; Kojima, "Ri Tsūgen ni okeru kōmyō shisō"; Koh, "Li Tongxuan."

20 There is one significant exception. According to Jietuo's account, after tirelessly searching for the vision of Mañjuśrī, Jietuo was said to have been visited by the bodhisattva himself, but Jietuo declined the opportunity to meet the bodhisattva, stating, "Mañjuśrī is Mañjuśrī, and Jietuo is Jietuo"; he was suggesting that enlightenment (i.e., *jietuo*) lies in the ultimate comprehension from within, and the perception from without is only the means, not the end itself; see *Gu Qingliang zhuan,* T.51: 2098.1096a19–20.

21 More specifically, they were termed "auspicious signs of Mount Qingliang" (*Qingliang ruixiang*), as in an account in *Gu Qingliang zhuan,* in T.51: 2098.1097.c2. In *Guang Qingliang zhuan,* Yanyi sometimes used the term "divine omens" (*lingrui*). The term "auspicious signs" was initially used in the context of omenology developed around the Han dynasties (202 BCE–220 CE), referring to extraordinary events or occurrences produced by heavenly mandate in response to the virtue and legitimacy of the ruler. In this case, the auspicious sign was also recorded in pictorial form, and catalogues of such pictorial images were compiled into collections (*ruitu*) as aids to observing and identifying them. See Wu Hung, *The Wu Liang Shrine,* 73–96. Unlike these omens, however, "auspicious signs" in the early history of Mount Wutai were more unusual, indicative of, as well as responding to, Mañjuśrī's divine presence.

22 Huize's visit at Mount Wutai is also recorded in *Ji shenzhou sanbao gantong lu,* compiled by Daoxuan in 664, T.52: 2106.422.c9–423a6. In this account, Huize made two separate visits to Mount Wutai. In 661, he was sent to Mount Wutai to repair aged pagodas, and in 662, he was dispatched to Mount Wutai to observe and record miraculous occurrences of the mountains and to repair dilapidated monastic buildings.

23 The term *zhenrong,* translated as "true presence" here, is highly suggestive in early Buddhist texts, referring to the true and unmediated presence or manifestation of the divine. In this sense, it is used in close relation to other comparable Chinese terms, such as *zhenxiang* 真相 (or *zhenxiang* 真像, lit. true image), *zhenshen* (true body), or *zhenyi* (true appearance). All these terms could also have particular specificities or emphases, based on the different or specific relationships of the divine with its manifestation(s) under investigation. Some of the distinctions among how these terms were applied historically will become important in my discussion of the iconic representation of Mañjuśrī in chapter 6. When used in reference to a person, *rong* can mean "face," and thus the term *zhenrong* is most often translated as "true visage" or "true countenance." In a medieval Buddhist context, however, the term *zhenrong* was almost without exception used to refer to the entire physical appearance or presence of the divine, rather than the face only. In Yang Xuanzhi's *Record of the Monasteries of Luoyang* (Luoyang qielan ji), dating from 547, the term *zhenrong* appears six times, all used in this latter sense. See Fan Xiangyong, *Luoyang qielan ji jiaozhu,* 1, 196, 200, 266, 272, 341. For this reason, I render *zhenrong* as "true presence." As will become clearer later in the chapter, the icon of Mañjuśrī called *zhenrong xiang,* created at Mount Wutai around 710–11, refers not only to the true

presence of the bodhisattva but more specifically to the true presence of Mañjuśrī on the back of his holy lion. I thank Michael Nylan for her insightful comments on my use of *zhenrong* in my paper "Locating Mañjuśrī at Early-Tang Mount Wutai," presented at 15th Annual Southeast Early China Roundtable, held at the University of the South, Oct. 7–9, 2011.

24 *Gu Qingliang zhuan,* T.51: 2098.1098c8–9.

25 Ibid., 1098c16. However, no details of the small screen (*xiaozhang*), nor its pictorial content, were provided by Huixiang.

26 Sacred traces (*shengji*) or numinous traces (*lingji*) in early accounts of Mount Wutai include, for example, holy footprints, sacred spots frequented by Mañjuśrī himself, or sites of important historical events or legends interpreted retrospectively as intervention by the bodhisattva.

27 For this observation of signs being embodied through sensory capacities, see Wei-Cheng Lin, "Sign."

28 For the altitudes of the mountains within the larger perimeter of Mount Wutai, see Hou Wenzheng, *Wutaishan zhi,* 17–22.

29 *Gu Qingliang zhuan,* T.51: 2098.1093c2–4.

30 *Guang Qingliang zhuan,* T. 51: 2099. Yanyi, an abbot of the Cloister of True Presence (Zhenrong Yuan) at Mount Wutai, compiled the historical records and miraculous accounts of the site, most of which are dated after the completion of Huixiang's *Ancient Records* in ca. 680; his compilation thus serves as the most detailed source for the history of Mount Wutai during the eighth through the tenth centuries.

31 About the earlier designation of the five peaks, Yanyi states in *Guang Qingliang zhuan,* "According to ancient maps, today's North Peak was the old Central Peak; Central Peak, the South Peak; and [Mount] Da Huangjian, the North Peak. Mount Kaolao is West Peak and [Mount] Mantianshi is East Peak. Only North and Central Peaks are different from the past; East and West Peaks are the same as the past" (T.51: 2099.1105b5–7).

32 For a notable example, see Robson, *Power of Place,* esp. chap. 2. Implications of the redesignation at Mount Wutai, though noted by scholars, thus far have not been discussed.

33 See Matsumoto, "The Iconography of Shaka's Sermon."

34 *Guang Qingliang zhuan,* T.51: 2099.1110a15–16.

35 This distinction between "auspicious sign" (*ruixiang*) and "exhibiting the body" (*xianshen*) is discussed in Choi Bok-hee, "Godaisan monju shinkō."

36 There is one notable exception, however. Daoxuan, writing in the first half of the seventh century, reports that the meditation master Jietuo was said to have observed, four times at the garden of Dafu Lingjiu Monastery, "Mañjuśrī surrounded by his retinue crowding the air, with a multitude of transcendents and extraordinary sages, who cannot be numbered or recorded" (*Ji shenzhou sanbao gantong lu,* T.52: 2106.425a9–a10). The translation is after Birnbaum, "The Manifestation of a Monastery," 121. Daoxuan's story, however, is not found in other sources related to Jietuo, and the terms of his description (e.g., his mention of transcendents) is different from those used to depict the vision of the bodhisattva in later periods.

37 This creation legend of the icon—Mañjśrī riding a lion—is one of the most critical historical components for the formation of the bodhisattva cult at Mount Wutai and its transmission elsewhere. There are three different versions of the legend.

The earliest one is by the Japanese pilgrim Ennin (794–864) in *Nittō guhō junrei gyōki*, dated about 847–58, in *NGJG*, vol. 3, 3–4. The second version is from the Dunhuang Manuscript, S529v, dating from the early tenth century (transcribed in Du, *Dunhuang Wutaishan wenxian*, 200–203). The third version from ca. 1060 is recorded in Yanyi's *Guang Qingliang zhuan*, in T.51: 2099.1110a13–a26. All three versions are transcribed and translated in appendix 1.

38 The discussion here is based on the account in *Guang Qingliang zhuan* (see appendix 1.3). Although Yanyi refers to the apparitional manifestation of Mañjuśrī as *zhenxiang*, literally "true image," the earliest record of the creation legend by Ennin used *zhenrong*, or "true presence," implying that this manifestation of the bodhisattva was Mañjuśrī himself, not an image of him. This is why the image hall built to house the icon was named Cloister of the True Presence (Zhenrong Yuan).

39 Although the Chinese term *yuan* is most often translated as "cloister," a translation I use in this book, *yuan* in traditional Chinese architecture does not necessarily refer to the cloister space, or open court, found in western monasteries, which is enclosed by a roofed or vaulted passage or ambulatory, often with an open arcade or colonnade facing the court. Rather, *yuan* more appropriately refers to a building compound, consisting of a courtyard and a main hall, enclosed by walls, roofed passages (*lang*), or subsidiary buildings (*fang*). A *yuan* compound could be large or small, but usually was a smaller precinct, unit, or subtemple inside a larger monastery.

40 *NGJG*, vol. 3, 4.

41 Of the two examples, the statue of Mañjuśrī at Nanchan Monastery is more publicized, as the image hall itself is the oldest surviving wooden structure in China today. The marble statue, however, is likely the older, and thus closer to the time of the legend. The statue was uncovered at the former site of Zhulin Monastery and now is in the collection of Shanxi Provincial Museum in Taiyuan. See Sun Xiaogang, *Wenshu pusa tuxiang xue*, 92–93.

42 The origin of the representational image of Mañjuśrī riding a lion is unclear but most certainly it goes back before the early eighth century, and maybe as early as the sixth century in China. See Sun, *Wenshu pusa tuxiang xue*, 36–45.

43 The idea of a "true image" imbued with the sacredness of the origin was not unique to medieval China. For instance, there is a Christian legend of Saint Luke, painting the image of the Virgin and Child, with the guidance of an angel, before an apparition of Mary holding the baby Jesus; this legend, also, touches on the concept of the authenticity and potency of an image made with divine intervention. See Belting, *Likeness and Presence*, 57–59; Freedberg, *The Power of Image*, 108–10. A similar instance in a Spanish context is given in Portús, "The Holy Depicting the Holy."

44 In medieval Christianity, religious cults tended to focus not on the place where the vision appeared but on the image that revealed the apparition. See, for example, Christian, *Apparitions in Late Medieval and Renaissance Spain*, 15–19. In comparison, as I argue in this book by examining the role of architecture, in medieval China both the place and image are brought together at a particular site.

45 *Guang Qingliang zhuan*, T.51: 2099.1110a26.

46 *Gu Qingliang zhuan*, T.51: 2098.1094a4–a6.

47 Ibid., 1094a28–a29.

48 For accounts of the three Mañjuśrī images, see ibid., 1098c4, 1094a13, and 1095b1.

49 This is observed in Yun-jo Lin, "Wutaishan yu Wenshu daochang," 106–10.

50 See *Ji shenzhou sanbao gantonglu,* T.52: 2106.425a6–a15, and *Daoxuan lüshi gantong lu,* T.52: 2017.437a21–b1.

51 See Yun-jo Lin, "Wutaishan yu Wenshu daochang," 98. Here, the "multicloistered complex" refers to more than one subunit (i.e., building compound) built inside the larger monastery. Usually termed *duoyuan shi siyuan* in modern scholarship, multiple compounds were already recorded as an element of monastic architecture in the fifth century, suggesting larger land properties, more complicated spatial layouts, and multiaxial organizations of Buddhist monasteries. During this early period, larger monasteries seemed to have been constructed on the model of nonreligious buildings, such as residences or palaces. Modern excavation has uncovered examples of large monasteries with multiple compounds in major urban centers. See Li Yuqun, "Sui Tang yiqian Zhongguo fojiao siyuan." In the Tang dynasty, most large monasteries in Chang'an, for instance, were multicloistered, and the monastic layout began to take on more doctrinal or symbolic meanings, a topic that is discussed later in this chapter. For a discussion on the submonastic units during the Tang, see Li Dehua, "Tangdai fojiao siyuan."

52 This name conferral is mentioned in two texts: Cui Zhiyuan, *Tang Da Jianfusi gu sizhu fanjing dade Fazang heshang zhuan,* T.50: 2054.284b10–11; and Chengguan (738–839), *Dafangguan fo Huayan jing suishu yanyi chao,* T.36: 1736.601c15–c16. This name change will be discussed in chapter 4.

53 In both *Gu Qingliang zhuan* and *Guang Qingliang zhuan,* all three monasteries were said to have been built during the time of Emperor Xiaowen (r. 471–99) of the Northern Wei, making them among the earliest Buddhist establishments built at Mount Wutai.

54 See *NGJG,* vol. 2, 460–61, vol. 3, 3–5. The Cloister of the True Presence was renamed around this time as Cloister of the Bodhisattva Hall (Pusa Tang Yuan).

55 About the pagoda, Ennin writes: "In front of the [Well-Abiding] Pavilion is a two-storied octagonal pagoda, [which is] dignified and magnificent. Under the pagoda, [relics of] Aśoka are deposited and buried underground. No one is allowed to see [the depository]. [The pagoda] is one of the eighty-four thousand pagodas constructed by King Aśoka" (*NGJG,* vol. 3, 5).

56 This is suggested in Ono and Hibino, *Godaisan,* 44–45.

57 The term "crown" is the translation of the Sanskrit term *uṣṇīṣa* (C: *ding*), referring to the topknot on the head of the Buddha. In Esoteric Buddhism, Mañjuśrī was usually visualized as a bodhisattva with a five-topknot crown, symbolizing the five kinds of wisdom, a topic that will be discussed in chapter 5.

58 See Puay-Peng Ho, "Building for Glitter and Eternity."

59 For Buddhism at Mount Wutai during the Ming, see Ono and Hibino, *Godaisan,* 92–128; Cui Zhengsen, *Wutaishan fojiao shi,* vol. 2, 580–95.

60 In particular, much of Daoxuan's doctrinal exegesis of this *vinaya* text was adapted from Daoan's monastic rules of the fourth century, discussed in chapter 1. The most influential version among Daoxuan's commentaries was the *Sifenlü shanfan buque xingshichao,* T.40: 1804. On Daoxuan's contribution to the formation of Chinese *vinaya,* see Yifa, *The Origins of Buddhist Monastic Codes in China,* 23–28. For a biography of Daoxuan, see *Song gaoseng zhuan,* T.50: 2061.790b7–791b26.

61 See Wright, "T'ang T'ai-tsung and Buddhism"; Weinstein, *Buddhism under the T'ang,* 17–21.

62 *Xu gaoseng zhuan,* T.50: 2060.621.a14–a15.

63 *Fayuan zhulin,* T.53: 2122.591a19–a24.

64 Daoxuan's tales of "resonant response" (*gantong*) can be divided into three categories: tales about places, objects, or humans, found respectively in his *Ji shenzhou sanbao gantong lu, Daoxuan lüshi gantong lu,* and the section on *gantong* aspiration in his *Xu gaoseng zhuan;* see Tan, "Daoxuan's Vision of Jetavana," 76.

65 *Ji shenzhou sanbao gantong lu,* T.52: 2106.424c22–425a15, trans. in Birnbaum, "The Manifestation of a Monastery," 120–21.

66 In his *Sifenlü shanfan buque xingshichao,* Daoxuan praises the Jetavana Monastery in the section "Methods for Building a Monastery" (Zaosi fa): "In *Illustrated Scripture of Jetavana Monastery*, buildings in either timber or stone all had their meanings in order to teach humans and deities to identify the [building] form, and consequently to understand the teachings. . . . But now, time has elapsed and the Buddha's teachings are often insulted. We still build, but the law of building is already obscure, thus causing us to err" (T.40: 1804.134c25–c27).

67 *Zhong tianzhu sheweiguo Qiyuansi tujing,* T.45: 1899. Jetavana *vihāra* was located outside the city of Śrāvastī during the Buddha's time. A parkland site, it was later purchased by Anāthapiṇḍada and Prince Jēta. The Buddha spent twenty-five years at this retreat and his preachings here are gathered in several important sutras, which made it an important pilgrimage center. Daoxuan had never been to India, but stated that he based his account on other texts, especially two by Lingyu (518–605) from Mount Bao, *Si gao* (Announcement of monasteries) and *Shengji ji* (Records of sacred sites), both no longer extant. The *Illustrated Scripture* (Zhong tianzhu sheweiguo Qiyuansi tujing), dating to 667, should have been accompanied by one or more illustrations of the monastic layout, as indicated in its title; however, no illustration is transmitted to the present along with this text. Daoxuan, nevertheless, composed another closely related text in the same year, titled *Guanzhong chuangli jietan tujing* (Illustrated scripture concerning the erection of the ordination platform in the Guanzhong Region, T.45: 1892), which describes the ordination altar inside a larger monastic layout resembling that of *Illustrated Scripture.* When reprinted in 1152, *Scripture Concerning the Ordination Platform* was accompanied by an illustration, showing a typical Chinese monastic layout surrounded by other cloisters on both sides. See Itō, *Tōyō kenchiku no kenkyū,* vol. 2, 365–406. A reconstruction of the monastic layouts described in both *Illustrated Scripture* and the *Scripture Concerning the Ordination Platform* are included in Fu Xinian, *Liangjin, Nanbeichao,* 478–79. For a discussion of the *Illustrated Scripture,* see Puay-Peng Ho, "The Ideal Monastery." The most comprehensive study, including the translation of the entire text, of *Illustrated Scripture* is Tan, "Daoxuan's Vision of Jetavana."

68 Faxian (337–422) visited the Jetavana Monastery during his stay in India from 399 to 414, and Xuanzang (600–664) came later, during his stay from 629 to 645. Both recorded their experience in writing, though the monastery was very much in ruins when Xuanzang arrived at the site. For a discussion of both Faxian's and Xuanzang's accounts about Jetavana Monastery, see Tan, "Daoxuan's Vision of Jetavana," 133–43. Also see Hazra, *Buddhism in India.*

69 *Zhong tianzhu sheweiguo Qiyuansi tujing,* T.45: 1899.883a23–a24.

70 See Steinhardt, *Chinese Imperial City Planning,* 101–9; Steinhardt, *Chinese Architecture,* 96–97.

71 Puay-Peng Ho, "The Ideal Monastery," 7.

72 The three emptinesses refer to "void or immateriality" (*kong*), "formlessness" (*wu-xiang*), and "inaction" (*wuzuo*), and the entrance gate to a monastery was often called "gate of the Three [Emptinesses]" (*sanmen*).

73 The crow-head gate, or *wutoumen*, refers to a style of gate in which the two lateral posts that support the crossbeam (and other horizontal components) project above the gate structure and turn into decorative finials. The projecting finials were often painted black, like crows stretching their heads upward. During the Tang, the crow-head gate was prescribed only for building complexes that belonged to mid-ranked, or higher, officials. See Qiao and Luo, "Paifang jianzhu."

74 *Zhong tianzhu sheweiguo Qiyuansi tujing,* T.45: 1899.886c20–c21. The translation is after Tan, "Daoxuan's Vision of Jetavana," 280.

75 *Zhong tianzhu sheweiguo Qiyuansi tujing,* T.45: 1899.890b4–b5. The translation is after Tan, "Daoxuan's Vision of Jetavana," 308.

76 For the murals at the Mogao caves that depict monastic architecture in a Pure Land setting, see Puay-Peng Ho, "Paradise on Earth"; Zhao Shengliang, "Dunhuang bi-hua yu Zhongguo hua."

77 For more discussion about the architectural complex as depicted in Dunhuang murals such as the one in fig. 3.4, see Xiao Mo, *Dunhuang jianzhu yanjiu,* 61–94.

78 *Jiaojie xinxue biqiu xinghu lüyi,* T.45: 1897. For a discussion of this text, see Reinders, "Ritual Topography."

79 See *Jiaojie xinxue biqiu xinghu lüyi,* T.45: 1897.869b21–869b28.

80 The term *shanmen* for the entrance gate to a monastery was applied rather late, probably not earlier than the end of the Tang dynasty, but as I suggest here, the notion that the monastic ground is like mountain topography must have arisen earlier. Ennin used the term *shanmen* in his diary to refer to points on the pilgrimage routes that led to Mount Wutai; see *NGJG,* vol. 3, 63.

81 *Gu Qingliang zhuan,* T.51: 2089.1098a29.

82 A later Japanese monk of the Huayan school (Kegon in Japanese), Myōe (1173–232), followed Jietuo and Mingyao by devising a similar meditation, known as Samādhi [Achieved by] Visualizing the Buddha's Radiance (*Butsu kōmyō zanmai kan*), as detailed in his *Kegon butsukō zanmai kan hihōzō* (Secret treasure of the samādhi [achieved by] visualizing the Buddha's radiance [based on] the *Flower Garland Sutra*), T.72: 2332. Although an anachronistic example, and although Myōe's meditative practice already included the esoteric components of the later Mañjuśrī cult, it is still suggestive that the vision to be attained through this meditation practice was the bodhisattva riding a lion and hovering in midair. After the true-presence icon was created in the early eighth century, the manifestation of the bodhisattva at Mount Wutai was recorded almost without exception as Mañjuśrī riding his flying lion. The iconic motif was transmitted to Japan most certainly no later than 845, when Ennin returned to Japan, bringing with him paintings of this iconic image. It is thus not a surprise that the iconic motif was integrated into the meditative practice that originated at Mount Wutai. See Shibasaki, "Myōe to bukkō zanmai kan."

83 *NGJG,* vol. 3, 3.

84 Eck, "Mountains," 6213.

85 This topic will be discussed in greater detail in chapter 6. For now, it suffices to note that in figure 6.8, a woodcut print pamphlet for devotional purposes, dating

from the first decades of the tenth century, the true-presence image of Mañjuśrī is identified as "Bodhisattva Mañjuśrī at Mount Wutai."

86 See, for example, Soper, *The Evolution of Buddhist Architecture,* 37, cited in Puay-Peng Ho, "The Ideal Monastery," 5.

87 See Steinhardt, "Early Chinese Buddhist Architecture." Although there is consensus among scholars about a general shift of focus from pagoda to main image hall in Tang monasteries, the shift was never straightforward, and building pagodas on the main north-south axis was not as unusual as one may expect, even in the example of urban monasteries in the Tang capital Chang'an. See useful textual materials discussed in Su Bai, "Shilun Tangdai Chang'an fojiao siyuan."

88 See Wong, "A Reassessment of the Representation of Mt. Wutai," 33.

FOUR. Mediating the Distance to Mount Wutai

The epigraph is taken from Zhang Chuzhen, *A Record of Mount Wutai and the [Stone] Lantern* (Wutaishan ji dengtai ji), ca. 713–39.

1 The shifting character of Mount Wutai as recorded in these two texts is briefly discussed in Choi Bok-hee, "Koseryōden kara kōseryōden e."

2 *Guang Qingliang zhuan,* T.51: 2099.1105b24–26. The monk in this account from the *Extended Records* is the Chan master Yan (Yan Chanshi), likely the same Master Yan in the *Ancient Records,* who was residing at Mount Wutai before he died in 673; see T.51: 2098.1095a28–1095b7.

3 This is pointed out in Birnbaum, "Light in the Wutai Mountains," 209.

4 *Guang Qingliang zhuan,* T.51: 2099.1105b28–1106c26.

5 For a brief reference on the structure of the stone lantern, see Fu Xinian, *Liangjin, Nanbeichao,* 526–27. According to Fu, there are at least four examples surviving from the Tang dynasty. A discussion on the use of lanterns made in bronze around this same period in Japan is in Matsuyama, "Tōdaiji dōzō hakkaku tōrō."

6 The pond, Yuhua Chi, is recorded in both *Gu Qingliang zhuan* (T.51: 2098.1093b22–25) and *Guang Qingliang zhuan* (T.51: 2099.1105b29–c3) as located on top of Central Peak.

7 The inscription itself is not dated, but the reign title Kaiyuan Shenwu (used by Emperor Xuanzong during 713–39), is mentioned in the inscription; see *Jiu Tangshu, juan* 8, 171, and *juan* 9, 210. The inscription and the stone lantern described in the inscription have not been published in any language other than Chinese. The entire inscription is transcribed in Fu Shumin, "Wutaishan shidengtai kao," and Cui and Wang, *Wutaishan beiwen xuanzhu,* 160–64, but both transcriptions have minor mistakes. The dedicatory inscription has twenty-six lines in all, carved on four sides of the octagonal shaft. The names of Tang donors on the other four sides were scratched out and carved over in 997 by those who donated to repair the lantern. My transcription and translation of the dedicatory inscription are in appendix 2. The quote in the epigraph is from lines 14–15 on side 3. The lantern has been removed from its original temple and is now in a small exhibition area inside the Drum Tower in Daixian, Shanxi.

8 The position of the town with respect to routes existing at the time is based on the pilgrimage routes to Mount Wutai reconstructed in Yan Gengwang, *Tangdai jiaotong tukao,* vol. 5, 1507–12; see also Du, *Dunhuang Wutaishan wenxian,* 191–92.

9 For Fazang, see Jinhua Chen, "More Than a Philosopher."

10 The translation sponsored by the empress is the eighty-fascicle *Flower Garland Sutra,* translated by the Khotanese monk Śikṣānanda in Luoyang in 669; see Weinstein, *Buddhism under the T'ang,* 44–47. For Wu Zetian, see Guisso, *Wu Tse-t'ien;* Fairbank and Twitchett, *The Cambridge History of China,* vol. 3, 242–332.

11 The visit by the delegation is discussed in chapter 3.

12 See *Gu Qingliang zhuan,* T.51: 2098.1098c11–17.

13 For instance, in 691, the year after Wu Zetian assumed the title of emperor (the male title) and renamed the dynasty as the Great Zhou, an imperial edict was promulgated to formally rank Buddhism above Daoism, thus inverting the religious priority set by the three preceding emperors. See Weinstein, *Buddhism under the T'ang,* 43.

14 The long journey required for a pilgrimage to Mount Wutai entails what Peter Brown terms "therapy of distance." As Brown explains, the distance to the pilgrimage site "is there to be overcome; the experience of pilgrimage activates a yearning for intimate closeness"; see Peter Brown, *The Cult of the Saints,* 87.

15 For more on my translation of the term *huasi* as "virtual monastery," see later in this chapter.

16 See, for example, Weinstein, *Buddhism under the T'ang,* 37–47; Jinhua Chen, *Monks and Monarchs,* 112–18.

17 See Forte, *Political Propaganda and Ideology;* Barrett, "Stūpa, Sūtra, and Śarīra"; Sen, *Buddhism Diplomacy, and Trade,* 79–86.

18 *Jiu Tangshu, juan* 20, 115; Guisso, *Wu Tse-t'ien,* 20.

19 See Wu Zetian's biography in *Jiu Tangshu, juan* 6, 115–34.

20 For Wu Zetian's building projects, see Puay-Peng Ho, "Architecture and Legitimacy." On the building of the Bright Hall, see Wang Guixiang, "Tang Luoyang gong Wushi Mingtang."

21 The gender reversal is proposed in Wu, "Wuyue de chongtu," 637.

22 Relics were taken on tour in 705, 756, 790, 819, and 873. For the reliquaries at Famen Monastery and its underground crypt (*digong*), see Shaanxisheng Kaogu Yanjiuyuan et al., *Famensi kaogu fajue baogao;* Chen, *Monks and Monarchs,* 118–26; Eugene Y. Wang, "Of the True Body."

23 For a detailed discussion on the relic distribution during the Renshou reign (601–4) of Emperor Wen, see Chen, *Monks and Monarchs,* chap. 2. See also Sonya Lee, *Surviving Nirvana,* 202–23.

24 The empress commissioned "golden caskets and silver encasements, nine altogether, with elaborate carving and decorations that are a source of marvel" (Daoxuan, *Ji shenzhou sanbao gantong lu,* T.52: 2106.407b17).

25 The distribution of the Guanzhai relics is recorded in *Song gaoseng zhuan, juan* 26, T.50: 2061.872c20–873a5.

26 The commentary is titled *Commentary on the Meaning of the Prophecy about the Divine Sovereign in* Dayun Jing (*Dayun jing* shenhuang shouji yishu), preserved in Dunhuang Manuscripts S2658 and S6502. See also Chen, *Monks and Monarchs,* 127.

27 The *fengshan* rite is documented in *Jiu Tangshu, juan* 23, 881–88; see the discussion in Wu, "Wuyue de chongtu," 634–37.

28 "[Emperor] Gaozong ascended to the throne, [and soon] officials and subjects requested [that the emperor] perform the *fengshan* rite. Zetian was named as the empress, supporting [the request] secretly" (*Jiu Tangshu, juan* 23, 884).

29 See *Jiu Tangshu, juan* 23, 891.

30 The empress's central position is discussed in Wu, "Wuyue de chongtu," 638–39.

31 Fazang, *Huayan jing zhuanji,* T.51: 2073.157a28–b1.

32 *Gu Qingliang zhuan,* T.51: 2098.1098c16. The work is discussed in chapter 3.

33 The account of Buddhapālita can be found in *Song gaosheng zhuan, juan* 2, T.50: 2061.717c15–718b7, and *Guang Qingliang zhuan,* T.51: 2099.1111a19–b23. The discussion here is based on Zhijing's preface included in T.19: 967. The preface is translated in Paul Copp, "Voice, Dust, Shadow, Stone," 45–47. For the Sanskrit rendering of the name, Buddhapālita, see Kroll, *Dharma Bell and Dhāraṇī Pillar,* 41–42.

34 *Foding zunsheng tuoluoni jing,* T.19: 967.349b13–15. The translation is after Copp, "Voice, Dust, Shadow, Stone," 46.

35 More is known about Divākara than about Du Xingyi. A Śramaṇa from central India, Divākara (612–87) was a prolific translator during his career in China, 676–87. His name was transliterated as Dipoheluo in Chinese, but he was also known by the Chinese name Rizhao.

36 The full Sanskrit title of the *Sutra of the Superlative Dhāraṇi* is *Uṣṇīṣavijāyā dhāraṇi sūtra* (Foding zunsheng tuoluoni jing). For the meaning of the Sanskrit title and its translation, see Copp, "Voice, Dust, Shadow, Stone," 41–44. The *Sutra of the Superlative Dhāraṇi* is available in eight different translations: T.19: 968, 969, 967, 970, 971, 973, 972, and 974. The most comprehensive study of this scripture, with an emphasis on the *dhāraṇi* pillar engraved with the scripture, is Liu Shufen, *Miezui yu duwang.* For the relation between this sutra and Mount Wutai, see Barrett, "Stūpa, Sūtra, and Śarīra," 25–30; Jinhua Chen, "Śarīra and Scepter," 103–17; and Lin Yun-jo, "Tangdai *Foding zunsheng tuoluoni jing.*"

37 *Foding zunsheng tuoluoni jing,* T.19: 967.349b4–c18.

38 See *Foding zunsheng tuoluoni jing,* trans. Du Xingyi, T.19: 968 (679 CE); trans. Divākara, T.19: 969 (682 CE).

39 Barrett, "Stūpa, Sūtra, and Śarīra," 28; Chen, "Śarīra and Scepter," 107–8; Copp, "Voice, Dust, Shadow, Stone," 48–49.

40 Forte, *Political Propaganda,* 97–100.

41 For example, Yijing (635–713), who traveled to India during 671–95, writes, "[Buddhists here] in the West expressed admiration that as Mañjuśrī is now residing in Bingzhou [where his sacred mountain is located], people there are blessed and should sing the praise of it" (*Nanhai jigui neifa zhuan,* T.54: 2125.228b14).

42 *Gu Qingliang zhuan,* T.51: 2098.1098c18–1099b8.

43 Antonino Forte argues that the legend should be considered "an integral part of a far-reaching political project whose aim was to transform China from a peripheral to a central area of Buddhist civilization." See Forte, "Hui-chih," 118.

44 *Jiu Tangshu, juan* 6, 123.

45 Degan was an important consultant of Wu Zetian for the construction of the Tower of Seven Jewels (Qibaotai), and also held the prestigious title "Venerable Translator" (*fanjing dade*); see Forte, *Political Propaganda,* 100–108.

46 *Guang Qingliang zhuan,* T.51: 2099.1107a24–28.

47 Fazang, *Huayan jing zhuanji,* T.51: 2073.157b1–2.

48 Peter Brown, *The Cult of the Saints,* 87.

49 *Guang Qingliang zhuan,* T.51: 2099.1107b7–8. In Zhencheng's *Gazetteer of Mount Qing-*

liang (Qingliangshan zhi), *juan* 4, Wu Zetian was described to have "spiritually journeyed" (*shenyou*) to the five peaks of the sacred mountain.

50 On the use of jade for a statue of the empress, see Barrett, "Stūpa, Sūtra, and Śarīra," 44–45; and Gu, "Tangdai Wutai Wenshu," 399–411. Sculpting a statue of an emperor or empress in jade was unprecedented, and the implications of the jade material are significant because jade was used in ritual or mortuary tradition and connotes the sense of transcending or transforming; for an example, see Wu, "The Jade Prince Revisited."

51 There is one significant exception: the building of Jin'ge Monastery (Monastery of Golden Pavilion), which will be discussed in chapter 5.

52 Liu Shufen, *Miezui yu duwang*, 33.

53 See *Foding zunsheng tuoluoni jing*, T.19: 967.351b9–18.

54 A dedicatory inscription dated 744, found in the Longmen cave site (niche 1720) outside Luoyang, attests to this soteriological aspect of the bodhisattva cult at Mount Wutai. The inscription reads: "[I], disciple Shang Shihui, have not done good deeds in this life, berating [people] whenever I opened my mouth. [I] hope [my] accrued bad karma may be removed along with my defilements of the past *kalpas* [for which I] wish to practice often at Mount Wutai and recite five hundred pages of scriptures daily." It is transcribed in Liu and Li, *Longmen shiku beike*, vol. 2, 580.

55 Since the column did not survive, it is not certain if the preface was the one written by Zhijing in 689 that included the legend of Buddhapālita and Mount Wutai.

56 Lu Zengxiang, *Baqiongshi jinshi buzheng*, *juan* 43, collected in Guojia Tushuguan Shanben Jinshizu, *Lidai shike shiliao*, vol. 3, 242–43.

57 The labels identify the images as "the [manifestation of] bodhisattva's hand" and "the [manifestation of] bodhisattva's presence."

58 *Guang Qingliang zhuan*, T.51: 2099.1112c23–24. The translation is after Birnbaum, "The Manifestation of a Monastery," 127. For Shenying's biography, see *Song gaoseng zhuan*, *juan* 21, T.50: 2061.843a7–b4.

59 Daoxuan, *Ji shenzhou sanbao gantong lu*, *juan* 2, T.52: 2106.422c22–23, also quoted in Birnbaum, "Manifestation of a Monastery," 128.

60 In his study of the story, Raoul Birnbaum writes: "In the case of [Shenying], there is a mysterious quality about his inner configurations, changed through long years of dedicated spiritual practice, such that by his nature he is closely attuned to the divine, and it correspondingly is made easy for such spirits to manifest themselves around him" (Birnbaum, "Manifestation of a Monastery," 137).

61 The four accounts are found in *Guang Qingliang zhuan*, T.51: 2099.1111b24–1116a22.

62 See Birnbaum, "The Manifestation of a Monastery"; Stevenson, "Visions of Mañjuśrī on Mount Wutai," 208.

63 For example, in *Fayuan zhulin*, *juan* 39, a monastery not fixed at one location was called *tiansi* (T.53: 2122.595b1–2). In the same text, *xiansi* was used for a monastery inhabited by immortals and seen sometimes but invisible at other times (T.53: 2122.596c5–15).

64 *Guang Qingliang zhuan*, T.51: 2099.1109a9–10.

65 Ibid., 1106b14; 1109a20. The quotation is from ibid., 1109a12.

66 For example, *Song gaoseng zhuan* contains two examples of *huasi* vision occurring at

sites other than Mount Wutai; in T.50: 2061.827b16–828a4 ("Biography of Faxiu") and T.50: 2061.801b03–28 ("Biography of Jianyuan").

67 For example, in Wuzhu's account, it is stated, "Although the way [of the Buddha] is not limited in place, at the efficacious site it is [nonetheless] easy [to follow the way]. [Wuzhu] thus decided to venerate Mount Wutai, determined to seek [the presence of] the Great Sage" (T.51: 2099.1111c4–5).

68 The concern with "dissolution of the Dharma" (*mofa*) or "end of the world" (*modai*) is expressed in the stories of Daoyi (*Guang Qingliang zhuan,* T.51: 2099.1113a23, c10) and of Fazhao (ibid., 1114b22).

69 In a sense, the virtual monastery can be understood as an architectural drawing, or virtual model or simulation used in modern architecture, to demonstrate in an abstract and immaterial way the critical ideas or concepts of the architecture. For a provocative discussion, see Evans, *Translations from Drawing to Building.*

70 The *huasi* account featuring Fazhao is the main topic of Stevenson, "Visions of Mañjuśrī," including the translation of the text, on pp. 212–20. Fazhao's biography can be found in *Song gaoseng zhuan, juan* 21, T.50: 2061.844a8–845b8. About Fazhao's position in Pure Land tradition, see Weinstein, *Buddhism under the T'ang,* 67–74; Tsukamoto, *Chūgoku jōdokyōshi,* 325–83. On Zhulin Monastery, see Saitō, *Chūgoku Godaisan Chikurin-ji.*

71 At Mount Lu, Fazhao practiced "samādhi in mindful recollection of the Buddha" (*Nianfo sanmei*), and it was during a period of intensive practice that Fazhao experienced a vision of Amitābha Buddha and received the method for intoning the Buddha's name in five tempos; this episode will be discussed later in this section. At Mount Heng, the South Sacred Peak, Fazhao, studying with a master named Chengyuan (712–802), likely learned to practice a form of intensive meditative visualization known as *Pratyutpanna samādhi* (Banzhou sanmei,) or meditation of direct encounter with the Buddhas of the present, discussed in chapter 1. See Stevenson, "Visions of Mañjuśrī," 206–7; for Fazhao's residency at Mount Heng, see Robson, *Power of Place,* 301–6.

72 *Guang Qingliang zhuan,* T.51: 2099.1114a12–15. Translation is after Stevenson, "Visions of Mañjuśrī," 212.

73 *Guang Qingliang zhuan,* T.51: 2099.1114a21–22.

74 Ibid., 1114.b16–21. Translation is after Stevenson, "Visions of Mañjuśrī," 214. See appendix 3, sec. 2, for Chinese text.

75 Daoxuan's vision of Jetavana Monastery is discussed in chapter 3.

76 *Guang Qingliang zhuan,* T.51: 2099.1114c9. Here rubbing the head (S: *vyākaraṇa;* C: *shouji*) is understood as a sign of Fazhao's future Buddhahood.

77 See the discussion of meditative visualization in chapter 1.

78 *Guang Qingliang zhuan,* T.51: 2099.1114b7. On the aspect of light as related to Mount Wutai, see Birnbaum, "Light in the Wutai Mountains."

79 The Diamond Grotto is discussed in chapter 3.

80 Fazhao justified his delayed circulation of the *huasi* account by stating that he initially did not want to publicize his visionary experience for fear that others might doubt and distrust him, but he finally did it only to benefit all who believed him; see *Guang Qingliang zhuan,* T.51: 2099.1115b24–1115c7.

81 The text is entitled *Rite for Intoning the Buddha's Name, Reciting Scripture, and Performing Meditation in the Five Tones of the Pure Land* (Jingtu wuhui nianfo songjing guan-

xingyi), collected incompletely in T.85.2827. The missing portion is partially made up by a manuscript of the same title found among the Dunhuang manuscripts. For the Dunhuang portion, see Hirokawa, "Reisan." Also see Stevenson, "Visions of Mañjuśrī," 205–6.

82 On the other hand, their circulation in the same year has also raised doubts about the circumstances surrounding the visionary accounts. As Daniel Stevenson reminds us, the early 770s was also the period when Fazhao began to make his way into the aristocratic and monastic circles in the capital of Chang'an to advocate his method of practice, as well as to solicit financial support to build a material counterpart of the virtual monastery at Mount Wutai. In other words, the visionary accounts might have been concocted with motives other than factual or spiritual experiences. See Stevenson, "Visions of Mañjuśrī," 210.

83 *Jingtu wuhui nianfo songjing guanxingyi,* T.85: 2827.1253c9–11. Translation is after Stevenson, "Visions of Mañjuśrī," 221.

84 *Foshuo wuliangshou jing,* T.12: 360.270a5–6. See Chappell, "Chinese Buddhist Interpretations of the Pure Lands"; Pas, *Visions of Sukhāvatī,* 149–62.

85 The term *jinse shijie,* used to mean the Pure Land of Mañjuśrī is found in Fazhao's biography in *Song gaoseng zhuan,* T.50: 2016.844a28. The canonical origin of the term is the chapter "Awakening by Light" of the *Flower Garland Sutra* (*Huayan jing,* T.10: 279.62b28–c8). When the term *jinse shijie* began to be used in China to mean the sacred realm of Mount Wutai is unclear, but should be no later than the last decades of the eighth century. In his diary, Ennin recorded a dedicatory inscription on a set of sutras in Jin'ge Monastery that reads: "Zheng Daojue, whose origin is in Chang'an, in the fourteenth day of the fifth month, the fourteenth year of the Dali reign [779], took a tour to venerate Mount Wutai and saw in person the Great Sage [Mañjuśrī], ten thousand bodhisattvas, and the Golden World" (*NGJG,* vol. 3, 94).

86 From *Eulogies of Mount Wutai* (Wutaishan zan), included in S5573, S4429, S5487, P3563, P3437, Beijing 8329, all dated to the first half of the tenth century; see Du, *Dunhuang Wutaishan wenxian,* 2–41. The translation is revised from Cartelli, *Five-Colored Clouds of Mount Wutai,* 117.

87 *Guang Qingliang zhuan,* T.51: 2099.1115c21–29.

88 *NGJG,* vol. 2, 428.

89 Birnbaum, "Light in the Wutai Mountains," 210.

90 The title reads *Wutaishan dasheng Zhulinsi shi Fazhao dejian taishan jingjie,* included in *Nyūtō shingū seikyō mokuroku* (Catalogue of the sacred teachings newly obtained in China), T.55: 2167.1085b4–5.

91 *Guang Qingliang zhuan,* T.51: 2099.1115b28–9, c2–3.

92 *Wutaishan dengtai ji,* app. 2, side 2.

93 For Chengguan's biography, see *Song gaoseng zhuan, juan* 5, T.50: 2061.737a2–c20.

94 Chengguan, *Dafangguang fo huayan jing suishu yanyi chao,* T.36: 1736.601c25–29.

95 It was called Monastery of Dharma Blossom of the Dali [Reign] (Dali Fahuasi) in Ennin's diary; see *NGJG,* vol. 3, 145. It is likely that the earlier name, Fahua Monastery, took Emperor Daizong's reign title Dali, used 766–79.

96 Yanyi listed seventy-two major monasteries at Mount Wutai, of which seventeen had been built since the Tang, while the remaining fifty-five were "ancient monasteries" (*gusi*), built before the Tang; see *Guang Qingliang zhuan,* T.51: 2099.1105b28–1106c26.

FIVE. Reconfiguring the Center

The epigraph is from Jonathan Z. Smith, *To Take Place: Toward Theory in Ritual* (Chicago: University of Chicago Press, 1987), 17. Reproduced with permission of University of Chicago Press.

1 T.52: 2120.834a9–a20, in *Daizong chao zeng Sikong da bianzheng guangzhi sanzang heshang biaozhi ji* (Collection of the memoranda on regulations bestowed by the court of Daizong to the minister of works, the greatly skillful and upright Guangzhi, the venerable Tripiṭaka master), compiled by Yuanzhao (d. 800), a disciple of Amoghavajra. The Chinese text is given in appendix 3, sec. 3.

2 Amoghavajra is also known as Bukong Jin'gang, or simply Bukong. Most of our knowledge about Amoghavajra's role in serving the court is based on his correspondence, documented in *Collection of the Memoranda*. For more on this document, see Orlando, "A Study of Chinese Documents." For titles and honors granted to Amoghavajra, see *Collection of the Memoranda*, T.52: 2120.845c23–846b2. On Amoghavajra, see Lehnert, "Amoghavajra"; Orzech, "The 'Great Teaching of Yoga.'"

3 For example, two such offerings were made in 740 and 748, recorded on a stele at Qingliang Monastery; the inscription, entitled *Stele of Qingliang Monastery at Mount Wutai* (Wutaishan Qingliangsi bei), is in *Quan Tangwen, juan* 264, 2,679–80. See also Cui and Wang, *Wutaishan beiwen*, 141–49.

4 *Jiu Tangshu, juan* 118, 3418.

5 The building of the Yuhua Monastery is recorded in *Collection of the Memoranda*, T.52: 2120.834b14–19.

6 See ibid., 835b17–c11. The sutras recited for this purpose were primarily the *Scripture for Humane Kings* and the *Lotus Sutra*.

7 Dali Fahua Monastery is discussed in chapter 4.

8 See, for example, Birnbaum, *Studies on the Mysteries of Mañjuśrī*, 25–38; Orzech, *Politics and Transcendent Wisdom*, 145–46; Jinhua Chen, *Crossfire*, 181–83.

9 *Wenshu shili fa baozang tuoluoni jing*, T.20: 1185A/1185B. Bodhiruci arrived in China in 693 and spent most of his career as a prolific translator, first in Luoyang and later at Chongfu Monastery in Chang'an. See Forte, "The South Indian Monk Bodhiruci"; Orzech, "Esoteric Buddhism in the Tang," 271–72. For this sutra in relation to Mount Wutai, see Lamotte, "Mañjuśrī," 85.

10 *Wenshu shili fa baozang tuoluoni jing*, T.20: 1185A.791c1–2, 791c12–14. The translation is modified based on Birnbaum, *Studies on the Mysteries of Mañjuśrī*, 11.

11 Birnbaum, *Studies on the Mysteries of Mañjuśrī*, 12–13; Osabe, *Tōdai mikkyōshi*, 118–19.

12 See Forte, "The South Indian Monk Bodhiruci," 89–90; Orzech, "Esoteric Buddhism in the Tang," 268, n. 17.

13 The name Wufeng was used in an otherwise lost passage quoted in Li Daoyuan's *Shuijing zhu*, cited in *Guang Qingliang zhuan*, T.51: 2099.1104a13.

14 See Copp, "Voice, Dust, Shadow, Stone," 41.

15 "Wheel-Turning King of One-Syllable Buddha's Crown" is a translation of the Sanskrit name *Ekākṣara-uṣṇīṣa-cakravartin*. For more on the Wheel-Turning King, see Misaki, "Bucchōkei no mikkyō," 483–85.

16 This text is *Yizi foding lunwang jing*, T.19: 951. For *homa*, see Payne and Orzech, "Homa."

17 For the different iconographic types of Mañjuśrī, see Inoue Akemi, "Kyōten to

zuzō"; Shimomatsu, "Monju bosatsu." In addition, quoting from a now lost *Records of Mañjuśrī* (Wenshu zhuan) written by Yuanxiao, a monk of Korean origin, Yanyi writes about this correlation: "Five peaks [of Mount Wutai] together is none other than the throne of the Tathāgatha of the five directions. It also resembles the five topknots on the bodhisattva's head" (*Guang Qingliang zhuan,* T.51:2099.1104a14–15). The translation is after Cartelli, *The Five-Colored Clouds of Mount Wutai,* 40.

18 Birnbaum, *Studies on the Mysteries of Mañjuśrī,* 24.

19 The print was discovered inside a statue of Śākyamuni brought to the Monastery Clear and Cool (Seiryōji) in Japan by Chōnen in 988; see Henderson and Hurvitz, "The Buddha of Seiryōji."

20 The text is translated in Birnbaum, *Studies on the Mysteries of Mañjuśrī,* 24.

21 This print has been dated to the Kamakura period (1185–333), although stylistically it is close to the surviving examples of Mañjuśrī with four attendants from the tenth century in China; see Sun Xiushen, "Zhongguo Xinyang Wenshu."

22 "Yoga," or *yuqie* in Chinese, is a technical term referring broadly to esoteric practices involving the use of hands (mudras), mouth (e.g., incantations), and mind (concentration), which enable practitioners to reach an ecstatic union of the individual mind and a deity, or to make mind and deity properly responsive to each other.

23 *Guang Qingliang zhuan,* T.51: 2099.1104b24–c7. The original Chinese text is given in appendix 3, sec. 4.

24 See Chiba, "Fukū no mikkyō ni okeru bucchōson." On the term *vajroṣṇīṣa* for *vajra* crown, Ronald M. Davidson has recently pointed out that *vajra-uṣṇīṣa* (i.e., *vajroṣṇīṣa*) has been misrendered by Japanese scholars as *vajraśekhara,* although the latter is a better-known term for the Chinese translation, *jin'gang ding. Vajra* refers to a thunderbolt, or diamond club, and has been used as a synonym for hardness, indestructibility, or power; the term "*vajra* crown," accordingly, implies the indestructible wisdom of the Buddha, a sign of his enlightenment. More specifically, "Vajra Crown" is the name of the esoteric doctrines, sutras, and tradition related to Vairocana Buddha. See Ronald M. Davidson, "Some Observations on the Uṣṇīṣa Abhiṣeka Rites." For Vajrabodhi, see Orzech, "Vajrabodhi."

25 This legend and the sutra (T.19: 967) are discussed in chapter 4.

26 For the use of the phrase "proto-esoteric Buddhism," see Strickmann, *Mantras et Mandarins,* 129–30; Sørensen, "On Esoteric Buddhism in China: A Working Definition."

27 See *Foding zunsheng tuoluoni jing,* T.19: 967.350b1–2.

28 For references on this sutra, see chapter 4, n. 36.

29 See Lin Yun-jo, "Tangdai 'Foding zusheng tuoluoni jing.'"

30 Divākara's translation of the *Sutra of the Superlative Dhāraṇī* is titled *Zuisheng foding tuoluoni jingchu yezhang zhou jing* (T.19: 970).

31 Yijing, *Sutra of the Superlative Dhāraṇī,* T.19: 971, has the same title as the sutra translated by Buddhapālita in T.19: 967.

32 For the three monks, also known as "three great masters of the Kaiyuan era [712–41]" (*Kaiyuan san dashi*) and their role in forming the esoteric practice in Tang China, see Yi-liang Chou, "Tantrism in China." For Śubhākarasiṃha, see Pinte, "Śubhākarasiṃha."

33 *Foding zunsheng tuoluoni niansong yigui fa,* T.19: 972. Śubhākarasiṃha's text is titled

Ritual Manual on the Yoga of the Superlative Buddha's Crown (Zunsheng foding xiu yuqiefa yigui) (T.19: 973). For a discussion and comparison of the two manuals, see Kuo, "Bucchōsonshō darani," 6–8; Michelle Wang, "Changing Conceptions of 'Maṇḍala.'"

34 The two events are from T.52: 2120.827c24–828a24 and T.52: 2120.829b18–c2.

35 See *Daizong chao,* T.52: 2120.829c17–830a11.

36 See *Fozu tongji,* T.49: 2035.377c25–378a14.

37 The two scriptures are rendered in Sanskrit by Kuo Liying as *Mahā-buddhoṣṇīṣa-dhāraṇī* and *Buddhoṣṇīṣa-dhāraṇī,* respectively; see Kuo, "Bucchōsonshō darani," 8; Paul Copp has suggested that both the scriptures might be the same as the *Sutra of the Superlative Dhāraṇī;* see Copp, "Voice, Dust, Shadow, Stone," 53–54, 135.

38 *Daizong chao,* T.52: 2120.852c10–13. The translation is after Yi-liang Chou, "Tantrism in China," 322.

39 Ibid., 840b1–6. The translation is after Orzech, "Esoteric Buddhism in the Tang," 282.

40 Copp makes a similar observation: "Bukong's [i.e., Amoghavajra's] interest in the spell . . . may in fact have been a direct result of his interest in Mañjuśrī" (Copp, "Voice, Dust, Shadow, Stone," 52–53).

41 For instance, in Amoghavajra's ritual manual (T.19: 972), Vairocana Buddha takes the position of the chief deity and is accompanied by eight great bodhisattvas to form a *maṇḍala* in which the mantra is to be chanted. See Michelle Wang, "From Dhāraṇī to Maṇḍala," 82–101. The *maṇḍala* based on Amoghavajra's instruction is discussed in Copp, "Voice, Dust, Shadow, Stone," 286–90.

42 Orzech, *Politics and Transcendent Wisdom,* 150.

43 About the related scriptures, see Osabe, *Tōdai mikkyōshi,* 114–15; Pan, "Bukong sanzang yu Wenshu pusa xinyang."

44 This observation is primarily based on the *Collection of the Memoranda;* see also Mukai, "Fukū sanzō no Monju bosatsu shinkō."

45 See *Daizong chao,* T.52: 2120.837a26–b10.

46 As Yifa points out, in the *Ten-Section Vinaya,* Piṇḍola was described as "forbidden by the Buddha to enter nirvana after he showed off his supernatural powers in front of laypeople" (Yifa, *The Origins of Buddhist Monastic Codes,* 14). See also Weinstein, *Buddhism under the T'ang,* 81. For the story of Piṇḍola, see Michihata, *Rakan shinkō shi,* 27–35; Strong, "The Legend of the Lion-Roarer."

47 *Daizong chao,* T.52: 2120.837b1–3.

48 Amoghavajra's request is recorded in ibid., 841c8–14; later, he sent another letter (ibid., 841c20–842a14) to express his gratitude after his earlier request was granted.

49 Although Amoghavajra did not use the term *cakravartin* in accounts discussed here, in 762 he had already employed the epithet Golden Wheel (Jinlun) for the emperor; see ibid., 829c28. The campaigns by Wendi of the Sui and Empress Wu are discussed in chapter 4.

50 See ibid., 842c13–29. The *Sutra [That Numerates] the Virtue and Magnificence of the Pure Land of the Great Sage Bodhisattva Mañjuśrī* (T.11: 319) is a retranslation by Amoghavajra of the same sutra that has two earlier translated versions in T.11: 318 (ca. 290) and T.11: 310.336c–341a (early 8th century). See Mukai, "Fukū sanzō no Monju bosatsu shinkō," 157–61.

51 *Daizong chao,* T.52: 2120.842a23–b21; on the construction of the Pavilion of Mañjuśrī,

see Iwamoto, "Fukū sanzō to Daikōzenji"; Li Ruoshui, "Tang Chang'an Da Xingshansi." For the general history of Great Xingshan Monastery, see Wang Yarong, *Da Xingshansi.* For its role as the headquarters of the esoteric practice in the Tang, see Jinhua Chen, *Crossfire,* 171–78.

52 The icons and images inside the pavilion, as well as the protective function of Mañjuśrī for the nation, are described in a report submitted to the throne in 777 by the monk Huisheng; see *Daizong chao,* T.52: 2120.857c24–858a10.

53 Ibid., 844c25–26.

54 Ibid., 851a21–24.

55 The name plaque of Jin'ge Monastery is first mentioned in the petition by Amoghavajra quoted at the beginning of the chapter, but exactly what name was inscribed on the plaque is not specified. The full name, Dasheng Jin'ge baoying zhenguo si, is first recorded in 779, in ibid., 859b3–b4.

56 *Guang Qingliang zhuan,* T.51: 2099.1113b28–b29.

57 About the legend, building, and history of Jin'ge Monastery, see a brief discussion in Xiao Yu, "Jin'gesi fojiao jianshi."

58 The *Collection of the Memoranda* (T.52: 2120.835a24–25) names Chuntuo as the architect of Jin'ge Monastery, as does the biography of monk Daoyi (T.50: 2061.844a5–7). Jinhua Chen identifies Chuntuo as the monk whose biography appears in Zanning, *Song gaoseng zhuan,* T.50: 2061.890c23–891a6; see Jinhua Chen, *Crossfire,* 181, n. 62.

59 For a detailed discussion of Hanguang, see Jinhua Chen, *Crossfire,* 142–45; Ono Genmyō, "Godaisan Kinkakuji."

60 Ryōzen was a Japanese monk who arrived in China in 804 and traveled to Mount Wutai, where he lived until his death ca. 825–28. According to Ennin, for an unspecified reason, he peeled the skin from his arm and painted a Buddha image on it, which was placed inside a gilded copper stupa; *NGJG,* vol. 3, 89. See also, Ono Genmyō, "Godaisan Kinkakuji," 33–35.

61 *NGJG,* vol. 3, 94. Full Chinese text in appendix 3, sec. 5.

62 See, for example, *NGJG,* vol. 3, 103–11; Chiba, "Fukū no mikkyō to Kinkakuji."

63 The true-presence (*zhenrong*) icon, is discussed in chapter 3.

64 *Jin'gang ding jing yuqie Wenshu shili pusa fa,* T.20: 1171. See *NGJG,* vol. 3, 103–6.

65 *Jin'gang ding jing yuqie Wenshu shili pusa fa,* T.20: 1171.705a21–24.

66 See Pan, "Bukong sanzang yu Wenshu pusa xinyang."

67 *Jin'gang ding jing yuqie Wenshu shili pusa fa,* T.20: 1171.705b21–23. The eight "offering bodhisattvas" are two sets of bodhisattvas found around the central five buddhas—the Vairocana Buddha and the four buddhas of the four cardinal directions—in the *Vajradhātu maṇḍala.* The first set comprises four "inner offering bodhisattvas," whom the Vairocana Buddha offers to the four directional buddhas; the four directional buddhas in turn offer the second set of bodhisattvas, the four "outer offering bodhisattvas," to the Vairocana Buddha. The four "bodhisattvas of attraction" appear in the *Vajradhātu maṇḍala,* each holding a tool (hook, rope, chain, and bell) to lead practitioners into the truth. See Ten Grotenhuis, *Japanese Mandalas,* 40–42.

68 For the Vajradhātu *maṇḍala,* see Toganoo, *Kongōchōkyō no kenkyū,* 20–32; Ten Grotenhuis, *Japanese Mandalas,* chap. 2.

69 *Jin'gang ding jing yuqie Wenshu shili pusa fa,* T.20: 1171.705c23–706a22.

70 Inoue Akemi, "Kyōten to zuzō," 45–51.

71 *Putichang suoshuo yizi ding lunwang jing,* T.19: 950. This is a new recension of the same

sutra previously translated by Bodhiruci in two different versions: *Wufoding sanmei tuoluoni jing* (T.19: 952) and *Yizi foding lunwang jing* (T.19: 951). For a comparison of the three translations, see Chiba, "Fukū no mikkyō ni okeru bucchōson."

72 For the four "perfection bodhisattvas" and sixteen "great bodhisattvas" and their positions in the Vajradhātu *maṇḍala*, see Ten Grotenhuis, *Japanese Mandalas,* 41.

73 The three texts are T.18: 870, 871, and 872, discussed in Osabe, *Tōdai mikkyōshi,* 163–79.

74 *Jin'gang ding yuqie sanshiqi zun chusheng yi,* T.18: 872.

75 Ibid., 298c8–9.

76 *Daizong chao,* T.52: 2120.835b29–c2.

77 On the expression "three times seven" to mean thirty-seven, see Orzech, *Politics and Transcendent Wisdom,* 161; Iwamoto, "Fukū sanzō to Daikōzenji," 73.

78 In this respect, Fu Xinian has argued that early monastic structures were built taking into consideration the view of the main icons provided at the entrance; see Fu, "Zhongguo zaoqi fojiao jianzhu."

79 See Chiba, "Fukū no mikkyō to Kinkakuji," 174.

80 When Ennin arrived at Jin'ge Monastery in the seventh month of 840, the Golden Pavilion had already been standing for sixty years, and thus the description of the colors still "not yet filled completely" should not be understood as due to incomplete construction. It is possible that the mural was in the middle of restoration or repainted, but still it is curious that it was only "colors" that were not filled in. In her recent study of paintings of *maṇḍala* used for the purpose of visualization, Michelle Wang suggests that the incompleteness of several liturgical diagrams from Dunhuang may indicate their use as visual cues for visualization of the deities concerned. See Michelle Wang, "Changing Conceptions of 'Maṇḍala,'" 202–4. The diagrams from Dunhuang have also been studied in a similar vein in Fraser, *Performing the Visual,* 152.

81 In regard to how the grid-like ground plan and modular system of traditional wooden structures were important in the spatial arrangement of the architectural interior, see Ledderose, *Ten Thousand Things,* 103–37; Wei-Cheng Lin, "Screening the Chinese Interior."

82 The two types of interior are proposed in Nancy Steinhardt's article on the excavation of a Tang building foundation, likely of a ritual hall for esoteric practices, inside Qinglong Monastery (Qinglongsi) in Chang'an. See Steinhardt, "The Mizong Hall of Qinglong Si," 38–40. The Qinglong monastery was also strongly associated with Amoghavajra; see Jinhua Chen, *Crossfire,* 178–80. For how the grid-like floor plan is related to the interior spatial arrangement in the traditional timber-frame structure around Tang times, see Fu Xinian, *Zhongguo kexue jishushi,* 310–11.

83 Chinese religious architecture contrasts quite drastically with its western counterpart in terms of "architectural iconology," as discussed in Crossley, "Medieval Architecture and Meaning." However, an exclusively iconographic approach may overlook the performative potential of buildings that could engage the viewer as she or he moves through the space, an understanding closer to what I am proposing here; see Camille, "Mouths and Meanings."

84 There are still no systematic studies specifically on the history of multilevel wooden architecture in China, although it seems to be the case that the multistoried image halls did not become more frequent until the early Song-Liao-Jin period (ca. 10th–13th century). See Fu, *Zhongguo kexue jishushi,* 460.

85 Both are discussed in detail in Steinhardt, *Liao Architecture,* chaps. 2 and 5.
86 See, for example, the essays included in Eade and Sallnow, *Contesting the Sacred.*
87 The two accounts are from *Collection of the Memoranda,* in T.52: 2120.858b24–c11 and T.52: 2120.858c15–859a3. See also Orlando, "A Study of Chinese Documents," 90–92.

SIX. Narrative, Visualization, and Transposition of Mount Wutai

The epigraph is from Jonathan Z. Smith, "Constructing a Small Place," in *Sacred Space: Shrine, City, Land,* ed. Joshua Prawer, Benjamin Kedar-Kopfstein, and R. J. Zwi Werblowsky (New York: New York University Press, 1998), 18. Reproduced with permission of the Israel Academy of Sciences and Humanities.

1 In general, Esoteric Buddhism in its late-Tang development was not as influential as it was during the time of Amoghavajra. The reasons for this shift have been speculated, but may have included such factors as the decline of institutional support and the emergence of other, stronger doctrinal emphases and esoteric cycles promulgated by other masters. For more discussion, see Orzech, "After Amoghavajra."
2 Lin Yun-jo, "Wutaishan yu Wenshu daochang," 199–210.
3 See *Jiu Tangshu, juan* 17, 512. For more discussion on the request for pictures of Mount Wutai from the Tibetan kingdom, see Zha, "Tufan qiu 'Wutaishan tu.'"
4 The earliest precedent, called "mountain picture" (*shantu*), was produced after Huize's visit at Mount Wutai between 661 and 663, as discussed in chapter 3.
5 This term is variably rendered as *taishan shisi* or *wutai shisi,* although all variants refer to the ten major monasteries of Mount Wutai; see *NGJG,* vol. 3, 76–77.
6 For Zhijun, see *Song gaoseng zhuan, juan* 27, T.50: 2061.881a21–b24; *Guang Qingliang zhuan,* T.51: 2099.1117c6–1118a9. The years during which Zhijun held the official title are recorded differently among texts. As this title is not seen elsewhere, it seems to have been an irregular post, assigned specifically at Mount Wutai during the ninth and tenth century. For the title Jianjiao, see Hucker, *A Dictionary of Official Titles,* 146.
7 The first explicit list of the ten monasteries, designated *wutai shisi,* was made officially in 980 during the early Northern Song; see *Fozu tongji, juan* 43, T.49: 2035.397c16–18.
8 For example, in his annotation for the *Commentaries on the* Flower Garland Sutra, Chengguan (738–839), the fourth patriarch of the Huayan lineage, explains that the reason why the number ten was frequently evoked in the *Flower Garland Sutra* is that "using [the number] ten as an example, [one could] demonstrate the comprehensiveness [of the Dharma]" (Chengguan, *Dafangguan fo huayan jing suishu yanyi chao,* T.36:1736.5c).
9 The list appears under the section "Names of Monasteries and Holy Traces in the Realm of Mount Wutai" (Wutai jingjie siming shengji), in *Guang Qingliang zhuan,* T.51: 2099.1105b28–1106c26.
10 Casey, *Representing Place,* 265.
11 The eulogy is translated and discussed in Cartelli, *The Five-Colored Clouds of Mount Wutai,* chap. 4; the quoted stanza is on page 96. For the dating of the eulogy, see Du, *Dunhuang Wutaishan wenxian,* 95–96.
12 See White, "The Value of Narrativity." Also, on the point about a "landscape" leading to "representation," Edward S. Casey argues, "To be a landscape is to be a *place*

already on the road to representation: at the very least, it is to be the more or less coherent setting of an embodied point of view" (Casey, *Representing Place,* xv).

13 The distinction between representation and visualization as used in the context of this discussion will be explicated in more detail in the section "Vision and Visualization," in this chapter.

14 For a survey of the cave, see Zhao Shengliang, *Dunhuang shiku yishu.*

15 Ennin, *Nittō guhō junrei gyōki,* in *Dai Nihon bukkyō zensho,* vol. 72, 84–133. The text is translated in Reischauer, *Ennin's Diary.* A recent investigation of Ennin's travel to China is in Palmer, "Searching for the Law," chap. 5.

16 As Michel de Certeau argues in another context, "the motions of walking are spatial creation" (De Certeau, "Practices of Space," 129); a slightly different version of his article appears in de Certeau, *The Practice of Everyday Life,* 91–110.

17 One of the purposes of Ennin's visit at Mount Wutai, in addition to venerating the sacred site, was to meet with an eminent monk, Zhiyan, residing at Huayan Monastery, for some questions he had about the Tiantai teaching in Japan; see *NGJG,* vol. 3, 4–5. See also Palmer, "Searching for the Law," 205–8.

18 These pilgrimage routes to Mount Wutai were called in textual records "roads to venerate [Mount Wu]tai" (*chaotai lu*) or "roads to present incense" (*jinxiang lu*); see Yang Chunyuan, "Tangdai Wutai jiaotong shulüe"; Du, *Dunhuang Wutaishan wenxian,* 191–97; Yan Gengwang, *Tangdai jiaotong tu kao,* vol. 5, 1507–12.

19 Putong Yuan refers to charitable monastic inns and facilities that were established specifically to assist pilgrims, both clergy and laity, in their travels to Mount Wutai after the mid-Tang; see *NGJG,* vol. 2, 405–9; Ye Luhua, "Tangdai Wutaishan putong yuan."

20 *NGJG,* vol. 2, 418–19; the English translation is after Reischauer, *Ennin's Diary,* 214.

21 The creation legend of the true-presence (*zhenrong*) icon is discussed in chapter 3; three different texts that recorded the legend are included and translated in appendix 1.

22 *NGJG,* vol. 3, 4.

23 The story of Buddhapālita's visit to Mount Wutai is discussed in chapter 4.

24 *NGJG,* vol. 3, 63.

25 Ibid., 64.

26 Ibid., 152.

27 Cf. Macauley, "Walking the Elemental Earth," 17.

28 See Dunhuang Manuscript P3931b. The translation is based on the transcription in Du, *Dunhuang Wutaishan wenxian,* 222. The original Chinese text is given in appendix 3, sec. 6. The manuscript is identified with the title "A Report on the Travel to Mount Wutai by the Indian Master Puhua" (Yindu Puhua dashi you Wutaishan qiwen); see Li Zhengyu, "Yindu Puhua dashi."

29 For instance, on the relation between narrative and reality, Hayden White writes, "In this world, reality wears the mask of a meaning, the completeness and fullness of which we can only imagine, never experience" (White, "The Value of Narrativity," 20).

30 See *NGJG,* vol. 3, 152. There is no other record of this southern gate. In their annotation to Ennin's text, Chen Yangjiong and Feng Qiaoying mention that there were four such *shanmen* located at the four routes to Mount Wutai in four cardinal

directions, without providing reference to these four gates; see Chen and Feng, *Gu Qingliang zhuan*, 177, n. 153.

31 *NGJG*, vol. 3, 178.

32 Ibid. Paintings or replications of Mount Wutai in Taiyuan, as in this example, are mentioned in an anonymous pilgrimage diary, P4648, dated to the eighth century; see Du, *Dunhuang Wutaishan wenxian*, 140–43.

33 The various forms of the bodhisattva's transformative manifestation are discussed in chapter 3.

34 *NGJG*, vol. 3, 181–82.

35 For a more elaborate discussion of religious vision, see Goodman, "Visions." Also for critical discussions of the significance of "vision" in the literature and religious practice of Mahayana Buddhism, see McMahan, *Empty Vision;* Faure, *Visions of Power.* A comparative study of vision in medieval West is Hourihane, *Looking Beyond.*

36 Scholars have recently become interested in "vision" as both a religious experience and visual practice and argued that instead of being analyzed only as esoteric or mythic, religious vision is necessarily socially and historically constructed. About this rising field concerned with religious vision, see Plate, *Religion, Art, and Visual Culture.* A more recent discussion in this same vein is Morgan, *The Sacred Gaze.*

37 Thus far in this chapter, "representation" has been used in a rather loose and uncritical way to mean a depiction or description that represents how an object appears. Here, however, I use "visualization," rather than "representation," to shift the focus from visual resemblance or mimetic quality often linked to representation to the capacity of an image able to serve such religious functions as visual invocation or icon worship, in which the presence of the deity may be enlivened or imagined through the image. For a discussion on representation, see Summers, "Representation."

38 For the Tibetan occupation of Dunhuang, see Beckwith, *The Tibetan Empire,* chap. 6. Also, Ma De, *Dunhuang Mogaoku shi,* 91–99.

39 The iconographic image of Samantabhadra riding an elephant was most certainly based on the description from the *Lotus Sutra* (T.9: 262), whereas Mañjuśrī riding a lion did not have a similar scriptural basis. Although the pairing of these two bodhisattvas was widespread, the early development of this iconographic pair is unclear, other than the examples appearing in the Mogao caves; see Sun Xiaogang, *Wenshu pusa tuxiang,* 45–49.

40 Although mostly painted on murals flanking the western niche, as in the case of Cave 220, the positions of the paired bodhisattvas in the cave could vary. Also, the paired murals depicting Mañjuśrī and Samantabhadra are usually called, respectively, "Wenshu bian" and "Puxian bian" in modern Chinese scholarship, although they may not carry the meaning denoted in the use of *bian*. The word *bian* is usually used in the sense of *bianxiang*, which, translated as "transformation tableau" or simply "sutra painting," in the Mogao caves often refers to the mural painting that has a textual basis in Buddhist canons, either narrative or exegetic. As the paired murals do not have a specific canonical basis, they cannot be considered sutra paintings, but they do allude to scenes of sermons as often described in sutras, in which both bodhisattvas usually serve as chief attendants of the Buddha, who is preaching. See

Pan Liangwen, "Dunhuang Tangdai de Wenshu pusa tuxiang"; Sun Xiaogang, *Wenshu pusa tuxiang,* 45–49. The concept and practice of *bian* and *bianxiang* have been much discussed and debated; for an example, see Wu Hung, "What Is *Bianxiang*?"

41 For more discussion on the paired murals of Mañjuśrī and Samantabhadra in Cave 159, see Li Yongning, "Dunhuang Mogaoku di 159 ku." Before Cave 159, two precedents of Mañjuśrī riding a lion flying on clouds over a mountain landscape can be found in Caves 172 and 222, but in both caves, the celestial group is only part of a larger mural composition.

42 For the history of Mount Emei and how it was developed into the sacred mountain of Samantabhadra, see Hargett, *Stairway to Heaven.*

43 Two recent articles that discuss the imagery of Mount Wutai produced during the period of Tibetan occupation are Zhao Xiaoxing, "Tufan tongzhi shiqi," and Wang Zhongxu, "Tufan shiqi Dunhuang."

44 Although a very important example, the condition of the mural in Cave 237 is the worst among all surviving murals of Mount Wutai. The inscriptions indicated in fig. 6.3b are based on Zhao Xiaoxing, "Tufan tongzhi shiqi," 121, and my own investigation in situ in 2009.

45 The suffix *shi* (lit. when, or the moment) was part of the standard phrasing formula used for mural inscriptions in Mogao during this period; but as *shi* was often employed to emphasize "timing," it could also have a temporal implication, as illustrated in our example. For more discussion and interpretation of the suffix *shi,* see Mair, *Tang Transformation Texts,* 82–86.

46 There is another similar example—a single mural that merges the bodhisattva surrounded by his entourage and Mañjuśrī riding a lion over the landscape of Mount Wutai—in Yulin Cave 32, dated from the tenth century.

47 Although not in the best condition, much of the writing in the cartouches on the mural is still decipherable, including the names of the peaks and buildings, as well as labels of divine manifestations and legends, such as Buddhapālita meeting Mañjuśrī. For a detailed discussion of the mural, see Zhao Xiaoxing, "Mogaoku di 361 ku."

48 For the history of Dunhuang under the rule of the military governor from the ninth through tenth centuries, see Rong, *Guiyijun shi yanjiu,* and Dohi, "Kigigun jidai."

49 The traffic that became more viable again between the Dunhuang region and Mount Wutai as documented in texts is discussed in Rong, "Dunhuang wenxian he huihua." Songs and eulogies related to the tales and legends of Mount Wutai are discussed in Cartelli, *The Five-Colored Clouds of Mount Wutai.* The most important study of this literary genre in Chinese is Du, *Dunhuang Wutaishan wenxian.*

50 For the official report on the uncovering of the mural by removal of the mural layer of the twelfth century, see Dunhuang Yanjiusuo, "Mogaoku di 220 ku." A comprehensive study of Cave 220, both historically and iconographically, can be found in Ning, *Art, Religion, and Politics in Medieval China.*

51 Dunhuang Yanjiusuo, "Mogaoku di 220 ku," 42.

52 This discussion and debate have been mostly among Chinese scholars; two notable recent related articles are Sha, "Dunhuang P. 4049 'Xinyang Wenshu' huagao" and Sun Xiaogang, *Wenshu pusa tuxiang,* 53–83.

53 One notable precedent for this front-facing Mañjuśrī riding a lion is from Cave 148, dated to 776. The Mañjuśrī riding a lion in Cave 148, however, was intended to look

as if both were moving forward inside the pictorial plane, rather than showing the dynamic tension between moving in the one and stillness in the other that can be observed in the mural from Cave 220.

54 See Roderick Whitfield, *The Art of Central Asia,* vol. 1, 323–24. On the topic, *Tejaprabhā Buddha and the Five Planets,* and its connection to "planet worship," see Takeda, *Hoshi mandara no kenkyū,* 105–26. A more recent discussion of this painting is in Russell-Smith, *Uygur Patronage in Dunhuang,* 104–10.

55 There are two important studies of *ruixiang* in Chinese: Sun Xiushen, "Mogao ku fojiao shiji gushi hua," and Zhang and Rong, "Dunhuang 'ruixiang ji,' ruixiang tu." In English, see Roderick Whitfield, "Ruixiang at Dunhuang." More recently, Ning Qiang discusses the *ruixiang* images painted inside Cave 220 (Ning, *Art, Religion, and Politics in Medieval China,* 81–105).

56 For the earlier use of *ruixiang* as "auspicious signs," see chapter 3. The use of *ruixiang* referring to Buddhist images can be traced back to the sixth and seventh centuries in China. In this case, *ruixiang* was reserved for statues possessing supernatural power in performing miracles and acting as if real deities; in some cases the miracle-performing statues were also recorded with extraordinary legends of origin, similar to what the term implies in the Mogao context. See Hida, "Ryōshō Bankaken zuizō."

57 Roderick Whitfield, "Ruixiang at Dunhuang," 149.

58 For the genesis of the Fanhe *ruixiang* as related to the legendary monk Liu Sahe and its imagery in Dunhuang, see Roderick Whitfield, "The Monk Liu Sahe"; Hida, "Ryōshō Bankaken zuizō"; Wu Hung, "Rethinking Liu Sahe"; Zhang Shanqing, "Liangzhou Jiande da dizhen."

59 It should be noted that the character *xiang* 相 of *ruixiang* in the inscription is different from the *xiang* 像 used in *ruixiang* imagery. However, in texts from this period, the two *xiangs* more often than not were used interchangeably; for example, the character *xiang* in the term *zhenxiang* could be either of the *xiangs* without changing the meaning of the term, "true image." In any case, I am not suggesting that the new-mode Mañjuśrī was one of the *ruixiang* images developed in the Dunhuang region around this time; rather, because the particular term *ruixiang* was evoked in the dedicatory inscription, I argue, the new-mode Mañjuśrī may have been considered similar to other *ruixiang* in terms of iconicity, function, and meaning.

60 All these phrases are included in the primary texts discussed and annotated in Zhang and Rong, "Dunhuang 'ruixiang ji,' ruixiang tu."

61 Because the cartouche is placed right next to the standing Mañjuśrī, some scholars question if the inscription inside the cartouche actually refers to the central Mañjuśrī riding a lion or to the standing Mañjuśrī to the right. Recently, based on an on-site investigation of the partially exposed underlayer of the mural at its corner, Sun Xiaogang has convincingly argued that the cartouche in question was intended for the central Mañjuśrī, but the entire composition, a central Mañjuśrī flanked by a standing Mañjuśrī on the right and a standing Avalokiteśvara on the left, may have been altered before the mural was completed, which contributed to the awkward position of the cartouche, which should have been placed closer to the central Mañjuśrī. See Sun Xiaogang, *Wenshu pusa tuxiang,* 56–57.

62 The creation legend was recorded in Dunhuang Manuscript S529v; see appendix 1 for a full translation of the account.

63 For this woodblock print, see Susan Whitfield, *The Silk Road*, 301; Cohen and Monnet, *Impressions de la Chine*, 50–51; Barrett, "On the Road to China," 50–52.

64 The entire inscription, except for the final two lines, is translated in Wong, "A Reassessment of the Representation of Mount Wutai," 40.

65 See Birnbaum, *Studies on the Mysteries of Mañjuśrī*, 24–25.

66 When discussing the difficulty of transposing a sacred space in medieval Christianity, Jonathan Z. Smith argues that a miniature replication of the space could elicit "a utopia, a theatre of mind, and imagination," in which the sacrality may still be experienced. Materials of Smith's research are from the Holy Sepulchre in Jerusalem, apparently different from the case of Mount Wutai, the sanctity of which did not lie in transportable and material objects such as relics. The holy presence, or *praesentia*, is nevertheless crucial in both cases. See Smith, "Constructing a Small Place."

67 The document is "List of Names of Caves and Niches Allotted the Lighting of Lamps on the Eighth Day of the Twelfth Month" (Laba randeng fenpei ku kan mingsu). The date 1011 is proposed in Jin, "Dunhuang ku kan mingsu kao," reprinted in Jin, *Zhongguo meishushi lunji*, 326–40.

68 See Rong, *Guiyijun shi yanjiu*, 113–22; Ma De, *Dunhuang Mogaoku shi*, 112–50.

69 The measurements of the cave are from Shi, *Mogao ku xing*, vol. 1, 130–34. For the archaeological investigation of the original timber structure that covered the cliff surface of the entrance leading into Cave 61, see Pan and Ma, *Mogaoku kuqian diantang yizhi*, 32–39.

70 About the set of icons on the altar, see Sha and Liang, "Mogaoku di 61 ku zhongxin fotan zaoxiang."

71 For an example, see Du, *Dunhuang Wutaishan wenxian*, 116–23.

72 I discuss the use of "visuality" in the case of making, seeing, and understanding religious imagery in more detail in Wei-Cheng Lin, "Relocating and Relocalizing Mount Wutai."

73 Duan, "Mogaoku wanqi de yishu." Recently Sonya S. Lee also discusses how Cave 61 shares many of its iconographic and artistic elements with several other contemporary and earlier caves in her "Repository of Ingenuity."

74 This is also observed in Kyan, "Family Space," 69, and app. 1.

75 Donor images before the tenth century were arranged to direct the attention to the central niche, as they were either located on the mural directly underneath the niche, or aligned along the lower registers of the north and south walls facing the niche. In Cave 61, they point to the entrance.

76 Scholarly research of this mural began in the 1950s with articles such as Su, "Dunhuang Mogaoku zhong de Wutaishan tu," and Hibino, "Tonkō no Godaisan zu." In English, Ernesta Marchand published the first article on this topic, "The Panorama of Wu-T'ai Shan as an Example of Tenth-Century Cartography," in 1976. The most important study of this mural to date is still Wong, "A Reassessment of the Representation of Mount Wutai." Most recently for a different purpose, Wen-shing Chou takes the mural as the prototype for the imagery of Mount Wutai produced in later periods in her "Ineffable Paths." From a different perspective, Natasha Heller explores the ways in which the pilgrim's experience was visualized in the mural in Heller, "Visualizing Pilgrimage and Mapping Experience."

77 For example, Wong, "A Reassessment of the Representation of Mount Wutai," 32; Birnbaum, "Light in the Wutai Mountains," 214.

78 See Ma De, *Dunhuang shiku quanji*, 56–59.

79 For the idea of "plot," Hayden White explains, "By 'plot' we mean a structure of relationships by which the events contained in the account are endowed with a meaning by being identified as parts of an integrated whole" (White, "The Value of Narrativity," 9).

80 For the term "chronotope," see M. Bakhtin, "Forms of Time and Chronotope in the Novel," in Bakhtin, *The Dialogic Imagination*, 84–258. For an application of "chronotope" in analyzing art historical materials, see Eugene Wang, *Shaping the Lotus Sutra*, 353–63.

81 The disposition of the peaks finds its precedent in Cave 237 (see fig. 6.3b), discussed earlier in the chapter.

82 The convention of adding a prefix *da* to the name of the grand and important monastery was already in practice in Chang'an during the early Tang; see Su, "Shilun Tangdai Chang'an fojiao siyuan," 31.

83 For a discussion of this perfect vision, see Wong, "The Mapping of Sacred Space."

84 Among the large caves built with a central altar during the tenth century, the altars in Caves 61, 55, and 146 were constructed with a screen, while those in Caves 108 and 256 were built without. Whether they had a back screen or not, the western murals in Cave 55, 108, and 46 all depict the "magic competition" between Raudrāksha and Śāriputra (*Laoducha dousheng jinbian*), a pictorial theme that features the competition between the two protagonists, whose images and actions are symmetrically distributed on the two opposite sides of the mural, rather than focused at the center. The content of the mural, furthermore, has no specific bearing on the group of icons on the altars. In contrast to these caves, where the back screen factors little in the overall reading of the cave, the one in Cave 61 serves to negotiate the space before and after it.

85 See Zhao Shengliang, *Dunhuang shiku yishu*, 28–30.

86 Ennin mentioned a South Mountain Gate of Mount Wutai (Wutai Nan Shanmen) in *NGJG*, vol. 3, 152, discussed earlier in this chapter.

87 For example, see Wong, "A Reassessment of the Representation of Mt. Wutai," 36–37.

88 The names as recorded in Chōnen's and Jōjin's accounts are discussed in *NGJG*, vol. 3, 9–11.

89 Jōjin described the various monastic complexes and buildings inside the Great Huayan Monastery at great length; see Jōjin, *San Tendai Godaisan ki*, in *Dai Nihon bukkyō zensho*, vol. 72, 267–68.

90 The spatial construction in the mural depicting the Pure Land through representing monastic architecture is analyzed in Zhao Shengliang, "Dunhuang bihua yu Zhongguo hua."

91 The divine triad of the Buddha and the two attending bodhisattvas, Mañjuśrī and Samantabhadra, based on the *Flower Garland Sutra*, is often referred to as the Three Holy Ones of the *Flower Garland [Sutra]* (*Huayan Sansheng*). It refers to the structure and intention of the *Flower Garland Sutra:* the words were preached by the Buddha, but one could comprehend the sutra only through the two primary bodhisattvas—through their wisdom to understand, their deeds to practice, and their bodhisattva vows to realize the words. For the notion of Three Holy Ones, see Gimello, "Ch'eng-kuan's Meditations."

92 For example, in the account of Zhulin Monastery in *Guang Qinglang zhuan*, Fazhao reported to have entered a virtual monastery, and after entering the monastery and arriving at the lecture hall, Fazhao described, "[I] saw the Great Sage Mañjuśrī in the west and Samantabhadra in the east, each seated on a lion seat, taking turns to lecture. . . . Surrounding Mañjuśrī are more than ten thousand fellow bodhisattvas, and likewise innumerable fellow bodhisattvas surround Samantabadhra" (T.51: 2099.1114b19–21).

93 These two different meanings of *zhenshen*, or true body, are exemplified in Dunhuang Manuscript S529v, which records the creation legend of the Mañjuśrī riding a lion statue. See appendix 1 for the translation of the manuscript. For a brief discussion of this term as to how it was applied in the cult of relics in medieval China, see Wei-Cheng Lin, "Bei 'shentihua' de sheli fozhi."

94 For a more elaborate discussion of the mural from Cave 172, see Wu, "Rethinking Liu Sahe," 40–42.

95 This proposed distinction between *zhenrong* and *zhenshen* appears to be particularly the case in the Dunhuang region. For instance, if one compares all three extant versions of the creation legend of Mañjuśrī riding a lion, it becomes evident that only the transmitted version in the Dunhuang Manuscript (S529v) employs both *zhenshen* and *zhenrong*, whereas the other two versions use only *zhenrong*. See appendix 1.

96 This is borrowed from Eugene Y. Wang; see Wang, "Watching the Steps."

97 I argue for this regional visual culture in a different version of this discussion on Mogao Cave 61; see Wei-Cheng Lin, "Relocating and Relocalizing Mount Wutai."

98 In fact, some scholars have suggested that Dunhuang caves built with a central platform were likely modeled after the wooden Buddhist image hall. See, for example, Xiao Mo, "Dunhuang Mogaoku de dongku xingzhi."

99 I use "metamonastery" to refer to the hermeneutics, that is, a more abstract and conceptual knowledge, of the monastery in its role of building Mount Wutai into a sacred mountain. For more discussion on the notion of *meta-*, see White, *Metahistory*.

CONCLUSION

The epigraph is from Chen Shunyu (d. 1074), *The Record of Mount Lu* (Lushan ji), T.51: 2095.1031a16–20.

1 This brief summary of the history of monastic architecture in relation to the construction of the sacred mountain follows Henri Lefebvre's conception of space. In his now classic work, *Production of Space*, Lefebvre analyzes space in three distinctive categories: perceived, conceived, and lived. Perceived space is defined by the "spatial practice" of daily routines and performances; conceived space is planned, administered, and to some extent, ideally constructed; and lived space, which Lefebvre also calls "representational space," is mediated through its associated images and symbols. The sacred site, I argue, among many things belongs foremost to these spatially constructed categories. Lefebvre does not conceive the three categories of space as developing in historical sequence, as my study suggests happened at Mount Wutai, but by characterizing the history of monastic architecture at Mount Wutai in three stages, I suggest that monastic architecture was conceived and built

to explore each of these three types of space at Mount Wutai during its early history. See Lefebvre, *The Production of Space*, esp. 31–44.

2 Ibid., 39.

3 Jietuo is discussed in chapter 3.

4 See *NGJG*, vol. 3, 145.

5 See chapter 4.

6 See *Fozu tongji*, *juan* 42, T.49: 2035.348b13–16. For Pei Du, see *Jiu Tangshu*, *juan* 170, 4413–35.

7 For Faxing's biography, see *Song gaoseng zhuan*, T.50: 2061.882c21–883a4; *Guang Qingliang zhuan*, T.51: 2099.1121b3–15.

8 *Guang Qingliang zhuan*, T.51: 2099.1121b9–11.

9 See note 12 on Faxing's official title.

10 See *Quan Tangwen*, *juan* 28, 862. For a discussion on Mount Wutai during the persecution and its rebuilding afterward, see Lin Yun-jo, "Wutaishan yu Wenshu daochang," 232–41.

11 *Guang Qingliang zhuan*, T.51: 2099.1121c29–a2. Yuancheng's biography is also in *Song gaoseng zhuan*, T.50: 2061.883a19–b10.

12 *Guang Qingliang zhuan*, T.51: 2099.1121a3. This title is different from the earlier "chief officer of the ten [major] monasteries at Mount Wutai" (*Wutaishan shisi dujianjiao*), first assigned to Zhijun (d. 853) of Huayan Monastery, who is discussed in chapter 6. In addition to Yuancheng, Faxing before him was also endowed with the title "chief officer (or inspector) of the Mountain Gate" (*Shanmen du* or *Shanmen dugang*), and both Faxing and Yuancheng were from Foguang Monastery. After the Tang, official titles for the monastic leader at Mount Wutai began with the term "Wutaishan" (Mount Wutai) or "*Wutai shisi*" (ten monasteries of Mount Wutai). This suggests that the term *shanmen* (mountain gate) was used specifically for Foguang Monastery, referring to its location outside the mountain range as the "mountain gate" of Mount Wutai. For the transition at Mount Wutai from the Tang to Song, including the official titles of monastic leaders, see Yang Zengwen, "Tang Song Wenshu pusa xinyang."

13 Although the ranked system in the use of brackets and bracketing style was not strictly regulated until the Northern Song (960–1127), by and large, it would have been the case already during the Tang that the grander a building was, the larger of the modular units and the more complex style of brackets would be applied. The Great Buddha Hall at Foguang Monastery contains the largest scale and most complex style of brackets surviving from the Tang period. Among the bracket sets, the most complicated bracketing is found across the exterior facade, a so-called seven-tier bracket set (*puzuo*), which includes two transversal brackets (*huagong*) and two downward-pointing cantilevered brackets (*xia ang*). See more discussion of the construction of Foguang Monastery as compared with other Tang structures in Steinhardt, "The Mizong Hall of Qinglong Si." For a discussion of Song architecture, see Tracy Miller, *The Divine Nature of Power*.

14 For the inscriptions, see Liang Sicheng, "Ji Wutaishan Foguangsi jianzhu," 21–23.

15 S397, part of which is translated in the introduction; see appendix 3.1 for the Chinese text. The whole of the surviving text is transcribed and annotated in Du, *Dunhuang Wutaishan wenxian*, 143–46.

16 Untitled manuscript, P3931b. See Li Zhengyu, "Yingdu Puhua dashi"; Du, *Dunhuang*

Wutaishan wenxian, 221–22. My transcription is based on Li's; Du's may have been transcribed incorrectly, as a few lines of the text cannot be deciphered meaningfully.

17 Fu Xinian, "Wutaishan Foguangsi jianzhu," 234.

18 See *NGJG*, vol. 2, 441–42.

19 Ono Katsutoshi, "Ennin no mita Tō no bukkyō girei," 199–200. As Ono Katustoshi points out, the ritual of the Seventy-Two Worthies may have been a rite specific to Mount Wutai, but Ennin also mentioned a similar rite dedicated to Forty-Two Worthies at Kaiyuan Monastery in Yangzhou; see *NGJG*, vol. 1, 354. Also, on the list of sutras brought back to Japan by Ennin is a related but now lost text, *Ritual Texts for Invoking Worthies and Other Miscellaneous Eulogies* (Qing xiansheng yiwen bing zhu za zan), in *Nyūtō shingū seikyō mokuroku,* T.55: 2167.1085a18.

20 See Chai, *Shanxi siguan bihua*, 15–17.

21 Du, *Dunhuang Wutaishan wenxian*, 144.

22 See Robert L. Brown, "Expected Miracles."

GLOSSARY

Abbreviations

C Chinese
J Japanese
S Sanskrit

abhijñā (S) or *shentong* 神通 (C) supernormal knowledge or supernatural power

abhiṣeka (S) or *guangding* 灌頂 (C) anointing, inaugurating, or consecrating

Ajātaśatru (S) or Asheshi wang 阿闍世王 (C) a prince who, according to a sutra (T.15: 626), murdered his father, Bimbisāra

Akṣobhya (S) or Ashan fo 阿閦佛 (C) the Immovable One; the Buddha associated with the east

Amitābha (S) or Amituo fo 阿彌陀佛 (C) the Buddha of the Pure Land of the west

Amoghasiddhi (S) or Bukong chengjiu fo 不空成就佛 (C) the Buddha of Infallible Accomplishment; the Buddha associated with the north

Amoghavajra (S) or Bukong 不空 (C) (705–74) master of Esoteric Buddhism

An Lushan 安祿山 (C) (703–57) general who rebelled against the Tang court

An Sheng 安生 (C) sculptor of the first icon of Mañjuśrī riding a lion at Mount Wutai

añjali (S) or hezhang 合掌 (C) two hands placed palm to palm, indicating reverence

apsara (S) or *feitian* 飛天 (C) celestial nymph

arhat (S) or *aluohan* 阿羅漢 (C) holy ascetic

Aśoka (S) or Ayuwang 阿育王 (C) (ca. 304–232) Indian Buddhist king

Avalokiteśvara (S) or Guanyin 觀音 (C) Mahayana Bodhisattva of Great Compassion

Ayuwang xiang 阿育王像 (C) Chinese Buddhist images of Aśoka, in Indian style

Ayuwangsi 阿育王寺 (C) Aśoka Monastery; monasteries founded where Aśoka relics were discovered

Bai Jian zhuan 白建傳 (C) "Biography of Bai Jian," included in *History of Northern Qi*

Banruosi 般若寺 (C) Monastery of Prajñā; a virtual monastery mentioned in Yanyi's *Extended Records*

Baodesi 報德寺 (C) Monastery of Returning Virtue

Baoshan 寶山 (C) Mount Bao, near Anyang, Henan province; site of Dazhusheng Cave

Baoshansi 寶山寺 (C) Monastery of Jeweled Mountains, at Mount Bao

Baoxiangsi 寶相寺 (C) Monastery of the Jeweled Image

beixing ku 碑型窟 (C) lit., stele cave, meditation cave with features common in steles

bhūmi (S) or di 地 (C) level or stage of spiritual development

bian 變 (C) or *bianxian* 變現 (C) transformative manifestation. *See huaxian*

bianxiang 變像 (C) lit., transformation tableau; painting of scenes from a sutra

Bingzhou 並州 (C) jurisdictional province, approximately today's Shanxi province

Binyang 賓陽 (C) name given to the caves in Longmen, near Luoyang, Henan province

bodhicitta (S) or *Puti xin* 菩提心 (C) lit., Bodhi mind; a mind set on enlightenment

Bodhidharma (S) or Putidamo 菩提達磨 (C) (ca. 461–534) Indian monk; established the Chan school of Buddhism

bodhimaṇḍa (S) or *daochang* 道場 (C) dharma field; a site of enlightenment

Bodhiruci (S) or Putiliuzhi 菩提流支 (C) (d. 527) Indian monk, translator of *Shidi jing lun*

Bodhiruci (S) or Putiliuzhi 菩提流志 (C) (672–727) Indian monk, translator of *Wenshu shili fa baozang tuoluoni jing*

Bolun 波崙 (C) Tang-era monk

buddhakṣetra (S) or fotu 佛土 (C) Buddha field; a land in which a buddha resides
buddhānusmṛti (S) or *nianfo* 念佛 (C) mindful recollection of the Buddha; meditation on the Buddha's perfections
Buddhapālita (S) or Fotuoboli 佛陀波利 (C) Indian monk, visited Mount Wutai in 676 and 683
buddhoṣṇīṣa (S) or *foding* 佛頂 (C) Buddha's crown; topknot or cranial protuberance of the Buddha
Bukong jin'gang 不空金剛 (C) or Bukong 不空 (C) (705–74) *See* Amoghavajra
busa 布薩 (C) or *posadha* (S) fasting; renewal of vows; confessional rite
Butsu kōmyō zanmai kan 仏光明三昧観 (J) *samādhi* [achieved by] visualizing the Buddha's radiance

caitya (S) worship hall
cakravartin(-rāja) (S) or *zhuan lunwang* 轉輪王 (C) wheel-turning sage king; universal monarch
Cao Yijin 曹議金 (C) (d. 935) military governor of the Return to Allegiance Army, 914–35
Cao Yuanzhong 曹元忠 (C) (d. 974) military governor of the Return to Allegiance Army, 944–74
chan 禪 (C) *dhyāna;* meditation; concentration
changzhu 常住 (C) constant abiding; neither to be born nor to end
chaotai lu 朝臺路 (C) lit., roads to venerate [Mount Wu]tai; pilgrim routes to Mount Wutai
Chengguan 澄觀 (C) (738–839) fourth patriarch of the Huayan lineage
Chengyuan 承遠 (C) (712–802) third patriarch of the Pure Land sect
chi 尺 (C) lit., foot; unit of measurement of length, approximately 30–35 cm.
Chinian Mantuluo Daochang 持念曼荼羅道場 (C) ritual arena set up as a *maṇḍala*, Jin'ge Monastery
Chōnen 奝然 (J) (938–1016) Japanese monk who visited Mount Wutai in 985
Chongfusi 崇福寺 (C) Monastery of Elevating Blessing, in Taiyuan, Shanxi
chongge 重閣 (C) multistory pavilion
Chuntuo 純陀 (C) (d. 767) disciple of Amoghavajra, responsible for the building of Jin'ge Monastery
ci 祠 (C) temple for indigenous Chinese religions
cichu 此處 (C) lit., the very spot
cidi 此地 (C) lit., the very place
Cui Guang 崔光 (C) (449–522) court official of the Northern Wei

Da Fodian 大佛殿 (C) Great Buddha Hall at Foguang Monastery
Da foding zhenyan 大佛頂真言 (C) *Great Dhāraṇī of the Buddha's Crown*, sutra presented to Emperor Daizong by Amoghavajra
Da Huangjianshan 大黄尖山 (C) Mount Da Huangjian, North Peak in earlier designation of Mount Wutai
Da Huayansi Pusa Zhenrong Yuan 大華嚴寺菩薩真容院 (C) Cloister of the Bodhisattva's True Presence at the Great Huayan Monastery
da jinqiao 大金橋 (C) great gold bridge
Da Xingshansi 大興善寺 (C) Great Monastery of Promoting Goodness, in Chang'an
da 大 (C) great
Dafu Lingjiusi 大孚靈鷲寺 (C) Monastery of Great Faith at Vulture Peak, at Mount Wutai
Dafusi 大孚寺 (C) Monastery of Great Faith; former name of Dafu Lingjiusi
Daigoji 醍醐寺 (J) Monastery of Perfect Buddha-Truth, in Kyoto
Daizhou 代州 (C) jurisdictional province where Mount Wutai is located, approximately present-day northern Shanxi
Daizong 代宗 (C) emperor of the Tang, r. 762–79
Dali Fahuasi 大曆法華寺 (C) Monastery of Dharma Blossom of the Dali [Reign]
Dali 大曆 (C) reign name (766–79) of Emperor Daizong of the Tang
dao 道 (C) circuit; administrative region of Tang China
Daoan 道安 (C) (312–85) eminent monk of the Eastern Jin; translator of monastery regulations
daochang 道場 (C) dharma field. *See bodhimaṇḍa*
Daohuan 道環 (C) (fl. mid-8th c.) Tang monk
Daoping 道憑 (C) (488–559) monk of the Northern Qi in the Ten Stage lineage; founded Baoshan Monastery

Daosengge 道僧格 (C) *Regulations for Daoist and Buddhist Clerics*, promulgated by Emperor Taizong in 637
Daoshi 道世 (C) (d. 683) author of *Fayuan zhulin*
Daoxuan 道宣 (C) (596–667) *vinaya* master and a well-known Buddhist scholar
Daoyi 道義 (C) (fl. early 8th c.) Tang monk who saw a virtual monastery at Mount Wutai
Dasheng Jin'ge Baoying Zhenguo Si 大聖金閣保應鎮國寺 (C) Monastery of the Great Sage's Golden Pavilion That Responds [the Call] to Protect the Nation; official name of Jin'ge Monastery
Dasheng Wenshu Shili Pusa Yuan 大聖文殊師利菩薩院 (C) Cloister of the Great Sage Bodhisattva Mañjuśrī
Dasheng Wenshu Zhenguo Zhi Ge 大聖文殊鎮國之閣 (C) Pavilion of the Great Holy Mañjuśrī for the Protection of the Nation, Da Xingshan Monastery
Dasheng Wenshu Zhenshen Dian 大聖文殊真身殿 (C) Hall of the True Body of the Great Sage Mañjuśrī
Dasheng Zhulin Zhi Si 大聖竹林之寺 (C) Bamboo Grove Monastery of the Great Sage, a virtual monastery
Dazhusheng 大住聖 (C) Great Abiding Holiness; meditation cave at Lingquan Monastery
Degan 德感 (C) (ca. 640–ca. 705) Tang monk, painted the marvels at Mount Wutai
dengtai 燈臺 (C) lantern
Dezong 德宗 (C) emperor of the Tang, r. 779–804
dhāraṇi (S) or *zhou* 咒 (C) incantation
dharmacakra (S) or *falun* 法輪 (C) Dharma wheel; Law established by the Buddha
dharmakāya (S) or *fashen* 法身 (C) Dharma body of Buddha; embodiment of Truth and Law
dhyāna (S) or *chan* 禪 (C) meditation
digong 地宮 (C) crypt inside the structure or foundation of a pagoda
dilun 地論 (C) lit., stage treatise; treatise on the Ten Stages path of the bodhisattva
Ding Lunwang Yuqiehui Wufo 頂輪王瑜伽會五佛 (C) Five Buddhas of the Yoga Assembly of the Wheel-Turning King of [the Buddha's] Crown; statues in the Golden Pavilion, Jin'ge Monastery
ding 頂 (C) peak; topknot; crown. *See uṣṇīṣa*
Dingzhou 定州 (C) Tang jurisdictional province, roughly southwest of present-day Hebei province
Divākara (S) or Dipoheluo 地婆訶羅 (C) (612–87) also known as Rizhao 日照; Central Asian monk and translator
dixian 地仙 (C) earthbound transcendents; divine humans who lived in the mountains
Dizang 地藏 (C) Kṣitigarbha, Mahayana bodhisattva associated with the underworld
Dong Dadian 東大殿 (C) Eastern Buddha Hall; Great Buddha Hall, Foguang Monastery
dongtian 洞天 (C) lit., grotto heaven; Daoist sacred site with caves or hollows
Dongyue 東嶽 (C) Eastern Sacred Peak, Mount Tai, in present-day Shandong province
Dongzhang 東張 (C) town in present-day Daixian, west of Mount Wutai
Du Guangting 杜光庭 (C) (850–933) eminent Daoist official and writer of the Tang
Du Xingyi 杜行顗 (C) (fl. 680s) translator of the *Sutra of the Superlative Dhāraṇī of the Buddha's Crown,* T.19: 968
du 睹 (C) see, have sight of
dujiang 都講 (C) reciter of a sutra lecture
Dulesi 獨樂寺 (C) Monastery of Solitary Joy, in Jixian, Hebei province
Dunhuang 敦煌 (C) town in the west of present-day Gansu province
Duobao Ta 多寶塔 (C) Many Treasures Pagoda
duoyuan shi siyuan 多院式寺院 (C) monastery with many cloisters or compounds

e 額 (C) name plaque
Ebang 阿房 (C) Qin dynasty palace, outside of present-day Xi'an
Emeishan 峨眉山 (C) Mount Emei, sacred mountain of Samantabhadra, Sichuan province
Ennin 円仁 (J) (794–864) Japanese pilgrim and diarist who traveled to Mount Wutai in 840

Fahua jingbian 法華經變 (C) sutra painting illustrating scenes from the *Lotus Sutra*
Fahua Yuan 法華院 (C) Cloister of Dharma Blossom, a virtual monastery
fahui 法會 (C) assembly of worship
Famensi 法門寺 (C) Monastery of the Dharma Gate, located outside present-day Xi'an

famie 法滅 (C) destruction of the true teaching; extinction of the Dharma; S: *saddharma-vipralopa. See mofa*

fang 房 (C) secondary buildings in a walled compound or cloister (*yuan* 院)

fangguang 放光 (C) to emit light

Fanhe *ruixiang* 番禾瑞像 (C) auspicious image from Fanhe, in Liangzhou, present-day Gansu province

fanjing dade 翻經大德 (C) venerable translator; honorific title given to sutra translators

Fanxianshan 梵仙山 (C) Mount of Buddhist Immortals, at Mount Wutai

fashi 法師 (C) dharma master

Faxian 法顯 (C) (337–422) eminent Chinese monk who traveled to India 399–414

Faxing 法興 (C) (d. 828) Tang monk, abbot of Foguang Monastery at Mount Wutai

Faxiu 法秀 (C) Tang monk

Fayun 法雲 (C) (fl. early 8th c.) Tang monk who commissioned the first icon of Mañjuśrī riding a lion

Fazang 法藏 (C) (643–713) chief Buddhist advisor to Empress Wu Zetian; third patriarch of the Huayan sect

Fazhao heshang ru hua Zhulinsi 法照和尚入化竹林寺 (C) "Monk Fazhao Entering Virtual Zulin Monastery"; section title in Yanyi's *Extended Records*

Fazhao 法照 (C) (fl. 8th c.) Tang monk who founded Zhulin Monastery

Fei Changfang 費長房 (C) (fl. 570s–80s) author of *Record of the Three Jewels through the Generations* (Lidai sanbao ji)

feilai 飛來 (C) to come flying; fly to arrive at a place

feilang 飛廊 (C) flying corridor; elevated corridors that join buildings

feiqiao 飛橋 (C) flying bridge

feitian 飛天 (C) celestial nymph

Feng 馮 (C) family name of Empress Wenming (442–90) before her marriage

fengshan 封禪 (C) state rite performed at Mount Tai to confer legitimacy on an imperial reign

fodian 佛殿 (C) Buddha hall

Foding zhou 佛頂呪 (C) Incantation of the Buddha's Crown, chanted 765 CE to protect the nation

foding 佛頂 (C) Buddha's crown. *See buddhoṣṇīṣa*

Fogongsi 佛宮寺 (C) Monastery of the Buddhist Palace, in Yingxian, Shanxi

foguang 佛光 (C) Buddha's radiance

foguang guan 佛光觀 (C) visualizing the Buddha's radiance

Foguang Zhenrong Chanyuan 佛光真容禪院 (C) Chan Monastery of the True Presence of Buddha's Radiance, name on plaque at entrance to the Great Buddha Hall, Foguang Monastery

Foguangsi 佛光寺 (C) Monastery of Buddha's Radiance, at Mount Wutai

fotu 佛土 (C) Buddha field. *See buddhakṣetra*

Fotuoboli 佛陀波利 (C) *See* Buddhapālita

Foying ming 佛影銘 (C) *Inscription on the Shadow of the Buddha,* by Huiyuan

fudi 福地 (C) auspicious terrain; Daoist sacred site

fuhui 赴會 (C) arriving to attend the [sermon] assembly

Fukou Xing 滏口陘 (C) Fukou Mountain Pass

Gaṇḍavyūha (S) or Ru fajie pin 入法界品 (C) chapter in the *Flower Garland Sutra*

gantong 感通 (C) spiritual resonance

ganying 感應 (C) spiritual resonance

Gao 高 (C) name of the ruling family of the Northern Qi, 550–77

Gaozong 高宗 (C) emperor of the Tang, r. 649–83; husband of Wu Zetian

gāthā (S) or *ji* 偈 (C) scriptural verse

Ge Hong 葛洪 (C) (283–343) author of *Master Who Embraces Simplicity* (Baopuzi)

gezhu 閣主 (C) main patron of the construction of a pavilion

Godaisan 五台山 (J) Mount Wutai

gongcheng 宮城 (C) palace-city

Gongxian 鞏縣 (C) cave site in present-day Henan province

gongyan bi 拱眼壁 (C) wooden board mounted between brackets above an architrave

gongyang pusa 供養菩薩 (C) lit., offering bodhisattvas; in depictions, bodhisattvas who are offered to the Buddha or buddhas

gongyang 供養 (C) to make offerings

Gṛdhrakūṭa (S) or Lingjiushan 靈鷲山 (C) Vulture Peak, near Rājagṛha, central India

Gu qielan zhuan 古伽藍傳 (C) *Ancient Records of Monasteries*

guan 觀 (C) to see, contemplate, discern
guancha chuzhi shi 觀察處置使 (C) surveillance and supervisory commissioner
guanglü 廣律 (C) the complete *vinaya*; regulations applied to monastics
Guangming jue pin 光明覺品 (C) "Awakening by Light," chapter in the *Flower Garland Sutra*
Guangzhai 光宅 (C) city ward in Tang-era Chang'an
guanjing 觀經 (C) visualization sutras, with instructions for practicing meditative visualization
Guanyin 觀音 (C) Mahayana Bodhisattva of Compassion. *See* Avalokiteśvara
Guiyijun jiedushi 歸義軍節度使 (C) military governor of the Return to Allegiance Army, a hereditary title
Guoqingsi 國清寺 (C) Monastery of National Purity, in Taizhou, Zhejiang province
guoshi 國師 (C) master of the state, honorific title
gusi 古寺 (C) ancient monastery
Guzang 姑藏 (C) town in present-day Wuwei, Gansu province

Hanguang 含光 (C) (d. after 774) disciple of Amoghavajra, supervised the building of Jin'ge Monastery
Hebei Dao Shanmen Dongnanlu 河北道山門東南路 (C) Mountain Gate of the Southeast Route in the Hebei Circuit
Hebei Dao Zhenzhou 河北道鎮州 (C) town of Zhenzhou in the Hebei Circuit
Hedong Dao Shanmen Xinan[lu] 河東道山門西南[路] (C) Mountain Gate of the Southwest Route in the Hedong Circuit
Hedong Dao Taiyuan 河東道太原 (C) town of Taiyuan in the Hedong Circuit
Hengshan 恆山 (C) Northern Sacred Peak, Shanxi province
Hengshan 衡山 (C) Southern Sacred Peak, Hunan province
Hexi 河西 (C) area to the west of the Yellow River, roughly present-day Gansu and Qinghai provinces
homa (S) or *humo* 護摩 (C) oblation, an esoteric ritual
Hongli 弘禮 (C) master of meditation (fl. 6th c.)
hongzhong zhi xiang 洪鐘之響 (C) lit., sounds of great resounding chimes

Hu 胡 (C) family name of Empress Ling (Empress Dowager Hu) before her marriage (d. 528)
Hua Wenshu Ta 化文殊臺 (C) Terrace of Mañjuśrī's Transformation; ancient name of the Vulture Peak, Huayan Monastery
huagong 華栱 (C) lit., flower bracket; bracket used in traditional timber-frame building
Hualinshan 花林山 (C) Mount of Flowery Woods, east of Mount Wutai
Huangfu 皇甫 (C) name of one of the caves at Longmen
Huangyou 皇祐 (C) reign name (1049–54) of Emperor Renzong of the Northern Song
huasi 化寺 (C) virtual monastery
huaxian 化現 (C) transformative manifestation of a buddha or bodhisattva
Huayan sansheng 華嚴三聖 (C) Three Holy Ones of the *Flower Garland [Sutra]*: Śākyamuni, Mañjuśrī, and Samantabhadra
Huayansi 華嚴寺 (C) Monastery of the *Flower Garland [Sutra]*
Huibin 慧斌 (C) (574–645) Buddhist monk who went to Mount Wutai
Huichang 會昌 (C) reign name (841–46) of Emperor Wu of the Tang
Huichangsi 會昌寺 (C) Monastery of the Current Flourish, in Chang'an
Huida 慧達 (C). *See* Liu Sahe
Huiguang 慧光 (C) (468–537) eminent monk who helped translate the *Commentary on Ten Stages Sutra* (Shidi jing lun)
huilangshi 迴廊式 (C) style of corridor
Huisheng 惠勝 (C) Tang monk, author of a description of iconic images at Da Xingshan Monastery, 777
Huisi 慧思 (C) (515–77) eminent monk, second patriarch of the Tiantai school
Huixiang 慧祥 (C) (fl. mid–late 7th c.) author of *Ancient Records of [Mount] Qingliang* (Gu Qingliang zhuan)
Huixiao 惠曉 (C) disciple of Amoghavajra
Huiyuan 慧遠 (C) (334–416) eminent monk; established monastic community at Mount Lu
Huize 會賾 (C) monk of Huichang Monastery, sent by the emperor to Mount Wutai, 661–63

Indra (S) or Dishi 帝釋 (C) king of the gods (devas); ancient Indian god of the sky

Jambudvīpa (S) one of the four great continents of traditional Buddhist mythology

jātaka (S) or bensheng 本生 (C) tales of the Buddha's previous lives

ji 偈 (C) scripture verse

jiadian 夾殿 (C) a smaller building built between two larger halls

jian 見 (C) to see

Jianchusi 建初寺 (C) Monastery of the First Built; first Buddhist monastery built south of the Yangzi River

jianfo 見佛 (C) to see the Buddha

jianjiao 檢校 (C) chief officer; a title of office

Jianye 建業 (C) present-day Nanjing; capital of the Southern Dynasties

Jianyuan 鑑源 (C) (fl. 1st half of the 8th c.) Tang monk

jiedushi 節度使 (C) regional military governor

Jietuo 解脫 (C) liberation; Huayan monk (561–642) who resided at Foguang Monastery during the early Tang

jin'gang ding 金剛頂 (C) *vajra* crown; *see ding*; the esoteric doctrines and sutras of Vairocana

Jin'gang Ding Yuqie 金剛頂瑜伽 (C) Yoga of the Vajra Crown; esoteric rites associated with Vairocana

Jin'gang ku 金剛窟 (C) Diamond Grotto, southeast of North Peak, Mount Wutai

Jin'gangxing Li Zhuchi Naluoyan Ku 金剛性力住持那羅延窟 (C) Cave of Nārāyaṇa, Upholder of the Power of the Adamantine Nature. *See* Dazhusheng

jin'ge 金閣 (C) golden pavilion, in Monastery of the Golden Pavilion, Mount Wutai

Jin'ge Yuan 金閣院 (C) Cloister of the Golden Pavilion, a virtual monastery

Jin'gesi 金閣寺 (C) Monastery of the Golden Pavilion, at Mount Wutai

Jindan 金丹 (C) "Golden Elixir"; section of a chapter of *Master Who Embraces Simplicity* (Baopuzi)

jingbian 經變 (C) sutra painting; esp. one of the Mogao caves murals

jingchuang 經幢 (C) sutra pillar or *dhāraṇī* pillar; pillar inscribed with sutra passages

Jingli fa 敬禮法 (C) Procedure for Offering Veneration

Jingmingsi 景明寺 (C) Monastery of Peaceful Prospect, in Luoyang

Jingtu 淨土 (C) Pure Land, in which a buddha or bodhisattva resides

Jingwan 靜琬 (C) (d. 639) Sui monk active at Yunju Monastery, in present-day Fangshan, Hebei province

Jingxing pin 淨行品 (C) "Pure Practices" chapter of the *Flower Garland Sutra*

Jingxing Xing 井陘陘 (C) Jingxing Mountain Pass

Jingyun 景雲 (C) reign name (710–11) of Emperor Ruizong of the Tang

jinlun 金輪 (C) golden wheel; emblem of sovereignty

Jinlun Shengshen Huangdi 金輪聖神皇帝 (C) Holy Emperor of the Golden Wheel; a title of Empress Wu Zetian

jinqiao 金橋 (C) golden bridge

jinse shijie 金色世界 (C) golden world; the Pure Land of Mañjuśrī

jinxiang lu 進香路 (C) "road to present incense"; pilgrimage route to Mount Wutai

Jinyang 晉陽 (C) town in present-day Taiyuan, Shanxi, about 200 km south of Mount Wutai; gateway on pilgrimage route

Jiuhuashan 九華山 (C) Mount Jiuhua, sacred mountain of the Bodhisattva Kṣitigarbha

Jōjin 成尋 (J) (1011–81) Japanese pilgrim who traveled in China 1072–81, author of *San Tendai Godaisan ki*

Kaihuasi 開化寺 (C) Monastery of Transforming the Character, at Mount Meng, outside present-day Taiyuan

Kaiyuan san dashi 開元三大士 (C) three great masters of the Kaiyuan era: Śubhākarasiṃha (637–735), Vajrabodhi (671–741), and Amoghavajra (705–74)

Kaiyuan Shenwu 開元神武 (C) an alternative reign name (713–39) of Emperor Xuanzong

Kaiyuan 開元 (C) reign name (713–41) of Emperor Xuanzong of the Tang

Kaiyuansi 開元寺 (C) Monastery of Kaiyuan [Reign]

Kamakura 鎌倉 (J) Japanese historical period, 1185–333

Kang Senghui 康僧會 (C) (d. 280) Sogdian monk who founded Jianchu Monastery

Kaolaoshan 栲栳山 (C) Mount Kaolao, West Peak of Mount Wutai

Kapila (S) or Jiapiluo 迦毗羅 (C) Indian deva king

karuṇā (S) or *bei* 悲 (C) compassion

Kegon 華厳 (J) or Huayan 華嚴 (C) or Avataṃsaka (S) Buddhist school or sect

kikō 紀行 (J) travel account

kong 空 (C) void or immateriality

Kuodizhi 括地志 (C) *Gazetteer Encompassing the Earth*, compiled ca. 640

Laba randeng fenpei ku kan mingshu 臘八燃燈分配窟龕名數 (C) List of Names of Caves and Niches Whose Lamps Are to Be Lit on the Eighth Day of the Twelfth Month

lang 廊 (C) roofed passages or corridors

Laoducha dousheng jingbian 勞度叉鬥聖經變 (C) Sutra Painting of the Magic Competition between Raudrāksha and Śāriputra

Li Daoyuan 酈道元 (C) (ca. 470–527) author of *Commentary on the Waterways Classic* (Shuijing zhu)

Li Tongxuan 李通玄 (C) (635–730 or 646–740) lay author of the *New Commentaries on the Flower Garland Sutra* (Xin Huayan jing lun)

Liang Sicheng 梁思成 (C) (1901–72) architectural historian who led expedition to Foguang Monastery, Mount Wutai in 1937

Liangzhou 涼州 (C) region in the northwest of present-day Gansu province

Liangzhou moshi 涼州模式 (C) lit., Liangzhou style; style of Buddhist practice, architecture, and iconography developed in the Liangzhou region

ling 靈 (C) efficacy

Lingbian 靈辯 (C) (fl. early 6th c.) monk said to have arrived at Mount Wutai in 516

lingji 靈跡 (C) numinous trace

Lingquansi 靈泉寺 (C) Monastery of the Numinous Spring, at Mount Bao, in Henan province

lingrui 靈瑞 (C) divine omen

lingshan 靈山 (C) sacred mountain; mountain with numinous qualities

Lingshansi 靈山寺 (C) Monastery of the Numinous/Sacred Mountain, outside present-day Anyang, Henan province

Lingyu 靈裕 (C) (518–605) eminent monk who built Dazhusheng Cave at Mount Bao

Linlüshan 林慮山 (C) Mount Linlü, near the Northern Qi capital, Ye

Liu Qianzhi 劉謙之 (C) (ca. mid-6th c.) eunuch of the Northern Qi, who visited Mount Wutai

Liu Sahe 劉薩訶 (C) (4th c.) legendary monk, also known as Huida

liushi lifo 六時禮佛 (C) daily ritual practiced at six designated times of the day

Liuzi Wenshu 六字文殊 (C) Six-Syllable Mañjuśrī; a six-syllable mantra

Lizhi fa shitiao 立制法十條 (C) "Rules in Ten Clauses"; monastic rules compiled by Zhiyi (538–98)

Longmen 龍門 (C) cave site outside Luoyang, Henan

Longshan 龍山 (C) Mount Long, site of Tongzi Monastery, outside present-day Taiyuan, Shanxi

Longshuo 龍朔 (C) reign name (661–63) of Emperor Gaozong of the Tang

Lu Taiyi 盧太翼 (C) (fl. ca. 600) Daoist practitioner, said to have traveled to Mount Wutai

Lu Zengxiang 陸增祥 (C) (1816–82) author of *Baqiongshi jinshi buzheng*

Lüe li qijie foming chanhui deng wen 略禮七階佛名懺悔等文 (C) text of the *Abridged Repentance for Venerating the Buddha Names of the Seven Registers*, inscribed on the wall outside Dazhusheng Cave

Lüezhuan 略傳 (C) *Abridged Record [of Mount Wutai]*, by Huize

Lushan ji 廬山記 (C) *The Record of Mount Lu*, by Chen Shunyu (d. 1074), ca. 1072

Lushan 廬山 (C) Mount Lu, in Jiujiang, Jiangxi province

lüshi 律師 (C) precept master; master or teacher in the rules of monastic discipline

Mahācīna (S) Great China; ancient Indian name for China

Maijishan 麥積山 (C) Mount Maiji; Buddhist cave site in present-day Gansu province

Maitreya (S) or Mile fo 彌勒佛 (C) the Future Buddha, who will succeed Śākyamuni as the next Buddha

maṇḍala (S) or *mantuoluo* 曼陀羅 (C) sacred circle; altar; ritual field

maṅgala (S) anything auspicious or of good omen, by virtue of association with the Buddha

Mañjuśrī (S) or Wenshu Pusa (C) Mahayana

Bodhisattva of Great Wisdom; believed to be present at Mount Wutai
mantra (S) or *zhou* 咒 (C) chant; sacred sound
mārga (S) the path or way; religious practice that leads to nirvana
Mengshan 蒙山 (C) Mount Meng, site of Kaihua Monastery
meppō 末法 (J) *See mofa*
Mijiao 密教 (C) Esoteric Buddhism
Mile Dage 彌勒大閣 (C) Grand Maitreya Pavilion, at Foguang Monastery
mingshan 名山 (C) lit., mountain of renown
Mingtang 明堂 (C) Bright Hall; ritual building designed to emulate the cosmos
Mingyao 明曜 (C) (b. 556) Buddhist monk residing at Mount Wutai
mingying 冥應 (C) profound response from a divinity
modai 末代 (C) end of the world; the latter days. *See mofa* and *famie*
mofa 末法 (C) dissolution of the Dharma, destruction of the true teachings; last of the three periods of transmission of the Dharma
Mogao 莫高 (C) cave site near Dunhuang in Gansu
mohou 末後 (C) ending; the last. *See mofa*
moshi 末世 (C) latter days; final age. *See mofa*
Myōe 明恵 (J) Japanese monk (1173–232)

nāga (S) or *long* 龍 (C) serpent-like being in Hindu and Buddhist mythology; dragon
Nanchansi 南禪寺 (C) Monastery of Southern Chan
Nanyue 南嶽 (C) Southern Sacred Peak. *See* Hengshan
Nārāyaṇa (S) or Naluoyan 那羅延 (C) Indian deva king
neicheng 內城 (C) inner city; area enclosed by the inner city wall, Luoyang. *See waicheng*
nian 念 (C) mindful recollection; mental concentration in meditative practice
nianfo sanmei 念佛三昧 (C) *samādhi* in mindful recollection of the Buddha; a meditative practice
nianfo 念佛 (C) Buddha-mindfulness (*buddhānusmṛti*); calling to mind the attributes or image of the Buddha
nirmāṇa (S) or *hua* 化 (C) to manifest through transformation

pañcaśikhin (S) or *wuji* 五髻 (C) five topknots; an esoteric form of Mañjuśrī
Pei Du 裴度 (C) (765–839) regional military governor (*jiedushi*) of the greater Shanxi area
Piṇḍola (S) or Bintoulu 賓頭盧 (C) eminent *arhat*, a statue of whom was often placed in refectories
Pingcheng 平城 (C) present-day Datong, first capital of the Northern Wei dynasty
posadha (S) confessional rite. *See busa*
Prabhūtaratna (S) or Duobao Fo 多寶佛 (C) the Buddha of Many Treasures; one of the ancient Buddhas
pradakśiṇā (S) or *raoxing* 繞行 or *xingdao* 行道 (C) ritual circumambulation
prajñā (S) or *zhi* 智 (C) wisdom; mental and moral wisdom
Pratyeka-buddha (S) or Pizhifo 辟支佛 (C) one of the Buddhas of the past
Puhua 普化 (C) Indian monk who visited Mount Wutai, early tenth century
Puli fa 普禮法 (C) Procedure for Offering Universal Veneration. *See Jingli fa*
Pusa Tang Yuan 菩薩堂院 (C) Cloister of the Bodhisattva Hall, former name of Cloister of the True Presence, Huayan Monastery
Pusa zhuchu pin 菩薩住處品 (C) the chapter "Dwelling Domicile of the Bodhisattvas" in the *Flower Garland Sutra*
Pusading Zhenrong Yuan 菩薩頂真容院 (C) Cloister of the True Presence of Bodhisattva's Crown; formerly, Cloister of the True Presence, Huayan Monastery
putong yuan 普通院 (C) way stations or lodges along pilgrim routes, common cloisters
Putuoshan 普陀山 (C) Mount Putuo; sacred mountain of the bodhisattva Avalokiteśvara
Puxian 普賢 (C). *See* Samantabhadra
Puxian bian 普賢變 (C) sutra painting of Samantabhadra
puzuo 鋪作 (C) set of brackets used in traditional timber-frame architecture

qi 氣 (C) potent energy
Qibaotai 七寶臺 (C) Tower of Seven Jewels; tower commissioned for the city of Chang'an
Qing xiansheng yiwen bing zhu za zan 請賢聖儀文並諸雜贊 (C) *Ritual Texts for Invoking Worthies*

and Other Miscellaneous Eulogies; a now-lost text taken to Japan by Ennin

Qingliang guoshi 清涼國師 (C) national master of [Mount] Qingliang; a title bestowed on Chengguan

Qingliang ruixiang 清涼瑞像 (C) auspicious signs of Mount Qingliang

Qingliangshan 清涼山 (C) Mount Clear and Cool, i.e., Mount Wutai

Qingliangsi 清涼寺 (C) Monastery Clear and Cold; an early monastery at Mount Wutai

Qinglongsi 青龍寺 (C) Monastery of the Azure Dragon, in Chang'an

qingyun 慶雲 (C) auspicious clouds

Qingzhou 青州 (C) jurisdictional province, approximately present-day Shandong

qixia chengyun 其下承雲 (C) to travel on the clouds

Qixiasi 棲霞寺 (C) Monastery of Residing in Colored Clouds; in present-day Nanjing, Jiangsu province

randeng ta 燃燈塔 (C) pagoda-shaped burner

raoxing 遶行 (C) ritual circumambulation

Ratnamati (S) or Lenabati 勒那跋提 (C) (d. ca. 513) Indian monk; helped translate the *Commentary on Ten Stages Sutra* (Shidi jing lun)

Ratnasaṃbhava (S) or Baosheng Fo 寶生佛 (C) the Jewel-born One; the Buddha associated with the south

rekishi 歴史 (J) history

Renshou 仁壽 (C) reign name (601–4) of Emperor Wen of the Sui

Rizhao 日照 (C) (612–87) *See* Divākara

rong 容 (C) presence; face; countenance; visage

ruitu 瑞圖 (C) picture of auspicious signs

ruixiang 瑞像 (C) auspicious images; icons or unusal sightings. *See* Qingliang *ruixiang*

rulai 如來 (C) lit., "thus come" or "thus gone"; one of the ten epithets of the Buddha

rumen 入門 (C) lit., entering the gate; entering the order or receiving initiation

rūpakāya (S) or *shengshen* 生身 (C) physical body; incarnated body

Rusi fa 入寺法 (C) "Norms for Entering the Monastery"; section of *Exhortation on Manners and Etiquette for Novices in Training* (Jiaojie xinxue biqiu xinghu lüyi), compiled by Daoxuan

Ryōzen 靈仙 (J) Japanese monk (d. Mount Wutai, 804)

saddharma-vipralopa (S) or *famie* 法滅 (C) destruction of the true doctrine. *See mofa*

sahā (S) or *suohe* 娑訶 (C) the world around us; the present world

Śākyamuni (S) or Shijia Mouni 釋迦牟尼 (C) the historical Buddha, "sage of the Śākya clan"

samādhi (S) or *sanmei* 三昧 (C) (mental) state of being firmly fixed; mental concentration in meditation

Samantabhadra (S) or Puxian Pusa 普賢菩薩 (C) Mahayana Bodhisattva of Great Conduct

samaya (S) or *sammeiye* 三昧耶 (C) mark, symbol, or emblem of the spiritual quality of a buddha or bodhisattva

San Tendai Godaisan ki 参天台五台山記 (J) *Records of Pilgrimage at Mount Tiantai and Wutai*, by Jōjin

Sanbao 三寶 (C) or Triratna (S) the Three Jewels, i.e., Buddha, Dharma, and Saṅgha

saṅgha (S) monastic order, assemblage, clergy

Sanjie 三階 (C) Three Stages [school]; founded by Xinxing (540–94)

Sanjie Jiao 三階教 (C) Three Stages sect

Sankong 三空 (C) the Three Emptinesses: "void or immateriality" (*kong*), "formlessness" (*wuxiang*), and "inaction" (*wuzuo*)

sanmei 三昧 (C) *samādhi*

sanmen 三門 (C) entrance to a monastery; Gate of the Three [Emptinesses]

Sanzigui 三自歸 (C) Threefold Refuge [in the Three Jewels]. *See* Sanbao

śarīra (S) or *sheli* 舍利 (C) relics; bodily frame; body remains

śarīra-pūjā (S) veneration of relics or stupas

Seiryōji 清涼寺 (J) Monastery Clear and Cool, in Kyoto

Sengchou 僧稠 (C) (480–560) leading Buddhist scholar-master of the Northern Qi

Sengfang 僧方 (C) (6th c.) Buddhist monk

Sengni guifan 僧尼規範 (C) *Regulations for Monastics*, a now-lost text, compiled by Daoan

sengzhi hu 僧祇戶 (C) lit., saṅgha household, one that could support the saṅgha's missions

shamen tong 沙門統 (C) controller of clergy; supervisor of national Buddhist affairs and communities

shan wenhua 山文化 (C) mountain culture
shan 山 (C) mountain
shangdu 上都 (C) lit. superior capital; first capital city, Ye, in present-day Linzhang, Hebei province. *See xiadu*
shanmen du[gang] 山門都[綱] (C) chief officer or inspector of the mountain gate [of Mount Wutai]
shanmen dujianjiao 山門都檢校 (C) chief officer of the mountain gate [of Mount Wutai]
shanshen 山神 (C) mountain lord
shantu 山圖 (C) lit., mountain picture; a painting of Mount Wutai
shanzhi 山志 (C) mountain gazetteer; geographical writing
shanzhu 善住 (C) abiding well; remaining content and joyful
Shanzhuge Yuan 善住閣院 (C) Cloister of the Well-Abiding Pavilion, at Huayan Monastery
Shazhou 沙州 (C) administrative area centered on present-day Dunhuang
shen 神 (C) lord; god; divine
Shendu 神都 (C) lit., divine capital; the capital city Luoyang
Shengji ji 聖跡記 (C) *Records of Sacred Sites*, a now-lost text by Lingyu
shengji 聖跡 (C) sacred trace
Shengmu Shenhuang 聖母神皇 (C) Holy Mother and Divine Sovereign; title adopted by Empress Wu Zetian
shengong 神功 (C) divine work
shengrong 聖容 (C) sacred presence; holy presence
Shengshen Huangdi 聖神皇帝 (C) Holy and Divine Sovereign; title adopted by Empress Wu Zetian
shenguang 神光 (C) divine radiance
Shengxing pin 聖行品 (C) "Sagely Practices," a chapter in the *Nirvana Sutra*
Shenhui 神會 (C) (668–760) eminent monk; one of the southern Chan patriarchs
shenling zhi yao 神靈之藥 (C) spirit-power herb
shenshan 神山 (C) divine mountain
shenta 身塔 (C) pagoda containing bodily relics, rather than dharma relics
shentong 神通 (C) supernormal knowledge or supernatural power
Shenying 神英 (C) (early 8th c.) Tiantai monk who saw a virtual monastery at Mount Wutai
shenyou 神遊 (C) spiritual journey
Shenyue 神岳 (C) Divine Peak; Mount Song, designated by Empress Wu in 695
shezhai 捨宅 (C) to donate one's residence for monastic use
shi 時 (C) when; the moment
Shijing 詩經 (C) *Book of Odes*; one of the ancient Chinese classics
shouji 授記 (C) or *vyākaraṇa* (S) predicting one's future buddhahood
Shuiyusi 水浴寺 (C) Monastery of Ablutions; caves in Handan, Henan, also known as the Little Xiangtangshan site
Si gao 寺誥 (C) *Announcement of Monasteries*, a now-lost text by Lingyu
Si nianchu 四念處 (C) the Four Foundations of Mindfulness; meditation practice involving a fourfold visualization procedure
si 寺 (C) monastery, esp. a Buddhist monastery
si'e 寺額 (C) official name plaque for a Buddhist monastery
sida mingshan 四大名山 (C) lit., four great and famous mountains [in Buddhism]: Mount Emei, Mount Putuo, Mount Jiuhua, and Mount Wutai
sifang shi 四方式 (C) four-sided style [of layout in early monasteries]
Śikṣānanda (S) or Shichanantuo 實叉難陀 (C) (652–710) Khotanese monk who translated the *Flower Garland Sutra*
Siliang 寺梁 (C) mountain site near Pingcheng, present-day Datong, site of Siyuan Fosi
Sima Chengzhen 司馬承禎 (C) (647–735) sixth patriarch of the Shangqing school of Daoism
Simenta 四門塔 (C) Four-Entry Stupa, in Shentong Monastery, Licheng, Shandong province
sishe pusa 四攝菩薩 (C) the "four bodhisattvas of attraction"; bodhisattvas who lead practitioners to the truth
sishi zuochan 四時坐禪 (C) sitting meditation at four designated periods of the day
Siyang Ling 思陽嶺 (C) Siyang Range; mountains south of Mount Wutai
Siyuan Fosi 思遠佛寺 (C) Buddhist Monastery of Contemplating the Past, at Siliang
Song Shaozu 宋紹祖 (C) (d. 477) tomb master of the Northern Wei
Songgao 崧高 (C) "Soaring Peak of Mount Song," poem in *Book of Odes*
Songshan 嵩山 (C) Mount Song; Central Sacred

Peak, near present-day Dengfeng, Henan province

Śubhākarasiṃha (S) or Shanweiwu 善無畏 (C) (637–735) Indian monk of the Esoteric school who came to China in 716

Sudhana (S) or Shancai tongzi 善財童子 (C) disciple pursuing the path, featured in the *Flower Garland Sutra*

Sukhāvatī (S) Pure Land of Amitābha Buddha; the blissful land

Sumeru (S) or Xumishan 須彌山 (C) lit., greatest of all mountains, at the center of the sacred geography of Buddhism

Sun Quan 孫權 (C) (182–252) founding emperor of the Wu of the Three Kingdoms

Suoren 筱人 (C) town near Yanmen, north of Mount Wutai, in present-day northern Shanxi

Suozigu 鏁子骨 (C) monk active at Mount Wutai during the sixth and seventh centuries

Suzong 肅宗 (C) emperor of the Tang, r. 756–62

Taihang ba xing 太行八陘 (C) eight mountain passes of [Mount] Taihang

Taihang 太行 (C) mountain range in present-day Shanxi province

Taihuai 臺懷 (C) town at the center of Mount Wutai area, site of Huayan Monastery

Taishan jingjie 臺山境界 (C) [sacred] realm of Mount [Wu]tai

Taishan shisi 臺山十寺 (C) ten [major] monasteries of Mount [Wu]tai. *See* Wutai *shisi*

Taiyuan 太原 (C) largest city in Shanxi province

Taizong 太宗 (C) emperor of the Tang, r. 626–49

Tanluan 曇鸞 (C) (ca. 476–ca. 542) eminent monk, a founder of the Pure Land school

Tanqian 曇遷 (C) (542–607) eminent monk of the Ten Stages school

Tanxisi 檀溪寺 (C) Monastery of Sandalwood Creek, in Xiangyang, in present-day Hubei

Tanyao 曇曜 (C) (fl. 450–90) eminent monk of the Northern Wei

Tanyun 曇韻 (C) (563–642) monk residing at Mount Wutai during the 580s

tathāgata (S) *See rulai*

Tayuansi 塔院寺 (C) White Pagoda Temple, at the former Huayan Monastery in Taihuai

Tendai 天台 (J) *See* Tiantai

tengkong er lai 騰空而來 (C) to come through the air

Tianbao 天保 (C) reign name (550–59) of Emperor Wenxuan of the Northern Qi

Tianbao 天寶 (C) reign name (742–55) of Emperor Xuanzong of the Tang dynasty

tiangong 天宮 (C) heavenly palace

Tianlongshan 天龍山 (C) Mount Tianlong; cave site near Jinyang, present-day Taiyuan

tiansi 天寺 (C) lit., heavenly monastery, a virtual monastery

Tiantai 天臺 (C) or Tendai (J) Buddhist school founded by Zhiyi

Tianzhong 天中 (C) lit., Heaven's Center; Mount Song. *See* Shenyue

Tongtuo Jie 銅駝街 (C) Bronze Camel Avenue; the Imperial Avenue (Yujie) that runs through Luoyang of the Northern Wei

tongzi 童子 (C) a boy, youth, son; a neophyte

Tongzisi 童子寺 (C) Monastery of Youths, at Mount Long, outside Jinyang, present-day Taiyuan

toutuo 頭陀 (C) austere ascetics

Trāyastriṃśas (S) or Sanshisan Tian 三十三天 (C) lit., Heavens of Thirty-Three; one of the six Buddhist Heavens of Desire

triśaraṇa (S) *See* Sanzigui

tu 圖 (C) image; picture; representation

Tuoba 拓拔 (C) clan of Xianbei people who founded the Northern Wei dynasty

Tuṣita (S) or Doushuai Tian 兜率天 (C) one of the heavens, from which Maitreya will descend in the future world

ūrṇā (S) or *baihao* 白毫 (C) white curls between the eyebrows; one of the thirty-two perfect marks of the Buddha

uṣṇīṣa (S) or *ding* 頂 (C) cranial protuberance; Buddha's crown. *See buddhoṣṇīṣa, foding*

Vairocana (S) or Piluzhena Fo 毗盧遮那佛 (C) Illuminator; Universal Buddha; the spiritual or essential body of the Buddha

Vaiśravaṇa (S) or Pishamentian 毘沙門天 (C) one of the four Heavenly Kings

vajra (S) or *jin'gang* 金剛 (C) thunderbolt wielded by Indra; diamond; the indivisible and imperishable nature of enlightenment

Vajrabodhi (S) or Jin'gangzhi 金剛智 (C) (671–741) eminent Indian monk of the esoteric school, arrived in China in 719

vajroṣṇīṣa (S) *See jin'gang ding*
vihāra (S) assembly hall; Buddhist monastery
Vimalakīrti (S) or Weimojie 維摩詰 (C) lit., Undefiled; lay practitioner contemporary to the Buddha
vinaya (S) or lü 律 (C) monastic discipline or behavioral codes
visionary monastery: monastery seen in a vision; virtual monastery. *See husi*
vyākaraṇa (S). *See shouji*

waicheng 外城 (C) outer city; area between the first and second city walls, Luoyang of the Northern Wei
Wan Pusa Lou 萬菩薩樓 (C) Pavilion of Ten Thousand Fellow Bodhisattvas, shown in a mural of Mount Wutai, Mogao Cave 61
wan pusa 萬菩薩 (C) ten thousand bodhisattvas; assembly of bodhisattvas
Wanli 萬曆 (C) reign name (1573–1615) of Emperor Shenzong
weijing 偽經 (C) apocrypha; sutras composed in China
weinuo 維那 (C) rector; second in command of a monastery
Wenming 文明 (C) Empress Feng of the Northern Wei, 442–90
Wenshu bian 文殊變 (C) sutra painting of Mañjuśrī
Wenshu Dian 文殊殿 (C) Hall of Mañjuśrī
Wenshu Pusa xian shi 文殊菩薩現時 (C) lit., the moment in which Bodhisattva Mañjuśrī manifests
Wenshu Pusa 文殊菩薩 (C) Bodhisattva Mañjuśrī. *See* Mañjuśrī
Wenshu Tang 文殊堂 (C) Hall of Mañjuśrī; a name for Mogao Cave 61
Wenshu zhenrong xiang 文殊真容像 (C) sculpture of the true presence of Mañjuśrī, in Huayan Monastery
Wenshu Zhenrong Yuan 文殊真容院 (C) Cloister of Mañjuśrī's True Presence
Wenshu zhuan 文殊傳 (C) *Records of Mañjuśrī*; a now-lost text
Wenxuan 文宣 (C) emperor of Northern Qi, r. 550–59
Wenzhao 文昭 (C) (469–497) concubine of Emperor Xiaowen (r. 471–99) of the Northern Wei
Wu Zetian 武則天 (C) (624–705) wife of Emperor Gaozong (r. 649–83), who later founded the Zhou dynasty
Wu 吳 (C) frontier state in the south of the Tang Empire
Wuding 五頂 (C) or Wufeng 五峰 (C) Five Peaks
wuhui nianfo 五會念佛 (C) Buddha recitation using five different tempos
wuse qingyun 五色慶雲 (C) five-color celebratory clouds
Wutai jingjie siming shengji 五臺境界寺名聖跡 (C) "Names of monasteries and holy traces in the realm of Mount Wutai," section title in Yanyi's *Extended Records of [Mount] Qingliang*
Wutai Nan Shanmen 五臺南山門 (C) South Mountain Gate of Mount Wutai
Wutai *shisi* 五臺十寺 (C) or Wutaishan *shisi* 五臺山十寺 (C) ten monasteries of [Mount] Wutai
Wutai *tu* 五臺圖 (C) or Wutaishan *tu* 五臺山圖 (C) picture of [Mount] Wutai
Wutaishan 五臺山 (C) or Godaisan 五台山 (J) lit., mount of five terraces; Mount Wutai
Wutaishan dasheng Zhulinsi shi Fazhao dejian taishan jingjie ji 五臺山大聖竹林寺釋法照得見臺山境界記 (C) *Records of Monk Fazhao from the Great Sage Zhulinsi at Mount Wutai Receiving the Vision of the [Sacred] Realm of Mount [Wu]tai*, a now-lost text
Wutaishan huaxian tu 五臺山化現圖 (C) "Picture of Transformative Manifestations at Mount Wutai"; painting commissioned by Yiyuan and presented to Ennin
Wutaishan Qingliangsi bei 五臺山清涼寺碑 (C) stele of Qingliang Monastery at Mount Wutai
Wutaishan shisi dujianjiao 五臺山十寺都檢校 (C) chief officer of the ten [major] monasteries at Mount Wutai
Wutaishan zan 五臺山贊 (C) eulogies on Mount Wutai; included in Dunhuang Manuscripts S5573, S4429, P3563, P3437, Beijing 8329
wutoumen 烏頭門 (C) crow-head gate; gate with projecting finials, often painted black
wuxiang 無相 (C) formlessness; absolute, undifferentiated truth
Wuyue 五嶽 (C) Five Sacred Peaks or the Five Marchmounts
Wuzhoushan 武州山 (C) Mount Wuzhou, in present-day Yungang

Wuzhu 無著 (C) (fl. ca. mid-8th c.) Tang monk who saw a virtual monastery at Mount Wutai

Wuzi Wenshu 五字文殊 (C) Five-Syllable Mañjuśrī; Mañjuśrī as a youth with five topknots

Wuzi yuqie guanmen 五字瑜伽觀門 (C) *Gate for Visualization of the Five-Syllable Yoga*, a now-lost text

Wuzong 武宗 (C) emperor of the Northern Zhou, r. 560–78; emperor of Tang, r. 840–46

wuzuo 無作 (C) inaction; state of being that is natural and intuitive

xia ang 下昂 (C) downward-pointing cantilever in a bracket

xiadu 下都 (C) lit., lower capital; the second capital city, Jinyang, in present-day Taiyuan, Shanxi province. *See shangdu*

xian 現 (C) to manifest

Xianbei 鮮卑 (C) nomadic people who lived in present-day Manchuria, Inner Mongolia, and Eastern Mongolia

xiangfa 像法 (C) semblance of Dharma; see *mofa*

Xiangtangshan 響堂山 (C) cave site near present-day Handan, Henan province

Xiangyang 襄陽 (C) city in present-day Hubei province

Xiangyun 祥雲 (C) monk of the Northern Qi who saw a virtual palace in the Diamond Grotto

Xiangzhou 相州 (C) administrative region near Ye, in present-day Linzhang, Hebei province

Xianhuashan 仙花山 (C) Mount of Immortal Flowers, near Taihua in the Mount Wutai area

Xianjing 仙經 (C) *Scriptures of Immortals*, a now-lost text

xianshen 現身 (C) to exhibit the true body; a transformative manifestation of a buddha or bodhisattva

xiansi 仙寺 (C) transcendent monasteries; monasteries inhabited by immortals

Xiantongsi 顯通寺 (C) Temple of Manifested Penetration; at the site of the former Huayan Monastery in Taihuai, Mount Wutai

xiansheng 賢聖 (C) worthies; those noted for goodness, wisdom, or insight

Xiaonanhai 小南海 (C) cave site near present-day Anyang, Henan province

Xiaowen 孝文 (C) emperor of the Northern Wei, r. 471–99

xiaozhang 小帳 (C) small screen

Ximingsi 西明寺 (C) Monastery of Western Illumination; a major monastery in Chang'an

xingdao 行道 (C) ritual circumambulation. *See pradakṣiṇā*

xingdao 陘道 (C) mountain pass

Xinggan 行感 (C) Tang monk

xingxiang 行香 (C) [act of] presenting incense

Xinxing 信行 (C) (540–94) eminent monk of the Three Stages sect. *See* Sanjie

Xinyang Wenshu 新樣文殊 (C) lit., new-mode Mañjuśrī; "new emanation" of the bodhisattva

Xuanwu 宣武 (C) emperor of the Northern Wei, r. 499–515

Xuanzang 玄奘 (C) (600–664) eminent monk of the Tang who traveled to India 629–45

Xuanzong 宣宗 (C) emperor of the Tang, r. 846–59

Xuanzong 玄宗 (C) emperor of the Tang, r. 712–56

yakṣa (S) nature spirit

Yan Chanshi 儼禪師 (C) (d. 673) Chan master Yan

Yang Xuanzhi 楊衒之 (C) (d. 555) author of *Luoyang jielan ji*

Yanmen 雁門 (C) Yanmen Pass, border town in northern Shanxi, north of Mount Wutai

Yanyi 延一 (C) (b. 999) author of *Extended Records of [Mount] Qingliang* (Guang Qingliang zhuan)

Yaoguangsi 瑤光寺 (C) Jade-Sparkle Monastery; founded for nuns, a convent

Ye or Yedu 鄴都 (C) capital of the Northern Qi, in present-day Linzhang, Hebei

Yifeng 儀鳳 (C) reign name (676–78) of Emperor Gaozong of the Tang

yigui 儀軌 (C) mode; style; manner; ritual manual

Yijing 義淨 (C) (635–713) eminent monk of the Tang who traveled to India in 671–695, a prolific translator

Yindu Puhua dashi you Wutaishan qiwen 印度普化大師游五臺山啟文 (C) *A Report on Traveling to Mount Wutai by the Indian Master Puhua*, a travel diary, 926–36

ying 應 (C) response

Yingzao fashi 營造法式 (C) *Treatise on Architectural Methods*, treatise (1103) compiled by Li Jie 李誡 (1035?–110)

yixiang zhi qi 異香之氣 (C) smell of unusual fragrance

yiyi 義邑 (C) Buddhist charitable society

Yiyuan 義圓 (C) Tang monk active at Mount Wutai in the mid-ninth century
Yongjia 永嘉 (C) reign name (307–12) of Emperor Huai of the Western Jin
Yongningsi 永寧寺 (C) Monastery of Eternal Peace; name of two different imperial monasteries of the Northern Wei
Youzhou 幽州 (C) jurisdictional state covering part of present-day Shanxi and Hebei
yü yürong 玉御容 (C) jade statue of the emperor
yuqie 瑜伽 (C) yoga; esoteric practices using mudras, incantations, and concentration
yuan 院 (C) cloister; hall
Yuancheng 願誠 (C) (d. 887) Tang monk, abbot of Foguang Monastery at Mount Wutai
Yuanxiao 元曉 (C) (fl. 617) monk of Korean origin, author of a now-lost text, *Records of Wenshu* (Wenshu zhuan)
Yue 嶽 (C) sacred peak; marchmount
Yue 越 (C) frontier state in the south of the Tang Empire
Yuhua Chi 玉華池 (C) Jade Floral Pond, at Central Peak, Mount Wutai
Yuhuasi 玉華(花)寺 (C) Monastery of Jade Floral, built ca. 758 at Mount Wutai
Yujie 御街 (C) Imperial Avenue. *See* Tongtuo Jie
Yunjusi 雲居寺 (C) Monastery of Cloud Dwelling, in present-day Fangshan, Hebei province. *See* Jingwan
Yunmensi 雲門寺 (C) Monastery of Cloud Gate; monastery associated with Sengchou

Zaosi Fa 造寺法 (C) "Methods for Building a Monastery," section in Daoxuan's notes on the *Four-Part Vinaya*
zaoxiang bei 造像碑 (C) image stele; stele carved with images
zase ruiguang 雜色瑞光 (C) multicolor auspicious blaze
Zezhou 澤州 (C) administrative region in present-day southern Shanxi and Henan
Zhai Fengda 翟奉達 (C) (883–961?) member of a prominent donor family in Dunhuang
Zhai Jiaku 翟家窟 (C) Cave of the Zhai Family
Zhang Chuzhen 張處貞 (C) author of the inscription "A Record of Mount Wutai and the [Stone] Lantern"
Zhang Yichao 張議潮 (C) (799–872) first military governor of the Return to Allegiance Army, 851–67
Zhencheng 鎮澄 (C) (d. 1617) author of the *Qingliangshan zhi*
Zhendan 震旦 (C) China, transliterated name used in ancient India
Zheng Daojue 鄭道覺 (C) lay person who visited Jin'ge Monastery in 779
zhengfa 正法 (C) correct Dharma
Zhenguan lü 貞觀律 (C) Code of the Zhenguan Reign, promulgated in 637
zhenjing 真境 (C) true domain
zhenrong 真容 (C) true presence
zhenrong xiang 真容像 (C) icon of true presence
Zhenrong Yuan 真容院 (C) Cloister of the True Presence, in Huayan Monastery
zhenshen 真身 (C) true body
zhenxiang 真像 (C) or *zhenxiang* 真相 (C) true image
zhenyi 真儀 (C) true appearance
Zhenzhou 鎮州 (C) city on the pilgrim route to Mount Wutai, in present-day Zhengding, Hebei province
zhiguai 志怪 (C) lit., recording the strange; a literary genre
Zhijing 志靜 (C) Tang monk, author of the preface to the *Superlative Dhāraṇī of the Buddha's Crown* attributed to Buddhapālita, T.19: 967
Zhijun 智頵 (C) (d. 853) Tang monk active at Mount Wutai during the ninth century
Zhiping 治平 (C) reign name (1064–67) of Emperor Yingzong of the Northern Song
Zhiyan 智儼 (C) eminent monk of Huayan Monastery at Mount Wutai during Ennin's visit
Zhiyi 智顗 (C) (538–98) founder of the Tiantai school
Zhongguo Yingzao Xueshe 中國營造學社 (C) Institute for Research in Chinese Architecture
Zhonghuangshan 中皇山 (C) Mount Zhonghuang; cave site in Shexian, Hebei province
Zhouye liushi fayuan wen 晝夜六時發願文 (C) "Vows Recited at the Six Periods of Day and Night," in *Confessional Rituals of Collected Sutras*, compiled by Zhisheng
Zhulinsi 竹林寺 (C) Monastery of the Bamboo Grove, founded by Fazhao, at Mount Wutai
zhuzuo 主座 (C) main deity installed in a monastic hall
Zifu 紫府 (C) lit., Purple Palace; the place where immortals reside; an early name of Mount Wutai

BIBLIOGRAPHY

PRIMARY SOURCES

Dunhuang Manuscripts

P.3931b (A report on traveling to Mount Wutai by the Indian master Puhua). Puhua 普化. Ca. 926–36.

P.4648 (Pilgrimage diary to Mount Wutai by an anonymous pilgrim). Ca. 8th century.

S.397 (Pilgrimage diary to Mount Wutai by an anonymous pilgrim). Ca. 10th century.

S.529v (The creation legend of the true-presence icon of bodhisattva Mañjuśrī at Huayan Monastery). Ca. early 10th century.

Primary Texts

Amituo jing 阿彌陀經 (Shorter *Sukhāvatīvyūha-sūtra*). T.12: 366. Translated by Kumārajīva 鳩摩羅什 (344–413).

Banzhou sanmei jing 般舟三昧經 (Pratyutpanna-samādhi-sūtra). T.13: 418. Translated by Lokakṣema 支婁迦讖 (fl. ca. 160s–180s). 2nd half of the 2nd century CE.

Baopuzi 抱朴子 (Master who embraces simplicity). By Ge Hong 葛洪 (283–343).

Baqiongshi jinshi buzheng 八瓊室金石補正 (Supplement to the stone and metal inscriptions from the Chamber of Eight Jewels). Compiled by Lu Zengxiang 陸增祥 (1816–82).

Beiqi shu 北齊書 (History of the Northern Qi). Compiled by Li Delin 李德林 (530–590) and Li Baiyao 李百藥 (565–648). 636 CE.

Beishi 北史 (History of the Northern Dynasties). Compiled by Li Yanshou 李延壽 (fl. 618–76). 659 CE.

Chongxiu Mengshan Kaihua zhuangyange ji 重修蒙山開化莊嚴閣記 (A record on the rebuilding of the Zhuangyan Pavilion at Kaihua[si]). In *Shanyou shike congbian* 山右石刻叢編, *juan* 10. By Su Yugui 蘇禹珪 (894–956). 945 CE.

Chu sanzang ji ji 出三藏記集 (Collection of notes on the translation of the Tripiṭaka). T.55: 2145. Compiled by Sengyou 僧佑 (445–518). 515 CE.

Dafangguang fo huayan jing suishu yanyi chao 大方廣佛華嚴經隨疏演義鈔 (Annotated commentaries on the *[Buddha]avataṃsaka-sūtra*). T.36: 1736. By Chengguan 澄觀 (738–839). Ca. 787 CE.

Daizong chao zeng Sikong da bianzheng guangzhi sanzang heshang biaozhi ji 代宗朝贈司空大辯正廣智三藏和尚表制集 (Collection of the memoranda on regulations bestowed by the court of Daizong to the minister of works, the greatly skillful and upright Guangzhi, the venerable Tripiṭaka master). T.52: 2120. Compiled by Yuanzhao 圓照 (d. 800).

Dai Nihon Bukkyō zensho 大日本佛教全書 (Complete Buddhist works of Japan). 100 vols. Edited by Suzuki gakujutsu zaidan. Tokyo: Kōdansha, 1970–73.

Daji jing 大集經 (Mahāsaṃnipāta-sūtra). T.13: 397. Translated by Dharmakṣema 曇無讖 (385–433) et al.

Daoxuan lüshi gantong lu 道宣律師感通錄 (Miraculous records of the Vinaya master Daoxuan). T.52: 2107. By Daoxuan 道宣 (596–667). 664 CE.

Dasheng Wenshu shili pusa fosha gongde zhuangyan jing 大聖文殊師利菩薩佛刹功德莊嚴經 (Sutra [that numerates] the virtue and magnificence of the Pure Land of the great sage bodhisattva Mañjuśrī). T.11: 319. Translated by Amoghavajra 不空金剛 (705–74). 773 CE.

Dayun jing 大雲經 (Mahāmegha-sūtra). Alternate title *Dafangdeng wuxiang jing* 大方等無想經. T.12: 387. Translated by Dharmakṣema (385–433).

Dayun jing shenhuang shouji yishu 大雲經神皇授記義疏 (Commentary on the meaning of the prophecy about the divine sovereign in *Dayun Jing*). S2658 and S6502. Ca. 691 CE.

Dongtian fudi yuedu mingshan ji 洞天福地嶽瀆名山記 (Record of grotto heavens, auspicious terrains, sacred peaks, rivers, and famous mountains). *Daozang, juan* 599. Compiled by Du Guangting 杜光庭 (850–933).

Fahua jing 法華經 (Lotus Sutra). Alternative title *Miaofa lianhua jing* 妙法蓮花經 (Saddharmapuṇḍarīka-sūtra). T.9: 262. Translated by Kumārajīva. 406 CE.

Fayuan zhulin 法苑珠林 (Jade grove of the dharma garden). T.53: 2122. Compiled by Daoshi 道世 (d. 683). 668 CE.

Foding zunsheng tuoluoni jing 佛頂尊勝陀羅尼經 (Uṣṇīṣavijāyā-dhāraṇi-sūtra, or Sutra of the superlative dhāraṇī of the Buddha's crown). T.19: 967. Translation attributed to Buddhapālita 佛陀波利, with preface by Zhijing 志靜 dated 689 CE.

Foding zunsheng tuoluoni niansong yigui fa 佛頂尊勝陀羅尼念誦儀軌法 (The rite for the recitation of the superlative dhāraṇī of the Buddha's crown). T.19: 972. By Amoghavajra. 764 CE.

Foshuo wuliangshou jing 佛說無量壽經 (Sukhāvatīvyūha-sūtra). T.12: 360. Translated by Saṁghavarman 僧伽跋摩 (fl. ca. 250 CE).

Fozu tongji 佛祖統紀 (Sequential record of the Buddha and patriarchs). T.49: 2035. Compiled by Zhipan 志磐. 1258 CE.

Gaoseng zhuan 高僧傳 (Biographies of eminent monks). T.50: 2059. Compiled by Huijiao 慧皎 (497–554). Ca. 530 CE.

Gu Qingliang zhuan 古清涼傳 (Ancient records of [Mount] Qingliang). T.51: 2098. By Huixiang 慧祥 (fl. mid- to late 7th century). 680–83 CE.

Guan wuliangshou fo jing 觀無量壽佛經 (Amitāyurdhyāna-sūtra). T.12: 365. Translated by Kālayaśas 畺良耶舍 (383–442). Ca. 424–42 CE.

Guanfo sanmei hai jing 觀佛三昧海經 (Ocean-like samādhi of Buddha visualization sutra). T.15: 643. Translated by Buddhabhadra 佛陀跋陀 (359–429).

Guang hongming ji 廣弘明集 (Expanded anthology of extended brilliance). T.52: 2103. By Daoxuan. Preface dated 664 CE.

Guang Qingliang zhuan 廣清涼傳 (Extended records of [Mount] Qingliang). T. 51: 2099. By Yanyi 延一. Ca. 1060.

Guanzhong chuangli jietan tujing 關中創立戒壇圖經 (Illustrated scripture concerning the erection of the ordination platform in the Guanzhong Region). T.45: 1892. By Daoxuan. 667 CE.

Guoqing bailu 國清百錄 (One hundred records of the Guoqin [Monastery]). T.46: 1934. By Zhiyi 智顗 (538–98). Ca. 595.

Hongzan fahua zhuan 弘贊法華傳 (Eulogizing the anthology of the *Lotus Sutra*). T.51: 2067. By Huixiang 慧祥 (fl. mid- to late 7th century).

Huayan jing zhuanji 華嚴經傳記 (Biographies and record [of those who promote] the *Flower Garland Sutra*). T.51: 2073. Compiled by Fazang 法藏 (643–712).

Huayan jing 華嚴經 (Flower Garland Sutra). Alternate title *Dafangguang fo huayan jing* 大方廣佛華嚴經 ([Buddha]avataṃsaka-sūtra). T.9: 278 (60-fascicle, translated by Buddhabhadra, ca. 420); T.10: 279 (80-fascicle, translated by Śikṣānanda 實叉難陀, 699); T.10: 293 (40-fascicle, translated by Prajñā 般若, ca. 798).

Ji shenzhou sanbao gantong lu 集神州三寶感通錄 (Collected records of miraculous experiences of the Three Jewels in China). T.52: 2106. Compiled by Daoxuan. 664 CE.

Ji zhujing lichan yi 集諸經禮懺儀 (Confessional rituals of collected sutras). T.47: 1982. By Zhisheng 智昇 (658–740). 730 CE.

Jiaojie xinxue biqiu xinghu lüyi 教戒新學比丘行護律儀 (Exhortation on manners and etiquette for novices in training). T.45: 1897. By Daoxuan (596–667).

Jin'gang ding jing yuqie Wenshu shili pusa fa 金剛頂經瑜伽文殊師利菩薩法 (Rite of the bodhisattva Mañjuśrī according to the *Vajraśekhara-sūtra*). T.20: 1171. Translated by Amoghavajra. 774 CE.

Jin'gang ding yuqie sanshiqi zun chusheng yi 金剛頂瑜伽三十七尊出生義 (Casual revelations of the thirty-seven divinities of the yoga of the *vajra* crown). T.18: 872. Translated by Amoghavajra (705–74).

Jin'gang jing 金剛經 (Diamond Sutra), or *Jin'gang banruo boluomi jing* 金剛般若波羅蜜經 (Vajracchedikā-prajñāpāramitā-sūtra). T.8: 235. Translated by Kumārajīva (343–413).

Jingtu wuhui nianfo songjing guanxingyi 淨土五會念佛誦經觀行儀 (Rite for intoning the Buddha's name, reciting scripture, and performing meditation in the five tones of the Pure Land). T.85: 2827. By Fazhao 法照 (fl. 8th century).

Jinshu 晉書 (History of the Jin). Compiled by Fang Xuanling 房玄齡 (578–648). 646 CE.

Jiu Tangshu 舊唐書 (Old history of the Tang). Compiled by Liu Xu 劉昫 (887–946). 945 CE.

Kegon butsukō zanmai kan hihōzō 華厳仏光三昧観秘宝蔵 (Secret treasure of the *samādhi* [achieved by] visualizing the Buddha's radiance [based on] the *Flower Garland Sutra*). T.72: 2332. By Myōe 明恵 (1173–232).

Lidai sanbao ji 歷代三寶記 (Record of the Three Jewels through the generations). T.49: 2034. Compiled by Fei Changfang 費長房 (fl. 560s–90s). Ca. 597.

Luoyang qielan ji 洛陽伽藍記 (Record of the monasteries of Luoyang). By Yang Xuanzhi 楊衒之 (d. 555). 547 CE.

Lushan Huiyuan fashi lei 廬山慧遠法師誄 (The eulogy for the *dhyāna* master Huiyuan at Mount Lu). T.52: 2103.267a12–b21. By Xie Lingyun 謝靈運 (385–433).
Lushan ji 廬山記 (The record of Mount Lu). T.51: 2095. By Chen Shunyu 陳舜俞 (d. 1074). Ca. 1074 CE.
Nanhai jigui neifa zhuan 南海寄歸内法傳 (Account of Buddhism sent home from the Southern Sea). T.54: 2125. By Yijing 義淨 (635–713). Ca. 690 CE.
Nanyue si dachanshi lishi yuanwen 南嶽思大禪師立誓願文 (Tract on the vow made by the great master [Hui]si of the Southern Sacred Peak). T.46: 1933. By Huisi 慧思 (515–77). 558 CE.
Niepan jing 涅槃經 (Nirvana Sutra), or *Dabanniepan jing* 大般涅槃經 (Mahāparinirvāṇa-sūtra). T. 12: 374. Translated by Dharmakṣema (385–433).
Nittō guhō junrei gyōki 入唐求法巡礼行記 (The record of a pilgrimage to China in search of the Law). In *Dai Nihon bukkyō zensho*, vol. 72, 84–133. By Ennin 円仁 (794–864). See Ono Katsutoshi, *Nittō guhō junrei gyōki no kenkyū* [*NGJG*].
Nyūtō shingū seikyō mokuroku 入唐新求聖教目錄 (Catalogue of the sacred teachings newly obtained in China). T.55: 2167. By Ennin. 847 CE.
Putichang suoshuo yizi ding lunwang jing 菩提場所說一字頂輪王經 (Scripture spoken at the Bodhimaṇḍa on the one-syllable wheel-turning king of [the Buddha's] crown). T.19: 950. Translated by Amoghavajra (705–74).
Qingliangshan zhi 清涼山志 (Gazetteer of Mount Qingliang). By Zhencheng 鎮澄 (d. 1617). 1596 CE.
Quan Tangwen 全唐文 (Complete prose literature of the Tang). Compiled by Dong Hao 董浩 (1740–1818) et al. 1814 CE.
Rizang fen jing 日藏分經 (Sūryagarbha-sūtra). T.13: 397.233–97. Translated by Narendrayaśas 那連提黎耶舍 (516–89).
San Tendai Godaisan ki 参天台五台山記 (Records of pilgrimage at Mount Tiantai and Wutai). In *Dai Nihon bukkyō zensho,* vol. 72, 267–68. By Jōjin 成尋 (1011–81). 1072 CE.
Shanyou shike congbian 山右石刻叢編 (Edited collection of stone inscriptions from areas to the east of [Taihang] mountains). Compiled by Hu Pinzhi 胡聘之 (1840–1912). 1898 CE.
Shidi jing 十地經 (Daśabhūmika-sūtra). T.10: 287. Translated by Shiluodamo 尸羅達摩. Ca. 799 CE.
Shidi jing lun 十地經論 (Daśabhūmikasūtra-śāstra). T.26: 1522. Translated by Bodhiruci 菩提留支 (d. 527).
Shizhu piposha lun 十住毘婆沙論 (Daśabhūmika-vibhāṣā-śāstra). T.26: 1521. Translated by Kumārajīva. Ca. 405 CE.
Shuijing zhu 水經注 (Commentary on the Waterways Classic). By Li Daoyuan 酈道元. 515–24 CE.
Shuowen jiezi 說文解字 (Explaining single-component graphs and analyzing compound characters). Compiled by Xu Shen 許慎. 100 CE.
Si Beiyue Hengshan Wen 祀北嶽恆山文 (Worship prayer to Mount Heng of the Northern Peak). By Emperor Taizong 太宗 (r. 626–49) of the Tang. *Quan Tangwen, juan* 10.

Sifenlü shanfan buque xingshichao 四分律刪繁補闕行事鈔 (Notes adding to and amending *Four-Part Vinaya*), T.40: 1804. By Daoxuan. 626–630 CE.
Siwei lüeyao fa 思維略要法 (Abridged method of meditation). T.15: 617. Translation attributed to Kumārajīva (344–413).
Song gaoseng zhuan 宋高僧傳 (Song dynasty biographies of eminent monks). T.50: 2061. Compiled by Zanning 贊寧 (919–1001). 988 CE.
Taiping yulan 太平御覽 (Imperially reviewed encyclopedia of the Taiping era). Compiled by Li Fang 李昉 (925–96) et al. 984 CE.
Tang Da Jianfusi gu sizhu fanjing dade Fazang heshang zhuan 唐大薦福寺故寺主翻經大德法藏和尚傳 (Biography of Mong Fazang, the former chief abbot and great-virtue translator of the Great Monastery of Advocating Blessings). T.50: 2054. By Cui Zhiyuan 崔致遠 (857–951). Ca. 904.
Tiwei boli jing 提謂波利經 (Scripture of Trapuṣa and Ballika). S2051, P3732.
Tuoluoni ji jing 陀羅尼集經 (Dhāraṇīsaṃgraha-sūtra). T.18: 901. By Atikūṭa 阿地瞿多. 653 CE.
Weishu 魏書 (History of the Northern Wei). Wei Shou 魏收 (506–72). 554 CE.
Wenshu shili ban niepan jing 文殊師利般涅槃經 (Mañjuśrī-parinirvāṇa-sūtra). T.14:463, Translated by Nie Daozhen 聶道真 (act. 265–317).
Wenshu shili fa baozang tuoluoni jing 文殊師利法寶藏陀羅尼經 (Mañjuśrī-dharma-ratnagarbha-dhāraṇī-sūtra). T.20: 1185A/1185B. Translated by Bodhiruci 菩提流志 (672–727). 710 CE.
Wenshu shili suoshuo mohe banruo boluomi jing 文殊師利所說摩訶般若波羅蜜經 (Saptaśatikā-prajñāpāramitā-sūtra). T.8: 233. Translated by Saṅghapāla 僧伽婆羅 (460–542).
Wufoding sanmei tuoluoni jing 五佛頂三昧陀羅尼經 (Dhāraṇī sutra of the five uṣṇīṣa wheel-turning kings). T.19: 952. Translated by Bodhiruci (672–727).
Wumen chanjing yaoyong fa 五門禪經要用法 (The essence of the meditation manual consisting of Five Gates of Chan). T.15: 619. Translated by Dharmamitra 曇摩蜜多 (356–422).
Wutaishan ji dengtai ji 五臺山及燈臺記 (A record of Mount Wutai and the [stone] lantern). By Zhang Chuzhen 張處貞. Referring to the reign period 713–39 CE.
Wutaishan zan 五臺山贊 (Eulogies of Mount Wutai). S5573, S4429, S5487, P3563, P3437, Beijing 8329. 10th century.
Xin Huayan jing lun 新華嚴經論 (New commentaries on the *Flower Garland Sutra*). T.36: 1739. By Li Tongxuan 李通玄 (635–730 or 646–740).
Xu gaoseng zhuan 續高僧傳 (Continued biographies of eminent monks). T.50: 2060. Compiled by Daoxuan. Ca. 664.
Yingzao fashi 營造法式 (Treatise on architectural methods). By Li Jie 李誡 (1065–110). 1103 CE.
Yizi foding lunwang jing 一字佛頂輪王經 (*Ekākṣara-uṣṇīṣa-cakravartin* scripture, or The wheel-turning king of the one-syllable Buddha's crown). T.19: 951, translated by Bodhiruci (672–727).
Yuezang fen jing 月藏分經 (Candragarbha-sūtra). T.13: 397.298a5–381c11. Translated by Narendrayaśas (516–89). 566 CE.

Zhong tianzhu sheweiguo Qiyuansi tujing 中天竺舍衛國祇洹寺圖經 (Illustrated scripture of Jetavana Monastery of Śrāvastī in Central India). T.45: 1899. By Daoxuan. 667 CE.
Zuisheng foding tuoluoni jingchu yezhang zhou jing 最勝佛頂陀羅尼淨除業障咒經 (Sutra of the superlative dhāraṇī of the Buddha's crown for eradicating karmic obstacles). T.19: 970. By Divākara 地婆訶羅 (612–87). 685 CE.
Zunsheng foding xiu yuqiefa yigui 尊勝佛頂脩瑜伽法儀軌 (Ritual manual on the yoga of the superlative Buddha's crown). T.19: 973. By Śubhākarasiṃha 善無畏 (637–735). 722 CE.

SECONDARY SOURCES

Abe, Stanley K. *Ordinary Images.* Chicago: University of Chicago Press, 2002.
Adamek, Wendi L. "Dimensions of Endtime at Bao Shan." In *Cultural Crossings: China and Beyond in the Medieval Period,* edited by Dorothy C. Wong and Gustav Heldt. Singapore: Institute of Southeast Asian Studies, forthcoming.
———. *The Mystique of Transmission: On an Early Chan History and Its Contexts.* New York: Columbia University Press, 2007.
Ambros, Barbara. *Emplacing a Pilgrimage: The Ōyama Cult and Regional Religion in Early Modern Japan.* Cambridge, Mass.: Harvard University Press, 2008.
Aramaki Tenshun. "Jōyō jidai no Dōan kyōdan ni okeru kōkyōkai no seiritsu ni tsuite" (On the mode of delivering sutra lectures established in Daoan's community during the time [it was based in] Xiangyang). In *Chūgoku chūsei no shūkyō to bunka,* 398–413. Kyoto: Kyoto daigaku jinbun kagaku kenkyūjo, 1982.
Bakhtin, M. M. *The Dialogic Imagination: Four Essays.* Translated by Caryl Emerson and Michael Holquist. Austin: University of Texas Press, 1981.
Barrett, T. H. "On the Road to China: The Continental Relocation of Sacred Space and Its Consequences for Mountains, Minds, and Texts." In *Images, Relics, and Legends*, edited by Benn, et al., 46–67.
———. "Stūpa, Sūtra, and Śarīra in China, c. 656–706 CE." *Buddhist Studies Review* 18, no. 1 (2001): 1–64.
Beckwith, Christopher I. *The Tibetan Empire in Central Asia.* Princeton, N.J.: Princeton University Press, 1987.
Belting, Hans. *Likeness and Presence: A History of the Image before the Era of Art.* Translated by Edmund Jephcott. Chicago: University of Chicago Press, 1994.
Benn, James, Jinhua Chen, and James Robson, eds. *Images, Relics, and Legends: The Formation and Transformation of Buddhist Sacred Sites.* Cheektowaga, N.Y.: Mosaic Press, 2012.
Benn, James, Lori Meeks, and James Robson, eds. *Buddhist Monasticism in East Asia: Places of Practice.* New York: Routledge, 2010.
Berger, Patricia. *Empire of Emptiness: Buddhist Art and Political Authority in Qing China.* Honolulu: University of Hawaiʻi Press, 2003.
Beyer, Stephan. "Notes on the Vision Quest in Early Mahāyāna." In *Prajñāpāramitā*

and Related Systems: Studies in Honor of Edward Conze, edited by Lewis Lancaster, 329–40. Berkeley: University of California, 1977.
Bielefeldt, Carl. "Practice." In *Critical Terms for the Study of Buddhism,* edited by Donald S. Lopez, 229–44. Chicago: University of Chicago Press, 2005.
Birnbaum, Raoul. "Light in the Wutai Mountains." In *The Presence of Light: Divine Radiance and Religious Experience,* edited by Matthew T. Kapstein, 195–226. Chicago: University of Chicago Press, 2004.
———. "Mañjuśrī." In *The Encyclopedia of Religion,* edited by Mircea Eliade, vol. 9, 174–75. New York: Macmillan, 1986.
———. "Secret Halls of the Mountain Lords: The Caves of Wu-t'ai Shan." *Cahiers d'Extrême-Asie* 5 (1989–90): 115–49.
———. *Studies on the Mysteries of Mañjuśrī: A Group of East Asian Mandalas and Their Traditional Symbolism.* Boulder, Colo.: Society for the Study of Chinese Religions, 1983.
———. "The Manifestation of a Monastery: Shen-Ying's Experiences on Mount Wu-t'ai in T'ang Context." *Journal of the American Oriental Society* 106, no. 1 (Jan.–March 1986): 119–37.
Blackburn, Anne. *Buddhist Learning and Textual Practice in Eighteenth-Century Lankan Monastic Culture.* Princeton, N.J.: Princeton University Press, 2001.
Bogel, Cynthea J. *With a Single Glance: Buddhist Icon and Early Mikkyō Vision.* Seattle: University of Washington, 2009.
Bourdieu, Pierre. *The Logics of Practice.* Translated by Richard Nice. Stanford: Stanford University Press, 1990.
Braudel, Fernand. *On History.* Translated by Sarah Matthews. Chicago: University of Chicago Press, 1980.
Brook, Timothy. *Geographical Sources of Ming-Qing History,* 2nd ed. Ann Arbor: Center for Chinese Studies, University of Michigan, 2002.
Brown, Peter. *The Cult of the Saints: Its Rise and Function in Latin Christianity.* Chicago: University of Chicago Press, 1981.
Brown, Robert L. "Expected Miracles: The Unsurprisingly Miraculous Nature of Buddhist Images and Relics." In *Images, Miracles, and Authority in Asian Religious Tradition,* edited by Richard H. Davis, 23–35. Boulder, Colo.: Westview Press, 1998.
Bynum, Caroline Walker. *Christian Materiality: An Essay on Religion in Late Medieval Europe.* New York: Zone Books, 2011.
Camille, Michael. "Mouths and Meanings: Towards an Anti-Iconography of Medieval Art." In *Iconography at the Crossroads: Papers from the Colloquium Sponsored by the Index of Christian Art, Princeton University, 23–24 March, 1990,* edited by Brendan Cassidy, 43–54. Princeton: Department of Art and Archaeology, Princeton University, 1993.
Campany, Robert F. *Strange Writing: Anomaly Accounts in Early Medieval China.* Albany: State University of New York Press, 1996.
———. "The Real Presence." *History of Religion* 32, no. 3 (February 1993): 233–72.

Cartelli, Mary Anne. "On a Five-Colored Cloud: The Songs of Mount Wutai." *Journal of the American Oriental Society* 124, no. 4 (2004): 735–57.

———. *The Five-Colored Clouds of Mount Wutai: Poems from Dunhuang.* Leiden: Brill, 2013.

———. "The Poetry of Mount Wutai: Chinese Buddhist Verse from Dunhuang." Ph.D. diss., Columbia University, 1999.

Casey, Edward S. *Getting Back into Space: Toward a Renewed Understanding of the Place-World.* 2nd ed. Bloomington: Indiana University Press, 2009.

———. *Representing Place: Landscape Painting and Maps.* Minneapolis: University of Minnesota Press, 2002.

———. *The Fate of Place: A Philosophical History.* Berkeley: University of California Press, 1998.

Caswell, James O. *Written and Unwritten: A New History of the Buddhist Caves at Yungang.* Vancouver: University of British Columbia Press, 1988.

Chai Zejun. *Chai Zejun gu jianzhu wenji* (Collection of papers by Chai Zejun on traditional architecture). Beijing: Wenwu Chubanshe, 1999.

———. "Foguangsi Dongdadian jianzhu xingzhi chuxi" (Preliminary analysis of the structure of the Great Eastern Hall of Foguang Monastery). In Chai, *Chai Zejun gu jianzhu wenji,* 90–95.

———. *Shanxi siguan bihua* (Temple murals in Shanxi). Beijing: Wenwu Chubanshe, 1997.

———. "Wutai Foguangsi" (Foguang Monastery at Wutai). In Chai, *Chai Zejun gu jianzhu wenji,* 78–89.

Chai Zejun and Chai Yumei. *Shanxi gudai caisu* (Painted clay statues in premodern Shanxi). Beijing: Wenwu Chubanshe, 2008.

Chappell, David W. "Chinese Buddhist Interpretations of the Pure Lands." In *Buddhist and Taoist Studies,* edited by Michael Saso and David W. Chappell, 23–53. Honolulu: University of Hawai'i Press, 1977.

———. "Early Forebodings of the Death of Buddhism." *Numen* 27 (1980): 122–53.

Chavannes, Edouard. *Le T'ai chan: Essai de monographie d'un culte chinois.* Paris: Ernest Leroux, 1910.

Chen, Huaiyu. *The Revival of Buddhist Monasticism in Medieval China.* New York: Peter Lang, 2007.

Chen, Jinhua. *Crossfire: Shingon-Tendai Strife as Seen in Two Twelfth-Century Polemics, with Special References to Their Background in Tang China.* Tokyo: International Institute for Buddhist Studies of the International College for Postgraduate Buddhist Studies, 2010.

———. *Monks and Monarchs, Kinship and Kingship: Tanqian in Sui Buddhism and Politics.* Kyoto: Scuola Italiana di Studi sull'Asia Orientale, 2002.

———. "More Than a Philosopher: Fazang (643–712) As a Politician and Miracle Worker," *History of Religion* 42, no. 4 (May 2003): 320–58.

———. "Śarīra and Scepter: Empress Wu's Political Use of Buddhist Relics." *Journal of the International Association of Buddhist Studies* 25, nos. 1–2 (2003): 33–150.

Chen Mingda, ed. *Gongxian, Tianlongshan, Xiangtangshan, Anyang shiku diaoke* (Sculp-

ture at Gongxian, Tianlongshan, Xiangtangshan, and Anyang caves). Beijing: Wenwu Chubanshe, 1986.
Chen Xiaolu. "Xiyu huizixing fosi yuanliu kao" (An investigation on the development of monasteries of the corridor style in the Western Region). *Kaogu*, no. 11 (2010): 79–90.
Chen Yangjiong and Feng Qiaoying, eds. *Gu Qingliang zhuan, Guang Qingliang zhuan, Xu Qingliang zhuan* (Ancient records of [Mount] Qingliang, Extended records of [Mount] Qingliang, and Continued records of [Mount] Qingliang). Taiyuan: Shanxi Renmin Chubanshe, 1989.
Chenru. "Dunhuang busa wen yu busa cidi xintan" (A new probe into the *busa* texts and *busa* procedures). *Dunhuang yanjiu*, no. 1 (1991): 120–132.
Chiba Shōkan. "Fukū no mikkyō ni okeru bucchōson no ichi zuke" (Positioning Amoghavajra's esoteric Buddhism in the [teachings of] the superlative Buddha's crown). *Taishō daigaku sōgō bukkyō kenkyūjo nenpō* 9 (1987): 33–48.
———. "Fukū no mikkyō to Kinkakuji" (Amoghavajra's Esoteric Buddism and Jin'ge Monastery). *Indogaku bukkyōgaku kenkyū* 35, no. 2 (1987): 173–75.
Choi Bok-hee. "Godaisan Monju shinkō ni okeru kagen" (Transformative manifestation in the Mañjuśrī cult at Mount Wutai). *Bukkyō daigaku daigakuin kiyō* 33 (March 2005): 15–29.
———. "Koseryōden kara kōseryōden e no Monju shinkō no hensen: Monju gainen o chūshin ni" (Changes in belief in Mañjuśrī as seen from the *Ancient Records* [compared] to the *Extended Records:* Centering on the concept of Mañjuśrī). *Indogaku bukkyōgaku kenkyū* 52, no. 1 (2003): 192–94.
Choi, Eung-chon. "Early Korean and Japanese Reliquaries in Relation to Pagoda Architecture," in *Transmitting the Forms of Divinity: Early Buddhist Art from Korea and Japan,* edited by Washizuka Hiromitsu, Park Youngbok, and Kang Woo-Bang, 178–89. New York: Japan Society Gallery, 2003.
Choi, Sun-ah. "Quest for the True Visage: Sacred Images in Medieval Chinese Buddhist Art and the Concept of *Zhen*." Ph.D. diss., University of Chicago, 2012.
Chou, Wen-shing. "Ineffable Paths: Mapping Wutaishan in Qing Dynasty China." *Art Bulletin* 89, no. 1 (March 2007): 108–29.
Chou, Yi-liang. "Tantrism in China." *Harvard Journal of Asiatic Studies* 8, nos. 3–4 (1945): 241–332.
Christian, William A., Jr. *Apparitions in Late Medieval and Renaissance Spain.* Princeton, N.J.: Princeton University Press, 1981.
Coakley, Sarah, ed. *Religion and the Body.* Cambridge: Cambridge University Press, 1997.
Cohen, Moique, and Nathalie Monnet. *Impressions de la Chine.* Paris: Bibliothèque Nationale, 1992.
Coleman, Simon, and John Elsner, eds. *Pilgrimage: Past and Present in the World Religions.* Cambridge, Mass.: Harvard University Press, 1995.
Collins, Steven. *Nirvana and Other Buddhist Felicities.* Cambridge: Cambridge University Press, 1998.
Conze, Edward. *Buddhism, Its Essence and Development.* New York: Harper, 1959.

Coomaraswamy, Ananda K. "The Origin of the Buddha Image." *Art Bulletin* 9, no. 4 (1927): 287–329.

Copp, Paul F. "Voice, Dust, Shadow, Stone: The Makings of Spells in Medieval Chinese Buddhism." Ph.D. diss., Princeton University, 2005.

Crossley, Paul. "Medieval Architecture and Meaning: The Limits of Iconography." *Burlington Magazine* 80 (Feb. 1988): 116–21.

Cui Zhengsen. *Wutaishan fojiao shi* (The history of Buddhism at Mount Wutai). 2 vols. Taiyuan: Shanxi Renmin Chubanshe, 2000.

Cui Zhengsen and Wang Zhichao, eds. *Wutaishan beiwen xuanzhu* (Selected stele inscriptions from Mount Wutai, with annotations). Taiyuan: Beiyue Wenyi, 1995.

Dallapiccola, Anna L., and Stephanie Zingel-Avé Lallemant, eds. *The Stūpa: Its Religious, Historical and Architectural Significance.* Wiesbaden: Franz Steiner, 1980.

Daozang (Daoist canon). 36 vols. Beijing: Wenwu Chubanshe; Shanghai: Shanghai Shuju; Tianjin: Tianjin Guji Chubanshe, 1988.

Datongshi Bowuguan. "Datong Beiwei Fangshan Siyuan Fosi yizhi fajue baogao" (The excavation report on the site of Siyuan Fosi of the Northern Wei at Mount Fang near Datong). *Wenwu*, no. 4 (2007): 4–26.

———. "Datong Fangshan Beiwei Yongguling" (Yongu Mausoleum of the Northern Wei at Mount Fang). *Wenwu*, no. 7 (1978): 29–35.

Davidson, J. Leroy. *The Lotus Sutra in Chinese Art: A Study in Buddhist Art to the Year 1000.* New Haven, Conn.: Yale University Press, 1954.

Davidson, Ronald M. "Some Observations on the Uṣṇīṣa Abhiṣeka Rites in Atikūṭa's Dhāraṇīsaṃgraha." In *Transformations and Transfer of Tantra: Tantrism in Asia and Beyond,* edited by István Keul, 77–97. Berlin: Walter de Gruyter, 2011.

Davies, Wendy et al., eds. *People and Space in the Middle Ages, 300–1300.* Turnhout: Brepols, 2006.

De Certeau, Michel. "Hagiographie." In *Encyclopedia Universalis*, vol. 11, 164. Paris: Encyclopædia Universalis France, 1992.

———. "Practices of Space." In *On Signs,* edited by Marshall Blonsky, 122–45. Baltimore, Md.: Johns Hopkins University Press, 1985.

———. *The Practice of Everyday Life.* Translated by Steven Rendall. Berkeley: University of California Press, 1984.

Debreczeny, Karl. "Wutaishan: Pilgrimage to Five Peak Mountain," *Journal of the International Association of Tibetan Studies* 6 (Dec. 2011): 1–133.

Dien, Albert E. *Six Dynasties Civilization.* New Haven, Conn.: Yale University Press, 2007.

———. "The Historical Background of the Eastern Wei and Northern Qi States." In Tsiang, *Echoes of the Past,* 80–91.

Dodgshon, Robert A. *Society in Time and Space: A Geographical Perspective on Change.* Cambridge: Cambridge University Press, 1998.

Dohi Yoshikazu. "Kigigun jidai" (The period of the Return to Allegiance Army). In *Tonkō no rekishi,* edited by Enoki Kazuo, 233–96. Tokyo: Daitō Shuppansha, 1980.

Dott, Brian R. *Identity Reflections: Pilgrimages to Mount Tai in Late Imperial China.* Cambridge, Mass.: Harvard University Press, 2004.

Du Doucheng. *Dunhuang Wutaishan wenxian jiaolu yanjiu* (Textual sources related to Mount Wutai from Dunhuang: Annotations and research). Taiyuan: Shanxi Renmin Chubanshe, 1991.

Du Jinpeng, and Qian Guoxiang, eds. *Han Wei Luoyang cheng yizhi yanjiu* (Research on the historical site of Luoyang during the Han and Wei Dynasties). Beijing: Kexue Chubanshe, 2007.

Duan Wenjie. "Mogaoku wanqi de yishu" (Art in the later-period Mogao caves). In Dunhuang Wenwu Yanjiusuo, *Dunhuang Mogao ku,* vol. 5, 161–74.

Dunhuang Wenwu Yanjiusuo. *Dunhuang Mogaoku* (Mogao caves in Dunhuang). 5 vols. Beijing: Wenwu Chubanshe, 1981.

Dunhuang Yanjiusuo. "Mogaoku di 220 ku xin faxian de fubi bihua" (The newly uncovered underlying mural inside Mogao Cave 220). *Wenwu,* no. 12 (1978): 41–46.

Durkheim, Emile. *The Elementary Forms of Religious Life.* Translated by Carol Cosman. Oxford: Oxford University Press, 2001.

Dutt, Sukumar. *Buddhist Monks and Monasteries of India.* London: G. Allen and Unwin, 1962.

Eade, John, and Michael J. Sallnow, eds. *Contesting the Sacred: The Anthropology of Pilgrimage.* Urbana: University of Illinois Press, 2000.

Eck, Diana L. "Mountains." In Jones, *Encyclopedia of Religion,* vol. 9, 6212–15.

Eckel, Malcolm David. *To See the Buddha: A Philosopher's Quest for the Meaning of Emptiness.* New York: HarperCollins, 1992.

Eliade, Mircea. *The Sacred and Profane: The Nature of Religion.* Translated by Willard R. Trask. New York: Harcourt, Brace and World, 1959.

Evans, Robin. *Translations from Drawing to Building.* Cambridge, Mass.: MIT Press, 1997.

Fairbank, John King, and Denis Crispin Twitchett, eds. *The Cambridge History of China.* 15 vols. Cambridge: Cambridge University Press, 1978.

Fairbank, Wilma. *Liang and Lin: Partners in Exploring China's Architectural Past.* Philadelphia: University of Pennsylvania Press, 1994.

Fan Peisong. "Zhongguo siyuan xingzhi ji buju tedian" (The forms and characteristics of arrangements of Chinese monasteries). *Kaogu yu wenwu,* no. 2 (2000): 82–88.

Fan Xiangyong, ed. *Luoyang qielan ji jiaozhu* (Annotations to the *Record of the Monasteries of Luoyang*). Shanghai: Shanghai Guji Chubanshe, 1958.

Farquhar, David M. "Emperor as Bodhisattva in the Governance of the Ch'ing Empire." *Harvard Journal of Asiatic Studies* 38, no. 1 (1978): 5–34.

Faure, Bernard. "Space and Place in Chinese Religious Traditions." *History of Religions* 26, no. 4 (1987): 337–56.

———. *Visions of Power: Imagining Medieval Japanese Buddhism.* Translated by Phyllis Brooks. Princeton, N.J.: Princeton University Press, 1996.

Feng, Jiren. *Chinese Architecture and Metaphor: Song Culture in the* Yingzao Fashi *Building Manual.* Honolulu: University of Hawai'i Press, 2012.

Forte, Antonino. "Hui-chih (fl. 676–703 AD), a Brahmin Born in China." *Annali dell'Istituto Universitario Orientale* 45 (1985): 106–34.

———. *Political Propaganda and Ideology in China at the end of the Seventh Century.* Naples: Istituto Universitario Orientale, 1976.

———. "The South Indian Monk Bodhiruci (d. 727): Biographic Evidence." In *A Life Journey to the East: Sinological Studies in Memory of Guiliano Bertuccioli (1923–2001),* edited by Antonino Forte and Federico Masini, 145–66. Kyoto: Italian School of East Asian Studies, 2002.

Foulk, T. Griffith. "Daily Life in the Assembly." In *Buddhism in Practice,* edited by Donald S. Lopez Jr, 455–72. Princeton, N.J.: Princeton University Press, 1995.

Fraser, Sarah E. *Performing the Visual: The Practice of Buddhist Wall Painting in China and Central Asia, 618–960.* Stanford, Calif.: Stanford University Press, 2004.

Freedberg, David. *The Power of Image: Studies in the History and Theory of Response.* Chicago: University of Chicago Press, 1989.

Fu Shumin. "Wutaishan shidengtai kao" (On the stone lantern from Mount Wutai). *Wutaishan yanjiu,* no. 1 (1987): 25–27.

Fu Xinian. *Fu Xinian jianzhu shi lunwen ji* (Paper collection of Fu Xinian's work on architectural history). Beijing: Wenwu Chubanshe, 1998.

———. *Liangjin, Nanbeichao, Sui Tang, Wudai Jianzhu* ([History of] architecture during the East Jin and West Jin, Northern and Southern dynasties, Sui and Tang, and Five Dynasties). Beijing: Jianzhu Gongye Chubanshe, 2001.

———. "Maijishan shiku zhong suo fanying chu de beichao jianzhu" (Architecture of the Northern Dynasties as reflected in the rock-cut caves at Mount Maiji). In Fu, *Fu Xinian jianzhu shi lunwen ji,* 103–35.

———. "The Three Kingdoms, Western and Eastern Jin, and Northern and Southern Dynasties," in Steinhardt, *Chinese Architecture,* 61–89.

———. "Wutaishan Foguangsi jianzhu" (Architecture of Foguang Monastery at Mount Wutai). In Fu, *Fu Xinian jianzhu shi lunwen ji,* 234–44.

———. *Zhongguo kexue jishushi: Jianzhu juan* (History of Chinese technology: Architecture). Beijing: Kexue Chubanshe, 2008.

———. "Zhongguo zaoqi fojiao jianzhu buju yanbian ji diannei xiangshe de buzhi" (The development of architectural dispositions in early Buddhist architecture and the arrangement of statues inside the [image] halls). In Fu, *Fu Xinian jianzhu shi lunwen ji,* 136–46.

Fujiyoshi Masumi. "Meppōka toshite no Narendaireiyasha—Shū Zui kakumei to tokugochōjakyō" (Narendrayaśas, an advocate of the *mofa*—[Northern] Zhou and Sui revolution and *Sutra of Candraprabha-kumāru*). *Tōyōshi kenkyū* 46, no. 1 (1987): 29–56.

Fukui Kōjun. "Butsuji no jigi" (Literal meanings of [the term] monastery). In *Tōyō shisōshi kenkyū,* 196–97. Tokyo: Shoseki Bunbutsu Ryūtsūkai, 1960.

Gernet, Jacques. *Buddhism in Chinese Society: An Economic History from the Fifth to the Tenth Centuries.* New York: Columbia University Press, 1995.

Gimello, Robert M. "Chang Shang-ying on Wu-t'ai Shan." In Naquin and Yü, eds., *Pilgrims and Sacred Sites in China,* 89–149.

———. "Ch'eng-kuan's Meditations on the 'Three Holy Ones.'" In *Kegongaku ronshū,* edited by Kamata Shigeo, 1066–148. Tokyo: Daizō shuppan, 1997.

———. "Li T'ung Hsüan and Practical Dimension of Hua-yen." In *Studies in Ch'an and Hua-yen*, eds. Robert M. Gimello and Peter N. Gregory, 323–61. Honolulu: University of Hawai'i, 1983.

———. "Wu-t'ai Shan during the Early Chin Dynasty: The Testimony of Chu Pien." *Chung-Hwa Buddhist Journal*, no. 7 (1994): 501–612.

Gjertson, Donald E. *Miraculous Retribution: A Study and Translation of T'ang Lin's Ming-pao chi.* Berkeley: University of California Press, 1989.

Glahn, Else. "On the Transmission of the Ying-Tsao Fa-Shih [*Yingzao fashi*]," *T'oung Pao* 61, nos. 4–5 (1974): 232–65.

Goodman, Felicitas D. "Visions." In Jones, *Encyclopedia of Religion*, vol. 14, 9611–17.

Goodson, Caroline, et al., eds. *Cities, Texts, and Social Networks, 400–1500: Experiences and Perceptions of Medieval Urban Space.* Burlington, Vt.: Ashgate, 2010.

Grapard, Allan G. *The Protocol of the Gods: A Study of the Kasuga Cult in Japanese History.* Berkeley: University of California Press, 1992.

Greene, Eric Matthew. "Meditation, Repentance, and Visionary Experience in Early Medieval Chinese Buddhism." Ph.D. diss., University of California, Berkeley, 2012.

Gu Zhengmei. "Tangdai Wutai Wenshu xinyang de dianji zhe: Wu Zetian" (Wu Zetian: The foundation builder of the Mañjuśrī cult at Mount Wutai during the Tang). In *Cong tianwang chuantong dao fowang chuantong: Zhongguo zhongshiji fojiao zhiguo yishi xingtai yanjiu*, 378–424. Taipei: Shangzhou Chubanshe, 2003.

Guisso, Richard. *Wu Tse-t'ien and the Politics of Legitimation in T'ang China.* Bellingham: University of Western Washington Press, 1978.

Guo, Qinghua. "Yingzao Fashi: Twelfth-Century Chinese Building Manual," *Architectural History* 41 (1998): 1–13.

Guo, Zhicheng. "Wutai Shan—A Museum of Chinese Temples." *Orientations* 27, no. 5 (May 1996): 64–66.

Guojia Tushuguan Shanben Jinshizu. *Lidai shike shiliao huibian* (A collection of historical documents from stone inscriptions of each of the dynasties). 6 vols. Beijing: Beijing Tushuguan, 2003.

Ha Lei. *Si nianchu yanjiu* (Research on *si nianchu*). Chendu: Bashu Shushe, 2006.

Hahn, Thomas H. "Daoist Sacred Sites." In *Daoism Handbook*, edited by Livia Kohn, 683–708. Leiden: Brill, 2000.

Hallisey, Charles Stephen. "Devotion in the Buddhist Literature of Medieval Sri Lanka." Ph.D. diss., University of Chicago, 1988.

Hanawalt, Barbara H., and Michal Kobialka, eds. *Medieval Practices of Space.* Minneapolis: University of Minnesota Press, 2000.

Handanshi Wenwu Baoguansuo. "Handan Gushan Shuiyusi shiku diaocha baogao" (Report on a survey of the Caves at Shuiyu Monastery at Mount Gu, Handan). *Wenwu*, no. 4 (1987): 1–23.

———. "Hebei Handan Gushan Changlesi yizhi qingli baogao" (Investigation report on the historical site of the former Changle Monastery at Mount Gu in Handan, Hebei). *Wenwu*, no. 10 (1982): 26–43.

Hargett, James M. *Stairway to Heaven: A Journey to the Summit of Mount Emei.* Albany: State University of New York Press, 2006.

Harrison, Paul, trans. *The Pratyutpanna Samādhi Sutra*. Berkeley, Calif.: Numata Center, 1998.

———. *The Samādhi of Direct Encounter with the Buddhas of the Present*. Tokyo: International Institute for Buddhist Studies, 1990.

Harrist, Robert E., Jr. *The Landscape of Words: Stone Inscriptions from Early and Medieval China*. Seattle: University of Washington Press, 2008.

Harvey, David. *Justice, Nature, and the Geography of Difference*. Cambridge, Mass.: Blackwell Publishers, 1996.

Hattori Hōshō. "Monju shūri hatsu Nehangyō to kangyōrui" (*Mañjuśrī-parinirvāṇa-sūtra* and the category of visualization sutras). *Indogaku bukkyōgaku kenkyū* 39, no. 1 (1990): 111–13.

Hazra, Kanai Lal. *Buddhism in India as Described by the Chinese Pilgrims,* AD *399–689*. New Delhi, Munshiram Manoharlal Publishers, 2002.

He Pingli. *Chongshan linian yu Zhongguo wenhua* (Ideas of mountain worship and Chinese culture). Ji'nan: Qilu Shushe, 2001.

He Yeju. *Zhongguo gudai chengshi guihuashi* (History of city planning in ancient China). Beijing: Zhongguo Gongye Chubanshe, 1996.

Heidegger, Martin. *Poetry, Language, Thought*. Translated by Albert Hofstadter. New York: Harper & Row, 1971.

Heller, Natasha. "Visualizing Pilgrimage and Mapping Experience: Mount Wutai on the Silk Road." In *The Journey of Maps and Images on the Silk Road,* edited by Philippe Forêt and Andreas Kaplony, 29–50. Leiden: Brill, 2008.

Henansheng Gudai Jianzhu Baohu Yanjiusuo. *Baoshan Lingquansi* (Lingquan Monastery at Mount Bao). Zhengzhou: Henan Renmin Chubanshe, 1991.

———. "Henan Anyang Lingquansi shiku ji Xiaonanhai shiku" (Caves at Lingquan Monastery and Xiaonanhai Caves in Anyang, Henan), *Wenwu,* no. 4 (1988): 1–20.

Henansheng Wenwu Yanjiusuo. *Gongxian shiku si* (Cave monasteries in Gongxian). Beijing: Wenwu Chubanshe, 1989.

Henderson, Gregory, and Leon Hurvitz. "The Buddha of Seiryōji: New Finds and New Theory." *Artibus Asiae* 19, no. 1 (1956): 4–55.

Hibino Takeo. "Tonkō no Godaisan zu ni tsuite" (On the representation of Mount Wutai in Dunhuang). *Bukkyō geijutsu,* no. 34 (May 1958): 75–86.

Hicks, Dan, and Mary C. Beaudry, eds. *The Oxford Handbook of Material Culture Studies*. Oxford: Oxford University Press, 2010.

Hida Romi. "Ryōshō Bankaken zuizō no setsuwa to zōkei" (Tales and forms of Fanhe *ruixiang* in Liangzhou). *Bukkyō bijutsu,* 217 (Nov. 1994): 33–54.

Hirokawa Takatoshi. "Reisan" (Ritual eulogy). In Makita and Fukui, *Tonkō to Chūgoku bukkyō,* 451–563.

Ho, Pingti. "Lo-yang, A.D. 495–534: A Study of Physical and Socio-Economic Planning of a Metropolitan Area." *Harvard Journal of Asiatic Studies* 26 (1966): 52–101.

Ho, Puay-Peng. "Architecture and Legitimacy in the Court of Wu Zhao." In *Politics and Religion in Ancient and Medieval Europe and China,* edited by Frederick Hok-ming Cheung and Ming-chiu Lai, 101–26. Hong Kong: Chinese University Press, 1999.

———. "Building for Glitter and Eternity: The Works of the Late Ming Master Builder Miaofeng on Wutai Shan." *Orientations* 27, no. 5 (May 1996): 67–73.

———. "Chinese Buddhist Monastic Architecture in the Sui and Tang Dynasties: A Study of the Spatial Conception." Ph.D. diss., University of London, 1992.

———. "The Ideal Monastery: Daoxuan's Description of the Central Indian Jetavana Vihāra." *East Asian History* 10 (Dec. 1995): 1–18.

———. "Paradise on Earth: Architectural Depiction in Pure Land Illustrations of High Tang Caves at Dunhuang." *Oriental Art* 41 (1995): 22–32.

———. "The Symbolism of the Central Pillars in Cave-Temples of Northwest China." *Cosmos: Sacred Architecture in the Traditions of India, China, Judaism, and Islam* 8 (1992): 59–70.

Holmgren, Jennifer. "Empress Dowager Ling of the Northern Wei and the T'o-pa Sinicization Question." *Papers on Far Eastern History* 18 (1978): 123–70.

Hou Wenzheng, ed. *Wutaishan zhi* (Gazetteer of Mount Wutai). Taiyuan: Shanxi Renmin Chubanshe, 2003.

Hou Xudong. *Wu liu shiji beifang minzhong fojiao xinyang: yi zaoxiang ji wei zhongxin de kaocha* (Buddhist beliefs among common people in northern China during the fifth and sixth centuries: an investigation centered around dedicatory inscriptions about making images). Beijing: Zhongguo Shehui Kexue Chubanshe, 1998.

Hourihane, Colum, ed. *Looking Beyond: Visions, Dreams, and Insights in Medieval Art and History.* Princeton: Index of Christian Art, Princeton University, 2010.

Howard, Angela F. "Liang Patronage of Buddhist Art in the Gansu Corridor during the Fourth Century and the Transformation of a Central Asian Style." In *Between Han and Tang: Religious Art and Archaeology in a Transformative Period,* edited by Wu Hung, 235–272. Beijing: Cultural Relics Publishing House, 2000.

Hsu, Eileen Hsiang-ling. "The Sengchou Cave and Early Imagery of Sukhāvatī." *Artibus Asiae* 72, no. 1 (2012): 283–323.

———. "The Xiaonanhai Cave-Chapel: Images of Deeds and Aspirations." Ph.D. diss., Columbia University, 1999.

Huang, Shi-shan Susan. *Picturing the True Form: Daoist Visual Culture in Traditional China.* Cambridge, Mass.: Harvard University Asia Center, 2012.

Hubbard, Jamie. *Absolute Delusion, Perfect Buddhahood: The Rise and Fall of a Chinese Heresy.* Honolulu: University of Hawai'i Press, 2001.

Huber, Toni. *The Holy Land Reborn: Pilgrimage and the Tibetan Reinvention of Buddhist India.* Chicago: University of Chicago Press, 2008.

Hucker, Charles O. *A Dictionary of Official Titles in Imperial China.* Stanford, Calif.: Stanford University Press, 1985.

Hurvitz, Leon. *Scripture of the Lotus Blossom of the Fine Dharma.* New York: Columbia University Press, 1976.

Ibuki Atsushi. "Tōsō Eshō ni tsuite" (Regarding the Tang monk Huixiang). *Waseta daigaku daigakuin bungaku kenkyūjo kiyō,* special issue no. 4 (1988): 33–45.

Inada Yasuo. "Shōnankai chūkutsu to Sōchū zenshi" (Xiaonanhai Central Cave and Chan Master Sengchou). In *Hokuchō Zui Tō Chūgoku bukkyō shisōshi,* edited by Aramaki Tenshun, 270–307. Kyoto: Hōzōkan, 2000.

Inoue Akemi. "Kyōten to zuzō: Monju bosatsu ni kanshite" (Scriptures and iconography: Regarding Bodhisattva Mañjuśrī). *Mikkyō zuzō* 3 (Dec. 1984): 41–58.

Inoue Ichii. "Godaisan shi no issetsu" (One section of the history of Mount Wutai). *Rekishi to chiri* 18, no. 2 (Feb. 1925): 7–19; 18, no. 4 (April 1925): 14–27; 19, no. 1 (Jan. 1926): 96–107; 20, no. 4 (April 1927): 32–47.

———. "Rosan bunka to Eon" (Mountain culture at Mount Lu and Huiyuan). *Shien*, no. 9 (1934): 1–34.

———. "Tōdai ni okeru Godaisan no bukkyō" (Tang Buddhism at Mount Wutai). *Rekishi to chiri* 21, no. 5 (May 1928): 1–19; 22, no. 6 (June 1929): 14–27; 24, no. 2 (Feb. 1931): 58–75; 24, no. 3 (March 1931): 33–39.

Itō Chūta. *Tōyō kenchiku no kenkyū* (Research on the history of oriental architecture). 2 vols. Tokyo: Ryūginsha, 1943.

Iwamoto Hiroshi. "Fukū sanzō to Daikōzenji Monjukaku ni tsuite" (Regarding Amoghavajra Tipiṭaka and the Mañjuśrī Pavilion at Da Xingshan Monastery). *Mikkyō gakkaihō*, no. 34 (1995): 61–80.

Jiang Fengrong. "Taishan Jingshigu moya kejing kao" (An investigation on *moya* carvings at Jingshigu of Mount Tai). In *Beichao moya kejing yanjiu*, 227–41. Jinan: Qilu Shushe, 1991.

Jin Weinuo. "Dunhuang ku kan mingsu kao" (A study of the list of names of Dunhuang caves and niches). *Wenwu*, no. 5 (1959): 50–54, 61.

———. *Zhongguo meishushi lunji* (Essays on Chinese art history). Beijing: Renmin Meishu Chubanshe, 1981.

Jones, Lindsay, ed. *Encyclopedia of Religion*, 2nd ed. 15 vols. Detroit: Macmillan Reference, 2005.

Juliano, Annette L. "Buddhist Art in Northwest China." In *Monks and Merchants: Silk Road Treasures from Northwest China*, edited by Annette L. Juliano and Judith A. Lerner, 119–43. New York: Harry N. Abrams and Asia Society, 2002.

Kajiyama, Yuichi. "Stūpa, the Mother of Buddhas, and Dharma-Body." In *New Paths in Buddhist Research*, edited by Anthony Kennedy Warder, 9–16. Durham, N.C.: Acorn, 1985.

Kanazawa Keimei. "Shoki Chūgoku bukkyō no sai ni tsuite" (On Buddhist ritual purification in early China). *Tōhō shūkyō*, no. 63 (May 1984): 55–63.

Karlsson, Klemens. *Face to Face with the Absent Buddha: The Formation of Buddhist Aniconic Art*. Uppsala, Sweden: Uppsala University, 1999.

Kieschnick, John. *The Eminent Monk: Buddhist Ideals in Medieval Chinese Hagiography*. Honolulu: University of Hawai'i Press, 1997.

———. *The Impact of Buddhism on Chinese Material Culture*. Princeton, N.J.: Princeton University Press, 2003.

King, Winston L. "Theravāda in Southeast Asia." In *Buddhist Spirituality: Indian, Southeast Asian, Tibetan, and Early Chinese*, edited by Yoshinori Takeuchi and Jan van Bragt, 79–92. New York: Crossroad, 1993.

Kleeman, Terry F. "Mountain Deities in China: The Domestication of the Mountain God and the Subjugation of the Margins." *Journal of the American Oriental Society* 114, no. 2 (April–June 1994): 226–38.

Knapp, Keith. "Did the Middle Kingdom Have a Middle Period? The Problem of 'Medieval' in China's History." *Education About Asia* 12, no. 2 (Fall 2007): 8–13.

Koh, Seunghak. "Li Tongxuan's (635–730) Thought and His Place in the Huayan Tradition of Chinese Buddhism." Ph.D. diss., University of California at Los Angeles, 2011.

Köhle, Natalie. "Why Did the Kangxi Emperor Go to Wutai Shan? Patronage, Pilgrimage, and the Place of Tibetan Buddhism at the Early Qing Court." *Late Imperial China* 29, no. 1 (June 2008): 73–119.

Kohn, Livia. *Monastic Life in Medieval Daoism: A Cross-Cultural Perspective.* Honolulu: University of Hawai'i Press, 2003.

Kojima Taisan. "Ri Tsūgen ni okeru kōmyō shisō no tenkai" (The development of the thoughts on light by Li Tongxuan). *Kegongaku kenkyū*, no. 2 (Oct. 1988): 189–282.

Kroll, Paul W. *Dharma Bell and Dhāraṇī Pillar: Li Po's Buddhist Inscriptions.* Kyoto: Scuola Italiana di Studi sull'Asia Orientale, 2001.

Kumoi Shōzen. "Hōmetsu shisō no genryū" (The origins and transmissions of the ideas of *mofa*). In *Hokugi bukkyō no kenkyū,* edited by Ōchō Enichi, 287–300. Kyoto: Heirakuji Shoten, 1970.

Kuo Liying. "Bucchōsonshō darani no denpa to gishiki" (The Dissemination and Rituals of the *Sutra of the Superlative Dhāraṇī of the Buddha's Crown*). *Tendai gakuhō* (October 2007): 1–39.

Kyan, Winston. "Family Space: Buddhist Materiality and Ancestral Fashioning in Mogao Cave 231." *Art Bulletin* 92, nos. 1–2 (March–June 2010): 61–82.

Lai, Whalen. "Society and the Sacred in the Secular City: Temple Legends of the Lo-yang Ch'ieh-lan-chi." In *State and Society in Early Medieval China,* edited by Albert E. Dien, 229–68. Stanford, Calif.: Stanford University Press, 1990.

Lamotte, Étienne. "Mañjuśrī." *T'oung Pao* 48, nos. 1–3 (1960): 1–96.

Lancaster, Lewis R. "An Early Mahayana Sermon about the Body of the Buddha and the Making of Images." *Artibus Asiae* 36, no. 4 (1974): 287–91.

Ledderose, Lothar. *Ten Thousand Things: Module and Mass Production in Chinese Art.* Princeton, N.J.: Princeton University Press, 2000.

———. "Thunder Sound Cave." In *Between Han and Tang: Visual and Material Culture in a Transformative Period,* edited by Wu Hung, 235–60. Beijing: Cultural Relics Publishing House, 2003.

Lee, Sonya S. "Repository of Ingenuity: Cave 61 and Artistic Appropriation in Tenth-Century Dunhuang." *Art Bulletin* 94, no. 2 (June 2012): 199–225.

———. *Surviving Nirvana: Death of the Buddha in Chinese Visual Culture.* Hong Kong: Hong Kong University Press, 2010.

———. "Transmitting Buddhism to a Future Age: The Leiyin Cave at Fangshan and Cave-Temples with Stone Scriptures in Sixth-Century China." *Archives of Asian Art* 60 (2010): 43–78.

Lee Yü-ming. "Baoshan Dazhusheng ku chutan" (An initial investigation on Dazhusheng Cave at Mount Bao). *Gugong xueshu jikan* 16, no. 2 (1998): 1–51.

Lefebvre, Henri. *The Production of Space.* Translated by Donald Nicholson-Smith. Cambridge, Mass.: Blackwell, 1991.

Lehnert, Martin. "Amoghavajra." In Orzech et al., *Esoteric Buddhism*, 351–59.

Lewis, Mark Edward. *The Construction of Space in Early China*. Albany: State University of New York Press, 2006.

———. "The *Feng* and *Shan* Sacrifices of Emperor Wu of the Han." In *State and Court Ritual in China*, edited by Joseph Peter McDermott, 50–80. Cambridge: Cambridge University Press, 1999.

Li Chongfeng. *Zhong Yin fojiao shikusi bijiao yanjiu: yi tamiao ku wei zhongxin* (Indian and Chinese Buddhist Chaityagharas: A comparative study). Xinzhu, Taiwan: Juefeng Fojiao Yishu Wenhua Jijinhui, 2001.

Li Dehua. "Tangdai fojiao siyuan zhi ziyuan qianxi: yi *Youyang zazu* weili" (An initial analysis of the subcloister in Tang monasteries: Taking *Miscellany of Youyang Mountains* as an example). *Zhongguo jianzhu shilun huikan* 6 (2013): 63–85.

Li, Li. "The Artistic and Period Characteristics of Sculptures Found at the Yongning Pagoda in Luoyang." In *Between Han and Tang:* Religious Art and Archaeology in a Transformative Period, edited by Wu Hung, 353–75. Beijing: Cultural Relics Publishing House, 2000.

Li Ping. *Beiwei Pingcheng shiqi* (The period of the Northern Wei in Pingcheng). Beijing: Shehui Kexue Wenxian Chubanshe, 2000.

Li Ruoshui. "Tang Chang'an Da Xingshansi Wenshu ge yingjian gongcheng fuyuan yanjiu" (Research to reconstruct the building project for the Mañjuśrī Pavilion of Da Xingshan Monastery in Chang'an of the Tang). *Zhongguo jianzhu shilun huikan* 6 (2013): 135–58.

Li Sheng. *Xianjing xinyang yanjiu* (Research on beliefs in the lands of immortals). Chengdu: Bashu Shushe, 2010.

Li Yongning. "Dunhuang Mogaoku di 159 ku Wensu, Puxian fuhui tu: Mogao ku di 159 ku chutan zhi yi" (Murals of Mañjuśrī and Samantabhadra arriving to attend the assembly in Mogao Cave 159, Dunhuang: Initial investigation of Mogao Cave 159, part 1). *Dunhuang yanjiu*, no. 4 (1993): 26–30.

Li Yuqun. "Sui Tang yiqian Zhongguo fojiao siyuan de kongjian buju jiqi yanbian" (The spatial arrangement of Chinese Buddhist monasteries and its development before the Sui-Tang period). *Bianjiang minzu kaogu yu minzu kaoguxue jikan* 1 (2009), 287–311.

———. "Jinyang Xishan dafo he Tongzisi dafo de chubu kaocha" (An initial investigation on the colossal Buddha at Xishan, Jinyang, and the colossal Buddha at Tongzi Monastery). *Wenwu jikan*, no. 1 (1998): 14–28.

Li Yuqun and Li Gang. *Tianlongshan shiku* (Caves at Mount Tianlong). Beijing: Kexue Chubanshe, 2003.

Li Yuqun and Yan Yaojin. "Taiyuanshi Longshan Tongzisi yizhi fajue jianbao" (A brief excavation report on the site of the former Tongzi Monastery at Longshan in the City of Taiyuan). *Kaogu*, no. 7 (2010): 43–56.

Li Zhengyu. "Yindu Puhua dashi Wutaishan xunliji" (Indian Master Puhua's pilgrimage at Mount Wutai). *Wutaishan yanjiu*, no. 1 (1990): 32–33.

Lian Kaowen. "Huixiang 'Langu shamen' yiduan" (Speculations on Huixiang, "the monk of Langu"). *Wutaishan yanjiu*, no. 2 (1992): 32–33.

Liang Sicheng. "Ji Wutaishan Foguangsi de jianzhu" (Notes on the architecture of Foguang Monastery at Mount Wutai). *Wenwu cankao ziliao* 5–6 (1953): 76–121.

———. "Ji Wutaishan Foguangsi jianzhu" (Notes on the architecture of Foguang Monastery at Mount Wutai). *Zhongguo yingzao xueshe huikan* 7, no. 1 (1944): 13–62, and no. 2 (1944): 1–20.

———. "Jixian Dulesi Guanyinge shanmen kao" (On the Guanyin Pavilion and entrance gate of Dule Monastery, Jixian). *Zhongguo yingzao xueshe huikan* 3, no. 2 (1932): 1–88.

Liang, Ssu-ch'eng (Sicheng). *A Pictorial History of Chinese Architecture: A Study of the Development of Its Structural System and Evolution of Its Types,* edited by Wilma Fairbank. Cambridge, Mass.: MIT Press, 1984).

Lin, Wei-Cheng. "Bei 'shentihua' de sheli fozhi: cong Famensi digong de 'zhenshen sheli' tang Zhongguo sheli yicang yu muzang" (Corporealized relics: Chinese relic depository and burial as seen from the "true body relics" uncovered from Famen Monastery). *Diancang gumeishu,* no. 218 (Nov. 2010): 162–69.

———. "Preserving China: Liang Sicheng's Survey Photos from 1930s and 1940s China," *Visual Resources* 27, no. 2 (June 2011): 129–45.

———. "Relocating and Relocalizing Mount Wutai: Vision and Visuality in Mogao Cave 61." *Artibus Asiae* 71, no. 1 (2013): 77–136.

———. "Screening the Chinese Interior: Architectonic and *Architecturesque.*" In *The Screen in East Asia and Beyond,* edited by Ping Foong and Chelsea Foxwell. Chicago: Center for the Art of East Asian, University of Chicago, forthcoming.

———. "Sign." In *Material Religion* 7, no. 1 (2011): 100–107.

———. "Untranslatable Iconicity in Liang Sicheng's Theory of Architectural Translatability," *Art in Translation* 5, no. 2 (June 2013): 219–50.

Lin Yun-jo. "Tangdai 'Foding zunsheng tuoluoni jing' de yichuan yu xinyang" (Translations, transmissions, and cults of *Sutra of the Superlative Dhāraṇī of the Buddha's Crown* during the Tang). *Fagu foxue xuebao* 3 (2008): 145–93.

———. "Wutaishan yu Wenshu daochang: Zhonggu fojiao shengshan xinyang de xingcheng yu fazhan" (Mount Wutai and Mañjuśrī's *bodhimaṇḍa:* The formation and development of a medieval Buddhist sacred mountain cult). Ph.D. diss., National Taiwan University, 2009.

Link, Arthur E. "Biography of Shi Tao-an." *T'oung Pao* 46 (1958): 1–48.

Little, Stephen, ed. *Taoism and the Arts of China*. Chicago: Art Institute of Chicago, 2000.

Liu Jinglong and Li Yukun, eds. *Longmen shiku beike tiji huilu* (Collection of stele inscriptions from the Longmen caves). 2 vols. Beijing: Zhongguo Dabaike Quanshu Chubanshe, 1998.

Liu Shufen. *Miezui yu duwang: Foding zunsheng tuoluoni jingchang zhi yanjiu* (Expiation and salvation: Research on the *dhāraṇi* pillar [carved with] the *Sutra of the Superlative Dhāraṇi of the Buddha's Crown*). Shanghai: Guji Chubanshe, 2008.

———. "Zhonggu fojiao zhengce yu sheyi de zhuanxing" (Buddhist policies and the transformation of *yiyi* society in the Middle Period). *Tang yanjiu* 13 (2007): 233–91.

Lopez, Donald S., ed. "Introduction" to *Critical Terms for the Study of Buddhism*, 1–11. Chicago: University of Chicago Press, 2005.

———. "Introduction" to *Religions of China in Practice*, 3–40. Princeton, N.J.: Princeton University Press, 1996.

Lü Tiegang, ed. *Fangshan shijing yanjiu* (Research articles on stone sutras at Mount Fang). 3 vols. Hong Kong: Zhongguo Fojiao Wenhua, 1999.

Lu Yaodong. *Cong Pingcheng dao Luoyang: Tuoba Wei wenhua zhuanbian de licheng* (From Pingcheng to Luoyang: The process and transformation of Northern Wei culture). Taipei: Lianjing Chubanshe, 1979.

Lü Zhou, ed. *Foguangsi Dongdadian jianzhu kancha yanjiu baogao* (Research report on the investigation of the Great Eastern Hall at Foguang Monastery). Beijing: Wenwu Chubanshe, 2011.

Ma De. *Dunhuang Mogaoku shi yanjiu* (Research on the history of Mogao caves in Dunhuang). Lanzhou: Gansu Jiaoyu Chubanshe, 1996.

———. *Dunhuang shiku quanji: Jiaotong hua juan* (Complete collection of Dunhuang caves: paintings of transportation). Hong Kong: Shangwu Chubanshe, 2000.

Ma Zhongli. "Yedu jinyi Beiqi fojiao kejing chutan" (An initial investigation on Buddhist sutra carvings around Yedu of the Northern Qi). In *Beichao moya kejing yanjiu*, edited by Zhongguo Shufajia Xiehui et al., 153–90. Jinan: Qilu Shushe, 1991.

Ma Zhongli, et al. "Shexian Zhonghuangshan Beiqi fojiao moya kejing diaocha" (Investigation on Buddhist *moya* carvings of the Northern Qi at Mount Zhonghuang in Shexian). *Wenwu*, no. 5 (1995): 66–76.

Macauley, David. "Walking the Elemental Earth: Phenomenological and Literary 'Foot Notes.'" *Analecta Husserliana* 71 (2001): 15–31.

Mair, Victor H. *Tang Transformation Texts: A Study on the Buddhist Contribution to the Rise of Vernacular Fiction and Drama in China*. Cambridge: Council on East Asian Studies, Harvard University, 1989.

Major, John S., et al. *The Huainanzi: A Guide to the Theory and Practice of Government in Early Han China*. New York: Columbia University Press, 2010.

Makita Tairyō. "Hōzanji Ryōyū ni tsuite" (On Lingyu of Baoshan Monastery). *Tōhō gakuhō* 36 (1964): 269–71.

Makita Tairyō and Fukui Fumimasa, eds. *Tonkō to Chūgoku bukkyō* (Dunhuang and Chinese Buddhism). Tokyo: Daitō Shuppansha, 1984.

Marchand, Ernesta. "The Panorama of Wu-T'ai Shan as an Example of Tenth-Century Cartography." *Oriental Art* 23 (Summer 1976): 158–73.

Matsumoto, Moritaka. "The Iconography of Shaka's Sermon on the Vulture Peak and Its Art Historical Meaning." *Artibus Asiae* 53, nos. 3–4 (1993): 358–411.

Matsuyama Tetsuo. "Tōdaiji dōzō hakkaku tōrō" (The octagonal lantern made in bronze at Tōdaiji). *Nanto bukkyō*, nos. 43–44 (1980): 172–93.

Mauss, Marcel. *Sociology and Psychology: Essays*. London: Routledge and Kegan Paul, 1979.

McMahan, David L. *Empty Vision: Metaphor and the Visionary Imagery in Mahāyāna Buddhism*. London: Routledge, 2002.

———. "Orality, Writing, and Authority in South Asian Buddhism: Visionary

Literature and the Struggle for Legitimacy in the Mahāyāna." *History of Religions* 37, no. 3 (1998): 249–74.

McNair, Amy. *Donors of Longmen: Faith, Politics, and Patronage in Medieval Chinese Buddhist Sculpture.* Honolulu: University of Hawai'i Press, 2007.

Michihata Ryōshū. *Rakan shinkō shi* (History of the cult of arhats). Tokyo: Daitō Shuppansha, 1983.

Miller, Patricia Cox. *The Corporeal Imagination: Signifying the Holy in Late Ancient Christianity.* Philadelphia: University of Pennsylvania Press, 2009.

Miller, Tracy. *The Divine Nature of Power: Chinese Ritual Architecture at the Sacred Site of Jinci.* Cambridge, Mass.: Harvard University Press, 2007.

Misaki Ryōshū. "Bucchōkei no mikkyō: Tōdai mikkyōshi no ichi shiten" (The *Buddha Crown* system in Esoteric Buddhism: A viewpoint of the history of Esoteric Buddhism during the Tang). In *Dōkyō kenkyū ronshū: Dōkyō no shisō to bunka,* 477–99. Tokyo: Kokusho Kankōkai, 1977.

Miura Kunio. "Dōten fukuchi shōron" (A brief essay on grotto heavens and auspicious terrains). *Tōhō shūkyō,* no. 61 (1983): 1–23.

Miyakawa Hisayuki. "Shindai oyobi sore ikō no Rosan" (Mount Lu from the Jin dynasty and thereafter). In *Rikuchōshi kenkyū: shūkyō hen,* 242–54. Kyoto: Heirakuji Shoten, 1964.

Mizuno Seiichi and Nagahiro Toshio. *Kanan Ryūmon sekkutsu no kenkyū* (Research on the Longmen caves, Henan). Tokyo: Zayuho Kankokai, 1941.

———. *Kyōdōsan sekkutsu* (The Xiangtangshan caves). Kyoto: Tōyō Bunkagaku Kyōto Kenkyūjo, 1937.

Mizuo Jakuhō. "Gyō-kō ni tsuide" (A study of Gyō-kō). *Tendai gakuhō,* no. 36 (October 1994): 111–17.

Moerman, D. Max. *Localizing Paradise: Kumano Pilgrimage and the Religious Landscape of Premodern Japan.* Cambridge, Mass.: Harvard University Asia Center, 2005.

Morgan, David. *The Sacred Gaze: Religious Visual Culture in Theory and Practice.* Berkeley: University of California Press, 2005.

Mukai Ryūken. "Fukū sanzō no Monju bosatsu shinkō" (Amoghavajra Tipiṭaka's Bodhisattva Mañjuśrī belief). *Taishō daigaku kenkyū kiyō,* no. 70 (1985): 1–23.

Müller, M. *The Sacred Books of the East,* vol. 49, 1st ed., 1894. New York: Dover, 1969.

Munakata, Kiyohiko. *Sacred Mountains in Chinese Art.* Urbana: University of Illinois Press, 1991.

Murata Jirō. *Chūgoku no teito* (China's imperial capitals). Kyoto: Sōgesha, 1978.

Nagahiro Toshio. "Unkō sekkutsu dai kyū, dai jū sekkutsu no tokuchō" (The characteristics of Yungang Caves 9 and 10). In *Chūgoku sekkutsu: Unkō sekkutsu,* 197–214. Tokyo: Heibonsha, 1989, vol. 2.

Nan, Shunxun, and Beverly Foit-Albert. *China's Sacred Sites.* Honesdale, Pa.: Himalayan Institute Press, 2007.

Naquin, Susan, and Chün-fang Yü, eds. *Pilgrims and Sacred Sites in China.* Berkeley: University of California Press, 1992.

Nara Kokuritsu Hakubutsukan. *Higashi Ajia no hotoke tachi* (Buddhist images of East Asia). Nara: Nara Kokuritus Hakubutsukan, 1996.

Nattier, Jan. *Once upon a Future Time: Studies in a Buddhist Prophecy of Decline.* Berkeley: University of California Press, 1991.

Ng, Zhiru. *The Making of a Savior Bodhisattva: Dizang in Medieval China.* Honolulu: University of Hawai'i Press, 2007.

Nietupski, Paul K. "Monasticism: Buddhist Monasticism." In Jones, ed., *Encyclopedia of Religion,* vol. 9, 6126–31.

Ning, Qiang. *Art, Religion, and Politics in Medieval China: The Dunhuang Cave of the Zhai Family.* Honolulu: University of Hawai'i Press, 2004.

Nishikawa Shinji, Yamane Yūzō, and Ariga Yoshitaga. *Daigoji taikan* (A survey of Daigoji). 2 vols. Tokyo: Iwaname Shoten, 2001.

Ñyanamoli, Bhikkhu, trans. *The Path of Purification.* Berkeley, Calif.: Shambhala, 1976.

O'Leary, Stephen D. *Arguing the Apocalypse: A Theory of Millennial Rhetoric.* Oxford: Oxford University Press, 1994.

Ogasawara Senshū. "Rankoku shamon Eshō ni tsuite" (About monk Huixiang of Langu). *Ryūkoku gakuhō,* no. 315 (1936): 231–51.

Ono Genmyō. "Godaisan dai Bukkōji no kobutsuzō ni tsuite" (About the ancient Buddha statue from the Great Foguang Monastery at Mount Wutai). *Tōyō tetsugaku* 30, no. 1 (1923): 41–47.

———. "Godaisan Kinkakuji Kankō daitoku to Reisen sanzō" (The Great Virtue Hanguang of Jin'ge Monastery at Mount Wutai and RyōzenTipiṭaka). *Mikkyō kenkyū,* no. 11 (1923): 17–35.

Ono Katsutoshi. "Ennin no mita Tō no bukkyō girei" (Buddhist rituals of the Tang as observed by Ennin). In *Jikaku daishi kenkyū,* edited by Fukui Kōjun, 171–208. Tokyo: Tendai gakkai, 1964.

———. *Nittō guhō junrei gyōki no kenkyū* (A study of the *Record of a Pilgrimage to China in Search of the Law*) [*NGJG*]. 4 vols. Tokyo: Suzuki Gakujutsu Zaidan, 1964–69.

Ono Katsutoshi and Hibino Takeo. *Godaisan* (Mount Wutai). Tokyo: Zauhō Kankōkai, 1942.

Orlando, Raffaello. "A Study of Chinese Documents Concerning the Life of the Tantric Buddhist Patriarch Amoghavajra (A.D. 705–774)." Ph.D. diss., Princeton University, 1981.

Orzech, Charles D. "After Amoghavajra: Esoteric Buddhism in the Late Tang." In Orzech et al., *Esoteric Buddhism,* 315–35.

———. "Esoteric Buddhism in the Tang." In Orzech et al., *Esoteric Buddhism,* 263–85.

———. *Politics and Transcendent Wisdom: The Scripture for Humane Kings in the Creation of Chinese Buddhism.* University Park: Pennsylvania State University Press, 1998.

———. "The 'Great Teaching of Yoga': The Chinese Appropriation of the Tantras, and the Question of Esoteric Buddhism." *Journal of Chinese Religion* 34 (2006): 29–78.

———. "Vajrabodhi." In Orzech et al., *Esoteric Buddhism,* 345–59.

Orzech, Charles D., Henrik H. Sørensen, and Richard K. Payne, eds. *Esoteric Buddhism and the Trantras in East Asia.* Leiden: Brill, 2011.

Osabe Kazuo. *Tōdai mikkyōshi zakkō* (Collection of research essays on Esoteric Buddhism of the Tang), 1st ed., 1982. Reprint, Tokyo: Keisuisha, 1990.

Palmer, Jesse Dalton. "Searching for the Law: Ennin's Journal as a Key to the Heian Appropriation of Tang Culture." Ph.D. diss., University of California, Irvine, 2009.

Pan Liangwen. "Bukong sanzang yu Wenshu pusa xinyang" (Amoghavajra Tipiṭaka and cult of the bodhisattva Mañjuśrī). *Taiwan zongjiao yanjiu* 7, no. 1 (June 2008): 1–28.

———. "Dunhuang Tangdai de Wenshu pusa tuxiang shixi" (An initial investigation on the iconography of Mañjuśrī from Dunhuang during the Tang). *Dunhuang yanjiu*, no. 3 (2013): 86–102.

Pan Yushan and Ma Shichang. *Mogaoku kuqian diantang yizhi* (Former sites of ante-halls to the Mogao caves). Beijing: Wenwu Chubanshe, 1985.

Pant, Sushila. *The Origin and Development of Stupa Architecture in India*. Varanasi: Bharata Manisha, 1976.

Pas, Julian F. "Six Daily Periods of Worship: Symbolic Meaning in Buddhist Liturgy and Eschatology." *Monumenta Serica*, no. 37 (1986–87): 49–82.

———. *Visions of Sukhāvatī: Shan-tao's Commentary on the Kuan Wu-Liang-Shou-Fo Ching*. Albany: State University of New York Press, 1995.

Payne, Richard K., and Charles D. Orzech. "Homa." In Orzech et al., *Esoteric Buddhism*, 133–40.

Pei Wenzhong, ed. *Yanbei wenwu kanchatuan baogao* (Report submitted by Yenbei region cultural relics investigation team). Beijing: Zhongyang Renmin Zhengfu Wenhuabu Wenhuaju, 1951.

Pinte, Klaus. "Śubhākarasiṃha." In Orzech et al., *Esoteric Buddhism*, 340–41.

Plate, S. Brent, ed. *Religion, Art, and Visual Culture: A Cross-Cultural Reader.* New York: Palgrave, 2002.

Portús, Javier. "The Holy Depicting the Holy: Social and Aesthetic Issues." In *Sacred Spain: Art and Belief in the Spanish World*, edited by Ronda Kasl, 37–53. New Haven: Yale University Press, 2009.

Qian Guoxiang. "Beiwei Luoyang Yongningsi suxiang de chubu yanjiu" (An initial research on the sculptures from Yongning Monastery of the Northern Wei in Luoyang). *Zhongyuan wenwu*, no. 1 (2005): 76–85.

Qiao Yunfei and Wei Luo. "Paifang jianzhu wenhua chutan" (A preliminary research on the architectural culture of memorial archways and gates). *Sichuan wenwu*, no. 3 (2003): 68–73.

Qin Mengxiao. *Sida mingshan: Wutaishan, Emeishan, Putuoshan, Jiuhuashan* (Four great mountains of renown: Mount Wutai, Mount Emei, Mount Putuo, Mount Jiuhua). Hong Kong: Heping tushu, 1987.

Quinter, David. "Visualizing the *Mañjuśrī Parinirvāṇa Sutra* as a Contemplation Sutra," *Asia Major*, 3rd ser., vol. 23, part 1 (2010): 97–128.

Rambelli, Fabio. *Buddhist Materiality: A Cultural History of Objects in Japanese Buddhism.* Stanford, Calif.: Stanford University Press, 2007.

Ray, Himanshu Prabha. "The Stūpa: Symbolizing Religious Architecture in Asia." In *Sacred Landscapes in Asia: Shared Traditions, Multiple Histories*, edited by Himanshu Prabha Ray, 63–80. Manohar: India International Center, 2007.

Reinders, Eric. "Ritual Topography: Embodiment and Vertical Space in Buddhist Monastic Practice." *History of Religions* 36, no. 3 (February 1997): 244–64.

Reischauer, Edwin O. *Ennin's Diary: The Record of a Pilgrimage to China in Search of the Law.* New York: Ronald Press, 1955.

Rhie, Marylin M. *The Fo-kuang ssu: Literary Evidences and Buddhist Images.* New York: Garland, 1977.

Robson, James. "Monastic Spaces and Sacred Traces: Facets of Chinese Buddhist Monastic Records." In James A. Benn et al., *Buddhist Monasticism in East Asia: Places of Practice,* 43–64.

———. *Power of Place: The Religious Landscape of the Southern Sacred Peak (Nanyue) in Medieval China.* Cambridge, Mass.: Harvard University Asia Center, 2009.

Rong Xinjiang. "Dunhuang wenxian he huihua fanying de Wudai Songchu zhongyuan yu xibei diqu de wenhua jiaowang" (Cultural interactions between central China and its northwest during the late Tang and early Song as reflected in Dunhuang texts and paintings). *Beijing daxue xuebao,* no. 2 (1988): 55–62.

———. *Guiyijun shi yanjiu: Tang Song shidai Dunhuang lishi kaosuo* (Study of the history of the Return to Allegiance Army: Investigation on the history of Dunhuang during the Tang-Song period). Shanghai: Guji Chubanshe, 1996.

Rotman, Andy. *Thus Have I Seen: Visualizing Faith in Early Indian Buddhism.* Oxford: Oxford University Press, 2009.

Ruan Yuan (1764–1849), ed. *Shisan jing zhushu* (Annotations of Thirteen Classics). Reprint, 2 vols. Beijing: Zhonghua Shuju, 1980.

Rujivacharakul, Vimalin, and Luo Deyin, ed. and trans. *Liang Sicheng and the Temple of Buddha's Light.* Singapore: Gale Asia, Cengage, 2013.

Russell-Smith, Lilla. *Uygur Patronage in Dunhuang: Regional Art Centers on the Northern Silk Road in the Tenth and Eleventh Centuries.* Leiden: Brill, 2005.

Saitō Tadashi. *Chūgoku Godaisan Chikurin-ji no kenkyū* (Research on Zhulin Monastery at Mount Wutai, China). Tokyo: Daiichi Shobō, 1998.

Schafer, Edward H. *Mao Shan in T'ang Times.* Boulder, Colo.: Society for the Study of Chinese Religions, 1980.

Schopen, Gregory. "The Phrase 'sa pṛthivīpradeśaś caityabhūto bhavet' in the Vajracchedikā: Notes on the Cult of the Book in Mahayana." *Indo-Iranian Journal* 17, nos. 3–4 (Nov.–Dec. 1975): 147–81.

Sekino Tadashi, and Tokiwa Daijō, eds. *Shina bukkyō shiseki* (Buddhist historical relics in China). 5 vols. Tokyo: Bukkyō Shiseki Kenkyūkai, 1928.

Sen, Tansen. *Buddhism, Diplomacy, and Trade: The Realignment of Sino-Indian Relations, 600–1400.* Honolulu: University of Hawai'i Press, 2003.

Sha Wutian. "Dunhuang P. 4049 'Xinyang Wenshu' huagao ji xiangguan wenti yanjiu" (A study of the sketch of the new-mode Mañjuśrī from Dunhuang Manuscript P4049 and its related issues). *Dunhuang yanjiu,* no. 3 (2005): 26–32.

Sha Wutian and Liang Hong. "Mogaoku di 61 ku zhongxin fotan zaoxiang wei huisu jiehe 'Xinyang Wenshu bian' shikao" (On the icons of the central altar inside Mogao Cave 61 as a new-mode Mañjuśrī transformation tableau combining sculpture and mural painting). In *2005 nian Yungang guoji xueshu yantao hui lunwen ji*, edited by Yungang Shiku Yanjiuyuan, 441–56. Beijing: Wenwu Chubanshe, 2005.

Shaanxisheng Kaogu Yanjiuyuan et al. *Famensi kaogu fajue baogao* (Report of the archaeological excavation at Faman monastery). 2 vols. Beijing: Wenwu Chubanshe, 2007.

Shanxi Lüyou Jingqu Zhi Congshu Bianweihui. *Wutaishan zhi* (Gazetteer of Mount Wutai). Taiyuan: Shanxi Renmin Chubanshe, 2003.

Shanxisheng Gu Jianzhu Baohu Yanjiusuo. *Wutaishan Foguangsi* (Foguang Monastery at Mount Wutai). Beijing: Wenwu Chubanshe, 2010.

Shanxisheng Kaogu Yanjiusuo and Datongshi Kaogu Yanjiusuo. "Datongshi Beiwei Song Shaozu mu fajue jianbao" (A brief excavation report on the tomb of Song Shaozu of the Northern Wei from Datong City). *Wenwu*, no. 7 (2001): 19–39.

Shi Zhangru. *Mogao ku xing* (Architectural structures of Mogao Caves). 3 vols. Taipei: Zhongyang Yanjiuyuan Lishi Yuyan Yanjiusuo, 1996.

Shibasaki Terukazu. "Myōe to bukkō zanmai kan: Jissen kan kara mita sono juyō no riyū oyobi haikei (2)" (Myōe and the *Samādhi [achieved by] Visualizing the Buddha's Radiance:* The reason and background of its reception from the perspective of practice [2]). *Nanto bukkyō*, no. 67 (Dec. 1992): 59–94.

Shimomatsu Tōru. "Monju bosatsu: sono katachi to shinkō" (Bodhisattva Mañjuśrī: The forms and belief). *Kōyasan mikkyō bunka kenkyōjo kiyō*, no. 8 (1994): 55–61.

Shinohara, Koichi. "Changing Roles for Miraculous Images in Medieval Chinese Buddhism: A Study of the Miracle Image Section in Daoxuan's 'Collected Records.'" In *Images, Miracles, and Authority in Asian Religious Traditions*, edited by Richard H. Davis, 143–88. Boulder, Colo.: Westview, 1998.

———. "Literary Construction of Buddhist Sacred Places: The Record of Mount Lu by Chen Shunyu." *Asiatische Studien: Zeitschrift der Schweizerischen Gesellschaft für Asienkunde* 53 (1999): 937–64.

———. "Story of the Buddha's Begging Bowl: Imaging a Biography and Sacred Places." In *Pilgrims, Patrons, and Place: Localizing Sanctity in Asian Religion*, edited by Phyllis Granoff and Koichi Shinohara, 58–107. Vancouver: University of British Columbia Press, 2003.

Shioiri Ryōdō. "Shaku Dōan no *Sōni Kihan* to kaikahō" (Monk Daoan's *Regulations for Monks and Nuns* and methods of repentance). *Taishō daigaku daigakuin kenkyū ronshū*, no. 1 (1977): 21–37.

Sickman, L. C. S., and Alexander Coburn Soper. *The Art and Architecture of China*. Harmondsworth: Penguin Books, 1971.

Smith, Jonathan Z. "Constructing a Small Place." In *Sacred Space: Shrine, City, Land*, edited by Joshua Prawer, Benjamin Kedar-Kopfstein, and R. J. Zwi Werblowsky, 18–31. New York: New York University Press, 1998.

———. *To Take Place: Toward Theory in Ritual*. Chicago: University of Chicago Press, 1987.

Snodgrass, Adrian. *The Symbolism of the Stupa*. Ithaca, N.Y.: Southeast Asia Program, Cornell University, 1985.

Sofugawa Hiroshi. "Kyōdōsan sekkutsu kō" (An investigation on Xiangtangshan Caves). *Tōhō gakuhō* 69 (1990): 165–206.

Sōma Kazui. "Godaisan kinpen no dōkyō teki huniki: roku seiki shotō no Hokugi bukkyō no ichimen" (The Daoist milieu around Mount Wutai: One aspect of Northern Wei Buddhism in the early decades of the sixth century). *Gyōshin gakuhō* 10 (May 1997): 85–105.

Soper, Alexander C. "Imperial Cave Chapels of the Northern Dynasties: Donors, Beneficiaries, Dates." *Artibus Asiae* 28, no. 4 (1966): 241–70.

———. *Literary Evidence for Early Buddhist Art in China.* Ascona, Switzerland: Artibus Asiae, 1959.

———. "Northern Liang and Northern Wei in Kansu." *Artibus Asiae* 21, no. 2 (1958): 131–64.

———. *The Evolution of Buddhist Architecture in Japan.* 1st ed., 1942. Reprint, Princeton, N.J.: Princeton University Press, 1978.

Sørensen, Henrik H. "On Esoteric Buddhism in China: A Working Definition." In Orzech et al., *Esoteric Buddhism,* 155–75.

Steinhardt, Nancy S., ed. *Chinese Architecture.* New Haven, Conn.: Yale University Press, 2002.

———. *Chinese Imperial City Planning.* Honolulu: University of Hawai'i Press, 1990.

———. "Early Chinese Buddhist Architecture and Its Indian Origins." In *The Flowering of a Foreign Faith: New Studies in Chinese Buddhist Art,* edited by Janet Baker, 38–53. New Delhi: Marg, 1998.

———. *Liao Architecture.* Honolulu: University of Hawai'i Press, 1997.

———. "Taoist Architecture." In *Taoism and the Arts of China,* edited by Stephen Little, 57–75. Chicago: Art Institute of Chicago, 2000.

———. "The Mizong Hall of Qinglong Si: Space, Ritual, and Classicism in Tang Architecture." *Archives of Asian Art* 44 (1991): 27–50.

———. "The Sixth Century in East Asian Architecture," *Ars Orientalis* 41 (2011): 27–71.

———. "The Tang Architectural Icon and the Politics of Chinese Architectural History." *Art Bulletin* 86, no. 2 (June 2004): 228–54.

———. "Xiangtangshan and Northern Qi Architecture." In Tsiang, *Echoes of the Past,* 60–77.

Stevenson, Daniel. "Pure Land Buddhist Worship and Meditation in China." In *Buddhism in Practice,* edited by Donald S. Lopez Jr, 359–79. Princeton, N.J.: Princeton University Press, 1995.

———. "The T'ien-T'ai Four Forms of Samādhi and Late North-South Dynasties, Sui, and Early T'ang Buddhist Devotionalism." Ph.D. diss., Columbia University, 1987.

———. "Visions of Mañjuśrī on Mount Wutai." In *Religions of China in Practice,* edited by Donald S. Lopez Jr, 203–22. Princeton, N.J.: Princeton University Press, 1996.

Strickmann, Michel. *Mantras et Mandarins: Le bouddhisme tantrique en Chine.* Paris: Éditions Gallimard, 1996.

Strong, John S. *The Legend of King Aśoka: A Study and Translation of the Aśokāvadāna.* Princeton, N.J.: Princeton University Press, 1983.

———. "The Legend of the Lion-Roarer." *Numen* 16, no. 1 (1979): 50–88.

Su Bai. "Donghan Wei Jin Nanbeichao fosi buju chutan" (An initial investigation on monastic layouts during the Eastern Han, Wei, Jin, and Northern and Southern dynasties). In *Qingzhu Deng Guangming jiaoshou jiushi huadan lunwenji*, 31–49. Shijiazhuang: Hebei Jiaoyu, 1997.

———. "Dunhuang Mogaoku zhong de Wutaishan tu" (Pictures of Mount Wutai in Mogaoku caves, Dunhuang). *Wenwu cankao ziliao* 5, no. 2 (1951): 49–71.

———. "Liangzhou shiku yiji he 'Liangzhou moshi'" (Remains of Liangzhou caves and "Liangzhou style"). *Kaogu xuebao,* no. 4 (1986): 435–45.

———. "Luoyang diqu Beichao shiku de chubu kaocha" (The initial investigation of the caves of the Northern dynasties in Luoyang area). In Su Bai, *Zhongguo shiku si yanjiu*, 153–75.

———. "Nanchao kanxiang yiji chutan" (An initial investigation on remains of niched images in the Southern dynasties). *Kaogu xuebao,* no. 4 (1989): 389–412.

———. "Pingcheng shili de jiju he 'Yungang moshi' de xingcheng yu fazhan" (The coalition of forces in Pingcheng and formation and development of "Yungang style"). In Su Bai, *Zhongguo shiku si yanjiu*, 114–44.

———. "Shilun Tangdai Chang'an fojiao siyuan de dengji wenti" (On issues of hierarchy among Buddhist monasteries in Tang Chang'an). *Wenwu,* no. 1 (2009): 27–40.

———. "Suidai fosi buju" (Monastic layouts of the Sui Dynasty). *Kaogu yu wenwu,* no. 2 (1997): 29–33.

———. "Yungang shiku fenqi shilun" (On the periodization of the Yungang caves). In Su Bai, *Zhongguo shiku si yanjiu*, 76–88.

———. *Zhongguo shiku si yanjiu* (Research papers on Chinese cave temples). Beijing: Wenwu Chubanshe, 1996.

Suguro Shinjō. *Hokekyō no seiritsu to shisō* (The formation and thoughts of the *Lotus Sutra*). Tokyo: Daitō shuppansha, 1993.

Summers, David. "Representation." In *Critical Terms for Art History,* 2nd ed., edited by Robert S. Nelson and Richard Shiff, 1–19. Chicago: University of Chicago Press, 2003.

Sun Xiaogang. *Wenshu pusa tuxiang xue yanjiu* (A study on the iconography of Bodhisattva Mañjuśrī). Lanzhou: Gansu Renmin Chubanshe, 2007.

Sun Xiushen. "Mogao ku fojiao shiji gushi hua jieshao (2)" (Introduction to paintings depicting stories of Buddhist history from Mogao caves [2]). *Dunhuang yanjiu,* no. 2 (1982): 98–110.

———. "Zhongguo Xinyang Wenshu yu Riben Wenshu sanzun wuzunxiang zhi bijiao" (The comparison between the Chinese new-mode Mañjuśrī and Japanese Monju triad and pentad). *Dunhuang yanjiu,* no. 1 (1996): 44–52.

Suwa Gijun. *Chūgoku chūsei bukkyōshi kenkyū* (A research on the history of Chinese medieval Buddhism). Tokyo: Daitō Shuppansha, 1988.

Takeda Kazuaki. *Hoshi mandara no kenkyū* (A study of star *maṇḍalas*). Tokyo: Hōzōkan, 1995.

Tamaki Koshirō. "Rosan Eon no shizen kannen" (Concept of nature of Huiyuan from Mount Lu). In *Bukkyō shisōshi ronshū: Yūki kyōju shōju kinen*, 379–96. Tokyo: Daizō Shuppan, 1964.

Tan, Zhihui. "Daoxuan's Vision of Jetavana: Imagining a Utopian Monastery in Early Tang." Ph.D. diss., University of Arizona, 2002.

Tanaka, Kenneth K. *The Dawn of Chinese Pure Land Buddhist Doctrine: Ching-ying Hui-yüan's Commentary on the* Visualization Sutra. Albany: State University of New York Press, 1990.

Tang Xiaofeng. "Wuyue dili shuo" (Theories of geography of the Five Sacred Peaks). In *Jiuzhou*, edited by Tang Xiaofeng and Li Ling, 60–70. Beijing: Zhongguo Huanjing Kexue, 1997.

Tang Yongtong. *Han Wei Liangjin Nanbeichao fojiaoshi* (History of Buddhism in the Han, Wei, East and West Jins, and Northern and Southern dynasties). 3 vols. Beijing: Zhonghua Shuju, 1983.

Teiser, Stephen F. *The Ghost Festival in Medieval China*. Princeton, N.J.: Princeton University Press, 1988.

Ten Grotenhuis, Elizabeth. *Japanese Mandalas: Representations of Sacred Geography*. Honolulu: University of Hawai'i Press, 1999.

Toganoo Shōun. *Kongōchōkyō no kenkyū* (Research on *Vajraśekhara Sūtra*). Kyoto: Rinsen Shoten, 1985.

Trainor, Kevin. *Relics, Ritual, and Representation in Buddhism: Rematerializing the Sri Lankan Theravāda Tradition*. Cambridge: Cambridge University Press, 1997.

Tsai, Julius Nanting. "In the Steps of Emperors and Immortals: Imperial Mountain Journeys and Daoist Meditation and Ritual." Ph.D. diss., Stanford University, 2003.

Tsiang, Katherine R. "Antiquarianism and Re-envisioning Empire in the Late Northern Wei." In *Reinventing the Past: Archaism and Antiquarianism in Chinese Art and Visual Culture*, edited by Wu Hung, 127–54. Chicago: Center for the Art of East Asia, Department of Art History, University of Chicago, 2010.

———. "Changing Patterns of Divinity and Reform in the Late Northern Wei." *Art Bulletin* 84, no. 2 (June 2002): 222–45.

———, ed. *Echoes of the Past: The Buddhist Cave Temples of Xiangtangshan*. Chicago: Smart Museum of Art, University of Chicago, 2011.

———. "Monumentalization of Buddhist Texts in the Northern Qi Dynasty: The Engraving of *Sūtras* in Stone at the Xiangtangshan Caves and Other Sites in the Sixth Century." *Artibus Asiae* 56, nos. 3–4 (1996): 233–61.

———. "Reconsidering Early Buddhist Cave-Making of the Northern Wei in Terms of Artistic Interactions with Gansu and the Western Regions." *Journal of Inner Asian Art and Archaeology* 4 (2009): 101–18.

Tsukamoto Zenryū. *Chūgoku jōdokyōshi kenkyū* (A study of the history of Chinese Pure Land Buddhism). Tokyo: Daitō Shuppansha, 1976.

———. *Hokuchō bukkyōshi kenkyū* (Research on the history of Buddhism in Northern dynasties). Tokyo: Daitō Shuppansha, 1974.

Tsuzuki Akiko. "Rokuchō kōhanki ni okeru dōkan no seiritsu: sanchū shudō" (The establishment of Daoist abbeys in the later half of the Six dynasties: Cultivating Dao in the mountains). In *Tōyōshi ronshū: Oda Yoshihisa hakushi kanreki kinen,* edited by Oda Yoshihisa Sensei Kanreki Kinen Jigyōkai, 317–51. Kyoto: Ryūkoku Daigaku, 1995.

Turner, Victor W. "Betwixt and Between: The Liminal Period in Rites of Passage." In *The Forest of Symbols: Aspects of Ndembu Ritual,* 93–111. Ithaca, N.Y.: Cornell University Press, 1967.

Tuttle, Gray, and Johan Elverskog, eds. *Wutai Shan and Qing Culture.* Special issue, *Journal of the International Association of Tibetan Studies* 6 (Dec. 2011).

Ui Hakuju. *Shaku Dōan kenkyū* (Research on Monk Daoan). Tokyo: Iwanami Shoten, 1956.

Vaidya, P. L., trans. *Gandavyūhasūtra.* Darbhanga, India: Mithila Institute of Post-graduate Studies and Research in Sanskrit Learning, 1960.

Van Gennep, Arnold. *The Rites of Passage.* Translated by Monika B. Vizedom and Gabrielle L. Caffee. Chicago: University of Chicago Press, 1960.

Verellen, Franciscus. "The Beyond Within: Grotto-Heavens (*Dongtian*) in Taoist Ritual and Cosmology." *Cahiers d'Extrême-Asie* 8 (1995): 265–90.

Wakae Kenzō. "Chūgoku ni okeru shōzōmatsu sanji no nendaikan" (The chronological concepts of the triple periods of the true, semblance, and final teachings in China). *Tōyō tetsugaku kenkyūjo kiyō,* no. 5 (1989): 1–23.

Wang, Eugene Y. "Of the True Body: The Famen Monastery Relics and Corporeal Transformation in Tang Imperial Culture." In *Body and Face in Chinese Visual Culture,* edited by Wu Hung and Katherine R. Tsiang, 79–118. Cambridge, Mass.: Harvard University Asia Center, 2005.

———. *Shaping the Lotus Sutra: Buddhist Visual Culture in Medieval China.* Seattle: University of Washington Press, 2005.

———. "Watching the Steps: Peripatetic Vision in Medieval China." In *Visuality Before and Beyond the Renaissance: Seeing as Others Saw,* edited by Robert S. Nelson, 116–42. Cambridge: Cambridge University Press, 2000.

Wang Guixiang, "Dongjin ji Nanchao shiqi nanfang fosi jianzhu gaishuo" (Survey of southern Buddhist architecture during the Eastern Jin and Southern Dynasties). *Zhongguo jianzhu shilun huikan* 6 (2013): 3–62.

———. "Fojiao chuchuan zhi Xijin mo Shiliuguo shiqi fosi jianzhu gaishuo" (Survey of Buddhist Architecture from Buddhism's arrival until the end of the Western Jin and Sixteen Dynasties). *Zhongguo jianzhu shilun huikan* 5 (2012): 3–35.

———. "Tang Luoyang gong Wushi Mingtang de jiangouxing fuyuan yanjiu" (Research on structural reconstruction of Wu [Zetian's] Bright Hall in the City of Luoyang of the Tang). *Zhongguo jianzhu shilun huikan* 4 (2011): 369–455.

Wang Huimin. "Mogaoku di 276 ku 'xingxiang shuoji wen' yu Daoan de xingxiang zhifa" (The verses recited at the rite of presenting incense from Mogaoku Cave 276 and Daoan's rite of presenting incense). *Dunhuang yanjiu,* no. 1 (2009): 16–21.

Wang, Michelle. "Changing Conceptions of 'Maṇḍala' in Tang China: Ritual and the Role of Images." *Material Religion* 9, no. 2 (June 2013): 186–217.

———. "From Dhāraṇī to Maṇḍala: A Study of Mogao Cave 14 and Esoteric Buddhist Art of the Tang Dynasty (618–907)." Ph.D. diss., Harvard University, 2008.

Wang Ming. *Baopuzi neipian jiaoshi* (Annotation on the Inner Chapter of *Baopuzi*). Beijing: Zhonghua Shuji, 1985.

Wang Shiren. "Han Chang'an cheng nanjiao lizhi jianzhu (Datumen cun yizhi) yuanzhuang de tuice" (Conjectured reconstruction of the ritual architecture in Han Chang'an's southern suburb [historical site at Datumen cun]). *Kaogu,* no. 9 (1963): 501–15.

Wang Yarong. *Da Xingshansi* (Great Xingshan Monastery). Xi'an: Shanqin Chubanshe, 1986.

Wang, Yi-t'ung. *A Record of Buddhist Monasteries in Lo-yang.* Princeton, N.J.: Princeton University Press, 1984.

Wang Zhongxu. "Tufan shiqi Dunhuang 'Wutaishan huaxian tu' yu Wutaishan xinyang" ("Picture of Transformative Manifestations at Mount Wutai" made in Dunhuang during the period of Tibetan occupation and the cult of Mount Wutai). *Meishu shi yanjiu,* no. 3 (2009): 53–60.

Watt, James C. Y. et al., eds. *China: Dawn of a Golden Age, 200–750 AD.* New York: Metropolitan Museum of Art, 2004.

Weidner, Marsha, ed. *Latter Days of the Law: Images of Chinese Buddhism 850–1850.* Lawrence: Spencer Museum of Art, University of Kansas, 1994.

Weinstein, Stanley. *Buddhism under the T'ang.* Cambridge: Cambridge University Press, 1987.

Weiss, Lucas. "Rectifying the Deep Structures of the Earth: Sima Chengzhen and the Standardization of Daoist Sacred Geography in the Tang." *Journal of Daoist Studies* 5 (2012): 31–60.

Wescoat, Bonna D., and Robert G. Ousterhout, eds. *Architecture of the Sacred: Space, Ritual, and Experience from Classical Greece to Byzantium.* New York: Cambridge University Press, 2012.

White, Hayden. *Metahistory: The Historical Imagination in Nineteenth-Century Europe.* Baltimore, Md.: Johns Hopkins University Press, 1973.

———. "The Value of Narrativity in the Representation of Reality." In *On Narration,* edited by W. J. T. Mitchell, 1–24. Chicago: University of Chicago Press, 1981.

Whitfield, Roderick. "Ruixiang at Dunhuang." In *Function and Meaning in Buddhist Art,* edited by K. R. van Kooij and H. van der Veere, 149–56. Groningen: Egbert Forsten, 1995.

———. *The Art of Central Asia: The Stein Collection in the British Museum.* 2 vols. Tokyo: Kodanssha International, 1982.

———. "The Monk Liu Sahe and the Dunhuang Paintings." *Orientations* 20, no. 3 (March 1989): 64–70.

Whitfield, Susan, ed. *The Silk Road: Trade, Travel, War and Faith.* Chicago: Serindia, 2004.

Williams, Bruce Charles. "Mea Maxima Vikalpa: Repentance, Meditation, and the Dynamics of Liberation in Medieval Chinese Buddhism, 500–650 CE." Ph.D. diss., University of California, Berkeley, 2002.

———. "Seeing through Images: Reconstructing Buddhist Meditative Visualization Practice in Sixth-Century Northeastern China." *Pacific World*, 3rd ser., no. 7 (Fall 2007): 33–89.

Williams, Paul. *Mahāyāna Buddhism: The Doctrinal Foundations.* New York: Routledge, 1989.

Wong, Dorothy C. "A Reassessment of the Representation of Mt. Wutai from Dunhuang Cave 61." *Archives of Asian Art* 46 (1993): 27–52.

———. *Chinese Steles: Pre-Buddhist and Buddhist Use of a Symbolic Form.* Honolulu: University of Hawai'i Press, 2004.

———. "The Mapping of Sacred Space: Images of Buddhist Cosmographies in Medieval China." In *The Journey of Maps and Images on the Silk Road,* edited by Philippe Forêt and Andreas Kaplony, 51–79. Leiden: Brill, 2008.

Wright, Arthur F. "T'ang T'ai-tsung and Buddhism." In *Perspectives on the T'ang,* edited by Arthur F. Wright and Denis Twitchett, 265–306. New Haven: Yale University Press, 1973.

Wu Hung. *Monumentality in Early Chinese Art and Architecture.* Stanford, Calif.: Stanford University Press, 1995.

———. "Rethinking Liu Sahe: The Creation of a Buddhist Saint and the Invention of a 'Miraculous Image.'" *Orientations* 27, no. 10 (Nov. 1996): 32–43.

———. "The Jade Prince Revisited." In *Chinese Jades,* edited by Rosemany E. Scott, 147–69. London: Percival David Foundation of Chinese Art, 1997.

———. *The Wu Liang Shrine: The Ideology of Early Chinese Pictorial Art.* Stanford: Stanford University Press, 1989.

———. "What Is *Bianxiang*? On the Relationship between Dunhuang Art and Dunhuang Literature." *Harvard Journal of Asiatic Studies* 52, no. 1 (June 1992): 111–92.

———. "Wuyue de chongtu: Lishi yu zhengzhi de jinianbei" (The Competing *Yue:* Sacred Mountains as Historical and Political Monuments). In Wu Hung, *Liyi zhong de meishu* (Art in Ritual), translated by Zheng Yan et al., vol. 2, 616–41. Beijing: Sanlian Chubanshe, 2005.

Xiao Mo. *Dunhuang jianzhu yanjiu* (Research on architecture [as seen in] Dunhuang). Beijing: Wenwu Chubanshe, 1989.

———. "Dunhuang Mogaoku de dongku xingzhi" (Structures of the Mogao caves in Dunhuang). In *Dunhuang Mogao ku,* edited by Dunhuang wenwu yanjiusuo, vol. 2, 187–199.

Xiao Yu. "Jin'gesi fojiao jianshi" (A brief Buddhist history of the Jin'ge Monastery), *Wutaishan yanjiu,* no. 3 (1997): 11–21.

Yabuki Keiki. *Sangaikyō no kenkyū* (Research on the Three Stages sect). Tokyo: Iwanami Shoten, 1927.

Yamabe, Nobuyoshi. "The Sūtra on the Ocean-Like Samādhi of the Visualization of the Buddha: The Interfusion of the Chinese and Indian Cultures in Central Asia

as Reflected in Fifth Century Apocryphal Sutra." Ph.D. diss., Yale University, 1999.
———. "Visionary Repentance and Visionary Ordination in the Brahmā Net Sūtra." In *Going Forth: Visions of Buddhist Vinaya,* edited by William M. Bodiford, 17–39. Honolulu: University of Hawai'i Press, 2005.
Yan Gengwang. *Tangdai jiaotong tukao* (Annotated maps of traffic routes in the Tang dynasty). 5 vols. Taipei: Zhongyang Yanjiuyuan Lishi Yuyan Yanjiusuo, 1985.
———. *Wei Jin Nanbeichao fojiao dili gao* (Draft of a Buddhist geography of the Wei, Jin, and Northern and Southern dynasties). Taipei: Zhongyang Yanjiuyuan Lishi Yuyuan Yanjiusuo, 2005.
Yang Chunyuan. "Tangdai Wutai jiaotong shulüe" (A brief essay on Mount Wutai's traffic during the Tang). *Wutaishan yanjiu,* no. 3 (1990): 39–41.
Yang Hongxun. "Guanyu Beiwei Luoyang Yongningsi ta fuyuan caotu de shuoming" (A note about the reconstructive sketch for Yongning Pagoda in Northern Wei Luoyang). *Wenwu,* no. 9 (1992): 82–87.
Yang, Xiaoneng, ed. *New Perspectives on China's Past: Chinese Archaeology in the Twentieth Century.* 2 vols. New Haven, Conn.: Yale University Press, 2004.
Yang Zengwen. "Tang Song Wenshu pusa xinyang he Wutaishan" (The cult of Mañjuśrī during the Tang and Song periods and Mount Wutai). *Wutaishan yanjiu,* no. 1 (1990): 13–19.
Ye Luhua. "Tangdai Wutaishan putong yuan" (Pilgrim way stations at Tang Mount Wutai). *Wutaishan yanjiu,* no. 1 (1992): 24–26.
Yen Chüan-ying. "Beiqi changuan ku de tuxiang kao: cong Xiaonanhai shiku dao Xiangtangshan shiku" (An iconographical investigation of meditation caves of the Northern Qi: From Xiaonanhai caves to Xiangtangshan caves). *Tōhō gakuhō* 70 (1998): 375–440.
———. "Beiqi Xiaonanhai shiku yu Sengchou" (Xiaonanhai caves of the Northern Qi and Sengchou). In *Fojiao sixiang de chuancheng yu fazhan,* edited by Shi Hengqing, 561–98. Taipei: Sanmin Shuju, 1995.
———. "Tianlongshan shiku de zai xingsi" (Rethinking caves at Mount Tianlong). In Zhongyang Yanjiuyuan Lishi Yuyan Yanjiusuo, *Zhongguo kaoguxue yu lishixue zhi zhenghe yanjiu,* edited by Cheng-hwa Tsang, 839–918. Taipei: Zhongyang Yanjiuyuan Lishi Yuyan Yanjiusuo, 1997.
Yifa. *The Origins of Buddhist Monastic Codes in China: An Annotated Translation and Study of the Chanyuan Qinggui.* Honolulu: University of Hawai'i Press, 2002.
Yin Guangming. *Beiliang shita yanjiu* (Stone stupas of the Northern Liang dynasty). Xinzhu, Taiwan: Juefeng Fojiao Yishu Wenhua Jijinhui, 2000.
———. "Shilun mofa sixiang yu Beiliang fojiao jiqi yingxiang" (On ideas of *mofa* and Northern Liang Buddhism and its influence). *Dunhuang yanjiu,* no. 2 (1998): 89–102.
Yü, Chün-fang. "P'u-t'o Shan: Pilgrimage and the Creation of the Chinese Potalaka." In Naquin and Yü, *Pilgrims and Sacred Sites in China,* 190–245.
Yungang Shiku Wenwu Baoguansuo. *Yungang shiku* (Yungang grottos). 2 vols. Beijing: Wenwu Chubanshe, 1991.

Yungang Shiku Yanjiuyuan. *Yungang shiku* (Yungang grottos). Beijing: Wenwu Chubanshe, 2008.

Zha Luo. "Tufan qiu Wutaishan tu shishi zakao" (Some notes on Tibet's request for a "Representation of Mount Wutai"). *Minzu yanjiu*, no. 1 (1998): 95–101.

Zhang Guangda and Rong Xinjiang. "Dunhuang 'ruixiang ji,' ruixiang tu jiqi fanying de Yutian" (Khotan as reflected in records and images of *ruixiang* from Dunhuang). *Tulufan wenxian yanjiu lunwen ji* 3 (1982): 69–147.

Zhang Rong et al. "Foguangsi Dongdadian shice shuju jiedu" (Explanation of the numerical and digital data from the on-site survey of the Great Eastern Hall at Foguang Monastery). *Gugong bowuyuan yuankan*, no. 2 (2007): 28–51.

Zhang Shanqing. "Liangzhou Jiande da dizhen yu Fanhe ruixiang xinyang de xingcheng" (The great earthquake in Jiande, Liangzhou, and the formation of the cult of Fanhe *ruixiang*). *Dunhuang xue jikan*, no. 3 (2011): 84–92.

Zhang Zong. "Northern Qi Inscribed Sutras and Buddha-Images: The Unique Case of the Inscribed-Sutra Cave at Mount Zhonghuang." *Asia Major*, 3rd ser., 23, no. 1 (2010): 285–305.

———. "Shandong Sculpture Tradition." Unpublished paper presented at the symposium "Art and Material Culture of the Northern Qi Period," at the Freer Gallery of Art, June 3–5, 2011.

Zhanru. "Dunhuang busa wen yu busa cidi xintan" (A new investigation on *posadha* texts from Dunhuang and *posadha* procedures). *Dunhuang yanjiu*, no. 1 (1999): 120–32.

Zhao Lichun. "Xiangtangshan Beiqi taxing ku lunshu" (On the stupa-shaped caves at Xiangtangshan of the Northern Qi). *Dunhuang yanjiu*, no. 2 (1993): 37–45.

Zhao Shengliang. "Dunhuang bihua yu Zhongguo hua kongjian goucheng" (Spatial structure of mural paintings in Dunhuang and Chinese paintings). In Zhao Shengliang, *Dunhuang yishu shijiang*, 167–86. Shanghai: Guji Chubanshe, 2007.

———, ed. *Dunhuang shiku yishu: Mogao ku di liushiyi ku* (Art of the Dunhuang caves: Mogao Cave 61). Nanjing: Jiangsu Meishu Chubanshe, 1995.

Zhao Xiaoxing. "Mogaoku di 361 ku de Wenshu xianxian yu Wutaishan tu: Mogaoku di 361 ku yanjiu zhi er" (Manifestations of Mañjuśrī and the picture of Mount Wutai inside Mogao Cave 361: Research on Mogao Cave 361, part 2). *Wutaishan yanjiu*, no. 4 (2010): 36–47.

———. "Tufan tongzhi shiqi chuanru Dunhuang de zhongtu tuxiang: yi Wutaishan tu weili" (Imageries transmitted from central China to Dunhuang during the period of Tibetan occupation: Regarding the picture of Mount Wutai). *Wenyi yanjiu*, no. 5 (2010): 118–26.

Zheng Guoquan. *Shan wenhua* (Mountain culture). Beijing: Zhongguo Renmin Daxue Chubanshe, 1996.

Zhong Xiaoqing. "Beiwei Luoyang Yongningsi ta fuyuan tantao" (A discussion on the reconstruction of Yongning Pagoda in Northern Wei Luoyang). *Wenwu*, no. 5 (1998): 51–64.

———. "Xiangtangshan shiku jianzhu lüexi" (A short analysis of the rock-cut cave architecture at Xiangtangshan). *Wenwu*, no. 5 (1992): 19–31.

Zhongguo Shehui Kexueyuan Kaogu Yanjiusuo. *Beiwei Luoyang Yongningsi: 1979–1994 nian kaogu fajue baogao* (Yongning Monastery of the Northern Wei in Luoyang: Excavation reports from 1974–1994). Beijing: Zhongguo Dabaike Quanshu Chubanshe, 1996.

———. "Hebei Linzhang xian Yecheng yizhi Zhaopeng cheng Beichao fosi yizhi de kantan yu fajue" (Investigation and excavation of the former Buddhist monastic site of the Northern Dynasties in Zhaopengcheng located in the former site of the capital Ye in Linzhang, Hebei). *Kaogu*, no. 7 (2010): 31–42.

Zürcher, E. *The Buddhist Conquest of China: The Spread and Adaptation of Buddhism in Early Medieval China*, 3rd ed. Leiden: Brill, 2007.

ILLUSTRATIONS

MAPS

PLATES *(follow page 50)*

FIGURES

Introduction

Chapter 1

Chapter 2

Chapter 6

Conclusion

INDEX